Residential Treatment of Adolescents and Children

Nelson-Hall Series in Social Work

Consulting Editor: Charles Zastrow
University of Wisconsin—Whitewater

Residential Treatment of Adolescents and Children
Issues, Principles, and Techniques

John A. Stein
Director of Adult Services, United Cerebral Palsy of Greater New Orleans, Inc.

Nelson-Hall Publishers/Chicago

Project Editor: Rachel Schick
Typesetter: Precision Typographers
Printer: Capital City Press
Cover Painting: *Coconuts 10* by Cynthia Hayes

Library of Congress Cataloging-in-Publication Data

Stein, John A.
    Residential treatment of adolescents and children : issues,
principles, and techniques / John A. Stein.
        p.   cm.
    Includes bibliographical references and index.
    ISBN 0-8304-1378-2
      1. Child psychotherapy—Residential treatment.   2. Adolescent
psychotherapy—Residential treatment. I. Title.
RJ504.5.S74   1995   94-26034
618.92′8914—dc20   CIP

Manufactured in the United States of America

10 9 8 7 6 5 4 3 2 1

™ The paper used in this book meets the minimum requirements of American National Standard for Information Sciences—Permanence of Paper for Printed Library Materials, ANSI Z39.48-1984.

CONTENTS

PREFACE

IF we teach someone electronics, we train them in all the things that have already been discovered so that they can go on and discover *new* things. What happens in psychotherapy, however, is that we send people to school instead. And when they come out of school, *then* they have to learn to do therapy. Not only do they have to learn to do therapy, but there's *no way* to learn to do therapy (Bandler & Grinder, 1979, pp. 13–14).

I have developed several concerns in my fifteen years of experience in residential treatment. Moreover, I have found that a number of my colleagues share these concerns. I have written this book to address those concerns.

First, I have rarely seen anyone new to residential treatment enter the field prepared to work in residential treatment, regardless of undergraduate or even graduate training. While they may know how to do some things that are beneficial in a residential setting, such as case management, counseling, education, applied behavior analysis, recreational therapy, or psychotherapy, they seldom know how to fit their helpful piece together with someone else's helpful piece.

There is not only a lack of coordination but also often conflict. Behaviorists argue for consequences; therapists argue for sympathetic understanding; child care counselors and supervisors seek stronger consequences—punishment. Case managers and therapists advocate for decisions based on the needs of individual residents; child care counselors, supervisors, and group workers advocate for decisions based on the effects an action may have on the group.

Residential treatment, in order to achieve its tremendous potential, requires the coordinated use of a variety of treatment modalities. Without a full utilization of all the potential treatment modalities available in the setting, residential treatment may be little more than a place where children reside while receiving therapy once or twice per week.

Second, once the newcomer begins working in residential treatment, there is little opportunity for learning more about the field. The work is intense and absorbing, affording little time to peruse professional literature. This is compounded by the fact that relevant professional literature is sparse. There are few books on the subject. Relevant articles are rare and scattered throughout numerous journals in psychology, social work, child welfare, corrections, psychiatry, and education. Many apparently relevant articles are so situation- or case-specific as to have little or no value for the average worker or a given residential setting. The chance of happening upon an article that is relevant to a current issue in a given setting is small.

Third, referrals are often inappropriate. Residential treatment is avoided, recommended only as a last resort. This not only delays needed treatment, sometimes for years, but also often compounds problems. Children are bounced from one ''less restrictive'' foster home to the next, experiencing one failure after another. During this process, the child learns that she or he can escape any unpleasant placement for a new one by misbehaving sufficiently to get thrown out.

By the time residential treatment is ordered, the child has become significantly more disturbed. Residential placement is avoided because it is restrictive and often seems to be so ineffective. Yet, by the time it is recommended or ordered, a child's problems may have become too severe for the recommended program. Nevertheless, the state agency having custody, now desperate to find placement for an exceptionally difficult child, applies pressure to a program to accept a child whose needs are beyond the program's capabilities, setting up yet another placement for failure.

Fourth, some persons who have responsibilities over residential facilities—administrators, governing boards, or state regulatory agencies—do not seem to have sufficiently high expectations for residential treatment programs or appropriate means to evaluate programs. They monitor and evaluate staff and programs based upon tasks or therapies that are documented and on the timeliness of reports—not on outcome or results achieved. We get what we pay for. State agencies contract and pay for "beds" and very often get beds rather than treatment.

Fifth, research is extremely difficult in the residential setting. Indeed, this is one of the reasons that relevant and significant literature is so rare. Research requires time for design, data collection, and analysis. Residential programs are intense. Professional and treatment staff have little or no time for anything beyond the pressing day-to-day needs and demands presented by the residents, not to mention those presented by licensing and funding agencies. Few programs have the personnel to spare for research. Moreover, it is difficult to hold other significant variables constant while the effects of an experimental variable are studied.

For example, shortly after assuming responsibility of a program for twelve adolescent boys, I changed the lighting from standard fluorescent to daylight fluorescent in the facility. During the three months following this change, the boys' performance on the program's token economy improved dramatically and major incidents declined. However, during these same three months, there were also significant changes in staff. Two difficult residents left the program and new residents were admitted. New scheduling patterns improved staff morale. Staff received training in new techniques.

Were improvements due to the change in lighting? Improved staff morale? New and possibly "less

disturbed" residents? Staff training and implementation of new techniques? Some or all of the above? Would it be desirable, fair, or even possible to hold all but one of these variables constant in order to secure experimentally valid data? If a change can be expected to improve treatment, then it is not ethical to delay that change for purposes of experimentation. Children come into placement for treatment, not to contribute data.

Sixth, I have seen no assessment and treatment planning process that readily facilitates the coordination of the many treatment modalities that may be available in the residential setting—individual therapy, behavior therapy, milieu therapy, family therapy, education, counseling, recreational therapy, art therapy, pharmacotherapy, medical and dental care, nutrition. A treatment plan should serve as a blueprint, a helpful guide to those involved in treatment—including the resident and the family. Too often it is only a document to meet licensing requirements.

Effective treatment requires effective assessment. Effective assessment must identify not only needs, problems, or weaknesses but also strengths that will enable the individual to learn and grow. Finally, responsibilities must be clearly assigned to therapists, child "care" staff or houseparents, the child, the family and, possibly, to others.

Most treatment plans that I have seen set appropriate goals. Some have made an attempt at assigning broad responsibilities. None has provided a clear indication as to how the goals will be accomplished, assigned clear responsibility and authority, or provided guidance for the coordination of efforts of the many people who are involved in the treatment of the child, including the child and the family.

Finally, practitioners in residential treatment complain of having to "reinvent the wheel," of having to do something from scratch that most probably someone, somewhere, possibly in the next county, has already done successfully. This is due to a combination of factors: the difficulties with research, the difficulties with professional literature, and the fact that other nearby programs with whom practitioners may have contact are in competition for children to "fill their beds." They are, understandably, guarded about anything that might give them a competitive edge.

I offer this book with some apologies. Most of the topics that are presented have warranted substantial books in their own right. Many are topics for a course or a major concentration of study at undergraduate or graduate levels. Many topics represent the life-work of noted theorists, experimenters, and practitioners. The brief treatment I have been able to give such topics is designed to provide the reader with some understanding of them rather than practicing knowledge or expertise. My purpose is not to create experts but rather to enable a reader who is pursuing or has expertise in one area to work more productively in coordination with practitioners who may have expertise in other areas.

I have experienced the problems with research. Many examples that are offered are anecdotal in nature. Although based upon careful observation and reflection, such examples lack the rigor of scientific research. They must be accepted for what they are, examples offered for illustration or argument, not as scientific proof.

Much that is presented in this text I have learned from years of experience with coworkers, children, and families in a variety of settings, not all residential. It is not possible to give these people specific credit. In most cases, I am unable to determine exactly how, when, or from whom a particular concept evolved.

My target audience is large, perhaps too large. I have been told, in attempting to market this book, that residential treatment will never amount to more than a chapter in an introductory social work text. The most powerful treatment modality should receive just a bit more attention than that.

I have attempted to include things I would have liked to have known when entering residential treatment nearly twenty years ago. I have included things I would have liked my staff to have known or understood during my years of service in residential treatment. I have included things I would like referring professionals and licensing workers and judges to know.

I have especially targeted undergraduate students in psychology, social work, sociology, and criminal justice. For those students, this book will provide a framework, a perspective for the integration of knowledge from the variety of advanced courses in their chosen fields. I have also attempted to write the book to be of use for graduate students, especially in psychology and social work. These students will find it a helpful review of a variety of significant topics. Moreover, I believe advanced students will derive even more from this book because of the greater depth of understanding they bring to much of the material presented.

Further, it is my hope that staff in residential treatment may derive some benefit from the book. I believe that it can facilitate the orientation of newer employees. I believe it may also assist experienced employees in refocusing their endeavors. Perhaps it may also serve as a reference for a given problem.

Lastly, I believe that the book will be helpful to practicing professionals outside of residential treatment who must evaluate children and make referrals. It is my hope that, rather than the alternative of last resort, residential treatment may be recommended and accessed when it can be most effective.

Because of the wide audience, some readers may find portions of this book to be a superficial treatment of areas in which they have expertise. For example, students in social work are likely to have a full course on the history of social services that treats the history and development of residential treatment in some detail. However, students in psychology are less likely to have access to such a course, while students in corrections may have a course treating such historical material from a purely correctional perspective.

Finally, much that is presented is my own, based on years of experiences, some successful, others not so successful, a few outright failures. I will be pleased to the extent that readers may find the contents of this book helpful. I will be just as pleased if the concepts in this book provoke disagreement and subsequent discussion, for I believe the issues, principles, and techniques presented are important and merit as much attention as they may receive.

INTRODUCTION

RESIDENTIAL treatment is one of the most powerful treatment resources available for children and youth with problems. Residential programs exist all around this country and the world for the purpose of treating children with a wide range of problems.

Some programs have evolved from orphanages or in hospital settings. Other programs have been developed as alternatives to hospitalization or incarceration. Some are relatively large, others very small. Some are operated by religious charities or churches, others by state, county, or municipal governments or non-profit agencies. Still others are operated for profit by private individuals, corporations, or national hospital management companies. Some are institutional in nature, others very personal, family-like, or community-based. Yet others are rural and isolated or wilderness-based; a few are sea-based, featuring sailing on tall ships.

Some work with children who are emotionally disturbed or who have behavior disorders, some with children who have developmental disabilities, others with children who are delinquent or "predelinquent"; still others work with youth with psychiatric disorders or autism, while others specialize in neglected or abused children or runaways.

Some are operated by foundations or have substantial endowments, others depend on charitable contributions or United Way funds, while others receive fees from state contracts or the health insurance policies of the families.

Nearly all residential treatment programs, however, have three things in common:

1. Twenty-four hour responsibility for children.
2. The goal of returning the child to the community in some way "better" and able to live a more normal life.
3. The potential to control or exert influence over virtually the total environment of the child.

I have organized the contents of this text into four sections: (1) orientation, (2) theory and concepts, (3) techniques and interventions, and (4) putting it all together. Part I, "An Orientation to Residential Treatment," is designed to provide the reader with an overall perspective. Chapter 1, "Introduction to Residential Treatment: What Makes it So Special?," deals with several important topics. The residential program has a responsibility like no other institution or treatment modality in our society—the near total responsibility for both the care and the treatment of a child. This responsibility gives the residential facility its tremendous power for treatment. Special legal, professional, and ethical accountibilities derive from this responsibility and power. Fulfilling these responsibilities is expensive. Residential treatment programs often exceed the cost of room, board, and tuition at a prestigious university. Finally, the children themselves are special; the attitudes of staff towards the children may be one of the most significant factors in their treatment.

Chapter 2, "History," traces the development of residential treatment in the United States in the context of some other related developments. Understanding the origins of practices and ideas may suggest solutions to situations and help us to avoid mistakes.

Chapter 3, "A Sampling of Programs," presents five programs that represent a variety of approaches to providing for children who cannot live at home.

Chapter 4, "Referral and the Continuum of Care," discusses the range of services and care that may be currently available in many communities and jurisdictions for children and families in need, from least intrusive to most restrictive. Alternatives may range from private counseling and special education services in the school to foster placement, psychiatric hospitalization, or incarceration in a juvenile correctional facility. Understanding where and how the residential program fits into this continuum is essential to understanding its role and the challenges facing residential treatment.

In Part II, "Theories and Concepts," I present some of the theories and concepts that have been influential in residential treatment, or that may be influential in a given program. Many of these concepts have degenerated in contemporary practice. For example, letting a child spend the night in detention for shoplifting has been referred to as Reality Therapy. This may be reality; it has little to do with Glasser's Reality Therapy, however. Structured systems of applying various punitive consequences for undesirable behaviors are sometimes referred to as behavior modification; sometimes a point system is viewed as the main component in the therapeutic milieu. Many times, these are oversimplifications of complex concepts of learning that do considerable disservice to the treatment potential of behavior modification and to the children.

I believe that everyone has some sort of theoretical orientation towards raising children, including parents. Some people have a systematic, carefully formulated theory. Others have a theoretical conceptualization that is mostly intuitive. Chapter 5, "Theory," presents some significant theories in psychology, psychiatry, social work, and sociology. Theories are presented as succinctly as possible and analyzed in terms of their implications for residential treatment, including how they might affect communication and practice.

Chapter 6, "The Milieu," presents a conceptualization of the treatment environment based primarily on the work of Fritz Redl. Redl was one of the more influential proponents of the concept of the treatment milieu in the United States during the mid-twentieth century.

Chapter 7, "Learning Theory and Controlling Behavior," presents principles of learning discovered and advanced by Ivan Pavlov, B.F. Skinner, and other behavior psychologists. Chapter 8, "Group Dynamics," discusses principles of group dynamics based on the perspectives of sociology and social psychology. These principles have countless implications in the treatment milieu.

Part III, "Techniques and Interventions," discusses the application of various techniques in the residential setting. Chapter 9, "Behavior Modification and the Application of Learning Principles," discusses issues relevant to defining behavior and choosing behaviors to change. It discusses choosing and using rewards and punishments with individuals and in the group setting. It concludes with some principles for the use of behavior modification in the residential setting.

Chapter 10, "Using Behavior Modification for Management, Treatment, and Therapy," proposes definitions for the concepts of behavior management, behavior treatment, and behavior therapy. When behavior modification is used primarily for management purposes, it is often erroneously assumed that treatment is taking place. Outcome sometimes indicates otherwise. Examples are offered of behavior modification for management, treatment, and therapy as used with individuals and in group settings.

Chapter 11, "Techniques and Interventions for Staff," offers some specific techniques that can be used by houseparents or shift personnel in a variety of often-encountered circumstances. Topics include normal activities, active communication, the teaching interaction, the life-space interview, and treatment of enuresis.

Chapter 12, "Therapeutic Crisis Intervention," discusses behavioral crisis as an opportunity for treatment. A model for conceptualizing crises is presented. Various techniques, including time-out, control rooms, five-point restraints, chemical restraints, and passive physical restraint are discussed and evaluated in terms of legal implications and long-term effects.

Many skilled professional interventions requiring formal advanced study and possibly professional licensure or certification may be available in a given residential setting. It is important that other staff and professionals have some understanding of such interventions. They must know what to expect from these interventions and their limitations. Further, such practitioners are dependent upon others for information and feedback, who must know what information to look for and communicate. Individual psychotherapy, art therapy, pharmacotherapy, group therapy, and education are presented in chapter 13, "Professional Interventions."

Historically, when children were removed from their families for institutional placement, families were discouraged from involvement with the child in residential placement. Family involvement, however, is now deemed important in more and more programs. A model for family involvement and some techniques for working with families are presented in chapter 14, "Family Interventions."

In Part IV, "Putting It All Together," I attempt to do just that. In chapter 15, "Assessment, Treatment Planning, and Progress Review," I offer a model for assessment that facilitates the identification of a child's strengths and needs in a format that will facilitate concurrent treatment in a number of modalities. Next, I offer a treatment planning format that facilitates the clear identification of

goals and strategies, including the clear assignment of responsibilities to various treatment modalities and personnel, as well as to the child and family. Finally, I present a format for progress reporting that simplifies this often dreaded task and facilitates the measurement and reporting of progress clearly and concisely for the child, family, staff, and courts.

Chapter 16, "Fine Tuning the Milieu," discusses the residential experience from preplacement through discharge and aftercare. It discusses relevant issues at each phase, identifies relevant principles, and suggests techniques. Other topics include runaways, staff burnout, and the hiring and orientation of staff.

Chapter 17, "Referral: The Continuum of Care Revisited," discusses the referral process. It reviews the continuum of care and suggests some guidelines that may be helpful in making placement recommendations and decisions. Indications and contraindictions are suggested for each component that may be available within the system of care.

I have included some additional material in appendices. Appendix A, "Multiple Placement Syndrome," is a description of a "disorder" I have encountered on several occasions. It is offered somewhat tongue-in-cheek in *DSM-III-R* format. Appendix B contains blank forms for assessment, treatment planning, and progress reporting as described in chapter 15. Appendix C, "Urine Screening for Substance Abuse," discusses some issues relevant to this procedure, which is gaining in popularity in a variety of settings.

PART I

Part I provides an orientation to residential treatment. Chapter 1, "Residential Treatment: What Makes It So Special?," is an introduction offered from the perspective of factors that set residential treatment apart from virtually all other fields of working with people: responsibility, accountability, cost, and the children themselves. Chapter 2, "History," provides a brief history of the development of residential treatment in the United States. Chapter 3, "A Sampling of Programs," presents some details about five specific programs that offer residential services from different perspectives. Chapter 4 places residential treatment within the continuum of care for children and discusses the processes by which children may come into care and, possibly, into residential treatment.

ORIENTATION TO

RESIDENTIAL

TREATMENT

Introduction to Residential Treatment: What Makes It So Special?

THIS chapter deals with six important issues that make residential treatment a unique treatment intervention and a unique place in which to work:

1. The residential treatment facility has nearly total responsibility for both the care and the treatment of each child.
2. The residential treatment facility has unique power for treatment that it derives from its nearly total responsibility for care.
3. The legal, civil, and ethical accountabilities of the residential facility, deriving from its responsibility and power, are unique.
4. There is irony in the residential program's responsibility—it has nearly total responsibility for the child, yet one of its main goals is to teach children to be more responsible for themselves.
5. Residential treatment is uniquely expensive.
6. Finally, and most importantly, the children themselves make residential treatment a unique environment. In spite of their problems, sometimes because of them, the children are exciting, invigorating, rewarding, and fun.

RESPONSIBILITY

"Billy hit me and I didn't do anything to him." "My shoes fell apart and it's the only pair I have." "My throat hurts." "I can't eat that. I'm allergic to seafood." "He said my mamma." "I need five dollars for school tomorrow." "Somebody took my English book." "I need a haircut." "We're out of toilet paper." "If she doesn't stop bugging me, I'm going to deck her." "Robert has a knife in his room." "I'm hungry, I wanna eat now." "Jennifer said she's going to run away tonight." "I went off because for the simple reason when Carl put me in my room, he threw me on the bed and slammed my head into the wall." "Can I go to the school dance this Friday?" "I called my mother and the phone's disconnected." "My uncle died and the funeral's tomorrow. Can I go?" "Betty has marijuana." "I'm not going to school because I'm not wearing the same clothes I wore yesterday. I told the staff I don't have any clothes." "Can I room with Darlene? I can't stand Elaine." "I'm better now. I want to go home."

The residential treatment center has nearly total control over the environment of a child. This provides the program with tremendous treatment potential. It also bestows tremendous responsibilities. In accepting a child for treatment, the program accepts the child for care. No other human service agency, from the mental health center or family guidance clinic to the boarding school or medical hospital, has the ethical, civil, or legal responsibilities of the residential treatment program.

Parents have been caring for children for as long as there have been people; therapists have been treating children and families for considerably less time, but nevertheless, for many years. Are the responsibilities of the residential treatment center for care and treatment different from those of the parent or the therapist? For a number of reasons, yes.

The Nature of Responsibility

Responsibility is a complex concept that depends on a number of related factors. Where does the responsibility come from? How is it acquired? Who shares it? What is the accountability? What are the consequences? The residential program derives its responsibilities from several sources.

Legal Responsibilities from State and Local Laws and Ordinances

Certain state and local statutes and ordinances relating to such things as school attendance, curfews, property damage, and alcohol and controlled substances apply to minors. These laws may hold parents or persons *in loco parentis* in some way responsible or accountable for the behavior of their children, e.g., for school attendance or property damage.

Responsibilities from Regulatory Agencies

Various federal, state, and local regulations apply to food service, sanitation, safety, building codes, child labor, wage and hour, etc. These regulations affect not only the program's responsibilities towards its residents but also its responsibilities towards its employees and the public.

Constitutional Responsibilities

Court decisions have found certain provisions of the Bill of Rights to apply to residents of institutions. These court decisions place some very specific responsibilities on residential treatment centers.

Responsibility from Licensing Authorities

With few exceptions, programs are required to be licensed. Licensing standards enumerate specific responsibilities for care and treatment.

Responsibilities from Funding Sources

Programs are likely to have contracts for funding with one or more state agencies. They may have agreements with other public agencies or private insurance companies. These contracts and agreements detail specific responsibilities for care and treatment.

Responsibility Deriving from Those Placing the Child

One aspect of a residential program's responsibility for a child is the responsibility the program accepts from the person or agency placing the child. A child may be placed by parents or by a state agency, either through welfare and child protection procedures or through juvenile justice procedures.

Voluntary Parental Placement. In voluntary placements, parents retain legal custody of the child but assign responsibility for care and treatment to the agency in an agreement at the time of placement. Normally, the parent can terminate the agreement at any time and remove the child. Thus, the parent retains ultimate responsibility for the child, assigning or delegating responsibility to the residential program.

Placement by a State Agency. When the state arranges placement, either for care and protection or for criminal or status offenses, an agency of the state usually retains custody. In these cases the facility accepts responsibility for care and treatment from the state agency at the time of placement.

Although the state can remove the child at any time, the facility is likely to have considerable influence with state workers in most decisions about the child's leaving. Thus, while the legal responsibilities of the residential program may be about the same as in a voluntary placement, ethically, the responsibilities may be greater to the extent that the program wields influence with the state agency for continued placement.

Responsibilities from Negotiated Agreements with the Family and Child

Programs usually negotiate agreements for service of individual children with the child, parents, and state workers at the time of placement. These agreements may detail specific responsibilities.

The Responsibility for Care

Care of a minor child for any period of time entails providing food and shelter. Clothing will have to be provided if the stay is for more than a few months and may be necessary upon admission for some children. Care requires providing for the child's education. When the care extends for several months, it also entails training in normal, age-appropriate, personal, social, and life skills, including training in hygiene, manners, care of clothes and other possessions, shopping, sex education, money management, job-seeking skills, apartment hunting, and other independent living skills. The care responsibility is to provide for the normal development of the child; correcting deficiencies in these areas is a treatment issue.

Care includes caring for the child's health, providing for treatment in the event of illness, injury, or toothache, providing for annual medical and dental checkups, and following through on recommended treatment. Care includes providing age-appropriate supervision to protect the child from dangers and situations the child is not prepared to handle.

Each responsibility for care can become more difficult in the residential setting. Care issues may not only require more time and effort than treatment issues but also, at times, conflict with treatment

issues. When properly managed, care issues can complement and support treatment.

Food

Schools that serve meals are expected to provide meals in accordance with dietary standards and to have a dietician review menus and other aspects of food service. Children usually have the option to pack lunch. Further, parents still have the primary responsibility for the child's nutrition, providing for more than half of the child's meals.

The residential program is likewise expected to provide meals in accordance with dietary standards and have a dietician review the food service program. Children do not have the option to bring lunch from home. Unlike the schools, however, the residential program has nearly total responsibility to ensure that its children are properly nourished. The program must be prepared to deal with the child who eats no vegetables, doesn't like anything that's served at tonight's supper, refuses to come to a meal, refuses to get up for breakfast, throws food necessitating removal from the meal, or overeats to the point of health-threatening obesity.

Allowing a child to suffer the natural consequences of behavior can be a reasonable means of teaching the child, depending on the consequences. It may be considered reasonable to allow a child to go hungry if the child refuses a food or a meal. Most of us have heard the maxim, "If you were really hungry, you'd be glad to eat that." But consider Jimmy.

> *Jimmy.* **Jimmy refused to get up for school in the morning and missed breakfast. Skillful counseling persuaded Jimmy to go to school in time for the second period. Remotivated, Jimmy rushed out the door, forgetting his lunch ticket. Rather than tell anyone, he spent the lunch period on the playground, skipping lunch. He could not be persuaded to eat the liver that was served that night. "If I have to eat that, I'll throw up."**

Food in the Group Setting. Nutrition may be further complicated by the group setting. A new child care worker quickly realizes the mistake in fixing Jimmy a sandwich because he "can't" eat liver when beans are served the next night and half the group wants peanut butter and jelly instead. But consider explaining to Tina that she can't have a substitute for liver when Jennifer gets a special plate whenever fish is served because Jennifer is allergic to seafood.

It may be reasonable to allow a child to choose to skip a meal for a number of reasons, knowing the consequence will be waiting until the next meal. Permitting a child to go without food for a full day is neglect. Consider the implications if the precipitating factor in this child's placement was parental neglect; his mother left him at home for days at a time with no food in the house. The social worker knows that Jimmy has to be fed; the counselor knows there will be a problem if Jimmy receives special consideration.

Food and Treatment. Treatment issues can further complicate the management of proper nutrition. In the following example, everything was going fine for William until he was ordered to be placed on a special diet.

> **William. William was a thirteen-year-old who was in placement because of serious behavior problems at home and in school, including fights, threatening teachers and his mother, and temper tantrums during which he threw things. He was 5′ 7″ tall and weighed 243 pounds. It was suspected that food was extremely significant in the family life. "Here is a boy who likes his meat and potatoes." "Look how much William has grown." "Here's a fine, big boy." Food had probably been associated with good behavior, withholding food with "bad" behavior.**
>
> **William made an excellent initial adjustment to the program. He responded well to the structured study hall after dinner and went to school every day with his homework completed. Problems at school decreased and William enjoyed the privileges and attention he earned upon return from school.**
>
> **His formal treatment plan was written during his first thirty days. The dietician had recommended that he lose sixty pounds; a diet was part of his treatment plan. William responded to attempts to limit his food with temper outbursts, which resulted in daily restrictions. He was angry in study hall after dinner and did not get his work done. He didn't accept criticism well in school about his incomplete homework and had problems nearly every day. Of course, he couldn't use any privileges he might earn for school behavior since he was already on restriction for several temper outbursts at mealtimes. Should the diet be discontinued or postponed until treatment gains in school have become more firmly established?**

Spoiled Food. Even an occasional full-time food service establishment whose primary function is the preparation and serving of food may serve something that is not fit to eat. Sometimes, especially in smaller programs and on weekends, staff whose primary responsibilities are for supervising and treating the children may have responsibilities for preparing and serving food. Their interest, talent, and abilities in cooking may be limited. Such staff may be faced with a refrigerator containing food bought or stored by other staff on other shifts. Unless such items are carefully dated and labelled, residents may be served food that has spoiled.

Food and Nurturing Care. A program may meet its responsibilities for feeding its residents very adequately and yet miss the potential that food has for contributing to the environment in which the child receives treatment. What is the message when a child sees her food being prepared with care and pride, with fresh ingredients and carefully prepared seasonings, sauces, and gravies? What is the message when meat is thrown in the oven and served with instant potatoes and canned beans? Or when the child is marched to a cafeteria to get institutional food served by cranky help who give larger servings to the staff? How the program meets the very basic responsibility of feeding its children says quite a bit about how much the program really "cares" for its children.

Clothing

The responsibility of the program is to ensure that the child is reasonably clothed for a given situation or activity such as school, court, swimming, an outing sponsored by a volunteer group, rain, snow, heat, or cold. The clothes must be neat, clean, and in good repair.

Children in residential settings may take clothes home on pass and give them to siblings, leave a jacket or shoes on the playground at school or on an outing, trade a pair of shoes for a skate board, or carelessly leave clothes lying around to be stolen. An encopretic may flush soiled underwear down the toilet (usually, only far enough to clog the line). Armed with an agency purchase order, a child care worker may be faced with a child refusing all of the clothes available in the designated store.

Sometimes parents, feeling badly about having had to place a child, try to make it up to the child by buying the best of designer clothes. Other times, parents complain when the program outfits their child with an adequate supply of fairly standard clothing. It creates problems for them when they cannot provide so well for the children at home, who must wear hand-me-downs and thrift store clothing.

Shelter

Finally, something easy. Providing shelter means providing a safe and reasonably comfortable environment. A roof over the head, a bed to sleep in, heat and, probably, air conditioning. Basic and simple. Until a child has a temper tantrum and breaks five windows on a cold night. Or gets scalded before getting the shower adjusted properly. Or shoots off a fire extinguisher to see how it works. Or gets into the medicine locker and takes some pills to get high—only they don't make him high; they produce convulsions. Or gets beat up in the bathroom while one staff is escorting a child to his room and the other staff is on the phone with a parent.

The physical environment must be safe in accordance with state and local health, sanitation, building, electrical, fire, and licensing codes applicable to businesses, public places, and institutions. It must be safe not only in terms of the ages of the children served but also with regard to the types of problems they can reasonably be expected to present, the social environment that exists within it, and the level of supervision the program provides. It must allow for reasonable privacy and acceptable comfort.

Implications for Supervision. The physical environment has significant implications for supervision. Shower areas for two or more, as opposed to private baths, provide opportunity for children to engage in impulsive sexual experimentation. Such behavior is relatively normal, but it is difficult or unpleasant to explain to parents or state workers. Congregate bath areas also provide opportunity for sexual battery. It is indeed unfortunate for a child to be removed from a home to protect him from sexual abuse only to be placed in a setting where he receives more abuse.

Other areas that are difficult to supervise may provide opportunities for strong-arm activities and intimidation to fleece a child out of money, a valued item of clothing, or a favorite toy or necklace. Such areas may also facilitate clique formations that may undermine treatment efforts on any number of levels.

Naturally, the more time and energy staff must spend on supervision to overcome problems caused by the facility's limitations, the less time and effort they have available for treatment and other activities that support treatment such as recording, report writing, and most importantly, simply enjoying kids. Shelter also has implications for intake. Is it ethical to accept a child with a known history of punching holes in walls and breaking windows only to transfer the child in a few months because of excessive damage? Is it ethical to accept a child who will pose a threat to other residents, or a child who will be at risk from other residents, if facility design and supervision can't protect vulnerable children?

Education

Just as parents are responsible for getting their children to go to school, and, sometimes, for their children's behavior in school, so is the residential program. However, the program often accepts a child knowing that school attendance and behavior are significant problems. Moreover, in many cases, the program provides the school. In other cases, the program may have significant influence with the public school system about which school the child might attend, or in what programs within the school the child might participate.

Finally, the program's reputation in the community may have significant effect on a child's attendance or behavior in school. One program made an annual Christmas appeal on the three local TV stations for donations of any type. The appeal embarrassed the residents, several of whom flatly refused to attend school after the appeal each year. The examples that follow belie the tremendous amount of time and energy devoted to education.

Pauline. **Pauline, a sixteen-year-old eighth grade student, wanted to drop out of school and attend Votech. It was reasonable, since she would be almost twenty-one upon high school graduation with no further setbacks, and past history suggested that there would be continuing setbacks. Mom and Dad, however, were dead set against her dropping out of school, which really meant they were dead set against her getting her own way.**

Barry. **Barry was in a similar situation. He wanted to drop out of school and work on his GED. This seemed reasonable, except that all he talked about was becoming a Marine. The Marine Corps requires formal high school graduation.**

Stanley. **Stanley was attending public school in a special education class for behaviorally disordered students. He was reportedly "doing well" and had done "well" in the class for nearly three years. He was performing on the second to third grade level when he was placed in the class. Three years later, he was still testing on the second to third grade level despite normal intelligence.**

Robert. **Robert was a fourteen-year-old sixth grade student. He failed his first year in the sixth grade. The next year, he was expelled in February. He failed his third year in the sixth grade because of too many absences, so he was repeating the sixth grade once again when he came into placement. However, he was performing on late seventh to mid-eighth grade levels on achievement tests in English, reading, and math. His scores, along with the tutoring the group home provided and Robert's strides in behavior and motivation, suggested that he could pass the eighth grade and have a reasonable chance of completing high school by the age of eighteen. The school, however, would not place him in the eighth grade, nor even in the seventh grade.**

Hygiene

Hygiene includes the basic care of one's body to maintain good body health and socially acceptable grooming. Many children come with excellent hygiene habits; others do not. The residential program is responsible for providing the necessities, bath and toilet facilities and supplies, laundry service or laundry facilities, and for providing the necessary supervision. It is also responsible for teaching the necessary skills and habits for those who do not have them or prefer not to use them.

In the group setting, this responsibility can become more difficult. A case of scabies, head lice, or pinworms may present special concerns. The following examples illustrate some aspects of meeting this responsibility in the residential setting.

A licensing violation. **A facility was cited in a licensing review for failure to have toilet paper on the holders in two of the three children's bathrooms. These adolescents of normal intelligence were responsible for maintaining their own living areas, including bathrooms. Toilet paper and other supplies were issued upon request from the staff office, which was located between the two bathrooms.**

Denny. **Denny came back from the barber without a haircut. The barber had refused to cut his hair because he had found head lice. The agency's physician prescribed a special shampoo and ordered that all boys wash their hair leaving the shampoo on for five minutes. He also ordered that all linens be washed with a cup of the shampoo added with the detergent. Richard refused to use the smelly stuff for two days and had to be isolated from the other boys. The program could not force him to comply. He finally acquiesced when told by the agency and his parents that he could not leave for his home pass without completing the treatment.**

Teaching Age-Appropriate Personal, Social, and Life Skills

Considering everything else with which the residential treatment program must contend, one might expect the teaching of normal, age-appropriate skills to be one of the least difficult areas of responsibility. Except, perhaps, that the program may have to contend with some poor role modeling by inappropriate peers. It is not unusual for parents to complain that their child's language has deteriorated since admission, for example. Or consider the implications if a fifteen-year-old "gets a girl pregnant." Then consider the implications if the girl is also a resident of the program.

The saddest aspect of this responsibility is in attempting to assist an eighteen-year-old to live on his or her own. The eighteen-year-old leaving a family to set up housekeeping is likely to receive some furniture and dishes and have the option to return home if things get too tough. The eighteen-year-old leaving residential treatment is likely to have little help and no chance to return. Programs can't afford to keep space available and states will not fund the cost of care for "adults." When a state-funded program allows such a young adult to return as a charity case, it means that funds the state is paying for other children are being diverted to an "adult." In many localities, the only residential services provided for adults are jails, mental hospitals, and emergency shelters.

Health and Dental Care

Again, this appears to be a fairly straightforward responsibility. The agency must simply find a good physician and a good dentist who accept Medicaid and get the child whatever checkups and care are required.

When to Seek Medicaid Care. Is the best course of action to secure professional care for any complaint? Obviously it is not reasonable to visit a physician at the first sign of a headache or upset stomach when there has been no injury and there is no other cause for additional concern. Few of us can afford the time or expense involved in seeking medical care indiscriminately. A number of children in residential treatment want to be taken to the doctor for every complaint and may put up quite a fuss when their complaint does not produce immediate action. What are the treatment implications of taking a child to the doctor or emergency room for every little complaint, then sending her home to a self-employed auto mechanic with no health insurance after she has "met all her treatment objectives"?

Barry. **Barry was a somewhat shy thirteen-year-old who had lost his mother a few years ago and was being raised by his maternal grandmother, whose husband had recently died. In addition to some shoplifting, Barry was failing in school. He came into placement through the Department of Corrections as a condition of his probation. At his initial dental exam, orthodontic treatment was recommended to correct a malocclusion. Further, Barry was somewhat embarrassed by his "buck" teeth. After eight months of letters and phone conversations, the state rendered the decision that it would not pay for "cosmetic" dentistry.**

Tom. **One Saturday while playing football on an outing at a nearby park, Tom hurt his foot. He sat out the remainder of the activity. Medical treatment was not indicated for what appeared to be a slight bruise or sprain. Tom did not want to interrupt the other boys. He also did not want to miss the outing** to an arcade that was to follow. Later that night, Tom mentioned his injury to his parents, who asked permission to take him to the emergency room where he was diagnosed as having a stress fracture.

The attending physician stated that no treatment was necessary, that the fracture would heal readily so long as Tom stayed off it as much as possible. Within two days, Tom was found playing basketball. A few days later, he failed to return from school and was found trying out for the basketball team.

A follow up x-ray two weeks later showed that the break had not yet begun to heal. The physician stated that a cast would be necessary if no healing were evident in two more weeks and that surgery might be indicated if all else failed. Tom's parents were not satisfied, felt that the doctor was incompetent, and wanted to take Tom to a doctor of their choice. Arrangements were made; the doctor put a walking cast on Tom's foot. Even with the cast, Tom had to be monitored constantly to keep him from running and jumping on the foot.

Sick call. In a large residential facility with a number of small units for children of different ages, children who complained of illness were sent to the nurse. There were "sick calls" at 7:30 A.M. and after school. The nurse determined whether or not children should be taken to the doctor, be put on bed rest, or be given aspirins or some other over-the-counter medication.

A few of the boys on the adolescent unit didn't like school and frequently complained of illness in the morning. When the nurse found nothing wrong and refused them an excuse for school, the boys became loud and verbally abusive. Staff were being summoned to the clinic almost daily to escort boys who should have been able to walk to and from the clinic on their own.

According to the boys, they got angry because they felt the nurse didn't believe them when they said they didn't feel well. Consultation with the nurse revealed that she felt intimidated by some of the older boys

and uncomfortable with the role of telling them they had to go to school.

A plan was worked out whereby the nurse would offer sympathy and appropriate medication while expressing confidence in their ability to "tough it out" and meet their responsibilities for the day despite the extra effort that would be required. Problems at the clinic decreased and, eventually, so did the number of visits to the clinic.

The Responsibility for Supervision

Parents and schools are expected to provide age-appropriate supervision. Young children require direct supervision; junior high and middle school children can be expected to play in a defined area that is free of obvious hazards when an adult is within distance to be readily summoned; older teens can be expected to be on their own in situations that are defined by reasonable limits.

In addition to age-appropriate supervision, the residential program is expected to provide supervision appropriate to the functioning level of children who have been identified as having problems of some kind. Moreover, the residential program has accepted the child into a setting with other children who have problems.

The residential program has a number of responsibilities with regard to supervision:

1. The residential program is responsible for the safety of residents in the program.
2. It is responsible for the behavior of residents in the program.
3. It is responsible for the behavior of residents under its supervision in the community.
4. It is responsible for the behavior of residents who are in the community with the program's permission.
5. It is responsible for the decisions and actions of its staff as well as their failure to act.

Sometimes these are legal responsibilities arising from criminal statutes, laws, or regulations that may carry legal penalties or allow for civil action;

other times the responsibilities are merely ethical. The following cases illustrate some aspects of the responsibility for protection. In the first case, supervision fails to protect a resident from other residents. In the second case, a staff member fails to take action to protect the child. In the third case, a supervisor decides to make an exception to policy, which results in a situation in which he could not provide the necessary supervision.

David. David was taken into protective custody because of several instances of sexual abuse by his mother's boyfriend, who lived off and on in the home for over ten years. David exhibited some effeminate mannerisms. One night after bed time, when the only staff on duty was distracted (in the bathroom, on the phone with a supervisor, asleep, or whatever), David was sexually assaulted by three other boys on the unit (possibly with his consent).

Richard and the missing relatives. Fourteen-year-old Richard had been in the custody of the state since he was three; no relatives had any interest in him. Several foster placements did not work out due to his aggressive responses to limits and criticism and his refusal of discipline. He had been in residential care for several years. One evening, he became angry with a staff person, lowered his head, and charged. The staff person disapproved of violence and stepped aside rather than engage Richard physically. Richard struck his head on a wall, broke his neck, and was paralyzed. Relatives came by plane to participate in legal action against the agency.

Shawn. Shawn was sentenced to residential placement for aggravated sexual battery. The victim had been an elderly woman. The charge was hard to believe; Shawn was mildly retarded and very timid. In horseplay one evening, Shawn bumped his head on the pool table. Staff felt that medical treatment was indicated and called for assistance. The supervisor on-call came in to take Shawn to the hospital.

Another boy with a cold requested treatment at the same time. The supervisor took both boys to the local hospital emergency room. At the hospital, the boy with the cold began using profanity and the supervisor remained with him in the emergency room while the x-ray technician took Shawn downstairs for x-rays. Shawn locked the door to the x-ray room and intimidated the technician into removing her clothes. He had her on the floor when police arrived to break down the door.

State regulations and agency policy required that two staff supervise whenever two or more residents were taken off grounds. The x-ray technician and her husband sued both the hospital and the program. The program's malpractice insurer successfully defended the case but refused the renewal of the agency's insurance, resulting in the agency's going out of business. (The hospital was found negligent. The x-ray room was in a corridor that was unoccupied at that time of night; the hospital should have had an orderly accompany the x-ray technician and the patient.)

The Responsibility for Protection

There is one other area of responsibility that warrants special attention, that of reporting abuse under child protection statutes. This responsibility is incumbent on anyone working with children, including doctors, private therapists, school teachers, and staff in residential centers.

The Smiths seek help. Mr. and Mrs. Smith came to the office to inquire about help with their son, who was totally unmanageable, cursing, making threats, punching holes in walls, and leaving the house without permission. He was in danger of being expelled from school. He had a bruise by his left eye. His father had disciplined him.

Judith. Judith returned from home pass with a swollen lip. She had cursed her mother, who slapped her.

Danny and a case of institutional abuse. Danny's state worker had promised to arrange a meeting with Danny and his parents that week to discuss Danny's discharge home. Danny had been in placement for over four years in several facilities. Danny thought the meeting was supposed to be on Wednesday. The meeting, however, had been arranged for Thursday at 1:00 P.M. As the program director approached Danny, Danny burst into a verbal tirade about being lied to once again, said he'd had it and was leaving. He had his jacket in his hand and put it on. The program director put his hand on Danny's shoulder and began to tell Danny that the meeting was set for tomorrow. Danny started for the stairs.

The program director held Danny, but Danny got to the stairs and managed to start down with the program director still holding on. Letting go would have caused Danny to lose his balance and fall. In the struggle on the stairs, Danny received a nasty brush burn on his cheek from rough paneling in the stair well. Staff came to assist and Danny was taken to the office without further incident. He attended the meeting and was discharged in two weeks.

The program director reported the incident to the child protection office. Abuse was substantiated; it was held that the program director should not have attempted to prevent this fourteen-year-old from leaving by physical intervention.

Bill's girlfriend. Bill seemed a little down for a few days. He eventually told his social worker that his girlfriend had told him that her father was having sex with her. When the social worker told Bill that the allegation had to be reported to authorities, Bill began to cry and begged the social worker not to report it.

The Responsibility for Treatment

Treatment is, after all, what the residential treatment center purports to do. "Patients are selected for the purpose of treatment" (Weber & Haberlein, 1972, p. 56). Child guidance centers, mental health clinics, family counseling agencies, day treatment centers, private practitioners, and others offer treatment to children. In what ways are the treatment responsibilities of the residential treatment center different?

Mental health and family counseling agencies, as well as private therapists, may see the child from one to several hours per week; they may also see the family. Therapists in such settings share their responsibilities for a child with the family and with the community. They are dependent on others for information—the child, the parents, possibly a school, state worker, or probation officer. Such therapists may devise strategies that involve the parents and, possibly, the school. They may recommend implementation of techniques that may be beneficial or the cessation of injurious techniques, but these matters are beyond their direct control; others are responsible for implementation. The child continues to be subject to a number of other influences: peers, teachers, television, movies, neighbors, etc. Parents and the child may often discontinue treatment at will. Day treatment programs accept considerably more responsibility for clients, but they are still far short of total responsibility.

The residential program, on the other hand, has the child twenty-four hours per day, seven days per week, except perhaps for community school, employment, or passes. Even so, the program may have considerable responsibility for deciding whether or not the child goes to outside school or work, or has a pass. The residential program is dependent on others for historical information about the child, but it is responsible for nearly all current information about the child.

The residential program is responsible not only for planning treatment strategies but also for implementing them. It is responsible not only for controlling the child's environment but also for creating it. It is responsible not only for maintaining the physical environment, directing its employees and controlling the child's peers, but also for having selected the facility, staff, and peers. In most cases, the program has the right to refuse to accept the child for treatment. Thus, whatever may be interfering with treatment is very likely to be the responsibility of the residential program.

The residential program incurs additional responsibilities for treatment to the extent that it limits the treatment choices of the child and the family. It may be responsible not only for the treatment that is provided but also for decisions about how and when that treatment will end. Many children in residential placement are in the custody of the state. In such cases, premature termination of treatment by the child or parent, even failure to return a child as scheduled from a pass, may result in the filing of a runaway report with the local police department. The child may then be returned by the police upon apprehension, even from home; the parents may face charges for harboring a runaway. The child's choices are even more limited when the child is on a locked unit and can't even run away. Ideally, many people will share in the responsibility for the treatment of a child: the child, parents, a probation officer, child protection worker, foster care worker, and family court judge. In reality, participation by others may be quite limited, and the residential treatment center is likely to have significant influence with those who do participate.

The Right to Treatment

A number of court decisions have implications for residential treatment that are primarily related to the extent to which the resident's placement is voluntary or the resident's freedom is restricted. *Lake v. Cameron* (1966) established the concept of the least restrictive alternative for persons committed by the state for protection, placing upon the state the obligation of showing that a placement that was less intrusive would not be effective (Heads, 1978).

Rouse v. Cameron (1966) established the right of persons who were confined involuntarily in public mental hospitals to receive adequate and appropriate treatment or to be released. This decision

was based on the constitutional guarantees of due process, of protection against cruel and unusual punishment, and of equal protection under the law as provided for in the Fifth, Eighth, and Fourteenth Amendments (Heads, 1978).

Morales v. Turman (1974) established the same right for juveniles. ''It is not sufficient . . . to contend that merely removing a child from his environment and placing him in a 'structured' situation constitutes constitutionally adequate treatment'' (Heads, 1978, p. 421). *Morales v. Turman* also established the precedent of an individualized plan of treatment. Providing a token economy with the same goals for everyone was not considered adequate. Neither was systematically structuring the environment and calling it a therapeutic milieu. Treatment by an untrained staff with poor supervision was likened to cruel and unusual punishment. Periodic progress reviews were also required (Heads, 1978).

The right to treatment for persons diagnosed as mentally ill without having committed a crime was established in *Donaldson v. O'Connor* (1975). It was held that it is justifiable to deprive a person of liberty because of danger to self or others only when treatment is provided. Two of the institution's psychiatrists were fined, having been held personally liable for depriving a person of his liberty (Heads, 1978).

The concept of ''protection from harm'' (Heads, 1978, p. 422) had previously been derived from the Eighth Amendment prohibition against cruel and unusual punishment. In *Wyatt v. Stickney* (1972), it was held that ''harm can result not only from neglect but from conditions which cause regression or which prevent development of an individual's capabilities'' (Head, 1978, p. 422). The formation of a human rights committee was mandated, and certain basic rights were established that could not be made contingent on behavior or used as privileges. The standards developed apply to retarded persons in institutions, but the relevance of the principles to other children in other residential settings is obvious (Heads, 1978).

Care versus Treatment: An Issue of Terminology

Treatment and care are both important. Both receive attention in the literature. In 1960, Alt emphasized treatment in *Residential Treatment for the Disturbed Child: Basic Principles in Planning and Design of Programs and Facilities.* Mayer, Richman, and Balcerzak, in 1978, emphasized care in *Group Care of Children: Crossroads and Transitions,* as did Adler in 1981 in *Fundamentals of Group Child Care: A Text Book and Instructional Guide for Child Care Workers.* Schaefer and Swanson's (1988) *Children in Residential Care: Critical Issues in Treatment* uses both terms in its title.

Unfortunately, the terms ''care'' and ''treatment'' sometimes seem to be used indiscriminately or interchangeably. Each is extremely important in the residential treatment setting. They are related; they are *not* different aspects of the same thing. We can provide residential care without providing treatment. We cannot provide residential treatment without providing care. For that reason, I use the term residential treatment throughout this book.

Likewise, the term ''child care worker'' belies the treatment contributions and potential for treatment of these staff. Whatever their capabilities for treatment, given their backgrounds and training, they spend nearly 168 hours per week with the children. The professionals, psychiatrists, social workers, and psychologists, on the other hand, may only spend minutes or hours with a child. By virtue of the time they spend with the children, they represent the strongest force for (or against) treatment in the residential program. For these reasons, I use the term child care counselor throughout this book.

Accountability

While providing care to a minor child in residential treatment is not always easy and may be complicated by a number of factors, the quality of care that is provided is fairly easy to assess—food, clothing, shelter, medical attention, supervision, etc., are either being provided in accordance with acceptable standards or they are not being provided in accordance with acceptable standards.

Licensing workers inspect facilities regularly, and protection workers investigate allegations of neglect or abuse. Significant violations may result in the issuing of a provisional license and/or a freeze on referrals until corrections have been made, or the facility's license may be revoked and the children removed.

Accountability for treatment is a much more complicated matter. Applicable standards tend to detail treatment services that must be provided and treatment processes that must be followed. They establish standards for the timeliness and content of treatment plans, for the amount of individual, group, and family therapy that must be provided and documented, and for periodic reviews of progress that must be documented. They do not deal with outcome or results. Agencies may be held accountable for failing to follow prescribed procedures or for failing to provide prescribed services; agencies are rarely held accountable for not getting results.

THE IRONY OF RESPONSIBILITY

One of the primary responsibilities in caring for children is to protect them from things and situations they cannot be expected to manage. Another equally important responsibility is to prepare them to be responsible for themselves by the time they reach adulthood. Helping children to assume age-appropriate responsibilities for themselves is always a care issue. It is most often an issue for treatment, as well, since many children in residential treatment have demonstrated a marked inability to assume age-appropriate responsibilities.

Preparing children to be responsible for themselves generally requires assisting them in acquiring the necessary knowledge, attitudes, resources, abilities, and skills to empower them to do so. This can rarely be accomplished well without some cooperation from the child. Thus, the child has some responsibility in the matter. Moreover, since people often learn best by doing, children should have increasing opportunities to practice responsibility, to assume responsibility for themselves in accordance with their developing abilities, and to experience consequences of their choices and decisions.

Allowing Children Increased Responsibility

Allowing children to practice responsibility may result in some problems. Children misbehave and make mistakes. Sometimes there are no consequences. Other times consequences may be minor: a scratch on a piece of furniture, a broken dish or window, a cut or a bruise. Occasionally consequences are more serious: a broken appliance, water damage, a fire, more serious injury, even loss of life. On the other hand, overprotection may result in a child's growing into an irresponsible adult. It is the proverbial thin line.

In the residential setting, however, it is a very significant line. Sensitivity on the part of the residential facility to the possible repercussions of a child's misbehavior in the community may result in a reluctance to allow the child to assume increasing responsibilities in the community. Sensitivity to the potential for lawsuits also results in hesitancy to allow residents to assume responsibilities. For example, I am aware of no program that can readily allow residents to practice the responsibility of driving, not only a very basic skill in our society but also a significant employment skill for many jobs.

Abuse Allegations and the Responsibility of the Child

There is at least one other area that may compromise a child's learning responsibility. When children provoke verbally or physically, there are sometimes questions about the appropriateness of the response by staff. Such questions invariably detract from the child's responsibility for his or her own behavior, despite the consequences that may be applied. It is extremely important for all personnel to maintain the highest standards when responding to a provoking child. It is therapeutically

important to give the child's responsibilities as full and as complete attention as possible before any questions about staff conduct are entertained with the child. This is sometimes very difficult to manage, as the following example illustrates.

Barthe. Barthe was admitted at the age of thirteen after a history of hospitalization and a failed residential placement in which he had incurred frequent discipline. He had problems with peer relations that resulted in teasing which he could not handle. Barthe did pretty well for about a year, then began to require frequent restraint, usually around problems with peers that he frequently set up.

After each restraint, when Barthe met with the program director, Barthe made allegations about staff misconduct—they threw him to the floor, banged his head when escorting to his room and placing him on the bed, banged him into the wall, etc. Although there were never any injuries, such allegations, of course, merited attention by the program director and were duly reported to child protection. Barthe, however, was never excused for his behavior and received the standard consequences, which were relatively mild.

Barthe's problems did not subside. Staff were tired of his frequent problems, which disrupted the program for hours at a time. Barthe was placed on an individualized anger management program. At the same time, the program director decided that he would no longer entertain any discussion by Barthe of staff conduct in response to his acting out behavior. The program director cut Barthe off if he raised any questions at all about staff conduct and redirected Barthe back to his own responsibility in each incident. (The program director did review each restraint carefully, but with no knowledge on Barthe's part.) Restraints decreased, eventually to zero. Barthe resumed progress and returned home successfully, based on a two-year follow up.

When children who frequently require physical intervention make frequent allegations about staff conduct, they are at increased risk of physical intervention that may exceed established guidelines. The frequent restraints are often annoying to staff and supervisors. So are the frequent allegations of abuse. As the patience of staff wears thin, so may their self-control. They may not be as careful with such a child when it has become obvious to everyone that the child has lost credibility, crying "wolf" once too often.

THE COST OF CARE
AND TREATMENT

Many people are shocked when they first learn of the cost of residential treatment. Programs may cost from $60 to $250 per day, $21,900 to $91,250 per year. Compare this, as some laymen occasionally do, to the cost of a year's room, board, and tuition at Yale University at $23,700 (Hoffman, 1992), or four years at $94,800.

The most significant cost is that of care and supervision of the children. To staff a unit for eight children requires, at a minimum, four full-time staff and a part-time staff to cover the 168 hours per week (or the necessary overtime for those working in excess of a forty-hour week). At $6 an hour, a minimal salary for such a responsible position, the annual salary for one staff comes to $12,480. With payroll taxes and reasonable benefits, the cost comes to about $15,500. Adding in the part-time person, the total for the unit comes to about $65,000 per year, or $22.26 per child per day.

Adding additional staff for the busy hours after school and a supervisor brings the cost to about $35.00 per child per day. To this must be added necessary costs for maintenance, laundry, food service, and administration. Record keeping requires secretarial work. And we have not yet entered any costs for treatment personnel, education, medical and dental care, the facility, and equipment. And given that the staff are very likely working with children that special education teachers with an aide

had difficulty managing in a setting for perhaps only four children, the $6.00 per hour salary indeed seems inadequate.

THE CHILDREN

Residential treatment is about children. People who genuinely like children—being around children, doing things with children, and sharing in children's lives, struggles, failures, and accomplishments—generally do well and are happy in residential treatment, regardless of their training or expertise. People who do not seem to like being with children, regardless of their training, expertise, or desire or need to help children, often do not do well in residential treatment and are not happy in such settings.

The children come in all shapes and sizes. They are cute, pretty, handsome, average, plain, disfigured, and ugly. There are twelve-year-olds who appear to be sixteen or seventeen; there are small fifteen-year-olds who look to be no more than twelve. Some are so smart one wonders why they can't solve any problem that comes up; others appear to be so slow one wonders how they got this far.

They come clean and neat; they come dirty and beat up. They come with manners and without. Some can change tires or sew an evening dress; some can't tie their own shoes. There are those who can't steal or lie and those who can't even tell the truth to themselves. There are those with an undauntable enthusiasm for life and those who are listless. There are those who don't know how to smile and those who never stop. I knew one teenager who awoke every morning smiling from ear-to-ear.

They come from the streets, from poor homes where everyone was too busy trying to make money, from well-to-do homes where everyone was too busy trying to make money. They come from poor homes where they shared a room and a bed; they come from well-to-do homes where they had their own rooms, stereos, and TVs; they come from poor homes where they had their own rooms, stereos, and TVs.

They come with histories of lying, stealing, fighting, truancy, breaking things, hurting people, and running away. They come with tales of sexual abuse by parents, stepparents, relatives, and live-ins. They come with tales of beatings and confinements in closets and being tied up. They come from parents who yell at them constantly but never discipline them, from homes in which they could do no wrong, and from homes in which they were barely noticed.

There are those who fight the program every step of the way, those who have to be pushed or dragged through the program, and those who are so proud of their accomplishments you think they're going to burst. There are those who seem to do everything right, but you wonder what's really going on in their heads.

There are those who leave the program with a triumphant sneer on the way to their next placement, having "won" again. There are those who are taken away in handcuffs, crying. There are those who leave with confidence—bigger, stronger, prettier, smarter, happier—on their way to families glad to have them back, and those who leave in the same condition but going to a world which, at best, will not be too kind to them. There are those who return over the years to share their accomplishments and memories and those you never hear from again; there are those you read about in the newspaper.

One of my favorite training exercises is to ask the staff of a residential program to describe the children with whom they work. In a short time, they invariably provide a list for the flip chart with items such as: aggressive, deceitful, devious, lie, can't delay gratification, selfish, steal, poor impulse control, poor values, poor temper control, lack of self control, disrespectful.

When I comment on the negative nature of their list, the staff quite quickly develop an equally impressive list of positives, often with more enthusiasm: energetic, humorous, enthusiastic, athletic,

pretty, kind, helpful, strong, talented, clever, funny, charming, cute, handsome, competitive, friendly, full of courage. To borrow a phrase from corrections, the children are not in treatment "for singing too loud in church." They come because of problems, but problems are not all they bring with them.

Residential treatment provides an opportunity to work with children that is unique, to work with them, to eat with them, to play and compete with them, to teach them, to show them, to watch them learn, achieve, and grow. The rewards are likewise unique.

SUMMARY

The residential treatment program is unique in its responsibilities for both care and treatment. It creates the environment in which treatment takes place and has significant responsibility for virtually every aspect of that environment. It has under its control not only most of the consequences of a child's behavior but also most of the antecedents of the child's behavior.

Its responsibilities derive from a variety of sources. Those having legal custody of the child, parents or a state agency, delegate responsibility for the care and treatment of the child to the facility. Licensing and other regulatory agencies also prescribe responsibilities for residential facilities, as do various federal, state, and local laws and ordinances. Courts have even determined that the Constitution prescribes certain responsibilities, especially for protection and treatment.

While both care and treatment are important, they are not different aspects of the same thing. We may speak of residential treatment and assume that care is provided. When we speak of residential care and child care workers, we cannot so readily assume any treatment.

The accountability of the residential treatment program is also unique. It can readily be held accountable for care by parents, a variety of state agencies and, at times, by courts. Residential programs may also be held accountable by licensing and funding agencies for following prescribed procedures in providing treatment. Accountability for treatment outcomes, however, is uniquely rare.

Responsibility in the residential setting poses some unique ironies. The child's responsibility for herself or himself is always a care issue and, most likely, a treatment issue as well. Yet, allowing children in residential settings to assume responsibilities for themselves poses risks. Misbehavior in the community may threaten the program's reputation and relationship with the community. The program is vulnerable to litigation. Finally, questions about staff conduct in responding to a verbally or physically provoking child invariably detract from the child's responsibility for her or his own behavior.

Residential treatment is a uniquely expensive intervention, largely because of the expense of the care and supervision of the children. Its cost may compare to the cost of a college education at a prestigious university. A successful outcome, however, may well offset the alternative of an adult who is a life-long dependent.

Finally, residential treatment offers a unique opportunity to work with troubled children. Along with the problems they bring with them, they bring the same qualities that make all children fun and enjoyable. Those who enjoy children do well in residential treatment; those who do not enjoy children do not do well, no matter how much they want to help.

History

R ESIDENTIAL treatment has historical roots dating back hundreds of years. These historical roots have led to practices, philosophy, and terminology that have, in some instances, achieved the status of tradition. Some traditions are good. They provide a sense of belonging, of stability. Others may be less beneficial, continuing well beyond their usefulness and interfering with creativity and initiative.

An understanding of history can provide a better understanding of the current state of affairs. It can assist us in avoiding mistakes of the past or suggest solutions that have been successful in the past.

Some readers may already have a more detailed knowledge of the history of child welfare than I can present here. Those readers may wish to proceed to the summary and chronology at the end of this chapter as a brief review. For those readers who have little background in the history of child welfare, I have attempted to include sufficient detail to provide some understanding of the historical trends and forces that have shaped residential treatment today.

A historical presentation can be organized chronologically, making trends difficult to follow, or by different trends, making chronology difficult to follow. This history is organized chronologically and broken down into periods that are significant because of characteristic or emerging trends. Periods, however, are subdivided according to those trends, which are then followed from preceding periods into subsequent periods. A strict chronology appears at the end of the chapter for reference. In addition to summarizing information from this chapter, the chronology also contains some relevant dates from programs presented in the following chapter.

COLONIAL TIMES THROUGH 1800

Colonial times were characterized by the lack of institutions. Early Americans believed that poverty and misfortune provided opportunities for the more fortunate to exercise their Christian charity; they responded to deviance with corporal punishment (Tiffin, 1982). Town fathers bound orphaned children over to tradesmen to serve as apprentices to work in exchange for room, board, and training, or to families to work as servants in exchange for room and board. If the children were crippled, idiotic, or too sickly to work, the town fathers boarded them out at the expense of the town or parish (Bremner, 1970). There were only six institutions catering to children prior to 1800 (Tiffin, 1982); information on them is sparse.

Early Institutions

The first children's institution within the current boundaries of the continental United States was in the French province of New Orleans (Whittaker, 1985). A trading company sent seven Ursuline nuns to New Orleans in 1727 to establish a school and a hospital. By the end of the year, the nuns were caring for an orphaned girl. A year later, they were caring for three girls. In 1730, they received female children orphaned in a Natchez Indian massacre. By 1731 the Ursulines were caring for forty-nine girls between the ages of three and twelve years (Bremner, 1970). The site, now a St. Anne Street hotel in the heart of New Orleans' French Quarter, is marked by a plaque.

German settlers established an orphans' home in Ebenezer, Georgia, in 1738. In the next year, George Whitefield established another orphanage ten miles north of Savannah. Many of the debtors sent to Georgia were unable to cope with the rigors of a new settlement and succumbed to a variety of hardships. Whitefield had become concerned about their orphaned children and had raised money privately throughout the colonies. He named his orphanage Bethesda, meaning house of mercy. Within two years, a civic leader documented his investigation of abuse at Bethesda in the case of a boy who had run away after a severe whipping. The administrator resented the intrusion, feeling that what went on within the orphanage was not the business of outsiders (Bremner, 1970). Bethesda continues in operation today "as a modern child care center for emotionally disturbed children" (Trattner, 1983, p. 113).

Charleston, South Carolina, established the first public orphanage in 1790 (Bremner, 1970).

THE NINETEENTH CENTURY

The 1800s were characterized by rapid social changes associated with a new and rapidly growing country and industrialization. People believed that major business and political scandals and debilitating conditions of slums contributed to the problems of dependents, defectives, and deviants. These indi-

viduals were removed from these conditions to institutions in which they could benefit from rehabilitation in a protected environment (Tiffin, 1982). Society and the institutions may have benefited more than the inmates. Almshouses, penitentiaries, juvenile reformatories, mental asylums, and orphan asylums appeared at an accelerating rate throughout the century. The dominant theme during the nineteenth century was rehabilitation through isolation, obedience, routine, and discipline, along with moral and religious training. Children were often treated the same as adults and cared for along with adults in large, congregate institutions (Tiffin, 1982).

1800 to 1850

Twenty-three institutions for children were established in the first thirty years of the nineteenth century, but for the most part, children were treated the same as adults and housed with adults. During the next twenty years, eighty-one additional children's institutions opened their doors (Tiffin, 1982).

Corrections

In March of 1787, four years after the end of the Revolutionary War and two years before the ratification of the Constitution, a group of Philadelphia citizens met at the home of Benjamin Franklin to discuss public punishment in Pennsylvania. Dr. Benjamin Rush, a signer of the Declaration of Independence, presented a paper proposing the establishment of a prison. He advocated classification of prisoners for housing, a rational system of prison labor to make the prison self-supporting, individualized treatment related to whether crimes arose from habit, passion, or temptation, and indeterminate periods of punishment. In the same year, the Philadelphia Society for Alleviating the Miseries of Public Prisons was organized (Gill, 1979).

On April 5, 1790, as a result of the efforts of the Philadelphia Society, the Pennsylvania legislature passed an act that is regarded as the beginning of the prison system in America. It provided for solitary confinement, the principle upon which the Pennsylvania and subsequent Auburn prison systems were based. During the 1790s, Pennsylvania abolished the corporal punishment, mutilation, and degradation that had been in vogue under English rule. By 1800, fines and imprisonment had replaced corporal punishment, and capital punishment was applicable only to the crimes of murder and treason. Other states followed suit by 1830 (Gill, 1979).

Early American society treated children who committed crimes the same as adults. It jailed children with adults to await trial and tried them with adults in court. It sentenced them to confinement with adults in prisons. New Jersey hanged a thirteen-year-old boy in 1828 for an offense he committed at the age of twelve (Cavan, 1969). In 1845, Massachusetts convicted ninety-seven children between the ages of six and sixteen and sentenced them to the House of Correction (Bremner, 1970).

Correctional institutions for juveniles began to appear in the 1820s. A reformatory was established in Elmira, New York, in 1824 (Levine & Levine, 1970). The Society for the Reformation of Juvenile Delinquents received state assistance to open the New York City House of Refuge in 1825. Its purpose was to care for and educate children picked up for vagrancy or other minor offenses. Such children had normally been sentenced to six months in the penitentiary. The children occupied a vacated military barracks (Cavan, 1969). Other juvenile reformatories were opened in Boston in 1826 and in Philadelphia two years later. Massachusetts was the first to establish a state reform school when it opened the Lyman School in Westborough in 1847 (Whittaker, 1985).

Care

During this period, philanthropists, civic groups, and municipalities established institutions for orphaned, dependent, or neglected children. Stephen Girard, a childless widower, provided a $6 million endowment in his will to found an orphanage for poor, white, male orphans. Girard College of Philadelphia opened in 1831; to this day it has the largest endowment of any institution for children in the United States. The racial restrictions of Girard's will became the subject of extensive litigation in the 1960s and were nullified by a federal appeals court in 1967, paving the way for the institution's first black orphans in 1968 (Bremner, 1970).

The Colored Orphan Asylum of New York City was founded in 1836. Draft rioters during the Civil War deliberately burned it to the ground in 1863. All 233 occupants, ranging in age from two to twelve years, escaped to find care in an almshouse (Bremner, 1970).

The fate of children in need of care, however, was most often the almshouse (Tiffin, 1982). Between 1800 and 1860, some 6 million immigrants came to the United States, mostly impoverished German and Irish Catholics who for the most part entered and remained in the Northeast. Civic leaders and the public became increasingly concerned that public relief to growing numbers of impoverished individuals and families added to the problem, encouraging the poor to rely on the public dole rather than their own initiative. Based on practice in England, work houses and almshouses, large congregate institutions, became the solution (Trattner, 1984).

In 1824, New York enacted the County Poorhouse Act. It called for the establishment of poorhouses in each county to which all recipients of public assistance were to be sent, except in cases of sickness or infirmity. The act assigned to counties the responsibility for maintaining the institutions out of tax revenue. Meanwhile, Massachusetts already had eighty-three almshouses, a number which grew to 180 by 1839 (Trattner, 1984).

Contemporary thought held great expectations for children in almshouses, which were to provide food, clothing, and education to the children. The reality was more often nakedness, filth, licentiousness, and degradation (Tiffin, 1982).

1850 to 1900

Institutions for children increased nearly tenfold during the latter half of the nineteenth century.

Beliefs about the values of isolation, routine, discipline, hard work, and moral and religious instruction continued. Congregate institutions contained everything the children needed. Children ate, worked, went to school, and played in the same building; they slept in large dormitories, sometimes two or three to a bed. Visitors, including relatives, were discouraged. Use of outside schools or churches was rare (Tiffin, 1982).

Military drills were a part of the routine, as often as three times per day. Staff emphasized industry, considering constant hard work to be a major agent of reform. The work, of course, was necessary to the running of the institution. Temperance meetings were a part of moral instruction, with pledges commonly extracted from the children. Staff used corporal punishment, extra work, and deprivation of food to discipline and coerce residents (Tiffin, 1982).

Juvenile reformatories during this period were patterned after adult prisons. Children wore prison garb and were confined by bars in prison cells. They performed prison labor and received prison discipline and prison punishments (Trattner, 1984).

Several factors contributed to the growth in numbers of institutions for children during the latter half of the century. Civic groups exposed abuses in almshouses; states began to pass laws abolishing almshouses and providing for children's institutions. Epidemics of cholera and other fatal diseases and the Civil War produced orphans.

Philanthropists and increasingly active women's organizations founded institutions. The Catholic Church and various Protestant and Jewish groups established orphanages so that children could retain the religious affiliation of their fathers (Mayer, Richman, & Balcerzak, 1978). States found it more economical to subsidize private institutions than to operate their own. Consequently, private persons could make a profit if they could care for children cheaply enough. They did so by providing the most minimal care (Trattner, 1984).

Several innovations also appeared during this period. Cottage care was introduced in the 1850s, with a matron cottage mother in charge of managing a home for twenty-five to fifty children, supposedly to simulate a family (Mayer et al., 1978). Foster care was also introduced in the 1850s. Later developments included farm schools, ship and industrial schools, separate hearings for juveniles, indeterminate sentencing, the first juvenile court, and student government.

Corrections

The Massachusetts Industrial School for Girls was founded in 1856. It housed its inmates in family-like cottages, as did the Ohio Reform School founded in 1857 (Bremner, 1970).

The state of Massachusetts established a ship school in 1860 to reform delinquents and contribute trained seamen to the merchant marine. Heavy operating expenses, disciplinary problems, and economic depression that put seamen out of work led to the abandonment of the school in 1877. Similar programs were established in New York and San Francisco and later closed for similar reasons (Bremner, 1971).

The New York State Reformatory at Elmira, opened in 1876, was the first children's institution to adopt the indeterminate sentence. Prison personnel set release dates based on performance and progress. Inmates received training and, upon release, were usually sent to prearranged places of employment for which they had been trained. They remained on parole after release. Results were impressive. Four out of five discharges remained out of prison over a ten-year period. By 1898, Massachusetts, Pennsylvania, Ohio, Michigan, Illinois, Minnesota, South Dakota, and Indiana had established similar programs (Trattner, 1984).

Massachusetts passed legislation during the 1870s that required separate hearings for juveniles, although the hearings continued to be conducted by adult judges in adult criminal courts (Trattner, 1984). In April of 1899, the Arizona legislature passed a law providing for separate treatment of juveniles in court. The law was not implemented until 1901. Meanwhile, the efforts of Jane Addams and her Hull House and Lucy Flowers and the Chicago Women's Club led to the founding of the first true juvenile court on July 1, 1899, in Chicago (Levine & Levine, 1970).

Care

Foster Care. Charles Loring Brace, a twenty-seven-year-old missionary in New York City, founded the Children's Aid Society in 1853. In the next year the society took forty-six boys and girls by train to a small town in Michigan and made an appeal in the church for families to take one or more children. By the following Saturday, all of the children had been placed. During the next twenty-five years, some 50,000 children were similarly removed from New York City (Trattner, 1984).

Ironically, the efforts of Brace and the Children's Aid Society to some extent promoted the development of Catholic institutions. Many of the children they relocated were descendants of Catholic immigrants; the families in the West were predominantly Protestant. The Catholic Church saw this as an effort to convert its children and sought to keep its children in the faith in Church-sponsored institutions (Trattner, 1984).

Brace's efforts met with other opposition. The poor objected to having their children sent so far from home. Recipient families, unscreened and unsupervised, commonly overworked the children and failed to provide proper food, clothing, and education. Children ran away and became public charges in their new states. States began to object. A study by Minnesota's State Board of Charities reported that close to 60 percent of these children became sources of trouble and public expense. States began passing prohibiting legislation or requiring a bond for each child in the event of problems (Trattner, 1984).

Brace's efforts are significant for two reasons. When others began to develop sound administrative control of placing children, notably the Boston Children's Aid Society, the New York State Charities Aid Society, and the Children's Aid Society of Pennsylvania, the practice of placing children with foster families gained credibility. By the turn of the century, foster care surpassed institutional placement in several cities (Trattner, 1984). Brace may also be credited with the first program that sent problem children out-of-state on a large scale.

Almshouses. The State Charities Aid Association of New York documented problems in the state's fourth largest almshouse, the Westchester County Poor House. The home cared for 370 people, including sixty children, along with men and women who were old, sick, insane, blind, deaf-and-dumb, or idiotic (Bremner, 1971).

The children were in the care of an elderly pauper woman whose daughter and grandchild had both been born in the poorhouse. Her daughter assisted her with the care of the children and had apparently communicated a contagious eye infection to them. There was no nursing for the sick. Children were badly clothed and fed, badly taken care of, and exposed to the degrading influences of the inmates who cared for them (Bremner, 1971).

The worst aspect, according to the association's *First Annual Report,* was that the children were joyless. The report cited the case of a respectable, widowed woman who had been admitted with her daughter. The woman was crippled by rheumatism and unable to care for the child. On a previous visit, the child had been noted to be a bright, smiling three-year-old. Within a year, the mother had died, and the child was found to have lost all expression, refusing to speak or smile (Bremner, 1971).

Charles Loring Brace was a member of the association, and offered to place the children in homes out West. The superintendents of the institution declined the offer. They wanted to keep the children where they could look after them and know what became of them (Bremner, 1971).

With legislation in 1861, Ohio became the first state to mandate the removal of children from almshouses (Trattner, 1984). Five years later Ohio passed a law permitting counties to establish children's homes, leading to fifty-six such homes in Ohio by the early twentieth century. Massachusetts opened the first state home for dependent children in 1866, followed by Michigan eight years later (Mayer et al., 1978). Most states passed laws abolishing almshouses between 1860 and 1900 (Adler, 1981), although almshouses and their care of children continued well into the twentieth century. Nearly 6,400 children were admitted to almshouses in 1910; there were still 1,900 children in almshouses in 1923. Available data does not allow accurate determination of how many of these children were admitted with a parent, admitted on their own, or born in the almshouse (Bremner, 1971).

Cottage Care. The Burnham Industrial Farm sought to capture the ideal of agrarian farm schools by implementing an authentic cottage system and farm routine. William M. F. Round, a journalist and reformer, and Frederick G. Burnham, a wealthy New York attorney, founded the program in 1887 on a farm owned by Burnham. Round borrowed the cottage program from European models. The name was changed to the Berkshire Industrial Farm in 1896 (Bremner, 1971).

Rudolph Reeder was appointed superintendent of the New York Orphan's Asylum in 1898 after a lengthy career in education. The asylum was a large, congregate institution founded earlier in the century. Within two years, Reeder moved the asylum to Hastings-on-Hudson to provide the children with the benefits of country life and restructured it on the cottage plan. Each cottage contained its own library, kitchen, dining room, bedrooms, toilets, etc. Fifteen to twenty-five residents and a matron lived in each cottage. The matron was described as a mother figure having a strong natural love of children. Obedience, industrial training, and daily mutual services were the significant features of daily living (Tiffin, 1982).

Student Government and a Token Economy (Money). William R. George was a New York businessman active in reform. In 1890, he opened the Fresh Air Camp in rural Freeville to provide city youths an opportunity for the benefits of country life. He became concerned that the program might be contributing to the laziness of the children and soon introduced a plan requiring children to work for everything they received (Tiffin, 1982).

By 1895 the Junior Republic was operating on a year-round basis. Children profited or failed according to their own industry. Each boy or girl was free to work or play but needed money at day's end for food and shelter. School programs allowed children to work at their own rate on subjects that interested them; emphasis was placed on spontaneity and exploration rather than regimentation. Members governed themselves according to republican principles. They elected their own legislative and executive officers, wrote their own constitution and laws, conducted their own courts, and punished offenders. Others established Junior Republics in other communities (Bremner, 1971; Tiffin, 1982).

Other Institutions. New York State provided a grant for the founding of the Thomas Asylum for Orphan and Destitute Indian Children. It was incorporated in 1855; twenty years later it was reorganized to become a state institution (Bremner, 1971).

THE TWENTIETH CENTURY

There were significant attempts throughout the twentieth century both to keep children out of institutions and to get children out of institutions. Foster care was more carefully regulated and used more extensively. States and later the federal government provided mother's aid, pension laws, and Aid to Families with Dependent Children to help keep children at home (Mayer et al., 1978). Toward the end of the century, states funded residential family care, which provided special training and a salary to foster parents to manage and treat more difficult children. States also began to fund family preservation programs, intensive treatment programs in the home, to help keep difficult children at home.

Institutions continued. However, they began an evolution from custodial care and rehabilitation into residential treatment programs. States developed standards for licensing programs in the early part of the century; professionals developed standards for accreditation later in the century. Professionals also developed procedures for detailed assessment and classification of childhood disorders. Programs began using principles of psychoanalytic theory, and later, principles of learning theory, to treat children with the goal of returning them to the community.

Institutional abuse also continued. Child care became big business toward the end of the century. The practice of sending problem children out-of-state reappeared on a large scale.

1900 to 1950

By 1923, the number of children receiving financial assistance to remain in their own homes far exceeded the number in foster care and approached the number in institutions. The number in almshouses had dropped to 1,900 from an estimated 9,000 in 1880 (Bremner, 1971).

Institutional care continued. There were an estimated 600 institutions caring for children in 1890 (Trattner, 1984). The number almost doubled to 1,151 in 1910, and reached nearly 1,600 in 1923 (Tiffin, 1982). The number of children in group care increased moderately between 1933 and 1966, from an estimated 144,000 to 155,905, not including correctional settings or institutions for the retarded. During the same period, the number of children in foster care increased from an estimated 105,000 to 249,000 (Mayer et al., 1978). States began to require that institutions be licensed and inspected. Administrators of public, private, and religious agencies resisted, resenting encroachments on their autonomy (Bremner, 1971). Emphasis gradually began to shift from rehabilitation to psychotherapeutic treatment.

Corrections

In the early 1900s, the major developments in institutional care occurred in corrections: separation of children from adults, detailed assessment and classification of childhood disorders, and a

model program that anticipated both the therapeutic milieu and the emphasis on learning.

Juvenile Courts. Twenty-two states had passed juvenile court legislation by 1912; within the next twenty years, all but Maine and Wyoming had such legislation, and Maine provided for separate hearings and probation (Bremner, 1971). Wyoming enacted its juvenile court legislation in 1945 (Cavan, 1969).

Assessment and Classification of Childhood Disorders. Chicago's juvenile court became concerned with the repeated stealing, lying, and sex offenses of too many children. It selected William Healy, M.D., to conduct scientific research into the causes of these problems. Healy established a research project into the causes of delinquency along with a clinic to treat the behavior problems of children. He founded his clinic in 1909; Jane Addams was a member of the executive committee. Healy chose the name Juvenile Psychopathic Institute because of a prevalent psychiatric opinion at the time that serious anti-social behavior implied serious pathology. Healy soon concluded that this opinion was incorrect (Levine & Levine, 1970).

Healy devised detailed and thorough procedures for examination, including histories of family, the social environment, mental and moral development, school, friends, interests, occupational efforts, bad habits, and contacts with law enforcement agencies or institutions. A complete medical examination from psychiatric and neurological standpoints and anthropometric and psychological studies were also completed (Levine & Levine, 1970).

Model for a Correctional Program. In 1913, Augusta F. Bronner joined Healy's clinic. She had a strong interest in educational problems as they related to delinquency. In 1915 Healy and Bronner published a remarkable outline for a model correctional program in the *Journal of Educational Psychology.* Although Healy did not operate a residential or correctional program at the time, he had studied and consulted at several. Levine and Levine (1970) found the outline of sufficient interest to warrant reproduction of a significant portion, as do I.

As Levine and Levine (1970) note, Healy and Bronner preceded their outline with discussions of goals, the plant and equipment, selection of staff, and the importance of follow-up after release. The outline is significant in its anticipation of the therapeutic milieu that began to appear in the late 1930s and achieved a dominant influence after 1950. It is also significant that I found no other references in the literature to Healy and Bronner's outline, although several writers referred to their contributions to assessment and classification of childhood disorders (Cavan, 1969; Trattner, 1984; Whittaker, 1985). Some contemporary programs might take a point or two from Healy and Bronner's outline (1915), as it was reprinted by Levine and Levine (1970):

Treatment in general: Before discussing specific phases of treatment, its general moods and aims should be taken up.

(a) The entire institutional life should be adjusted with the ideal that it is treatment, that it is educational, and all to the end that the delinquent shall be better fitted to meet an outside environment.

(b) This requires high individualization. One of the arguments against the advisability of a set system is found in the successes which are actually obtained by a rational and understanding approach to the problem of the individual. Both education and work must be adapted to the individual needs.

(c) Three things to avoid are any kind of deceit, the show of pedantry, and any demonstration of irrationality. It is most desirous to make the individual rational and honest, and this can only be done by showing a good example in these respects.

(d) The method should be elastic in all ways, particularly in institutions for girls, where allowance must be made for outbreaks and explosions of pent-up emotions and energies, either occasional or periodic. Of course, physical fluctuations must be allowed for.

(e) Punishments: These must be highly individualized according to personalities involved. There is no doubt that stimulus to doing better is more apt to result from the promise of rewards than the administering of penalties. There must be goals toward which the delinquent is to work as the reward of good behavior. With constructive treatment the problems of discipline largely tend to disappear. It should be remembered that coercion and punishment by inflicting pain are the lowest levels of control.

(f) Above all things, mental vacuities, either on weekdays or Sundays, must be prevented. "The empty mind is the devil's workshop." There should be abundant opportunity for good conversational reactions. This may be as important as formal instruction, and always the mental life should be the first and foremost consideration.

(g) The whole institutional equipment should be used with the sole idea of its social and moral worth.

(h) General and social life should include the planning of service and of rendering helpfulness to others in the institution. Cultivation of this is worth much, and from it can be built up larger ideas of social relationships. Perhaps the best way to avoid jealousies is to inculcate the idea of service, one to the other in the institution.

(i) Inmate social life: One of the best helps toward a better life is an understanding friend and advisor with whom the cause and the help for trouble may be discussed.

(j) In considering treatment in general it must not be thought that building up is always the point, or that positive habits are the only good; the inhibitions of bad impulses must also be considered. In some cases excessive physical vigor, or obstinancy of will, make special forms of modification necessary.

Dress: A moot question is over the dress of institutional inmates. One point stands out clearly proven; namely, that any self-expression that is practicable in this matter should be cultivated.

Work: The arrangement of work to be done by the inmates has its economic and also its social and moral values. The immediate economies must not conflict with the aims of the institution. If the work has a deteriorating effect, or is interferring with treatment, it should be done by outsiders. But this does not mean that difficult or even so-called menial work should be neglected. The idea of duty . . . may be cultivated, although perhaps with difficulty in early adolescence, through the understanding that the institution ought to be largely self-sustaining. Work of all kinds is done, chiefly for common welfare. If it is merely assigned as a matter of routine or punishment without this feeling, work is apt to be detrimental and cause a grudge.

Very much of housework and other work can be done in the spirit of scientific training. There may be attention to skill and success in many household occupations. It must be shrewdly recognized that there may be great benefits accruing to selected individuals through their engaging in hard labor, either physical or mental, or both.

Religion: Religious training would be out of place to discuss here. In general, we may say that religious training which takes the individual as one of a group and does not meet special problems is not apt to get results. Then it must be remembered, in all common sense, that natures differ greatly. The religious appeal is very strong in some, and others are oblivious to it (Healy & Bronner, 1915, pp. 307–309).

The balance of the outline contains a detailed school curriculum centered around the male and female roles and likely vocations. It also discusses political organizations, social welfare agencies, and other community resources including recreation (Levine & Levine, 1970).

Camps. Riverside County in California opened a forestry camp for probationers in 1927 as a project of the probation office. The camp closed due to a lack of funds in 1932, the same year that Los Angeles County opened a forestry camp for transient boys. In 1943, the California Youth Authority opened its first state camp. In 1944, the Youth Authority contracted with the United States Army for camps to produce war materials at Benecia Arsenal and Stockton Ordnance Depot. Each camp housed 150 boys transferred from county jails. The Federal Bureau of Prisons operated the Natural Bridge Camp from 1944 to the mid-1960s. By 1967, twenty states were operating a total of forty-nine camps (Cavan, 1969).

Care

During the first thirty years of the twentieth century, government agencies developed programs for visiting and inspecting institutions; licensing raised standards and increased control (Bremner, 1971). The next twenty years saw the beginnings of the evolution to treatment (Mayer et al, 1978).

The Jewish Protectory and Aid Society was incorporated in 1902 to take boys from the streets and place them in a wholesome setting where they could be instructed in the Jewish faith. Five years later, the society opened a school based on the cottage plan in the village of Hawthorne. In 1935, the school implemented a new treatment program to create a total therapeutic situation with increased use of a psychiatrist and social worker (Alt, 1960).

Father Edward J. Flanagan opened Boys Town in rural Nebraska in 1917; it provided a congregate home and education for homeless, neglected, abused, or handicapped boys of any faith (Boys Town, undated). Boys Town is summarized in the next chapter.

Evolution to Residential Treatment. Under the influence of Aichhorn, first published in English in 1935, a form of group care began to appear that avoided much of the opposition to the traditional institution. Based on psychoanalytic theories, it gained prestige among professionals and introduced the concept of the therapeutic milieu. Many custodial programs became residential treatment centers, and new treatment centers opened. With no firm criteria, almost every institution serving children could lay claim to the title (Mayer et al., 1978).

Meanwhile, during the 1940s, Jacob Kepec of the Jewish Children's Bureau in Chicago began using group homes to replace institutions. He was one of the first administrators to do so (Mayer et al., 1978).

1950 to the Present

The evolution of residential treatment continued. Bruno Bettelheim and Fritz Redl, both proponents of the therapeutic milieu and psychoanalytic principles, published extensively beginning in 1949 and 1951, respectively (Mayer et al., 1978). Beginning in the 1960s, behavior modification began to appear in residential programs (Adler, 1981). Considerable literature described individual techniques as well as token economies and point systems for entire wards or living units. Some programs complemented psychoanalytic approaches with behavioral approaches; others replaced them.

Trends towards cottage living continued and cottages became smaller; trends away from larger institutions in favor of smaller, more community-based programs and group homes evolved. The concept of the benefits of country living expanded into wilderness programming, featuring accomplishment in the wilderness as a means of building a sense of achievement, self-reliance, and self-confidence. Maritime programs featured similar concepts at sea in sailing ships.

States imposed tougher licensing standards and included standards for treatment. Professional associations developed standards for accreditation, and agencies began to pursue accreditation voluntarily.

Abuses of children also continued. Child care continued to be profitable and, by the 1970s, had become big business. The practice of sending children out-of-state reappeared. By the 1970s, according to the Children's Defense Fund, only four of the fifty states neither accepted children from other states nor shipped their children to other states. Twenty-seven states were accepting children from states to which they were sending their own children. In states with lax licensing laws, entrepreneurs were willing to accept any kind of problem child for a price. Directors not only made a good salary but also made money in lease-back schemes by renting property to the programs they operated. Programs in Texas, accepting children from Cook County, Illinois, expanded their capacities by sending children on extended camping trips that lasted as long as three years (Taylor, 1981).

In the 1970s, the Federal government began providing grants through the Law Enforcement As-

sistance Administration. States began funding new programs to keep children out of institutions, or to get them out. Federal legislation during the 1980s required states to make reasonable efforts to keep families together or terminate parental rights and develop a permanency plan; other legislation required states to develop a community-based system of care for children.

Therapeutic foster family care provided salaries, training, and support to foster parents to enable them to manage more difficult children in specialized foster homes. Family preservation programs provided intensive therapy in the home in an attempt to avoid the removal of children. Courts referred juvenile offenders to residential programs in increasing numbers as a condition of probation in lieu of incarceration. Although some programs continued to specialize, the distinction between corrections and care began to disappear; some programs served both populations.

It is difficult to assess accurately the number of children in group care because of differences in definitions and placement procedures, but the number appears to have dropped dramatically during this period. While the number of children in foster care rose from 249,000 in 1966 to 617,000 in 1990, the number of children in group care fell from 155,905 in 1966 to 25,335 in 1986 (Mayer et al., 1978; Yelton, 1993).

Corrections

Diversion, Deinstitutionalization, and Treatment. In the mid-1960s, a group of psychologists affiliated with the University of Kansas opened Achievement Place, a group home that employed principles of behavioral psychology to treat young offenders. The home was staffed by a married couple called Teaching Parents. They were trained in behavioral science and implemented a program of shaping productive behavior that was incompatible with delinquent behavior. The program spread to other localities. The University of Kansas provided a year-long training program; six other regional training sites were developed. A national Teaching Family Association was founded (Stumphauzer, 1986).

The Commission on Law Enforcement and Criminal Administration concluded in 1967 that institutionalizing juveniles did not work (Stumphauzer, 1986). The Juvenile Justice and Delinquency Prevention Act of 1974 mandated that status offenders, youths convicted of offenses that would not be criminal for an adult such as truancy or running away, may not be detained or sentenced to correctional facilities (Sarri, 1985).

Federal grants became available to communities to establish alternative programs, including group homes, to facilitate diversion. Deinstitutionalization became the byword of the 1970s. In 1969, Massachusetts Governor Francis Seargent brought in Dr. Jerome Miller to reform the state's archaic reform schools. A year later, having met with considerable resistance from personnel, Miller concluded that he could not reform the schools. He began closing the ten institutions then operating, including the aforementioned Lyman School, the nation's oldest state reform school, opened in 1847 (Taylor, 1981).

By 1973, the Massachusetts Department of Youth Services had 250 juveniles in foster homes, 750 in group homes, and 120 in residential treatment centers. Miller then left to accept a similar position in Illinois (Taylor, 1981) and moved to Pennsylvania in 1975 to close the state's juvenile institution at Camp Hill.

By the late 1970s, the Massachusetts Department of Youth Services had approximately 1,500 juveniles committed to some form of community care (550 in residential care, 500 at home under supervision of a parole officer, 500 more at home under intensive supervision and in counseling, job training, or an alternative school) and 300 on informal probation. Massachusetts no longer sent 200 to 300 children out-of-state (Taylor, 1981, p. 192).

Miller's efforts met with considerable opposition from state correctional personnel as well as others. Criticisms included moving too fast with a lack of planning, the inability to monitor 200 private providers, and a failure to provide security for those children who required it (Taylor, 1981).

Evaluation of diversion programs suggests that diversion can only be effective for minor and first offenders when adequate community resources in education, employment, recreation, and child welfare are available. Federal Child Welfare funding was available for residential treatment so that many youth became reinstitionalized in public and private residential centers or psychiatric hospitals (Sarri, 1985).

Perhaps the most recent innovation is in-home probation. The probationer is given a strict curfew and closely monitored for compliance. The probationer may be fitted with an electronic bracelet that facilitates monitoring of violations.

Care and Residential Treatment

The transition from custodial care accelerated; existing programs changed and new programs opened. Psychoanalytic theory and the therapeutic milieu dominated residential treatment until the introduction of behavior modification techniques in the 1960s. Subsequently, other approaches have appeared. Positive Peer Culture, based on techniques of guided group interaction, focuses on the role of the peer group in effecting change in attitude and behavior. Presently, no single theory dominates the field of residential treatment (Adler, 1981).

Other programs focus on the overcoming of obstacles in the wilderness or at sea as a means of developing self-confidence, self-reliance, and trust in others. Many programs employ a variety of theories, principles, and techniques. Mayer et al. (1978) argue that, with no firm criteria as to what constitutes a residential treatment center, virtually any program caring for children can lay claim to the title.

Weber and Haberlein (1972) suggest twelve criteria to serve as guidelines for identifying residential treatment centers. Residential treatment centers:

1. have some theory or technique to deal with children's maladaptive behaviors.
2. deal with children who are defined as deviant by some behavioral or psychiatric criterion.
3. select children using some diagnostic procedure.

4. select children for the purpose of treatment.
5. purposefully integrate a variety of program activities into daily life.
6. pay attention to individual needs.
7. are flexible in planning length of stay.
8. employ clinically trained personnel.
9. have child care workers with a high level of skill.
10. require parents to participate in the program.
11. provide a relatively open setting.
12. have procedures to evaluate their work and make adjustments as needed.

It is interesting to compare these points with Healy and Bronner's model for a correctional program.

Classification of Facilities

Mayer et al. (1978) suggest a classification of six types of residential programs, three for group homes and three for institutions. They distinguish group homes from foster care in that the facility is owned by an agency, so that children can remain in the home despite any changes in staff that may occur. The facility should fit into the community, and the staff and residents should participate in community life including schools, churches, social and political activities. They identify three categories:

1. *Family Group Home.* Foster parents, single people, or married couples, with or without relief staff, care for four to six children.
2. *Peer Group Home.* Child care staff take care of five to ten children.
3. *Group Residence.* Child care staff care for ten to fifteen children.

Mayer et al. (1978) define an institution as "one or more buildings especially established for the purpose of housing and caring for groups of children who cannot live with their families" (p. 52). Institutions may be within or outside of a residential community. They identify three categories:

1. *The Child Care Center.* It may also be known as an institution for dependent and neglected children. Fifteen or more children who cannot live at home through no fault of their own are cared for by child care staff. They usually attend community schools and churches and are expected to behave normally for their ages except for any reactions to their separation. There is a full-time administrator with training in education, social work, or a related field. A professional staff is available to assist with intake, discharge, and crises. Group living is the major form of social interaction.

2. *Children's Service Center.* Fifteen or more children whose homes are not available to them and who have problems in adapting to their environment live in a specially built institution. They live in groups under supervision of child care staff. Many of them require a high degree of "social stimulation and control" (Mayer et al., 1978, p. 53). Many have serious behavior problems but can function age-appropriately most of the time. There is an experienced administrator with training in social work, psychology, or education. Professionally trained staff are available during admission, discharge, crisis, and, to some children, on a weekly basis. Most therapeutic intervention is part of the daily living program, and staff work with parents to assist them in making the best possible long-range plans for their children.

3. *Child Therapy Center.* Fifteen or more children with serious emotional problems live in a residential program where residential therapy is the "planned integration of all social, educational and psychotherapeutic activities so that all daily experiences can become important ingredients to growth and rehabilitation" (Mayer et al., 1978, p. 54). The administrator or a clinical director is experienced and trained in social work, psychology, psychiatry, or special education. A therapeutic milieu is developed by a staff of trained case workers, group workers, psychologists, psychiatrists, and spe-

cial educators who work closely with child care staff. There are individual, group, and family therapy sessions and a special school on campus. Group living is usually the major form of socialization, but the program is highly individualized (Mayer et al, 1978).

Court Decisions and the Right to Treatment. A number of court decisions beginning with *Rouse v. Cameron* (1966) have implications for residential treatment. In this case, that of a convicted criminal confined in a psychiatric facility, the right was established to either be provided adequate and appropriate treatment or be released. *Lake v. Cameron* (1966) established the right to be treated in the least restrictive setting. The decision placed the burden on states to demonstrate that less intrusive treatment or lesser infringement on liberty would not be effective when it places an individual for purposes of protection (Heads, 1978).

Morales v. Turman (1974) established the right to treatment for children. Further, the federal court warned that merely placing a child in a structured environment, or even providing a token economy with similar provisions for all residents and labeling it a therapeutic milieu, does not constitute adequate treatment (Heads, 1978).

Federal Legislation. The Adoption Assistance and Child Welfare Act of 1980, Public Law 96-272, requires states to make "reasonable" efforts to keep families together. It also requires states to work for a prompt reunification of families when removal of a child is necessary. If the child cannot be returned home, the state is required to develop a permanency plan for the child's future, including termination of parental rights and pursuit of adoption. The law requires timely periodic judicial review (Yelton, 1993).

PL 96-272 led to expansion and increased use of emergent family preservation programs. These programs send trained therapists into homes to work with families intensively on a variety of problems. Therapists work with two or three families at a time for four to eight weeks on crisis, therapeutic, and practical issues.

Community mental health began to get more involved with children during the 1980s. With Federal funding, the National Institute of Mental Health instituted the Child and Adolescent Service System Program (CASSP) in 1984, with pilot projects in several states (Yelton, 1993). By the end of the decade, forty-eight states had CASSP programs. Through grants, CASSP provides for the establishment of coalitions of agencies at state and local levels to discuss services and bring about system change. The goal of the program is the development of local community-based continuums of care for children with severe emotional disturbance. CASSP participants include mental health, child welfare, juvenile justice, special education, and family advocacy agencies (Stroul, 1989).

The Mental Health Act of 1989, Public Law 99-660, as amended by PL 101-639, further increases the involvement of community mental health in child welfare. This law requires states to develop and implement plans for comprehensive community-based systems of care for children with serious emotional disturbance. It also requires interagency service coordination among various agencies and resources serving individual children and families in especially difficult cases (Yelton, 1993). Mental health began offering family preservation, case management, and mobile in-home emergency crisis services to assist families of children with severe emotional disturbance in their homes.

SUMMARY

In colonial America, communities handled their own problems locally with little reliance on institutions. Needy children were boarded out or apprenticed to families or tradesmen. The poor were dependent upon the Christian charity of those who were better off. Criminals and deviants received corporal punishment or were executed.

FIGURE 2.1: Chronological Summary of Important and Interesting Events in the Development of Residential Treatment for Adolescents and Children

1728	Ursuline Nuns opened the first orphanage within the present boundaries of the United States in the French Province of New Orleans. It was for girls.
1738	German settlers established the first orphanage in the colonies in Ebenezer, GA.
1739	George Whitefield established Bethesda, an orphanage near Savannah, GA.
1741	A case of abuse was investigated at Bethesda.
1790	The City Council of Charleston, SC, established the first public orphanage.
1800	There were six institutions for children.
1800–1830	Twenty-three institutions for children were opened.
1824	First juvenile reformatory, Elmira, NY.
1825	New York City House of Refuge was opened for youths committing minor offenses.
1826	Juvenile reformatory opened in Boston.
1828	Philadelphia opened a juvenile reformatory.
	New Jersey hanged a thirteen-year-old boy.
1830–1850	81 institutions for juveniles opened.
1831	Girard College, a home for poor white orphans, opened in Philadelphia as per provisions of Stephen Girard's will.
1836	The Colored Orphan Asylum of New York City was founded.
1845	Massachusetts convicted and sentenced ninety-seven children between the ages of six and sixteen to the House of Correction, an adult prison.
1847	Massachusetts opened the first state reform school in Lyman, MA.
1850–1900	Concerns with conditions in almshouses led to increasing numbers of institutions for children, state laws abolishing almshouses, and attempts to keep children out of institutions through foster care.
1850s	Charles Loring Brace promoted foster care over institutions and indenture for New York City's children, sending them to foster homes in the Midwest.
1855	The Thomas Asylum for Orphan and Destitute Indian Children was incorporated.
1860	Massachusetts opened a ship school to train seamen for the merchant marine.
1863	Rioters burned the Colored Orphan Asylum to the ground in New York City.
1877	Massachusetts closed its ship school.
1880	9,000 children were being served in the nation's almshouses.
1882	William Thurston established a home for children in Pennsylvania's Lehigh Valley (see chapter 3).
1887	Frederick Burnham and William Round founded The Burnham Industrial Farm for New York City's inner-city children, stressing ideals of agrarian farm schools and the cottage system.
1895	William R. George developed his Junior Republic in Freeville, NY.
	Captain James Wiley purchased land and built a residence for Thurston's home in the Lehigh Valley, eventually to become known as Wiley House (see chapter 3).
1898	Rudolph Reeder, an experienced educator, was appointed superintendent of the New York Orphan's Asylum.
1899	Arizona passed a law providing for separate treatment of juveniles in April. It was not implemented until 1901.
	The first true juvenile court was founded in Chicago through efforts of Jane Addams' Hull House.
1900–1950	Separation of children from adults.
	Juvenile courts.
	Detailed assessment and classification of childhood disorders.
	Use of psychoanalytic principles in treatment.
	State regulation and licensing of placement agencies and institutions.
	Increased use of foster care.
	Attempts to keep children at home through mother's aid and aid to dependent children.
1900	Reeder moved the New York Orphan's Asylum to Hastings-on-Hudson and restructured it on the cottage plan.
	Sigmund Freud published *The Interpretation of Dreams*.
1901	Ben Lindsey founded Arizona's first juvenile court using the 1899 legislation.
	Freud published *The Psychopathology of Everyday Life*.
1902	The Jewish Protectory and Aid Society was incorporated to take Jewish boys from the streets of New York City.
1904	Pavlov received the Nobel Prize for his work on the digestive reflexes. On the occasion, he delivered an address in which he discussed conditioned reflexes.
1907	The Jewish Protectory and Aid Society opened a cottage institution for boys in Hawthorne, NY.
1909	William Healy founded his Juvenile Psychopathic Institute in response to recidivism in Chicago's juvenile court. He developed a plan for detailed and comprehensive assessment of juveniles.
1910	1,151 institutions for children were in operation.
	6,400 children were admitted to almshouses.

FIGURE 2.1 *(continued)*

1915	Healy and Augusta F. Bronner published a detailed outline for a model correctional program in the *Journal of Educational Psychology.*
1917	Father Flanagan opened Boys Town in Nebraska to care for homeless, neglected boys (see chapter 3).
1923	Nineteen hundred children were still being cared for in almshouses.
1927	Riverside County, CA, opened a forestry camp for probationers.
	Pavlov first published in English.
1932	Los Angeles County opened a forestry camp; Riverside county closed its forestry camp for lack of funds.
1935	Aichhorn published in English on the therapeutic milieu.
	The Hawthorne Cedar Knolls School implemented a new treatment program to create a total therapeutic situation with increased use of psychiatrists and psychiatric social workers.
1938	Skinner published *The Behavior of Organisms.*
1943	The California Youth Authority opened its first state work camp.
1944	The California Youth Authority contracted with the U.S. Army to operate camps at Benecia Arsenal and Stockton Ordnance Depot to produce war materials.
1944	The Federal Bureau of Prisons opened the Natural Bridge Camp and operated it for twenty years.
1950–1990	Deinstitutionalization.
	Group homes.
	Residential treatment centers.
	Therapeutic milieus.
	Behavior modification.
	Abuse continued.
1951	Both Fritz Redl and Bruno Bettelheim published on the therapeutic milieu.
1966	The right to treatment was established in *Rouse v. Cameron.*
	The least restrictive alternative was established in *Lake v. Cameron.*
1967	Federal court nullified the racial provisions of Stephen Girard's will.
1968	The first black was admitted to Girard College.
1969	Governor Francis Seargent brought Dr. Jerome Miller to Massachusetts to reform the reform schools.
1970	Dr. Miller closed the nation's first state reform school in Lyman, MA.
	Wiley House began a program of expansion to offer a full continuum of services (see chapter 3).
1973	Dr. Miller went to Illinois.
	Boys Town began conversion to family-based care (see chapter 3).
	Steven R. Rogers and R. Ledger Burton founded VisionQuest, a wilderness program based on aspects of Plains Indian culture, in Tucson, AZ (see chapter 3).
	Kaleidoscope founded in Chicago to treat children returning from out-of-state placement in Texas (see chapter 3).
1975	Dr. Miller went to Pennsylvania and began moving juveniles out of the State Correctional Institution, Camp Hill, by opening small, regional facilities for twelve boys for short-term, secure treatment of hard-core offenders.
1978	Herman Fountain founded the Bethel Baptist Home in Lucedale, MS (see chapter 3).
1980	PL 96-272, the Adoption Assistance and Child Welfare Act, required significant efforts to keep families together or terminate parental rights.
1984	National Institute of Mental Health funded demonstration projects for its Child and Adolescent Service System Program (CASSP).
1989	PL 99-660, the Community Mental Health Act, required states to develop plans for establishing community-based systems of care for children.
1992	Wiley House changed its name to KidsPeace National Centers for Kids in Crisis (see chapter 3).
1993	KidsPeace opened a newly-constructed psychiatric facility for children on 300 acres in nearby Orefield, Pennsylvania, and relocated its national office to the site.

With increasing industrialization and immigration came larger communities and increased poverty. Wars and epidemics added to the problem. Public corporal punishment and execution lost favor, as did public relief. Institutions became the solution of choice for the poor, the dependent, and the deviant.

Institutions came into being at an ever-increasing rate during the nineteenth century. For the most part, they were operated on the principles of isolation, regimentation, hard work, and harsh discipline. While orphanages and reformatories for children appeared at a steadily increasing rate, large numbers of children continued to receive care or confinement in almshouses and adult prisons. Foster care appeared as an attempt to keep children in the community. Ironically, Catholic, Protestant, and Jewish groups established additional institutions, in part in response to foster care, in hopes of exposing their children to the religious traditions of their heritage. Cottage care appeared, initially in corrections, in an attempt to provide a more normal setting within the institution.

At the turn of the twentieth century, advances in social work, psychiatry, and psychology began to influence the care and treatment of children. In 1899, largely through the efforts of Jane Addams' Hull House, the first juvenile court was established in Chicago. It advanced the principle of separation of children from adults. William Healy, in response to concerns about recidivism in that court, established an outpatient clinic to treat children. He developed principles and procedures for the detailed assessment of children, including detailed social history and medical, psychiatric, neurological, and psychiatric examinations, and offered a model for treatment in juvenile correctional programs.

Aid to Families with Dependent Children appeared and served to keep more children at home.

Use of foster care continued to grow. States began procedures for licensing and regulating institutions.

Stemming from the work of Freud, Aichhorn, and others, advances in psychiatry led to a shift from residential care to residential treatment in the 1930s as psychiatrists and psychiatric social workers were added to staff. The concept of the therapeutic milieu appeared in the 1950s based on the work of Redl and Bettelheim. In the next decade, advances in psychology based on the work of Pavlov and Skinner led to the application of principles of learning in the treatment of behavior.

Trends away from both care and treatment in institutions mark the latter part of the twentieth century. Federal courts established the principles of the right to treatment and the least restrictive alternative in the 1960s. Miller began closing reform schools in Massachusetts in 1970 in favor of group homes, intensive family care, and increased probation services. Others developed programs for intensive in-home services to prevent removal of children, and intensive therapeutic foster care with specially trained families and clinical and crisis support to serve difficult children in family settings. Federal legislation required community mental health to get into the act as the twentieth century drew to a close.

Consequently, there has been a shift in the types of children referred to residential treatment. No longer styled as a refuge for orphans or dependent and neglected children, residential settings have become the placement of last resort for children who not only cannot be treated in other settings but also cannot be managed in any other setting. See figure 2.1 for a chronology of events in the development of residential treatment of adolescents and children.

A Sampling of Programs

For those who are more comfortable with concrete examples, I have selected five programs for presentation in this chapter. I have avoided presenting any programs in which I have had any involvement. The programs are presented in order of their founding dates, oldest to most recent. In most cases, the presentations are limited by material provided to me upon request by the program. The exception is the Bethel Baptist Home, which received some attention in the news media.

The programs are presented solely for the purposes of example and illustration. With the exception of the Bethel Baptist Home, the presentations are provided with the permission of the programs. Nothing in this chapter should be taken as an endorsement of any program or an advocacy for any particular style, approach, treatment, or intervention.

I chose the first, KidsPeace (formerly Wiley House), for two reasons. It is an example of a fairly traditional model of a residential treatment program with a history dating back to 1882, and it has some name recognition because it advertises nationally. It also offers a variety of nonresidential services. Although I lived in that community for a number of years in the late 1960s and early 1970s, I knew no more about the program than its name and location. The material comes primarily from their promotional package. No information was provided on cost.

I selected Father Flanagan's Boys' Home for several reasons. It has name recognition—it has been the subject of three movies; it operates programs in several parts of the country; it conducts a national fund drive. Moreover, several other agencies around the nation operate programs based on its treatment model, the Family-Teacher Model, and send their staff to Boys Town for training and certification. It, too, offers a variety of nonresidential services. Boys Town provided promotional material, an annual report, and a training manual.

VisionQuest is presented as an example of a nontraditional model for residential treatment. It is a for-profit agency that offers both wilderness programming and a sea-based program, as well as some nonresidential services. VisionQuest provided promotional material and portions of their program manual.

Kaleidoscope is an example of noninstitutional care and treatment that has achieved some national recognition through the consultation it provides to state agencies in a number of states and its leadership in several national conferences. I learned of Kaleidoscope through its consultation to mental health in Louisiana. Kaleidoscope provided promotional and training material. No outcome data is available.

The Bethel Baptist Home is presented for contrast. It is a religious program that was exempt from state licensing regulation. Material is based on coverage by the local press.

KIDSPEACE/WILEY HOUSE

William Thurston opened a home for the needy children of the Lehigh Valley in 1882. The Lehigh Valley is comprised of Allentown, Bethlehem, and Easton, Pennsylvania, about sixty miles from Philadelphia and 120 miles from New York City. Thurston operated his home at his own expense until it was incorporated in 1886. In 1895, Captain James Wiley purchased six acres of land just outside Bethlehem where he constructed a residence that served children for over seventy-five years (Wiley House, undated b).

In the early 1970s, Wiley House began to expand existing programs and develop an integrated continuum of treatment programs to meet the need for a continuity of care (Wiley House, undated b). Wiley House currently maintains accreditation with three agencies and membership in some eighteen professional associations at local, state, regional, national, and international levels:

1. Accreditation.
   a. Joint Commission on Accreditation of Healthcare Organizations.
   b. Middle States Association of Colleges and Schools.
      1. Elementary accreditation.
      2. Institution-wide accreditation of elementary and secondary schools.
   c. The American Association of Psychiatric Services for Children—Accreditation for Interdisciplinary Services for Emotionally Disturbed and Mentally Ill.
2. Membership.
   a. International Association of Psychological Rehabilitation Services.
   b. Psychiatric Outpatient Centers of the Americas, Inc.
   c. American Association of Children's Residential Centers.
   d. American Association for Partial Hospitalization.
   e. Association of Private Schools for Exceptional Children.
   f. Child Welfare League of America.
   g. Council for Exceptional Children.
   h. Crisis Prevention Institute.
   i. National Association for the Education of the Young Child.
   j. National Association of Homes for Children.
   k. Northeastern and Central Partial Hospitalization Providers Association.
   l. Pennsylvania Association of Community MH/MR Providers.
   m. Pennsylvania Association of Federal Program Coordinators.
   n. Pennsylvania Council of Children's Services.
   o. Pennsylvania Council of Voluntary Child Care Agencies.
   p. West Virginia Child Care Association.
   q. Delaware Valley Adoption Council (Wiley House, undated a).

Treatment Philosophy

Wiley House operates under the philosophy that an agency should provide a full continuum of programs for children and adolescents in need of psychiatric treatment and that their needs should be met in as normal a setting as possible. The treatment needs of seriously emotionally disturbed children are best served in a structured and supervised milieu. The natural family plays an important role in the treatment process. An eclectic approach is guided by highly individualized treatment plans (Wiley House, undated b).

Population Served

Wiley House serves boys and girls with severe emotional and behavioral problems, including mood disorders, adjustment disorders, sexual disorders, and personality disorders. Children are screened as to their potential for growth and change to determine their appropriateness for admission (Wiley House, undated b).

Residential Care and Treatment

The Long Term Residential Treatment Program serves boys and girls aged twelve to seventeen who have moderate to severe behavioral problems. The overall focus of the program is "improvement in emotional, social, and behavioral health" (Wiley House, undated b, p. 10).

The treatment team is composed of board certified child and adult psychiatrists, licensed clinical psychologists, pediatricians, registered nurses, licensed clinical social workers, child care workers, mental health workers, teachers certified in special education, and recreation therapists. The team develops individualized treatment plans with the child, family, and referral source. Plans are "problem specific and time-limited" (Wiley House, undated b, p. 10) and designed to help residents achieve age-appropriate behavior to facilitate return to a less restrictive environment. The Quality Assurance Program ensures that goals are being met through periodic reviews of treatment. Discharge planning begins at intake; the average length of stay is twelve months (Wiley House, undated b).

Treatment Modalities

Major treatment modalities include individual therapy, group therapy, family therapy, reality therapy, life space counseling, behavior modification, recreational therapy, and speech therapy. Treatment plans are reviewed monthly and formally developed every three months. Three hours of individual therapy are provided weekly, along with two hours of group therapy, a unit group, and a problem specific group. One hour of family therapy is provided weekly for local families; ongoing consultation is provided to therapists of out-of-town families. A board certified child psychiatrist reviews

treatment weekly. When psychotropic medication is indicated, it is prescribed and monitored by psychiatrists and administered by psychiatrists or nursing staff (Wiley House, undated b).

Range of Programs and Services

Wiley House presently offers some twenty-three different programs and services.

1. *Residential services.*
   a. Three residential programs provide treatment to boys aged thirteen to eighteen, girls of the same age, and boys aged seven to eleven.
   b. Community Residential Care provides transition for boys coming out of structured settings.
   c. Specialized Community Residential Care provides services to boys who need residential treatment but can manage open community settings.
   d. Emergency Shelter Care provides temporary care until a suitable placement can be arranged.
   e. A Diagnostic/Acute Care Program for children in acute crisis serves to stabilize the child, provide a complete diagnostic evaluation, and develop a plan for placement to help avoid multiple placements that may often occur in especially difficult cases.
2. *Intensive Treatment Family Program.* This program provides a consistent and caring family for children who cannot live in their own homes.
3. *In-Home Youth/Parent Sponsorship.* An intensive in-home program is provided for children at risk of placement to maintain them in the home. The program is also available to assist children with return home from a structured setting.
4. *Day Treatment.* Both day treatment and afternoon treatment are offered to help children prepare to participate in community life. Programs

are offered for preschool and primary school-aged children and older boys and girls.

5. *Special Education.* Schools in several localities serve children who cannot function in public schools.

6. *Outpatient Services.* Several programs are offered for children, individuals, and families, including professional counseling, outpatient psychiatric services, and treatment for children and adolescents who have been sexually abused.

7. *National Conferences.* Wiley House provides training and development for professionals involved in the care of children, adolescents, and families (Wiley House, undated b; undated c).

In 1992, Wiley House changed its name to KidsPeace National Centers for Kids in Crisis. In January of 1993, KidsPeace opened a newly-constructed psychiatric hospital for seventy-two children on a 300-acre site in nearby Orefield, Pennsylvnia, and relocated its national headquarters there. Since 1989, KidsPeace boasts an 80 percent success rate measured one year after discharge and defined as the child's continuing in a less restrictive environment with no new legal charges. KidsPeace presently operates foster care offices in the states of Georgia, New York, and Indiana, and a residential program in Maine (Powers, 1994).

FATHER FLANAGAN'S BOYS TOWN

Father Edward J. Flanagan opened his Boys Town in Nebraska in 1917 (Boys Town, undated a). His purpose was to provide care to homeless, neglected, abused, and handicapped boys (Boys Town, undated c). Initially, he started his program in a house in town, later acquiring a rural site where he began construction of Boys Town (Considine & Taurog, 1938). Boys lived in large dormitories except for a few cottages for groups of twenty that were constructed by Father Flanagan before his death in 1948. Boys Town is an incorporated village in Nebraska, managed by a Board of Trustees, with its own police and fire departments, two churches, and three schools. It maintains its own roads, sewers, and water (Boys Town, undated c). In 1934, Boys Town was granted its own U.S. Post Office (Boys Town, undated a).

Treatment Philosophy

Beginning in 1973, Boys Town converted to a philosophy of family-based care. Six years later, the first girls were accepted. By 1987, youth were living in seventy-one homes of from six to ten children under the supervision of trained married couples called Family-Teachers. Family-Teachers are trained and certified to provide all treatment the children receive, guiding and instructing them on a twenty-four-hour basis. Boys Town developed a training and certification process for Family-Teachers in the late 1970s. (Boys Town, undated c). (Compare to the Teaching Parents of Achievement Place.)

Population Served

About 700 youths, of whom some 35 percent are minorities, reside at Boys Town. Children may come from anywhere in the country and even foreign countries such as Canada or Saudi Arabia. The normal age of admission ranges from nine to sixteen years; exceptions may be made for siblings. Protestants and Catholics are about equally divided; a few are Jewish. Boys Town has always been nonsectarian and employs Protestant and Catholic chaplains; Jewish youths attend services at a local synagogue. According to Father Flanagan: "Every boy must learn to pray . . . how he prays is up to him" (Boys Town, undated c, no pagination).

Residential Care and Treatment

Family-Teachers are responsible for the care, treatment, and improvement of children in their home. The treatment modality is a teaching system with continual feedback and review coupled with a motivational system. A structured technique called a teaching interaction is used to teach social and communication skills, such as following instructions, disagreeing appropriately, accepting criticism, and accepting no for an answer. Moral and religious values are also taught along with good study, work, and grooming habits and problem-solving skills. Initially, children acquire privileges on a point system; eventually they move to a schedule of more real rewards and consequences (Boys Town, undated b).

Outcome

The average stay is twenty-two months. Of the 7 percent who run away, most return within a day or two. Children graduate when they have corrected their problem behaviors and have a place to go, or when they graduate high school. Those who qualify are provided with scholarship assistance. Graduates include doctors, lawyers, state senators, professional football players, and businessmen (Boys Town, undated c).

Range of Programs and Services

In addition to the main residential campus, Boys Town operates several other programs. A diagnostic, treatment, and research hospital for children with speech, hearing, and learning disorders, founded in 1977, serves 8,500 children annually (Boys Town, undated c). Father Flanagan High School opened in Omaha in 1983 for inner city high-risk students. It maintains an enrollment of 300, providing alternative school services, an on-site parole officer, nursery, and substance abuse services.

In addition to the many independent agencies around the country operating on the Family-Teacher model, Boys Town operated programs in San Antonio, New Orleans, Tallahassee, and Orlando in 1989. Boys Town plans to be in seventeen metropolitan areas by 1993, including Las Vegas, Brooklyn, New England, and California (Boys

Town, undated a). In addition, Boys Town offers training and certification for staff of other agencies operating the Family-Teacher model. In 1989, sixty-two other child care agencies in ten other states received training, technical assistance, certification, or recertification from the Boys Town National Training Center (Boys Town, undated c.)

Nonresidential Services

Nonresidential programs on the main campus and other sites around the country include:

1. *Parent Training.* Parents attend a series of eight two-hour sessions and receive training in techniques developed at Boys Town.
2. *Shelter Care.* A shelter, opened in March of 1989 in Grand Island, Nebraska, provides a safety net to children and families in crisis by developing a plan utilizing community resources to avoid breaking up the family.
3. *Home-Based Services.* Boys Town techniques are provided through intensive in-home treatment to empower the family and keep it together.
4. *Treatment Foster Care.* Boys Town Foster Parents in several of the communities in which Boys Town operates receive forty hours of training prior to receiving a child. Training continues after a child is placed, along with consultation, respite care, and twenty-four-hour on-call service for crises (Boys Town, undated a).

VISIONQUEST

Steven R. Rogers and R. Ledger Burton, corrections professionals who had become discouraged with the lack of success of traditional programs, founded VisionQuest in 1973. Currently licensed to serve 963 youth, VisionQuest is a for-profit corporation owned by stockholders. In addition to its office in Tucson, VisionQuest has offices in Easton, Pennsylvania, and Stockton, California (L. Buckel, 1990; VisionQuest, undated b).

Treatment Philosophy

VisionQuest takes its name from the Native American rite of passage to adulthood. Its programs are based on a philosophy with several key premises:

1. *Tradition and Ceremony.* Negative traditions and ceremonies, e.g., gang behavior, shared drug use, and court appearances, are replaced with positive traditions and ceremonies that are based on those of the Plains Indians and emphasize accomplishments and cooperation, e.g., circle meetings.
2. *Success.* Successes at challenging yet attainable experiences increase self-esteem and provide a sense of mastery that generalize to other areas of life.
3. *Supportive Intervention.* VisionQuest holds youths accountable and responsible for behavior and decisions, but confrontation is balanced with empathy and support.
4. *Commitment.* Youth and their families are presumed to be basically honorable. Youth are asked to commit to VisionQuest for a minimum of one year, to abstain from drugs, tobacco, and alcohol, to not run away from the program or family issues, and to complete three high-impact programs or quests. Parents, when involved, are asked to face family issues honestly and discuss problems that arise with their child.
5. *Parenting.* Staff view their job as one of parenting and build a close and trusting relationship with youth. Within that relationship they set limits and expectations and explore treatment issues.
6. *Personal Safety.* VisionQuest views a physically and emotionally safe environment as essential. Staff are clearly in charge and provide structure and supervision to minimize intimidation, physical and sexual harassment, and bullying. "In providing treatment, no consideration will be placed above the safety of youth in the program" (VisionQuest, 1990, p. 2).
7. *Redirecting the Family.* Three primary treatment issues are frequently the result of family patterns: abuse, abandonment, and control. VisionQuest works with the family in individual, conjoint, and group meetings as established in the youth's individual plan. Parents are encouraged to visit and to participate in planning (VisionQuest, 1990).

Population Served

VisionQuest serves difficult children. In Pennsylvania, 33 percent of its children had arrest histories for crimes against the person; in California, 43 percent had histories of violent crimes. The youth range in age from ten to twenty-one years. Most have been adjudicated delinquent, although referrals from social service agencies and parents or guardians are also accepted (VisionQuest, undated a; VisionQuest, undated b).

Residential Care and Treatment

Youths normally begin at an Impact Camp near their home. Impact camps consist of a tipi village with tipis on platforms arranged in a semi-circle. Tipis are licensed by local authorities for twelve to fifteen youths and are used primarily for sleeping. Tipi staff consist of a tipi foreman and three tipi parents. Youth and staff form a tipi family who eat, sleep, work, and participate in activities together. At least two staff in the village remain awake at night (VisionQuest, 1989d).

Classrooms, kitchen and dining areas, offices, playing fields, wilderness courses, and enclosed exercise areas in cold climates complete the village. Impact camps are devoted to assessment, orientation, physical conditioning, building relationships, and training skills necessary to participate in quests. Orientation may take from a few days to over a month, depending on the needs and history of individual youth. A psychologist, nurse, teacher, and senior staff comprise a multi-disciplinary team that completes the assessment and develops a plan with the youth, and with parents and placement agency as available (VisionQuest, 1989d).

Tipi staff lead their families in work projects

and chores. Staff promote a competitive spirit between families to build team spirit and abilities as youth compete to achieve recognition. Physical training to build strength and endurance and develop the youth's awareness of his or her own body becomes an important part of programming after medical clearance. Youths are prepared for quests according to the four-directional approach of the Native American medicine wheel: physically, emotionally, mentally, and spiritually (VisionQuest, 1989d).

Education

School is provided in accordance with local standards. An individual plan is developed for each youth. Confidence and self-esteem gained from achievements in physical training, sports, work projects, and other areas can be observed to generalize to the classroom.

Quests

Quests, periods of stress and intensive learning, become reference points for each youth. Milestones and difficult moments are shared and memorialized in circle meetings. Quests are carefully planned and highly structured activities with specific goals. Central to each are teamwork and individual accomplishment. Quests are staffed by trained personnel on a staff-to-child ratio of about one to two. One of the staff is an emergency medical technician; a vehicle is always nearby and available by radio. Youths are selected for quests based on need, ability to benefit, and accomplishment; some quests must be earned. All youth receive training beforehand in the specific skills they will need (VisionQuest, 1989d).

1. *The Hiking Quest.* Five to seven staff accompany from ten to twelve youth on a hike that lasts from fourteen to twenty-one days. It begins with a stress hike to reach the food drop; slower and faster youths must strive together to reach a common goal. Youths then spend about three days alone in their own individual camps, visited daily by staff and monitored by binoculars. "Alone, they cannot define themselves in terms of their relationships with others; nor can they escape the reality of their own thoughts and feelings" (VisionQuest, 1989f, pp. 3–4).

The students then undertake a trek on their own; staff monitor but do not interfere except for safety. The group must manage a trek of several days that includes rock climbing and rappelling. "These activities provide dramatic opportunities for each youth to test his own limits, and to confront his fears with courage and determination. Once again, each youth is forced to recognize his responsibility to his peers as well as his own need to trust others" (VisionQuest, 1989f, p. 4).

2. *The Bicycle Quest.* Similar to the hiking quest, bicycle quests may last from several weeks to two months. Ten to twelve youth and about six staff tour back roads and national parks (VisionQuest, 1989f).

3. *Buffalo Soldiers Quest.* The Buffalo Soldiers commemorate all-black units of the U.S. Army who overcame adversity, including racial prejudice, and fought in Indian wars to help open the West. From twenty to forty youth and ten to thirty staff participate. The quest features the contributions made by black Americans; it is open to all youth regardless of race or sex. Buffalo Soldiers travel on a horseback pack trip and perform precision drills at community events. They have performed at the U.S. Capitol, at Disneyland, at military bases, and in parades (VisionQuest, 1989f).

4. *The Winter Quest.* The East Coast VisionQuest program conducts a seven- to ten-day Winter Quest, which features cross country skiing and igloo construction in addition to wilderness hiking (VisionQuest, 1989f).

5. *The Canoe Quest.* Seven to ten youth and a minimum of three staff participate in canoe quests that last from seven to ten days on lakes or rivers with no noticeable current. A quest may operate from a base camp or travel and establish new camps daily (VisionQuest, 1989f).

6. *The Wagon Train Program.* Fifty to seventy-five youth and thirty-five to sixty-five staff travel in nine to twelve wagons with horses and mules for individual riders. Staff work ahead to set up camps; a specially equipped bus accompanies the train to allow youths to continue their educational program (VisionQuest, 1989g).

7. *OceanQuest.* VisionQuest owns and operates two tall ships, the *New Way* and the *Bill of Rights.* Ships' captains and mates are licensed by the Coast Guard. The quest promotes self-discipline and respect for authority, closeness, teamwork, interpersonal involvement, and introspection. "The vastness and capriciousness of the sea is a teacher in the VisionQuest sailing programs. . . . Youths develop the ability to accept the inevitable changes that life brings and to be thankful for periods of smooth sailing" (VisionQuest, 1989e, p. 1).

Outcome

In California, where 43 percent of their clients had committed violent crimes before placement, 69 percent remained out of incarceration and only 16 percent had committed violent offenses two years after release. In Pennsylvania, where 33 percent of their clients had been arrested for crimes against people before admission, only 9 percent had been arrested for violent crimes and 86 percent remained unincarcerated six to eighteen months after release, although 44 percent had been rearrested. VisionQuest is moving to provide aftercare services in Pennsylvania's inner cities to improve these results and currently offers aftercare in Erie and Pittsburgh (VisionQuest, undated a).

Range of Programs and Services

VisionQuest also offers a group home program and two HomeQuest Programs. The group home program assists youths in returning to the community from VisionQuest. HomeQuest provides aftercare services to youths returning home from Vi-

sionQuest and is also available to selected youth to help them remain in their own homes. HomeQuest Plus is a more intensive in-home program that monitors youths regularly and provides on-call assistance after 9:00 P.M. (VisionQuest, 1989a; 1989c; 1989e).

KALEIDOSCOPE

Kaleidoscope was founded in Chicago in 1973 by child care workers who felt they could do a better job than the agency with whom they were employed. Eventually, they decided to stop complaining and do something. In founding their own agency, they agreed on two fundamental principles. Just as parents do not screen their child in the hospital nursery before deciding to take the new baby home, Kaleidoscope founders decided on a policy of taking all comers, a no-decline policy for referrals. Just as natural parents do not usually throw their children out of the home for misbehavior or for completing the program, Kaleidoscope founders decided on a policy of commitment to the child regardless of behavior, a no-punitive discharge policy for all children (Dennis, 1992).

They began at about the same time that Illinois began returning hundreds of children from out-of-state placements all across the country. The children presented especially difficult problems that many private agencies were reluctant to serve. Kaleidoscope started with small group homes staffed with shift personnel. They decided that several children in one setting posed more issues of control than of treatment and evolved to a foster family model (Dennis, 1992).

Treatment Philosophy

Kaleidoscope offers a different approach to serving especially difficult or "seriously unique" children (Kaleidoscope, undated a, no pagination). Kaleidoscope:

1. Accepts full responsibility for each child:
   a. turning down no child who is referred.
   b. putting no child out because of bad or good behavior.
2. Serves all of its children in family settings or independent apartments in the community. Family settings include:
   a. the natural family when possible.
   b. placement with other family members if possible and necessary, and
   c. placement in paid foster family placement when natural family placement cannot be made to work (Dennis, 1992).

Two basic principles, normalization and unconditional care, underlie its service philosophy. Normalization holds "that children can best learn to become normal, competent adults if they live in and learn from a normal environment—a family, a neighborhood, community" (Kaleidoscope, undated b, no pagination). Unconditional care "asserts that children need loving care regardless of their behavior, and rejecting them from care for misbehavior worsens their condition and our society's burden" (Kaleidoscope, undated b, no pagination).

Population Served

Kaleidoscope serves the most difficult to place youth—those with a history of multiple placements, institutionalized children, and children with multiple handicaps or severe mental illness. It also serves children who have their own child or children, keeping mother and child together, and children born with AIDS (Kaleidoscope, undated d).

Residential Care and Treatment

Kaleidoscope serves all of its children in the community. Two basic program models serve children in placement: Therapeutic Foster Family Homes and The Youth Development Program (Kaleidoscope, undated b).

Therapeutic Foster Family Homes

Therapeutic Foster Family Homes serve about seventy children. Foster parents are paid and trained to provide full-time care to a child. There are two recent additions:

1. *The Adolescent Parent Program.* This program serves wards of the state who are pregnant, or who are parents, along with the children.
2. *The STAR Program (Specialized Team for AIDS).* This program serves babies born with AIDS (Kaleidoscope, undated d).

Adoption or return home for the children served is seldom an option. The program is, consequently, long-term. Foster families seek to provide "acceptance, structure and nurturing" (Kaleidoscope, undated d, no pagination).

Foster parents are carefully recruited, trained, matched with a child, and then paid to provide specialized services. Foster parents are supported by teams of social workers (who have either a bachelor's degree or a master's degree), a vocational counselor, a therapeutic recreation specialist, and administrators. Only one child is placed with a family unless an exception is made in the case of siblings or a child-parent with her own child or children (Kaleidoscope, undated d).

While children may occasionally be reunited with natural family, most often they are graduated to independent living in the Youth Development Program. Terminally ill children "live out their short lives in the loving environment of the foster home" (Kaleidoscope, undated d, no pagination).

Children receive care in a nurturing family environment, with twenty-four-hour supervision, discipline that encourages responsibility and caring, transportation to appointments and youth activities, foster parent participation in school and community activities, advocacy, and role modeling. Foster parents receive support that includes at least one home visit per week, twenty-four-hour emergency consultation, support and crisis intervention in addition to orientation, pre-service and in-service training, and compensation. Biological families are included in treatment planning, supervised visits, and referral to the Satellite Family Outreach Program for reunification, when appropriate (Kaleidoscope, undated d).

Agency personnel provide treatment planning; casework services; a minimum of two treatment sessions per month; individual, group, or family therapy with qualified professionals; educational and vocational planning and placement services; and structured recreation. Agency staff arrange necessary medical and dental evaluations and care. They provide support with educational and job placements and other community resources such as church and youth groups (Kaleidoscope, undated d).

The treatment team consists of a case manager (who generally has an MSW), a Foster Family Worker (an experienced staff with a bachelor's degree) and a supervisor. Formal treatment planning conferences are held quarterly; plans are updated at least monthly (Kaleidoscope, undated d).

The Youth Development Program

The Youth Development Program serves an often neglected population—older children and young adults who have grown up in institutions and foster care. The program places over forty such youth in apartments in the community and provides supervision to help them become independent. Most youths are eighteen or nineteen years old, although some may be as young as sixteen or as old as twenty. Youths typically have a history of physical or sexual abuse. Skirmishes with legal authorities are common, as is drug or alcohol abuse. They are educationally behind, often functionally illiterate. They lack work skills (Kaleidoscope, undated e).

Two staff teams serve groups of twenty-two youths. Each team is composed of a supervisor, two social workers with master's degrees, three youth workers with bachelor's degrees, and an adolescent parent specialist. Administration and the agency's recreation, employment, and housing specialists are also available (Kaleidoscope, undated e).

Only one youth is placed in an apartment. Each youth visits the agency once per week to meet with staff and pick up her or his allowance. Staff visit each youth at least four times per month (Kaleidoscope, undated e).

Youths receive an apartment in a residential neighborhood, casework, supervision, twenty-four–hour crisis intervention, advocacy with community resources, individual counseling or therapy, therapeutic recreation, group counseling, educational planning, vocational assessment, job development, sex and drug education, and assistance with independent living skills. Medical and dental care are also provided. Formal treatment conferences occur semi-annually, with treatment plans updated at least monthly (Kaleidoscope, undated e).

Range of Programs and Services

Kaleidoscope also works hard to preserve families. Its Satellite Family Outreach Program works to keep children from being removed from their families to prevent institutionalization and to reunite children who are already in residential treatment with their families. It serves nearly fifty families (Kaleidoscope, undated c).

Families receive eighty to 125 hours of service per month, mostly in the home. Services include help with basics—food, housing, child and home management, recreation—along with counseling and therapy. Most families are urban and low income, dependent on AFDC, with about two-thirds headed by women. Family heads are typically unskilled, lacking high school diplomas. About two-thirds are seeking work unsuccessfully. Severe relationship disturbances, including violence, sexual abuse, substance abuse, and depression, complicate problems in providing food and shelter. Role and boundary problems are also typical, including the parental child (Kaleidoscope, undated c).

Teams of four family workers with bachelor's degrees and a social worker with a master's degree serve up to twelve families. Family workers provide direct and collateral services while the social worker coordinates clinical services. Agency administration and specialists in housing, recreation, and employment are available (Kaleidoscope, undated c).

Services include twenty-four–hour crisis intervention, individual counseling, group counseling, homemaker services, financial planning, assistance with home maintenance, therapeutic recreation, food assistance, diagnostic and assessment services, individualized educational planning, social work, job placement, first aid education, sex and drug education, and nutritional consultation. Formal treatment planning conferences occur every six months, but plans are updated monthly by workers. Staff participate in treatment planning done by other agencies, including courts (Kaleidoscope, undated c).

THE BETHEL BAPTIST HOME

Herman Fountain arrived in Lucedale, Mississippi, in 1978. A former heroin addict, Fountain was travelling in a camper with his wife, their four children, and three other children. He started his Bethel Baptist Home that same year. Within ten years the home was serving about 130 children and youths, of whom about thirty were over the age of eighteen. During those ten years approximately 150 children had run away, many complaining about abuse (Snyder, 1988a), while the home grew to several dormitories, barns, a stable, staff housing, and a swimming pool on twenty-eight acres (Snyder, 1988d).

In addition to the abuse, there were allegations of child labor law violations. According to former residents and members of the community, Fountain contracted for construction and demolition projects and used residents without paying them. A local minister reported contracting with Fountain to have a roof torn off a building. About eighteen boys showed up to do the work. A property officer at the Keesler Air Force Base reported that the base contracted with Fountain to have some buildings torn down. Busloads of children arrived, including some seven- and eight-year-olds. The youngest children didn't do much. Fountain supervised the work. Former residents reported that they were forced to work fourteen hours per day (Snyder, 1988b).

Girls reported that a room about the size of a bathroom with no windows was used for discipline. It was called the revival room. Children were allowed out for showers and meals. One girl was confined in the room for two weeks; another spent six weeks in the revival room (Snyder, 1988e).

A hearing of alleged abuse and neglect was held on June 10, 1988, in the case of a boy who had run away about thirty days before. A physician testified that the boy had not received treatment for an eye condition that would eventually produce blindness. At the conclusion of the hearing, the judge ordered state officials to remove all children from the home. Officials went for the children that same evening. Many of the children fled into the woods—Fountain had told them they were going to be put in a mental hospital (Snyder, 1988a). Police finished rounding up the children on June 13 and arrested Fountain (Snyder, 1988c).

A year later, Fountain admitted to being in financial trouble; he had only ten children. Contempt of court fines in the amount of $1,500 per day had mounted to $450,000. Three boys aged twelve, fifteen, and seventeen had recently been removed by Mississippi officials. The twelve-year-old had bruises on his buttocks that he alleged to have received for failing to eat his breakfast. The fifteen-year-old alleged that he had been beaten for failure to memorize Bible verses. The seventeen-year-old alleged that he missed a whole year of school in seventh grade to work on the boys' dormitory. Boys got ten "licks" for looking at the girls (Snyder, 1989).

When asked about the abuse alleged by the boys, Fountain replied: "They got their licks just like anybody else did" (Snyder, 1989e, p. A–6). When asked if he would comply with court orders, Fountain replied: "No way. I'll take the same stand I took before, separation of church and state" (Snyder, 1989, p. A–6). Mississippi was moving to change licensing regulations that exempted homes giving care without charge. Fountain accepted monthly donations from parents, many of whom sent their children from out of state (Snyder, 1989).

SUMMARY

This chapter presented a variety of programs and approaches to treating troubled children. The presentations were limited by available material—in most cases, material provided by the programs themselves.

KidsPeace is an example of a traditional residential treatment program that evolved from an orphanage established near the turn of the century into a multiservice agency. KidsPeace lists numerous professional affiliations. Its residential treatment component consists of three residential programs, group homes, shelter care, and an acute diagnostic and care program. Residential programs stress a multidisciplinary team approach with individual, group, and family therapies, life-space counseling, behavior modification, and recreational therapy. Psychotropic medication, when indicated, is administered and monitored under the close supervision of the attending psychiatrist. Both professional staff and child care counselors are given significant roles in treatment.

In addition, KidsPeace offers an array of community-based services, including therapeutic foster family care, intensive in-home therapy, day treatment, and special education for nonresident children, along with a variety of outpatient services.

Boys Town developed from a large, congregate-style orphanage into a cottage-style program and multiservice agency with programs nationwide. The main campus is, in actuality, an incorporated village in which residents have significant responsibilities for self-governance. The present cottage-style program places specially trained house parents, Family-Teachers, in full charge of treatment. The treatment system emphasizes continuous teaching of social skills, with feedback and reinforcement on a point system.

In addition, Boys Town offers a hospital for children, an inner city high school, parent training, shelter care, intensive in-home services, intensive foster family care, and a national 1-800 hot line for troubled youths and families. Boys Town and several other agencies operate group homes based on the Family-Teacher Model in numerous cities around the country.

VisionQuest began operations in 1973 as an alternative to corrections and traditional residential treatment. It is based on the traditions and ceremonies of the Plains Indians and stresses commitment, success in a variety of challenging experiences, supportive intervention by tipi staff who view their role as one of parenting, personal safety, and family intervention aimed at redirecting the family. A multidisciplinary team evaluates youth and develops a plan with the youth. Tipi staff have primary responsibility for treatment. A variety of Quests play a significant role in treatment: hiking, bicycling, canoeing, sailing, a winter quest, wagon train, and a cavalry unit. VisionQuest offers programs in Arizona, California, and Pennsylvania. It also offers a group home program and an in-home program, along with aftercare. It reports favorable outcome statistics, although recent runaways have been high.

Kaleidoscope was also founded in 1973. Kaleidoscope rejects no child that a referring agency chooses to refer for an available opening; it discharges no child for bad behavior. Its philosophy is to provide whatever it takes to serve the child. Initially, it operated on the group home model with staff working shifts and progressed to a therapeutic foster family model with clinical, program, and crisis support for families. Kaleidoscope serves especially difficult children, including teens with families and children with AIDS.

In addition to its therapeutic foster family program, Kaleidoscope serves children in the natural family, including the extended family, whenever possible through an intensive in-home program. It also offers a program for children who have grown up in placement to assist them in establishing themselves independently in their own apartments.

The Bethel Baptist Home, founded in 1978, is an example of a return to the past. I suspect that the founding philosophy was one of wanting to help children in spite of themselves. Its treatment philosophy appears to be ''spare the rod and spoil the child.'' Its outcome statistics are not favorable; runaways were extremely high.

Referral and the Continuum of Care

Two related topics remain in providing an orientation to residential treatment: the means by which children come into residential treatment and the continuum of services and care in which residential facilities exist. Some knowledge of these topics is essential to an understanding of residential treatment today.

At one time, institutional placement was very likely the first or the only option to be considered for a child in need. Today, that is seldom the case. The continuum of services and care that may be available to children and families in need is extensive.

It begins with special services that may be available in the schools and the community. It may include intensive in-home services in some localities. It progresses through foster care and therapeutic foster care to group home care, residential treatment, psychiatric hospitalization, and incarceration in a state juvenile correctional facility.

The decision to utilize residential treatment often depends on what other services may be available in the community instead of residential treatment and on the quality of those services. Residential treatment is often not pursued until other services have failed.

In this chapter, each component of the system of care is described briefly. Not all are available in every community or jurisdiction. Next, with some knowledge of the continuum of services and care as a perspective, we will review the means by which children come into the continuum of care and, possibly, into residential treatment. There are four possibilities:

1. A parent may take the initiative in seeking help.
2. A child may ask for help or run away from an abusive setting.
3. A child protective agency may take initiative because of neglect, abuse, or abandonment.
4. A juvenile court may take initiative because of a child's misconduct or criminal behavior.

A brief description of child protective services, along with its legal base, is followed by a presentation on the juvenile court and misconduct by juveniles. Parents or children seeking help must often approach one of these agencies, since they serve as the gatekeepers and funding sources for many of the more expensive services. Finally, this chapter looks at the decision-making process and some of the factors that govern decisions about children and families in need.

THE CONTINUUM OF CARE

The continuum of care has evolved from binding children out to families and tradesmen, through reliance on institutions, to a return to foster care as an alternative to institutions, to a variety of services to keep the child and family together. The current system of care includes all of these, and ranges from the natural family with services and supervision to commitment to a juvenile correctional facility. A knowledge of the continuum of services and care that may be available in a community is essential to an understanding of residential treatment for several reasons:

1. Children may enter the system of care at any point. Likewise, they may enter residential treatment from any other point in the continuum.
2. Knowing that a child has had some success or failure with some aspect of the continuum of care tells much more about the child's needs when one understands the capabilities and limitations of that resource.
3. It is necessary for formulating treatment goals and determining readiness for discharge. A child who is going to a group home with capabilities for continued treatment may need less treatment in the restrictive residential setting than a child who will return to a family who does not have access to continued therapy after discharge, or who will not participate in therapy that may be available.
4. It is necessary in determining the appropriateness of the child for placement. The child should not be accepted if the child's needs for care and treatment can reasonably be expected to be provided for with less restrictive interventions. The child should also not be accepted if the child's treatment needs can reasonably be expected to require capabilities beyond those of the residential program.
5. The residential facility and other components of the system of care may interface during treatment. The program may utilize other services in the continuum during treatment, such as services in the public schools or a mental health clinic. Parents may be referred to other resources in the community for support or treatment for themselves or for other children remaining at home. Protective services may be concerned about issues of care and treatment and allegations of abuse within the residential program. Probation officers and courts may monitor a child's compliance with the program.

The Natural Family

Growing up in the natural family is the ideal. For children who cannot live at home because of the inability of their parents to care for them (possibly due to the parents' physical or mental disabilities or illness, their severe substance abuse, or their physical abuse or neglect of their children), the natural family remains the ideal for many of them. Some seem to be obsessed with returning home, no matter how bad the home was for them when they were there, no matter how frequent and intense the arguments or fights, no matter how frequently the parent fails to show for a visit, for therapy, or to pick the child up for a scheduled pass. The home often improves magically in the child's thinking during his or her placement and becomes idealized, as with Todd.

Todd. **Todd had been raised by his grandmother until he was eight years old. She died. He went to live with his mother, who had little time for him; she went out nearly every night with her boyfriend. Todd, at the age of nine, attempted suicide twice. During his hospitalization following his second very serious attempt, he was informed that he would be placed with a foster family upon discharge. He cried. He wanted to go home. The psychiatrist decided that returning home would be the best for Todd and proceeded with plans to discharge him to his mother.**

Two weeks prior to his discharge, his mother left her boyfriend's home at mid-

night. Her boyfriend had gone out drinking earlier and had not yet returned. Her fourteen-year-old daughter was left alone in the boyfriend's home. The mother called later to tell her daughter that she was staying with a friend. The boyfriend returned very late. The next day, he took the daughter to her mother's apartment and dropped her off. The apartment had been without electricity for several days. A neighbor called the police. They picked the girl up later that night. The police could not locate the mother and turned Todd's older sister over to protective services. The hospital also called protective services to assume responsibility for Todd.

The Natural Family with Services

Sometimes the ideal seems within reach. A number of traditional as well as recent innovative services can help children and families reach this ideal in some cases.

Outpatient Services—Education, Counseling, or Therapy

A number of services are available in the community to which children and families in need can go for help. Some are public, others private for a fee or on a sliding fee.

Education. Many schools offer counseling to children and extra support to teachers who have a difficult child in their class. These services may be offered prior to, or in addition to, special education services, which may range from partial-day placement in resource classes for remediation to placement in special self-contained classes for children with behavior disorders, emotional disturbance, learning disabilities, or developmental disabilities.

Some school districts provide special schools with programs for especially difficult children, programs that include point and level systems, time-out or control rooms, intensive work with social workers, and other extraordinary interventions. Private agencies, such as KidsPeace, may also offer special schools and day treatment programs to provide ser-

vices for special children who otherwise could not remain at home and go to school.

Parenting Help. "Parent education" or "parent training" may be offered by various agencies to improve the parenting skills of parents. Parent support groups may also be available for parents who are having problems in the home. These services may be helpful to parents who are experiencing minor problems or in conjunction with other services.

Counseling or Therapy. Community mental health centers and a variety of charitable or for-profit social service agencies offer a range of services that include individual and family counseling or therapy, groups, and psychological and psychiatric treatment, either free or on a sliding fee. Private practitioners offer similar services that may be covered through a family's health insurance.

Probation Services for the Child. Children who have either committed a "real" crime or a status offense (truancy, ungovernable behavior, runaway, curfew violations, and the like) may be placed on probation. Probation may be used to coerce improved behavior and participation in treatment. The child is assigned a probation officer who monitors the child's behavior in accordance with conditions of probation and offers some assistance, including referral for service. Children and families may be court-ordered into treatment or therapy as a condition of a child's probation. Children may also be ordered into placement as a condition of probation.

In-Home Services

Recent Federal legislation requires states to develop plans for community-based systems of care for children in need. The emphasis is on keeping children at home (Yelton, 1993). This has given impetus to recent trends to provide in-home services to help maintain families and has led to expansion of several emergent programs to other communities.

Case Management. Various state agencies offer case management service to children and their families. While traditional child welfare agencies may have case managers who are overburdened with large case loads of perhaps thirty to sixty or more cases, they may also have special units with smaller case loads and more intensive services.

Recent developments in community mental heath have resulted in the establishment of units in several states in which case managers carry case loads of from ten to twenty. Medicaid may pay for such services if the family is eligible for Medicaid benefits. While such case managers do not provide therapy per se, they offer hands-on support and assistance to the child and family in accessing the full range of benefits and services that may be available in the community, along with encouragement and perhaps the counseling necessary to support the family's efforts and participation.

Family Preservation. Family preservation programs provide intensive, usually short-term crisis intervention in the home by a trained professional in cases where placement of a child appears imminent. The professional usually maintains a small case load of perhaps two or three families. Intervention is usually several days and evenings per week for four to six weeks up to three months. Family preservation workers provide hands-on assistance and therapy in the home in all areas of family living—teaching, counseling, and modeling in appropriate areas, and working to resolve family conflicts and restructure family relationships that may be dysfunctional. Most programs rely heavily on linkage of the family with other resources for continuing long-term treatment and support (Hartman, 1993). A few models of intensive in-home services may be long-term, up to one or two years, as with Kaleidoscope.

In-Home Crisis Intervention. Twenty-four hour per day, seven day per week, in-home crisis services are available in some communities. Crisis workers may be sent to a home in which a child is acting out seriously—suicidal, physically aggressive towards others, or destructive of property. Crisis workers calm or subdue the child and calm the family. They can remain on the scene for several hours, even being relieved by other workers so that assistance may be continued for several days. Crisis workers may make referrals for additional services and may arrange temporary placement of the child or emergency psychiatric hospitalization if necessary.

Temporary Out-of-Home Placement

There are a number of temporary placement resources for children who cannot stay at home for one reason or another. They can serve one or more of several purposes:

1. To provide respite for the child or family, to deescalate a situation that has temporarily become difficult or dangerous, and to prevent longer term removal.
2. To allow time for a full assessment when it has not been determined whether or not a child can or should return home, for example, while allegations of abuse are being investigated.
3. To provide intensive treatment for a child in crisis to promote a prompt return home or to a previous placement.
4. To provide for a child who cannot or should not return home or to a previous placement when it has not yet been decided where the child should go or while more permanent placement is being arranged.
5. To provide for a thorough evaluation of a child to determine the most appropriate placement.

Temporary placements serve various needs well. However, when more permanent arrangements are delayed, temporary placements that are not equipped to provide for long-term needs may become problematic when a child gets stuck for an extended period.

Respite Care

Respite care is designed to maintain in-home placement of the child. It provides temporary placement of one or more children with a specially trained family for one to five days. Respite care is helpful for children or families in crisis. It provides an alternative to the child's running away and to the parents' use of overly harsh or severe discipline. It often provides an alternative to more permanent placement outside the home. The family and child may be referred for crisis counseling prior to the return of the child.

Placement with Relatives

Placing a child with relatives can serve much the same purpose as respite care for a short term, temporary "vacation" for the child, family, or both. It may also be used as an alternative to foster care or other more restrictive placement outside the home for a longer term or permanent placement when the child cannot remain at home for whatever reason. Sometimes relatives may qualify for and be certified for foster care benefits and support.

Shelter Care

Shelter care is temporary placement in a residential facility that may range from group home size and style to small residential size. Such facilities offer twenty-four-hour staff and some counseling. School is usually provided in public school, although some larger facilities may provide their own schools.

While shelter care is designed to be short term, problems may be encountered with returning a child home or in finding other placement, resulting in longer residence in the shelter. Children in temporary placement may not be motivated to invest fully in their school placement. Further, such facilities may not be staffed to provide intensive supervision or long-term treatment. Children may be somewhat intimidated by other children, or they may take advantage of the opportunity to intimidate others. Meanwhile, many treatment needs may be on hold until more permanent arrangements are made.

Runaway Shelter

Runaway shelters provide safety, room, board, and crisis services to walk-in children. They may or may not accept referrals or otherwise assist children in state custody. They normally require some contact with the family to inform them that the child

is all right and work to return the child home or make appropriate referrals for the child's future.

Inpatient Crisis Intervention for the Child in an Inpatient Acute Care Unit

Brief hospitalization may be useful for severe situational reactions or fairly recent problems of brief duration when a child is suicidal or seriously out of control in the community. Hospitalization on an intensive, acute brief stay unit provides an opportunity for the child to "stabilize," to regroup in a safe and secure environment with counseling and support, brief psychotherapy, and pharmacotherapy. At the same time, parents may get a much-needed break and receive counseling, brief family therapy, and some training.

Diagnostic Units

Some agencies offer intensive diagnostic units whose primary purpose is to thoroughly assess the child and his or her treatment needs and make appropriate placement recommendations. They also stabilize a child in crisis prior to placement. Kids-Peace, summarized in chapter 3, offers such a resource. Sometimes, acute care units in psychiatric hospitals may serve the same purpose.

Detention

Juvenile detention facilities are usually small and local, although in larger urban areas they may be quite large. They are designed to provide for children awaiting court action for status offenses, for children who have violated conditions of their probation, and for those accused of some act that would be criminal for an adult. They are secure, provide a teacher for remedial education, and may provide for some short-term counseling.

Placement in detention is usually short term, from less than one day to several days or a few weeks. Occasionally, placement may be longer—as with a shelter—when the child cannot be returned home or to a previous placement, and problems arise in finding a new placement for the child. In some jurisdictions, placement may be extended when a child is awaiting transfer to an overcrowded correctional system.

Long-Term Out-of-Home Placement

Adoption

Adoption is an alternative only when the natural parents are out of the picture, either through death, voluntary surrender of the child for adoption, or court action that terminates parental rights. Termination of parental rights usually has to do with neglect, abuse, abandonment, or long-term incarceration of the parent.

Foster Care

Foster care is a means of providing a home for a child who needs one. Foster parents are recruited, usually by a state welfare agency, to provide care for children who cannot remain at home or who cannot return home for an extended period. Foster families are provided with financial compensation that usually amounts to little more than cost of care, and with training that covers some parenting and technical areas along with how to fill out various forms for the various types of reimbursement available.

Therapeutic Family Care

Therapeutic family care, residential family care, or therapeutic foster care involves placement of a child or two with specially recruited and trained families who are expected to manage more difficult children. States may contract with private agencies to recruit, train, and support such families, including the provision of an on-call supervisor or therapist who can provide specific training, treatment planning, and crisis support. Kaleidoscope, summarized in chapter 3, provides most of its services with this model; KidsPeace and VisionQuest also offer the service.

While therapeutic family care can offer some significant treatment for the child, it may also suggest to the child's family that they are seriously at fault. The child and family do not require the professional intervention of some "institution," but rather the child merely needs to be placed with a better family. Therapeutic family care may be very good for a child who will not return home, but may be less successful for a child who could return home with successful treatment for the child and family.

Group Home

Some group homes provide a safe and nurturing environment for residents with a live-in married couple providing consistent care. Others have nearly all of the capabilities of a residential treatment program, with awake staff twenty-four hours a day on shift assignment, full-time social workers, family therapy, and psychiatric consultation and treatment. Any combination of services between these two extremes is possible. For example, in the Family-Teacher model of Boys Town, Family-Teachers are trained to provide behavior treatment. Group homes are community-based and utilize community resources, especially public schools. They rarely have an on-grounds school or locked doors.

Residential Treatment

The variety of residential treatment programs may be endless. They may be small or large, rural or urban—even wilderness. They may follow a behavioral or psychoanalytical model, or both, or have some other orientation, as does VisionQuest. They may work with families or primarily with the child. They may use public schools, have their own schools, or utilize a combination of both resources. They may or may not have secure (locked) units. Treatment capabilities may be led by social workers, psychologists, or psychiatrists.

Hospitalization

Psychiatric hospitalization most often provides the most intensive intervention, with locked units, behavioral programming, secure schooling, individual and group therapy offered by social workers and sometimes by psychologists or psychiatrists, intensive physical control capabilities, and pharmacotherapy.

Unfortunately, psychiatric care is not always

used only for those who need it but also for those children for whom other resources are not available. Not all children who are referred for psychiatric care are homicidal, suicidal, or psychotic. Some are merely too aggressive to be accepted by or managed by existing resources (Dalton & Forman, 1992).

Private psychiatric hospitals accept children from families who have medical insurance. Medical insurance may limit benefits to from thirty to sixty days. Sometimes this is enough. When longer term hospitalization is needed, placement in a public psychiatric hospital is indicated. When the need for longer term hospitalization can be determined in advance, the child should be placed in a public facility initially. Otherwise, unless the private hospital agrees to continue treating the child after benefits have expired, the child must be moved to a state facility or discharged without completing treatment.

Corrections

Correctional placement is the most restrictive placement. It usually requires that the child be convicted in a juvenile court of an act that would be a crime if committed by an adult. It is even more restrictive than the hospital in that the child's release is often not determined by the child's behavior or the child's mental state. In many cases, the release date is determined by judicial order that sentences the child for some specified period of time, irrespective of the child's progress or performance. Many juvenile correctional facilities offer counseling, behavioral management or behavioral treatment, education and vocational training, and some forms of therapy. Few offer family therapy or transitional services, although probation and parole services may help somewhat upon release.

COMING INTO CARE

In 1988, twenty-nine states had provisions for parents to agree to out-of-home placement while re-

taining full legal custody. Placement, however, was limited to thirty, forty-five, sixty, ninety or, at most, 180 days. Twenty-two states had provisions for parents voluntarily placing custody with the state. Four states had no provisions for out-of-home treatment at public expense (Yelton, 1993). Some private insurance carriers will also pay for treatment in residential facilities that meet their approval, which normally requires accreditation by the Joint Commission on Accreditation of Healthcare Organizations. Finally, there are a few residential programs such as Boys Town that accept charity cases without the parent's surrendering custody to the state. These programs usually have substantial endowments to cover the cost of care and treatment.

Psychiatric hospitalization in a state facility does not usually require that custody be taken away from parents. Hospitalization in a private psychiatric hospital when parents have insurance that will cover the cost allows parents to retain custody.

There is very little that a child can do to get help without parental consent or state involvement. Treatment requires the consent of the person or agency having custody of the child. Either the parents must give their consent to the placement, or the child must come into state custody and the state agency must consent to the placement. Notable exceptions are the runaway shelter, which offers temporary care, and psychiatric hospitalization for children who have passed their sixteenth birthday, at which point, for the purposes of psychiatric hospitalization, the child's consent may be recognized.

Long term out-of-home treatment, consequently, is very often possible only at public expense and most often requires that the child become a ward of the state (Yelton, 1993). Although procedures may vary from state to state, there are two processes by which custody of a child may be placed with the state. One involves finding the parents at fault; the other involves finding the child at fault. Both require action by a juvenile court judge. The first involves taking the child into custody under child protective statutes as a child in need of care. The other involves taking the child into custody under juvenile statutes as unruly or ungovernable—a child in need of supervision—or as a delinquent. Even when the family is seeking help and placement, the first labels the family; the latter labels the child.

Protective Custody and Children in Need of Care

Generally, children coming into state custody through juvenile courts by way of protective or child welfare agencies are considered as children in need of care. The implication is that the child has need of care through no fault of her or his own, but rather due to problems within the family or other circumstances for which the child has no responsibility. We shall see later that it is not always so simple.

Legal Perspectives

The right of the state to intervene between a parent and child developed from the English common law doctrine of *parens patriae,* which established the right of the king, as *parens patriae,* to protect the children of his realm. Originally, this doctrine had more to do with supervising the estate of a minor child. In early America, this doctrine came to be applied to justify intervening with the parent in an attempt to enforce parental duty or provide substitute care. In 1678, a child was removed because the father failed to attend public worship and failed to submit to authority in other ways. The poor laws also provided legal basis for placing children out of the home (Costin, 1985).

Prior to the nineteenth century, however, the doctrine of *parens patriae* was used primarily in cases of dependency and delinquency, rather than for cruelty or abuse. It was generally accepted that parents could control their children without interference. During the nineteenth century, a few cases limited parental discipline. In 1869, an Illinois court ruled in *Fletcher et al. v. Illinois* that parental authority "must be exercised within the bounds of reason and humanity." A few years later, in North Carolina, a father was charged with assault and battery on his daughter. The court established "permanent injury or malice" as a test of excessive discipline in *State v. Jones* (Costin, 1985).

In 1874 in New York, Elbridge T. Gerry founded the first Society for the Prevention of Cruelty to Children (SPCC). Gerry prosecuted a case of child abuse which had been brought to the attention of the director of the SPCA (although not under cruelty to animal statutes as is sometimes implied). By 1900, there were 250 such societies in the United States and others in Europe. They investigated and prosecuted cases of cruelty and abuse, usually working for the removal of the children. They also advocated for a system of children's rights and legislation to prevent exploitation of children. Prior to this time, children had the legal status of the property of their parents (Costin, 1985).

As the nineteenth century drew to a close, laws dealing with the physical neglect of children began to appear. States did not begin enacting laws dealing with emotional abuse until the latter half of the twentieth century. Meanwhile, the SPCC began to expand its philosophy to providing services in an attempt to prevent removal of children from neglectful or abusive homes. During the 1950s and 1960s, the Society began to decline as the public sector assumed responsibility for its enforcement and service functions. The 1960s also saw the enactment of the mandatory reporting laws that require certain professionals to report instances of neglect and abuse to appropriate authorities (Giovannoni, 1985).

Public Law 96-272, the Adoption Assistance and Child Welfare Act of 1980, establishes principles that guide current practices in cases of neglect and abuse. When possible, services to resolve problems related to neglect and abuse should be provided to prevent removal of the child. When removal is necessary because the home environment is too unsafe, then services to reunify the family are required while the child is in placement. If reunification is not possible or fails within a reasonable period of time, then a permanent plan should be developed for the child, preferably through termination of parental rights and adoption (Giovannoni, 1985).

Practice

The actual practice of child protective services in any locality is dependent on the specific state legislation, the precedents and procedures established by the courts, and the structure and policy of the state agency providing the services. Terminology may very from state to state, as well. Nevertheless, the general procedures that follow are fairly typical.

Emergency Removal. When a worker with the agency charged with child protective services feels that a child is in danger or at risk of serious harm, emergency removal of the child is indicated. In some jurisdictions, workers may have limited authority to remove a child in limited circumstances before securing a court order; the requisite court order must then be obtained within a limited time. In other jurisdictions, the court order may be required prior to removal, in which case the worker may need to reach a judge at home.

In nearly all states, an emergency hearing is required within seventy-two hours or less following an emergency removal to determine whether the child can safely return home or stay with a relative or should remain in the care of the state agency (Hardin, 1985).

Adjudication. The adjudication is a trial at which it is decided by the court, based on the case presented by the state agency, whether or not the child has been abused or neglected by the parents or guardians. If the court finds that abuse or neglect has occurred, the court can assume jurisdiction over the case and exercise powers that it does not have over other children and families (Hardin, 1985).

Disposition. The disposition is the action taken by the court if charges are substantiated in the adjudication. The timing of the disposition depends on state law and the practice of the court. Disposition may immediately follow the adjudication or occur in a separate hearing scheduled at a later date (Hardin, 1985).

At the disposition hearing, the court may order continued custody of the child and order the type of placement that it deems in the best interest of the child. It may establish conditions for visitation. It may establish conditions under which a child may return home. It may order specific evaluations of the parents or the child, or specific therapies for the parents, child, or family. It may order the child returned home under the supervision of the state agency with conditions for evaluation or treatment.

While juvenile courts may order families into treatment and children into custody for a certain type of placement, they rarely have the authority to order a particular facility or program to treat the family or accept the child, except for specific state agencies such as the child welfare agency or a state institution. Judges generally have no specific authority over a program until a program accepts a child or family into treatment or care.

Court Review. After disposition, the court conducts periodic reviews of the case. Practices again vary, based on state law and the procedures of the particular court. Reviews may be annual or quarterly, or more frequently if the judge decides. Either party, the state or the family, sometimes even the child, can request a review. Reviews may be formal in open court, less formal in chambers, or simply the submission of a written report (Hardin, 1985).

Federal law requires a final hearing within eighteen months of placement in which it must be decided to return the child home or continue placement. If placement is to be continued, a long-term plan must determine whether the child is to be continued in foster care for a specified period, placed for adoption, or be continued in foster care for a long term because of the child's special needs (Hardin, 1985). The court usually has the authority to require any treating agencies or facility caring for the child to participate in the review.

Termination of Parental Rights. The central issue in termination of parental rights should be whether or not a reasonable possibility exists for the child's safe return home. A decision to terminate parental rights obviously has serious implications for both the child and the family. The purpose is to enhance the possibilities for long-term placement for the child, primarily adoption. The hearing to terminate parental rights is a separate hearing. Some states require that it be in a different court than the child protection hearings (Hardin, 1985).

Hardin (1985) suggests five indicators for termination of parental rights:

1. The parent's extreme lack of interest in the child, evidenced by failure to visit or communicate with the child while in placement and a history of leaving the child with others and failing to return as scheduled.
2. The parent has failed to make necessary or court-ordered adjustments, such as securing appropriate housing or completing ordered therapy or substance abuse treatment.
3. The abuse may have been so severe and repetitive that work with the parent does not appear to be reasonable.
4. A diagnosis of pervasive mental illness, mental retardation, chronic substance abuse or, in some cases, severe medical disability may indicate that return home is not practical.
5. Because of the parent's past involvement with the child, the child is unalterably and adamantly opposed to return.

In addition, inability to locate the parents or the long-term incarceration of the parents may be grounds for termination of parental rights.

Probation, Correctional Custody, and Children in Need of Supervision

Children coming into state custody through the juvenile court by way of correctional services are generally considered to be either children in need of supervision or juvenile offenders. Children in need of supervision (CINS) are usually guilty of status offenses, violations of juvenile law that are not crimes and that would not be illegal if committed by an adult.

Examples include curfew violations, drinking, running away, sexual promiscuity, truancy, and expulsion from school. Minor criminal offenses such as shoplifting, minor theft, theft from a parent, driving without a license, driving a vehicle without permission, fighting with another juvenile, minor assault (threatening bodily harm), or battery (unlawful touching) may also be handled under CINS procedures. The terms unruly, ungovernable, or incorrigible may be used.

CINS children may be placed on probation but generally do not face sentencing to a juvenile correctional facility. They may be placed in detention for a few days or weeks for contempt of court if they do not comply with conditions of probation, and they may be ordered into custody for placement in a residential program.

Children answering more serious criminal charges in juvenile court generally face conviction and more formal sentencing, including sentencing to a juvenile correctional facility for a specified or indeterminate period of time. When crimes are serious, children may be bound over for trial as adults in some jurisdictions. Criteria, based on age and the ability of the child to form a criminal intent, prior record, and the nature of the alleged crime, vary from state to state.

Legal Perspectives

Prior to the twentieth century, children were treated much the same as adults, based on the traditions of English common law. According to English common law, children under the age of seven could not be held accountable for criminal acts. Between the ages of eight and fourteen, they could be held accountable if the state could show that the child was intelligent enough to understand the difference between right and wrong and the nature and consequences of his or her misdeed (Cavan, 1969).

Generally, children were handled by adult judges in adult courts, although during the nineteenth century some adult courts heard cases involving children in separate sessions. Children were frequently sentenced the same as adults to adult institutions. Those jurisdictions that had juvenile institutions generally modeled them after adult institutions. The doctrine of *parens patriae* was perhaps applied more to delinquent and troublesome children than in cases of neglect or abuse.

Based on the precedent that children under a certain age could not be held accountable for their criminal acts, the age of responsibility was eventually raised from seven to sixteen (Cavan, 1969). The juvenile courts established in Chicago and Colorado at the turn of the century began the practice of handling children separately and differently from adults. The state was viewed as the best agent to determine what was in the child's best interest; its involvement was viewed as benevolent. Little attention was paid to the rights of the child, since such proceedings were not viewed as criminal proceedings. All but two states established juvenile courts by 1925 (Sarri, 1985).

Juvenile courts and juvenile corrections failed to meet expectations for the rehabilitation of delinquent juveniles. Dissatisfaction with outcome, along with several Supreme Court decisions in the late 1960s and early 1970s, led to more attention to due process and formal control in juvenile proceedings and less emphasis on rehabilitation. State laws were changed and court proceedings became more formal—children received the right of counsel and rules of evidence were followed. Meanwhile, Federal grants offered incentives for decriminalization, diversion, and deinstitutionalization (Sarri, 1985).

Practice

The practice of juvenile justice in any locality is dependent upon specific state legislation, court procedures and precedents, and available resources. Terminology may vary. Still, the procedures and practices that follow are fairly typical.

Children in Need of Supervision. Children have to do things that adults do not have to do: go to school, come home at a reasonable hour, follow reasonable requests of their parents, abstain from sex and alcohol. When they do not, they may come to the attention of the juvenile court. The proceedings are not criminal proceedings.

Initial Petition. Schools may report children for truancy, police may pick them up after curfew or in response to a complaint, or parents may file charges against children they cannot control. Such children may be referred to the court through a probation officer or the district attorney's office. A petition alleging noncriminal offenses is filed with the court, which schedules an adjudication hearing.

Detention. When the police pick up a child, the child may be placed in detention if the police cannot contact the parents to return the child, or if parents refuse to accept the child. A detention hearing is then scheduled by the court within seventy-two hours or less, depending on statute, to determine whether the child can return home.

Adjudication. Those alleging the misconduct, the parents, and the child appear at the adjudication hearing. This hearing may be relatively informal or more formal, including legal representation for the child. The court determines whether or not the child is guilty of the misconduct. If the child is guilty, the court may warn or reprimand the child, adjudicate the child, or order evaluations of the child and family pending disposition. Of course, if the child is not guilty, the child goes home.

Disposition. At disposition, the court may order the child placed on probation and order conditions of probation. Conditions of probation may include reporting regularly to a probation officer, attending school, being home by a particular time, attending therapy, doing community service work, or anything else determined to be of possible benefit to the child. The court may order the family to participate in therapy or to attend parent training. The court may place the child in state custody for placement in a treatment program and order the child's cooperation with the program.

Generally, the court may not order placement in a juvenile correctional facility. However, failure of the child to comply with conditions of probation, or with the residential placement, may result in sentencing to the local juvenile detention facility for contempt of court for a period of up to fifteen days.

Judicial Review. Reviews may be quarterly, annual, or as requested by the child, family, or probation officer. The court may simply review reports or require that parties attend.

Delinquency. Children accused of crimes almost always come to the attention of the court through the police and the district attorney. The district attorney files formal charges based on police investigation and reports and any subsequent investigation by the district attorney's office.

Detention. A child who is arrested for a crime, either in the act or on a warrant, may be returned to his family or placed in detention. If placed in detention, the juvenile court must conduct a detention hearing within seventy-two hours or less to determine if the child is to be bound over for trial, and if so, whether the child is to continue in detention or return home.

Adjudication. The adjudication hearing for a minor criminal offense, in some jurisdictions, may be similar to the adjudication for CINS cases. For more serious crimes, the adjudication hearing is more formal. Usually, the child has the same rights as an adult, except for trial by jury. Evidence is presented according to the rules of evidence. The judge decides guilt or innocence. If the child is found guilty of a criminal act, the judge may order a pre-sentence investigation by the probation officer and/or a psychosocial and psychiatric evaluation of the child and family prior to disposition. The child may be placed in or continue in detention pending disposition.

Disposition. Options for disposition for criminal offenses differ from the options for status offenses and CINS. If the child is adjudicated delinquent, the child may be sentenced to a juvenile correctional facility for a specified or indeterminate period. State laws vary. Laws in many states now set guidelines for specific sentences (determinate sentences) to eliminate judicial discretion (Sarri, 1985). The sentence may be suspended and the child placed on probation for a specified period of time with specified conditions for behavior and participation in treatment by the child and family. The child may be placed into state custody for placement in a treatment facility, either as a sentence or as a condition of probation.

Probation. When a sentence to a juvenile correctional facility for a criminal offense is suspended and probation is ordered, the probation is different from probation for a CINS child. If a child with a suspended sentence violates conditions of probation, the court may revoke the probation and invoke the sentence. Credit for time served on probation may not apply. For less serious charges, a child may receive a ninety-day sentence, suspended, and two years' probation. The child may violate the probation after eighteen months, be revoked, and serve the ninety days. For a more serious offense, a sixteen-year-old may receive a two-year sentence, suspended, and two years' probation. The child may violate the probation after eighteen months, be revoked, and be required to serve two years in the correctional facility.

Parole. Parole is supervision in the community with conditions very much like probation, except that it occurs following early release from a correctional facility. Early release may be offered for a number of reasons, including good behavior or overcrowding. When a child is released from the correctional facility before the end of the sentence, the child may spend the remainder of the sentence on parole, with a parole officer and conditions of parole much like those of probation. Violation of parole may result in revocation, in which case the child is returned to the correctional facility until the end of his or her sentence. Successful time served on parole is counted towards the sentence; unsuccessful time on parole, such as time spent on runaway, might not be counted.

REFERRAL

The two systems, child welfare and juvenile corrections, appear to be separate and distinct, designed to serve very different types of children in different circumstances with different needs. In reality, this distinction often becomes very blurred, especially when the children's needs for treatment are considered. Children who come into the system for care often have treatment needs that go unnoticed or unattended for too long. Children in the child welfare system who have problems with unruly, ungovernable, or criminal behavior continue to be handled within the care system—they are already in state custody and, consequently, are sometimes protected from the usual consequences for all but the most serious criminal behavior.

Meanwhile, children who come into custody through the correctional system may have needs for care that do not get adequately addressed. They, too, are already in state custody, but in a system that provides correction and, in many jurisdictions, is ill-equipped or unable to arrange foster care when they cannot or should not return home following treatment.

GUIDELINES AND DECISION MAKING

There may be fewer guidelines for referral of children to the various components of the continuum of care than for any other aspect of child welfare. This is unfortunate. Needed services are delayed when children are referred to inappropriate placements. Such children do not enter a holding pattern until they get needed services. Rather, they tend to deteriorate. Problems worsen. New and more serious problems appear.

Reasons for Referral

Placing a child outside the home is a serious responsibility. There are two basic reasons that a child may be considered for out-of-home placement:

1. There is something wrong with the home of a serious enough nature that the child cannot or should not stay there.

2. There is something wrong with the child of a serious enough nature that the child cannot or should not stay in the home.

There are obvious implications:

1. If there is something wrong with the home, then the child needs a new home, at least until the old one is improved (child in need of care).
2. If there is something wrong with the child, then the child needs to be treated (child in need of supervision).

Unfortunately, the obvious does not always bear up under further analysis. In most cases, it is not so simple as an either-or proposition, not so simple as finding a new home, improving the natural home, or treating the child.

If there is something substantially wrong with the home, one can expect that the child will be experiencing some difficulties. If the child is experiencing some difficulties, one can expect some problems in the home. It is rare that one finds a case in which the problems are solely the child's. It is equally rare that one finds a case in which the problems of the family have not resulted in a child with problems.

Moreover, removing a child from the home does not necessarily result in an improvement for the child. Children have been removed from abusive homes only to be placed in other settings in which they received more abuse. Children who have been abused seem sometimes to invite abuse, if not from staff or foster parents, then from other children or from others in the home or community.

There Is Something Wrong with the Home

What could be wrong with a home such that one or more children could not stay there?

1. Death, injury, or illness prevent a parent or other guardian from properly caring for the child.
2. A parent or other guardian is so neglectful in meeting the child's basic physical and emotional needs that the child is in some danger

of coming to harm, or is suffering developmentally to such an extent that intervention seems necessary.

3. A parent or other guardian is abusing the child psychologically, physically, or sexually and the child is in danger.
4. A parent or guardian has become so frustrated with the child's behavior, and consequently with the child, that the child is no longer "welcome" in the home. "You better take him before I kill him."

Death or Disability of Parent(s) or Other Caretaker. In the following cases, the children are clearly in need of homes through no fault of their own. A relative may provide the needed home; adoption may be possible; a foster family may be found. Siblings may be kept together, but they may be separated. Residential care or treatment is not an option likely to be needed or considered. However, even in such cases, the issue is not fully as simple as finding a suitable family. Each situation is traumatic for the child or children involved. Grief issues and other effects of the trauma might be resolved in the new home, or professional counseling or treatment may be needed.

> *A traffic accident.* **Both parents were killed in an automobile accident; their two children, a son aged four and a daughter aged two, survived the crash but had to be hospitalized for serious injuries. There were no other surviving relatives.**

> *A fire.* **A mother and three children died in a fire in their apartment. They were survived by their ten-year-old son who was staying with a friend.**

> *Cancer.* **A grandmother, raising her daughter's children, was hospitalized with terminal cancer. Her daughter had shown little interest in the children. She was a cocaine addict who lived with one boyfriend after another. The grandmother was not expected to come home from the hospital.**

Neglect. Neglect, the failure to provide for a child's basic physical or emotional needs or to provide appropriate supervision and protection, usually does damage to children by the time it reaches the proportions that bring it to the attention of state agencies. By the time it reaches the proportions that justify the removal of a child, it often does even more damage.

> *Poverty.* **Ernestine received $436 per month in welfare and $535 in food stamps. She had three children ages seven, six, and two. When her family came to the attention of child protective services, her electricity had been off for two days due to nonpayment; food had spoiled; she was two months behind in her rent, and eviction proceedings had begun.**

> *Imposing on a babysitter.* **Mary was a working mother with an eight-year-old daughter and a six-year-old son at home. She worked as a bartender in the evening and made good tips. Her neighbor across the hall looked in on the children while she worked. Occasionally, Mary would go out after work and not return home until the next day. The neighbor, tired of being taken for granted, called protective services; they found the children at home alone, unwashed, partly clothed, with little food in the house. The apartment was extremely hot; the thermostat was set at 90 degrees.**

> *A mother's good times.* **Susie, fourteen, and her brother, Tommie, eight, had been raised by their grandmother in a nurturing home until her death. They then went to live with their mother, Arlene. Arlene liked to party. At fourteen, Susie was old enough to watch her brother when her mother went out. One Friday night, Tommie tried to hang himself while his mother was out. He was hospitalized briefly and responded well.**
> **Two weeks after his return home, his mother went out on a Monday night and left him at home with his sister and one of her friends. While his sister and friend were**

watching TV, he took his medicine out of the refrigerator and took 84 pills. His mother came home unusually early and found him unconscious. She called 911. He was rushed to the emergency room and admitted to intensive care in the pediatric ward. After five days, he was transferred to a psychiatric hospital for a longer stay.

Abuse. Some of the previously accepted child rearing practices of our Puritan heritage are no longer in vogue. When practiced, they may prompt some sort of intervention by a state protective agency. Herman Fountain's Bethel Baptist Home, described in part in chapter 3, provides a recent example of a state agency's response to an institutional example of such child rearing practices. It also details some of the children's responses—150 runaways in ten years of operation. Abusive physical treatment, for punishment or any other purpose, is not good for children. Stopping the abuse, removing the abuser, or removing the child may not be enough—some treatment may be needed.

The literature indicates that sexual abuse in childhood may play a more significant role in adult psychiatric patients than previously credited (Mason, 1991). This is consistent with my own recent experience with adult female psychiatric patients. Kohan, Pothier, and Norbeck (1987) found that 48 percent of girls and 16 percent of boys admitted to child psychiatric units had been sexually abused. Such abuse may require specialized treatment (Mason, 1991). The earlier effective treatment may be provided, the sooner the child's development may resume a more normal course.

Abuse in placement. **Johny was a difficult ten-year-old. He had been in special education since the second grade. He was diagnosed with Attention-Deficit Hyperactivity Disorder. Both at home and at school, he was often defiant and loud. He threw things. He attacked his mother and his teacher. His parents would occasionally resort to corporal punishment, which the school dutifully reported to the appropriate authorities.**

The resources offered to the family included a family preservation worker who came into the home several evenings per week, crisis intervention staff who could be called twenty-four hours per day, seven days per week, and respite care for several days if they needed a break from Johny. It was subsequently found that the father in the respite family had engaged in sexual activities with several of the children who had been placed there.

Games at bathtime. **Erlita had a chronic urinary infection for years. Her pediatrician issued a standing prescription for a persistent vaginal rash. Her father bathed her regularly because of her persistent rash (her mother worked evenings as a waitress). After a special class in school (second grade, she was an honor student) called Good Touch-Bad Touch, she told her teacher about the special game her father played with her at bath time.**

The Child Is No Longer Welcome. Power struggles in the home are traumatic. Sometimes the escalation of problems in the home reaches the point at which the child runs away; other times it may reach the point at which a parent demands relief.

A big girl. **Tonya was big for her age—165 pounds at thirteen years of age. She frequently refused to attend school. When she did go, her behavior got her sent home as often as not. Her mother wanted Tonya to do better. She didn't know what to do. She yelled a lot. Tonya responded by cursing her mother horribly, pushing her, breaking things, or walking out of the house to stay gone for hours. Her mother, at 130 pounds, felt powerless to control Tonya. She was at her wits' end. She filed child in need of supervision charges against Tonya with the local probation office. Later, Tonya was placed in detention when picked up on runaway. Her mother refused to accept her back home.**

Twins. **Earl and Gary were twins, although not identical. Earl had always done ex-**

tremely well in school. Gary had done well at times, but never extremely well, and never consistently so. Their mother, Earline, had divorced when the twins were four and remarried by the time they were six. She and their stepfather had two children of their own. By tenth grade, Earl had become a consistent honor roll student and was president of his class. Although Gary had had a bad year in sixth grade and repeated, Gary was in two honors courses in ninth grade.

When Gary reached adolescence, discipline with him had become somewhat problematic. Earline told him that, if he couldn't "listen," he could get out. One night, Gary came home over an hour late with alcohol on his breath. Earline threw his clothes onto the front lawn and demanded that he leave.

An understanding family on the next street took Gary in for a few days. They notified the police of the circumstances. Two days later, Earline filed charges against them with a magistrate for harboring a runaway. The state protective agency removed Gary and placed him in a temporary foster home, then moved him to a group home while the legal system worked to resolve the matter.

During the next nine months, Earline became involved in therapy at the group home and began to take Gary for home visits. On one of those visits, she found out that Gary had spent time with a friend she had forbidden him to see. She returned him to the group home and once again "disowned him."

Eventually, the court approved placement with the family who had taken Gary in on the previous occasion. The family underwent training to become an approved foster home. Within six months of discharge to that family, Gary's disrespect of property in the home, although not violent and aggressive, had resulted in damage on more than one occasion. The family asked that he be placed elsewhere.

There Is Something Wrong with the Child

Sometimes, the behavior of the child warrants removal from the home. The behavior may be such that the child is dangerous to herself or himself or to others. Other times, the family is simply concerned and seeks help because of some problems with a child who is not progressing according to their expectations and desires. No matter what the problems with the child, and no matter how responsible and healthy the family may seem, workers must always be sensitive to the possibility of problems in the home.

A concerned mother. Troy had been in placement for about eight months. A small twelve-year-old, he had been extremely disrespectful to his mother for some time, often leaving the house without permission. His mother's main concern, however, was his school performance. Once an A student, he had begun earning failing grades in several subjects. When he failed for the year, his mother sought placement in a nearby group home.

Troy was a needy child who did well in placement. His mother likewise participated fully. Staff, however, felt that there was something they were missing. One day, following a suspicion of marijuana use by several of the boys, a urine screen for all boys was announced. Troy became extremely anxious. He eventually asked his counselor if it would show in his urine if he had been with someone who was smoking marijuana. At first, he refused to say who it was, but denied that it was any of the other boys. He finally confided that it was his mother. No drugs were found in his urine.

Issues

If the situation is serious enough to warrant consideration of removing the child, then one should expect problems to exist both in the home and with the child. A focus on the obvious problems with one to the neglect of the less obvious problems with the other often leads to some disservice to the child. Consideration of removing a child, then, must include:

1. the needs of the child.
2. whether or not the child is to be returned home.

3. what the family needs if the child is to return home successfully in the future.
4. what will happen to the child if the child is not to return home.

Must the Child Be Removed? If the child is in clear and present danger in the home, then either the danger must be removed from the home or the child must be removed from the home. If the child is a danger to herself or himself, or to someone else in the home, and if the home cannot provide the necessary supervision to protect whoever is in danger, then the child must be removed. The state, or the state agency removing the child, then assumes responsibility for the child's safety.

While the decision to remove the child may be fairly clear cut, the decision about what to do with the child after removal depends on several issues:

1. Is the child to be returned home?
   a. What does the child need in order for the return home to be successful?
   b. What does the home need in order for the return of the child to be successful?
2. If the child is not to be returned home, then what is the plan for the child's future? Where will the child grow up?

How these issues are managed should depend upon what resources are available, and on the continuum of care that is available.

Should the Child Be Removed?

This is a much more difficult question. It hinges on three basic issues:

1. Is the situation bad enough to warrant intervention by the state?
2. What resources are available to improve the situation without removing the child?
3. If the child is removed, are resources available that can be expected to result in an improvement for those involved, especially the child?

Thus, the decision as to whether or not a child *should* be removed depends upon the resources available for both in-home and out-of-home intervention, i.e., on the continuum of care that is available to address problems.

SUMMARY

There is an extensive continuum of care with a multitude of interventions. Some interventions are designed to keep children at home and families together. Examples include special services in the schools, community mental health centers, outpatient services in private agencies (sometimes with public contracts and sliding fees), day treatment programs, parent education and training programs, intensive in-home therapy, case management, probation services, respite services, programs to promote early intervention in cases of mistreatment of the child or child misconduct, even brief psychiatric hospitalization to prevent long-term out-of-home placement. These programs may also be used to promote a child's early return home and support the return.

Not all programs and services are available in all communities. Available services may lack the capacity to serve the numbers of children and families needing the service. The capabilities of an available service may not be quite up to the needs of certain children or families. When available services cannot ensure the necessary care, supervision, and safety of a child in the natural home, or meet the treatment needs of the child, then out-of-home care is indicated.

The continuum of out-of-home care and services is also extensive. Possibilities include placement with relatives or friends, foster care, intensive therapeutic foster family care, group home placement, residential treatment, psychiatric hospitalization, and the juvenile correctional facility. The intent is to provide a setting that is as natural and family-like as possible for a given child.

Although the state's right to intervene with children was established in the doctrine of *parens patriae,* legal precedent also viewed children as the property of their parents, with few if any rights. Historically, states did not often intervene between parent and child. Legal precedent also established the principle that children under a certain age were not responsible for their actions. These precedents, along with social pressures, led to the establishment of juvenile courts, public agencies for child welfare, and juvenile corrections during the early 1900s.

During recent decades, dissatisfaction increased with the results of the ''benevolent'' intervention of these agencies and juvenile courts on behalf of children. This resulted in the establishment and protection of rights for children, movements for deinstitutionalization and diversion, efforts to keep families together, and the principle of permanency planning.

Welfare and corrections agencies may become involved with children and families as a result of complaints filed by citizens, professionals, schools, police, the child, or parents. Their initial involvement is investigatory. They may take action only by an order of the juvenile court. Emergency action to take the child into custody or place the child in detention is temporary. More permanent action requires formal adjudication and disposition by the court.

Disposition in cases of caretaker neglect or abuse may result in the return home of the child under court ordered supervision by the child welfare agency, with court-ordered treatment for the family and/or child, or placement of the child in state custody for placement in foster care or treatment. Dis-

position in cases of minor misconduct by the child may likewise order the child home, but under the supervision of a probation officer with conditions of behavior for the child and of treatment for the child and family. Such disposition may also order the child into custody for placement for treatment.

Disposition in cases of criminal behavior of the child may result in a sentence to a juvenile correctional facility, or the child placed in custody for placement in a treatment program. The sentence may be suspended and the child ordered on probation, as above, with conditions, except that violation may result in the child's loss of probation and incarceration for the full sentence.

The decision to remove a child from the family may be fairly clear in cases in which the child is in danger: from the family directly, due to the family's inability to protect, or from himself or herself. The decision as to what may be the best placement for the child is not so clear. The need for care is obvious; the need for treatment may not be so obvious.

The decision to remove the child from the home for treatment can be very difficult. It depends not only on the problems within the family but also on the availability and efficacy of treatment services that may be available in the continuum of care. The probabilities of arranging successful services for the child in the home must be weighed against the probabilities of success in out-of-home placement. There is a clear dilemma: delaying needed treatment makes matters worse; placement that exceeds the child's needs violates the principle of the least restrictive alternative.

PART II

In Part II we consider some theories and concepts that may be significant or influential in a given residential treatment program. In the residential setting, people with a variety of backgrounds and orientations come together, sometimes with a clash, to care for and to treat children. Personnel must work with each other as well as with people outside of the program—parents, teachers, judges, state workers, and neighbors. Each has expectations of what the program should do and how it should be done. The potential for misunderstanding abounds within the program and in the program's interactions with others. The better people understand each other's perspectives and potential, the better they are able to work together. The better they work together, the better the care and treatment of the children.

Chapter 5, ''Theory,'' discusses the importance of theory in the residential setting and the implications of one's theoretical orientation for managing information, communication, and decision making. It then summarizes briefly some theories from psychiatry, psychology, and sociology that one might encounter in a given program, discussing the implications that each may have for managing information, communications, and decision making. The remaining three chapters discuss concepts that have special significance in contemporary residential treatment settings: chapter 6, ''The Milieu,'' chapter 7, ''Learning Theory and Controlling Behavior,'' and chapter 8, ''Group Dynamics.''

THEORIES AND

CONCEPTS

Theory

I F there is a "correct" theory of human behavior, personality, child development, or treatment, there is no agreement on what it is. Theories have focused on development of psychological constructs, personality, neurological or biological factors, cognitive functioning, learning, treatment, or on combinations of these. All seem to have their good points and their successes. Many practitioners employ a variety of theories or a number of techniques developed or suggested by a variety of theories. Other practitioners seem to avoid theory altogether and concentrate only on what works.

Practitioners and workers in residential treatment come from a variety of backgrounds. They must not only work together but also work regularly with persons outside of the residential setting—parents, school personnel, state workers, probation officers, police, judges, neighbors, business people, financial contributors—whose backgrounds may be even more diverse. Each has some idea as to what the residential program should do and how it should do it. In the residential setting, the theoretical orientations of these people come together. Sometimes sparks fly.

This chapter will first consider the role of theory in the residential setting, then highlight briefly some of the theories that are significant in contemporary residential treatment. Based on my experience with encountering various theoretical orientations in the residential setting, I have chosen to present briefly on psychoanalysis, biopsychiatry, learning psychol-

ogy, cognitive theories of therapy, systems theory, eclectic approaches, personality, and "everyone knows how to raise kids." I have summarized these theories as fairly, accurately, and concisely as I was able. I am by no means an expert. It is not my intent to advocate for one over another, but rather to better enable the reader to work with those who may work from different theoretical orientations.

THE ROLE OF THEORY IN RESIDENTIAL TREATMENT

Theories meet certain basic needs that people seem to have:

1. The need to focus their attention, since they are usually unable to attend to everything at once.
2. The need to organize information into categories.
3. The need to understand things in their environment.
4. The need to control or influence their environment.
5. The need to communicate.

In addition to meeting these needs, which may be substantial in the residential setting, theory has implications for decision making and possible theoretical conflicts.

Focusing Attention

People do not appear capable of perceiving everything that is going on around them; there is just too much. There is a need for discrimination. People tend to focus on the kinds of information they consider important and to ignore information they consider to be irrelevant. The information they consider to be important is, therefore, more likely to be perceived to the exclusion of other information and more likely to be remembered to the exclusion of other perceptions.

For a given event, it is not at all unusual for one staff member to be focused on a child's behavior while the social worker is attending to what the child may be feeling and another staff is focused on the group's reactions to the whole thing. In a staffing on another child, one team member may emphasize trauma during the child's formative years while another emphasizes recent behavior problems with peers. Meanwhile, others may be focused on the lack of consequences for the child while yet others speak about the child's motivation.

Organizing Knowledge and Information

There is a tremendous amount of knowledge and information to be gained about human beings from history, religion, philosophy, anecdotes, parables, personal experience, scientific study, and observation in psychiatry, psychology, sociology, social psychology, and education. Within the residential setting, there is usually a considerable amount of information available about individual children. It is normal for humans to organize such information into categories in some way. Race, ethnicity, gender, age, religion, economic status, and occupation provide some obvious and ready categories.

Obviously, there are other categories. *The Diagnostic and Statistical Manual of Mental Disorders,* 3rd ed.—revised (DSM-III-R) provides ready categories such as Conduct Disorder, Oppositional Defiant Disorder, Attention Deficit-Hyperactivity Disorder, and Major Depression. The legal system provides other categories such as child in need of supervision, truant, arsonist, shoplifter, runaway, burglar, and juvenile delinquent. Different theories provide different categories for organizing information. Some will stress categories of behavior, others of historical and developmental events; yet others will stress categories related to personality or biological heritage.

The categories we create have indications for how we focus our attention. We are set to attend to information that fits the categories we use.

Understanding Our Environment

The human desire to organize information has purpose beyond that of categorizing quantities of information. We seek to understand phenomena in our environment by identifying relationships between or among phenomena. When we identify correlations, we are in a position to make predictions. Again, human nature being what it is, it is likely that workers in residential treatment programs will have some beliefs about the relationships among the various bits of information they have about children in general and about specific children in particular.

One of the easiest predictions to make is that past behavior is a very good predictor of future behavior. Other predictions may relate to the likelihood of a child with a given background or diagnosis having a successful treatment outcome in a given program or with a given therapy. Theoretical orientation will determine what kinds of information will be identified and used in making predictions.

Influence and Control

When correlations suggest a relationship of cause and effect, we are in position to attempt to exert influence or control over phenomena in our environment. Control is an important issue in the residential setting. The need to control children's behavior may be almost obsessive. The ability to influence, however, also has implications for treatment. Theoretical beliefs determine what interventions may be employed to control and treat the children.

Communication

One's theoretical orientation has several implications for communication. Obviously, to the extent that theory affects what is considered to be important, what is attended to, perceived, and remembered, theory affects what one is able to communicate. Staff cannot communicate what they did not notice or remember. Similarly, one is less likely to accurately receive and process communication that does not fit into one's theoretical orientation. Workers who are cognitively oriented may not be in a position to receive information about a child's feelings that are interfering with rational thought. Persons with a psychoanalytic orientation may have little interest in a child's present behavior, once a diagnosis has been made.

Theory also provides specific definitions of words that describe phenomena and concepts. When different theories use words in different ways, communication between persons of differing orientations may be hindered. A behavioral psychologist may speak of a child as being unmotivated, referring to a given situation for a specific task, with the implication that the treatment team must find some way of motivating the child. A probation officer may quickly agree that the child is unmotivated, referring to the child's personality and character, with the implication that the child is chronically lazy and worthless.

Finally, not all communication is verbal. Facial expression and voice tone may communicate much more than words. Our feelings and beliefs occasionally betray us in our attempts to communicate verbally. This is especially important in communications with children. Belief in retribution, in just punishment for misdeeds, is very much a part of American heritage and culture, possibly even of human nature. No matter how carefully thought out our own personal theories of child development or treatment, underlying feelings about what the child

"deserves" may very well betray our best cognitive effort to respond therapeutically to a child who has just hurt someone or damaged something in a seemingly cruel or vicious manner.

Decision Making

Decisions may be based on any number of factors and made in any number of ways. Some of the factors used by people in decision making may include:

1. The information that is available either through recall or perception.
2. Identification of alternative choices.
3. Beliefs about the expected outcomes of identified alternative choices.
4. Feelings about alternative choices.
5. Feelings about alternative outcomes.

Some of the ways in which people make decisions may include:

1. Deliberate, with careful consideration of all factors, including available information, identified alternatives, and projected outcomes, with a reasonable expectation that the decision made will produce the desired outcome.
2. Intuitive, based on much available information, some consideration of possible alternatives and outcomes, and some consideration of feelings, but without complete deliberation perhaps due to time constraints, lack of complete information, or uncertainty about possible outcomes.
3. Impulsive, with little deliberation, based on feelings, beliefs, or habits.
4. Arbitrary, a random choice perhaps due to lack of effort or ability to consider alternatives or outcome.

No matter how we make a given decision, the process will be affected by the information we consider, our predictions, and our beliefs about cause and effect. Even in arbitrary decision making, the alternatives we identify from which to randomly choose will be limited by information and beliefs. Alternatives, however briefly considered in impulsive decisions, will be similarly limited. In deliberate decision making, theory will affect the information that is perceived and recalled, the identification and evaluation of alternatives and outcomes, and our feelings and beliefs about alternatives and outcomes. When we are not so sure of our theoretical orientation in a given situation, then deliberate decision making becomes very difficult, prompting decision making on some other level.

Conflict

The issue of abortion may provide the best illustration of theoretical conflict in contemporary society. Just a few of the theoretical concepts involved include:

1. When human ''life'' begins—at conception, at viability of the fetus, or at birth.
2. What rights a woman has over her own pregnancy.
3. What rights society has over a woman's pregnancy.
4. What right society has to know about a woman's pregnancy.
5. What responsibilities society has towards a fetus.
6. What rights a father has towards an unborn child.
7. What rights a father has towards a fetus.
8. What responsibilities a father has towards a fetus.
9. What rights or responsibilities parents have towards the pregnancy of a minor child.
10. What rights a fetus has.

There are, of course, many more concepts. Terminology and definitions become very important, as is evidenced by words such as fetus, the unborn, pro-life, anti-choice, pro-abortion, right-to-life, abortionists, baby-killers, etc. The conflicts among persons with different theoretical orientations is obvious.

Consider also the internal conflicts of:

1. The woman who had an abortion and became an avid pro-lifer.
2. The pro-life student who became pregnant despite proper precautions and could not tell her parents.
3. The husband and father who campaigns enthusiastically against abortion with his family but has an affair that results in pregnancy.
4. The ardent pro-life supporter who does not adopt any children or vote for taxes needed to improve services to dependent or neglected children.

In residential treatment, theoretical differences may lead to conflicts among workers. Further, the worker who is uncertain about her or his own theoretical orientation may develop internal conflicts or uncertainties about theoretical issues, leading to intuitive, arbitrary, or impulsive decision making.

One of the most significant theoretical issues for residential treatment is the extent to which the child is responsible for his or her own behavior. On one level, this is first a legal issue. It is generally held that children are not fully responsible for themselves or their own behavior prior to the age of sixteen. By legal definition, a child cannot have the criminal intent necessary to commit a crime. This is part of the foundation of the juvenile court.

Some theories view people as being largely under the influence of their environments, either in the development of their personalities or through their learning of behaviors. Other theories view people as more responsible for themselves. There are theories that seek to improve the individual's control over self and environment, to empower the individual.

The abused, then abandoned child who sits alone in her room in a state of depression may readily arouse sympathy. Meanwhile, it may be difficult to feel sympathy for the bully who just bloodied a younger child's nose, then defiantly told the counselor he'd gladly do it again. These are the kinds of issues that may cause theoretical conflicts for workers in residential treatment who are faced not only with the problems of the child but also with the problems the child causes for others. Sympathetic understanding may be in order for both children, but expression of sympathy may be a counter-productive treatment strategy in both cases as well.

Conclusions

I wonder whether there is anyone who does not have a theory or theories about the raising of children, if not formal and carefully thought out, then partially considered or on an intuitive level. Having been children, we all have some personal experience with the raising of children. As adults, we have seen other children being raised and, perhaps, have raised or begun to raise our own. Residential treatment provides an even greater exposure to the phenomena surrounding adults having responsibilities for children.

The issue is not whether to have a theory or not, for everyone will have a theory or theories from which she or he operates. Nor is the issue as simple as deciding what one's theoretical orientation(s) will be, which is not in itself a simple task. Within the residential setting, one must be aware of one's own theoretical orientation, its strengths and limitations. One must also be aware of the theoretical orientations of the program and of others with whom one must work, communicate, and share responsibility.

Theory will influence what is perceived, remembered, and reported; it will either assist or hinder the communication of information; it will influence decisions that are made about treatment; it may lead to conflicts among staff or within individuals; it will affect attitudes about clients.

In the following presentation, a number of complex theories or categories of theories are summarized very briefly. For each, I have attempted to touch on the following points:

1. How the theory organizes information about people.
2. The relationships the theory proposes, correlational for assessment and prediction, of cause and effect for treatment.
3. The types of information on which the theory focuses as important.
4. The kinds of decisions the theory will suggest in terms of treatment, specifically goals and strategies.
5. The implications for communication.
6. Locus of control and any other implications for possible conflict.

Finally, I suggest some possible implications the theory may have for residential treatment.

PSYCHOANALYTIC THEORIES

Psychoanalytical theories began to appear in residential facilities in the 1930s, enjoyed predominance into the 1960s, and continue to be significant to the present day. Such theories may be held by some social workers, psychologists, psychiatrists, and bachelor's level staff.

Most simply, psychoanalytic theories are largely concerned with the unconscious (Glasser, 1975). Freudians concern themselves with the primal drives of the id, the development of the ego as a rational control of the id's primal drives, and the development of the superego as a mediator or conscience. Later theorists emphasized different aspects of the individual's developmental history with resultant deficiencies or conflicts.

Problems with behavior are viewed as arising from problems within these hypothetical constructs of the unconscious, either deficiencies or conflicts. Behavior is important to the extent that it serves as a key to assessing the unconscious, to classifying disorders. Since the unconscious problems cause the problem behaviors, correcting problems in the unconscious will enable the patient to improve functioning. Helping the patient find the psychological roots of the problem and gain understanding and insight into her or his unconscious is considered more important than conscious problems (Glasser, 1975).

Treatment consists of exploring the patient's unconscious and helping her or him to understand it. Techniques may include taking the patient back through the patient's developmental history to points in which problems were experienced, analysis of dreams, free association, and transference (Glasser, 1975). Goals of treatment may be expressed in terms of increased ego strength, of resolving conflicts among superego, ego, and the id, or of helping the patient to understand the sources of these unconscious problems.

Traditional psychoanalysis holds that mental illness exists, can be classified, and should be treated in accordance with the diagnosis (Glasser, 1975). Consequently, diagnostic classifications will have a significant import on communications, as will terminology related to specific theoretical constructs or stages of development, such as id, ego, superego, and oedipal complex.

Traditional psychoanalytic theory views deviant behavior as the product of mental illness; the patient should not be held morally accountable. Further, improving behavior is not considered an important part of therapy; once cured of the illness, the patient will be able to behave (Glasser, 1975). Although the locus of control, the patient's unconscious, is internal, the locus of control for the development of the unconscious is external and not the responsibility of the patient. A likely source of conflict in residential treatment is the theory's position on responsibility and current behavior (read "misbehavior").

Summary

Psychoanalytic theory organizes information about people in terms of mental health and mental illness. Current behaviors, including verbal self-disclosure and dreams, are related to underlying constructs and serve as a means of assessing the problem(s). Deep-seated psychological problems are seen as causal to current problems with functioning. Understanding the etiology is critical to treatment. While current behavior is important for assessment and as an indicator of progress, more emphasis will be placed on historical events than on present events and their consequences.

Treatment will focus on identifying and defining psychological problems and their causes and on correcting deficiencies or resolving conflicts by helping the patient to understand their sources or causes. Communication will thus emphasize historical events rather than current events and consequences.

The present locus of control is internal and psychological in nature, but the locus of control for the development of hypothetical psychological constructs is external. The patient is blameless, but parents may not be.

Implications for Residential Treatment

From time to time in residential treatment, one encounters children who seem to suffer from internal conflicts that appear to affect behavior. Consider the child with an early history of abuse and extreme neglect who has an underlying anger that seems pervasive across a variety of situations. In some such cases behavior is very resistant to behavioral interventions that have worked well with others, while problems with thought processes seem to be very resistant to rational interventions.

When such a child fails to respond to treatment interventions that are effective with other children, some may label the child as unmotivated, resistant to treatment, untreatable in this environment, or as "having derived maximum benefit from treatment." A psychoanalytic approach in such cases, coupled with behavioral and cognitive interventions, may be most effective. A purely psychoanalytic therapist, however, is less likely to be concerned with present functioning and may not be especially interested in what is going on in the rest of the program setting. The therapist may readily expect additional acting out as unconscious material begins to emerge in therapy. Staff may undermine therapy in such situations while the therapist may undermine other treatment when a child distorts what others are ''doing'' to her or him. This can be especially problematic with outside therapists.

BIOPSYCHIATRIC THEORIES

Those with a biopsychiatric orientation view problems with functioning as resulting from biological or neurological malfunctions that affect thoughts, feelings, learning, and behavior. Behavior will provide clues for diagnosis and assessment. Information from physical and neurological examinations and tests will be important. Goals of treatment will be to correctly diagnose the illness and to prescribe and administer the appropriate treatment. Medication is a primary treatment modality (Gelman, 1990). Electroconvulsive therapy may be employed by some therapists (Staff, 1990); psychosurgery is still practiced quietly on consenting patients (Beck and Cowley, 1990).

Such theorists will be interested in current behavior as an indication of the progress of treatment and indications for changing dosage or medication. The locus of control is internal, but the patient is not morally responsible for behavior, which is due to some neurobiological problem.

There are cases in which medication has allowed the patient a much improved level of functioning, or served to significantly reduce serious problem behaviors. There are other cases in which medication has served to improve the patient to the point where she or he is more receptive to other therapies (Wishik, Bachman, and Beitsch, 1989). There are cases in which medication has had little beneficial effect and other cases in which medication seems to retard levels of responding on undesirable as well as on desirable levels. There are those for whom

medication seems to be effective, but who discontinue their medication or refuse to take it.

Implications for Residential Treatment

Psychotropic medication can have an almost immediate, dramatic, and profound effect on some children. Problem behaviors may virtually disappear. Seriously depressed mood may be normalized. Seriously aggressive behavior may be brought under control. When medication has such profound effects, normal, age-appropriate learning may resume in school, and treatment in other modalities may be greatly enhanced and facilitated.

There are other implications that have to do with the potential for abuse of psychotropic medications, which can occur in several ways. Child care staff faced with difficult children see medication as a means of eliminating the difficulty. Supervisors and professional staff feel pressure to advocate for medication. There may be a tendency to embellish reports of problems to influence the psychiatrist to prescribe. Other interventions may be neglected. If medication proves effective, it is continued indefinitely; if medication proves ineffective, it may still be continued indefinitely.

I have seen ''hyperactive'' children on Ritalin so hyper that one cannot imagine their being any worse without it. I have seen aggressive children on thorazine so drugged that other interventions are meaningless. In the first case, it is possible that the overactive behavior of the child does not have an organic origin and that treatment other than medication is indicated. In the second case, thorazine is very likely to be discontinued by the child or family at some point after discharge with full return of aggressive behaviors that were otherwise untreated because they were controlled by the medication.

A second concern for abuse with psychotropic medication is the potential for misuse by residents. Residents may on occasion get over on staff, pretending to take a dose but saving pills for a later time, possibly sharing with or selling to others. Residents are also capable of elaborate and successful plans to breach the security of the medical supply. We will consider pharmacotherapy in more detail in chapter 13, "Professional Interventions."

BEHAVIORAL THEORY

Behavioral or learning theory began to compete with psychoanalytic theory in the 1960s and has gained considerably in influence since then. A behavioral orientation may be influential with some social workers, psychologists, and bachelor's level staff.

Those with a behavioral or learning orientation will focus on present behavior and the antecedents and consequences of that behavior. They will have less interest in historical development except as it may have implications for selecting reinforcements or other consequences of behavior. They will view the locus of control as external to the client or resident. Goals of treatment will be in terms of changing specific behaviors. Treatment will involve the manipulation of consequences for targeted behaviors.

Behaviorists will organize information about people in terms of specific behaviors and the consequences of those behaviors. Some may focus in addition upon emotions and events that may correlate with behaviors. Assessment will involve identifying problem behaviors, their precipitating events, and their reinforcements; treatment will entail changing situations and reinforcements to change behavior. Behaviors and reinforcements, therefore, are the primary information on which behaviorists focus. Treatment decisions will evolve around types and schedules of reinforcement and possible use of punishment. Behaviorists will not be likely to communicate about historical events or constructs of the personality.

The locus of control is external to the client, who is not likely to be blamed. Parents and society might have some blame, but behaviorists are not as likely to focus on etiology—their interest is in the present.

Implications for Residential Treatment

Virtually all children who come to residential treatment come because of problems with behavior. Further, like other children, they still have much to learn. Whatever other treatment might be employed, learning theory and principles of learning can play an important role in maintaining desirable behaviors, reducing or eliminating undesirable behaviors, and teaching new behaviors. Principles of learning can also be helpful in working with emotional disturbances, extinguishing inappropriate feelings, and teaching more appropriate ones in their place. Behavioral and learning approaches may be used as the primary intervention; these approaches may also be used effectively in support of or in addition to virtually any other interventions that may be employed.

There is also danger in the application of the principles of learning in the residential setting. Effective behavior management, deceptively effective in managing behavior within the setting, may produce a compliance that appears to be successful treatment, but that has little chance of generalizing to settings outside the residential program. We will consider learning theory and the application of learning principles in more detail in chapters 7, 9, and 10.

COGNITIVE THEORIES

Cognitive theories focus on the strength of the human intellect and the relationship of thinking to feelings, attitudes, and behavior in the present. Theories of development are not significant for treatment and are left to others. Goals of treatment will be expressed in terms of changing thinking to change behavior, feelings, emotions, and/or attitudes. Treatment involves exploration of thoughts and may include instruction, verbal self-instruction, and verbal self-reinforcement. Such theories view the locus of control as internal, with the client fully responsible for his or her own behavior and happiness.

Cognitive therapists will be concerned with present behavior and its effects on others, since that is important to how others respond to the client. Cognitive therapists will not be interested in historical development, excusing behavior, or blaming others; they may have some interest in principles of learning, especially cognitive learning, and may use some behavior therapy along with cognitive techniques (Ellis, 1977; Glasser, 1975). Ellis' Rational Emotive Therapy and Glasser's Reality Therapy are summarized briefly in chapter 13, "Professional Interventions."

Implications for Residential Treatment

Because of their emphasis on the individual's taking responsibility for her or his own behavior and happiness, cognitive theories and techniques can be very popular with other residential personnel, especially those with no strong formal theoretical orientation of their own, such as some child care counselors and support staff. Further, child care counselors can be taught some of the basics of whatever cognitive techniques are being used to support the therapy on a twenty-four-hour basis, reminding children of the techniques and reminding them to use the techniques. Thus, cognitive techniques become a part of the environment that the child encounters daily, rather than weekly in the therapist's office.

SYSTEMS THEORY

Anderson and Carter (1984) propose a systems model for viewing human behavior. They quote Buckley's definition of a system: "a complex of elements or components directly or indirectly related in a causal network, such that each component is related to at least some others in a more or less stable way within a particular period of time" (p.

3). The systems model is a way of looking at elements and the whole, and of "dynamic patterns of relatedness . . ." (p. 3).

Both the micro and macro levels of conceptualization are important; society is constructed from the behavior of individuals, and society has implications for individual functioning or behavior. Further, each social entity is made up of parts to which it is the whole while itself being a part of a larger whole. Thus, each social entity must look inward to its parts and outward to the system of which it is a part (Anderson & Carter, 1984).

Focal System

The systems approach requires the designation of a focal system, which sets the perspective. Attention must be paid both to its parts and to the environment in which it exists. With the family as the focal system, one would attend to individual members as well as to community, neighborhood, employment, schools, politics, friends, etc. (Anderson & Carter, 1984). Rather than dealing with cause and effect, the systems approach suggests that we be concerned with action and interaction.

Energy

Anderson and Carter (1984) suggest that the basic consideration in the systems approach is energy, although they acknowledge some disagreement on this point among systems theorists. Energy and information move within a system and between a system and its environment. Energy of a military organization might include hardware, appropriations, and public support. Individual energy sources might include nutrition, physical conditioning, education, support, and cultural sanctioning of one's beliefs, to name a few.

Entropy and Synergy

The concept of energy suggests several related concepts borrowed from systems applications in the physical sciences. Entropy refers to the tendency of an untended system to move towards an unorganized state of decreased interactions among members, followed by a decrease in usable energy. Synergy refers to increased energy due to increased interactions (Anderson & Carter, 1984).

Organization

Systems theory also requires focus on the organization. In highly organized systems, such as many families, components are strongly interdependent. In systems of lower organization, such as a large city and some families, components are much more independent and autonomous. If there is no organization, there is no system. Disorganization refers to insufficient organization to meet the system's goals. Possible reasons for family disorganization may include: members are in opposition to goals, elements of organization are unclear (roles, feedback, communication), insufficient energy is available within the system, energy is denied by the suprasystem, or environmental pressures are causing disorganization (Anderson & Carter, 1984).

Boundaries

Systems must have some form of boundary to enable them to be distinguished from the environment. Boundaries differentiate interactions within the system from those outside the system. Systems may be open or closed, relating to flow of energy across boundaries. Linkage refers to the transfer of energy across boundaries between systems. Employment, for example, is a vital linkage between a family and the economic system. Organization within a boundary may be hierarchical, related to energy distribution, authority, and power. Organization may also be based on specialization (Anderson & Carter, 1984).

Control and Feedback

The systems approach also requires notice of certain behavioral aspects. Socialization and control occur in all systems. Control may be coercive, based on power, or cooperative, based on the system's supporting the goals of components in exchange for contributions to the system's goals. Socialization is another form of social control. The transfer of energy to further system goals is called communication. Feedback is a term borrowed from systems theory and corrupted in popular use (Anderson & Carter, 1984), often to avoid the negative connotations of the term "criticism." Feedback is the means by which a system gets information about the effects or results of its functioning and adjusts itself to meet its goals.

Equilibrium and Homeostasis

The concept of equilibrium refers to a system that is in balance internally and externally, but relatively precariously, such that a change causes an imbalance that results in a malfunction. Homeostasis, on the other hand, denotes a balance that is more variable, wherein the system can make adjustments within a range of limits to maintain balance. Steady state denotes a system that can make a wide range of adjustments to maintain itself (Anderson & Carter, 1984).

Summary

Those utilizing a systems approach to theorizing about human behavior will be organizing information in terms of social systems and the individual as both a part of various social systems, and as a system herself or himself, made up of genetic, biological, psychological, and behavioral components. Relationships are of an interactional nature, each affecting the other and being affected in turn. All information is likely to be important. Treatment will focus not only on the individual but also on changes in family, schools, peers, and others whenever possible. Although systems theorists might talk about things that other theorists might not focus upon as important, systems theorists are likely to view contributions from any other theorists as at least relevant, although possibly not as primary. The locus of control is likely to be seen as both internal and external, with the individual sharing responsibility with others.

Implications for Residential Treatment

Systems theory is especially consistent with the concept of the treatment milieu and the significance of staff, family, schools, peers, the community, supervision, management, and virtually everything else in the treatment environment. It should generate little conflict. It is, however, complex and may not provide the specificity of clear, concise answers and concrete ideology that many of us require.

ECLECTIC APPROACHES

Those subscribing to eclectic approaches may attempt to integrate a variety of theories, use different theories at different times as deemed relevant, or eschew all theory and merely use techniques that seem appropriate. Any of the above may apply in terms of focus, locus of control, goals of treatment, or treatment modalities.

Implications for Residential Treatment

An eclectic approach can be very effective in the residential setting. Its strongest point is its emphasis on results and whatever works. Those using an eclectic approach should be able to communicate with those using other, more traditional approaches. Possible conflicts may occur when the eclectic practitioner challenges a particular approach as not working well enough and advocates an alternative. As with systems theory, the eclectic approach may not provide clear answers needed by some staff, clients, and families.

PERSONALITY THEORY

If "attitude" is defined as a predisposition to act or feel a certain way in a given situation, "personality" can be conceived of as a more pervasive or global predisposition to act or feel a certain way in a variety of settings, as a way of approaching life in general. Millon (1990) conceives of personality "as a complex of psychic structures and functions" (p. 111) that operate within three basic polarities: pleasure-pain, active-passive, and self-other.

The Pleasure-Pain Polarity

Pleasure and pain may be conceived of as two dimensions, as bipolar, in Millon's terminology. That is, pleasure is not merely the absence of pain; both can occur together. Pleasure is life-enhancing, while pain is life-threatening. In terms of personality, the pleasure and pain are related to interpersonal relationships and social interactions as opposed to ice cream sundaes or bee stings.

For the sake of conceptualizing the model, think of the X and Y axes of a graph, the upper right-hand quadrant, where X and Y may each have values of zero, or any positive values above zero. A given situation may be evaluated as high on one of these dimensions, while at the same time being zero, low, or high on the other (see figure 5.1). Personalities, according to Millon's model, can be assessed in terms of their orientation in the bipolar polarities of pleasure and pain, that is, the extent to which they are motivated to seek pleasure or to avoid pain. Millon sees this as analogous to the basic struggle of life versus death.

The Active-Passive Polarity

The polarity of active-passive is unidimensional, or in Millon's terminology, unipolar. It can be conceptualized as a continuum ranging from totally passive on the one extreme to totally active at the other extreme (see figure 5.2). The passive extreme describes a style in which the organism or species accommodates itself to its environment, making adjustments or changes to enhance its survival according to whatever the environment might offer. The active pole refers to a style in which the organism or species acts upon its environment, moving about and producing changes in its environ-

FIGURE 5.1: The Pleasure-Pain Polarity

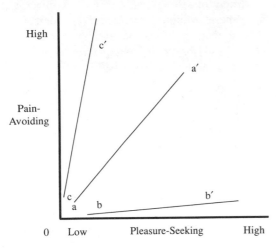

a, a′ Points along this line are characterized by the relative balance in motivations to seek pleasure and avoid pain through interpersonal relationships.

b, b′ Points along this line are characterized by the predominance of the motivation to seek pleasure through interpersonal relationships and relatively little concern with the possible pain from such relationships.

c, c′ Points along this line are characterized by the predominance of the motivation to avoid the pain that may occur in interpersonal relationships (high sensitivity to such pain) with little motivation to seek pleasure from interpersonal relationships (relative inability to experience pleasure through interpersonal relationships).

Of course, any other points on the graph are possible in terms of the Pleasure-Pain Polarity.

ment. Millon notes that both styles have been extremely successful modes of adaptation as evidenced by the evolutionary success of both the plant kingdom (passive-accommodating) and the animal kingdom (active).

The Self-Other Polarity

As with pleasure-pain, the self-other polarity is bipolar. Concern for others does not preclude self-interest. Personalities may be assessed in terms of the individual's orientation within the dimen-

sions of self and other, the extent to which the individual requires others to fulfill his or her own needs. This polarity, according to Millon's model, is analogous to the two basic strategies of reproduction.

One successful reproductive strategy entails the production of large numbers of offspring with relatively minimal effort or investment by adult members of the species. The most important aspect of this strategy is the self-interest of the adults that produces matings. The more matings, the more offspring. The more offspring, the more that survive. This strategy is successful for the plant kingdom and for many species of egg-laying animals. In some species of aquatic animals, the female does not even prepare a nest. She merely deposits the eggs in the water to be fertilized after they are laid. The young are completely on their own after hatching.

In the other successful reproductive strategy, relatively few offspring are produced because of gestation periods and the amount of care the young require until they can survive on their own. With this strategy, survival of the species is dependent upon other-interest, the interest of the adults—most often the mother—in the care, feeding, protection, and raising of the young. This strategy is successful with mammals and some species of egg-laying animals.

In humans, as with many other animals, survival of the species has depended upon the female's nurturance of the young. Gestation, along with the period of time during which young are dependent upon adults for care, means that relatively few young can be produced by a given female. Males, on the other hand, can produce a significantly higher number of offspring through multiple matings. Survival of the species requires that females be other-oriented; it does not require such an orientation of the male to the same extent that it does of the female. Millon cites studies that indicate that human females in infancy tend to be more other-oriented than males.

However, as with the active-passive polarity, the self-other polarity is bipolar (see figure 5.3). That is, while some individuals may place high on the "self" pole and low on the "other" pole, or vice versa, other individuals may place relatively

FIGURE 5.2: The Active-Passive Polarity

<table>
<tr><td>c</td><td>a</td><td>b</td></tr>
<tr><td>Active</td><td></td><td>Passive-Accommodating</td></tr>
</table>

a—Indicates a style in which the person is relatively well-balanced in his or her style or ability in accommodating himself or herself to others as well as in actively pursuing his or her own interests.

b—Indicates a style in which the individual primarily accommodates himself or herself to others.

c—Indicates a style in which the individual actively pursues her or his own interests with little accommodation to others.

A given personality may occupy any point on the Active-Passive Polarity (a continuum) from totally Active to totally Passive-Accommodating.

FIGURE 5.3: The Self-Other Polarity

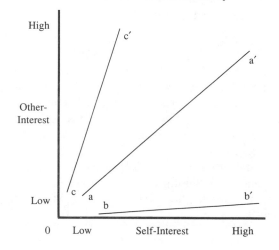

a, a′ Points along this line are characterized by the relative balance in Self-Interest and Other-Interest.

b, b′ Points along this line are characterized by the predominance of Self-Interest over Other-Interest.

c, c′ Points along this line are characterized by the predominance of Other-Interest over Self-Interest.

Of course, any other points on the graph are possible in terms of the Self-Other Polarity.

high (or low) on both poles. Survival of some species of animals may be best advanced by multiple matings of males with the raising of the young left exclusively to the females. In other species, including humans, the survival of the species requires at least some "other" interest on the part of males.

The Personality

According to Millon, well-functioning individuals will exhibit a harmonic balance among the polarities. Dysfunction results from deficiencies, imbalances, or conflicts within or between polarities. Deficient personalities lack the ability or capacity to enact or experience one or more aspects of the polarities. Imbalanced personalities lean towards one or another extreme of a polarity. Personalities that are in conflict struggle with ambivalence towards opposing ends of a polarity.

Millon's model is consistent with the Axis II disorders of the *DSM-III-R.* It organizes them into a conceptual framework that has implications for treatment. Further, it has implications for Axis I disorders as well, suggesting that these disorders will be consistent with the individual's personality style.

Disorders in the Pleasure-Pain Polarity

There are four personality disorders that arise primarily from dysfunction in the pleasure-pain polarity.

The Passive-Detached Personality

According to the model, the passive-detached personality (*DSM-III-R* 301.20 Schizoid Personality Disorder) is deficient in its capacity to experience either pleasure or pain in social situations. It is passive in its approach. Schizoids tend to be apathetic, listless, and distant, with minimal emotions or needs for affection. Some may lack the constitutional makeup for seeking, discriminating, or sensing pleasurable or painful events in social situations. Others may have been deprived of the nurturance necessary for the maturations of such capacities. A third group may have been exposed for a time to irrational or confusing family dynamics resulting in "cognitive perplexities or motivational apathies" (Millon, 1990, p. 116).

The Active-Detached Personality

The active-detached personality (*DSM-III-R* 301.82 Avoidant Personality Disorder) is relatively deficient in its ability to experience pleasure but is unusually sensitive to pain in interpersonal relationships. This personality is active in its avoidance of events that appear threatening. Like the passive-detached schizoid, the active-detached avoidant lacks the capacity to experience much pleasure, either from self or from others. However, the active-detached personality is marked by extreme sensitivity to psychic pain, to feel sad or threatened. While there may be some biological substrates, more likely there will be a history of harsh, rejecting early experiences and a deprivation of experiences that strengthen feelings of self-worth and competence.

The Passive-Discordant Personality

The passive-discordant personality (*DSM-III-R* 301.90 Personality Disorder not Otherwise Specified), or self-defeating personality, experiences a reversal in the pleasure-pain polarity, such that pain may be the preferred experience. Such personalities are passive in their style. They are likely to have a history in which physical brutality or other anguish was followed by intimacy and love, in which self-abasement produced absolution from guilt.

The Active-Discordant Personality

The active-discordant personality (*DSM-III-R* 301.90 Personality Disorder not Otherwise Specified), or sadistic personality, also experiences a reversal in the pleasure-pain polarity, experiencing pleasure at the social or physical discomfort or pain of others. This personality is active in style, seeking and using power to inflict pain on others. Stress, fear, humiliation, and cruelty are the preferred modes of interpersonal relations.

Disorders in the Self-Other Polarity

Millon characterizes six personality disorders by their dysfunction in the self-other polarity.

The Passive-Dependent Personality

The passive-dependent personality (*DSM-III-R* 301.60 Dependent Personality Disorder) is imbalanced in that it turns almost exclusively towards others to experience pleasure or avoid pain. This personality type is passive, waiting for others to take initiative. Such persons may have failed to learn autonomy or initiative due to a history with overprotective parents. They may have experienced peer failures that contributed to low self-esteem such that they have given up on attempts at self-assertion and self-gratification. They have failed to develop initiative but are dependent on others for affection, protection, and leadership. They accept whatever relationships they may find and submit to the wishes of others to maintain them.

The Active-Dependent Personality

The active-dependent personality (*DSM-III-R* 301.50 Histrionic Personality Disorder) also turns almost exclusively towards others, but in active style. This personality is seductive, manipulative, gregarious, and often employs attention-getting behaviors in interaction with others. Such personalities differ from the passive-dependent in their active pursuit of relationships. They require almost constant tribute and affection from others and fear genuine autonomy.

The Passive-Independent Personality

The passive-independent personality (*DSM-III-R* 301.81 Narcissistic Personality Disorder) is extremely self-oriented with little interest in or need for others. There is an unrealistic belief in self-worth, an inflated self-esteem. They passively await what is their due, expecting it as a right that requires no effort on their part. The history is often that of admiring and doting parents.

The Active-Independent Personality

The active-independent personality (*DSM-III-R* 301.70 Antisocial Personality Disorder) is also extremely self-oriented but skeptical of others. Such personalities are active in pursuit of self-interest, insensitive, and ruthless towards others, often pursuing retribution for perceived injustices in the past.

The Active-Ambivalent Personality

The active-ambivalent personality (*DSM-III-R* 301.84 Passive-Aggressive Personality Disorder) is characterized by intense conflict in the self-other polarity. Active-ambivalents vacillate between compliance and rebellion, experiencing conflicts in daily life between pursuing their own desires and rewards and meeting expectations or needs of others.

The Passive-Ambivalent Personality

The passive-ambivalent (*DSM-III-R* 301.40 Obsessive-Compulsive Personality Disorder) is also characterized by intense conflict in the self-other polarity. However, this personality represses or denies the desires, wishes, and emotions of the individual, conforming to the values or needs of others. They are likely to have a history of intimidation and coercion to accept the standards of others, with a resultant conflict between hostility towards others and fear of social disapproval.

Severe Personality Disorders

Three remaining personality disorders in the *DSM-III-R* are formulated in Millon's theory as severely dysfunctional.

The Schizotypal Personality

The schizotypal personality (*DSM-III-R* 301.22 Schizotypal Personality Disorder) experiences minimal pleasure, has difficulty differentiating between self and other strategies, and also experiences difficulties with active versus passive styles. Such persons may be confused cognitively or autistic, being self-absorbed and ruminative. They may have notable behavioral eccentricities.

The Borderline Personality

The borderline personality (*DSM-III-R* 301.83 Borderline Personality Disorder) experiences conflicts in all three polarities, fluctuating from one extreme to the other. They experience intense mood swings, with periods of dejection and apathy interspersed with spells of anxiety, anger, or euphoria. Simultaneous feelings of rage, guilt, and love are common. They repeatedly reverse what they have already done.

The Paranoid Personality

The paranoid personality (*DSM-III-R* 301.00 Paranoid Personality Disorder) is driven by a high sensitivity to pain and is strongly self-oriented. This personality tends to be dysfunctional in the active-passive polarity as well; it is actively assertive but often in an inner world of beliefs and assumptions. Such persons are fearful of losing autonomy and vigorously resist external influence and control.

Implications for Residential Treatment

Millon's theory has significant implications for residential treatment. Going beyond an eclectic approach, Millon proposes integrated treatment utilizing the concepts of potentiated pairings and catalytic sequences. The eclectic approach involves a knowledgeable selection of an approach or intervention. In an integrative approach, the therapist uses more than one approach. Approaches are timed (catalytic sequences) or paired (potentiated pairings) to produce therapeutic arrangements that promote balances in polarities and changes in attributes that would not occur from the use of one technique alone. Integrative therapy requires more than diagnosis. It requires a detailed assessment (Millon, 1990).

In catalytic sequences, one intervention is used to set up or enhance a subsequent intervention. For example, with a child suffering from low self-esteem and poor peer relations, one might first employ behavior modification to teach improved social skills, followed by individual therapy, possibly Reality Therapy, to improve peer relations and self-esteem. With a child experiencing depression, one might employ pharmacotherapy to directly affect the child's mood, followed by behavior modification to improve functioning in a variety of life areas so that the child has a number of accomplishments about which to feel good. Individual or group therapy may then help the child focus on accomplishments and feelings. With things going better for the child, medication may no longer be necessary and may be phased out.

In potentiated pairings, two interventions are used simultaneously. In cognitive behavioral therapy, cognitive techniques are combined with learning theory and behavior modification to both control feelings and change behavior. Examples of cognitive behavioral therapy for anger management are presented in chapter 10. Residential treatment has the potential to combine group forces in the milieu with behavior modification and individual therapy to change attitudes, feelings, and behavior. Residential treatment also has the potential to work with the family, producing changes in communications and approaches to discipline while at the same time working with the child to produce changes in behavior.

EVERYONE KNOWS HOW TO RAISE KIDS

This may be one of the most significant theories in residential treatment. Administrators with degrees in business or management and child care counselors with high school educations or college educations in fields other than human services may have no formal theoretical background. Nevertheless, they can be expected to have some theoretical orientation about the raising of children. Likewise, parents and members of the community with whom the

residential program interacts regularly are likely to have some informal but nevertheless potentially strong opinions on the subject of raising and disciplining children. Moreover, secretaries, clerks, cooks, accountants, maintenance people, and others in residential treatment can be expected to have theories about the rearing, management, or treatment of children.

Those operating from this orientation will organize information about people based on personal experience, moral values, religion, personal biases and prejudice, and good old common sense. Relationships among phenomena may be in terms of "good" and "bad," "spare the rod and spoil the child," getting one's "comeuppance," and "nothing's too good for my baby." This orientation is most likely to focus on behavior and the results of that behavior, not in terms of consequences for the individual, but in terms of its effects on others—making more work for maintenance, disrupting the living unit, creating the need to write a report, causing expense or waste, making a mess to clean up, etc.

If treatment decisions are influenced by this "perspective," they are likely to be inconsistent, possibly overly sympathetic at times but more likely overly punitive. Communication may be of a "gossip" nature. Some may view the locus of control as external, blaming parents, schools, or peers, while others may view the locus of control as internal, leading to labeling of the child.

Implications for Residential Treatment

This "theoretical" orientation is real. It is this orientation with which the child must contend outside of residential treatment whenever he or she leaves, on pass, on activities, in school, or in the community. It is the orientation with which the child must contend after discharge. This "orientation" is so much a part of us that it probably has some significance for every worker in the residential environment, even the most professional. Some children are experts at finding chinks in the armor of our professional theoretical orientation and exploiting them to get to our more personal selves beneath.

An attentive milieu will be able to derive some benefit from persons with such orientations, be they child care staff, clerical staff, cooks, maintenance personnel, volunteers, or others. Those rare individuals who seem to have an almost unconditional love for children, regardless of their behavior, provide a respite for a child under constant pressure and criticism from the treatment environment. Others may provide some doses of reality for children who have mastered the treatment environment but who are not competent in the real world.

On the other hand, those operating from the ''everyone knows how to raise children'' orientation may gain too much influence in some residential settings. Turnover among clerical, maintenance, dietary, and business management positions may be much lower than the turnover among child care or professional staff in some facilities. As staff come and go, a program's theoretical orientation may change, sometimes dramatically, while the support staff and their opinions remain relatively stable. Persons in these positions have considerable influence due both to their longevity and to the power they derive from the considerable resources they control. The following examples illustrate the intrusion of this orientation into the treatment milieu.

Tyrone. **Tyrone said something to John, and John got angry. John hit Tyrone and a brief fight erupted. By the time staff intervened, Tyrone's jaw was broken. Two weeks later, the bookkeeping department received a bill for $35 that was not covered by Medicaid. They attached the allowances of both boys, each to pay $17.50 towards the cost. Tyrone's behavior deteriorated so that he earned only the minimum allowance of $1. It took him almost four months to clear his bill with the bookkeeper.**

Missing recreation funds. **A new supervisor took over two units that shared a building and recreation area. The supervisor, in planning activities for a weekend, learned that weekend activity funds were not available for either unit. Both units had been assessed over the past several months for clogged sew-ers outside the unit (two times), damages to recreation equipment, and damages to the entryway. With $200 left to pay, and activity funds of $50 per unit, it would be two months until the bill was paid and three months until funds were available. And damages were continuing.**

When called for service or a repair, the maintenance supervisor would determine if residents were accountable for the item and submit the bill to the bookkeeper. Sometimes the supervisor scheduled repairs promptly; other times, he would put them off. Neither the bookkeeper nor the maintenance supervisor thought it necessary to inform unit supervisors of damage assessments to their units until they requested activity funds. Most units were far in debt with damages continuing faster than activity funds were allowed. Nevertheless, children were receiving "appropriate" consequences for their behavior.

CONCLUSIONS

At what point does a child become responsible for his or her own behavior and happiness? To what extent is the child responsible? What is the nature of that responsibility? With whom is that responsibility shared?

A child receives a genetic heritage at conception. This genetic heritage endows the child with physical, mental, and psychological characteristics and abilities that include strengths, weaknesses, and sometimes handicaps. From conception, the child begins to grow within the context of her or his environment. At first, the environment is the prenatal environment, which is primarily a physical environment. It acts upon the fetus in various ways, and the fetus responds in various ways.

At birth, the environment begins to add a social context in addition to the physical context. Moreover, the child begins to have an impact upon the environment. Action and reaction give way to interaction. As the child grows, the social context takes on increasing significance, as does the child's impact on his or her environment. In addition to physical development and growth, learning begins to take on ever-increasing significance. Not only does the environment affect the child but the child also learns how to influence, even control, her or his environment.

In the prenatal environment, the child is very much like a prisoner, at the mercy of the mother's physical health. Such things as her nutrition and whether or not she smokes, drinks, or uses drugs or medications affect the growth that conception has set in motion, enhancing or retarding the physical and mental development of the fetus.

From birth, such things as nurturance, nutrition, exercise, teaching, safety, security, consistency, and predictability—to name but a few—have effects on the child's growth. Children can overcome handicaps with which they were born, or develop new handicaps—physical, mental, sociological, psychological. A child with the genetic heritage to become an Olympic athlete may fail to develop due to malnutrition, or be crippled by disease, substance abuse, or injury; a "90 pound weakling" may become a star body builder. Likewise, mental, social, and psychological development may be enhanced or retarded by interaction with the environment. Just as genetic heritage and early nutrition lay the foundation for later physical growth and adult health, so do genetic attributes and early learning lay the foundation for what comes after.

Few, including theorists and laypeople, will disagree that genetics, nutrition, the family, and the broader sociocultural environment all have an impact on the growth and development of a child. Disagreement arises on the relative importance of each at different stages of development. It is not unusual to hear a distraught divorcee state that a difficult child has bad genes, that he's "just like his father." Nor is it unusual to hear professionals in residential treatment blame the child who "refuses" to cooperate with "the Program": "We gave him every opportunity," or "She's just not motivated." It is also not unusual to hear others—

laypeople, professionals, and children—blame society or "the System" for a child's problems—the housing projects, the schools, welfare, foster care drift, corrections, or the system of institutional placement.

The task of residential treatment is not to assign blame but to fix the problem. If identifying causes helps to identify a solution, then identifying causes is helpful. If assigning responsibility helps to implement a solution, then assigning responsibility is helpful. Unfortunately, assigning responsibility often amounts to a means of relieving the residential treatment program of the responsibility it acquired when it accepted the child for treatment: the responsibility for treating the child successfully so that he or she can return to the community ready and able to resume growth and development.

SUMMARY

Psychoanalytic theories tend to emphasize the unconscious and possible deficiencies or internal conflicts resulting from the individual's developmental history. The individual is not at fault. The therapist seeks to improve deficiencies and reduce or eliminate internal conflicts through psychotherapy.

Biopsychiatric theories emphasize neurobiological substrates that may have effects on the individual's activity level, perception, mood, disposition, orientation, thought processes, etc. Again, the individual is not at fault. Medication is the primary treatment modality.

Behavioral theories emphasize learned behavior and, possibly, learned feelings. Focus is on antecedents and consequences of behavior. Treatment involves arranging reinforcements and punishments to teach new behaviors or the use of available behaviors in new situations. Again, the individual is not at fault.

Cognitive theories view the individual as responsible for his or her own thoughts, feelings, and behavior. Therapy most often involves techniques to change rational thoughts that affect feelings and behavior.

Systems theories emphasize the individual as part of a variety of social systems—family, peers, community. Treatment often involves attempts to rearrange patterns of relationships between and among individuals and other social units.

Those taking an eclectic approach will often attempt to identify the best theory and intervention for the specific individual and the specific problem. The emphasis of an eclectic approach will most likely be on whatever works.

Personality can be conceived of as a predisposition to feel and act in a certain way across a variety of settings. Millon conceptualizes personality within three basic polarities: Pleasure-pain, active-passive, and self-other. Individuals have different styles on each axis that contribute to their basic style of existing within their social environment. They may be more oriented to seeking pleasure, or more oriented towards avoiding pain. They may tend more towards active interaction with others to get others to behave in certain ways, or more passively adjust themselves to accommodate oth-

ers. They may be more focused on meeting their own needs, or more focused on meeting the needs of others to gain fulfillment.

Excesses or incapacities in any polarity may be problematic. Millon allows for a variety of interventions. Rather than an eclectic approach, however, he proposes the concept of integrative therapy. In catalytic sequences, one intervention is used to set up or enhance the effectiveness of a subsequent intervention. In potentiated pairings, two or more interventions are used simultaneously. The goal of therapy is to promote the balance among and within the three polarities. In residential treatment, the opportunities to sequence and pair interventions are countless.

More often than not, the "everyone knows how to raise kids" orientation has an impact on residential treatment. It affects most of us. We "know" that people must be held accountable for their actions. We "know" that good deeds should be rewarded; we "know" that bad deeds must be punished. Further, this is the orientation the child is most likely to encounter outside the residential facility during and after placement.

6

The Milieu

CREATING a treatment milieu is not too difficult. Every residential treatment center has one. Making the treatment milieu therapeutic is quite another matter. The treatment milieu is the environment in which treatment occurs. When that environment is specifically selected or designed to accomplish one or more specific treatment objectives, it is a therapeutic milieu. When aspects of that environment are deliberately manipulated to accomplish one or more specific treatment objectives, milieu therapy is being employed.

VisionQuest selects specific environments to accomplish specific treatment objectives: the various Quests have each been selected or established as therapeutic milieus with specific treatment objectives clearly defined. The Teaching-Parents of Achievement Place and the Family-Teachers of Boys Town both employ structured environments with point systems that are carefully designed therapeutic milieus.

The manipulation of the environment in milieu therapy is a much more difficult technique to employ. It requires a high level of communication among all treatment personnel to identify specific objectives to be targeted, then to plan and implement the strategies to be employed. It requires highly trained professional staff with the time to plan manipulations to accomplish specific objectives, and it requires well-trained staff with a rela-

tively small population of clients to implement strategies with sufficient consistency to be effective. It appears that Redl's (1972) therapeutic milieu in his children's psychiatric unit for six boys had the capability of conducting milieu therapy.

Although Freud originated the concept of milieu (Dalton & Forman, 1992), the concept that a residential environment could be beneficial was certainly not new. It dates back to at least the almshouses and orphanages of the 1800s when children were removed from the streets to an environment where routine, industry, and discipline were believed to be of considerable benefit.

During Freud's era, the role of the milieu in a psychiatric setting was primarily containment. In the early 1930s, Harry Stack Sullivan stressed a supportive function for the milieu. Staff were trained to treat patients with warmth and respect to protect the patient from deterioration between therapy sessions. Aichhorn advanced the concept during the next decade. In 1949, Bruno Bettelheim proposed the principle of the social environment as a primary therapeutic agent; his Orthogenic School coined the term ''milieu therapy'' (Feist, Slowiak, & Colligan, 1985).

Fritz Redl furthered the concept of the milieu beginning in the late 1950s, identifying components of the milieu that have effects on treatment (Dalton & Forman, 1992). ''No one since has had Redl's clarity of vision combined with the descriptive power to illuminate the meaning of events we live with every day'' (Morse, 1991). In this chapter, I have chosen to look at the treatment milieu from the perspective offered by Redl. He identifies twelve items that he considers important. In his own words (1972, pp. 134–144):

1. The social structure.
2. The value system that oozes out of our pores.
3. Routines, rituals, and behavioral regulations.
4. The impact of the group process.
5. The trait clusters that other people whirl around within a five-yard stretch.
6. The staff, their attitudes and feelings—but please let's not call it all ''transference.''
7. Behavior received.
8. Activity structure and nature of constituent performances.
9. Space, equipment, time, and props.
10. The seepage from the outside world.
11. The system of umpiring services and traffic regulation between environment and child.
12. The thermostat for the regulation of clinical resilience.

THE SOCIAL STRUCTURE

The social structure includes, at a minimum, the unit staff and the children. Secretaries, supervisors, therapists, nurses, maintenance personnel, and cooks may also play a part.

Redl (1972) modeled his hospital ward after a summer camp as a pattern with which the children might be familiar. Group homes or cottages with house parents have a social structure that is designed to be family-like. Other structures may bear some similarity to a college dormitory, fraternity, or sorority, except that supervision should be a good deal more intense.

Redl (1972) discusses three aspects of the social structure: role distribution, the pecking order, and the communication network. He cautions, however, that there are many more aspects

and argues against oversimplification or attention to one aspect to the exclusion of others. The important issues are the relevance for treatment goals and implications for choice of techniques, with a recognition that an aspect of the social structure may be beneficial at one point of treatment, a major obstacle at another.

Houseparents versus Shift Personnel

Some programs make a deliberate attempt to establish a family-like setting using stable married couples to staff group homes in the community or cottages on a campus. Other programs staff group homes, cottages, wards, or living units with staff working different shifts. Each has advantages and disadvantages.

Houseparents

In a typical houseparent model, a married couple lives in the residential unit with a separate apartment or bedroom and bath. Provisions are sometimes made for the children of the houseparents. A relief worker may be provided to assist the houseparents a few days during the week and relieve them on weekends. A night supervisor may be provided to remain awake while children and houseparents sleep. One of the houseparents may be permitted to have another job or attend school.

The houseparent model provides both male and female role models, the modeling of a strong husband-wife relationship, and a high level of consistency in implementation of treatment strategies while promoting strong attachments between children and houseparents, all of which may be advantageous for many children in treatment. With but two houseparents having the major responsibility for decisions and implementation of treatment, problems with role distribution, pecking order, and communications are minimized.

In some programs, psychiatrists and psychiatric social workers provide treatment while houseparents provide care. In contrast, the Teaching-Parents of Achievement Place and the Family-

Teachers of Boys Town are specially trained to provide all treatment and care.

The houseparent model may be more economical to operate than the shift model and may allow for higher salaries to attract better qualified personnel. Houseparents typically receive room and board and possibly the use of a vehicle in addition to salary; they can save a major portion of their salary, which allows them the opportunity to save or invest nearly all of their earnings.

On the other hand, with little time off, job stress is high. Marital problems may have adverse effects on treatment. A child's behavior that threatens or injures one of the family, either a spouse or one of their children, may pose more difficulty than in other models when such behavior does not endanger family. Hiring two qualified staff as a team for a vacancy may be more difficult than hiring one, or even two separate individuals. The facility must be equipped to provide adequate living space for houseparents and relief staff.

Ironically, other disadvantages are related to the model's strengths. The departure of the houseparents causes a major disruption in care and treatment, affecting stability and consistency. The close attachments formed and broken may pose significant problems for new houseparents and the children. The model works well for children who begin and complete treatment with one couple, less well for children who are faced with a change in couples during their treatment.

Shift Personnel

The shift model entails the staffing of three eight-hour shifts on a daily basis with personnel who normally work a forty-hour week. This requires four full-time personnel and one part-time person for eight hours, since there are 168 hours in a calendar week. To have more than one person on duty during busy times, such as evenings or during the daytime on weekends and in the summer, additional personnel are required. Typically, a supervisor is required to provide leadership and to promote consistency.

The shift model can provide a variety of different individuals with whom children may form attachments, including staff of both sexes, different races, and varied ethnic backgrounds. It can also provide personnel with a variety of interests, talents, and abilities in treatment, music, athletics, dance, and academics. Attachments may be just as intense as in the houseparent model, but attachments do not need to be intense, an advantage for children who experience difficulties with close attachments. There may be less disruption when a staff person leaves.

The shift model also offers strength in its ability to manage children who pose especially difficult problems. A child who requires physical intervention five times in a given month may be restrained by five different people; in the houseparent model, the male member is likely to have performed all five restraints.

On the other hand, the model is more expensive to operate. Low staff salaries may limit the selection of qualified staff and contribute to high turnover. Programs serving girls are often hesitant to hire male staff because of concerns over sexual abuse, not only the possibility of its occurring but also the problems associated with false allegations. Programs serving boys are often hesitant to hire female staff out of concern that they may be unable to control or manage aggressive or violent residents. Programs may have nearly all white or all black staff depending on a variety of factors. In a relatively stable staff, the resignation of one staff to accept a better position may trigger several more resignations.

Further, communication among different persons on different shifts may be difficult. Different styles among workers may lead to disagreement. With several people responsible for the same tasks, accountability may be difficult to assign and important tasks may be overlooked as each staff leaves them for another.

Supervision. With the shift model, supervision is extremely important. It is necessary to promote communication, assign responsibility for tasks, and resolve differences among personnel. With a supervisor present much of the time when staff are on duty, role distribution becomes significant. Children often prefer to go "right to the top" and bypass staff who have less status and authority, as in the following example.

> *Access to petty cash.* **A supervisor of a unit for twelve boys, with five staff on rotating shifts, maintained control of petty cash, which was used for school supplies and clothing, among other things. Each counselor was assigned a "primary" case load of two or three boys for case management. A boy needing clothing was supposed to ask his primary counselor, who was supposed to get the money from the supervisor and take the boy shopping.**
>
> **In practice, the supervisor rarely gave counselors money when they requested it. Sometimes there was not enough money in petty cash; other times the supervisor had assignments for the counselor that made the shopping trip inconvenient at that time. The boys recognized that the supervisor made the decisions and began approaching the supervisor directly. Eventually, the supervisor would take the boys shopping himself. The counselor's role soon became little more than that of trying to get the boys to meet their responsibilities and passing out consequences when they did not.**

Consistency. Consistency is dependent on communication, which may be problematic in the shift model. The scheduling of days off usually requires that staff work with different partners and be relieved by different people on different days. Staff have different levels of tolerance. One staff may be very comfortable with a lot of noisy activity and radios playing while another may be every uncomfortable with higher noise levels. One staff may be very strict about all rules and regulations while another may be strict on some and less interested in others; a third staff may be very permissive.

"Ron never makes us do that." "He wouldn't get away with that if Jean was here."

Individual differences lead to different approaches to situations. One staff may be quick to identify that a child is about to lose self-control and intervene promptly to successfully head off a problem; another staff may be less able to anticipate a problem but move aggressively with physical control when the problem begins; a third staff may get the child to regain control through verbal intervention during a crisis; a fourth staff may have to call for help.

Different staff also tend to have different priorities. This becomes significant when the number of demands and responsibilities become such that not everything that may be desired can be accomplished: housekeeping, chores, study hall, reports, a trip to get supplies a child needs for a school project due tomorrow, a child in crisis, a child wanting to talk about a problem, a child wanting to play a game of checkers, a medical appointment, etc.

While virtually everyone will agree that a child in crisis is a high priority, agreement thereafter is far from universal. Administrators, and consequently supervisors and staff, tend to place a very high priority on reports and housekeeping, and for good reason. Therapists may tend to place a very high priority on a child wanting to talk, play a game of checkers, or get supplies for a special school project.

When a treatment plan calls for a specific intervention to be done consistently, it must be remembered that there are a great many other things, perhaps too many, that must also be done consistently. A special program designed to teach a child the habit of brushing his teeth every day may have a relatively high priority on the treatment plan, especially with respect to the implications it may have for peer relations at school. Consistent attention to the brushing of teeth, however, may be a relatively low priority in the living unit in competition with getting ten children up, dressed, fed, given medication for a cold, and ready for school with their books, homework, notes, and library fines, coupled with the problem behaviors that occur from time to time.

Program Residents

The social structure among residents is very likely to have implications for treatment. It will definitely have implications for the lives of the children.

Some programs may have committees of residents, either appointed by staff or elected by the residents, to participate in various aspects of the program. Committees may participate in planning or conducting activities; reviewing privileges, rules, or chores; planning menus; or even hiring staff. Such procedures help residents to learn responsibility and promote their investment in the program. As with any political body, such procedures also allow for persons to gain power and to abuse it.

Or consider the implications of rooms for one, two, and three children. Should a girl with poor self-esteem and little ability to interact with peers be placed by herself, be placed with a roommate, or be placed in a room with two other girls? It depends on who else is going to be in the room. By herself, she will be safe from conflict and harm, but she will have less opportunity to practice and develop interpersonal skills. With the right roommate, she may well have such opportunity, but with the wrong roommate, she may be in constant trouble or may be victimized. If placed in a room with two roommates who get along well, she is likely to find herself always the one to be laughed at, ridiculed, or excluded.

VALUE SYSTEMS

There are any number of value systems in a residential setting that require attention. Administration, professional treatment personnel, staff or houseparents, support personnel, the residents, parents, and the community all have value systems that may be significant for treatment, including moral values, ethical values, and clinical values. Ideally, these value systems will be similar, with few conflicts. In reality there may not only be conflicts between individuals but also internal conflicts within an individual.

Conflicts Within Individuals

Children are masters at testing adults. They are well noted for the testing of limits within the residential setting. However, much of what passes for testing of limits may be a more healthy testing of the values of the adults who supervise and treat them.

There is considerable diversity of values in contemporary society. So much so, in fact, that many adults are not clear on what their own values may be. Children who are searching for their own values look to the adults around them. Sometimes, those adults may fool themselves about their values; they seldom fool the children. The following examples are but a sample of value conflicts within individuals that may be readily encountered in a residential setting.

Administrative values. **An administrator verbalizes the highest ideals of individualized treatment but all comments and memos seem to be on the subjects of unmade beds, overflowing garbage cans, damage to equipment, staff punctuality, and overdue reports.**

A therapist's values. **A social worker stresses the importance of honest communication, then doesn't tell a child that she has cancelled his pass for the weekend.**

School attendance. **A staff member tells a child about the importance of going to school every day and meeting responsibilities, then calls in sick the next day with a headache.**

Respect for the law. **A staff member explains to children consistently that, whatever one may say about marijuana, it's still illegal. The staff member also drives consistently at fifty miles per hour in the thirty-five miles per hour speed zone on the way back from school with the residents. Of course, all the other traffic is also moving at fifty miles per hour or better.**

Needs and procedures. **The bookkeeper believes in helping children but refuses to pro-**

cess a last minute request for an advance on a child's allowance for a special outing because staff didn't make the request twenty-four hours in advance.

Who hurt whom? A child complains that she was injured during a restraint in which she bit a staff's finger through to the bone.

Honor among thieves. Children repeatedly complain about theft on the unit but don't believe in "ratting."

Violence and power. A parent tells a child it is wrong to hit his little sister, then spanks him so he won't do it again.

School attendance. A school stresses the value of attendance and getting an education, then suspends a child for cursing under his breath while walking away from a fight.

Conflicts Between Groups

Given the diversity of values within our culture, the diversity of groups within the residential setting, and the diversity of groups outside the residential setting with which the program may have contact, it is not at all surprising that value differences between various groups impact treatment. Within the residential setting, staff will have different backgrounds, cultural as well as clinical. Children, likewise, will come from different backgrounds. Further, the program must deal with various groups outside the setting.

Selection procedures for staff should be designed to identify possible areas of conflict in values. Professional staff should explore ethical and clinical values of a prospective employee. Further, communications must be open and frequent to identify and manage possible discrepancies in values that may develop over time among program components and personnel. The value systems of individual children will be, of course, a matter for treatment and will be impacted critically by any confusion around values among the adults. Conflicting values of the peer group may be a topic for group work. Conflicting parental values may be addressed with some success in treatment, but they are often highly resistant to change. Good liaison work with the school and community may eventually improve problems with values in those settings, but it requires considerable time and consistent effort. The following examples serve to illustrate a few potential problematic differences between groups in the residential setting.

A new point system. The administration and professional staff developed a new point system that replaced the former list of rules and restrictions. Staff went along with the presentation of the package in training, but they "knew" that it would not work. They needed more "control" over the residents or they would take over the institution.

Johnny. Johnny, a 220-pound fourteen-year-old, had been having trouble with his peers. He had had several arguments and had to be held back a few times to prevent him from hitting another boy. After one of his problems, which occurred just before a family visit, a staff overheard his father telling him, "If it happens again, put him in the hospital like you did that other boy."

A home pass. The social worker had been working very hard on some problems between Julie and her mother. A home pass was critical at one point in treatment. Meanwhile, Julie had refused to do her chore all week and efforts to get her to do it resulted in her cursing of staff on four occasions. Staff were strongly opposed to the pass.

Community relations. A rural community strongly resented a residential program that had been operating for several years, serving primarily black inner city youth from the nearby metropolis.

ROUTINES, RITUALS, AND BEHAVIORAL REGULATIONS

Routines

''The sequence of events and the conditions under which people undergo certain repetitive maneuvers in their life space can have a strong impact on whether they can keep themselves under control, or whether their impulse-control balance breaks down'' (Redl, 1972, p. 136). It can be a joy to work in a program in which routine responsibilities are handled routinely. There is plenty of time left over for what everyone wants to do: observe kids, talk to kids, counsel kids, play with kids, share in their accomplishments. A program with few routines is a nightmare for everyone—even the children, who will set up some of their own routines, such as not going to bed on time, getting up after they're in bed, coming to supper late, or always being the last one ready for school.

Only a few procedures can be established as routines at any given time. Close and consistent supervisory attention is required along with reasonable reinforcements and possible sanctions. Formalizing procedures in written terms provides little help in establishing routines, since routines are established by other means. It is the routines that exist in practice, not the ones that are posted, that are important.

Establishment of routines requires a bit more than the printing and posting of rules, schedules, and procedures. In fact, it is not at all unusual to find firmly established routines in violation of posted schedules and procedures. When children ask why, which they sometimes do, and a rule has been posted, the answer is likely to be, ''Because that's the rule.'' Some of us don't like rules very much. This seems to apply to staff on occasion, as well as to residents. Posting a rule may invite trouble rather than help to establish a procedure. Sanctions for failing to follow posted procedures sometimes help and sometimes seem to do very little good. The following example illustrates the successful establishment of a routine without sanctions or posted regulations.

Fire Drills. **A new supervisor conducted a fire drill and found the response of the residents to be undisciplined and too slow. The supervisor brought the residents and staff back inside and calmly explained to the residents the importance of cooperating during fire drills. Staff would have to return to the burning building if they couldn't promptly account for any resident during an actual fire.**

The next day, another fire drill was held. The response was better but not good enough. Another short and informal group was held. Two days later, a drill was held and the response was good. A group was held again. Residents were thanked for their cooperation and were sent with staff on an outing for ice cream. A drill a month later met with prompt response and cola was served at dinner. The next drill met with virtually instantaneous response and was also followed up with a treat. Somehow, treats for drills were overlooked from that point onward, but for four years, fire drills continued to be answered with instantaneous response.

Rituals

Rituals, the performance of one or more behaviors in a ceremonial fashion, can be important in determining behavior. VisionQuest utilizes the ceremonies of the Plains Indians as a formal part of its therapeutic milieu. Other ritualistic behavior may be established by residents.

The fighting ritual is an interesting example. It involves a snide remark, followed by an exchange of verbal insults, followed by remarks about lineage, usually maternal. It proceeds to a finger in the face, knocking the finger away, a push on the shoulder, a fist drawn back by one party, and a defensive posture by the other. The first blow may now be struck. Failure of one party to follow the ritual of escalation, even up to the point of assuming the defensive posture, will usually prevent the fight.

A short cut to the fighting ritual. On one campus of thirty-five children in four cottages, the boys had evolved a short cut to the fighting ritual. One simply had to say something about someone's mother to start a fight. Occasionally a child would come running to staff yelling, "He said my mamma! He said my mamma!" The phrase was offered up as explanation and justification for virtually every fight or near fight that occurred. One supervisor, in consultation with a distraught child, told the child, "Your mamma's a nice lady." The child ran from the office crying, "He said my mamma!"

Traditions

Traditions may also contribute to the treatment milieu. They provide children with a sense of security and a sense of belonging. Traditions can provide everyone with something to which they can look forward. Talking about traditions provides legitimate opportunities for older residents to impress some of their peers with talk about something other than their exploits on home pass. Newer residents can not only look forward to upcoming activities, but also to becoming "experienced residents" with something to one day share with newer residents.

It is difficult to measure the effects of traditions experimentally, but the following program, which developed a strong sense of tradition around its summer program and a few other traditions during the year, had few problems with runaways or children unable to complete treatment objectives. While there were certainly other factors at work, the traditions were a contributing part of the milieu.

Traditions in a small group home. A group home with rotating shift personnel serving twelve boys had established numerous traditions. A few traditions were observed during the school year. Wednesday evening was spaghetti night; guests were frequently invited for dinner, including former residents and their families, community people, former staff, and special guest speakers including body builders, school personnel, and musicians. Thursday morning was French toast for breakfast.

The major traditions, however, developed primarily around the summer program. Several activities during the summer took on the status of tradition, including visits to a foreign consulate and a local children's hospital, trips to an out-of-state military museum, ocean-side camping trips, and a special out-of-state camping trip at the end of summer to luxury cabins in a state park during which professional staff relieved child care counselors and children from all responsibilities around cooking, clean up, and chores.

The summer ended with an awards banquet in which residents performed and were recognized for their accomplishments during the preceding year. The banquet was attended by families, community leaders, volunteers, public school counselors, teachers, and principals.

There was but one runaway in four years, a boy who left during his first weekend and was not accepted back due to a firearms offense while on runaway. Eighty percent of program residents during those four years completed treatment objectives successfully, and of those, 80 percent continued to do well after discharge during those four years.

Behavioral Regulations

When people live together in groups, the need for regulating behavior increases. Some behaviors are inappropriate just about any time and any place—stealing, fighting, hurting someone, intimidation. (Please note that a few children may be at a distinct disadvantage in their home communities if they cannot fight or otherwise respond effectively to the aggressive or provocative behavior of others.) Other behaviors must be regulated because of the group setting. There must be regulations about eating, bed time, noise, chores, laundry, dress, even showers, when and how often to take them. Some children don't bathe often enough; a rare child will bathe and change clothes several times a day. Yet other behaviors must be regulated because of licensing requirements and general safety, such as participation in fire drills.

Children who come to residential settings often have a history of problems with rules and regulations. The residential setting, rather than providing them with relief from rules and regulations, imposes more rules and regulations. Children may be used to going into the kitchen at will at home to get drinks and snacks. Few programs can accommodate such behavior. Children used to bathing in the morning before school may need to adjust their schedule to bathing at night before bed. Children used to bathing just before bedtime may need to bathe during their favorite TV show so that others can use the showers. Children used to unlimited hot water may need to limit their showers. The following illustrates some problems with regulating behavior in the supervised group setting.

> *Kitchen regulations.* **A group home had a rule that, after one was finished eating, one was to scrape any uneaten food from one's plate into the garbage, then rinse the plate and leave it in the sink to be washed. A new resident had learned this rule. One weekend, when the resident was assigned the chore of washing dishes, a staff failed to rinse his plate as prescribed. The resident refused to wash the dishes. The staff confronted the resident. Eventually, the police had to be called to subdue the resident, who had armed himself with a fire extinguisher.**
>
> **In another group home, residents were not allowed in the kitchen unless they had specific chores. Staff, meanwhile, had access to coffee, leftovers, juice, snacks, and soft drinks.**

THE IMPACT OF GROUP PROCESS

Children have many very basic needs; two of them are the need for adult approval and the need for peer approval. For younger children, the former may be the stronger; for older children, the latter. Earrings for boys, heavy makeup for girls, special hair styles, eccentric clothing, smoking, tattoos, and defiant attitudes for both boys and girls are likely to indicate not only the need for peer approval, but also a possible disdain for adult approval.

Granted, a certain amount of self-assertion and rebellion are normal as adolescents mature, but residents of residential treatment programs are seldom noted for their maturity. Such behaviors cause problems for these children at home, in the school, in the community, and in court. One may comment on but not be too concerned with the "eccentricities" of an "A" student who is also a star athlete; one should have considerably more concern for such "eccentricities" on the part of a child who is making few good decisions.

For some children, such behaviors may be signs of self-confidence, maturity, and growing independence; for many children in residential treatment, they are signs of low self-esteem and insecurity. Evaluation of such behaviors must, of course, be tempered by consideration of prevailing community standards. Such behaviors are more significant in a community that has strict dress codes in its schools than in a community that is more tolerant. The extent to which such behaviors are identifiable symbols of deviant or delinquent groups is the key.

The most significant factor is the extent to which the peer group within the residential program supports program goals and objectives. The more similar the goals and values of administration, the staff, and the residents, the smoother and more successful the treatment; the more divergent, the greater the conflict and the less successful the treatment.

All the processes of "group dynamics, group psychology, and sociology" are at work, and they are as real as "the unbreakable room in which a boy screams off his tantrum" (Redl, 1972, p. 137). The following example illustrates a possible problem with group standards in a small setting. We shall consider group dynamics in more detail in chapter 8.

Dress and group process. A program for adolescent boys that consistently enjoyed the cooperation of residents (except for impulsive outbursts) and a high rate of success up to four years after discharge maintained a standard of dress: no earrings, no tattoos, no beards or mustaches, and hair above the collar. Any preexisting tattoos had to remain covered at all times. Boys over the age of thirteen who smoked regularly when they came into the program were allowed to continue smoking with written parental consent. No other boys were allowed to smoke.

The program's dress standards were carefully reviewed during intake. Questions about these standards were met with consistent replies at intake and throughout treatment to the effect that there was nothing wrong with long hair, earrings, tattoos, etc. On the other hand, children who were uncomfortable without such trappings were unlikely to be comfortable with them. Further, these things were very likely to cause problems in school, and none of the residents needed any more problems in school than they had already.

Personnel believed that these standards helped to prevent the emergence of subgroup cultures that might undermine treatment. Unfortunately, such beliefs are difficult, if not impossible, to verify experimentally. One attempt to relax standards for boys on the highest level just prior to discharge was not successful. The first boy to be allowed a mustache and longer hair regressed markedly and was unable to complete the program. No other attempts were made to relax standards.

TRAIT CLUSTERS

The traits of the residents in the program are significant not only as matters for treatment but also as real things to the other children who have to live with them. They comprise a significant aspect of the milieu in which residents live. Sometimes residents must merely tolerate the traits of other residents. On occasion, they emulate them or learn from them. The following examples illustrate a few of the problems the traits of a resident may cause for peers.

Terry and Danny. Terry was a particularly neat fourteen-year-old boy who always kept his room immaculate. His clothes were folded neatly in drawers or hung in his half of the closet. His bed was made so that you could "bounce a quarter on it." Danny was a new resident assigned to Terry's room. Staff were pleased to see Terry sometimes helping Danny with his bed. Danny had some problems with hygiene. After three weeks, staff discovered that Danny had numerous dirty clothes piled in his half of the closet with the doors closed. They smelled strongly and some had mildewed, adding to the odor.

Tina and Denise. Tina was a large, personable but aggressive girl while Denise was personable and extremely helpful to everyone. They got along well as roommates. One day, Denise was found doing Tina's chore. After a little investigation, staff learned that Denise had been doing all the housekeeping in the room, including making Tina's bed.

Jerome. Jerome had some problems with temper. After a few unpleasant confrontations with staff, Jerome developed the technique of walking away to his room, returning after awhile in a more reasonable frame of mind. Staff considered this an improvement for Jerome, especially since two other boys were being carefully coached in a similar technique to begin managing their tempers.

After several weeks, staff discovered that many of Jerome's posters covered holes in the wall, and the one over his bed covered a hole in the ceiling. Two dresser drawers were split from being slammed shut. Staff also learned that Jerome's roommate had begun venting his temper in a similar way out of frustration with Jerome's behavior.

Barry and John. Although Barry, a sixteen-year-old, had refused to go to school for an entire semester of the tenth grade before coming into the group home, he had a history of doing well in school and was only one year behind. He became almost obsessive in his desire to catch up and graduate on time. He spent long hours in his room studying and took three correspondence courses for high school credit to catch up.

His roommate, John, also sixteen and in the tenth grade, had had a very checkered academic career. He had done quite well some years and poorly other years. He had failed once. Like Barry, John also worked hard after coming into the group home.

Barry completed his treatment program in just over a year and was discharged home, where he continued to do well. He graduated with his class. John, meanwhile, had earned placement in several advanced classes. After Barry's discharge, John again began experiencing problems in school. The school reported that John was frequently late for class and did not have assignments completed. He began to cut classes. John failed several subjects and eventually had to pursue a GED. It was believed that Barry's positive traits had contributed significantly to John's school performance.

STAFF ATTITUDES AND FEELINGS

The attitudes of professional staff and child care staff have some serious implications for treatment. It is relatively normal for parents to become frustrated with their children and get angry. It is just as normal for most of us to become angry with our cars when they don't start. On the other hand, we would most likely be suspicious of a mechanic who became exceedingly angry with a car, yelling and cursing at it and slamming its doors shut, especially on our own car. Mechanics are not supposed to get angry with broken cars; they're supposed to fix them. It's their job.

One should also have some doubts about people who work with children with problems and then get angry because of the children's problems. A mechanic should be able to fix a broken car in a day or two, and maybe a week for a major repair. It takes much longer to help a child with problems to improve those problems. The mechanic should enjoy the process: the diagnosis, the turning of nuts and bolts, the taking apart and putting back together. The mechanic should not mind dirty hands and crawling under things too much.

People working with children should likewise enjoy the process; observing children, defining problems, talking with children, working with children, taking control when children are out of control. They should not too much mind getting cursed out, or swung at or spit at. The mechanic may occasionally get angry over a stubborn bolt that keeps him from finishing a car as promised, or with himself because an improperly propped hood fell on his head; the child care worker or therapist may likewise occasionally become angry at a stubborn problem that resists interventions, or an attack that really wasn't personal.

We would counsel a mechanic who is always angry at broken cars to get another job. Unfortunately, we tend to take a different approach with staff who seem too often angry with disturbed children. While it would seem very inappropriate to blame the car for failing to be fixed after the mechanic works on it, it seems somehow much less inappropriate to blame the child for failing to respond to our ministrations or treatment.

I don't mean to imply that staff should tolerate being swung at or spit at, any more than a mechanic should tolerate things falling on his head. Just as the mechanic should take precautions, so should staff. On the other hand, I have never seen a mechanic provoke a car into closing its hood on his head. I have seen staff provoke children and have done so myself. It is not appropriate to blame the child, however. There is a subtle difference between blaming the child and teaching the child responsibility.

BEHAVIOR RECEIVED

We focus so much on the behaviors that the children do in a day that we may sometimes lose focus on the behaviors that are done to them. It could be as interesting to list the behaviors a child receives in the course of a day as it is to list the behaviors performed (Redl, 1972). The following is not untypical.

> *Behaviors received in a typical day.* **Awakened by having the covers pulled off, pushed out of the way by another trying to get into the bathroom first, had French toast for breakfast, instructed to take out the garbage, reminded of goals for school, got a math test back with an F on it, the class laughed at a clever response to the teacher in English class, laughed at by the class when the teacher's come-back was even more clever, a hug from Patricia when she came on duty, criticized by John for the F, complimented on a nice shot in basketball, soundly beaten in basketball, cursed at during supper, got bonus points, received a "Thank you," had a pair of shoes "borrowed," criticized in front of the group for tipping a chair back on two legs, complimented on homework, had the channel switched in the middle of a favorite TV show, sent for a shower, given shampoo, given milk and cookies, sent to bed, yelled at to turn off the light and be quiet.**

ACTIVITY STRUCTURE

Few programs have the capability of filling waking hours with school, psychotherapy, and chores.

They offer a wide range of activities to children, sometimes seemingly as much for survival as for treatment—"Idle hands are the devil's workshop." Careful attention to the therapeutic potential of various activities can enhance treatment considerably.

Games and Athletics

People seem to need to play. For adults, it's recreation and may provide a release of tension. For children, it's more. It's how they learn certain things, not only motor skills and eye-hand coordination, but also about feelings, emotions, identification, and getting along with others. Children can play at how it feels to be a princess, a rock star, a basketball star, a parent, a teacher, a police officer, or a bank robber.

Games or athletics in which staff participate provide opportunities for staff to model good competition, proper aggressive behavior, good winning, and good losing. Most important of all, they can model how to have fun with the game. Especially for boys, athletic contests sometimes take on the level of a life and death struggle in which fragile egos are on the line and no smiles are on their faces.

In games, children will most assuredly learn what it feels like to lose; hopefully, they will occasionally learn what it feels like to win. With luck, or careful planning by staff, they may even learn what it feels like to hang tough, to overcome obstacles, and come from behind to win.

> *Eddie.* **Eddie was a twelve-year-old who was easily discouraged. When he got behind in anything, he would quit in disgust. Bob and Carl, two staff, began talking about how good they were at basketball. They taunted each other; a serious challenge developed. Bob said he wanted Jim on his side; Carl said, "In that case, I'll take Eddie." Carl had a good relationship with Eddie. They got the basketball and went outside.**
>
> **The other kids were really hyped up for the game and came out to watch. Before too long, Carl and Eddie fell behind nine to four**

in a game of twelve. Carl and Bob were playing each other so close that Eddie and Jim had to take most of the shots. Carl seemed a bit frustrated, but Eddie was just standing around. Carl called a time out and took Eddie aside. Eddie had given up. Carl said, "I can't let Bob see me give up. He'll never let me live that down. Just try to finish the game for me." Eddie said, "OK."

Carl blocked one of Bob's shots and got the ball to Eddie under the basket. Eddie missed, but Carl got the rebound. Bob was right on him and Carl got the ball to Eddie, who made the shot. Eventually, Carl and Eddie won the game by one point. Carl really rubbed it in to Bob, and Eddie joined in with an ear-to-ear smile that lasted all night.

Carl and Bob had set the whole thing up. They knew they could control the course of the game and make it look real, especially if they talked it up, although at the end, Carl began to have some doubts about whether Bob was going to follow through and let Eddie and him win. (Jim was a better basketball player than Eddie and won more than his share of games.)

Movies and Stories

Movies and stories can also serve purposes beyond simple entertainment, such as catharsis for aggressive feelings and possible emotional turmoil from previous traumas, identification with a variety of role models, teaching moral values, and broadening horizons with basic information, possibly in concert with something at school. Local video stores can provide an inventory of their movies that will allow for some advance planning. Consider the movies "Witness," "Chariots of Fire," "The Poseidon Adventure," "The Last Emperor," or biographies of entertainment, sports, or historical figures. Consider telling stories like Aesop's Fables or fairy tales over snacks prior to bedtime.

The king. Once upon a time, a king, wanting to study human nature, placed a large boulder in the middle of a narrow road. Travelers could only get around the boulder with some difficulty, having to go off the road into a soggy marsh on one side or brave a steep drop off on the other side. For years, travelers suffered the hardships and went around the boulder.

One day, a young man, on the way to the city to seek his fortune, saw the difficulty the boulder posed for everyone. He put his shoulder to it, and he was able to roll it a little. He rested and tried again. Travelers passed by and shook their heads at his efforts. Finally, after more than an hour, he got the boulder rolling and pushed it off the road into the marsh. Underneath the boulder the king had buried a chest of gold and jewels.

Tours

Children also have a need to be stimulated. Most enjoy learning even if they don't seem to want to learn what adults think is good for them. School holidays and the summer provide excellent opportunities to broaden their horizons.

Many adults take their communities for granted; many children never get to learn enough about their communities to take them for granted. Tours—of dairies, newspapers, bakeries, the local soft drink plant, clothing factories, city hall, hospitals, colleges, the county jail, nursing homes, farms, special local industries, museums, cultural events, ethnic centers, churches, military installations, TV or radio stations, national parks, local or state police headquarters, the water plant, a power plant, the sewage treatment plant—can begin to stimulate awareness that may carry over to school.

Many children have such a limited view of the world and such a deficiency of knowledge that it is difficult for them to integrate much that is available for them to learn, including the treatment that is offered with such dedication. When left to their own devices, they have little to think about except what they've learned from other kids and what they've learned from TV. One may be unhealthy; the other may be unreal.

A Christmas tour. **Boys and girls were amazed at their Christmas-time tour of an insurance company in a high-rise office building. The company choir sang Christmas carols in the lobby. Attractive and well-dressed men and women sat behind desks answering phones, writing, typing, and working with computers. The company cafeteria served freshly grilled sandwiches made to order, seafood, pasta, and fancy salads; it had an ice cream sundae bar and served freshly baked pies and cakes. An exercise room had personnel to assist with aerobics, weight machines, treadmills, and exercise bikes, as well as whirlpools and saunas. An auditorium was staffed with video and audio technicians who developed training and advertising materials. The views from many offices were breathtaking.**

The children were treated with courtesy and respect. They were allowed an hour in the exercise room with the three trainers; they were fed lunch in the company cafeteria. Their behavior and the questions they asked surprised some of the staff. The tour guide told the children that they had conducted themselves better than many school and Scout groups who had toured. Upon reflection, the boys and girls realized that the company offered opportunities for everyone from accountants, lawyers, and public relations professionals to maintenance and repair people, physical education instructors, security people, drivers, janitors, receptionists, cooks, and dishwashers.

SPACE, EQUIPMENT, TIME, AND PROPS

The design and layout of the facility, the available equipment and its condition, the timing of events and activities, and the props that may be available are significant parts of the treatment milieu. They can support treatment objectives or compromise them.

Space

Ideally, all facilities would be designed with particular programs in mind. Practically, many programs have to be designed to fit available facilities. Programs that have areas that are difficult for staff to supervise, or too many activity areas for staff to supervise, create problems for the staff as well as for the children. Some activity areas may be fairly noisy—a game room with a pool table, pinball, and video games, a gym or outdoor activity area. Others should be relatively quiet—a TV room or an area for table games such as cards and Monopoly. Children must be afforded some opportunity for privacy (individual, not group). Staff should be afforded some privacy for dealing with a child, so that not all instruction, criticism, counseling, and disclosure must occur in the group context.

The ability of staff to supervise the facility has several implications. Some programs will provide service both to children who tend to take advantage of others and children who are vulnerable. Vulnerable children who too frequently find themselves with others in areas that are difficult for staff to supervise are at special risk. Staff may counsel the vulnerable child that he or she does not have to be afraid and to come to staff with any problems. The fact of the matter is, if the child has a problem about which staff are ignorant, the child can be intimidated by the fear that something will happen before he or she can get to staff. Consequences to the bully after a beating or a sexual assault do little for the victim.

Further, areas that allow residents to get together too frequently for too long a time away from staff supervision diminish the program's ability to monitor and direct the group process. Hours of therapy to work with an adolescent on how to accept criticism from a disliked teacher rather than cursing and threatening the teacher can be undone with just a few minutes of impressing a peer with how she told the teacher where to go and what to do to himself when he got there. A resident who just received counseling and consequences for striking another resident may end up convincing a third resident and, consequently, himself, that the victim only got what he deserved and that "I'd do it again!"

The end result can be some rather interesting and clever plots.

The fight. Two boys who had been having problems all week were at it again—another fight. The counselor ran from the office to break it up. The boys were really at it hot and heavy, but with the help of another staff, he was able to break up the fight. Together, he and the other staff counselled the boys. The staff found out what the problem had been; the boys apologized, shook hands, and accepted their consequences. Staff felt they might have finally gotten through to these boys.

Later that night, the two boys who had been fighting and two other boys became quite ill. Someone had gotten into the medicine cabinet. They had all taken some of a prescription medication that made them sick rather than high. When the boys returned from the hospital, staff learned that the fight had been staged. While the fight was going on, a third boy slipped into the office and jimmied the medicine cabinet while a fourth served as lookout. The thief relocked the cabinet; the boys shared their "goodies" just before bedtime.

Equipment

Residents of residential treatment programs tend to be a little hard on property. Some damage is deliberate; other damage is normal wear and tear, which can be expected to be considerable with six or more hopefully active and energetic children about. A program that is not prepared to make needed repairs in a reasonable time can expect damages to accelerate.

Broken windows. An elderly man complained about the number of windows the neighborhood kids had broken out of his garage. It had been going on for years. He hardly ever went out of his house and never saw the kids who did it. The garage was on an alley behind his house. The old man used

it only for storage—he no longer had a car. Shrubbery around the garage had grown a bit wild. The garage was in need of paint. Most of the fifteen windows in the garage door had been broken and never repaired.

Not one other broken window was in evidence on nineteen other garages on the alley, all of which were in good repair. Moral? Perhaps it is that kids don't have much chance to see what it feels like to break a window. When they happen upon a window that no one seems to care about, some will take the opportunity to find out how it feels to toss a stone through it.

The pool table. There had been some problems recently with children playing catch, and even dodge ball, with the balls on the pool table; pool sticks had been used to poke holes in the ceiling. The pool sticks had obviously not had tips for some time. Consequently, the sticks tended to slide off the cue ball when residents tried to make a shot. The sticks had also begun to drop splinters all over the table; the splinters became stuck in the fabric. Two of the bumpers were broken, the fabric was torn and one of the pockets was broken— balls went under the table. Residents couldn't play much of a game of pool, so they had found something else to do. Behavior in the rec room was not much of a problem after the program repaired the pool table and provided properly tipped pool cues.

Acoustics

Hard walls and tile floors, perhaps easier to maintain than carpet, tend to increase echoes. This may make it more difficult to hear when a group is being addressed. It may also tend to not only increase the noise during activities, but also to make the children get louder. "Remember what a bunch of boys do when running through a viaduct with an echo effect?" (Redl, 1972, p. 141).

Lighting

Ott (1976) studied the effects of lighting on the children in four first-grade classes in Sarasota, Florida, using time-lapse photography. He mounted hidden cameras in each classroom. In two of the classrooms, he replaced the standard cool-white fluorescent tubes with full-spectrum fluorescent tubes that more closely approximated natural daylight. He also covered the cathode ends of the tubes with lead foil shields to stop suspected soft x-rays. He left the standard fluorescent fixtures unchanged in the other two classrooms.

The time-lapse photographs showed children in the classrooms with the standard unshielded lights fidgeting excessively, leaping from their seats, flailing their arms, climbing on tables, and paying little attention to their teachers. In the experimental classrooms, the photographs showed children settling down more quickly, paying more attention to their teachers. They were less nervous and their overall performance was better.

Later, full-spectrum shielded tubes were installed in the remaining two classrooms. These children were photographed two and three months later. They were found to be more calm and more interested in their work. One boy who stood out in earlier photographs because he was constantly in motion had become more quiet and able to sit still. His teacher reported that he was able to study independently and had learned to read during the three-month period.

Another study in Sarasota schools reported that hyperactive children in the Adjustive Education Center improved after defective television sets in their homes were either repaired or replaced. These sets had been found to emit measurable amounts of x radiation (Ott, 1976).

I recall a facility for adolescent girls that I visited on occasion. The girls appeared to be somewhat more active than staff desired. Each time I visited, I was annoyed by the intermittent flickering of several of the fluorescent fixtures that were in need of having tubes replaced.

Time

The timing of the various events in the milieu can be very important. Attention to treatment objectives, the needs of the children, and the needs of the program can enhance the effectiveness of scheduled events. On the other hand, spontaneity can also enhance the milieu on occasion.

Scheduling

Effective scheduling requires attention to the needs, abilities, and limitations of both staff and residents. It also requires attention to programmatic needs and objectives. The timing of events in the schedule can enhance or undermine staff control. Timing can also enhance or detract from the effectiveness of scheduled activities, such as therapy. Further, the timing of a particular child's participation in an event or activity, such as a home pass, can have significant implications for treatment. In the following example, a simple rearrangement of the schedule solved a daily problem with getting chores done.

> **Chores.** **The program schedule called for chores to be completed immediately after study hall at 7:00 P.M. and prior to the opening up of privileges—pool, pinball, TV or Nintendo, and basketball in the yard. Of course, every night there were some boys who had failed to earn privileges and weren't too concerned with completion of chores.**
>
> **The schedule was changed. Privileges were opened immediately after study hall and closed fifteen minutes before snacks were served at 9:00 P.M., during which time chores were to be done. As soon as staff were finished checking everyone's chores, they would set out snacks. Since snacks were not contingent on behavior and were given to everyone, everyone was usually cooperative, even enthusiastic, about completing chores.**

Therapy

For children who are in public school, therapy sessions must usually be scheduled after 4:00 P.M. Therapy after 9:00 P.M. is seldom productive; although some children are unusually alert until 10:00 P.M., few therapists are. Friday seems to be a poor day for therapy for therapists, families, and children; everyone is focused on weekend activities. This leaves twenty hours from 4:00 P.M. to 9:00 P.M., Monday through Thursday for individual, group, and family therapy. With ten children for individual sessions, ten families on a bi-weekly schedule for five families per week, and two groups of five children, there are at least seventeen hours of therapy to be conducted during the twenty hours available. Supper and study hall need to occur during these same twenty hours, as does recreation.

Who cannot concentrate while others are playing basketball? Who needs as much time with peers as can be provided in order to work on peer relations? Who can be productive during the normal dinner time and have a plate held? Who can be productive if she brings her plate to therapy? Who will benefit from having dinner with the therapist? Who can attend therapy during the normal study hall and be depended upon to complete homework with limited supervision? Or who is in special education and not likely to have significant homework? The following examples illustrate a few issues with timing.

Debra's home pass. Debra had not seemed very interested in going home lately, until one week. It was her mother's birthday. She had made her a card and bought her a cigarette case that she had already wrapped. Unfortunately, Debra also got a three-day suspension from school on Thursday for fighting. She had a minor argument with another girl, but she really lost her temper when the other girl told Debra that her mother was a prostitute. Nobody goes on a pass if she's not in school because of a disciplinary problem.

An activity. With fairly new staff on duty for the weekend, a supervisor had scheduled a Saturday outing to a new gym early in the week. He had visited with the owner of the gym, who was donating the use of the facility to the program. He had reviewed with the staff concerns about supervision and setting limits. He had met with the boys and set some expectations. An administrator, working a bit late on Friday evening, asked someone about the weekend schedule after the supervisor had left. The administrator was not

familiar with the gym or what had gone into the arrangements. He cancelled the activity, told the new staff to plan something else, then went home.

Spontaneity

While scheduling is important, providing both staff and residents with a sense of security and routine, the timing of events in the schedule may not always be appropriate to the needs of the program or the children at a given time. The ability of the staff to adjust, amend, or change the schedule within limits can enhance treatment objectives; blind adherence to a schedule may be counterproductive at times. The following provides an example of spontaneity versus adherence to a schedule.

A tale of two programs. An agency operated two group homes. One program director insisted on strict adherence to the schedule; the other allowed staff to use their judgment in making changes in scheduled activities.

One day, the more flexible program director scheduled a major clean-up—attention to chores had not been good recently. The boys pitched in and worked hard, despite the fact that one of the air conditioners was down and the home was quite warm. After lunch, the staff decided to cancel the outing to the track where the boys would run and exercise and to take the boys swimming instead.

At another time, the staff at the more structured home had been having a difficult morning with their boys. This followed a difficult evening. Nevertheless, they took the boys to the scheduled swimming activity at the nearby gym where the program had a membership. Due to the behavior of some of the boys at this activity, the program's membership was cancelled for the remainder of the year.

Props

Teachers are familiar with the technique of placing an unusual or out-of-place object on the desk at the beginning of class; it will hold attention for a time as the children listen, waiting for some clue as to its reason for being there. Child care counselors are aware of the difficulty in trying to sort out a problem with a group of youngsters when a coworker walks in with the duffle bag filled with balls, gloves, and bats for a baseball game (Redl, 1972).

SEEPAGE FROM THE OUTSIDE WORLD

No matter how secluded or secure the program, events in the real world intrude into the milieu. They may have serious impacts on the milieu itself, or impact the treatment of a particular child, as follows.

Troy. Troy liked to keep staff off guard. She was also very good at setting her parents and the program at odds. On a night during a week in which her behavior had been barely passable, she became very defiant about her chores. Staff reminded her that her points for the week were awfully close and that she really couldn't afford to have any problems if she wanted a home pass. Troy immediately informed the staff with a toss of her head that she was going home this weekend, "Just you wait and see!"

Her problems increased during the night and she taunted the staff with her defiance, while confidently assuring them, in spite of all their warnings, that she would have her pass no matter what they said. Of course, she fell far short of the points necessary for a home pass when the week's points were totalled the next day after school.

Troy knew from a phone call from her father that her grandmother had died and that the funeral was this weekend. The program always let children attend funerals of close relatives, no matter what, and her father was going to request a special pass for her in family therapy that evening.

Tony. Tony got a call from his girlfriend, as he did every night. Tonight she told him of a fight with her mother and her plans to run away. She wanted Tony to meet her.

Bernice. Bernice hadn't heard from her mother in over a year. Her mother had moved to another state three years ago with Bernice's two younger brothers and younger sister; they had been without a phone for eighteen months, so Bernice couldn't call. After eighteen months, her mother called one Saturday morning to tell Bernice about her new baby sister.

School. There was a fight at school during the week. One combatant was black and the other was white. The white boy's father came to school the next day and was so disruptive that police had to be called to have him removed. Rumors ran rampant around the school. A big fight was supposed to "go down" on Monday. Several boys made clubs while on home pass and managed to hide them on the grounds upon returning. They got them to school on Monday.

There really was no racial tension except for the rumors, and school officials had everything well in hand. Nevertheless, two boys who didn't know what to do with their clubs were caught with them in their lockers.

Renee. Renee's boyfriend called and said that he just had to see her tonight. He also had a friend who wanted to meet her roommate, Tammy.

UMPIRING AND TRAFFIC REGULATION

Children occasionally need adults to mediate their disagreements and regulate their activities. These are normal needs that can take on added dimensions when children with problems live together in close proximity.

Umpiring

In the normal give-and-take of human interaction, occasional disagreements arise. With children, even when other children react appropriately, the child may not fully understand what may be occurring. "Some 'milieu impacts' hit the children directly; nobody needs to interpret or translate. Others hit the child all right, but to have their proper impact someone has to do some explaining" (Redl, 1972, p. 143).

Donnie and Jim. Donnie and Jim were in the TV room. An argument developed over what channel to watch. Donnie pushed Jim. Jim punched Donnie in the nose and bloodied it. Jim couldn't understand why he was being punished. He was only defending himself.

Tony. Tony liked the bigger kids and tried to play basketball with them. He was little, young, and uncoordinated. He tried to steal the ball just like the big kids did, slapping and fouling incessantly. The bigger boys put him out of the game. Tony came running in crying.

Traffic Regulation

"Depending on the amount of their disturbance . . . some social interactions that normal life leaves to the children's own resources require traffic supervision by an adult" (Redl, 1972, p. 143). The teasing and horseplay that occur in some residential settings may be considerably less than may be seen at a summer camp for Girl Scouts or Boy Scouts, and far less than can be observed in a college dormitory. Even a little bit of teasing or horseplay may result in a child's running away screaming and crying or a full-blown fight.

Children who don't do very well with instructions and rules and who aren't very good at losing can have difficulties with even the simplest of games such as pinball. Games with detailed instructions and rules, such as Monopoly, can pose even more problems.

New residents wanting to be accepted by the group are especially vulnerable to pressures to share their prized possessions with other residents who have relatively little, and who have less opportunity to get new clothes, jewelry, cosmetics, or toys than they would like. The following illustrate two of the constant problems children in residential programs experience over their possessions that often require adult attention.

Mark. Mark often borrowed other children's toys and clothes. For Christmas, Mark received his heart's desire, a radio-controlled car. With such a long history of borrowing and never having anything that other boys wanted to borrow, Mark was under a lot of pressure to share his car. By the time he got to play with it himself, the batteries were dead and he had to wait two days until he could get his allowance and go shopping for new batteries.

Donna. The girls were always borrowing each others' clothing. Donna loaned her best and favorite sweater to Bonnie for her weekend pass. Bonnie didn't return from the pass and was put on runaway status. By the time Bonnie returned, no one could figure out what may have happened to the sweater.

THE CLINICAL RESILIENCE THERMOSTAT

Rather than debate the merits of rigidity versus flexibility, Redl (1972) is interested in the ability of the treatment environment to be resilient—to tighten controls in early phases of treatment or when impulses threaten, and to loosen up during later phases of treatment to provide opportunities to practice self-control. There are definite benefits to control. A well-run correctional institution has few problems. It teaches inmates to follow its rules and say "Yes, sir," and "No, sir" in appropriate tones with a success that residential programs may some-times envy. Some correctional programs may teach very little else.

It is difficult to treat shoplifting, and even more difficult to determine whether or not it has been treated, if a resident never gets into a store, or only gets into a store under strict supervision. On the other hand, a program cannot tolerate repeated shoplifting at local businesses, especially if staff are accompanying residents when it occurs.

SUMMARY

Many unpleasant things happen to children in resi-dential treatment centers. They get criticized, in-structed, questioned, confronted, and punished (some programs now use the word ''con-sequated''). They get controlled when they have been used to being in control. They live with other children who may be unpleasant or downright dan-gerous. They may have painful experiences brought out in therapy.

With care, planning, and hard work, many pleasant things can also happen to children in resi-dential treatment. They can get some, most, or all of their needs met. They can learn new and rewarding ways of relating to peers and adults. They can learn to live with and control tempers that may be even more frightening to them than to others. They can learn more about the world around them. They can learn to experience some success at school. They can gain some confidence that maybe they can have some control over their lives and even their futures.

Virtually every aspect of the treatment environ-ment is significant. Each aspect can have positive impacts on treatment. Likewise, each aspect can undermine treatment in some way.

The social structure impacts residents' rela-tions to staff and to other residents. It has signifi-cance for how staff work together or fail to work together. The houseparent model offers consistency and a strong family model, but a turnover in houseparents during treatment can be disastrous. The shift model offers children a variety of staff, but communications and consistency are problematic. Meanwhile, the structure among residents, formal and informal groups, and room assignments may also support treatment objectives or exacerbate problems.

Value systems—ethical, moral, and clinical—of staff, clinicians, support personnel, administra-tors, schools, probation officers, courts, and the community meet in the milieu. Children naturally test the values of adults with whom they interact. They readily detect internal conflicts and inconsis-tencies, as well as differences between various groups. Some children exploit these differences. Adults must be clear on their own values and just as clear on how they present these values to the children.

The routines of the program are those that exist in practice, not those that exist on paper. They, too, are a significant part of the milieu. While the milieu may have its own rituals, so may the children develop certain ritualistic behaviors. Traditions may be significant in providing the children with a sense of security and of belonging. Behavioral regulations, not only those related to immoral acts but also those necessary for the orderly operation of the program or institution, are significant. Children who have problems with rules and regulations are most often faced with even more rules and regula-tions than they experienced previously.

Group processes are a very significant part of the milieu. While children have some need of adult approval, their needs for peer acceptance increase with age. Peer group dynamics form a powerful component of the milieu that requires constant vigil and attention. We will consider some principles of group dynamics in chapter 8.

The traits of other residents comprise an aspect of the milieu that also merits attention. These traits may be positive or negative, merely unpleasant or downright dangerous.

Staff attitudes can contribute significantly to

treatment or compromise treatment just as significantly. Staff attitudes require careful attention during the hiring process and merit considerable attention thereafter.

While we are most often occupied with the behaviors that a child exhibits, we should not lose sight of the behaviors the child receives from peers, staff, and others. These behaviors can support or undermine treatment significantly as they reinforce or fail to reinforce the behaviors of the child.

With 168 hours in a week, of which perhaps thirty-five may be spent in school and but a few in therapy, the activity structure on the unit becomes especially significant for treatment. Activities may simply fill up time, or they can support or undermine treatment in a variety of ways. Games, athletics, movies, stories, and tours can provide much in support of overall treatment objectives.

Likewise, the facility itself, its equipment, and the timing of events and activities can support treatment or add to the difficulties of providing for the children. Areas that are difficult to supervise can endanger vulnerable children and lead to group activities that are counterproductive. Poorly maintained equipment may add to problems of supervision, as may acoustics and lighting. Scheduling of activities versus spontaneity may also contribute to or compromise treatment.

The normal interactions of children require the occasional umpiring of an adult, someone to call the fouls, to interpret what is taking place. The normal interactions of children also require the occasional regulation of an adult to keep things from getting out of hand.

The thermostat for clinical resilience is significant for milieu therapy. It allows the milieu to be flexible, to respond to the treatment needs of a given child or of the group at a given time. It allows flexibility when appropriate, and provides structure when necessary.

Children are by nature needy; residents of treatment programs are often especially so. Only a few of the children's needs are treatment needs, and only a few are basic needs. The more needs the program is able to meet, the more successful the program is likely to be.

Learning Theory and Controlling Behavior

Virtually anyone working with children in any setting has some interest in controlling behavior: a parent wanting a child to eat her broccoli; a barber wanting a child to hold still; a school teacher wanting a child to pay attention and learn; a counselor wanting a child to learn to manage certain problems; a child care counselor knowing a child is going to lose his temper when he receives his restriction.

The behavior of children is a major concern in residential treatment and likely to consume considerable time and effort, regardless of the philosophical or treatment orientation of the program. No matter what their other problems may be, it is problems with their behavior that most often bring children into residential treatment. In those rare cases where a child comes into residential treatment because no other more suitable placement can be found, behavior may still become an issue should the child begin to exhibit some of the behaviors of his or her new peers.

Enter the psychology of learning, stage left. The learning and controlling of behavior has been a major focus of psychology. Psychologists have proposed theories of learning and proposed principles for controlling behavior. Behavior modification has grown from a novel, almost taboo approach in the 1960s to *status quo* in the present day.

Rewards and punishments have been a part of our culture for thousands of years. Now, educators, therapists, and others apply rewards and punishments under the banner of psychology, often calling them reinforcements and negative reinforcements. They create systems for rewarding and punishing children's behavior and claim that they are doing behavior modification. Psychology, however, tells us much more about learning than to reward behaviors that we want and to punish behaviors that we don't want. In fact, psychology suggests that this approach may not be producing the results that we desire.

In this chapter, we will look at some of the concepts and principles of learning and behavior that have been proposed by the psychology of learning. Psychology has proposed principles that apply both to overt behavior and to underlying feelings and emotions. In humans, most feelings, emotions, and behavior appear to be subject to learning.

The psychology of learning offers principles that relate to controlling behavior in a given setting. This is most desirable in residential treatment. However, the psychology of learning offers much more. It offers insight into the learning of new behaviors, the use of behaviors in different settings, and the learning and experiencing of feelings and emotions. From a treatment perspective, these may be even more desirable.

First, we will look at some issues of control. Then we will look at learning as the psychologist views it. We will define carefully some of the concepts psychologists use, then proceed to consider two basic types of learning—Pavlov's classical conditioning and Skinner's operant conditioning. Finally, we will look at some of the principles of learning that have been established by each of these fields.

The concepts, principles, and processes are complex. I have attempted to make this presentation clear and concise. Space does not allow details of the tremendous amount of experimental and other research that has gone into the development of these fields. In the next section, we will look at the application of these principles in the residential setting to accomplish specific objectives.

SOME ISSUES OF CONTROL

When adults exhibit socially unacceptable, impractical, and sometimes even dangerous behavior, they are often referred to as childish, especially if the behavior falls short of psychotic or criminal. Lack of self-control is a childlike quality. Children are not expected to exhibit socially acceptable, practical, or even safe behavior in all settings. This is why they require supervision. It is also why they are sometimes refreshingly funny and enjoyable.

Children have to be taught. While they are being taught, they have to be supervised; sometimes they have to be physically controlled. As they get older, expectations increase. Their self-control is supposed to get better in more and more situations. They are supposed to require less supervision, less control by others.

We can control a child by physically holding the child, as in preventing a three-year-old from running into the street, in stopping a fight, or in taking a child out of a dangerous area. We can also control a child for longer times by locking the child in a cell or padded room, by lashing the child to a bed, by placing the child in a straight jacket, or by drugging the child into oblivion, or nearly so. All of these techniques have been used in correctional facilities and psychiatric hospitals. These techniques prevent behavior. The threat of these techniques may elicit behavior.

Most often, what is meant by controlling a child's behavior is influencing the child's behavior with threats of punishment or offers of rewards. Many children who end up in residential treatment come from backgrounds in which one of these techniques was used almost exclusively to the exclusion of the other, or in which both techniques were used with a great deal of inconsistency.

The earliest myths tell of gods rewarding and punishing mortals and other gods for all sorts of deeds. Reward and punishment have been topics of heated debate for social and moral philosophers, theologians, judges, psychoanalysts, and now, social and behavioral scientists. Contemporary religion offers eternal life over eternal damnation— quite a clear choice. And yet newspapers carry stories of the sins of clergy, even in their service to children.

Psychologists interested in learning theory and behavior modification have very specific definitions for the concepts of "reward" and "punishment." These concepts, however, are so much a part of Western Civilization that it is sometimes difficult for even the clinician or scientist to lay aside some of the connotations, especially of "punishment." When working with children, we must be very clear of our own values and feelings; our children will read these despite what we may tell them, or what we may be telling ourselves.

Ultimately, we want to teach the child to control himself or herself. Rewards and punishments are very powerful teaching agents. In fact, they are much more effective in teaching than they are in controlling. Sometimes, when we're using them in an attempt to control a child, we forget to look at what we may be teaching the child. It is important to keep purpose clearly in mind.

Behavioral psychologists, with principles and theories of learning, have introduced behavior modification. Terms such as behavior therapy, behavior treatment, and behavior management have appeared in the vocabulary of residential treatment. Whatever one's interest or theoretical orientation in working with children, it is likely that one will be using rewards and punishments in some way, although one may choose to use terms such as consequences or "negative reinforcements." However, as we shall see, negative reinforcement is not the same as punishment. Learning psychologists have developed much that can contribute to a better understanding of how rewards and punishments work to affect present and future behavior, as well as feelings and emotions.

UNDERSTANDING LEARNING AS THE PSYCHOLOGIST VIEWS IT

Scientists use the scientific method of observation, formulation of hypotheses, and experimental testing of hypotheses to attempt to identify relationships between phenomena that can be expressed as laws. They attempt to formulate theories that organize these laws into conceptual frameworks that explain various laws and suggest new hypotheses. Engineers and others apply scientific principles to make things and to do things.

Learning psychologists are scientists who have been studying learning in the laboratory since before Pavlov's classic work on the reflex salivation of dogs was first published in English in 1927. They have defined various aspects of learning and have discovered relationships that they have expressed as principles of learning. They have formulated theories to explain those principles and have tested new hypotheses suggested by those theories. While some theories attempt to explain a great deal, no

theory explains learning to everyone's satisfaction (Hill, 1963). Behavior modifiers have applied principles of learning in various situations to change behavior (Neuringer, 1970).

The applications of scientific principles by engineers have become increasingly remarkable. They have designed automobiles that last longer and require less routine maintenance. They have sent people to the moon and launched space shuttles to repair satellites in orbit.

Nevertheless, cars get recalled for components that do not perform as expected, a space shuttle exploded, and the expensive Hubble Telescope at first did not function as well as expected. Some of the problems have been with engineering design, others with manufacture by technicians. New designs are tested under a variety of conditions, but unanticipated conditions during use may require modifications in design. The better the engineer understands the principles involved, the better she will be at avoiding problems or correcting them when she encounters them. In the final analysis, components must be properly installed if they are to perform as designed.

Likewise, application of the scientific principles of learning in behavior modification have met with both success and failure. In addition to the problems faced by the physical scientist and the engineer, the application of learning principles faces additional problems in at least three areas.

First, like the physician, those dealing with behavior are dealing with organisms that have individual differences. Principles dealing with individual organisms are not nearly so precise as those governing the flow of electrons through a circuit or the interaction of a precise mixture of chemicals at a given temperature. The prescribed treatment may work as expected most of the time, but not all patients respond the same. Some will respond quickly, others slowly; there may be a few who do not appear to respond at all, and others who have an allergic or other aversive reaction. The better the physician understands relevant principles and theories, the better able she will be to adjust the treatment or select other treatments.

Second, like the meteorologist, those dealing with behavior deal with an incredible number of variables in the environment. The meteorologist may have an excellent understanding of the effects of a high pressure in a given location, sun spots, humidity, temperature, the jet stream, and many other relevant variables that affect the weather. However, the continuing effects of all of the above on each of the above as each changes sets up more variables than the human brain can conceptualize at one time. The accuracy of the meteorologist's forecasts depends not only on her understanding of theory and principles, but also on the number of variables she can consider for a given forecast.

Third, principles of learning are not nearly so precise as principles in other sciences, and theories are not nearly so well developed. There is not "a theory of learning" that is totally accepted. Many theories have been proposed. Some attempt to explain all learning for all organisms, others attempt to explain some aspect of learning (Deese & Hulse, 1967).

People dealing with behavior, then, are dealing with individual organisms with individual differences in a complex environment in which countless variables operate. Further, they are doing so with principles and theory that provide guidance that is, at times, less than precise. Like the engineer, those dealing with behavior can expect failures due to problems with design and failures due to the use of that design by "technicians" who are responsible for application. There will be "recalls." As with the physician treating a patient, there may be a need to adjust a technique for individual differences. As with the meteorologist, something in the interplay of countless variables may have been missed.

With all of the above, however, the scientific principles involved are rarely in dispute. The problems are encountered in design and application. Those dealing with behavior are faced with an additional problem: a principle shown to be valid in a particular situation may not apply in the situation for which it has been chosen. In any case, the better one understands the principles and theories of learning, the better one will be at changing behavior.

Definitions

Psychology uses a number of fairly common terms, such as reward, punishment, and reinforcement. It uses them, however, with very precise definitions that are different from the many meanings and rich connotations such words may have in everyday use. Other terms, such as learning, are defined by psychologists much more broadly than in common use. And, of course, psychologists have their own special terms for their own special concepts, such as negative reinforcement. It is necessary, therefore, to carefully define terms and concepts as used by psychologists and as used in this text.

Behavioral Definitions

Psychologists who study behavior attempt to define things in terms of behavior. "A behavioral approach emphasizes the importance of a functional analysis of the behavioral referents involved as well as related antecedent and consequent factors" (Gambrill, 1977, p. 664). "Depression" may be defined in terms of reduced levels of behavior, reduced food intake, excessive sleeping or insomnia, and statements the person makes about being unhappy rather than in terms of mood or feelings. "Fear" is likely to be defined in terms of the glandular secretion of adrenaline, increased heart rate, or increased or decreased level of activity ("freezing").

Operational Definitions

Words that cannot be defined in terms of behavior may be defined in terms of the "operation" used. "Hunger" may be defined in terms of how long the subject has gone without food (Deese & Hulse, 1967).

Learning

Different psychologists define learning in somewhat different ways; some do not offer a precise definition. Learning is used by psychologists in a broader sense than it is used colloquially or in other fields such as education. It is often defined in behavioral terms, but it also includes emotions, feelings, and attitudes. Learning involves some change that is more than temporary. Learning may be conscious or unconscious. It includes simple habits, complex motor skills, problem solving, concept formation, verbal skills, emotions, feelings, attitudes, knowledge, and superstitions. There is no "right" or "wrong" (Hill, 1963).

Habit

Any kind of learned behavior is called a habit (Lawson, 1960).

Instinct

An instinct is an unlearned behavior that is elicited by an identifiable stimulus or pattern of stimuli (Verhave, 1966). Instincts are ". . . fairly complete sequences of species characteristic responses usually performed frequently in the normal existence of the individual" (Burghardt, 1973, p. 361). Instinctive behavior involves the skeletal muscles and the skeletal somatic nervous system. While a wide range of simple and complex instinctive behavior patterns may be displayed by other species, most human behavior is learned (Deese and Hulse, 1967). While certain drives are instinctive and unlearned, these drives do not produce in humans the kinds of patterned behavior characteristic in other species (Burghardt, 1973).

Colloquially, we often speak of "reacting on instinct" in the same way we speak of reflex reactions, as in catching something that is about to hit us, or in swerving our car to avoid an obstacle. We may argue an "instinct" for self-preservation, but the behavior with which we respond is learned.

Reflex

A reflex is an unlearned response that an organism makes to a given stimulation whenever that stimulation occurs. With few exceptions, reflexes involve one or more of the following: the autonomic nervous system, the smooth or visceral muscles, and glandular secretions. Some examples are the galvanic skin response to an electrical shock (increased conductivity of the skin due to increased perspiration, measured by electrodes, as used in polygraph examinations), the knee kick reflex to a tap on the patellar tendon, the blinking of the eye to a puff of air, and the salivation to food or salt water in the mouth. The organism may or may not be conscious of the reflex response, but the response is not under conscious control (Verhave, 1966).

The driver who swerves a car to avoid a small animal and hits a tree destroying the car speaks of an "unconscious reflex reaction," but this response does not involve the autonomic nervous system, visceral musculature, or glandular secretions; such may occur simultaneously as separate responses, but they are not the response that wrecked the car. The response that wrecks the car is a learned motor skill, even if it is initiated unconsciously and accompanied by reflex responses related to fear or anxiety.

Conditioned Reflex

Reflexes can be conditioned to stimulations that do not naturally produce them. When so conditioned, they are called conditioned reflexes (Deese & Hulse, 1967). Salivation to food in the mouth is a reflex; salivation to the charcoal aroma when passing a fast food restaurant is a learned behavior. As natural as it seems to modern Americans, one would not expect infants or prehistoric man to salivate to the aroma without some prior experience. In the same way, Pavlov used experience with sounds and food to condition dogs to salivate to sounds and other stimuli, including the passage of a fixed interval of time as the only stimulus.

Stimulus

A stimulus is something that may somehow affect the organism. It may be external, such as a sound, light, color, smell, or physical touching; it may be internal, such as the effect of a hormone or the sensation of a muscle contraction. The term is obviously related to the word "stimulation" but should not carry quite the same implications. Stimulation implies excitement; stimulus should not. A barely noticed light bulb or a casual nod of approval may be stimuli (Deese & Hulse, 1967).

Unconditioned Stimulus

The stimulation that naturally produces a reflex response is called an unconditioned stimulus (Deese & Hulse, 1967). Food in the mouth and a tap on the patellar tendon are unconditioned stimuli for salivation and the knee jerk response, respectively (Verhave, 1966).

Conditioned Stimulus

When a neutral stimulus that does not normally produce a reflex begins to produce that reflex, it is called a conditioned stimulus (Hill, 1963). The aroma of a fast food restaurant is a conditioned stimulus for many Americans.

Classical Conditioning

Classical conditioning is the process by which an organism learns to make a reflex response to a stimulus that previously did not elicit that response. The process can be demonstrated in the laboratory. The stimulus that naturally produces the reflex is presented at the same time as a stimulus that does not normally produce the reflex. After a number of repetitions, the previously neutral stimulus will be found to produce the reflex when presented alone. The organism has *learned* to make the reflex response to a new stimulation and will continue to do so for some time, i.e., a previously neutral stimulus has become a conditioned stimulus through pairing with an unconditioned stimulus. The process has received considerable attention since Pavlov discovered it in the early 1900s in his classic work in conditioning the salivation of dogs to various sounds and other stimuli (Hill, 1963).

Operant Conditioning

Operant conditioning is one of the means by which organisms learn to make responses in their environment, responses that involve the skeletal muscles and the skeletal somatic nervous system. A wide range of behaviors and stimulations may be involved. Unlike classical conditioning, it is not always possible to identify stimuli that elicit responses. Behaviors are often conscious, but may be unconscious as well. Unconscious behaviors,

however, can be brought under conscious control much more easily than can reflexes such as the patellar knee kick, the eye blink, salivation, or the galvanic skin response (Deese & Hulse, 1967).

B. F. Skinner's work, beginning in the 1930s, has resulted in much attention to this type of learning. Perhaps his best-known technique involves the training of the white laboratory rat to press a bar to receive food or escape electric shock.

Response

A response is anything that an organism does, simple or complex, conscious or unconscious, external or internal, motor, instinct, or reflex. The implication is that the response is "to" something, which implies one or more stimuli, but it is not always possible to identify a stimulus that produces a response. The response itself generates a number of stimuli for the organism (Deese & Hulse, 1967; Lawson, 1960; Verhave, 1966).

Independent Variable

ındependent variable is a term used in research. An independent variable is something the researcher uses to make a prediction. In experimental research, the independent variable is controlled and manipulated by the experimenter, who observes what happens. When the independent variable cannot be controlled by the researcher, the research is not experimental. The researcher observes differences in the natural occurrence of the independent variable, and observes what else occurs along with it (Hill, 1963).

Dependent Variable

Dependent variable is also a term used in research. The dependent variable is something about which the researcher makes a prediction (Hill, 1963). To determine the effects of lighting on production output of workers in a factory, some measure of light would be the independent variable, while some measure of work, such as units produced in a given time, would be the dependent variable. Units produced per unit of time (day, week, or month) would then be measured for different levels of lighting.

Extraneous Variable

Extraneous variable is a term used in research to describe a thing about which the researcher is not making a prediction. Extraneous variables must, therefore, be controlled and held constant so that they do not vary with changes in the independent variable. In a study about the effects of lighting on productivity in a factory, the researcher is not studying the effects of pay, temperature, morale, or anything else; all must be held constant so that only the lighting varies.

Intervening Variable

An intervening variable is a theoretical concept used to describe something that occurs between the independent variable and the dependent variable to explain their relationship (Hill, 1963). In a study of hunger on the effects of learning in a laboratory rat, hunger is an independent variable that is manipulated by the experimenter and measured by the amount of time the rat has been without food. Some measure of the rat's performance, such as the amount of time to correctly run a maze to get to food at the end, is the dependent variable. The concept of motivation is an intervening variable used to explain the fact that hungry rats learn faster when food is used as a reward.

Hypothetical Construct

A hypothetical construct is a theoretical concept most often used to describe an intervening variable that cannot be seen, touched, or otherwise "proven" to exist by the senses, such as motivation (Deese & Hulse, 1967).

Scientific Theory

Scientific theory is an attempt to explain how and why things happen. The pure scientist is interested in understanding rather than doing. In some sciences, there is little practical application at present. There seems to be little that can be done with

the astronomer's discovery of a distant quasar (Lawson, 1960).

Scientific Research

Scientific research is the application of the scientific method to identify relationships between and among phenomena.

Scientific Method

The scientific method is the application of the following steps:

1. Formulation of a hypothesis about the relationship between or among phenomena.
2. Careful design of research to test the hypothesis.
3. Observation and collection of data.
4. Analysis of data.
5. Drawing conclusions, either accepting or rejecting the hypothesis (Horton & Hunt, 1976).

Experimental Research

Experimental research is a study in which the experimenter is able to manipulate and control the independent variable and to control extraneous variables, allowing conclusions of cause and effect with considerable confidence. Experimental research may be done in the laboratory, allowing great control of extraneous variables, or outside the laboratory where extraneous variables may not be as readily controlled (Hill, 1963).

Consider the Hawthorne Effect. A series of studies were conducted at the Hawthorne Works of the Western Electric Company during the 1930s to test the effects of increased pay, shorter hours, improved lighting and ventilation, rest pauses, and refreshment periods on women producing electric relays. Each incentive resulted in an increase in production. A return to normal working conditions, rather than producing a return to the pre-experimental levels of production, also produced an increase in production (Munn, 1961).

Researchers concluded that the workers were responding not only to the specific changes but also to the increased attention they were receiving. Morale was much improved and workers in the study were noted to have a special esprit de corps (Munn, 1961).

There was another variable that was not controlled: perceptions of management interest, an extraneous variable. Had the experiment not been designed to include a return to normal working conditions, the conclusion that the various changes caused increased output would likely have been drawn and an important factor would have gone unnoticed (Munn, 1961).

Although studies in the laboratory sometimes seem to have little relationship to the real world, such studies provide the best opportunity to control for extraneous variables (Hill, 1963). Would a laboratory study of lighting and other factors on work output have provided more information? Would those results have translated to the much more complex work environment? Does lighting have any effect on the behavior of children in residential treatment? Do other factors?

Nonexperimental Research

In nonexperimental research, the researcher cannot manipulate the independent variable, but must observe naturally occurring variations. Some variables, like sunspots or the IQ of a subject, are beyond our ability to manipulate at present. We do not manipulate other variables such as oil spills, harsh punishment of children, or sexual abuse because of ethical considerations. Nonexperimental research may be conducted in the laboratory or in the natural setting (Hill, 1963).

While nonexperimental research may lead to valid conclusions of relationships between phenomena, conclusions of cause and effect cannot always be drawn with confidence (Hill, 1963). One might conclude from Sheldon's study on the relationship between physical characteristics and personality that certain body types produce certain personality characteristics. One might also conclude that certain personalities lead to certain physiological characteristics. Or one might conclude that some other factors in the history of the subjects produced both the physiological and psychological traits that were observed to be correlated. One might even conclude

that the researcher was predisposed to certain conclusions and biased in the design or the application of criteria (Munn, 1961).

Reinforcement

A reinforcement is something that increases the probability of a response when it is in some way contingent on that response. The reinforcement for behavior in classical conditioning does not have to be rewarding—while meat powder reinforces the salivation to the sound of the bell, salt water or sand will also produce the salivation necessary to reinforce conditioning (Deese and Hulse, 1967).

Conditioned Reinforcement

A conditioned reinforcement is a neutral stimulus that initially has no effect on the probability of a response, but comes to have an effect on that response after it has occurred in the presence of a stimulus that is a reinforcement for that response (Deese & Hulse, 1967). Letters of the alphabet written on little sheets of paper have very little significance for children until they move along in school; for many, A's and B's become conditioned reinforcements when those grades occur along with praise from parents and teachers.

Reward

Reward is a term sometimes used in operant conditioning to refer to a reinforcement. Reward has theoretical implications, since it implies the involvement of some hypothetical construct such as pleasure or satisfaction. No matter how satisfying or pleasurable, however, a stimulus is a reward only if it increases a response (Deese & Hulse, 1967).

Punishment

Punishment is a stimulus that decreases a response when contingent upon that response (Deese & Hulse, 1967). As with a reward, a stimulus is a punishment only when it reduces a response in some way.

Conditioned Punishment

When a stimulus that previously failed to reduce the probability of a response acquires the effect of reducing that response due to pairing with a punishment, it is called a conditioned punishment (Hill, 1963). An F on a test paper may come to have the effect of changing a student's social life for a time, as the student forgoes some pleasurable evening activity to study. Some students, teased by peers for A's, may come to give fewer correct responses on tests or in class. Even a stimulus that serves as a reinforcement can become a conditioned punishment.

Negative Reinforcement

A negative reinforcement is something that increases the probability of a response when it is removed (Deese & Hulse, 1967). When a rat receives an electric shock in a maze, then learns how to run out of the maze to escape the shock, the shock is a negative reinforcement. In effect, the termination of a negative reinforcement acts to reinforce learning.

Negative reinforcement is not a euphemism for punishment. Although both are likely to be aversive, a stimulus is a punishment only when it reduces a response; negative reinforcements increase responses by their removal (Deese & Hulse, 1967).

Acquisition

Acquisition is an increase in the occurrence of a particular response, or chain of responses, due to reinforcement or negative reinforcement (Deese & Hulse, 1967).

Extinction

Extinction is the decrease in the occurrence of a response that occurs when the reinforcement is no longer available or when punishment is made contingent on that response. Extinguished responses seldom disappear completely, but rather fall to some random level of occurrence. Researchers, therefore, must define the criteria for extinction in some way (Lawson, 1960).

Spontaneous Recovery

Spontaneous recovery is the reoccurrence of an extinguished response even though reinforcement continues to be unavailable (Lawson, 1960) or punishment continues to result from the response (Deese & Hulse, 1967).

Performance

Performance is the way psychologists determine if learning has occurred. Observation of the kinds of responses made is qualitative; psychologists will try to make quantitative observations whenever possible (Deese & Hulse, 1967).

Response Strength

Response strength refers to quantitative measures of performance, such as the probability of a response, the amount of saliva produced, or the number of bar presses in an hour (Deese & Hulse, 1967).

Rate of Responding

Rate of responding is a means of quantifying performance; it is the number of responses made in a given period of time (Deese & Hulse, 1967).

Resistance to Extinction

Resistance to extinction is another quantitative measure of response strength. It is the number of responses made until the predetermined criterion for extinction is reached (Deese & Hulse, 1967).

Stimulus Generalization

When a subject learns to respond to a particular stimulus, then makes a similar response to a different but similar stimulus, stimulus generalization is said to occur (Deese & Hulse, 1967). For example, a child who has been bitten by one dog may learn to fear all dogs.

Discrimination Learning

When stimulus generalization is occurring, subjects may learn to discriminate between or among stimuli with considerable precision. The reinforcement is made contingent on a given stimulus.

Similar stimuli are presented without reinforcement. The subject learns to respond to the appropriate stimulus, but learns to discriminate between the reinforced stimulus and other stimuli. In effect, generalized responses are extinguished (Verhave, 1966).

Cue

A cue is a stimulus, or group of stimuli, used in some types of discrimination learning to signal different learning situations. A cue such as a light may signal that reinforcement is available when the light is on, unavailable when the light is off (Deese & Hulse, 1967).

Escape Learning

Escape learning is a situation in which a subject learns to make a response to escape from or turn off a negative reinforcement (Deese & Hulse, 1967).

Avoidance Learning

Avoidance learning is a situation in which a subject learns a response to avoid an unpleasant stimulus (Deese & Hulse, 1967).

Reinforcement Schedule

Reinforcement schedule refers to the way in which reinforcements are available (Hill, 1963).

Continuous Reinforcement

Continuous reinforcement is a schedule wherein every appropriate response is reinforced (Lawson, 1960).

Partial Reinforcement

When only some but not all appropriate responses receive a reinforcement, a partial reinforcement schedule is in use (Deese & Hulse, 1967).

Fixed Ratio Reinforcement

A fixed ratio reinforcement schedule is when reinforcement is provided for every so many responses on a fixed ratio, such as every fifth, or every twentieth response (Deese & Hulse, 1967).

Variable Ratio Reinforcement

Variable ratio reinforcement is a partial reinforcement schedule in which a predetermined average number of responses is reinforced, but the number of responses for a given reinforcement is varied randomly. For example, with a variable ratio of five, the subject may receive reinforcements for the first response, then for the second response, then not until the tenth, the third, and the ninth responses, averaging one reinforcement for every five responses (Deese & Hulse, 1967).

Fixed Interval Reinforcement

In fixed interval reinforcement the subject receives reinforcement for a response only after a fixed interval of time has elapsed after the last response (Deese & Hulse, 1967). For example, when the rat presses the bar and receives a pellet of food, another pellet will not be dispensed for another response until two minutes have elapsed, no matter how many responses the rat makes during that time.

Variable Interval Reinforcement

In variable interval reinforcement the subject receives reinforcements only after a period of time has elapsed, but the period of time varies randomly after each response (Deese & Hulse, 1967).

Classical Conditioning and the Learning of Feelings

What, exactly, is anger? Why does a fourteen-year-old, who has spent hours in group therapy learning about temper control, get into a fight and lose a valued pass only three hours after his most successful session? What makes a child get so angry that he is beyond reason? How do emotions affect behavior? Does behavior affect feelings? The concepts and principles of classical conditioning contribute substantially to our understanding of feelings and emotions.

Pavlov was a scientist, specifically a physiologist, who won the Nobel Prize for his work on digestion, yet he is best remembered for his work on learning (Lawson, 1960). He was especially interested in the role of salivation in digestion. Saliva was not only produced by the introduction of food, acid, or even grains of sand into the mouth, but also by the sight of food or acid under certain conditions (Pavlov, 1928/1966). Pavlov and his colleagues are credited with the introduction of the concepts of conditioned reflexes, stimulus generalization, extinction, and spontaneous recovery. Their work was extensive by the time it was discovered in the United States in 1927 (Lawson, 1960).

Pavlov's classic design involved placing dogs in a harness with a vial attached to collect and measure saliva. A neutral stimulus such as the ticking of a metronome, or a tone, was then presented along with an unconditioned stimulus, such as meat powder or acid introduced into the mouth. After several pairings, the neutral stimulus became a conditioned stimulus: it elicited salivation, a conditioned response, in the absence of the unconditioned stimulus, the meat powder or acid. The unconditioned response and the conditioned response are fundamentally the same except for the stimulus by which they are elicited. They are not, however, identical, differing in response strength in certain situations, in this case, volume of saliva (Lawson, 1960).

The unconditioned stimulus is considered to be a reinforcement. Several trials in the absence of reinforcement will eventually result in extinction of the conditioned response. After extinction, the conditioned response may reoccur; this is called spontaneous recovery. Reinforcement during spontaneous recovery strengthens the conditioned response (Lawson, 1960).

When a tone of 1,000 cycles per second has become a conditioned stimulus, and a tone of 800 cycles per second is presented for the first time, a weakened conditioned response is observed, and stimulus generalization is said to have occurred. Furthermore, if meat powder is placed into the dog's mouth every thirty minutes, with careful control to ensure that no other stimuli are associated with the introduction of the meat powder except for the passage of time, the dog will be found to begin to salivate just prior to the end of the thirty-minute period. This suggests that the dog is re-

sponding to some internal stimuli associated with the passage of time, and that these internal stimuli become conditioned stimuli (Lawson, 1960).

Classical conditioning has been demonstrated in animals ranging from the single-celled protozoa to human infants and adults. In mammals it has been demonstrated to affect a number of organic functions, including heart rate, respiration, gastric secretions, the volume of the arteries, and the passage of urine from the kidneys to the bladder (Verhave, 1966). In 1920, Watson and Raynor (cited in Deese & Hulse, 1967) conditioned fear in a one-year-old baby boy. The boy showed no signs of fear to a variety of stimuli, including a white rat and burning newspaper. He did, however, exhibit a startle reaction to a loud sound—he cried and showed other signs of emotional activity. After a few pairings of the white rat with a loud sound, the white rat by itself elicited the full-scale emotional response. Moreover, the emotional response generalized to other animals and furry objects, including a wad of cotton.

Operant Conditioning

There has been a tremendous body of work on various aspects of operant conditioning, including research, theory, and practical application. Numerous learning situations have been studied, including simple habit acquisition, the learning of complex motor skills, discrimination learning, verbal learning, concept formation, and problem solving (Deese & Hulse, 1967; Lawson, 1960; Neuringer & Michael, 1970; Verhave, 1966). The number of possible responses to study may be infinite. Practical applications have also been extensive, from the bell and pad for treating enuresis (Houts & Mellon, 1989) to teaching machines (Hill, 1963) and token economies (Krasner, 1970).

Not long after the first appearance of Pavlov's work in English in the late 1920s, B. F. Skinner introduced some of his principles of operant learning in 1933. The body of knowledge and writings he and his colleagues have contributed since then has been voluminous.

In classical conditioning, there is a clearly identified stimulus that produces a clearly identified response. A clearly identified second stimulus is then conditioned to produce that same response. The unconditioned stimulus is a clear reinforcement (Deese & Hulse, 1967).

In operant conditioning, there is no unconditioned stimulus to produce and reinforce an unconditioned response. The experimenter (teacher or therapist) must first identify something that can serve as a reinforcement for the desired response. Then the experimenter must either await a random occurrence of the desired response (Deese & Hulse, 1967) or attempt to produce the response by shaping with successive approximations (Hill, 1963). The appropriate behavior is then reinforced. With repetition, the organism learns to make the appropriate response and receive the reinforcement (Hill, 1963).

Perhaps the best-known example of Skinner's operant conditioning is that of the white laboratory rat in a Skinner box, a small cage with a bar that activates a food magazine (Deese & Hulse, 1967). The food magazine dispenses one pellet of food with an audible click when the bar is pressed. The rat is deprived of food for a twenty-two-hour period, then placed in the box for a one-hour session. The experimenter waits patiently as the hungry animal explores the cage. if the animal happens to press the bar during exploration, learning is under way.

If the animal does not press the bar, the experimenter activates the food magazine manually by remote when the animal approaches the bar. As the animal begins to "hang around" the bar, the experimenter awaits the animal's standing on its hind legs near the bar and reinforces this behavior by manually activating the food magazine, then reinforces the animal's touching the bar, etc., until the animal is rapidly pressing the bar and consuming pellets of food. The animal is allowed a predetermined number of reinforcements in the experimental situation, then returned to its cage where food is available for one hour prior to beginning deprivation for the next session.

The bar is wired to a recording device that automatically graphs the number of responses per minute. A Skinner box may also contain a light above the bar, a switch that turns the click of the food magazine on and off, and a grid floor that can be electrified with a mild electric current.

Once acquisition has occurred to a continuous reinforcement schedule, a variety of independent variables and dependent variables can be studied. Independent variables that can be manipulated by the experimenter include the amount of food deprivation prior to learning, reinforcement schedule (fixed rate, variable rate, fixed interval, variable interval), click of the magazine on or off, light on or off, and shock on or off. Dependent variables that can be measured include length of time to acquisition, rate of responding, and length of time or number of responses to extinction (resistance to extinction).

The experimenter can study the effects of different reinforcement schedules on acquisition, rate of responding after acquisition, and resistance to extinction. The effects of punishment on extinction can be studied by arranging the bar to turn on a mild electric shock rather that activating the food magazine. The effects of the "click" of the food magazine as a conditioned reinforcement can be studied using resistance to extinction as a dependent variable, with the rat receiving the click but no food for each bar press.

After acquisition, it can readily be demonstrated that the rat generalizes the experimental condition of light off and light on. The rat can then be taught to discriminate between the light on and light off situations, by reinforcing responses in one situation and turning off the food magazine in the other. The rat can be taught to turn off the electrical shock by pressing the bar (escape learning). By turning on the light for a brief period prior to turning on the shock, the experimenter can teach the rat to press the bar to prevent the shock (avoidance learning).

The effects of an aversive stimulus as a discriminative cue can be studied by using the electrical shock to signal the condition that reinforcements are available, with reinforcement not being available when the shock is off. The effects of an aversive stimulus along with reinforcement can be studied by arranging for the bar press to produce both the food and the shock, and different schedules may be used for the contingency of the reinforcement or the shock, i.e., the food may be given on a continuous schedule with the shock on a partial schedule, or vice versa.

Skinner has also done extensive study of learning with other animals, including pigeons using a similar apparatus, with the pigeon being trained to peck at a disk. He has studied learning in humans extensively, as well. He has demonstrated practical applications, including teaching machines (Hill, 1963).

The use of animals has both advantages and drawbacks. Animals are easy and economical to maintain. The smaller setting that animals require allows for easier control of a number of extraneous variables (Lawson, 1960). Deprivation and use of aversive stimuli do not meet with the same ethical complications as do such procedures when used with humans. Other extraneous variables, such as preoccupation with personal matters or an upcoming exam, are not present. On the other hand, generalization from an animal in the simple laboratory setting to humans in their complex sociocultural environment is far from precise.

SOME PRINCIPLES OF LEARNING

A thorough understanding of the principles of the internal combustion engine will not allow an inexperienced person much success in tearing a motor apart and rebuilding it, setting timing chains, fitting bearings, and adjusting complicated fuel injection systems, let alone allow the designing and building of such a motor from scratch. A good understanding will, however, promote better maintenance, allow for some simple troubleshooting, and prevent some abuse by an unscrupulous or incompetent mechanic; at the least, it may lead to the seeking of

additional opinions before questionable procedures are approved.

A full text on the subject of learning would not do justice to the vast amount of laboratory and field data, the contributions of numerous theorists, and the many practical applications. The few basic principles that are presented here will not create learning or behavioral treatment specialists. Rather, this section should provide an understanding of the complexity of behavior. It should stimulate professionals to learn more, to appreciate the potential contributions of behavioral specialists in treating behavior if a given program is fortunate enough to be able to employ such a person. It should allow professionals to make better decisions about behavior and to avoid some errors.

Classical Conditioning

Classical conditioning involves reflexes that are not under conscious control and the conditioning of those reflexes to stimuli that do not normally produce them. Principles of classical conditioning, therefore, have implications for emotions, feelings, and attitudes, and how people learn to feel certain ways in different situations (Deese & Hulse, 1967; Hill, 1963). These principles have been demonstrated repeatedly in experimental and nonexperimental research, both in and out of the laboratory. They have been found to have some validity for humans.

1. Classical conditioning may occur whenever there exists a stimulus (unconditioned stimulus) that nearly always produces a given reflex response (unconditioned response) (Deese & Hulse, 1967; Lawson, 1960; Verhave, 1966).

   Example: A loud noise producing a startle response in an infant, resulting in fear, which includes increased adrenaline flow, increased heart rate, and increased rate of respiration.

   a. There may be more than one unconditioned stimulus that produces a given unconditioned response (Verhave, 1966).

   b. A given unconditioned stimulus may produce more than one unconditioned response, although responses are likely to be closely related (Deese & Hulse, 1967).

   Example: A camera flash producing both a startle response and fear in an infant.

2. Other stimuli that occur at about the same time as the unconditioned stimulus may become conditioned to elicit a similar response, which then becomes a conditioned response to the previously neutral stimulus, depending on a number of factors:

   a. Proximity in time. The strongest conditioning takes place when pairing is virtually simultaneous, when the neutral stimulus precedes the unconditioned stimulus only briefly, especially when the neutral stimulus continues until the onset of the unconditioned stimulus (Deese & Hulse, 1967; Lawson, 1960).

   b. Number of pairings. The more times it happens, the more likely conditioning will take place (Lawson, 1960).

   c. Intensity of the stimuli. More intense unconditioned stimuli tend to produce more intense unconditioned responses (Lawson, 1960; Verhave, 1966).

   d. The significance of the conditioned response for the organism's well-being, survival, or any other practical consideration is irrelevant (Hill, 1963).

3. The conditioned response usually extinguishes when the conditioned stimulus appears sufficiently often in the absence of the unconditioned stimulus, which is viewed as a reinforcement (Lawson 1960; Verhave, 1966).

   a. Corollary: No conditioned response can continue without periodic reinforcement.

   b. Caution: The reinforcement in classical conditioning does not have to be "rewarding." Weak acid may serve as a reinforcement for conditioning salivation; electric shocks may reinforce conditioning of the galvanic skin response (Deese & Hulse, 1967).

4. Extinction can also be accomplished when responses incompatible with the conditioned response are elicited by a new unconditioned stimulus during extinction in a process called counter-conditioning. In effect, a new unconditioned response is produced by the new unconditioned stimulus and conditioned to the former conditioned stimulus. Thus, the organism learns to make a different response to the previously conditioned stimulus (Lawson, 1960).

5. A response that has undergone extinction can be expected to reoccur to the conditioned stimulus at some time in the future. Should reinforcement (the unconditioned stimulus) occur during spontaneous recovery, reacquisition can be expected (Deese & Hulse, 1967).

6. A partial schedule of reinforcement can be expected to impede acquisition. If pairings of the unconditioned stimulus are sufficiently infrequent, acquisition may not occur at all (Lawson, 1960).

7. A partial schedule of reinforcement can be expected to increase resistance to extinction and increase responses in spontaneous recovery (Deese & Hulse, 1967).

8. The learning can be expected to generalize to stimuli that are similar to the conditioned stimulus. The strength of the conditioned response in stimulus generalization depends on the degree of similarity (Deese & Hulse, 1967).

9. The organism can be expected to learn to discriminate between the conditioned stimulus and other similar stimuli if the unconditioned stimulus continues to appear to reinforce the conditioned stimulus, and if the unconditioned stimulus does not appear when the similar stimuli undergo extinction (Verhave, 1966).

10. A formerly neutral stimulus, once it has become a conditioned stimulus, may be used to elicit the conditioned response in the presence of other neutral stimuli to produce other conditioned stimuli (Lawson, 1960).

11. More than one stimulus may become a conditioned stimulus during the learning situation, so that more than one conditioned stimulus may elicit the conditioned response (Lawson, 1960).

12. Internal stimuli (glandular secretions, heart rate, visceral reactions, stimuli from receptors in muscles) may become conditioned stimuli (Lawson, 1960).
13. Operant behaviors may be learned along with conditioned responses (Lawson, 1960).

Operant Learning

Operant learning involves the full range of voluntary behavior, from the simple nodding of the head to baking a cake, flying a jet, conducting a therapy session, taking a test, and repairing an automobile. Principles of operant conditioning, therefore, have implications for virtually every situation in which people may find themselves and others. A number of principles have been demonstrated in a number of situations. Many have been shown to have considerable validity, even in complex situations. No theorist, however, seems to have been able to propose an all-encompassing theory that is generally accepted. Rather, certain principles and theories have been able to help us understand behavior better. Some of the more basic of these are presented here.

1. Operant learning may occur whenever contingencies follow a behavior with sufficient regularity (Lawson, 1960).
2. When reinforcements follow a given behavior, the occurrence of that behavior is likely to increase (Lawson, 1960).
   a. Corollary: Anything that increases a behavior is a reinforcement for that behavior (Lawson, 1960).
   b. Corollary: The more reinforcements the behavior has received, the stronger the behavior (Lawson, 1960).
   c. Corollary: If the termination of an unpleasant or aversive stimulus serves to increase a behavior, then that termination is a reinforcement (Lawson, 1960).
   d. Definition: A negative reinforcement is anything that increases behavior by its termination (Deese & Hulse, 1967).

3. Nonreinforcements that occur sufficiently in the presence of, or near the same time as, reinforcements may become conditioned or secondary reinforcers (Lawson, 1960).
   a. Corollary: A conditioned reinforcement may serve as a reinforcement for the acquisition of a new behavior (Lawson, 1960).
   b. Corollary: A conditioned reinforcement does not have to have any inherent properties of reward; a somewhat aversive stimulus may become a conditioned reinforcement.
4. Extinction of a behavior may occur when reinforcements stop. However, extinction in operant learning does not necessarily mean that the behavior will fall to zero. Rather, the occurrence will fall to a "chance" level of occurrence and the criteria for extinction must be established by definition (Lawson, 1960).
   a. Corollary: A behavior is unlikely to persist at a high level without reinforcement.
   b. Corollary: An operant or voluntary behavior may never disappear completely (Lawson, 1960).
   c. Corollary: A conditioned or secondary reinforcement, when available during extinction, may increase resistance to extinction in the absence of the original reinforcement (Lawson, 1960).
   d. Corollary: More than one, and perhaps many, repetitions of the behavior can be expected during extinction, depending on the reinforcement schedule (Deese & Hulse, 1967).
5. A behavior that has undergone extinction can be expected to reoccur at some level in the future (Deese & Hulse, 1967). If reinforcement occurs during this spontaneous recovery, reacquisition can be expected.
6. Classical conditioning may occur during operant learning whenever reflex responses occur with any regularity in the operant situation (Lawson, 1960).
   a. Negative reinforcements may produce classically conditioned responses, such as

those associated with the fear emotion (Deese & Hulse, 1967).

b. Positive reinforcements may produce classically conditioned responses, such as salivation (Verhave, 1966).

c. Any number of stimuli present may become conditioned stimuli, including stimuli in the environment and internal stimuli in the organism (Deese & Hulse, 1967).

7. Learning, including rate of responding and resistance to extinction, depends significantly on the schedule of reinforcement (Deese & Hulse, 1967; Lawson, 1960).

a. When reinforcement is available on a continuous schedule, acquisition can be expected to be fairly rapid, performance to be at a relatively moderate rate, and resistance to extinction relatively low (Tighe, 1982).

b. Acquisition may not occur when reinforcement is not available at or near a continuous schedule (Lawson, 1960).

c. A fixed ratio of reinforcement, especially when it occurs early during acquisition, can be expected to produce a higher rate of response, brief pauses after responses, and a high resistance to extinction (Tighe, 1982).

d. A variable ratio of reinforcement can be expected to produce a very high rate of response, with periods of extremely intense responding, and a resistance to extinction that is "almost pathological" (Tighe, 1982, p. 268).

e. Reinforcement at a fixed interval of time can be expected to produce performance at a low rate following reinforcement, with responses increasing towards the time the reinforcement is available; resistance to extinction will be considerable (Tighe, 1982).

f. Reinforcement on a schedule of variable intervals can be expected to produce a steady and stable rate of responding and persistence during extinction (Tighe, 1982).

g. Reinforcement that is not contingent on behavior, such as reinforcement that is delivered on a fixed time interval, sometimes leads to acquisition of some random behavior (Lawson, 1960). This is called superstition. Superstitious behaviors can be expected to be highly resistant to extinction, depending on which reinforcement schedule is approximated. Note that the availability of reinforcement is not contingent on the acquired behavior. Increases in the behavior, however, make it increasingly likely that a reinforcement will occur in conjunction with the behavior on other than a continuous schedule (Tighe, 1982).

h. Repetition of the behavior and the reinforcement may be expected to strengthen learning, depending on the schedule of reinforcement (Deese & Hulse, 1967; Lawson, 1960).

i. Once a behavior has been acquired, a continuous schedule of reinforcement may not be the most efficient means of maintaining the behavior (Lawson, 1960).

8. When rewards do not promptly follow behavior, there is a chance that some other behavior may occur before the reward is delivered (Lawson, 1960).

9. Behavior learned in one situation can be expected to generalize to similar situations (Deese & Hulse, 1967).

10. When a generalized behavior does not meet with reinforcement in new situations, extinction can be expected in the new setting (Deese & Hulse, 1967).

a. Stimuli that are different between the situation in which reinforcement is available, and situations in which it is not available, become cues for discrimination (Deese & Hulse, 1967).

b. Conditioned reinforcements may increase resistance to extinction and impede discrimination learning (Deese & Hulse, 1967).

11. When any stimulus reduces the occurrence of a behavior that precedes it, that stimulus is a punishment for that behavior (Birnbrauer, 1978).
    a. The effects of punishment are not nearly so clear as are the effects of positive and negative reinforcement (Deese & Hulse, 1967; Lawson, 1960).
    b. Corollary: If something does not reduce the occurrence of a behavior, then it is not a punishment for that behavior, no matter how aversive or noxious.
    c. Punishment may only delay extinction in certain situations. That is, if employed during extinction, punishment may suppress the response while the punishment is in effect, only to have the behavior resume to undergo relatively normal extinction after the punishment is discontinued, with little difference in the total number of responses during extinction (Deese & Hulse, 1967).
        1. Corollary: A behavior may have to occur in the absence of reinforcement to actually undergo extinction.
        2. Corollary: A behavior may not extinguish if it is prevented from occurring by some means.
    d. An aversive stimulus may serve as a discrimination cue between situations when reinforcement is available and when it is not (Deese & Hulse, 1967).
    e. Stimuli associated with the punishment may become conditioned punishments. When conditioned punishments have developed, avoiding the punished response may remove the conditioned punishments and thus reinforce behavior that is incompatible with the punished behavior (Hill, 1963). For example, the growl of a dog when you reach out your hand may become a conditioned punishment through its association with the bite of the dog. Withdrawing your hand stops the growl, reinforcing behavior that is incompatible with touching the dog and getting bitten.

    In the same way, a person's angry expression may become associated with punishment and reinforce an apology that is incompatible with verbally aggressive behavior.
    f. Unconditioned reflex responses (e.g., adrenaline) to the punishment may become classically conditioned to other stimuli present during punishment (Hill, 1963; Lawson, 1960). In this way, we learn to become anxious or fearful in situations that have produced punishment in the past.
    g. Punishment may be more effective when it closely follows a response (Lawson, 1960).
    h. Punishment is most effective in the absence of reinforcement (Lawson, 1960).
    i. Punishment may only suppress a response temporarily (Deese & Hulse, 1967). It may be effective in stopping a behavior, but not as effective at preventing the behavior from reoccurring (Hill, 1963).
    j. Responding may appear at a higher rate when punishment is removed (Deese & Hulse, 1967; Hill, 1963).
    k. Learning may occur in the presence of punishment if rewards are also present; punishment, when it accompanies the reward, may even produce more rapid acquisition than the reward alone (Deese & Hulse, 1967).
    l. While severe punishment may be more effective than mild punishment in suppressing the targeted response, it is also likely to suppress other responses that are not targeted (Deese & Hulse, 1967).
    m. Punishment is deceptive; it appears to be dramatically effective but its effects are short-lived (Hill, 1963).
12. A response is most likely to extinguish when other incompatible responses are being reinforced (Lawson, 1960).
13. Complex behaviors can be learned (or taught) by operant principles; several behaviors can be chained (Deese & Hulse, 1967).

14. Denial of expected reinforcements (extinction) can be expected to produce some emotional response (Deese & Hulse, 1967).

15. A wide variety of stimuli can serve as primary reinforcements, including those that satisfy basic needs, visual or tactile stimulation, a change in environment, and objects such as toys (Deese & Hulse, 1967; Munn, 1961; Tighe, 1982).

16. An almost infinite variety of stimuli can become conditioned reinforcements, including money, tokens, words, a nod of approval, places, situations, and various internal stimuli associated with feelings (Deese & Hulse, 1967).

17. A wide variety of stimuli can serve as punishments, including unpleasant or painful stimuli and the loss of reinforcing stimuli (Nevin, 1973).

18. A wide variety of stimuli may become conditioned punishments, including objects, words, shaking of the head in disapproval, stimuli associated with places, situations, and people, and various internal stimuli associated with feelings (Hill, 1963).

19. People learn best through practice and experience (Hill, 1963).

20. People can learn from watching others (Hill, 1963).

21. People can learn from verbal instruction (Deese & Hulse, 1967; Taber, 1981).

22. Satiation with a reward may occur, in which case the reward may no longer serve as a reinforcement.

SUMMARY

The behavior of children can be controlled by many means. Sometimes physical controls are necessary for the protection of the child or the protection of others. Rewards and punishments may control children's behavior in some situations, especially when most aspects of their environment are able to be controlled, or when their access to rewards is able to be tightly controlled. Controlling children or their behavior in a given setting, however, may not be teaching children what we want them to learn: self-control.

Practice and experience are the best "teachers." Children must learn not only appropriate behaviors, but also appropriate feelings—about themselves and about others. Both are learned through experience with the consequences of behavior—reinforcements, rewards, negative reinforcements, and punishments—all of which operate on complex individuals in a complex environment in which they come to take on new meanings with experience.

In the classical conditioning of emotions, reinforcements do not have to be rewarding. The only requirement is that the reinforcement must produce (elicit) the reflex. Conditioning to other stimuli can then occur. In the operant conditioning of behavior, reinforcements also do not have to be especially rewarding, at least not in the colloquial sense. They merely have to increase the likelihood of the behavior. Many stimuli can be conditioned to serve as reinforcements, even stimuli that have no intrinsic value for the organism, or stimuli that may have some negative value. Being yelled at by an adult, rather than serving as a warning that punishment is about to ensue, may actually become a conditioned reinforcement if it is often enough associated with peer approval or increased status with peers.

Reinforcements may have more implications for stronger learning when not delivered consistently. On the other hand, reinforcements, especially those with high intrinsic reward value, may have some emotional impact, especially when withheld or not delivered as expected.

Punishment, while it may clearly affect behavior in a given and specific situation, does not seem to have long-term effects. It may merely delay the extinction of a response. Punishment also has clear implications for feelings and emotions.

The ability of children to discriminate and

generalize has special significance for residential treatment. If we want behavior learned in the residential setting to generalize outside the setting, we must be attentive to the cues that may be present to promote generalization and discrimination. We must also attend to the likelihood that generalized behavior will be reinforced outside of the residential setting.

The principles are indeed more complex than consistently rewarding desirable behavior or punishing undesirable behavior. In chapter 9, ''Behavior Modification and the Application of Learning Principles,'' we will consider issues relating to the application of these principles in the treatment environment to accomplish specific objectives. Specific examples are presented in chapter 10.

Group Dynamics

M ANY residential treatment facilities use groups as a part of their treatment program. Groups may be organized in various ways and for various purposes. They may include therapy groups, parent support groups, activity groups, staff meetings, multi-disciplinary team meetings, house meetings, and student government councils. Such groups may occupy several hours of resident and staff time each week and be highly significant in treatment.

On the other hand, there are 168 hours in a seven-day week. Group dynamics do not stop operating when a group leader is not present. Group forces act upon residents and staff each and every waking hour. Psychoanalytic theorists and others might argue that they are even at work during sleep and dreams. Some of the group forces originate within the residential program, others from outside. Some of the forces are initiated or controlled by the program; other forces may be initiated by the children; yet other forces may be beyond the control or influence of anyone affiliated with the program.

At least three basic groups can be expected to be a part of every treatment program: residents, child care staff, and administration. Intergroup forces become important. Sometimes, one finds residents aligned against staff in an ''us'' and ''them'' situation. Such situations readily promote cohesiveness among residents as well as staff: they rarely promote treatment.

In a similar manner, one occasionally finds the child care staff aligned against administration in an ''us'' and ''them'' situation. Again, cohesiveness is promoted among staff and among management. Again, this cohesiveness does not necessarily promote the goals of the institution. Moreover, with three distinct and cohesive groups, one may find residents aligned against staff and administration, against the institution. Occasionally, one may find residents and staff aligned against administration.

In larger institutions, other groups may form, possibly among treatment personnel—psychiatrists, psychologists, social workers, teachers; possibly among support personnel—cooks, maintenance, housekeeping, clerical. There may be a board of directors or an advisory board. Other groups of residents may include recreation groups, living groups when residents live in separate units, and groups in the community to which the resident may belong. Residents may form their own groups based on age, sex, race, or interest.

If the goal of the institution is the treatment of children, then subgroups of the institution should be aligned together towards the accomplishment of the objectives of the institution. This rarely happens by accident. One or more people must make it happen. This requires some appreciation of the processes within groups as well as among groups.

As with other topics I have presented, group dynamics is a vast and complex field. There are many theorists and theories. As the reader shall see, there are many relevant principles. I do not expect readers to memorize them but, rather, to develop an appreciation and an understanding of the importance of group dynamics in almost every phase of residential treatment. It seems that each and every decision has some impact on one or more groups in a residential program, and that one or more groups can be expected to have some impact on virtually every decision.

This chapter will touch briefly on historical and theoretical perspectives of group dynamics as a field. Next it will introduce some of the key concepts and terms, followed by some principles that have relevance for the residential setting. There are a lot of them. I have attempted to organize them into a conceptual framework: how groups work, the deliberate use of groups, forming groups and group size, undesirable groups and, finally, leadership. Lastly, the chapter will consider some aspects of team building, with some suggestions about how individuals and various subgroups may be pulled together and focused towards some common objectives. Some aspects of group therapy as a specific treatment intervention in the residential setting will be considered in chapter 13, "Professional Interventions."

HISTORICAL AND THEORETICAL PERSPECTIVES

Our knowledge about groups has come from two basic sources, practitioners and scientists. Practitioners began working with groups at the turn of the twentieth century. Scientists began studying groups using scientific methods in natural and laboratory settings at about the same time (Toseland & Rivas, 1984).

Group Work Practice

Group work practice had its origins in settlement houses and youth agencies with those who led socialization, education, and recreation groups. Be-

tween 1910 and 1920, workers began to realize that groups could help people to participate in their communities, enrich lives, and provide support to members. They could facilitate development of problem-solving and social skills. Activities such as recreation often provided the group setting in which these outcomes occurred (Toseland & Rivas, 1984).

Freud's *Group Psychology and the Analysis of the Ego* set the tone for group psychotherapy. Others, drawing from social group work, contributed much to techniques and the use of group process. Psychodrama and sociodrama added additional techniques. Education, influenced by Dewey, broadened purposes and methods—group projects, student government, and extracurricular activities became important. Administrators began to develop information about groups and the management of larger organizations. From all of these, group dynamics began to emerge as a discipline in the social sciences in the 1930s (Cartwright & Zander, 1960).

During the 1940s and 1950s, workers began to use groups more for therapy in mental health, including child guidance programs and hospitals. Rather than activities, such groups focused more on diagnosis and treatment of problems. Groups were also used during this period for social action in neighborhood centers and community agencies (Toseland & Rivas, 1984).

The popularity of group services declined during the 1960s and 1970s. Colleges trained people more generically, moving away from specializations in community organization, group work, and case work. Much of the contemporary focus on social group work practice is on therapy—problem identification, assessment, and treatment (Toseland & Rivas, 1984).

Social Science Research

Scientific research into groups began at the turn of the century. Much of the focus has been on how groups influence their members. Studies increased after World War I. Allport (1924) studied the effects of a laboratory group on members' performance; Thrasher (1927) studied Chicago gangs in their natural environment, observing roles, status, and a common code enforced by group opinion, coercion, and punishment. Sherif (1936) studied the effects of a laboratory group on members' perceptions. Extensive studies on groups of workers and production were conducted at Western Electric's Hawthorne Plant in Chicago. There were also studies of combat units during World War II (Toseland & Rivas, 1984).

The 1950s was the golden age of groups in both practice and scientific study, leading to an explosion of knowledge. Attention to groups declined somewhat since then in both areas (Toseland & Rivas, 1984).

Theory

Many theories have been developed about the relationships of individuals within the groups in which they are members. Full exploration of those theories is beyond the scope of this text. Systems theory, considered briefly in chapter 5, is one example. Psychoanalytic theory works with insight, ego-strength, and defense mechanisms. Members identify with the group leader and form transference reactions with the leader and each other based on early life experiences. The group leader helps members work through unresolved conflicts by exploring past behavior and linking it to the present, interpreting and helping members gain insight (Toseland & Rivas, 1984).

Kurt Lewin (1951) proposed a field theory developed out of his work in the 1930s and his Research Center for Group Dynamics at the Massachusetts Institute of Technology in the 1940s. The theory views a group as a gestalt that is constantly changing to cope with its social situation. He contributed the concepts of role, status, norm, power, cohesion, and valence (see "Concepts and Definitions" below). The theory uses vectors to describe forces within and outside the group (Toseland & Rivas, 1984).

Social exchange theory emphasizes individual behavior, postulating that people in groups act to maximize rewards and minimize punishments in their interactions. Interaction is influenced by the amount of social power and social dependence in any situation (Toseland & Rivas, 1984).

Learning theory contributes principles of classical and operant conditioning to understanding and manipulating behavior within the group. Members learn cues and receive verbal and, possibly, token reinforcements to increase (or decrease) communications and change behavior. Bandura (1977) contributed social learning theory to group practice in the 1970s. In the group setting, a majority of learning takes place through observational learning, including vicarious reinforcement and punishment. When members see another being praised for a behavior, they repeat the behavior later, hoping for similar praise. They likewise learn to avoid behavior that has been ignored or punished. Cognitive theories of learning may also be applied in the group setting (Toseland & Rivas, 1984).

We shall consider some of the effects of rewards and punishments in the group setting, as well as some of the effects of the group on rewards and punishments, in chapter 9, "Behavior Modification and the Application of Learning Principles." In chapter 10, "Using Behavior Modification for Management, Treatment, and Therapy," we shall consider some applications of learning principles in group settings.

CONCEPTS AND DEFINITIONS

As with other scientific study, group dynamics has developed its own concepts and definitions. In the following, I have presented those I consider to have some significance in the residential setting. I have attempted to define them concisely, beginning with broader and more basic concepts, proceeding to more specific concepts.

A *group* is "any number of persons who share a consciousness of membership and of interaction" (Horton & Hunt, 1976, p. 536).

In addition to interaction, the following may be expected as the group develops:

1. Shared motives for membership.
2. Shared goals for the group.
3. Shared norms.
4. A stabilized set of roles, formal or informal.
5. A network of interpersonal attraction based on likes and dislikes (Hare, 1962).

A *formed group* comes together through some outside influence or intervention. Formed groups are generally convened for a specific purpose and generally require some outside sponsorship. Examples include athletic teams, businesses, classrooms, therapy groups (Toseland & Rivas, 1984), and residential programs.

A *natural group* comes together spontaneously from naturally-occurring events, mutual attraction, or mutual need. Examples include family, peer groups, and cliques (Toseland & Rivas, 1984).

An *in group* is a group in which one is a member.

An *out group* is a group in which one is not a member.

A *primary group* is a group that is especially important or significant (salient) for an individual, such as a family or a peer group. Primary groups are usually small (Hare, 1962). They are usually informal and natural groups that have marked influence on the values and normative behavior of members (Toseland & Rivas, 1984).

A *secondary group* is a group which, when compared to a primary group, is usually larger and of less salience (Hare, 1962). A peer group may be of especially high salience to adolescent residents of an institution when compared to their membership in their therapy group or school.

A *reference group* serves as a model or guide (Horton & Hunt, 1976), whether or not one is a member; a group in which an individual "aspires to attain or maintain membership" (Siegel & Siegel, 1960, p. 232).

A *treatment group* is a formed group characterized by bonds based on members' personal needs, roles developed through interaction, open communication, high self-disclosure, and evaluation based on members' meeting treatment goals. Examples

include educational groups, growth groups, remedial groups, and socialization groups (Toseland & Rivas, 1984).

A *task group* is a formed group characterized by bonding based on the task to be completed, assigned or developed roles, focused communication with a minimum of self-disclosure, and evaluation based on task completion. Task groups may include administrative groups, committees, treatment teams, athletic teams, and social action groups (Toseland & Rivas, 1984).

A *subgroup* is a group within a group.

A *cabal* is a subgroup with the same values as the larger group, which seeks to provide advantage to its members in their advancement in the larger group. Cabals are concerned with access to secret information, power, and status (Cartwright & Zander, 1960).

A *clique* is a subgroup that ridicules the roles and standards of the larger group. It is a small and especially cohesive group based on common interests. It may be differentiated from a cabal in that its members do not seek to advance themselves, but rather to excuse their failures in the larger group by criticism of the larger group (Cartwright & Zander, 1960).

Group *cohesiveness* may be defined in behavioral terms. Possibilities include:

1. The extent to which members talk of "we" rather than in terms of "I."
2. The extent to which members share the same norms.
3. The extent to which members are willing to work together for a common goal.
4. The extent to which members defend the group from attack.
5. The willingness of members to endure adversity for the group (Cartwright & Zander, 1960).

Cartwright and Zander (1960) prefer to limit the term to phenomena related to the attractiveness of the group to members. Schachter defines cohesiveness as: "the total field of forces acting on members to remain in the group'' (1960, p. 260).

Salience refers to the importance of a group to an individual; a group with high salience is significantly important to the individual (Cartwright & Zander, 1960).

Valence relates to the attractiveness of a group. If one is especially attracted to a group, it has a high valence (Cartwright & Zander, 1960).

A group has *structure* when it has acquired some stability in the relationships among its members (Cartwright & Zander, 1960).

Formal structure is the most visible, reflected in tables of organization, job descriptions, offices, assignments, and the like (Hare, 1962).

Informal structure can become visible through sociometric tests that identify positions such as best liked, most helpful, or scapegoat (Hare, 1962).

Status is a collection of rights, responsibilities, and duties that belong to a position as opposed to belonging to a person (Cartwright & Zander, 1960). The person who occupies the position enjoys the status until she or he leaves the position. Status does not have to be "high." Both "leader" and "member" may be clearly defined statuses within a given group.

A *norm* is a rule of behavior, an way of acting that has been accepted by a group (Hare, 1962).

Role refers to the norms for a person who occupies a particular status, the expected behavior of a person who occupies a particular status in a group (Hare, 1962). When one performs the duties and responsibilities of his or her status, one is performing a role (Cartwright & Zander, 1960).

Role collision refers to the conflict that may develop when two or more people within a group have roles which overlap (Hare, 1962).

Role confusion occurs when an individual holds a role for which there are inconsistent and incompatible expectations. There are three possible sources.

1. There is agreement within the group about expected behavior, but the expectations are difficult to satisfy at the same time (Hare, 1962). For example, a supervisor may be faced with the need to dismiss two staff for inappropriately punishing a difficult child as well as the need to schedule sufficient staff to work on the weekend to meet licensing requirements for coverage.

2. There is disagreement within the group about expected behavior (Hare, 1962). For example, staff expect their supervisors to advocate raises; administration expects supervisors to explain to staff why the company cannot afford raises at this time.

3. The individual belongs to other groups that disagree about his or her role (Cartwright & Zander, 1960). For example, residential treatment programs occasionally exert pressures on children to gain information about some misconduct while peers exert pressure to keep residents from "ratting."

A state of *dissonance* exists when one makes a choice that, despite its positive aspects, also has negative aspects (Secord & Backman, 1964). For example, children in residential programs who may be victimized by a bullying peer may often find themselves in a state of dissonance. If they talk to staff about the problem, they may lose face or have other problems with peers; if they keep quiet, they face continued bullying or abuse.

Power is the ability to significantly influence the attitudes, opinions, decisions, and especially the behavior of others (Cartwright & Zander, 1960). Five bases of social power are relevant to groups. All are based on the members' perception of an individual or the group's having certain abilities, whether or not the ability is real:

1. *Coercive power* is based on the perception that one has control or influence over punishment.

2. *Expert power* is based on the perception that one has special knowledge.

3. *Legitimate power* is based on the perception that one has the right to prescribe behavior.

4. *Referent power* is based on the fact that one serves as a model with which someone identifies.

5. *Reward power* is based on the perception that

one has the ability to grant or to influence rewards (Cartwright & Zander, 1960).

Social control is "the process by which the individual manipulates the behavior of others or by which group members bring pressure on the individual" (Hare, 1962, p. 25). There may be formal rules and formal exercise of power; there may be informal pressures in small and intimate peer groups. While social control may be applied forcibly, most often it occurs from self-control when the individual anticipates the responses of others (Hare, 1962).

Social reality refers to the opinions of people in a social setting. Social reality is especially important when empirical references are limited or confusing (Schachter, 1960). For example, a few hundred years ago, the social reality was that the sun travelled across the sky each day. Consider ethnic prejudice in terms of empirical evidence and social reality in any social setting. Consider values.

PRINCIPLES

There are a number of groups that may be expected to be of significance in the residential treatment program. The program itself is an identifiable group; residents, employees, and volunteers are members.

Any variety of subgroups may exist within the larger group. Residents may be grouped by age, by sex, by living unit, by diagnosis, by seniority, by performance or achievement, or by discharge plan (whether or not they will be going home or remain until adulthood, for example). They may be formed into groups based on interest or activity—baseball, football, basketball, dance, music, Scouting, work assignments. Educational assignments may lead to the formation of groups: public school or on-grounds school; elementary, middle, or high school; votech; or adult education.

Room assignments lead to the formation of groups among roommates. Therapeutic groups may be created: sexual abuse survivors group, offenders group, young boys group, adolescent girls group, discharge planning group, career planning group, and so on. Some programs divide residents into teams for purposes of treatment—randomly or by some plan.

Moreover, residents will form their own informal groups, possibly along the lines of interests: those who smoke, those who like basketball, those who use drugs, even those who study together. They may also form groups along ethnic or racial lines.

Staff may be grouped formally or informally: administration, staff, professional staff, clerical staff, support staff, maintenance, or food service, to name a few. They may be grouped by living unit assignment or by shift assignment.

Staff may also form their own groups informally. Social workers from a particular graduate school may form a group; staff who have an interest in basketball may group at work or after work, or the agency may have a bowling team. Staff can also be expected to form informal groups according to sex, race, or ethnic similarities.

Volunteers, too, may be formed into groups. Formal examples include advisory boards and boards of directors. Subgroups or committees may be formed.

Moreover, groups may be formed across other subgroup lines. A treatment group consists not only of the residents who form the group but also the staff who lead the group. Living groups or treatment "teams" include both the residents and the staff assigned to the groups. Staff may also be assigned to a committee of the board (advisory or governing).

Groups outside of the agency have relevance as well. Residents may be members of a family or a peer group; they may be involved with some activity group in the community. Staff, likewise, have families and other groups of which they are members. Moreover, such groups may play some role as reference groups even when the individual does not seem to have significant membership.

In the following section, I will present a number of principles that relate to groups. Each principle may apply to any number of groups of residents, staff, families, or the community. Rather than attempt to discuss each, which would be a monumental task, I have chosen to state each principle as clearly and concisely as possible and ask the reader to think a bit about how each principle might apply to various groups or situations.

I have attempted to organize the principles into some categories:

1. How groups apply pressures and standards to their members.
2. The deliberate use of groups within the program.
3. Principles relating to formation of groups and group size.
4. Undesirable groups.
5. Leadership.

How Do Groups Work? Group Pressures and Standards

"For some groups it is recognized by all that they may legitimately exert pressures for uniformity of behavior and attitudes among their members. . . . Other more informal groups may also exert an influence over their members, but often without anyone's consciously intending to do so and without the awareness of the members that it is happening" (Cartwright & Zander, 1960, p. 166). I ask the reader to consider each of these principles first in terms of a resident's membership in the living/treatment unit and then in terms of a resident's membership in a clique that is not fully in support of treatment objectives.

1. Forces toward uniformity tend from two sources:
   a. Forces within the individual when the person realizes that her or his behavior or opinions are different from those of others.
   b. Forces induced by others in an attempt to change the behavior or beliefs of another (Cartwright & Zander, 1960).

2. An individual whose behavior does not conform to group norms has four alternatives:
   a. Conform.
   b. Change the norms of the group.
   c. Remain deviant.
   d. Leave the group (Hare, 1962).
      Consider the child who either cannot or will not conform to standards within the program and either runs away or gets discharged as "untreatable in this milieu."
3. When deviants fail to respond to pressures to conform, groups may:
   a. Redefine the boundaries of the group to exclude the individual.
   b. Reinterpret the behavior of the deviant in such a way that it is no longer viewed as threatening to the group.
   c. Change group standards (Cartwright & Zander, 1960).
4. Group standards can be changed, but "the more striking character about them is their enduring quality" (Cartwright & Zander, 1960, p. 181).
5. The opinion of an individual is more likely to conform to that of the group when:
   a. The subject matter is ambiguous.
   b. The opinion of the individual is to become public.
   c. There is a large majority holding a contrary opinion.
   d. The group is friendly or otherwise close knit (Hare, 1962).
6. Primary groups tend to have greater influence on an individual than do secondary groups (Hare, 1962). When residents form their own groups, they are likely to become primary groups and, as such, have more influence than the treatment unit or other groups. For many residents, the family also continues to be a primary group. When such groups support deviant values, treatment may be especially difficult.
7. The greater the ambiguity of an issue, the greater the influence of other group members (Hare, 1962). Consider the influence of

groups on values, and just how ambiguous values may be.

8. The higher the status of a group member, the greater that member's influence on another member's judgment or opinion (Hare, 1962). Sometimes, a child is admitted who is so "cool," whose personality is so strong, that other residents are immediately drawn to her or him. Sometimes, the behavior of residents changes dramatically when such a "super star" arrives.

9. High-status members tend to communicate with all group members. Members with lower status tend to communicate with other members of equal or lesser status (Toseland & Rivas, 1984).

10. Group members with low status are the least likely to conform—they have little to lose unless they seek to gain higher status (Toseland & Rivas, 1984). This suggests that programs should be especially attentive to the status of children in the program.

11. Those who conform tend to be the most popular members of a group (Hare, 1962).

12. Individuals who conform to the larger group tend to be labeled as over-conformists—teacher's pets (Hare, 1962) or brown-nosers.

13. Leaders also conform. It is often difficult to determine whether a leader is conforming to the group or the group is conforming to the leadership (Hare, 1962).

14. When the individual is unsure of herself or himself, the individual is almost completely dependent upon the group (Cartwright & Zander, 1960).

15. Membership in a group determines much of what the individual may see, experience, learn, think about, and do (Cartwright & Zander, 1960).

16. Individual members or groups may influence members by exercising:
    a. Legitimate power. (Consider the program's rules, regulations, and enforcement.)
    b. Reward power. (Consider point systems,

for example. Also consider the social rewards that may be offered by staff or by other residents.)
    c. Coercive power. (Consider threats of loss of privileges, as well as coercion by other children.)
    d. Referent power. Referent power is based on identification, on wanting to be like someone and therefore behaving like her or him without regard to reward or punishment. (Both staff and residents may enjoy referent power. Consider the "cool" or highly personable resident.)
    e. Expert power. (Staff certainly have expert power in certain matters. So do other residents who may know how to get over, or know what is "in." [Cartwright & Zander, 1960].)

17. Members tend to conform when:
    a. The group is cohesive and has a high valence.
    b. Goals are important and meaningful.
    c. Membership is desired because of the individual's own needs or outside forces.
    d. Rewards and sanctions are present.
    e. There is freedom within the limits imposed by the group (Toseland & Rivas, 1984).

18. Conformity may be expected to be directly proportional to the certainty of sanctions for deviation (Cartwright & Zander, 1960). Programs have certain sanctions that they apply for misbehavior; so do peers, as in prohibitions against informing on others.

19. When the achievement of the group is important, pressures toward uniformity depend directly upon:
    a. The clarity of the group's goal to the members.
    b. The clarity of the path to the goal.
    c. The extent to which the members of the group value the goal.
    d. The extent to which the members see the goal as attainable (Cartwright & Zander, 1960).

Consider each of the above for a residential treatment program whose goal is the "treatment" of children. When the agency's goal is vague, when the path to the goal is unclear, when children do not especially value being "treated," when "treating children" does not appear to be readily attainable, then we may expect some problems with conformity within the group, both among children and among employees.

20. Public behavior may be expected to be more conforming to group standards than private behavior (Cartwright & Zander, 1960). Some residents do an excellent job of conforming overtly, yet other residents suggest that they may not be doing so well as they may seem.

21. When persons succumb to group pressures, their confidence in their own beliefs decreases, which further reduces their resistance to group pressures (Cartwright & Zander, 1960).

22. A state of cognitive dissonance is produced when a person conforms but maintains some reservations about his or her decision (Cartwright & Zander, 1960).

23. Cognitive dissonance is directly proportional to the attractiveness of the alternatives the individual has rejected (Cartwright & Zander, 1960).

24. Persons seek to reduce dissonance. Possible means of reducing dissonance include:
    a. Convincing oneself that the chosen alternative is even more attractive than previously thought.
    b. Distortion.
    c. Denial.
    d. Degrading the opinions of others.
    e. Denouncing the opinions of others.
    f. Degrading those who hold different opinions.
    g. Deciding that the differences are not that important (Cartwright & Zander, 1960).

25. The tendency to reject a deviant is directly proportional to the cohesiveness of the group (Cartwright & Zander, 1960).

26. The tendency to reject a deviant is directly proportional to the extent to which the deviance is relevant to the purposes of the group (Cartwright & Zander, 1960). Consider the readiness with which some programs discharge "untreatable" children.

27. The tendency to reject a deviant is inversely proportional to the importance of the deviant to the group (Cartwright & Zander, 1960). When each child is highly valued and considered to be important, there is less tendency to reject her or him because of problems with behavior.

28. An individual who belongs to different groups with conflicting standards may struggle with dilemmas and conflicts (Cartwright & Zander, 1960).

29. An individual who belongs to different groups with conflicting standards may behave in accordance with the standards of the group that is most salient at the time, often seemingly unaware of any inconsistencies in his or her beliefs (Cartwright & Zander, 1960). Thus, children may behave quite differently within the program, at home, at school, and in the community.

Using Groups

Given the influence that groups may have over their members, the residential program certainly wants to use groups to further its objectives. I ask the reader to consider the following principles both in terms of residents on a treatment unit and in terms of staff on a unit.

30. Group pressures may influence an individual member's:
    a. Attitudes.
    b. Perceptions.
    c. Opinions.
    d. Behavior.
    e. Decisions.
    f. Personality (Hare, 1962). Thus, groups may be highly significant for many difficult treatment objectives.

31. Where membership is voluntary, the power of a group over an individual member is a function of the valence of the group for a given member (Cartwright & Zander, 1960).

32. When the group is able to restrain the individual from leaving (as in the military, prison, or some residential treatment centers), the power of the group is a function of the restraining forces rather than the group's valence (Cartwright & Zander, 1960).

33. When the power of the group is based on restraining forces, superficial changes in compliant, public behavior can be expected to occur without internalization or long-term effect (Cartwright & Zander, 1960). This suggests that apparent changes occurring in secure or locked facilities may not continue after discharge.

34. When the power of the group is based on its valence, longer lasting changes in attitudes and motivation are much more likely to accompany changes in overt behavior (Cartwright & Zander, 1960). This suggests very strongly that the relative attractiveness of the residential treatment program has highly significant implications for long-term change.

35. Norms as to what is valued, preferred, and accepted behavior develop as the group develops (Toseland & Rivas, 1984).

36. One of the processes by which norms develop is through members' observations of others receiving rewards and punishments (Toseland & Rivas, 1984).

37. Norms may be changed by:
    a. Discussion.
    b. Intervention of someone with high status.
    c. External forces that produce pressure for change (Toseland & Rivas, 1984).

38. When members participate as an entire group in a decision to change behavior, the agreed upon behavior can be expected to occur even outside of the group. The extent to which a change may occur depends on the extent to which group consensus is reached (Cartwright & Zander, 1960).

39. Group discussion is more likely to produce a change than a lecture or a directive (Hare, 1962).

40. When individuals are *forced* to behave in public in a manner contrary to their beliefs, their beliefs are not likely to change (Cartwright & Zander, 1960).

41. When individuals *agree* to act publicly in a manner that is inconsistent with their beliefs, they tend to modify their beliefs to come into conformity with their overt behavior (Cartwright & Zander, 1960). We shall consider some applications of points 37 through 41 along with principles of learning to change group norms and attitudes about theft and fighting in chapter 10, "Using Behavior Modification for Management, Treatment, and Therapy."

42. Group cohesiveness only serves to improve productivity (treatment) of the group when the pressures of the members are towards increased productivity (treatment) (Cartwright & Zander, 1960).

43. Group cohesiveness can be expected to lead to reduced productivity (treatment) when the pressures of the members are in the opposite direction (Cartwright & Zander, 1960). When a cohesive group of staff does not fully support the treatment programs, rules, regulations, and consequences officially "in place" in the milieu, there will be pressure in another direction. This can be especially evident when staff believe that they need more control, that children are not receiving sufficient consequences for their behavior. The actual program in operation may be quite different from the program described in the program manual or brochure.

44. The ability of a group to exert influence over its membership is directly proportional to the cohesiveness of the group (Cartwright & Zander, 1960).

45. The ability of a group to influence a given member is directly proportional to the salience of the group to that member (Toseland & Rivas, 1984).

46. The ability of a group to exert influence over a given member is directly proportional to the group's valence to that member (Cartwright & Zander, 1960).

Strengthening Existing Groups—Building Group Cohesiveness

To use group pressures, it may be necessary or desirable to strengthen natural groups or groups that already exist, such as groups of roommates, peer groups, staff, living groups, and the larger group—the institution itself. Cartwright and Zander (1960) prefer to consider group cohesiveness in relation to the attractiveness of the group to its members, its valence. Principles relating to group cohesiveness provide insight into ways in which the influence of a group may be enhanced. Conversely, such principles give clues as to how undesirable groups might be discouraged from forming, weakened, or disbanded. I ask the reader to consider these principles in terms of residents' membership in a living unit and in terms of attempting to disband or diffuse the influence of a disruptive clique.

47. Persons for whom a group has a high valence are more likely to:
    a. Accept responsibilities.
    b. Participate actively in meetings.
    c. Persist at difficult tasks.
    d. Try to influence others.
    e. Listen to others.
    f. Modify their own views to those of fellow members.
    g. Value the group's goals.
    h. Adhere to the group's standards.
    i. Exert pressures on those who do not accept the group's standards.
    j. Be more secure, comfortable, and relaxed in group activities.
    k. Find release from tension in group activities (Cartwright & Zander, 1960).
48. Valence depends on both the properties of the group and the needs and wants of the individual (Cartwright & Zander, 1960).

Properties of the Group

49. Properties of the group that may affect valence include:
    a. Its goals.
    b. Its size.
    c. Its type of organization.
    d. Its position in the community (Cartwright & Zander, 1960). Consider the reputation that a residential treatment program may have in the community. For some programs, its children are not welcome in stores, businesses, or schools. Other programs have received publicity for abuse or neglect. Yet other programs receive publicity and recognition for activities and the achievement of their residents.
50. Groups have higher valences the more they:
    a. Meet the needs of members. (Children have many needs beyond treatment.)
    b. Meet members' expectations. (In my experience, one of the most important factors for both new residents and new staff is that expectations be accurately and fully set prior to admission or employment. Children who don't know what to expect or have misconceptions when they walk in the door most often do very poorly. Staff who believe they are going to counsel and treat children soon become disillusioned when faced with supervising chores, completing reports, and maintaining the facility and equipment.)
    c. Increase members' prestige and status. (Again, consider the program's reputation. Few children gain status by entering treatment. Also, consider the status of the "child care worker.")
    d. Produce access to rewards and resources (Toseland & Rivas, 1984). Consider the activities and access to the community for the children. Many residential treatment programs reduce considerably the access to rewards and resources. Others may increase them, especially for children who had little access to rewards at home or school.

51. Properties of the group affect the valence of the group only to the extent that those properties are perceived by one or more members (Cartwright & Zander, 1960). A member may perceive properties that do not in fact exist.

52. A change in a member's perception of one or more properties of a group can be expected to have an effect on the valence of the group for that individual (Cartwright & Zander, 1960). Perceptions of the group's properties, and therefore its valence, may change for a member even when the group's properties have not changed.

53. Properties of a group related to cohesiveness exist "if, and only if, the group exists" (Cartwright & Zander, 1960, p. 72). Disbanding a group can be expected to eliminate cohesiveness. Room assignments, activity schedules, living units, and school assignments may all be changed to weaken or disband undesirable groups.

Individual Needs

54. Needs of the individual that may impact the valence of a group include needs for:
    a. Affiliation.
    b. Recognition.
    c. Security.
    d. Any other need that the group might mediate (Cartwright & Zander, 1960).

55. Needs and wants can have an effect on the valence of a group for an individual only to the extent that the individual perceives them (Cartwright & Zander, 1960). Children sometimes do not fully appreciate their needs for education or treatment.

56. The needs of the individual can be expected to change over time due to any number of influences, including participation in the group (Cartwright & Zander, 1960).

57. Both the needs of the individual and the abilities of the groups to meet needs can be expected to change over time (Cartwright & Zander, 1960).

58. When one or more members perceive that the group has improved its abilities to meet their needs, then its valence for those members can be expected to increase (Cartwright & Zander, 1960).

59. The valence of the group can be expected to change as the needs of the individual change (Cartwright & Zander, 1960).

60. Groups may satisfy needs outside the group, for example:
    a. The need for status or prestige.
    b. The need for security in a threatening environment (Cartwright & Zander, 1960).

61. Anxiety increases the need for affiliation (Cartwright & Zander, 1960). New children can be expected to be anxious. Some children know this instinctively and seek out new residents. Staff must use this initial time to engage new residents before they are otherwise engaged.

62. A given group may satisfy different needs for different people (Cartwright & Zander, 1960).

Other Factors

63. Groups have higher valences for those members who are clear on the group's goal and their own role in moving the group towards that goal (Cartwright & Zander, 1960).

64. Forces outside the group may increase the group's valence, such as:
    a. A raise in pay to a particular group of workers.
    b. The improvement of the group's position in relation to other groups.
    c. An attack on the group (Cartwright & Zander, 1960).

65. An increase in hostility towards an out-group tends to be associated with an increase in affection for members of the in-group.

66. Working with an out-group on a common goal tends to improve intergroup harmony and reduce feelings of hostility towards the out-group and its members (Hare, 1962). This suggests that when aggression becomes problematic between two groups, such as between two living

units or between groups of Anglo-Americans and Hispanic-Americans, a cooperative work project might be set up for which each group may earn rewards when it is completed.

67. When the goals of a subgroup are consistent with or supportive of the goals of the larger group, valence of the large group can be expected to increase (Cartwright & Zander, 1960).

68. The valence of the group is higher for individuals who are made to feel well accepted than for those who feel poorly accepted (Cartwright & Zander, 1960).

Forming New Groups: Principles Relating to Structure and Process

Residential programs are always forming and changing groups. The most obvious example is the admission of a new resident. Principles of group dynamics suggest some things for consideration prior to and during intake. Decisions must be made about room assignments. More than one resident may have to have her or his room assignment changed.

When a program seeks to form a new group, the program should attend to the proposed reasons or purposes for the group and structure it for maximum benefit. I ask the reader to consider these principles in terms of a resident's acceptance into the program and the assignment of residents to living groups and therapy groups.

69. Groups wherein members join based on their own forces tend to be more cohesive than groups wherein members join based on induced or external forces (Cartwright & Zander, 1960). This suggests that the residential program may be more cohesive if residents have some choice in whether or not they will enter the program. It further suggests that voluntary therapy groups may be more cohesive, and therefore more influential, than therapy groups to which residents are assigned. It also suggests that informal peer groups of children

may be more influential than the living unit or other treatment groups.

70. The valence of the group is higher when the member must pay some "price" for membership, such as a difficult screening process or some form of initiation (Cartwright & Zander, 1960), or payment for a service. Many programs utilize some sort of initial adjustment period that new residents must complete before achieving the status of full membership in the program, with full privileges. Some programs also use a very confrontive preplacement process in which the child must convince a staffing group of his or her worthiness for acceptance into the program.

71. When an individual has alternative groups from which to choose, the valence of the various groups will be directly related to the individual's perception of her or "his relative social worth in the groups considered" (Jackson, 1960, p. 138).

72. Smaller groups tend to be more cohesive than larger groups (Cartwright & Zander, 1960).

73. Groups wherein members are cooperating tend to have higher valences than groups in which members are in competition (Cartwright & Zander, 1960). Children in residential programs tend to be in competition for a variety of scarce commodities, such as the highest points for the day or week, staff approval or attention, and peer approval.

Friendly competition for highest points has benefit. Not only does the competition help to motivate some children, it also helps to establish point-earning behaviors as a means of gaining status with peers. Competition for staff attention and approval can become problematic. Staff must be especially vigilant as to how, to whom, and how often they give attention and approval. The potential adverse effects that natural and healthy competition may have on group cohesion can be offset by a sufficient number of objectives within the milieu that require cooperation. Even competition for high points can be made a more cooperative endeavor when there is some celebration or bonus when everyone meets or exceeds a certain minimum point total.

74. Members of cooperative groups tend to welcome a talented member as a potential contributor; members of competitive groups tend to view a talented newcomer as a rival (Cartwright & Zander, 1960). Consider this in terms of new staff.

75. Groups with more interpersonal interaction tend to have higher valences for members than groups with minimal interpersonal interaction (Cartwright & Zander, 1960).

76. Groups in which members share certain common traits or similarities tend to have higher valences than groups in which members have little in common (Cartwright & Zander, 1960).

77. Competition with other groups tends to increase cohesion (Toseland & Rivas, 1984). Thus, a competitive series of activities may be used to increase cohesion among a group of residents, among a group of staff, or among some group of staff and residents together.

78. Larger groups tend to:
    a. Show less tension over differences of opinion.
    b. Use more humor when differences of opinion occur.
    c. Be better able to tolerate differences of opinion.
    d. Use more mechanical means of introducing information (less personal).
    e. Make more of an attempt to control others to reach a majority decision rather than influencing others to reach a consensus (Hare, 1962).

79. Smaller groups tend to:
    a. Be more sensitive to differences of opinion.
    b. Work harder to resolve differences of opinion.
    c. Be more sensitive to the feelings of members in processing information.
    d. Be less tolerant of differences of opinion (Hare, 1962).

80. The tendency for the formation of subgroups increases with the size of the group (Hare, 1962). Smaller living units may be expected to have fewer problems with cliques, while cliques on large units that are difficult for staff to supervise may end up "running the program."

Dyads

A dyad is a group of two members. I ask the reader to consider these principles from three perspectives: semi-private rooms, an only child with a single parent, and two staff working the same shift.

81. In a dyad, either member can disband the group by withdrawing (Hare, 1962).

82. Dyads are characterized by a seeking of limits to avoid the withdrawal of either member (Hare, 1962).

83. Dyads tend to:
    a. Have high rates of showing tension.
    b. Have high rates of asking for opinions.
    c. Have low rates of expressing opinions.
    d. Concentrate on exchange of information, acknowledgment, and agreement (Hare, 1962).

84. Over time, dyads tend to be characterized by one member exercising the power of initiative while the other member exercises the power of veto (Hare, 1962).

Triads

A triad is a group with three members. I ask the reader to consider these principles from the perspective of a three-person room, a single parent with two children, two parents with an only child, and three staff on a shift.

85. Triads tend to be characterized by the power of majority over minority since the minority in a triad is isolated without the support of even one other group member (Hare, 1962).

86. The weakest member of a triad has unique power in his or her ability to form a majority with either the strongest or the second strong-

est member, unless the strongest member can prevail against a coalition of the other two (Hare, 1962).

87. In more permanent triads, e.g., family, the coalition may be found to shift, avoiding the permanent exclusion of any one member (Hare, 1962).

88. It is also possible in a triad that one member may be permanently in the minority (Hare, 1962).

Mid-Sized Groups

Mid-sized groups are small groups with four or more members. I ask the reader to consider these in terms of therapy groups for residents.

89. Even-numbered groups of four or more members have less potential to have a majority and a minority and tend to:
    a. Have higher rates of showing disagreement.
    b. Have higher rates of showing antagonism.
    c. Have lower rates of asking for suggestions.
    d. Have lower rates of showing agreement.
    e. Have higher rates of deadlock (Hare, 1962).

90. Odd-numbered groups have more likelihood of having majorities and minorities (Hare, 1962).

91. Members of five-member discussion groups tend to be more satisfied than members of smaller or larger groups (Hare, 1962).

Some Principles Relating to Undesirable Subgroups

A few principles relate directly to the influence of undesirable groups as a force in the institution over one or more individuals or to the weakening or disbanding of such groups. I ask the reader to consider these principles with first a resident clique and then a staff clique in mind.

92. When the goals of a subgroup are in conflict with the objectives of a larger group, the va-

lence of the larger group for all members may be decreased (Cartwright & Zander, 1960). Cliques tend to decrease the valence of the larger group.

93. Subgroups tend to challenge authority and substitute their own goals and methods (Toseland & Rivas, 1984).

94. Valence decreases when there is disagreement among members on how to solve a group problem (Cartwright & Zander, 1960).

95. An unpleasant experience in the group can be expected to reduce the valence of the group for that member (Cartwright & Zander, 1960).

96. The valence of a group may be expected to decrease if the group makes excessive or unreasonable demands on members (Cartwright & Zander, 1960).

97. When one or more members perceive that the group's ability to meet their needs has decreased, then the group's valence for those members can be expected to decrease (Cartwright & Zander, 1960).

98. The actual influence of a group over a given member can be expected to be reduced by the opposition a member may develop towards group standards based on:
    a. The individual's own perceived wants and needs.
    b. The demands of other groups in which the individual may be a member (Cartwright & Zander, 1960).

99. Individuals may be more resistant to group pressures to conform when:
    a. The individual's personality is such that the individual has a tendency against conformity.
    b. The individual has skill or previous success with the subject under consideration.
    c. The individual has preconceptions that are anchored in some other group (Hare, 1962).

100. Persons who have been encouraged to stand on their own principles, make up their own minds, and resist the pressures of others are

more resistant to group pressures to conform than are persons who have not been so encouraged (Cartwright & Zander, 1960).

101. Members are constantly weighing the benefits of membership in comparison to the benefits of membership in other groups that may be available (Toseland & Rivas, 1984).

Individual Motives and Group Goals

"The essential feature of a goal is that it specifies a preferred state and guides action toward the attainment of this state. . . . A group goal might be conceived of as some sort of composite of *individual goals for the same group*" (Cartwright & Zander, 1960, pp. 348–49). I ask the reader to consider these principles in terms of decision making and staff morale in a small program or unit.

102. Most group objectives fall under one of two categories:
    a. The achievement of some group goal.
    b. The maintenance or strengthening of the group (Cartwright & Zander, 1960).
103. Goals may be operational or nonoperational (Cartwright & Zander, 1960).
104. Nonoperational goals are safe in that activities cannot be termed a failure when goals are vague (Cartwright & Zander, 1960).
105. When the basic goals of a group are nonoperational, one may expect operational subgoals to be developed to steer group activities (Cartwright & Zander, 1960).

    The goal of one residential program was to provide local children with "an alternative to incarceration." Subgoals included such things as keeping the beds filled and hiring qualified staff. Seventeen unsuccessful discharges (pregnancies, runaways, psychiatric hospitalizations, and premature removal by parents) over a twelve-month period with no successful discharges was not in conflict with the agency's goal—children did have an alternative to juvenile incarceration.

106. "When a group has a clear and accepted operational goal, a basis is provided for evaluating success" (Cartwright & Zander, 1960, p. 366).
107. Members who are perceived as contributing towards the group's goal are valued (Cartwright & Zander, 1960). Consider the child who is "responding to treatment."
108. Members who are unwilling or unable to contribute towards the group's goal tend to stimulate negative feelings towards them in others (Cartwright & Zander, 1960). Consider the difficult-to-treat child.
109. When the main group goal is operational in nature, differences of opinion about subgoals are likely to be evaluated analytically (Cartwright & Zander, 1960).
110. When the main group goal is nonoperational, differences of opinion about subgoals are likely to be resolved through bargaining processes (Cartwright & Zander, 1960). This was especially evident in the above program with the goal of providing an alternative to incarceration.

Leadership

While experimental studies have shown "that the same group of people will behave in markedly different ways when operating under leaders who behave differently" (Cartwright & Zander, 1960, p. 487), "the belief that a high level of group effectiveness can be achieved simply by the provision of 'good' leaders . . . appears naive in the light of research findings" (p. 487). "Leadership is viewed as the performance of those acts which help the group achieve its preferred outcomes" (p. 492).

Leadership involves the ability to influence other people, and through them, the group process and the outcome of group efforts. It involves the use of power, either formal or social. Leadership includes actions that aid in:

1. Setting group goals.
2. Moving the group towards goals.

3. Improving interactions among members.
4. Building cohesiveness.
5. Making resources available to the group (Cartwright & Zander, 1960).

I ask the reader to consider principles relating to leadership in terms of the leadership of a treatment team on a living unit.

111. Hare (1962) identifies five functions of leaders:
    a. Advancing the purpose of the group.
    b. Administration.
    c. Setting the pace of the group, inspiring greater activity.
    d. Making members feel secure.
    e. Acting without regard to self-interest.
112. One or more members may perform leadership functions (Cartwright & Zander, 1960).
113. Leadership functions may be performed by members who do not hold rank or office as leaders (Cartwright & Zander, 1960).
114. When the designated leader fails to perform certain leadership functions, other members may perform them (Cartwright & Zander, 1960).
115. The purpose of the group may affect the types of leadership functions that are needed (Cartwright & Zander, 1960).
116. In order for a member to perform a leadership function (or any other group function), the member must be aware that the function is needed (Cartwright & Zander, 1960).
117. In order for a member to perform a leadership function (or any other function within the group), the member must either:
    a. Be confident that she or he has the skill or ability to perform the function successfully, or
    b. Feel that it is safe for her or him to make the attempt, i.e., feel safe to fail (Cartwright & Zander, 1960).
118. Leaders who fail to meet expectations may lose support (Cartwright & Zander, 1960).

In some programs, administrators and professionals enjoy very little support from child care counselors, perhaps because they have in some way failed to meet expectations for discipline, treatment, or support.

119. In some groups, the concentration of leadership functions in one or a few offices facilitates efficiency (Cartwright & Zander, 1960).
120. In some groups, concentration of leadership functions without delegation may produce conflict and reduce enthusiasm, creativity, morale, and motivation (Cartwright & Zander, 1960).
121. Autocratic leadership tends to produce greater
    a. Dependency.
    b. Scapegoating.
    c. Hostility.
    d. Aggression, or a submissive reaction with little aggression.
    e. Quantity of work.
    f. Underlying discontent, including persons leaving the group.
    g. Attention-seeking behavior.
    h. Acting out behavior following release (Kirscht, Lodahl, & Haire, 1960), as when a ''successfully treated'' child acts out shortly after discharge from a secure unit or psychiatric hospital.
122. Democratic leadership tends to produce greater
    a. Work motivation.
    b. Continued work in the absence of the leader.
    c. Originality.
    d. Friendly interactions, including play.
    e. Mutual praise.
    f. Sharing of group property (Kirscht, Lodahl, & Haire, 1960).
123. Laissez-faire leadership tends to produce:
    a. Less work.
    b. Poorer work.
    c. More play (Kirscht, Lodahl, & Haire, 1960).

TEAM-BUILDING

The contemporary American football team provides an excellent example of an organization of many individuals and many diverse units working together. There is an offense and a defense. There are special teams for kickoffs and kickoff returns, punts and punt returns, and place kicking. On each team there are subgroups. There are many different roles. There are offensive linemen, defensive linemen, receivers, a defensive secondary, running backs and linebackers, quarterbacks, kickers and safeties, and more. There are high status starters and lower status backup players. Some players play more than one position or on different special teams. There are also many coaches, trainers, equipment personnel, a head coach, general manager, and owner or group of owners.

The mission of the organization is to win games. For most professional teams, it may be to win the Super Bowl. This may be broken down into subgoals, such as winning the next game. The offense seeks to keep the ball and score points, the defense to prevent points and get the ball back. But what unites all of these highly competitive people is the mission. The performance of each unit and each individual is measured in terms of the mission.

Of course, it doesn't always work out perfectly. Frictions develop, as when the offense turns the ball over too much, or when the offense scores lots of points, but the defense allows more points. Or when players become jealous over relative salaries and status. There may be disagreements on play selection or strategy.

In residential treatment centers, there are likewise many teams and subteams, many roles, people playing different positions at different times or under differing circumstances. There are child care counselors, social workers, supervisors, cooks, clerical personnel, and many others, in addition to the children.

The problem with professional football is that there are twenty-seven other teams with the same mission. There must be losers. Only one team can win the Super Bowl. But the mission remains clear. Everything may be evaluated as to how it may contribute to the mission.

Residential treatment centers, on the other hand, are not so fully in competition with others. There do not have to be any losers. The problem with residential treatment is that the mission is not always so clear or so measurable. If the goal is to treat children, many programs do not have the capacities to check with a child two or three years later to find out if she has indeed been treated. But a more serious problem may be that some very important people in the residential setting—the children—have very little knowledge about or investment in the agency's mission.

To build an effective treatment program in which all members, including the children, may work together, this first requires the adoption of a mission statement that all members of the agency can wholeheartedly endorse without reservation. Without it, such things as keeping the beds filled, making enough money to cover expenses, and maintaining the facility and equipment tend to take on a life of their own while the needs of children get lost. All of these things and many others are important, but they are only important to the extent that they contribute to the agency's mission.

To be accepted by everyone, the agency's mission should be developed with input by everyone: staff, children, professionals, support personnel, administrators, board members, and families. Or it must be so readily apparent and acceptable, like winning the Super Bowl, that everyone can embrace it despite having no input.

I much prefer the participation of everyone to the attempt to propose a statement that could be universally embraceable. Just for illustration, however, I suggest that a possible statement might look something like this:

1. It is our mission to help children to become happy, competent, and independent adults.
2. Children are the most valued part of our program. Each child is important. We strive for excellence in both care and treatment.

3. Staff are our most important resource. Each staff member is important. We are committed to the development and well-being of each employee.
4. Our families and our community are our customers. Their satisfaction is very important.
5. We strive to provide our children with every possible opportunity to learn and to grow, and to provide every possible support to enable our children to take advantage of those opportunities.
6. We expect to have fun pursuing our mission.
7. Everything that we do will be evaluated in terms of the above.

Whatever the mission statement, it must be something that each employee, child, and family may embrace. Each program, policy, strategy, and individual behavior by a child or employee may be evaluated in terms of the mission statement. Whenever something is in conflict with the mission statement, including policy, procedure, practice, or the behavior of residents or employees, it should be questioned. In this way, the various groups that make up the agency may be focused as to their role, their potential for contribution to the agency's mission. The mission should pervade the milieu, from preplacement and intake to discharge and aftercare.

Creativity in accordance with the mission should be actively encouraged. Responsibilities should be assigned, even some to the children, with the authority to carry out assigned responsibilities. Each success should be recognized. Honest failure need not be criticized, let alone punished. Rather, it should be recognized and evaluated in terms of what can be learned to help the agency fulfill its mission. Children can learn to pursue learning, independence, and excellence, especially when these are modeled by the adults around them. When a common purpose prevails, people achieve success. This is the power of the group.

SUMMARY

Knowledge about groups has come from two major sources, practitioners working with groups and scientists studying groups in the laboratory and in natural settings. Both began just prior to the turn of the twentieth century.

Practitioners initially worked in settlement houses and with youth groups where activities provided the medium for using groups for socialization, social action, and support. Later, psychoanalytic influences led to group practice in mental health settings to provide treatment.

Scientists studied groups for a variety of purposes in a variety of settings. Their interests have included street gangs, industrial settings, educational settings, children's camps, and the military, among others.

Both scientists and practitioners produced increasing information about groups until the 1950s, the golden age of groups. Following the 1950s, interest in groups declined in both fields. While much recent work has focused on formally structured groups, residential treatment needs to pay considerable attention to natural groups that may form in the treatment setting. They may be more powerful and influential than groups that are deliberately formed and utilized.

Groups exert considerable pressure on members towards conformity. These pressures affect not only behavior but also attitudes, perceptions, opinions, and beliefs. The more uncertain the individual about a matter, the greater the influence of the group. Moreover, as members give in to group pressures, they become even less certain of themselves and more susceptible to the group.

The influence of the group is dependent on its valence (attractiveness), salience (importance), and cohesiveness. Members who do not conform are under considerable pressure, either from themselves or from the group, to conform or to leave. Groups are difficult to change, with norms more difficult to change than roles or status.

Persons for whom the group has high valence (attractiveness) are more likely to accept responsibilities, persist at difficult tasks, try to influence others, listen to others, modify their own views towards other members, adhere to standards, and be more comfortable. Groups are more attractive to members who feel well accepted, and to members who must pay some price for admission. Groups with voluntary membership tend to be more cohesive than groups with members who were somehow forced into joining.

When members join groups because of external forces rather than their own volition, the group tends to be less cohesive. When members are restrained from leaving the group, the group's influence is a function of the restraining forces. Such groups may produce superficial changes in behavior without long-term effect. Groups with higher valence may be expected to produce more long-term changes in attitudes and motivation and longer term changes in behavior.

When residents first come to a residential program, their anxiety produces a need for affiliation. They are likely to affiliate with the first groups that appear capable of meeting some of their needs as they perceive them at the time. The extent to which they pay a price for membership and receive acceptance in these groups may well determine which groups have the highest valence and salience, and, consequently, the most influence.

When forming groups deliberately, cooperative groups rather than competitive groups have advantages. Larger groups are not so satisfying for some purposes. A group of five members may be most rewarding for many purposes. Groups of two or three have special dynamics. In dyads, either member can dissolve the group; members tend to seek opinion rather than offer opinions. Triads are characterized by the shifts of power or by the exclusion of one member. Groups of four tend to deadlock on issues. Groups that have objectives that are in conflict with a larger group tend to decrease the valence of the larger group for *all* members.

People who experience conflicting demands from two or more groups develop a state called cognitive dissonance. They may reduce the dissonance by distortion or denial, by degrading the opinions of others or the people who hold them. To decrease the effectiveness of a clique or group

that is undermining the program, one might attempt to change members' perceptions of the ability of the clique to meet their needs, change the perception of members as to their own needs, or disband the group by assigning members to different living units or putting some out of the program.

Clear operational goals have implications for groups, especially for staff in the residential setting. Nonoperational goals are safe—there can be no failure. Nonoperational goals tend to produce operational subgoals; they may have little to do with meaningful treatment, however.

Leadership has less to do with the functioning of groups than we might think. Leaders are also under considerable pressure to conform to the group; it is sometimes difficult to determine who is following whom. Any group member may perform a leadership function if the member perceives the need and feels safe to try. Democratic leadership tends to produce the best motivation, work in the absence of the leader, friendly interactions, play, praise, and sharing. Autocratic leadership tends to produce dependency, scapegoating, hostility, aggression, more persons leaving the group, attention-seeking behavior, and acting out behavior after a person leaves the group, all significant problems for residential treatment programs.

Team-building depends on establishing a common purpose or mission that all members of the team may embrace. This is best done democratically, with input from all members. A common mission or purpose may do much to reduce the effects of cliques.

If this chapter has convinced the reader of the complexity and importance of groups in the residential setting, then it has done its job. Hopefully, it will stimulate some to pursue further study of group dynamics. It is a field that does not receive sufficient attention in competition with individual and group therapy and behavior modification. In fact, when we consider the application of principles of behavior modification in the next chapter, we shall see that group processes may have a significant effect on that much-touted treatment modality.

PART III

TECHNIQUES AND INTERVENTIONS

In Part III we will look at the application of specific techniques and interventions in the residential setting. These techniques and interventions fall into six conceptual categories: therapy, treatment, remediation, counseling, management, and normal developmental activities. For the purposes of this text, I propose the following definitions:

1. *Therapy*. Therapy is a concept that has its origins in medicine. Therapeutic techniques and interventions are designed to change the individual. They are concerned with constructs or substrates of personality, and unconscious thoughts, feelings, and attitudes.
2. *Treatment*. Treatment is also a concept with medical origins. Treatment techniques and interventions are focused on producing lasting changes in the way in which the individual functions. They are concerned with overt behavior and more conscious thoughts, feelings, and attitudes.
3. *Remediation*. Remediation is a concept that has its origins in education. Remedial activities are designed to correct deficiencies that result from a previous failure to learn. The failure to learn may have been due to a lack of opportunity or some failure to respond to a previous opportunity to learn.
4. *Counseling*. Counseling has to do with the provision of information, the identification of al-

ternatives, guidance, advice, and decision making. It does not have to do with changing the individual or the individual's general functioning but rather with the individual's decision making in a given circumstance or type of situation.
5. *Management*. Management-oriented techniques and interventions are focused on the individual's functioning within a specific setting and the needs of the institution, other residents, and staff. Such techniques are little concerned with the individual's performance outside the setting.
6. *Normal developmental activities*. Normal developmental interventions and techniques are focused on the age-appropriate normal needs of the child for supervision, education, recreation, nutrition, etc.

I have not seen others make these distinctions. In practice, these distinctions are not always clear. However, they are not arbitrary distinctions. I believe that they are not only useful but also necessary. Therapy and treatment are much more effective when purposes and objectives are clear. When

147

therapeutic and treatment objectives become mixed with management and normal developmental objectives, I believe that therapy and treatment suffer.

Further, I believe that management and normal developmental activities also suffer when they become confused with treatment and therapy. Moreover, when the need is for remediation or counseling, therapeutic and treatment techniques may not be productive.

Finally, when we label simple activities as therapy when they are not, I believe that the client suffers. The more normal activities we provide, the more normal the child may feel. When a child cannot play until it is time for "recreational therapy," we heighten the child's awareness of his or her differences and detract from whatever normalcy may be present and healthy.

For example, theft, for some children, is a matter for therapy and treatment. When it occurs with too much frequency on a unit or within the institution, theft becomes a management issue and is best dealt with as such.

In addition, a child who is out of control needs to be controlled. It is required for the child's own safety, for the safety of other residents and staff, and for the maintenance of the institution. All of these management needs can be met by placing the child in a padded room and closing and locking the door until the child is calm. While this meets the management needs of the institution, it may not meet the treatment or therapeutic goals for the child. It may even be counterproductive for treatment.

A child who has not learned how to accept limits, criticism, or instructions may be more apt to respond to techniques designed to remediate these deficiencies rather than to therapy or treatment. Meanwhile, children who cannot control their tempers may sometimes need therapy for their excessive and inappropriate anger or rage. However, when their anger is relatively appropriate but their expression of their anger is not, they may need treatment, counseling, or remediation to learn to control their behavior.

Children need activities. Making wallets is useful and productive. It can be instructional. It can also be fun. It may even be therapeutic in some cases. But calling such activities occupational therapy when they have no clear therapeutic purpose and no other purpose than occupying some time with a structured activity detracts from the potential of real treatment and therapy activities.

Therapeutic objectives can be accomplished during recreational activities. This becomes much less likely, however, when all recreation is called recreational therapy simply because recreation is good for the child (or because insurance companies may pay for recreational therapy but not for recreation). Recreation is good for all of us.

By all means, if the recreational, art, or "occupational" programs have specific therapy or treatment (as opposed to normal developmental) goals for each individual child, along with clear and specific strategies for meeting each such goal, call them therapy. They are. If they do not have clear and specific goals and clear and specific strategies, let them go as recreation or arts and crafts and let the kids play, enjoy themselves, and improve their skills normally.

A multitude of interventions and techniques are available to child care counselors and professional staff. When the strengths and problems of children are well identified and appropriate goals are set for the interventions that are most likely to be effective, residential treatment can be extremely powerful. It is not nearly so effective when some appropriate interventions are underutilized and other interventions are expected to address goals for which they are not designed.

In chapter 9, "Behavior Modification and the Application of Learning Principles," we will look at issues related to the application of the principles of learning to change behavior—from choosing and defining behaviors to change to choosing reinforcements and punishments or negative consequences. We will also consider motivation. In chapter 10, "Using Behavior Modification for Management, Treatment, and Therapy," we will consider the concepts of behavior management, behavior treatment, and behavior therapy as they may apply in the residential setting, along with examples of each as used with individuals and groups.

In chapter 11, ''Techniques and Interventions for Staff,'' we will consider techniques and interventions that staff can employ for remediation, counseling, treatment, and management. In chapter 12, ''Therapeutic Crisis Intervention,'' techniques for managing crises that meet the management

needs of the institution *and* the treatment needs of the child will be considered. Chapter 13, ''Professional Interventions,'' considers techniques and interventions that professionally trained staff may employ to accomplish therapeutic and treatment objectives. Chapter 14, ''Family Interventions,'' proposes a model for family involvement and considers therapeutic, treatment, and remedial interventions that may be employed with families.

9

Behavior Modification and the Application of Learning Principles

USING the principles of learning to deliberately change behavior is called behavior modification. The use of behavior modification in residential settings began in the 1960s. It conjured up images of brainwashing or mind control, of controlling people against their will. Behavior modification is now commonplace; control seems just as elusive as ever.

Behavior modification uses rewards and punishments in accordance with the principles of learning, but not all use of rewards and punishments is behavior modification. The use of rewards and punishments to influence behavior is not new. At the least, evidence of their use dates back to ancient mythology. Successful behavior modification involves more than simply rewarding desirable behaviors and punishing undesirable behaviors.

In this chapter, we will consider issues related to the use of behavior modification in the residential setting. We shall begin with a brief overview. We shall then consider issues in three key areas that have considerable significance for effective behavior modification in the residential setting:

1. Developing and implementing a plan to change behavior.
2. Choosing and defining behaviors to be changed.
3. Motivation and choosing rewards and punishments.

In chapter 10, we will define the concepts of behavior management, behavior treatment, and behavior therapy and consider examples of each for individuals and groups.

BEHAVIOR MODIFICATION

Definition: Behavior modification is the deliberate attempt to change behavior in a desired direction using principles of learning from psychology.

Behavior modification has gained considerable respectability. Federal guidelines for special education require individual educational plans (IEPs) to have objectives stated in behavioral terms that are

151

measurable. State licensing requirements for residential programs require treatment plans with objectives defined in measurable behavioral terms. Some agencies advertise for child care counselors for "implementation of behavior modification programs" (Help Wanted, 1991, p. I-16). Colleges of education offer courses in behavior modification in their curricula for teachers.

Behavior modification did not always enjoy such acceptance. There was both public and professional controversy about its use. Public controversy centered primarily around two issues: claims of "controlling behavior" and use of aversive techniques. Professional controversy centered around these same two issues, as well as the criticism that the behavior modifier is treating only symptoms and not causes (Neuringer, 1970).

Behavior Control Controversy

Early proponents of behavior modification talked of using principles of learning to "control" behavior. This conjures up images of people being made to do things against their will that they would not normally do, of "brainwashing." While there are some applications of behavior modification techniques that do give the appearance of "controlling behavior," in most applications "influencing behavior," "teaching new behavior," or "helping the individual to change behavior" would more accurately describe what is occurring.

Control of behavior is approached only as the behavior modifier approaches total control of all of the positive and negative consequences of the specific behavior in question. This most readily occurs for specific and less complex behaviors and often requires the subject's cooperation. Control of more diverse and complex behaviors can be approached in institutional settings where the behavior modifier can make a wide variety of reinforcements and punishments, even basic necessities, contingent on specific behaviors. Control is even further enhanced when the institution is locked, as in a correctional facility or psychiatric hospital. As with any intervention in a person's life, abuse is possible. It has occurred on more than one occasion, often when unqualified practitioners claimed to be using behavior modification to justify their use of excessive or unusually aversive punishments. Ethical considerations are extremely important.

Professional Controversy

Other professionals have criticized behavior modification techniques for neglecting the underlying causes of problem behaviors. Behavior modifiers argue that it is often the behavior that causes the problem, not the emotion or personality. It may take years of psychotherapy to uncover and sort through emotional problems and their causes. Even after therapy, problem behaviors may continue (Neuringer, 1970).

Behavior, on the other hand, can be changed in a relatively shorter time. People who cannot afford the commitment that psychotherapy requires can be helped by behavior modification with much less investment of time or money. Further, improved behavior can be expected to improve the emotional state of the client, who will have fewer problems with which to cope, and who can relate to situations and people in better and more meaningful ways (Neuringer, 1970).

Recent Controversy

Gardner (1988) believes "that behavior modification programs—as the primary, if not the exclusive, modality for antisocial acting out—do more harm than good" (p. 739). Gardner emphasizes that he means the use of behavior modification for treatment of antisocial disorders and that he is not criticizing its use for the treatment of other disorders, such as phobias.

Gardner (1988) argues that children with antisocial behavior disorders, in anticipating a misbehavior, calculate the chances of being caught and the consequences. In a behavior modification program, the child knows exactly what will happen. Moreover, the child is often allowed to work off the consequences of the misbehavior, thus learning various kinds of manipulation.

The problem, according to Gardner, is that such children have defects in their internal guilt-evoking mechanisms—guilt not in the legal sense of whether the child committed the act, but guilt in the sense of conscience. Behavior modification tends to stress guilt in the sense of whether or not the child committed the act, ignoring the conscience. It teaches children to avoid misbehavior because of the consequences, not because of the rightness or wrongness or the problems caused for the victim or for others.

Once the child's behavior improves under behavior modification, the child is pronounced "cured" and discharged. Rather than extinguishing problem behaviors, however, the effect is just the opposite and the behavior becomes more entrenched. When the child leaves the setting, away from the monitoring and structured consequences, such children often become even worse than they were before (Gardner, 1988).

I suspect that a great many behavior modification programs function very much as Gardner suggests. Many such programs involve the oversimplified application of minor rewards and punishments for behavior, perhaps serving the purpose of controlling behavior on the unit. On the other hand, I have seen behavior modification programs that have contributed to lasting changes in behavior with antisocial children, changes that continued for years after discharge. These programs attended to feelings as well as behavior—both are learned—and paid more careful attention to the effects of rewards and punishments and the social setting.

PLANNING TO CHANGE BEHAVIOR

The deliberate attempt to change behavior using principles of learning involves a great deal more than the intuitive application of consequences to behavior. Deliberation implies planning. Someone must identify behaviors to be changed and establish criteria for success. When more than one behavior is involved, priorities must be set. Decisions must be made about rewards and punishments. Strategies must be developed, then carried out. There are both ethical and practical considerations concerning who is involved in this process and how decisions are made.

Residential treatment programs may take a number of different approaches to changing behavior. A program may choose to develop a specific plan for a specific behavior of an individual child. It may choose to develop a comprehensive plan for an individual child treating a number of behaviors. It may develop a behavioral system such as a token economy or point system to treat a number of behaviors that are typically in need of treatment among the types of children served. It may have a system that treats fairly typical behaviors but allows for some individualization. And finally, a program with a system in place may decide to develop a specific plan for a child or for a child's specific behavior that does not seem to be responding to the system. Whatever the approach, certain principles apply.

Ethical Considerations

Ethics dictate that the child should be involved in the planning, as should others responsible for the child—parents, or a state worker *in loco parentis*. They should support the objectives and outcome criteria. There can be little concern about unethical practice with the informed endorsement of the plan by the child and the parent.

Practical Considerations

Practicality dictates that the child and those responsible for implementation of the plan should be involved in the planning—it will promote their cooperation and their understanding when interpretations or decisions are required. Parents, teachers, child care counselors, and the child can do a lot to undermine a plan they do not fully support or understand.

Most importantly, someone who is skilled in behavior and learning must be involved. If not, the plan is likely to amount to little more than attempting to bribe the child to do good and threatening punishment if the child doesn't, followed by considerable exasperation with the child when the plan doesn't work.

Finally, all persons involved in the implementation of a plan must have some training on the behaviors being treated. They must be able to observe the behaviors and to report or record their observations. They must have reasonable expectations. They must be able to understand when the plan is not working as well as when the plan is working. They must be comfortable with any rewards or punishments they have to apply. They must understand how to apply them and apply them correctly. It is not at all uncommon for a parent, teacher, or staff member, concerned about controlling a child rather than teaching a child self-control, to increase negative consequences, to apply additional punishments, or to indicate that the child is getting off much too lightly. On the other hand, giving out reinforcements with an unpleasant expression because another duty has been interrupted can turn a positive reinforcement into a punishment.

CHOOSING AND DEFINING BEHAVIORS

Residential treatment programs deal with all kinds of behavior, from simple habits like brushing teeth and combing hair to complex behaviors such as a child picking up a weapon or a group of adolescents engaging in armed robberies on their way to school. All are subject to principles of learning.

Criteria and the Conceptualization of Behavior

How the different parties to the plan conceptualize behavior may have a significant effect on the way in which they identify behaviors to be changed and set priorities, as well as on their participation in the implementation of the plan. There are many ways to conceptualize behavior.

Good and Bad

Perhaps the most common way of conceptualizing behavior is in terms of good and bad. Many of those involved in residential treatment may conceptualize behavior in this way: children, parents, some child care counselors, support staff, teachers, and the community. These concepts may mean different things to different people. Conceptualizing behavior in terms of good and bad requires value judgments. Some will base these judgments primarily on practical values, others on moral values, and still others on some combination. Agreement on which behaviors are "bad" may be problematic.

Consider fighting. While most residential and school personnel consistently treat fighting as an undesirable behavior to be eliminated, some children seem to believe that fighting is a necessity, almost an inalienable right, to protect themselves and their fragile egos from harm. One occasionally encounters parents who encourage their children to assert themselves by fighting.

Use of marijuana, masturbation, or drawing dirty pictures pose similar problems for determining whether or not such behaviors are "bad." Obviously, there will be some disagreements. Further, this method of conceptualization has implications for labeling the child and decreasing the child's self-esteem.

Finally, this method of conceptualization has implications for what behaviors may receive attention. Bad behaviors are more likely to receive attention than are good behaviors. People *may* attend to good behaviors when there are no bad behaviors with which to contend; when the two occur together, people are most likely to attend to the bad behaviors instead of the good behaviors.

Positive and Negative

Viewing behavior on a continuum from positive to negative avoids some of the moral value judgments of good and bad and emphasizes the practical outcomes of the behavior, both for the child and for others. As with good and bad behaviors, negative behaviors are still more likely to receive attention. Teachers are very good at reinforcing positive behaviors, from good grooming and polite manners to correct answers during recitation and pretty drawings. But consider the child who has few positive behaviors to gain the teacher's attention, has poor clothes and hygiene, can't draw, is awkward when talking to adults, and has few correct answers. The teacher may be impressed with Donna's recitation until Johnny starts throwing spitballs across the room. Johnny finally gets attention while Donna's recitation gets ignored.

Adaptive and Maladaptive

Professionals are likely to view behavior in terms of what purpose it may serve for the child. Again, the concept of a continuum is possible. Lying is maladaptive to the extent that it prevents those who have the best interests of the child in mind from making sound decisions about the child and because of its effects on trust and relationships. However, for a child who regularly receives severe beatings from an abusive parent, lying may be very adaptive. Stealing is maladaptive because of the negative consequences that others place on the child and the implications it has for the child's future and probable imprisonment if it continues. The emphasis is on the outcome of the behavior for the child with less moralizing. This method of conceptualization may also promote more equal attention to adaptive and maladaptive behaviors. However, it may do little to promote the development of guilt as an internal control.

Defining Behaviors

Behaviors to change will fall into two categories: those someone wants the child to do and those someone wants the child to stop.

Behaviors to Extinguish

Argues, fights with sister, talks in class, gets out of seat, steals, lies, curses, hits parents, hits siblings, breaks things, runs out of the house, stays out all night, screams and yells, bangs head, wets the bed, is having sex, smokes cigarettes, drinks, uses drugs, has a bad attitude, talks back, makes threats, fights in school—these are some of the complaints that intake workers hear about children being referred for treatment.

Behaviors to be extinguished should be defined with two objectives clearly in mind:

1. The definition must facilitate the arrangement of contingencies to extinguish the behavior.
2. The definition should facilitate generalization to other settings.

Learning theory suggests that punishment contingent on a behavior may reduce the behavior, as may lack of reinforcement. Learning theory suggests with much more conviction that reinforcement is the best teacher and that acquisition of a competing behavior will extinguish another behavior.

Behaviors to Acquire

Most behaviors to be extinguished can be defined in terms of competing behaviors to be acquired. In the case of a child who lies compulsively about everything, is the problem behavior "lying," or is it "not telling the truth"? If we punish lying, we may end up with a child who talks very little. If we reinforce telling the truth, we may end up with a child who tells the truth instead of lying. A child who pays attention in class and completes assignments is not likely to disrupt the class. A child who follows instructions is less likely to get angry when receiving an instruction. A child who talks about what is causing the anger and attempts to change it is less likely to hit a wall or a person.

Consider the following:

1. Follow instructions.
   a. Look at the person giving the instruction.
   b. Listen to the instruction.
   c. Ask questions if you don't understand.
   d. State any objections calmly no more than once.

    e. Listen to the reply.

    f. Say "OK."

    g. Go do the instruction.

    h. Check back.

2. Accept criticism.

    a. Look at the person giving criticism.

    b. Listen to the criticism.

    c. Ask necessary questions if you don't understand.

    d. Say "OK."

    e. Refrain from making excuses.

3. Control temper.

    a. Tell someone in a calm voice tone why you are angry.

    b. Listen to the reply.

    c. Express any disagreement calmly.

    d. Refrain from hitting.

    e. Refrain from throwing or breaking things.

    f. Refrain from cursing.

    g. Refrain from yelling.

    h. Refrain from stomping away and slamming doors.

4. Accept "no."

    a. State objections clearly in a calm manner one time.

    b. Maintain pleasant voice tone.

    c. Control temper.

5. Relate well with adults.

    a. Maintain eye contact.

    b. Maintain pleasant voice tone.

    c. Answer when spoken to.

    d. Use appropriate language.

    e. Speak clearly and distinctly.

    f. Refrain from using slang.

6. Relate well with peers.

    a. Speak respectfully.

    b. Use appropriate voice tones and language.

    c. Refrain from teasing.

    d. Refrain from name-calling.

    e. Ask permission to use something that belongs to another.

7. Pay attention in class.

    a. Remain in seat.

    b. Look at the teacher when the teacher is talking.

    c. Raise hand to speak.

    d. Look at the teacher when you are talking.

    e. Refrain from talking to others.

8. Complete class work.

    a. Be prepared.

    b. Take all needed material to class.

    c. Work on assignments when instructed.

    d. Ask questions or ask for help when you don't understand.

9. Complete homework.

    a. Write down all assignments completely and accurately.

    b. Bring home all needed material and books.

    c. Plan adequate time to study.

    d. Ask for help if needed.

    e. Avoid making excuses.

A child who is performing these behaviors can do very few of the problem behaviors listed above. Notable exceptions are smoking, drinking, using drugs, and engaging in sexual activity. Smoking and other substance abuse pose special problems even in cases in which the client wants to stop. Consenting sexual behavior involves moral considerations beyond the scope of this text.

Teaching appropriate behaviors offers several advantages. While it is certainly advantageous to attempt to minimize reinforcement for undesirable behaviors, and while punishments are still likely to be issued, elimination of undesirable behaviors does not guarantee that the child will replace them with desirable behaviors. Helping the child to acquire social skills such as the above not only teaches desirable behaviors but also helps with the extinction of many undesirable behaviors. Further, appropriate behaviors such as social skills are much more likely to generalize to other settings and to be sustained by reinforcements in those settings.

MOTIVATION

Our society tends to believe that rewards and punishments motivate people, and they do. A person who is in a position to be concerned about a child's behavior, and who is faced with a behavior that is not what is desired, may very well try to explain to the child what the consequences of that behavior are likely to be. The expectation is that understanding the consequences, the child will change behavior in the desired direction:

If you don't improve your grades, you won't get promoted.
If you don't clean up your room, people will think you're sloppy.
If you don't eat your broccoli, you won't grow up to be big and strong like your daddy.
If you don't improve your behavior, the judge won't let you go home.

When this proves effective, all is well. When it does not, the adult may conclude that the child is unmotivated. Being unmotivated may imply that there is something wrong with the child who doesn't do what everyone else does, doesn't want to be like everyone else, or doesn't want the things that everyone else wants. The child may simply be labeled as lazy.

The next step, then, may be to attempt to motivate the child with something else, offering a reward or threatening a punishment:

I'll give you $2 for every A on your report card and $1 for every B.
I'll give you 25 cents a day for every day your bed is made.
If you don't make your bed, you will not be allowed to watch TV.
If you don't clean your plate, you won't get dessert.
If you don't earn your points, you won't get a home pass this weekend.

Should all of this fail, the adult may up the ante by combining or increasing rewards or punishments. Eventually, the adult may give up, which may earn the child a label that goes beyond "lazy," possibly to "bad."

What is motivation? Most simply, it is having a need or want that causes some behavior. There are several ingredients:

1. *Desire.* There must be a need or a want.
2. *Effort.* The desire must be strong enough to be worth the effort to satisfy it.
3. *Competition.* The desire must compete with other needs and wants.
4. *Self-confidence.* The individual must believe that she or he can accomplish the behavior necessary to satisfy the desire.
5. *World view.* The individual must have sufficient confidence in the order of things to believe that when she or he accomplishes the behavior, the desire is likely to be satisfied and the reward delivered.

Desire

Basic needs are most often associated with biological drives, such as hunger, thirst, or sex, or drives for self-preservation or to escape pain. There are also social needs, such as the need for contact with others, and psychological needs, such as the need to protect one's self-esteem. Wants, too, may be associated with biological drives, social, or psychological factors. A thirsty person *needs* a drink but may *want* a Coke. Children may sacrifice their biological need for safety in taking a dangerous dare to impress a peer. Not everyone feels the same needs to the same extent; we do not all want the same things.

Effort

The need or want must be strong enough to be worth the effort required to achieve it. Many of us want things that are just too much trouble: a clean car for the weekend, a Ph.D. or law degree. One person may have a car that can be cleaned up in thirty minutes, another's car may require three hours of work to remove bugs and tar from the finish, dog hair and trash from the interior. One person may have to earn money and support a family while pursuing a Ph.D.; another may have a family that can help. Some children must expend considerably more effort than other children to do the same thing, such as being neat, studying, or remaining calm.

Competition

A need or want must compete with other needs and wants in order to affect behavior. One person may have to forgo a tennis match to clean the car for the weekend, another may have nothing else to do, while a third may have to complete a term paper. One Ph.D. aspirant may have to postpone marriage; another may have to sacrifice time from spouse and children. Some children sacrifice considerable reinforcements from sports or other peer activities to do their homework; other children seem to get little reinforcement from athletics or peers no matter what they do.

Self-Confidence

The individual must have some reason to believe that he or she can accomplish the necessary behavior. Many who have dabbled in music or sports have at some time entertained fantasies of stardom, but stardom very often requires performance at an exceptional level that we may not believe we can attain. Our recently cleaned automobile may have a flat tire. Some people have so little confidence in their abilities that they will not attempt to change the tire. Some children have little confidence in their ability to achieve in school while others have a history of success.

World View

The individual must have some reason to believe that, if he or she does what is necessary, it will result in that which will satisfy the want or need. The musician or athlete may know an extremely gifted and talented person, possibly the music teacher or high school coach, who failed to achieve stardom. The child may know many high school graduates, even college graduates, out of

work or in low-paying jobs, possibly even the agency's child care counselors. The child may have little confidence that a parent or staff member will deliver a reward as promised. What is the motivation for a black male from an inner city neighborhood with a high murder rate if he does not expect to live to the age of twenty?

Summary of Motivation

Few children are unmotivated or lazy; many children are unmotivated to do some of the things adults want them to do. More often, assessment will show one or more of the following conditions to exist:

1. The child isn't as interested in available rewards as we think she or he should be.
2. The child may have to expend more effort than we realized, and the reward isn't worth it.
3. The child is more interested in other things and is unwilling to give them up.
4. The child is not confident that he or she is capable of doing what is necessary.
5. The child doesn't really believe he or she will get the reward in the end.

CHOOSING REWARDS AND PUNISHMENTS

A good deal of the study of learning has involved very clear, precise definitions and application of rewards and punishments in "sterile" laboratory settings. Rewards have often been basic necessities, with motivation for the reward controlled by some sort of deprivation; punishments have been naturally aversive, even painful stimuli.

We might expect a sentient rat to be especially fond of an experimenter who placed it in a nice clean cage every day so it could get all it wanted to eat by simply pressing a bar. On the other hand, we might expect a sentient rat that really knew what was going on to be extremely resentful of the experimenter who held it in captivity, deprived it of food, then capriciously manipulated it for purposes about which the rat couldn't care less. This rat might just decide it wasn't going to press any bars for anybody, no matter what. Of course, the experimenter just might come up with some contingencies to get even a sentient rat to change its mind.

Outside the laboratory, the use of reinforcements and punishments and the manipulation of motivation become more difficult. The needs and wants of people are varied and complex. They not only have basic physiological needs and wants but also complex psychological and social needs and wants.

Rewards

Rewards used in research are often basic necessities. The researcher may control motivation for a given reward by some schedule of deprivation. Finding rewards in dealing with children can be a little more complicated than merely finding something the child needs or wants badly enough:

1. People have feelings and beliefs about specific rewards that are unrelated to their intrinsic value.
2. People have feelings about those in control of rewards that affect the value of rewards.
3. The feelings of those in control of a reward are usually evident and affect the value of a reward.
4. The social context in which the reward is given and received affect the reward's value.
5. The effect of the reward on others in the social context may be as important in the residential setting as the effect of the reward on the individual receiving it.
6. The use of specific rewards can be symbolic of adult approval, or it may detract from adult approval as a reinforcement for behavior.

Beliefs or Feelings About the Reward

The effect of a reward that the child clearly wants may be influenced by how the child thinks or feels about that reward. Principles of learning tell us that rewards given on an intermittent schedule may produce the strongest learning. However, when a child works for a reward that has been agreed upon, the child is not likely to appreciate the employment of an intermittent schedule of reinforcement. Expect some rebellion when this occurs. The same may occur if we attempt to make something that the child believes to be a ''right'' to which she is entitled contingent on some behavior.

Moreover, feelings about things used as rewards change. Use of food as a reward may lead to food taking on some associations with goodness and possible eating disorders.

Feelings About Those in Control

When dressed up for a special occasion, ''Wow!'' from your date is not nearly the same as ''Wow!'' from your father or mother. Likewise, occasional praise or reward from an abusive parent may mean much more than praise from a teacher or a peer; praise from a music teacher or coach may carry more impact than praise from a parent for achievement in music or athletics. A child may cut grass for $10 at home and want $20 for a similar job in the neighborhood. Even more likely, a child may cut grass for $10 in the neighborhood and hardly ever cut it at home.

Many parents are amazed, astounded, miffed, or chagrined at the rapid changes in the behavior of their children following their placement in a residential treatment program. Some children respond surprisingly quickly to some very simple reinforcements that are initially available. The staff, however, are not encumbered by years of feelings that have been built up for parents.

Conversely, ''You're not my father!'' and ''You can keep your point system!'' are heard often enough to indicate that many children have feelings about the personnel or a whole agency or the system that have significance for any rewards that may be attempted as contingencies. In any case, it is clear that different children have different feelings about different people who may be in control of rewards and that these feelings are very relevant to the effectiveness of these rewards in motivating or reinforcing behavior.

Feelings of Those in Control

The feelings of those giving out rewards are exceedingly important. When a reward is given in conjunction with a clear communication of adult approval, one may condition the other. In this way, letter grades for school work may become conditioned reinforcements. Just the opposite is also true. When receiving a reward in the presence of adult approval, the adult approval may, in time, become a conditioned reinforcement. This can be especially significant for children in treatment who have not had much positive experience with adult approval.

On the other hand, the feelings of those in control may also detract from a reward. When staff, annoyed at having to interrupt some other activity to reward a child, issue the reward with an expression of irritation, they may readily turn the reward into a punishment.

Rewards in the Social Context

In a group setting, the attitudes of the group or subgroups toward something used as a reward may have a significant effect on the value of the reward as a reinforcement. An A on a test or term paper may mean more to some of us than to others. One student may be in competition with peers. Another student may have peers who get C's, D's, and F's for whatever reasons. In the first case, the peer group adds considerably to the value of an A; the A confers status on the recipient. In the second case, if the student is lucky, the peer group will not have much effect on the value of an A; more likely, an A will be a source of embarrassment or grounds for teasing and ridicule. Too many A's may result in ostracism. Perhaps the student should choose another peer group, but possibly this peer group is important because of sports, music, or other nonacademic interests.

Effects of Rewards on Others

Because people learn by observation and mimicking, rewards can have additional effects in the group, especially in establishing and reaffirming norms and values within the group. Members seeing others receive rewards may feel punished for not exhibiting the same behavior and missing out on the reward. They may later mimic the rewarded behavior. They may also attempt to devalue the reward.

Adult Approval as a Reinforcement

For many children, the approval of adults may be an extremely powerful reinforcement. Other reinforcements, such as an A on a test, a favored dessert, or money, may be merely symbols of that coveted adult approval. Children also covet the approval of peers, a commodity often in competition or conflict with the approval of adults. Anything that may undermine the value of the approval of adults increases the relative value of peer approval. Excessive rewards given too frequently may focus the child more on the reward, less on the approval that goes with it.

Consider the rewards often offered for grades on report cards—$2 for an A, $1 for a B, etc. When given as an unannounced reward by a genuinely pleased parent, this money may communicate some measure of parental approval and help to add to the value of grades as conditioned reinforcements in the future. However, the situation may be very different in the case of a distraught parent attempting to get a child to improve grades. In this case, the parent is likely to be frequently reminding the child of the potential to earn money and the things the child might want to do with that money. The child may do better in school for a variety of reasons, possibly the parent's increased attention to homework and daily grades, possibly the money. When the money comes, however, it comes as something to which the child is entitled, having earned it; its symbolic value has been lost. The parental approval is still there, but the child is focused on the money.

Children who seem virtually immune to the approval or disapproval of adults come into residential treatment every day. They can work effectively for long periods for any number of material rewards or privileges, so long as the behavior required does not jeopardize peer approval.

Punishment

One could make a career out of the study of punishment. Moreover, one could do so in any number of fields: psychology, psychiatry, sociology, social psychology, criminology, corrections, anthropology, history, or theology. One might even be able to do so in law, personnel management, or education. Punishment in the social environment is a great deal more than merely an aversive or unpleasant stimulus that affects behavior. In fact, some ''punishment'' doesn't seem to affect behavior very much at all.

The definition of punishment in the psychological laboratory, like that of reward, is neat and clean—free from the clutter of feelings, judgments, and social values. But what do we *really* mean by punishment? Everything—from a disapproving look or a one word verbal reprimand to capital punishment in modern Western culture, from public ridicule and ostracism, to disfigurement and death by torture in ''less modern'' times and cultures. Most often, we want to change behavior *now*. Punishment in the popular sense is something that is designed to change behavior through inflicting discomfort or pain, or through causing fear.

We really expect the threat of punishment to control behavior. When it doesn't, we are likely to conclude that there is something wrong with our ''arithmetic''—something must have gone wrong when we ''assigned value'' to the ''crime'' and selected an ''appropriate'' punishment. Obviously, the punishment is too lenient. If the punishment isn't working, we must do more of it.

But punishment does work. It controls or at least influences some of us, probably most of us. The threat of a life sentence is not what keeps most of us from shooting the person who rudely cuts in line in front of us, but the threat of a parking ticket makes many of us drive around the block, pay at the lot, or walk a few extra blocks in the cold.

As with rewards, choosing punishments is not a simple matter of finding something unpleasant that the child dislikes enough to avoid. There are a number of considerations:

1. People have feelings and beliefs about specific punishments that are unrelated to their intrinsic value.
2. Punishment creates feelings that may require attention.
3. Punishment relieves guilt.
4. Feelings about those in control of a punishment may affect the value of a punishment.
5. The feelings of those in control of a punishment are usually apparent and may affect the value of the punishment.
6. When punishment occurs in a group setting, the group may influence the effects of the punishment.
7. The effect of the punishment on others in the social context may be as important in the residential setting as the effect of the punishment on the individual receiving it.
8. The use of punishment may distract the child from adult disapproval.

Feelings About a Punishment

Few of us are purely rational. Emotions come into play in most of our decisions. Individual differences are always a factor. Consider the effects of some ''natural punishments'': gravity leads to maiming or death for those who fall from high places; wild animals kill; fire burns; speeding cars kill and maim occupants when they crash. Humans climb mountains because they are there; they hunt or tame wild animals, twirl flaming batons at high school football games, race autos, and drive too fast on the way home from work or school. They embezzle money, burgle houses, rob banks, steal the answers to exams, and do any number of other things for which consequences are serious. Danger is exciting.

Feelings Created by Punishment

Punishment produces feelings. Those feelings are rarely good. If feelings of remorse occur, they are more likely the result of perceived adult disapproval, of which the punishment is but a symbol. The punishment itself it more likely to produce feelings of pain, humiliation, powerlessness, worthlessness, and anger, and distract the child from the adult disapproval.

The residential program must frequently contend with the residual effects of punitive practices with children in the home and, unfortunately, in our schools. Those residual effects are often matters for treatment. Consider Larry.

> *Larry.* **Five-year-old Larry put a candy bar in his pocket one day while shopping with his father. His father caught him eating the candy bar later that day and quickly got to the bottom of the matter. Larry's father was morally outraged that his son was a thief. He called Larry names and loudly criticized him for the theft. He then gave Larry a good spanking to teach him to "never do that again." Larry never did.**
>
> **Six months later, Larry and a playmate found themselves playing doctor on a rainy afternoon. So did his playmate's mother, who told Larry's mother. Larry got a good (real "loud") talking to and a good spanking. Larry hasn't played doctor since.**
>
> **Larry is a good boy who tries to do everything right and usually does. However, when his parents try to tell him that he didn't do something right, Larry's stomach begins to churn, his hands get sweaty, and his knees start to shake; he can't seem to think clearly about what his parents are telling him. He yells at his parents. They yell back. Sometimes it gets physical. Larry also has trouble with criticism at school.**

Punishment Relieves Guilt

The sentenced convict serving time and "paying his debt to society" is likely to feel little need to make amends to his victim. The ability to experience the feeling of guilt is a potential punishment of future behavior, one of the means by which a child develops self-control. The ability to feel guilt must be taught. Rather than facilitating feelings of guilt, harsh punishments often relieve such feelings. We get a number of children in residential treatment who seem to feel no remorse for injuring another.

Feelings Blocked by Punishment

Some punishments interfere with the child's ability to feel good by interfering with the child's ability to do good. Punishment may not only relieve the child from the responsibility of making amends for a misbehavior, but also actually prevent the child from doing so. This may be especially true of restrictions. Moreover, a restriction may actually prevent the child from practicing the desired behavior and receiving reinforcement for it, as the following example illustrates.

> *Darlene.* **Darlene can't seem to get her mouth under control. She says things to other kids that get her in trouble. She says things to the staff in the program that get her in trouble. Staff send her to the table for five minutes to get her behavior under control. This is a time-out procedure that is supposed to interrupt the child's behavior, give her a few moments to think, then rejoin the activity. Darlene's behavior is so annoying to the other kids and the staff, however, that five minutes doesn't seem to be enough "punishment." So Darlene gets thirty minutes at the table the next time.**
>
> **Darlene knows her problem. When she is at the table, she thinks about what she has done wrong and what she must do to become better, for the first ten minutes. Then she starts thinking about Chad at school. He's cute, and she thinks he likes her. Then she starts thinking about what's for snacks tonight, then how she's going to treat her kids when she grows up. Somehow she forgets everything staff told her about controlling her mouth when she rejoins the group. She's sent back to the table again in a few minutes. Staff know the procedure isn't working, so they put her at the table for an hour this time.**

Feelings About Those in Control

Another aspect of punishment is the meaning attached to it by the fact that it has to be applied or, more accurately, inflicted by someone. Most of us very quickly learn to approach a rose bush with caution, possibly even wearing heavy gloves. The prick of the thorn is quite painful and produces rapid learning.

Harsh punishments inflicted by someone whose authority we do not accept, who seems vindictive or capricious, does not always produce the desired learning. History is replete with martyrs who accepted punishment nobly from authorities they did not accept. Punishment from authorities we do not trust may readily produce rebellion. I have often seen children rebel against punishments; I have never seen anyone rebel against a rose bush.

Feelings of Those in Control

Punishment often includes an aspect of retribution. It can actually be quite funny to hear a child run a string of profanity at a set of building blocks that will not behave the way he wants them to. When he loudly uses the same language on his sister in the grocery store, it becomes quite a different matter. Some of the most serious punishments a child receives come not from the inherent wrongness or danger in the act, but from the embarrassment or inconvenience caused to adults. It sometimes appears that school officials demand a parent conference more to inconvenience the parent than to engage the parent in a cooperative solution. Do we teach a child that it is proper to hurt others when things don't go the way we want them to?

Some people don't enjoy inflicting punishment. When they use punishment as a threat, they are inclined to make the threat serious out of the hope or expectation that it will not have to be carried out. They make the decision to threaten the punishment, but not the decision to apply it, expecting the threat to be effective. The child, sensing indecision, pleads an admirable case. Instead of learning to control behavior to avoid punishment, the child learns that it is easier to get out of consequences than it is to avoid them by appropriate behavior in the first place.

Punishment in the Group Setting

Sometimes punishment in the group setting produces a state of dissonance in the individual.

Sometimes individuals resolve dissonance with distortion and denial.

In its mildest form, punishment implies unpleasantness or discomfort. Often, punishment involves pain. Sometimes, it involves humiliation. A criticism given in private may be almost a matter of instruction, if handled that way; in public, it may become a serious punishment due to the humiliation the recipient feels. One child may feel à severe humiliation from the mildest criticism in front of the class, while another may gain status among peers from a much more serious dressing down.

Corporal punishment is still permitted and practiced in some of our nation's schools. Sometimes it produces the desired change in behavior. Other times it earns the individual status among peers of being a tough guy, able to handle all that may be dished out and then some.

The Effects of Punishment on Others

Punishment may actually have more beneficial effects on the behavior of others than it does on the individual on whom it is inflicted. It helps to establish and validate norms. The infliction of some sanction on a transgressor may be reinforcing to others who have expended some effort in avoiding the same undesirable behavior. It reduces the urge for retribution. Consider your own feelings when on a rainy day at the mall you have to park fifty yards from the entrance. As you approach, cold and damp, you observe an expensive car with no handicapped plates parked in the handicapped zone near the entrance. Do you feel some satisfaction if the driver returns, rips a parking ticket from under the wiper blade, and begins cursing?

Punishment also reduces the need for retribution in the social setting. This can be especially important in the residential setting. Consider Donnell.

Donnell. **Donnell was a small ten-year-old with a ''mouth like a sailor.'' He frequently talked tough to older boys when staff was nearby. Donnell received counseling along with consequences for his inappropriate language and improper peer relations, but the** behavior continued. Everyone knew he wouldn't be able to talk like that to older boys if staff wasn't there to protect him.

One day, he spit on a burly fifteen-year-old. His mother couldn't understand that little Donny received the same restriction as was given for hitting, especially since the program did not even have spitting on their list of rules and consequences. His restriction cost him a home pass. On the other hand, failure of the program to respond seriously to this incident could have resulted in retaliation by one or more boys who were outraged by the incident.

Adult Disapproval

The approval and disapproval of others may be the best reinforcements and punishments to sustain behavior outside of the residential treatment setting. A mild sanction or punishment serves to communicate adult disapproval, perhaps along with understanding and compassion. A harsh punishment may indicate very strong adult disapproval, but it may not communicate it very well. The child's physical or emotional pain takes so much of the child's attention that there is little attention left for consideration of how others might be feeling. The punishing adult, appearing harsh, vindictive, or vengeful, may seem to care very little about the child's feelings. "This is going to hurt me more than it hurts you," applies only if the child is able to consider more than his or her own suffering.

Summary of Punishment

1. The threat of a strong punishment increases the risk inherent in the act, the danger, and the excitement.
2. Punishment must be applied or inflicted by someone. This brings in the issues of whether or not we accept the authority of the agent applying the punishment, and whether or not the punishment is perceived as fair and just. It allows the recipient to mitigate the punishment by attaching nobility to serving it, to be martyred.
3. The severity of a punishment may have more to do with the inconvenience caused than the

"badness" or maladaptiveness of the behavior being punished.
4. Punishment may be unpleasant for the person administering it. Consequently, it may be threatened but never administered. The child does not learn to anticipate consequences; rather, the child learns to become a skilled defense lawyer.
5. The humiliation may be more significant than the actual punishment for some.
6. Punishment of an offender serves as a reinforcement to other members of the group who have expended some effort at refraining from similar transgressions.
7. Punishment relieves the victim of having to deal with thoughts and consequences of retaliation.
8. Punishment relieves guilt.
9. Some punishments, especially long ones like restrictions, make it awfully difficult to be "good" or to practice doing good.
10. Disapproval of others, especially adults, may be one of the strongest deterrents for a child. A strong punishment focuses the child on his or her own suffering rather than the disapproval of others. It may produce thoughts, but not the thoughts that are desired.

ALTERNATIVES TO REWARDS AND PUNISHMENTS

Perhaps the greatest obstacle I have seen to the successful application of behavior modification is the obsession with the need to control a child. Psychology teaches us that learning requires practice. Common sense and experience tell us that practice requires patience. Desired behaviors must occur frequently in the presence of appropriate reinforcement to be learned and strengthened. Undesired behaviors must occur sufficiently in the absence of reinforcement to become extinguished (to some minimal level). When we suppress undesired behaviors by other means, we should expect them to recur when the "other means" are no longer available, i.e., after discharge.

How can we avoid the problems with rewards and punishments? First, we must think in psychological terms of reinforcing behavior as opposed to rewarding behavior.

Second, we must avoid our own desire to "appropriately" punish a child, to effect a dramatic change in behavior through unpleasant or painful consequences. We can approach this ideal by thinking in terms of preventing or removing reinforcements when negative behavior occurs and in terms of negative consequences (not negative reinforcements) rather than punishment. We can attend more carefully to the child's feelings as well as to the child's behavior. We can also attend more carefully to our own feelings.

Thinking in terms of reinforcements and negative consequences, then, may enable us to focus more on teaching children appropriate behaviors and self-control, rather that on motivating and controlling children with artificially contrived rewards and punishments. There are several methods that if properly used may minimize some of the pitfalls of rewards and punishments. One alternative is to focus on natural and logical consequences. Another alternative is the point system.

Natural and Logical Consequences

Natural consequences are those that occur naturally, without any need for action on our part. Some of these consequences occur in nature; others are applied by other people. Logical consequences are consequences that we apply in logical response to a child's behavior (Popkin, 1993).

Natural Consequences

Natural consequences include such things as getting stuck by a thorn on a rose bush, falling and getting a bruise if running too fast on the stairs, burning a hand on a hot pan, cutting a finger with a knife, getting hit by a car when running into the street without looking, and getting punched in the nose when provoking an aggressive bully. Some of these natural consequences may be very good teachers; others are very dangerous. When the natural consequence may be dangerous, obviously, we must protect the child.

When natural consequences are not too dangerous, we should not only let them teach but also help them teach. We can let them teach by doing nothing. We can help them teach by empathizing with the child, by helping the child interpret what occurred, and by helping the child identify alternatives.

We can prevent natural consequences from teaching by taking away from the child's responsibility, by saying "I told you so," by applying our own consequences (punishments), and by trying to fix the problem for the child.

Of course, natural consequences may also be positive. Again, we can let them teach, help them teach, or we can interfere. We let them teach by doing nothing. We help them teach by sharing in the child's feelings, by interpreting, and by letting the child describe what happened. We can minimize the teaching of natural consequences by taking away from the child's responsibility, by taking credit for ourselves ("I told you you could do it"), and by offering additional rewards.

Negative Logical Consequences

When natural consequences may be too severe, when there are no natural consequences, or when the natural consequences do not affect the child, then we must intervene if we are to have an effect on behavior. Logical consequences are logically related to the behavior in question (Popkin, 1993). As with natural consequences, logical consequences may be positive or negative. Of course, we know that logical reinforcements for positive behavior will teach more than negative consequences for negative behavior.

Properly applied logical consequences that are negative do not convey punishment in the popular sense, although they do punish behavior in the learning sense. Moreover, when properly applied, they not only do not interfere with the child's sensitivity to adult disapproval, but also they augment it. In the following example, staff does not punish the child, but rather has the child think about the possible consequences of his behavior for others. This underscores the staff's disapproval by emphasizing the natural consequence of the loss of staff trust. It also prepares the child for a time in the future when the child might practice appropriate behavior.

> *Shoplifting.* **Upon returning from a trip to the grocery store with two boys, a staff member sees one of the boys, Bobby, with a candy bar. The staff knows that Bobby did not have any money.**

Staff: **Bobby, where did you get that candy?**

Bobby: **At the store.**

Staff: **I know you didn't have any money. How did you pay for it?**

Bobby: **I found some money.**

Staff: **I didn't see you find any money and I didn't see you buy anything. You stole the candy bar, didn't you?**

Bobby: **(Looks at floor, doesn't say anything.)**

Staff: **Well?**

Bobby: **Yeah.**

Staff: **I'm really sorry to hear that. How do you think that clerk feels?**

Bobby: **(Looks puzzled.) I don't know. He probably doesn't even miss it.**

Staff: **Well, my guess is that he just works there. The owner, however, probably has some sort of inventory system. He can tell when things are being stolen. Then he will ask the clerk what's happening to his profits. He might even think the clerk is stealing and fire him.**

Bobby: **You mean he would fire the clerk over one candy bar?**

Staff: **Well, maybe not one. But I'm not sure you haven't taken others, or that you won't do it again. Eventually, the owner is going to realize something is wrong.**

Bobby: **Yeah, I guess so. I guess I never thought much about it.**

Staff: **Well, you'll have to take it back, and I expect you'll want to apologize.**

Bobby: **. . . I guess so.**

Staff: **You guess so?**

Bobby: **OK. I'll apologize.**

Staff: **That's good. You know, it will be some time before I'm comfortable trusting you in the community again, so you won't be able to go to the store with us any more this week.**

Bobby: **Yeah. I understand. But I won't do it again.**

Staff: **Well, I hope not. We'll talk about it some more this weekend, and then maybe you can try again next week.**

Bobby: **(Dejectedly.) OK.**

Positive Logical Consequences

When positive logical consequences are used properly, we can minimize the appearance of bribing the child, trying to buy the child's cooperation, or using a perceived right as a reward. We can also minimize the contamination of the reinforcement through its taking on the status of an earned right.

> There will be no dessert if you don't clean your plate.

> versus

> I'll get the ice cream as soon as you've finished everything else.

> If you don't have any fights this week, you can have a home pass.

> versus

> If you can settle differences with the other kids this week without fighting, I'll get you a home pass so you can practice these same skills with your sister.

> If you go to school every day next week, you can earn a home pass this weekend.

> versus

> If you make it through school this week without any absences or suspensions, I'll get you a home pass so you can tell your folks how well you're doing. I'll bet they'll be pleased.

Girls who get up on time without any problems can have an extra snack.

versus

The normal bedtime is 9:00 P.M. However, girls who can get themselves up on time without any problems may stay up until 10:00.

The differences are subtle. The results may not be so subtle. These techniques require a sensitive and well-trained staff with the responsibility and authority to employ them, as well as a milieu that has the flexibility to allow them.

Point Systems

Properly designed point systems, when they are also properly used, can minimize some of the problems inherent in trying to motivate and control children with rewards and punishments. Point systems award or subtract points for specific behaviors. Specific privileges are awarded based on the number of points each child earns. Points, then, become conditioned reinforcements; when they are taken away, points can also serve as conditioned punishments.

Thus, points can be used to avoid some of the pitfalls of more traditional rewards and punishments. They can avoid the contamination of feelings or beliefs that a child might have about more specific rewards and punishments. Since the points are used in conjunction with a pre-defined system, the point system can also avoid some of the feelings a child might have about those in control of rewards and punishments. The system is in control. The only decision those in control need to make is whether or not a particular behavior has occurred. The system awards or takes away the points based on children's, not an individual's, behavior. Points are also less likely to distract from adult approval or disapproval and may even enhance their effects for the child, provided adult anger is kept under control. Excessive anger by staff may actually undermine the effectiveness of the points.

There are several keys to the effective design and use of a point system:

1. The logic behind the behaviors that are selected and designed for reinforcement or punishment.
2. The logic behind the reinforcements that are available for points and, consequently, denied to those who do not have the points.
3. The extent to which the staff accept the system; their ability to apply the system consistently, to be patient, and to allow the system to "do the work."
4. The extent to which residents accept the system as fair and reasonable.

The Logic Behind the Behaviors Selected

Most point systems I have seen identify desirable behaviors and assign points to each based on some judgement as to the relative value of each behavior. Behaviors such as getting up on time, making beds, hygiene, doing chores, coming to meals on time, going to therapy appointments and groups, participating in activities, behavior on outings, going to bed on time, brushing teeth, going to school, completing homework, keeping rooms clean, etc., are given point values. Children earn points for each.

Undesirable behaviors are listed, sometimes as rules, and assigned negative values. Behaviors such as cursing, fighting, stealing, lying, going into unauthorized areas, refusing to do chores, refusing to go to therapy, refusing to go to school, running away, cursing staff, assaulting staff, etc., are also given point values. When points are deducted or "fined," it will result in a restriction from some or all privileges for a period of time until enough positive points can be earned to offset the fine or deduction.

The logic of such a system is obvious. However, the logic is as much related to the orderly running of the unit or the institution as it is to the treatment of the child—perhaps even more related to the orderly running of the unit. Such systems, when they work, establish the children into routines and schedules, get them to meet certain responsibilities in the institution, and get them to therapy. Such systems result in fairly long lists of desirable behaviors and even longer lists of rules about undesirable behaviors so that each behavior may be assigned appropriate point values. However, since the specific behaviors that are defined for reinforcement and sanctions are so closely related to life in the institution, there is frequently little generalization to life outside the institution.

An Alternative. Behaviors such as following instructions, accepting criticism, using appropriate language, peer relations, adult relations, temper control, and accepting "no" can eliminate the long lists of institution-specific behaviors and get to the heart of the behaviors that typically cause problems for the types of children who come into residential treatment. Focusing on such behaviors allows staff (and residents) to focus on the acquisition and use of social skills that may readily generalize to home, school, jobs, and the community in general.

Rather than rewarding a child for doing a menial chore, this system rewards the child for following an instruction to do the chore. In order to receive the points, the child must listen to the instruction, acknowledge the instruction by saying something like "OK," maintain a pleasant affect, avoid grumbling, do the instruction, and check back after the task is complete.

Rather than following detailed schedules and obeying long lists of rules, children are reinforced for following instructions to either do things or to stop undesirable behaviors, to accept criticism when behavior is inappropriate, etc.

The Logic Behind the Selection of Reinforcements

The reinforcements most often used with point systems are privileges such as pool, TV, video games, outside activities, going to the store, outings, home passes, and allowances. Most often, these are viewed as rewards for earning points. When they are not earned, or when point fines are applied for misbehavior, the loss of privileges is often perceived of as a punishment in the colloquial

sense of inflicting pain, or at least unpleasantness, in a desire to change the child's behavior.

When the attitude can be established in the milieu that the point system is a measure of the child's responsibility and current level of functioning, that it is a measure, or at least some indication, of the child's ability to handle certain privileges at a given time, then the system appears less arbitrary. Children who have achieved certain point totals have demonstrated that they can manage the responsibilities of interacting with peers in the TV room, recreation areas, etc. They have demonstrated that they can be trusted to act responsibly on outings. They have evidenced progress in treatment in preparation for discharge; consequently, home passes are indicated as they move towards discharge. They have demonstrated skills that need to be practiced at home.

Conversely, residents whose behavior is not up to standards as evidenced by their point earnings are not presently welcome in recreation areas. Their behavior may disrupt others who are enjoying activities. They cannot be trusted to behave responsibly in the community. Since they are not progressing on goals as necessary for eventual discharge, providing a home pass without improved behavior is pointless—the child needs as much treatment as possible and needs to stay in treatment for the weekend. (When using this approach, I generally allow a "free" pass at the end of the month—most children also need time at home with parents and siblings, regardless of behavior.)

The Logic Behind the Selection of Negative Consequences

Despite the emphasis on positive social behaviors, it is necessary to list a few behaviors that require point fines. Point fines result in the loss of the opportunity to earn points towards privileges until the fine is paid off. The list of behaviors is kept to a minimum—aggression, theft, destroying property that the resident cannot pay for, substance abuse. Fines amount to a one- or a two-day restriction, if the resident recovers and resumes earning points. The restrictions are minimal, a maximum of two days, even for aggression against staff. Of course, a fine also means that the resident most likely cannot earn sufficient points for a weekend pass or community activities. But logically, such residents cannot be trusted in the community so soon after such behavior.

Antisocial children do not have to do much arithmetic to calculate whether or not the fine is worth the risk. The effects of the point fines are too insignificant. Consequently, negative behavior occasionally occurs. Should such residents complain about the consequences, it can almost always be demonstrated that others, staff and residents, have experienced more consequences from the misbehavior than the resident. The resident can almost always be focused on the amount of staff time devoted to investigation, the reports, the pain of another child who was hit. The resident can also usually be focused on the natural consequences of loss of trust, loss of affection from peers, or loss of status. The resident can hardly ever feel that he or she has "paid" for the transgression.

Staff Acceptance and Understanding

The strength of the point system stems from two things:

1. The point system clearly communicates in a systematized way what is expected.
2. The point system minimizes the contamination of reinforcements and negative consequences from all the various factors that may affect them.

Maximizing these two strengths requires staff support and their understanding of the system. When the system does not deal with behaviors or problems that the staff consider to be important, then staff are strongly influenced to circumvent the system, to go outside the system to deal with such problem behaviors.

The purpose of a properly defined point system is not to control the behavior of residents. Rather, it is to teach residents to control their own behavior. Teaching takes time. Residents learn through repetition of behaviors and the repetition of the positive and negative consequences of those behaviors. Staff must therefore be patient and consistent. They must let the system "do the work."

Staff can augment the point system in several ways. They can offer encouragment. Sometimes, but not always, expressing approval for positive behavior and accomplishments may be helpful. Occasionally, one encounters a child for whom expression of adult approval seems to serve more as a negative consequence than as a reinforcement. Staff can also augment the system by being empathetic with residents who fail to earn desired privileges, especially when they have expended some effort yet have still failed. This may serve to reduce the appearance of a punitive response in the sense of wishing to cause the child discomfort or pain.

Staff can also undermine the system in countless ways. Staff often feel a need to assert their authority, threatening to "take points" in a punitive way instead of stating something like "You're losing points" or "If your behavior doesn't improve, you'll lose points," in a calm tone. They may stray from strict definitions of behavior, feeling a need for stronger consequences, and attempt to fit a behavior into a category that will result in a higher point fine. They may seek to augment consequences with verbal punishment or humiliation. They may also undermine positive consequences, giving earned points begrudgingly or telling the child she doesn't really deserve an earned privilege. They may simply fail to attend fully to behavior, fail to award positive points, or overlook or excuse certain negative behaviors.

It is important that communication about the point system be open at all times. No point system can fit all contingencies that may arise. When too many things occur with which the point system cannot deal effectively, then changes are indicated.

Resident Acceptance

It is not unusual for a resident to tell staff to "take all my points. I don't care." This is usually an indication that the system is effective and meaningful, rather than the contrary. The same resident two weeks later may argue at length over an interpretation that involves but one or two points. Residents also sometimes complain that another resident has gotten off too lightly. It is carefully explained that the purpose of the program is to teach responsible behavior, not to punish children. Consequently, misbehaving children seldom gain status with peers for suffering a punishment with nobility. And if they complain, they lose even more status with peers.

SUMMARY

Certain principles apply in behavior modification, in whatever form it is attempted:

1. The behavior modifier must decide who is to be involved in choosing behaviors to change.
2. Behaviors to be changed must be clearly defined to facilitate desired changes. While undesirable behaviors that are to be extinguished often appear to be most important, it is nearly always best to identify behaviors to be acquired that will interfere with undesirable behaviors. It is easier to teach new behaviors than to extinguish established behaviors. Further, results are more likely to generalize to other settings and to last longer.
3. Reinforcements must be selected. They should not be too large or they will interfere with the effectiveness of adult approval as a possible reinforcement.
4. If punishments are to be used, they must be selected carefully. Severe punishments are likely to have undesirable effects.

5. Naturally occurring reinforcements or punishments are also important. For example, withdrawal of a reinforcement may have a punishing effect. Consider loss of peer approval.
6. Many of the negative aspects of punishment can be avoided if naturally occurring consequences are allowed to work without additional negative consequences being applied.
7. When negative consequences must be applied, many of the negative aspects of punishment can be avoided if the negative consequences are logically related to the behavior rather than merely designed to hurt the child in proportion to the misbehavior.
8. Motivation is dependent upon a number of factors, only some of which are related to contingent rewards or punishments.
9. Environmental cues that precede behavior may be very important.
10. Feelings may be changed along with (or instead of) behavior.
11. If behavior does not change as desired, either something is wrong with the plan, or something is going wrong in the implementation of the plan.
12. Behavioral systems such as token economies or point systems, when properly designed and implemented, can be effective in changing behavior. Targeted behaviors may or may not generalize to settings outside the residential setting, depending on how they are defined.
13. It is difficult to teach children self-control, but teaching self-control is usually easier than controlling the child, which is often impossible to do with rewards and punishments.

Using Behavior Modification for Management, Treatment, and Therapy

TERMS like behavior management, behavior treatment, and behavior therapy have appeared, perhaps in an attempt to avoid the negative associations of behavior modification, perhaps in an attempt to sound more professional or more therapeutic. Some behavior modifiers might object to the association with disease or medical models implied by therapy or treatment. Behavior modifiers have argued against viewing clients as "sick" or in need of a "cure"; problem behaviors are learned just like any other behaviors in accordance with principles of learning, and they can be corrected in accordance with those same principles (Neuringer, 1970).

Nevertheless, I believe that the terms "behavior management," "behavior treatment," and "behavior therapy" can be used to differentiate three concepts that represent somewhat separate and distinct uses of behavior modification. In this chapter, I will propose definitions for these concepts and illustrate uses of each, both with individuals and in group settings.

BEHAVIOR MANAGEMENT

Definition: Behavior management is the deliberate attempt to improve behavior in a specific setting using principles of learning without regard to the effects on behavior outside the setting. The behavior within the setting is the primary focus.

The residential treatment program may be very concerned with prompt response to fire drills, safety in vehicles, staying out of the kitchen, housekeeping, schedules for meals, showers, study hall, and bedtime. The more time staff spend on routines, the less time they have for other things, such as treatment and having fun with the kids, which may be one of the most important requisites for treatment. The therapist needs to have the child come to sessions before anything can happen and needs to have certain rules followed in the group, as well as to establish certain attitudes in the group.

The teacher requires certain behaviors in the classroom that are not necessary on the playground.

Applications of principles of learning can be extremely effective in establishing desirable behavior in given settings with a minimum of effort so that time and energy can be devoted to more important matters. When used in conjunction with principles of group dynamics, principles of learning may also be used to establish desired norms in the residential milieu. Unfortunately, much of what is passed off as behavior therapy or behavior treatment is behavior management, with little chance for behaviors to generalize to other settings, or for treatment or therapy to occur.

BEHAVIOR TREATMENT

Definition: Behavior treatment is the deliberate attempt to improve one or more problems with overt behavior using principles of learning. It is recognized that there may be some reduction in emotional problems as behaviors improve, but emotional problems are not specifically targeted.

For some children, feelings are relatively appropriate, but inappropriate behaviors or lack of appropriate behaviors get them into trouble. It is sometimes appropriate to get very angry when frustrated with others, oneself, or a situation. It is rarely appropriate to curse others, slam doors, punch walls, scream and yell, throw things, hit things, or hit people. Treatment of behavior can solve a lot of problems for such a child and the family.

When severe emotional problems are being successfully treated through more traditional therapeutic interventions, treatment of behavioral problems is usually still indicated. The child with the unmanageable rage may still need to learn behaviors other than smashing things or hitting people while the therapist works with her rage.

There may be additional problems with behavior that are not seriously related to emotional problems, such as the need to improve manners or hygiene.

BEHAVIOR THERAPY

Definition: Behavior therapy is the deliberate attempt to improve one or more serious emotional problems and associated behaviors using principles of learning.

While behavioral treatment may improve the behaviors of children with severe emotional disturbances, resulting in fewer problems because of improvements in behavior, it is also possible to apply principles of learning to change inappropriate feelings or feelings that occur at inappropriate times. It is sometimes possible to teach new feelings. It does not appear that children are born with a concern for others; such feelings are learned and may be taught.

Some children have quite simply never learned to control their tempers; other children may feel a rage that is so intense that it is virtually uncontrollable. Some children feel genuinely sorry when they cause a problem or an injury to someone else, others feel no remorse at all, still others feel so much guilt that they cannot function. Some children seem genuinely fond of others, while other children seem to use others for whatever they can get, ignoring people until they need something. Some children simply don't do what they're told to do, others get into such a state of excitement when they're given an instruction that further communication is impossible.

Wolpe has been using principles of learning to change emotions for over thirty years. He concluded that (1962): "neurotic behavior consists of *persistent habits of learned (conditioned) unadaptive behavior acquired in anxiety-generating situations*, and that therapy depends upon the unlearning of this behavior'' (p. 555). Anxiety refers to responses of the autonomic nervous system to painful or noxious stimuli: rapid breathing, rapid pulse, raised blood pressure, perspiration, and muscular tension. Anxiety is unadaptive when it occurs when there is no real danger.

Of 210 neurotic patients treated by Wolpe using behavioral methods, nearly 90 percent were either cured or much improved after an average of thirty sessions. Forty-five of them were followed for from two to seven years with only one relapse. Wolpe hypothesized (1962):

> If a response inhibitory to anxiety can be made to occur in the presence of anxiety-evoking stimuli, it will weaken the connection between these stimuli and the anxiety response (p. 562).
>
> The autonomic effects of relaxation are the opposite of those of anxiety (p. 564).

Systematic desensitization therapy is among the techniques employed by Wolpe. He found it especially effective in treating phobias and habits of responding with anxiety to complex situations such as being rejected. ''Relaxation can counteract anxiety only if the latter is relatively weak'' (1962, p. 564). He employed three sets of operations. First, he trained the patient in relaxation. Next, he and the patient identified themes of the patterns of stimuli that produced the anxiety, e.g., situations of rejection, then listed and ranked different situations that might produce that anxiety. Finally, he had the patient imagine the least disturbing situation while undergoing relaxation until the patient could do so without anxiety, then proceeded through the list over several sessions until the patient could manage the most anxiety-producing situation on the list without anxiety (Wolpe, 1962).

It is not at all unusual to treat children who do not follow instructions or who do not accept criticism in ways that increase their anxiety in hope of coercing their cooperation—raised voice, angry facial expression, reminders (read ''threats'') of consequences, etc. Consider the consequences of

this if one of the problems the child has with instructions or criticism is the anxiety that such situations produce.

BEHAVIOR MANAGEMENT FOR AN INDIVIDUAL

In the following example, a program was designed for a fifteen-year-old boy who was unable to complete even one day of school because of uncooperative and argumentative behavior. Since the residential program depended on public schools for all education services, his failure to stay in school would eventually result in his being referred to another program with an on-grounds school. The goal was very clearly a management goal—for Roland to stay in school so that he could continue in the treatment program.

> *Roland.* **Roland was a fifteen-year-old ninth grade special education student. Prior to placement, Roland posed so many problems in school that he was placed on home bound instruction in November. (His special education status prohibited him from being expelled.) He had been involved in three fights and was most recently caught in the girls' bathroom.**
>
> **His biggest problem, however, was a habit of anticipating what adults were going to say and interrupting before they finished to explain why a criticism was unfair, why he shouldn't follow an instruction, etc. This occurred in any and every situation in which Roland thought he was going to receive an instruction or a criticism. He argued so incessantly that it was extremely difficult for any adult to communicate anything to him.**
>
> **Following placement, Roland was placed in a new school. During his first two weeks in his new school, the school called every day to have Roland picked up,**

sometimes before the driver who dropped him off could return to the facility. On one occasion, during instructions for state-wide standardized testing, Roland asked to go to the bathroom. While the teacher was trying to tell him that the test procedures required that everyone start together, Roland interrupted to explain why he had to go and left. He was surprised to learn that he couldn't attend school for the remainder of the day and the next two days because he had missed the beginning of three days of testing.

When asked where his free lunch form was, he launched into a lengthy account of how it wasn't his fault and that staff had failed to give it to him. When told to get off the principal's desk on which he sat, he explained to the principal why he had a right to be there and why she had no right to tell him to get off.

No one expected Roland to be able to resolve his problems in school in time to have a reasonable chance to graduate high school or that he had much of an educational future. However, Roland's being sent back from school every day was a serious problem for the program, which did not normally schedule staff during school hours. Moreover, it was a serious problem for Roland. If he got put out of school permanently again, he would have to be transferred to a program with an on-grounds school; there were none close to his home.

The program supervisor met with the principal and special education teacher and worked out a plan. They agreed that when Roland had a problem, the teacher would warn him one time. If he failed to correct his behavior, he would be sent to the office to call the program. Program staff would counsel Roland by phone to attempt to keep him in school. If Roland had a second problem that day, the school would call the program to have Roland picked up.

The plan was reviewed carefully with Roland, who was comfortable with the plan and objectives. Roland was motivated to stay in school. Consequences of being back from school for disciplinary reasons were fairly serious—no interaction with staff, an unappetizing but nutritious cheese sandwich, milk, and fruit for lunch, and the day devoted to either school work or chores. The major consequence, however, was that Roland was the only boy who could not complete a full day of school, which cost him status not only with staff but also with peers.

Although motivated to stay in school, Roland was unable to stop his compulsive verbal behavior when receiving instructions or criticism. School personnel were unable to manage the behavior he presented, even though they, too, wanted very much to work with Roland. The plan gave both Roland and the school something to do to interrupt Roland's compulsive behavior—send him to make a phone call. Once his behavior was interrupted (stopped), staff reinforced Roland verbally for making the phone call, then reviewed with him the steps for following instructions and accepting criticism. When Roland got sent back later, staff reinforced Roland verbally for the amount of time he had completed in school for the day and applied consequences for being sent back in a matter-of-fact manner.

The first three days the plan was in effect, Roland called before 10:00 A.M. each day and the school called before lunch to have him removed. On one occasion, the school's call followed within five minutes of Roland's call. On Thursday, Roland called at 11:00 A.M. and finished his first day. Within three weeks, Roland was calling only three times per week and getting sent back only once per week. By the end of the quarter, Roland was calling only once or twice per week and being sent back only once or twice per month.

Roland was able to continue in the treatment program. He improved his social skills markedly. The next year, Roland enrolled in a half-day GED VoTech program and continued to make progress with his compulsive verbal behaviors. Following discharge, Roland subsequently completed his GED, enlisted in the military, and successfully completed basic training.

BEHAVIOR TREATMENT WITH
AN INDIVIDUAL

In this example, nine-year-old Donna failed to respond to the program's point system and other available reinforcements to perform satisfactorily in school. Even when she had a strong desire to pass for the year, Donna failed to complete the daily behaviors necessary to earn passing grades—completing class work, completing homework, and passing tests. The social worker was able to arrange daily reinforcements and nonpunitive negative consequences which changed school behavior. Whereas the goal for Roland was simply to keep him in school, the goal for Donna in this example is for long-term improvement in academic performance.

> *Donna.* **Donna was a nine-year-old whose father and stepmother could not manage her at home. Her temper tantrums were frequent and disruptive to the rest of the household. School problems, however, were the major concern: class disruption, refusing to do class work and homework, frequent suspensions, and failing grades. Donna was above average in intelligence but had been in danger of failing and a "behavior problem" since the first grade.**
>
> **Donna entered the group home in February; she continued to attend the same class in the same school. Problems with behavior, class work, and homework improved just enough so that she could pass if she passed two classes in summer school. She passed them with D's.**
>
> **Donna realized how much she missed during the group home's summer program of local and out-of-town tours, swimming, and athletics; she did not want to have to go to summer school again and got off to a good start in the fourth grade. It didn't last. Linking school goals to the program's point system didn't help. Staff would check her homework to be sure it was done, make sure she had it in the morning, then get a note from the teacher that she hadn't handed it in.**

> **Nothing seemed to work. Donna didn't seem to care much about any of the privileges or about home passes, either. Although her desire to participate in the next summer program appeared to remain high, it had little or no effect on her daily performance in school.**
>
> **For the start of the second semester, the social worker arranged with Donna's parents for them to provide twenty-five cents per day to be awarded to Donna for her school performance. Donna would report to the social worker's office every day after school and show her school sheet. If she had homework and class work checked off as having been completed for four out of six classes, she would get a quarter. Whether she had a good school sheet or not, she would be allowed to call her stepmother, who would ask how she had done. If Donna failed to meet the criteria, her stepmother would say OK and hang up. If Donna met the criteria, her stepmother would chat with her for five minutes.**
>
> **Donna's school performance improved gradually but steadily. The criteria were later raised to five out of six classes. Donna passed for the year. Moreover, Donna's relationship with her stepmother appeared to have improved, as did the stepmother's feelings about Donna.**

BEHAVIOR THERAPY FOR
AN INDIVIDUAL

When strong emotions interfere with learning, the emotions must be addressed if behavior is to change. Taber (1981) reports on Steve, an eleven-year-old who was unable to control his temper despite verbal interventions and the reinforcements and negative consequences of the treatment facility's point system. Darlene is a similar example from my own experience. In both cases, a plan to address the anger itself was necessary before problems with behavior could be treated. Taber's study also highlights one of the problems with research in the residential setting—Steve relocated so that follow-up data was not available.

Steve. Steve was an eleven-year-old boy who had been placed in a small residential treatment center because of temper outbursts that included screaming, swearing, and fighting at the slightest provocation. The problems persisted for one year of placement despite verbal interventions by child care workers, the use of time-out, and the token economy, in which privileges were contingent on temper control. Problems included such things as fights over another boy's taking his seat or pen, and attacks on staff that required physical intervention when told to put his bike away and come for dinner. Steve had a history of abuse, neglect, and abandonment by both parents. He was motivated to solve his temper problems so that he could go to a foster home.

The target behaviors of swearing, hitting, and fighting were carefully defined. Child care workers recorded base lines for each behavior for nine weekdays over a two-week period prior to the intervention, recording seven fights, twenty-two instances of hitting, and seventeen instances of swearing.

The intervention included self-monitoring, cognitive preparation for verbal self-instruction, practice of verbal self-instruction, and application of verbal self-instruction. For self-monitoring, Steve carried a notebook in which he checked off each time he stopped himself from one of the target behaviors.

Cognitive preparation for verbal self-instruction included six elements. Steve was taught to identify situations and people that triggered his anger, to identify the difference between anger and aggression, and that he could become angry without hitting someone. He began to explore the cues that were present when he became angry, what his body felt like, his stomach, etc. Steve learned to recognize cues early, that he was going to get into trouble when his stomach got tight.

He was taught to discriminate between justified and unjustified anger, and that sometimes it was all right to get angry. He was introduced to the concepts of managing his anger, controlling himself, and substituting other behaviors for hitting and swearing.

For practice of the verbal self-instruction, Taber first modeled the process of self-instruction out loud for a particular anger-producing circumstance or person and had Steve practice. She then modeled the process with whispered self-instructions and had Steve practice. Finally, she modeled the process silently with gestures of thinking and had Steve practice. The process included defining the problem, deciding to not get angry, deciding on something that could solve the problem, trying it, then giving himself reinforcement. Steve was then sent out to the unit to practice. Taber met with him before bedtime to review.

Finally, the verbal self-instruction was conceptualized and generalized to all situations that might get Steve angry. Over a five-week period, two fights were recorded, twenty-nine instances of hitting, and twenty instances of swearing. Fighting, which had been occurring almost daily, was virtually eliminated. Swearing and hitting were reduced by 41 and 47 percent. Child care workers reported that Steve was handling his anger more appropriately. Follow-up data was not possible because Steve relocated (Taber, 1981).

Darlene. Darline was a fourteen-year-old girl who did not get along well with the other girls. She shared few interests with them, was extremely ineffectual in conversation, and had such poor hygiene that the other girls teased her. Frequently a victim of pranks or teasing, she occasionally became violently angry, throwing and breaking things. She then attacked staff who attempted to calm her down. Darlene had a history of physical abuse and had been in two prior placements, including a psychiatric hospital. She said she wanted to go home and visited with her parents regularly, but staff had some doubts over her feelings about going home.

After a year in the program, Darlene's temper tantrums began to increase to the point that she had to be physically controlled several times per month, sometimes several times per week, and once four times in one day. Since she was on a point system that awarded points for temper control and fined points for property damage, she failed to earn privileges and home passes.

In sessions with a supervisor, Darlene was helped to understand that, when she "felt bad," she did something "bad," which made her feel worse, which made her do more "bad" things, a vicious circle. It often took her several hours in the supervisor's office until she could calm down and return to the program, at which point she always cleaned up all that she had done, accepted consequences, and felt good for several days. She agreed that when she did "good," she felt good.

Since she didn't like getting angry, Darlene agreed to try a plan. When she started getting angry, she would stop what she was doing and start doing something that would make her feel good. Darlene and the supervisor made a list of things that made Darlene feel good. Since Darlene liked to help people, many items on the list had to do with helping other girls or staff with chores. Other items were paying someone a compliment and brushing her teeth, which was a goal on her service plan.

Darlene also agreed that when she got angry, she very quickly reached the point where she wasn't thinking clearly. She would therefore have to act quickly at the first signs of becoming angry if the plan were to work. Later she would talk to staff about whatever she felt angry about. She agreed to report to the supervisor daily on her use of the plan.

For several weeks, Darlene reported with some pride on things that she did to help her feel good when she was about to get

angry. Restraints decreased dramatically. She returned home nine months later. Two years after discharge, she appeared happy and well. She had a summer job and was looking forward to her sophomore year at high school.

BEHAVIOR MANAGEMENT WITH GROUPS

Management of behavior in the group setting is of special concern in residential treatment. The first example, wearing seat belts in the agency van, illustrates the use of principles of learning in conjunction with principles of group dynamics to establish a simple routine. The next two examples, violence and theft, illustrate the uses of learning theory in conjunction with principles of group dynamics to address more serious but all-too-common problems. While violence and theft may be treatment issues for individual children, when they occur too frequently in the residential setting they quickly become management issues and are most effectively approached as such.

Seat Belts—Establishment of a Simple Routine

In the following example, negative consequences failed to establish a behavior of wearing seat belts in the agency van. Reinforcement in the group setting was successfully employed to produce vicarious learning.

Seat belts. Getting the kids to wear their seat belts in the van was always a problem. A few would put their belts on when they got in the van; some would put them on when instructed to do so; others would buckle them but not pull them tight; those who sat in the back wouldn't put them on unless the driver refused to move until they complied.

Occasionally, a staff would stop the van, instruct everyone to put his hands on the ceiling, then walk through the van to see who had his belt on; those who did not lost points for not "following instructions." Seat belts, however, continued to be a hassle.

One morning, the driver instructed the boys in normal tones to put on their seat belts, then started the van and drove away. At the end of the driveway, rather than pulling out into traffic, he turned the van off and instructed everyone to put his hands on the ceiling. He went carefully through the van, noting who had his seat belt properly fastened and who did not. Without saying a word, he took the boys to school.

When he picked them up after school, he had a crisp one dollar bill for each of the six boys who had his seat belt properly buckled. The next morning, twelve buckles snapped almost in unison and straps were pulled tight. A repeat was given in a few days; twelve boys received one dollar.

Occasional repeats of about once per month by different drivers resulted in a marked decrease in the amount of effort required to have children properly buckled in. Both staff and residents had fun with the procedure.

Violence—Changing Group Norms

Norms for aggressive and violent behavior are fairly normal among some groups of children, especially boys. In the following example, the daily routine of the group (school) was interrupted by an external force (program staff) to produce pressure for change of the norm for aggressive behavior. Principles of avoidance learning (the threat that the interruption of normal routine might continue through the weekend) were used to motivate all members of the group. Except for this threat, however, no other coercion was used. Free discussion, with verbal reinforcement for participants, was the primary intervention, with the goal of having group pressures get individuals to agree publicly to change their behavior.

Violence. Incidents of violence towards peers had shown an alarming increase in a group home for twelve boys ranging in age from ten to sixteen years. Jerome had little history of behavior problems. He was in placement primarily for school refusal since going to live with an aunt and because, at fifteen, he was too old to place in available foster homes. After a few weeks in the program, a thirteen-year-old made a snide comment about Jerome's breath, not because there was a problem with Jerome's breath, but merely as a taunt. Jerome turned away, then turned back and struck the boy in the face without warning. The boy suffered cuts around the eye.

Two weeks later, Jerome hit another younger boy in the face. The boy's glasses broke, and he was cut near the eye. Again, the provocation was only verbal and the blow came without warning.

Moreover, several other boys were saying that the latter boy had finally gotten "what he deserved." Yet another boy was talking about what he was going to do if he ever found out who took his favorite rock music tape. Finally, two other boys were involved in a fight; staff had some difficulty breaking it up, and both boys were saying that it wasn't over.

The treatment team leader made the decision to keep the boys out of school on Thursday. On Thursday morning, a supervisor arrived at wake-up time and told the boys that they would not be going to school. Instead, he informed them of the day's scheduled activities. After breakfast and chores, there would be a group to discuss violence in the program. The group would continue until the team leader was satisfied that the boys, as a group, understood the concepts that would be taught. If necessary, the group would continue on Friday. The team leader emphasized his willingness to change his personal plans so that they could continue through the weekend, if necessary.

The team leader explained carefully that this was not punishment but concern. Smoking would be permitted; regular meals would be served. **Even the boys who were not involved were affected by having to witness the violence and by having their home disrupted. Most of the boys were attentive to the group activities; a few seemed to have a somewhat cavalier attitude. The team leader made little attempt to control attitudes or participation but verbally reinforced active participants.**

Concepts of living without rules were explored, as well as living by violence. Legal concepts of first- and second-degree murder and of voluntary and involuntary manslaughter were covered, along with legal concepts of self-defense, which covers only protection, not retaliation.

After a nice lunch, an oral "test" was given. Boys who gave correct answers received positive reinforcement. Several boys had trouble with some of the concepts that had been covered. They were not criticized. The team leader stated calmly that he would continue until everyone fully understood the issues and concepts.

The team leader presented the material again, still informally, and followed with another oral test. More boys paid attention. Those who occasionally got off task were encouraged by their peers to get down to business. By 4:30 P.M., the team leader was able to announce that he was satisfied with the group's understanding and attitudes and return the home to regular programming. Violence in the program was not a problem for over one year.

Changing Group Norms Towards Theft

I have used a similar approach for dealing with theft on a larger unit for thirty adolescent male children. The goal was clearly a management goal: to stop rampant theft on the unit. The external pressure on the group interrupted the group's normal weekend schedule, not for punishment but rather for treatment. Again, this was done out of concern. Children's complaints about "punishment" were mitigated by the fact that all administrative, supervisory, and treatment personnel, who were nor-

mally off duty on weekends, were also present for the "treatment weekend."

Again, discussion was the primary intervention, coupled with attempts to build cohesiveness among residents and staff through cooperative work details to improve security on the unit. Again, verbal reinforcement was used to promote vicarious learning and group pressures for public statements to the effect that theft would no longer be accepted in the living unit. Change was reinforced by return to normal programming (escape learning).

Theft. **In a unit for thirty adolescents from mixed inner city and rural backgrounds, theft had escalated to the point that it was obvious that even the boys who were not participating were at least condoning it. Rooms were entered; lockers were broken into; clothes, radios, and jewelry were taken. Incidents were occurring once or twice per week. Kids lost valuables; staff spent lots of time looking for stolen property that was never recovered, and the dangers of violent retaliation if a boy ever caught someone stealing from him seemed very real. After a radio was stolen, it was announced that a treatment weekend would be held to deal with theft from residents in the program. Passes would be rescheduled for the following weekend.**

On Saturday, supervisors and social workers arrived with tools and hardware to repair lockers and damaged door locks. Each took a group of six boys to discuss issues around theft—the boys' not caring about thieves taking the possessions of others so long as they didn't catch the thief with their own possessions, prohibitions against "ratting," feelings of the victim, the fact that no one could feel secure about his possessions, etc. Although theft in the community (shoplifting) was also a problem, it was not discussed. The focus was kept strictly on theft from residents on the unit.

Appropriate statements were verbally reinforced. Then work details were established to repair lockers. Groups were reconvened later in the afternoon. The radio

turned up without having been requested. Problems with theft on the unit disappeared for about three months. The next treatment weekend for theft put the matter to rest for over six months.

BEHAVIOR TREATMENT WITH GROUPS: A SAMPLE POINT SYSTEM

While many point systems seem to be primarily related to managing behavior within the treatment setting, including chores, routines, participation in activities and school, and various disruptive behaviors, it is also possible to use a point system to teach behavior skills and to treat behaviors that are typically problematic for children in the program. In the following example, the emphasis is placed on social skills rather than schedules, routines, and chores. I have chosen to present it as it might appear in an agency's Policy and Procedures Manual or Program Manual.

A Sample Point System

I. Purpose:
    A. To teach residents appropriate pro-social skills that will empower them to function more successfully in a variety of settings.
    B. To reinforce residents for using those skills.
    C. To provide logically appropriate sanctions for selected inappropriate behaviors.
    D. To individualize learning according to the specific needs of individual residents.
    E. To allow residents to accept responsibility for their own behavior.
    F. To gradually reduce the resident's dependence on more immediate reinforcements and provide a means by which natural reinforcements replace points and privileges as reinforcements for the use of prosocial skills.

G. To provide a mechanism by which residents may gain status with staff and peers for appropriate behavior.
H. To provide a record of behavior and progress.

II. Philosophy:
    A. Many residents coming into treatment have problems with behavior in a variety of settings. This point system is designed to assist in the teaching of social skills and to reinforce residents for using those skills. It is designed to promote learning and to teach responsibility. It is not designed to control behavior. Learning requires practice and repetition. Residents learn best as they either use skills and receive reinforcements or fail to use skills and miss out on reinforcements.

    Likewise, residents who exhibit inappropriate behaviors learn as they produce those behaviors and receive the consequences. For most residents, several repetitions may be necessary. The fact that a consequence is prescribed, threatened, or applied is not expected to control behavior. Most often, it is the repeated application of the consequence for the repetition of the behavior that eventually teaches or helps the resident to learn.

    B. Home passes are most important. Since eventual discharge depends on the resident's progress in treatment, most home passes are made contingent on progress in treatment. Residents who are experiencing difficulties in treatment generally benefit from the additional treatment available on weekends. However, since each resident needs time at home with his or her family regardless of progress in the program, each resident will receive at least one home pass per month regardless of behavior or progress.

III. Policy:
    A. The point system provides the primary means for formal reinforcement or sanc-

tion of behavior. Use of other reinforcements or sanctions (except for verbal praise or criticism) is to be avoided unless, in unusual circumstances, the treatment team or the Director of Treatment prescribe special sanctions or reinforcements.

B. Prior to discharge, each resident must complete ninety days off the point system. Behavior during the thirty days immediately preceding discharge must be at a level that would merit full privileges for points on any previous level.

IV. Procedures:

A. Levels: There are five levels with increasing responsibilities and privileges.

1. *Adjustment*. Residents begin the program on Adjustment. Residents on Adjustment are responsible for learning the expectations of the program; staff are responsible for teaching expectations, getting to know the resident, and completing an assessment.

Residents on Adjustment are on ''eyesight.'' They must remain under the direct supervision of staff at all times. Eyesight:

a. protects new residents from possible exploitation by others.

b. protects others from victimization by new residents who have not yet been fully assessed.

c. facilitates the assessment of new residents and promotes their attachment to staff rather than other residents.

Residents on Adjustment are able to earn most daily privileges and limited weekly privileges. Adjustment is designed to last approximately thirty days, depending on the performance of the individual resident. The completion of the Individual Treatment Plan with staff and their families is a requisite for advancement to Level 1.

2. *Level 1*. Residents on Level 1 are responsible for responding appropriately to staff and for beginning to work on their treatment goals. Residents receive reminders from staff as to expectations and problems. They may earn points in virtually all areas if they respond appropriately to correction.

Residents on Level 1 may earn most daily and weekly privileges, including two home passes per month. Level 1 is designed to last approximately ninety days. This allows staff time to get to know a resident well enough to make decisions about the resident's ability to handle the responsibilities of the unsupervised privileges that are available on Level 2.

3. *Level 2*. Most treatment takes place while the resident is on Level 2. The resident is responsible for his or her own behavior and is expected to meet program and individual treatment expectations without reminders or prompting from staff.

Residents on Level 2 may earn all available daily and weekly privileges, including unsupervised outings and one extra home pass per month. Level 2 is expected to last approximately twelve months, depending on the individual resident's progress on specific treatment goals.

4. *PreTerm*. Residents on PreTerm have met nearly all treatment objectives. PreTerm residents are expected to exhibit appropriate behavior without the reinforcement of daily privileges for daily points. Points are totalled weekly rather than daily. Residents earn daily and weekly privileges for the coming

week based on their weekly point total for the preceding week.

Residents on PreTerm are beginning the transition to home and the community. They may earn home passes every week. They are responsible for maintaining treatment gains and appropriate behavior without daily reinforcements from daily points. PreTerm is designed to last approximately ninety days.

5. *Term.* Residents on Term are responsible for their behavior without the daily or weekly reinforcement of points and privileges. All privileges are available.

Residents on Term receive home passes of forty-eight hours on weekdays. If they meet responsibilities while on weekday passes and when at the program, they may receive weekend passes every weekend as well. Term residents also receive one or more two-week trial discharges in preparation for return home.

B. Advancement criteria.

1. Residents earn advancement from Adjustment to Level 1 upon meeting all of the following conditions:

   a. A total of 2,500 points earned while on Adjustment (may be accomplished in four weeks).

   b. A total of 600 points earned for the week immediately preceding advancement to Level 1 (to insure ability to perform at an acceptable level).

   c. A completed Treatment Plan.

2. Residents earn advancement from Level 1 to Level 2 upon meeting all of the following criteria:

   a. A total of at least 7,500 points earned while on Level 1 (to

insure that staff have ample opportunity to get to know the resident and assess the resident's ability to handle unsupervised activities available on Level 2; may be accomplished in as little as ten weeks, but can generally be expected to require three to four months).

   b. A total of at least 2,500 points for the four weeks immediately preceding advancement to Level 2 (to insure the resident's ability to perform consistently over a period of time).

   c. A total of at least 600 points for the week immediately preceding advancement to Level 2 (to insure that the resident does not receive reinforcement following a problem week).

3. Residents earn advancement from Level 2 to PreTerm upon completing the following:

   a. All treatment goals established for advancement to PreTerm in their Individual Treatment Plans (indicates readiness to begin preparing for discharge).

   b. Formulation of goals with staff and family to be accomplished during PreTerm prior to advancement to Term.

4. Residents earn advancement from PreTerm to Term upon completing the following:

   a. All goals established for PreTerm as established above.

   b. Formulation of goals with staff and family to be accomplished while on Term prior to discharge.

5. Residents are discharged upon successful completion of goals during Term, which will normally include the successful completion of a two-

week trial discharge during which the resident is expected to meet home and school responsibilities.

C. Scoring.

1. Earning points.

   a. 100 points per day or 700 points per week are available to be earned.

   b. Bonus points are also available for extraordinary behaviors.

   c. Categories and point values differ somewhat from level to level, as indicated on point sheets.

   d. Residents are considered to have earned their points for any category when they complete the twenty-four-hour period without a negative entry for that category.

   e. Behavioral definitions establishing criteria for each behavioral category are attached (see below).

   f. Bonus points may be awarded at the discretion of staff for any behavior that is considered to be extraordinary for a given resident. Bonus points may not exceed more than 50 percent of the point value for the behavioral category in which the points are awarded.

2. Personal goals (PG) and personal school goals (PSG).

   a. Residents on Levels 1, 2, and PreTerm have personal goals that are handwritten on their point sheets in accordance with their Individual Treatment Plans. Goals may also be established in individual staffings to address specific problems that may arise.

   b. Personal goals may relate to behaviors not covered by the system. Personal goals may also relate to behaviors covered by the system to tailor behaviors to the individual needs of individual children, e.g., "follow instructions with one reminder" (for children on Level 2 with unusual difficulties); "control temper without hitting"; "control temper without breaking things"; "control temper without profanity" (in progression to allow a child to earn points for temper control according to his or her increasing abilities).

3. Point fines.

   a. A few selected behaviors may result in point fines of from fifty to 200 points for each occurrence. Definitions for these behaviors and prescribed point fines are attached (see below).

   b. When a point fine is recorded, the resident loses any privileges previously earned and may not earn points towards privileges until earning sufficient points to pay off the fine.

4. Totaling points.

   a. Staff total daily points for each resident between the hours of 3:00 and 4:00 P.M., after school or activities.

   b. Staff total weekly points on Thursdays between the hours of 3:00 and 4:00 P.M. along with the daily points for Thursday.

   c. Points earned towards point fines do not count towards daily or weekly totals. Thus, a 100-point fine will result in loss of privileges for two or more days, one day to pay off the fine, and one day in which to earn points towards privileges. Point fines also affect weekly privileges.

5. Privileges.
  a. Daily and weekly privileges differ from level to level. A schedule of privileges is attached (see below).
  b. For Adjustment, Level 1, and Level 2, daily privileges are awarded as earned after daily points have been totalled. Residents on PreTerm receive daily privileges for the coming week based on their previous weekly point total.
  c. Weekly privileges are awarded when weekly points have been totalled on Thursdays. Weekly privileges require a point total of at least seventy-five points for the day the privilege is to be used. Many weekly privileges such as home passes and unsupervised outings may also require staff and parental permission.

V. Daily Privileges
  A. 0–69 points, or restriction
    1. Basic privileges: The following privileges are available to any resident, regardless of points or restrictions, as long as the resident handles the privilege responsibly.
      a. Table games: cards, checkers, chess, Monopoly, etc., in the dining room.
      b. Telephone: five minutes to or from parents.
      c. Outside: one hour under staff supervision
  B. 70–79 points
    1. TV room and television
  C. 80–89 points
    1. Rec room: pool table, table tennis, fooseball
    2. Telephone: in addition to five minute call to or from parents:
      a. Adjustment: ten minutes to or from parents

      b. Level 1 and Level 2: fifteen minutes to or from any approved family member or friend
    3. Outside: All residents with the points may have unlimited time with staff supervision
  D. 90 points and above
    1. Rec room: pinball and video games
    2. Telephone:
      a. Level 2: Additional fifteen minutes of telephone time, as available, up to thirty minutes total for the day, in addition to five minute call with parents
    3. Outside:
      a. Level 2:
        1. May request permission to go outside without staff supervision
        2. May request permission for a thirty-minute walk to the store without staff supervision

VI. Weekly Privileges
  A. 0–549 points, or when on restriction
    1. Basic privileges: The following privileges are available to anyone, regardless of points or restrictions, as long as the resident handles the privilege responsibly.
      a. Allowance: $1
      b. Weekend activities: Daytime activities on Saturdays and Sundays, and Saturday evening activities
      c. Extra jobs for pay: Any resident may work an extra job for pay with staff permission. If the resident does not have the privilege of receiving pay, the pay will be placed into an account to be collected later according to the resident's level and weekly point totals. Any balance in the account will be given upon discharge.

d. Home passes: Any resident who has completed Adjustment but who has failed to earn a home pass during the month may have a "free" home pass on the last weekend of the month.

B. 550–599 points
1. Adjustment: $3 allowance
2. Level 1: $3 allowance
3. Level 2: $3 allowance
4. PreTerm: Daily privileges for the following week include:
   a. TV room and television
   b. Rec room: pool, table tennis, and fooseball
   c. Fifteen minutes of telephone time
   d. $3 allowance
   e. Friday night activity
   f. Home pass (limit, two per month)

C. 600–649 points
1. Adjustment:
   a. $4 allowance
   b. Friday night supervised outing
2. Level 1:
   a. $4 allowance
   b. May receive pay for any extra jobs worked during the week
   c. Friday night supervised outing
   d. Home pass (limit, two per month)
3. Level 2:
   a. $4 allowance
   b. May receive pay for any extra jobs worked during the week
   c. May request up to $5 from personal account for an approved purpose
   d. Friday night supervised outing
   e. Home pass (limit, two per month)
4. PreTerm:
   a. All daily privileges, including thirty minutes phone

   b. $4 allowance
   c. May receive pay for any extra jobs worked during the week
   d. May request up to $10 from personal account for an approved purpose
   e. Home pass that does not count towards two-pass limit

D. 650–699 points
1. Adjustment: $5 allowance
2. Level 1:
   a. $5 allowance
   b. May request up to $5 from personal account for an approved purpose
3. Level 2:
   a. $5 allowance
   b. May request up to $10 from personal account for an approved purpose
   c. May request permission for an unsupervised outing in the community of up to eight hours
   d. May have a home pass that does not count towards the two-pass limit
4. PreTerm:
   a. $5 allowance
   b. May request any amount from personal account for an approved purpose
   c. May request permission for an unsupervised outing in the community of up to twelve hours
   d. May have a fourth home pass for the month

E. 700 points or more
1. $7 allowance

VII. Inappropriate Behaviors and Consequences: The following behaviors are inappropriate almost anywhere in our society. There are usually consequences beyond the restriction specified, such as loss of trust, loss of respect, loss of affection or friendship, or even possible criminal charges.

A. 50 point restriction
   1. Being in another resident's room.
   2. Being in the kitchen or an office when no staff is present and without permission.
B. 100 point restriction
   1. Hitting another person, when occurring within the program.
   2. Brandishing or wielding an object as a weapon, when occurring within the program.
   3. Verbally threatening to harm someone or something.
   4. Threatening to harm oneself to gain advantage or avoid responsibility or consequences.
   5. Lying to gain advantage or to avoid responsibility or consequences.
   6. Theft, when occurring within the program.
   7. Use of alcohol or drugs, when occurring while on pass.
   8. Absence from the program or an assigned activity without permission for more than thirty minutes (100 points for each additional twenty-four-hour period).
C. 200 point restriction
   1. Hitting another person while in the community.
   2. Brandishing or wielding an object as a weapon in the community.
   3. Threatening with a weapon in the community.
   4. Theft in the community.
   5. Possession or use of alcohol or drugs in the program.
   6. Possession of an object designed primarily for use as a weapon.
VIII. Behavior Definitions: The following definitions of expected behavior are offered for the guidance of residents and staff. On higher levels, some of these categories are combined into point categories.
   A. Eyesight:
      1. It is the resident's responsibility to be within eyesight of staff at all times when on "eyesight."
      2. Remain within eyesight of staff at all times unless clearly given permission to leave the area for a specific purpose, or remain in an area when staff leaves.
   B. Getting up on time:
      1. Out of bed on second wakeup call
      2. Refrain from complaining
      3. Refrain from returning to bed
   C. Hygiene:
      1. Teeth brushed
      2. Face and hands clean
      3. Hair appropriately cut and neatly combed
   D. Manners at meals:
      1. Properly dressed
      2. Properly groomed
      3. Hands washed
      4. On time
      5. Napkin on lap
      6. Refrain from loud talking
      7. Refrain from reaching in front of others
      8. Refrain from taking more food than you can eat
      9. Ask politely
      10. Ask to be excused
   E. School on time:
      1. On time
      2. All books, papers, homework, supplies, and any fees
   F. Chore:
      1. Completed on time
      2. Completed to specifications for the chore
      3. Checked and approved by staff
   G. Study hall behavior:
      1. Bring needed books and materials home from school
      2. Write down homework and study assignments
      3. Arrive on time

4. Refrain from disturbing others
5. Ask for help when needed
6. Complete assignments

H. Bed on time:
1. In sleep wear
2. Under covers
3. Lights out
4. Radio may play softly
5. Refrain from disturbing others
6. Refrain from getting up for one hour after retiring

I. School all day:
1. On time in the morning
2. No classes missed
3. Not sent back for any reason

J. No discipline at school:
1. No detentions
2. No punishwork
3. No suspensions
4. Being sent to the office does not count as discipline

K. Following instructions:
1. Look at the person giving the instruction
2. Listen to the instruction
3. Ask questions if you don't understand
4. State any objections calmly no more than once
5. Listen to the reply
6. Say "OK"
7. Go do the instruction
8. Check back

L. Accepting criticism:
1. Look at the person giving criticism
2. Listen to the criticism
3. Ask necessary questions if you don't understand
4. Say "OK"
5. Maintain appropriate voice tone
6. Refrain from pouting, muttering, profanity
7. It seldom helps, and almost always makes things worse, to attempt to explain yourself or to object

M. Accepting "no":
1. State objections clearly in a calm manner one time
2. Maintain pleasant voice tone
3. Refrain from whining
4. Refrain from complaining
5. Refrain from making threats
6. Control temper

N. Asking permission:
1. Ask politely to see or to touch property belonging to another
2. Ask politely to use property belonging to another
3. Ask politely to enter an office or room
4. Ask politely to be excused from a meal, an activity, or a responsibility
5. Ask politely to join in an activity
6. Ask politely to change the TV channel
7. Ask politely to use a privilege
8. State any disagreement appropriately one time and listen to reply
9. Refrain from demanding
10. Refrain from making threats
11. Accept "no"

O. Temper control:
1. Tell someone in a calm voice tone why you are angry
2. Listen to the reply
3. Express any disagreement calmly
4. Refrain from hitting
5. Refrain from throwing or breaking things
6. Refrain from cursing
7. Refrain from yelling
8. Refrain from stomping away and slamming doors

P. Peer relations:
1. Speak respectfully
2. Use appropriate voice tone
3. Use appropriate language
4. Ask permission to use another's property
5. Refrain from name-calling

6. Refrain from teasing
7. Refrain from insulting
8. Refrain from cursing
9. Refrain from touching
10. Refrain from hitting
11. Refrain from pushing
12. Refrain from throwing things

Q. Adult relations:
1. Maintain eye contact
2. Maintain pleasant voice tone
3. Answer when spoken to
4. Use appropriate language
5. Speak clearly and distinctly
6. Refrain from using slang
7. Refrain from name-calling
8. Refrain from cursing
9. Refrain from touching
10. Refrain from hitting
11. Refrain from pushing
12. Refrain from throwing things

R. Respecting property:
1. Ask permission to use property of others
2. Use property for the purpose intended
3. Put things away when finished
4. Return things in the condition in which received
5. Report any problems or damage promptly

S. Completing homework:
1. Write down all assignments completely and accurately
2. Bring home all needed material and books
3. Plan adequate time to study
4. Ask for help if needed
5. Turn in assignments on time
6. Avoid making excuses

T. Completing class work:
1. Be prepared
2. Take all needed material to class
3. Work on assignments when instructed
4. Ask questions or ask for help when you don't understand

5. Remain in seat
6. Look at the teacher when the teacher is talking
7. Raise hand to speak
8. Refrain from talking to others

Discussion

A point system virtually identical to this evolved over a five-year period in a group home for twelve boys ranging in age from ten to seventeen years. Most boys were between the ages of thirteen and fifteen. Most had diagnoses of Oppositional Defiant Disorder or Conduct Disorder. There was an occasional diagnosis of Depression or Attention Deficit Hyperactivity Disorder. Most boys were refusing parental supervision and experiencing major problems in school. A few boys had criminal charges. All boys had families with which to visit on weekends. Most boys were expected to return home upon completion of the program. A few boys came from other programs or foster care with some history of prior placement.

The system was implemented by well-trained child care counselors with college degrees under the direction of a full-time supervisor. It was used in conjunction with teaching interactions and life space interviews, with routines established in practice by staff direction rather than by posted schedules and lists of rules.

Point sheets were posted on the wall outside of the staff office on clips that were fastened to the wall and labeled with each boy's name. Sheets were posted in descending order, from Term to Adjustment, with sheets in each level descending by the length of time or seniority on each level. Term sheets were simply white sheets of paper on which staff could make notes; PreTerm sheets were yellow; Level 2 sheets, green; Level 1, blue; and Adjustment, pink. This contributed to the status of each level.

Occasionally, a point sheet would disappear or get torn up by an angry resident. When this happened, the resident could not earn points until he requested a new point sheet from staff. Torn point

FIGURE 10.1: Adjustment

Adjustment

Name: _____   Week ending date: _____

Points last week: _____   Points towards
Level 1 to date: _____

	Fri	Sat	Sun	Mon	Tue	Wed	Thr
dinner manners 2							
evening chore 2							
study hall 2							
homework 2							
shower 2							
laundry 2							
bedtime 2							
up on time 2							
hygiene 2							
proper dress 2							
breakfast manners 2							
room 2							
bed 2							
morning chore 2							
ready for school 2							
school all day 10							
no discipline at school 10							
proper use of property 5							
proper verbal with peers 5							
proper verbal with adults 5							
proper physical/peers 5							
proper physical/adults 5							
followed instructions 5							
accepted criticism 5							
accepted "no" 5							
temper control 5							
eyesight 5							
points earned 100							
point fines							
Daily Total							

Weekly Total _____   Points towards Level 1 _____

Level 1

Name: _____   Week ending date: _____

Points last week:_____   Points towards
                                  Level 2 to date: _____

Points last 3 weeks:_____

		Fri	Sat	Sun	Mon	Tue	Wed	Thr
polite manners	5							
respected property	5							
good hygiene	5							
completed chores	5							
asked permission	5							
good study hall	5							
good peer relations	5							
good adult relations	5							
followed instructions	5							
accepted criticism	5							
accepted "no"	5							
controlled temper	5							
PG _____	5							
PG _____	5							
homework, 3/5 classes	5							
homework, 5/5 classes	5							
class work, 3/5 classes	5							
class work, 5/5 classes	5							
followed instructions	5							
PSG _____	5							
points earned	100							
point fines								
Daily Total								

Weekly Total _____   Points towards Level 2 _____

                                 Points last four weeks _____

FIGURE 10.3: Level 2

Level 2

Name: _____   Week ending date: _____

Points last week:_____

		Fri	Sat	Sun	Mon	Tue	Wed	Thr
polite manners	5							
respected property	5							
good hygiene	5							
completed chores	5							
asked permission	5							
good study hall	5							
good peer relations	5							
good adult relations	5							
followed instructions	5							
accepted criticism	5							
accepted "no"	5							
controlled temper	5							
PG _____	5							
PG _____	5							
homework, 4/5 classes	5							
homework, 5/5 classes	5							
class work, 4/5 classes	5							
class work, 5/5 classes	5							
followed instructions	5							
PSG _____	5							
points earned	100							
point fines								
Daily Total								

Weekly Total _____

191

FIGURE 10.4: PreTerm

PreTerm

Name: _____   Week ending date: _____

Points last week:_____

home responsibilities	10	
school responsibilities	10	
peer relations	10	
adult relations	10	
following instructions	10	
accepting criticism	10	
accepting "no"	10	
temper control	10	
personal goal (specify)	10	
personal goal (specify)	10	

Total this week _____

sheets could not be taped back together for use—they were not neat enough for posting in public. Consequently, boys lost whatever points had been earned up to the time the new sheet was posted. Unfortunately, this did not apply to restrictions, since any restrictions were also posted in the office until completed. Thus, restrictions continued in force until a boy requested a new point sheet and began earning points towards the restriction. Instances of point sheets being mishandled were rare.

During the last three years of this point system's operation, 83.3 percent of discharges successfully completed the program; 80 percent of the successful discharges were considered to be doing well on follow-up during these three years (still in school, graduated, or employed). Ten percent remained in the community, but were not doing well; 10 percent were either returned to placement or incarcerated. Of the unsuccessful discharges, 12.5 percent were transferred due to a lack of progress; 4.2 percent (one boy) were discharged on runaway.

Boys often experienced problems following level advancement, evidencing difficulties with the new criteria and reinforcement schedules of new levels before adjusting. Most boys completed Adjustment in four or five weeks. A few required five or six weeks. One boy required over two months. Nearly all boys completed Level 1 within three or four months, Level 2 in as few as six or as many as twelve months. PreTerm and Term generally required three months each. Boys required between fifteen and twenty-three months to complete the program, with an average of about nineteen months. The system had to be substantially modified when state funding sources limited the length of stay to twelve months.

This system has several advantages over others I have used:

1. Its primary advantage is its simplicity. It is easy to understand and easy to use. It communicates a considerable amount of information with ease.
2. It focuses on social skills that readily generalize to and receive reinforcement in other settings.

3. It is relatively nonpunitive.
4. It offers flexibility and individualization.
5. It contributes to status for appropriate behavior.
6. It contributes towards competition, which can be healthy with careful attention by treatment personnel.

It also had disadvantages:

1. It does not provide for immediate reinforcement for expected behavior, although the use of bonus points provides immediate reinforcement for exceptional behavior.
2. A negative entry in any point category means that a resident cannot earn his points in that category for the day. This creates the potential that a boy who lost his points for not following instructions early in the day might refuse further instructions without consequence.
3. It did not seem to work as effectively with the occasional ten-year-old who was accepted into the program.

Simplicity

With daily points based on 100, the system uses a number scale with which everyone is familiar. It is similar to grades in school, percentage, money, etc.

The posted point sheets contrast with systems in which residents carry point cards and present them upon request. With the posted point sheets, staff may make entries at their convenience after counseling a resident about a problem behavior, without interrupting ongoing activities. Staff make and initial brief notations ("Not at dinner," "not with Danny," etc.)

Each sheet provides at a glance a graphic indication as to how each boy is doing for the day and for the week. Relatively "clean" point sheets—few entries—indicate excellent performance. Sheets with a few entries for the day or the week indicate satisfactory performance. Sheets with more entries indicate problems for the day or for the week. Moreover, the system readily facilitates the identification of patterns. Specific problem areas are clearly exposed when a child has a problem with a specific behavior, such as following instructions or accepting no. Patterns of "bad days" readily appear also—Mondays, Fridays, weekends, etc. A review of the file of point sheets for an individual resident may also indicate cyclical problems, such as problems for the week immediately following a home pass.

Social Skills

The social skills on which the system focuses serve residents well at school, on home pass, and after discharge. The skills were taught by the child care counselors using teaching interactions. The Teaching Interaction is a remedial technique that teaches social skills to established criteria—it is presented in the next chapter, "Techniques and Interventions for Staff." Within a few months, boys could recite the steps to social skills such as are described above under "Behavior Definitions"; they could use the skills at will. Graduated residents who returned for visits spoke of how their skills helped them in job and family situations.

Nonpunitive

The maximum restriction of 200 points is certainly mild for such things as theft in the community, bringing drugs into the program, or hitting someone with an object used as a weapon. Occasionally, residents or newer staff would remark about the leniency. Generally, someone would respond that we were not there to punish, but rather to teach, and that we felt that the restriction was sufficient to facilitate learning. Someone would then talk about consequences other than the restriction, such as the loss of respect or trust, the pain or injury caused to another, or the program's reputation in the community. Possible ways in which the guilty party might make amends would also be discussed. The program had significantly fewer problems with violence, theft, or drugs than other programs with which I have been acquainted, all of which had more severe sanctions.

Flexibility and Individualization

The use of Personal Goals and Personal School Goals allows considerable flexibility in meeting the individual treatment needs of residents. No one area carries sufficient weight to keep a resident from earning privileges. On the other hand, residents who continue to have problems with a specific area and fail to progress, yet continue to earn privileges, may have personal goals established in that particular area, for example, "following instructions," "peer relations," "bedtime," or "brushing teeth," such that fifteen points per day may be based on such behavior. Behaviors that are not covered by the system may also be similarly addressed, for example, "accepting limits," "following rules," "phoning parents," "attending therapy," or "following physician's orders."

Status and Competition

Posting of point sheets contributed to generally healthy competition. Occasionally, to promote cooperation as well, staff would announce a "bonus week." Examples include a pizza party for Thursday night, a special outing, or double allowances when every boy earned at least 600 points. Staff would then encourage other residents to support and encourage residents who were experiencing continuing difficulties.

Boys were allowed to sign up for certain privileges based on their point rank, boys with the highest points having first opportunity to sign up. A telephone sign-up sheet with fifteen-minute increments of phone time was based on daily points. Opportunity to sign up for extra jobs for pay, such as cleaning offices or cutting grass, was based on weekly point rankings at first come, first served availability. Boys also picked their household chores for the week from ten chores based on point rankings. Thus, the two boys with the highest points for the week could avoid weekly chores when the program had twelve residents; boys with lowest points were left the less popular chores.

Lack of Prompt Reinforcement

Expected behavior merited verbal recognition from staff but not an entry on the point sheet. Expected behavior, then, did not receive formal recognition until point sheets were totalled at the end of the day. Although this would appear to be contrary to principles of learning, the system was remarkably effective with adolescents in the program. Perhaps the continuing "clean" point sheet served as some form of ongoing positive reinforcement. Whatever the reasons, any means of providing more prompt reinforcements would have detracted substantially from the simplicity of the system, which appeared to be one of its main strengths.

Loss of Points for the Day in a Category

If, after points for the day were totalled at 4:00 P.M., a resident experienced a problem with instructions resulting in a point sheet entry, the resident could not earn points for instructions for the remainder of the twenty-four-hour period. It would seem likely that residents in such a situation would refuse further instructions since there would appear to be no consequences. In practice, this seldom happened. When it did, staff were generally patient, allowing the system to work over a period of days or weeks.

Instructions about chores or other routine responsibilities were not viewed as critical. Other means of getting things done, such as paying another resident to complete a chore, were utilized. Occasional natural or logical consequences were used. "When you finish cleaning your room, you may leave on your home pass," or "You may have snacks after your shower." Personal goals could also be used to address such problems, for example, "peer relations second time" and "peer relations third time" after the original entry had been made.

Effectiveness with Younger Children

Perhaps because of the above two disadvantages, perhaps due to other factors, the system was only marginally effective with the occasional preadolescent who was accepted into the program. Reinforcements should probably have been available more frequently and more promptly than daily and weekly, with more opportunities to earn (or fail to earn) points for each behavior each day.

Additionally, the privileges were not as meaningful. Ten-year-olds were inept at most of the recreational activities that were available, not as appreciative of telephone time, and not nearly so motivated by weekly allowances. Competition with older residents was not motivating; "peer" support from older residents, who were not really peers, was perhaps not so helpful. Nevertheless, all younger children returned home relatively successfully, perhaps because of gains made by their families during treatment.

BEHAVIOR THERAPY WITH GROUPS

Behavior therapy in the group setting is probably the most difficult application of behavior modification. I have never attempted this approach. Feindler, Ecton, Kingsley, and Dubey (1986) have. They conducted a twelve-session group anger control program for male adolescents in a psychiatric setting.

Anger Control in a Group Setting

Psychiatric staff identified boys on two units who were in need of anger control training. Feindler et al. (1986) made thirty-minute presentations about the program to these boys. Twenty-one boys volunteered.

Ten boys from one unit were selected for the first group; the remaining eleven boys were placed on a waiting list and served as a control group. Sixteen of the subjects were classified as having conduct disorders, either undersocialized aggressive type (10) or undersocialized nonaggressive type (6); the five remaining boys had other clinical diagnoses. Four subjects were classified in the normal range of intelligence while the remaining seventeen were classified in lower ranges; the mean IQ scores were 83.7 for treatment subjects and 80.2 for control subjects. Boys ranged in age from 13.2 to 18.8 years (Feindler et al., 1986).

Treatment

Feindler et al. (1986) conducted twelve sessions during eight weeks. Boys received training in "relaxation, self-instructions, use of coping statements, more assertive social interactions, the evaluation of one's own behavior, the self-monitoring of anger and conflict experiences, and problem-solving training" (p. 114). Teaching strategies included "live modeling, behavioral rehearsal and practice, role playing, negative and positive symbolic modeling [videotape presentations] . . . and role playing utilizing videotape equipment and videotape feedback" (p. 114). Residents received points during sessions for cooperation and participation; sodas were awarded for points at the end of each session.

Session 1. The introductory session consisted of a discussion of the program's rationale and rules. The boys received training in relaxation techniques, specifically deep breaths, counting backwards, and pleasant imagery. These techniques reduce physiological tension, refocus attention from provocative external stimuli to internal control, and provide a time delay before choosing how to respond.

Session 2. Two homework assignments on self-monitoring devices were presented. These devices were used for the remainder of the group. The first was the daily Hassle Sheet. It provided each boy with an accurate picture of how he handled conflicts during the week. The second was a self-assessment of anger-provoking and aggression-provoking situations. It analyzed situations according to the behavioral concepts of antecedents, actual behavioral response, and consequences.

Session 3. The boys were taught to identify situational variables that triggered their angry responses. They also received training in progressive muscle relaxation.

Sessions 4 and 5. The boys discussed the rights of adolescents and the rights of others. They discussed various assertion techniques including friendly or empathetic assertion and escalating assertion as alternative responses to aggression. They were taught how to deescalate conflicts while maintaining their rights and self-control. They viewed videotapes of appropriate and inappropriate uses of these techniques (positive and negative symbolic modeling).

Sessions 6 and 7. Boys were introduced to self-instruction techniques and trained in their use. They were prompted in generating a list of reminders that they could use for themselves in pressure situations. They viewed videotapes on the appropriate and inappropriate uses of these techniques.

Sessions 8 and 9. The boys were taught to think ahead using self-instructions and problem solving to anticipate future negative consequences for inappropriate responses to conflicts. They practised "the contingency statement: 'If I (*misbehavior*) now, then I will (*future negative consequence*)' " (p. 115). They viewed videotapes on the appropriate and inappropriate uses of this technique.

Session 10. The boys were trained to give themselves immediate feedback after conflict situations—self-evaluation responses. Hassle Sheets from each boy were evaluated for resolved and unresolved conflicts.

Session 11. The boys were taught to choose and use the best self-control technique according to a problem-solving sequence:

1. What is the problem?
2. What can I do?
3. What will happen if . . .?
4. What will I do?
5. How did it work?

Session 12. The boys reviewed definitions and procedures for the seven major self-control techniques that they learned.

Results

Feindler et al. (1986) administered a battery of assessment tests to both the experimental group and the control group as pretest and posttest conditions. The experimental group showed significant increases in reflective and correct responding on the Matching Familiar Figure Test whereas the control group did not. Child care staff, rating both groups on the Behavior Rating Scale for Children, noted significant improvement in the experimental group's self-control while the control group showed some decrement.

> From reviewing the results, it is clear that participation in group anger-control training resulted in improved performance by treatment subjects on the MFFT in terms of reduced error rates and increased response latencies; improved changes in treatment of subjects' self-control capabilities as perceived by child care staff; increased use of more appropriate verbal and nonverbal anger-control techniques by treatment subjects in dealing with various anger-provoking stimuli; and a decreased frequency in treatment subjects' on-ward restrictions for physical aggression and general rule violations (Feindler et al., 1986, p. 121).

Control subjects received the group training beginning three weeks after the experimental group completed the training. A three year follow-up indicates positive discharge results. Of the twenty-one boys, eighteen were discharged from the psychiatric facility. Of those eighteen boys, only three required further psychiatric hospitalization or incarceration.

This study indicates some of the problems inherent in evaluating the effectiveness of various treatment strategies in the residential setting. Ethical considerations (right to treatment) affect the assignment of residents to control groups and preclude the establishment of control groups for an extended period of time. Thus, it was not possible to compare the results of treatment three years after discharge with a group that had not received treatment.

SUMMARY

Behavior modification, the application of principles of learning to change behavior, can be used for three distinctly different purposes: to change behavior in a given setting (behavior management), to produce a more pervasive change in behavior (behavior treatment), and to produce emotional changes that facilitate desired changes in behavior (behavior therapy). These distinctions facilitate the identification of behaviors (or emotions) to change, the clear identification of goals, the identification of reinforcements and negative consequences, and development of a plan, increasing the probability of a successful outcome. Plans can be devised to utilize principles of learning to change behavior or emotions for individuals and in group settings.

Techniques and Interventions for Staff

CHILDREN in residential treatment have a variety of needs. They have normal developmental needs. They also need help with special problems. Normal developmental needs can be met in a variety of ways. Needs for help can also be met in a variety of ways. Residential treatment centers should be able to meet both types of needs.

While normal developmental needs might be met by providing age-appropriate, normal developmental activities, it must be remembered that the child is not in a normal environment of age-appropriate peers. Children in residential treatment are there because of problems. Problems can be addressed in a variety of ways: remediation, counseling, treatment, and therapy.

Since the child care counselors spend more time with children than any other personnel in the program, they are most often in the best position to address the various needs of the child. They readily address normal developmental needs and provide counseling and remediation; they routinely deal with issues related to management of the children. While they are usually not trained for therapy or treatment, they may be trained to complement treatment or therapy that may be provided, especially behavioral treatment or behavioral therapy when offered.

In this chapter, we will examine some of the techniques and interventions that child care counselors may use in working with children in placement. We will consider their involvement in normal activities, active communication (a counseling technique), the teaching interaction (a remedial technique), the life-space interview (a counseling technique), and treatment of enuresis (a remedial technique employing behavioral treatment). In chapter 12, we will consider how child care counselors can be trained to perform therapeutic crisis intervention (a technique that must meet *both* management *and* treatment objectives).

ACTIVITIES

Activities are normal. They meet normal needs and contribute to normal learning and development. Activities in residential settings pose some special problems. Age-appropriate "normal" behaviors of children do not always produce age-appropriate normal responses from peers. Horseplay may be a fairly typical behavior among adolescent males, for example, at a Boy Scout summer camp. In the residential setting, innocent horseplay may produce a violent response, provoke a fight, or produce withdrawal of the recipient from the group.

Choosing up sides for an athletic contest may also pose problems. Excluded residents may withdraw, suffering further damage to self-esteem that is already too weak.

Staff must be able to identify what is normal, both in terms of the initial behavior and the response of the other children. Normal age-appropriate behavior that produces normal age-appropriate responses is generally healthy. When normal age-appropriate behavior produces unhealthy responses, intervention is indicated.

One of my staff once told me how he dealt with noise levels during free time in a group home for adolescents. Rather than attending to the level of noise—music, loud talk, laughter—he attended to the facial expressions of the boys. When facial expressions indicated everyone was having a good time, everything was fine. When a facial expression indicated that someone was not having a good time or was out of control, he intervened, set limits, and enforced them.

ACTIVE COMMUNICATION

Popkin's (1993) active communication is primarily a counseling technique. In the residential setting, it has both management and therapeutic potential. It is used to help the child identify alternatives and possible consequences. This facilitates decision making (counseling). However, it also promotes the child's talking about issues, especially feelings. To the extent that it promotes a child's talking about feelings, it provides him or her with the alternative of expressing feelings verbally rather than behaviorally, a clear management benefit. Further, when it promotes verbal communication about issues and feelings that are important to the child, it provides information for therapy.

According to Popkin, active communication involves five skills:

1. Listening actively.
2. Listening for feelings.
3. Connecting feelings to content.
4. Looking for alternatives and evaluating consequences.
5. Following up.

Listening Actively

To listen actively, staff must keep their own talk to a minimum. They must give full attention. This means stopping what they are doing, looking at the child, getting on the child's level, leaning closer, possibly putting an arm around the child. They must acknowledge what they are hearing with nods, brief verbal responses such as "I see" or even "Uh-huh." They must ask relevant questions or offer brief summaries. The staff must also demonstrate appropriate affect for the communication. This requires some understanding of the child's feelings—empathy.

Listening for Feelings

Helping, or just allowing children to express their feelings verbally, may avert many a crisis. Feelings are not right or wrong, they just are. Acknowledging a child's feelings and accepting them often reduces the child's need to act on them.

Connecting Feelings to Content

Connecting feelings to content is perhaps the most powerful part of the technique. The skill is simple, but like any skill, it requires practice. Staff simply try to identify the feeling, then state it clearly, simply, and non-judgmentally, relating the feeling to what the child is saying. "That seemed to make you angry." "That must have made you mad." "I guess you were embarrassed when the teacher told you that in front of the class." "Wow, that must have hurt!" "I'll bet that made you feel good." The staff does not even have to get the feeling right; if the staff guesses wrong, the child will often make the necessary correction. "I guess I was a little embarrassed, but I was really pissed off."

As the staff and child together identify the child's feelings, the child begins to really open up. When we go to a friend with a problem we do not so often go with the desire for or expectation of a solution as we do for a sympathetic ear, for empathy and understanding—to share. When the child gets the non-judgmental empathy, the communication actually accelerates. The child often cannot stop talking when he or she gets a sympathetic ear. Talking is not compatible with running away, slamming doors, or hitting people.

Looking for Alternatives, Evaluating Consequences

If the child is allowed to express feelings verbally, rather than through behavior, the battle is half won. The child is then more able to listen and to think rationally. After feelings have been shared, the child is often ready to think about alternatives, and the consequences of alternatives. "What can you do?" "What else could you do?" "What do you think will happen if you do that?" "What do you think would happen if you did. . . ?" Moreover, the staff who appears to understand the child's feelings often seems to acquire a special quality of wisdom in the child's eyes, even when the staff does not condone the behavior.

To the extent that staff allows the child to choose an alternative, the staff allows the child to accept responsibility, not only for the decision but also for the consequences. To the extent that staff attempts to influence or direct the child, the staff assumes responsibility, detracting from the child's responsibility.

Following Up

Following up later the same day or a day or two later confirms the staff's interest in the child, the child's problem, and the child's decisions about the problem. It often provides excellent opportunity for reinforcement (and occasionally for further active communication if the child did not make the best choice).

Example

Tyrone. **Staff heard some shouting in the TV room and went to find Tyrone and Gilbert bracing up to each other. The staff stepped between the two boys. Gilbert quickly calmed down, but Tyrone, screaming profanity, tried to push past the staff to get at Gilbert. The staff took firm hold of Tyrone and escorted him to the office. Tyrone offered minimal resistance, but continued to hurl threats, complete with expletives, at Gilbert. In the office:**

Staff: **(Empathetically) You seem angry.**
Tyrone: **You're damn right I'm angry! I'll kill that motherfucker!**
Staff: **(Sitting down and leaning towards Tyrone) Tell me what happened.**
Tyrone: **(Pacing) Man . . . I was watching the basketball game. Gilbert came right in and turned the channel to MTV.**
Staff: **Boy. That must have made you mad.**
Tyrone: **(Nodding) Man! Jordan had the ball and was driving. I said, "Hey mother . . ." Well, you know. Gilbert said to F my own mother. Man! Nobody talks about my mother!**
Staff: **It makes you really angry when someone talks about your mother.**
Tyrone: **Yeah. I mean, you can't let someone talk about your mother.**
Staff: **You feel like you have to do something when someone says something about your mother.**
Tyrone: **(Hesitates) Well, you can't let them get away with that.**
Staff: **You seem to believe that that's a challenge you can't back down from.**
Tyrone: **Well, it's not right.**
Staff: **You must have felt that Gilbert was being really unfair. First he turned off what you were watching. Then he said something about your mom.**
Tyrone: **You got it. I was so mad. I just wanted to kill him?**
Staff: **Did you really?**
Tyrone: **Well, no, not really . . . you know.**

Staff: I'm not sure I do.

Tyrone: Well, I just got mad. I wanted to do something. I mean, I had to do something.

Staff: Well, what could you have done?

Tyrone: Man, I could've decked him!

Staff: What do you think would have happened if you did that?

Tyrone: Well, I'd have gotten a restriction.

Staff: Yes. I wouldn't have had any choice about that.

Tyrone: Well, he shouldn't talk about my mom like that.

Staff: Why do you think he did that.

Tyrone: (Thinks) To get me mad?

Staff: Are you guessing?

Tyrone: No. He wanted to get me mad.

Staff: So what else could you have done?

Tyrone: Come and told staff.

Staff: Well, that's one thing you could do. What do you think would have happened?

Tyrone: He'd 'a' called me a chicken, running to staff.

Staff: What else would have happened?

Tyrone: You'd have gone to talk to Gilbert?

Staff: I might have. I don't know for sure. If I did, what would you be doing right now?

Tyrone: Watching the ball game.

Staff: That would be your decision, wouldn't it?

Tyrone: Yeah.

Staff: What else could you have done?

Tyrone: (Thinks, can't answer)

Staff: Could you have asked him to put the game back on?

Tyrone: Yeah, I guess so.

Staff: You guess so?

Tyrone: I could have asked him to put the game back on.

Staff: Yes, you could have. What do you think would have happened?

Tyrone: (Thinks again) I don't know.

Staff: Neither do I. Do you think he might have put the game back on?

Tyrone: I don't know.

Staff: Neither do I. What do you think would have happened if you just got up and walked out?

Tyrone: I don't know.

Staff: How do you think Gilbert would have felt?

Tyrone: Well, glad, I guess, that he could watch the TV.

Staff: Do you think he wanted to watch TV alone?

Tyrone: I don't know.

Staff: Where is Gilbert, now?

Tyrone: I don't know.

Staff: Go look, then come and tell me.

Tyrone: Okay. (Leaves and returns) He's on the phone.

Staff: So what was it that you want?

Tyrone: I want to see the game.

Staff: Did attacking Gilbert help you to see the game?

Tyrone: No.

Staff: So which alternative would have helped you see the game?

Tyrone: I guess I could have told him I really wanted to see the game and asked him to put it back on.

Staff: You guess?

Tyrone: I could have asked him to put the game back on.

Staff: And if he refused?

Tyrone: I guess I could have left and waited for him to leave.

Staff: Yes. And you could have come to talk to me. What do you think would have happened then?

Tyrone: You'd have made him put the game back on?

Staff: I don't know. Maybe by the time we got done talking, he would have been on the phone. Then we could go watch the rest of the game together.

Tyrone: Yeah.

Staff: Well, let's go watch the rest of the game.

THE TEACHING INTERACTION

The teaching interaction is designed to teach skills, specifically social skills. It is primarily a remedial technique designed to correct deficiencies in previous learning. It can be used to teach a specific skill in planned and scheduled individual sessions or in problem situations. It is also useful in situations in which a child is having a problem with a particular skill (Weber & Burke, 1986). Moreover, the technique can be somewhat aversive without being punitive, thus serving as a logical consequence for a misbehavior.

The staff who work with the children on a daily basis will be the primary personnel to employ the technique. However, all program personnel who have responsibilities for interacting with children should be skilled in the use of this technique if it is to be used effectively. Supervisors must be in a position to model the technique and to hold staff accountable for its use on a consistent basis; case managers and therapists must understand its use and be able to use the teaching interaction in individual and group sessions in support of staff. Even more importantly, therapists working with families must be in a position to coordinate with families as their child learns new skills. Families must know what to expect, and the family therapist must be in a position to evaluate generalization of treatment to the home setting during passes as well as in aftercare.

There are nine components of the Teaching Interaction. Each component is made relevant and specific to the individual child, the given social skill, and the particular setting.

1. An initial statement of praise or empathy.
2. A description of the inappropriate behavior.
3. Consequences for the inappropriate behavior.
4. A description of the appropriate behavior.
5. Rationale for the appropriate behavior.
6. Requests are made for acknowledgment throughout.
7. Practice.
8. Feedback, additional practice, and reinforcement.
9. General praise (Weber and Burke, 1986).

A Sample Teaching Interaction

Staff: **Jimmy, you had a really good day today. You had a good school sheet, and you** got a C on that spelling test you were so worried about.

Jimmy: **The test wasn't as hard as I thought it would be.**

Staff: **No test is hard if you know the answers. I think this is a good time to teach you what some of the other kids know about following instructions.**

Jimmy: **OK.**

Staff: **There are several steps to following instructions.**

First, you have to look at the person giving the instruction. You know, make eye contact.

Next, you have to listen to the instruction carefully and try to understand it.

If you don't understand the instruction, what do you think you should do?

Jimmy: **Uh, I guess you should ask about it.**

Staff: **That's very good. You should ask questions whenever you don't understand something. When you do understand the instruction, what should you do?**

Jimmy: **I don't know, go and do it, I guess.**

Staff: **Of course, it's usually good to do an instruction. . . . Let me ask you this. Do you find your parents lecture you a lot when they want you to do something?**

Jimmy: **Yeah. My mom's always doing that.**

Staff: **Kind of like nagging you?**

Jimmy: **Yeah. All the time.**

Staff: **Well, there's a magic word that can help sometimes. When you understand the instruction, you say "OK." That will very often stop all the nagging. Then, after you say "OK," you go and do the instruction, and then there's just one more step. I'll bet you thought if you did the instruction, you were all finished.**

Jimmy: **(Looks puzzled)**

Staff: **After you've done the instruction, you report back to see if what you did was OK. Now, let's review. First you look at the person. While you're looking, you listen carefully. If you don't understand, you ask questions. When you do understand, you say "OK." Then you go and do it. Finally, you check back. Got it?**

Jimmy: **I think so.**

Staff: OK. What are the steps?

Jimmy: Uh, . . . look at the person, . . . listen, . . . ask questions, go and do it, and check back.

Staff: That's real good, but don't forget to say OK. Let's practice. Hand me that pencil. (Staff points to a pencil on the desk)

Jimmy: (Picks up the pencil and holds it out to the staff)

Staff: Thank you. That was good. You looked at me, and you gave me the right pencil. Do you know what you forgot?

Jimmy: . . . To ask questions?

Staff: Well, you seemed to know which pencil I wanted, so you didn't have to ask questions.

Jimmy: Well, I didn't check back.

Staff: That's true. You also didn't say "OK." Don't forget, saying "OK" helps to stop the lectures, and lets people know you understand the instruction. It also helps them to believe you're going to do it. Let's try again. Take your time. Will you give me that piece of paper?

Jimmy: (Looks around the desk) Which one?

Staff: That one over there. (Points)

Jimmy: You mean this one?

Staff: Yes.

Jimmy: (Pauses and thinks) OK. (Hands staff the paper)

Staff: (Takes the paper and looks at Jimmy without saying anything)

Jimmy: (Looks puzzled, then a light goes on) Is that the one you meant?

Staff: (With enthusiasm) Yes, it was! That was perfect! You got all the steps! How did that feel?

Jimmy: OK, I guess.

Staff: It will take some time till you get all the steps automatically, and some practice. Not all instructions are so easy, but if you follow these steps, they usually won't be as bad as you sometimes think they will be. Just be sure to remember to say "OK."

Jimmy: (Smiling a little) OK.

Staff: The way you're going, I think you're going to have your pass this weekend. I'll be looking forward to hearing from you about how it goes. I bet your mom will be surprised if you try these steps on her over the weekend.

Jimmy: Yeah! I guess so.

Staff: Let's go and see about snacks.

Jimmy: OK.

Initial Praise or Empathy

Mastery of a new skill is a positive experience for most people when the skill is something in which they are interested. On the other hand, for many of the children in residential treatment, teaching situations have often been unpleasant events in which little learning has occurred. First, a teaching interaction is a teaching event that in itself may be perceived as aversive by some. Second, when used simply to teach in a neutral setting, it implies a deficiency. Third, when used to correct a problem with behavior, it becomes criticism. Fourth, it very often interrupts or otherwise keeps a child from doing something that may be more reinforcing.

It is absolutely imperative that staff employing this technique avoid the appearace of "inflicting" a punishment. The initial component of beginning with a statement of praise or empathy is therefore critical. The initial praise should be genuine, specific, and related to the individual child and the particular skill being taught. When a staff can identify no behavior for praise, she or he should offer an empathetic statement showing positive feelings for the child. Statements should be delivered with a pleasant voice tone, appropriate facial expression, and nonthreatening posture (Weber & Burke, 1986). For example, in a case in which a child has had a problem with peer relations and temper control resulting in a fight, staff might initiate the teaching interaction by saying: "I know it's really hard for you when the other kids tease you so much."

Describing the Inappropriate Behavior

The staff person describes the inappropriate behavior in specific behavioral terms and may even choose to demonstrate the inappropriate behavior. The staff also asks questions to insure that the child understands (Weber & Burke, 1986). I have seen humor used with effect when used with sensitivity. Humor can be a very effective tool in promoting insight. Learning, after all, can be fun for both teacher and student. Humor can also be damaging to fragile egos, especially in the presence of peers. It depends on the individual child and the circumstances.

Delivering Consequences

If the staff is using the Teaching Interaction in response to a problem behavior, the staff calmly announces the established consequences for that behavior according to whatever system is in place (Weber & Burke, 1986). The staff must avoid the appearance of inflicting a punishment. A phrase from an old job description comes to mind: ". . . gives sympathetic understanding without necessarily condoning behavior" (Family Service Society of the Lehigh Valley, job description for a street worker in 1971). If the Teaching Interaction is being used in a neutral, purely instructional setting, the consequences for related inappropriate behaviors may be reviewed or this step may be skipped.

Describing the Appropriate Behavior

The staff describes the appropriate behavior in behaviorally specific terms and asks questions or requests acknowledgment to insure the child understands. The staff may choose to demonstrate the appropriate behavior (Weber & Burke, 1986).

Rationale

The staff relates how the appropriate behavior may benefit the child, requesting acknowledgment of the relevance and clarity of the rationale (Weber & Burke, 1986). This component of the Teaching Interaction is designed to show the child that the skill is worth learning or acquiring. Social skills empower individuals to be more effective in social settings. Without social skills, children have little choice but to behave inappropriately. With the skills, children have the choice to behave appropriately or to behave inappropriately, and to observe the effects of a wider repertoire of behaviors on staff, parents, teachers, and peers.

Requests for Acknowledgment

Requests for acknowledgment are separate components of the Teaching Interaction that are used throughout the process (Weber & Burke, 1986). One of the "social skills" that many children have learned is to meet the needs of adults for an "attentive" listener to their wisdom. Many children are quite competent at maintaining eye contact with appropriate facial expression and nods of the head while thinking about other things, (such as, "How many times have I heard this before?")

Practice

Many social skills are complex. The staff may use a role reversal to demonstrate the appropriate behavior for the child before having the child practice. Then the child practices the behavior to criteria (Weber & Burke, 1986). For example, following instructions involves much more than walking away mumbling to take out the garbage with a scowl that is unrelated to the odor emanating from the can.

Children with a history of problems with instructions are used to lengthy lectures that accompany instructions from parents, teachers, and staff. Even when they complete the instruction, there is little for them to feel good about. Simple acknowledgment of an instruction with an "OK" or "I'd be glad to" will go a long way towards cutting off demeaning or belittling lectures.

Many of the social skills in real life must be performed in less than pleasant situations. Instructions are seldom given for things we already plan to do; the situation may be even worse when instructions are given for something we already planned to do. Consider Jennifer.

Jennifer. **Jennifer decided during supper that she would do the dishes; it was obvious that her mother had had a hard day. During dessert, Jennifer's mother told her: "After** supper you're going to do the dishes before you leave this kitchen and I don't want any lip. You have it too good around here and it's time you started pulling your own weight. I'm sick and tired of being taken for granted. I deserve some time to myself, too.''

Accepting criticism, temper control, and accepting "no" also tend to be called for in emotionally charged situations. These skills can be learned and strengthened by practice in neutral and, occasionally, in fun situations.

General Praise

The staff member ends the Teaching Interaction on a positive note, praising the child's mastery of the skill: "Jim, you're learning skills so fast! You went through the practice of that skill perfectly the first time, with all the components included. It's sure fun to teach someone who learns as quickly as you do" (Weber & Burke, 1986, p. 77).

Feedback

The staff provides specific feedback on the practice: (1) positive feedback on what the child performed correctly, and (2) corrective feedback on whatever was missed. Practice and feedback continue until the child is able to perform the skill to criteria. The staff may reward the child for successful mastery of the skill with a reduction in the negative consequences the child received for the problem behavior, up to a 50 percent reduction in those consequences (Weber & Burke, 1986).

Examples

Jimmy. Jimmy has not been having a good week. He received a point restriction for hitting another boy on Sunday. On Tuesday he got sent back from school; he didn't have his homework and cursed the teacher when he asked Jimmy about it.

Staff: Jimmy, it's time for you to take out the garbage.

Jimmy: (Continues talking to another boy)
Staff: (A little bit louder) Jimmy, it's . . .
Jimmy: I ain't takin' out no fuckin' garbage!
Staff: (Calm voice tone) Jimmy, you're having a problem with the instruction I just gave you.
Jimmy: (Looking around at peers) I'm having a whole lot of problems around here!
Staff: (Calm, almost apologetic voice tone) You're losing points right now.
Jimmy: Fuck your points!
Staff: Let's go and talk about it.
Jimmy: Fuck you!
Staff: Let's go to your room. (Turns and walks to Jimmy's room)
Jimmy: (Hesitates, then follows kind of slowly)
Staff: (In Jimmy's room, sitting on his roommate's bed) You've had a pretty rough week. (No praise seems appropriate, hence, empathetic statements.) You're not going to earn your home pass, and I know that's important for you. Do you think there's any way you can get a home pass this week?
Jimmy: (Dejectedly) No.
Staff: Tomorrow starts the points for a new week. You can earn a pass next weekend.
Jimmy: Yeah, I know.
Staff: I know you want that pass. But if you don't start soon, you're going to have problems next week, too. You should practice with what's left of this week so you're all set for next week.
Jimmy: I guess so.
Staff: I know instructions are hard for you. They're hard for me, too, sometimes. (More empathy)
Jimmy: (Makes eye contact)
Staff: Sometimes you're really good with instructions. How does your mother feel when you follow instructions at home?
Jimmy: She's surprised. She really likes it.
Staff: Sometimes you really like to surprise your mother.
Jimmy: Yeah.
Staff: You know, when I asked you to take out the garbage, you didn't say "OK." You can't earn your points for following instructions when you have a problem like that. You

also had a problem with staff relations. Do you remember what that was?

Jimmy: Yeah. I cursed.

Staff: That's right. So you also lost points for adult relations. Do you remember the steps of following instructions?

Jimmy: Look at the person, ask questions, say "OK," do it, and check back.

Staff: Very good. You didn't mention the part about listening, but I know you remembered it. Take off your shoe.

Jimmy: Which one.

Staff: Good! The left one.

Jimmy: OK. (Takes off left shoe. Looks at staff) Is that all?

Staff: That's great. This stuff we're trying to teach you, it helps at home and at school, doesn't it?

Jimmy: Yeah, when I use it.

Staff: You don't feel like people are on your back so much, do you?

Jimmy: Not when I use it.

Staff: OK. That's what it's for. Now, if you want to have a good week next week, like you did last week, you have to get started so you're in a good frame of mind.

Jimmy: I guess so.

Staff: Are you guessing?

Jimmy: No, I know it.

Staff: OK. Right now, I really need for you to take out the trash.

Jimmy: OK. Can I put my shoe back on?

Staff: (Laughs) Sure.

Jimmy: (Puts his shoe on and says "Thank you." Leaves to take out the garbage)

Staff: Don't forget to check back.

Jimmy: OK.

Later . . .

Jimmy: I took out the garbage and put a new bag in the can.

Staff: Very good. I'm going to give you five bonus points. You had a problem, but you worked hard to correct it. I think you'll be off to a good start for the new week when it starts tomorrow.

Bernadette: Bernadette is yelling at Tamika about something.

Staff: Bernadette, you're too loud.

Bernadette: (Still yelling) She got on the phone and it's my turn!

Staff: You're having a problem with criticism right now.

Bernadette: (Shrieking) It's my turn for the phone.

Staff: Let's go to the office. (Turns and goes to the office)

Bernadette: (Follows)

Staff: (Sitting in the chair, which she pulled from behind the desk to the side) Earlier today, Tanya was having a problem with Tamika, and you talked to her and helped her to calm down.

Bernadette: (Surprised) I didn't think you noticed.

Staff: Well, I did. That was very good. Now, when I gave you criticism in the living room, what should you have done?

Bernadette: I know. I should have looked at you, listened, and said "OK." Then I should have stopped yelling.

Staff: Right. Then I could have asked what the problem was.

Bernadette: Tamika jumped my turn on the phone.

Staff: I know. That was wrong. It wasn't polite and it wasn't fair. You know, when you have problems with criticism, it costs you points.

Bernadette: I know.

Staff: There are also other consequences besides points.

Bernadette: (Looks puzzled)

Staff: Well, if you had accepted my criticism, then I would probably be talking with Tamika about her peer relations right now. What would you be doing?

Bernadette: Using the phone?

Staff: Are you asking me?

Bernadette: Using the phone.

Staff: That's right. So, there are consequences besides points. Don't you sometimes have problems with criticism in school?

Bernadette: I guess so.

Staff: Guess?

Bernadette: Yes, sometimes I have problems in school.

Staff: Do you remember what you got detention for last week?

Bernadette: I was late to math class.

Staff: Yes, you were. What happened?

Bernadette: I was getting a drink when the bell rang. I was only a minute late.

Staff: True, but you were still late.

Bernadette: Yeah.

Staff: Then what happened?

Bernadette: The teacher sent me to the office.

Staff: Why?

Bernadette: She told me something. I told her I was only getting a drink.

Staff: You made an excuse.

Bernadette: It was true.

Staff: Yes it was. What do you think would have happened if you had just said "OK" when she criticized you?

Bernadette: Nothing, I guess. I mean, nothing.

Staff: Well we can't know for sure. But I don't think you'd have been sent to the office or gotten detention if you had accepted the criticism. So, what are the steps to accepting criticism?

Bernadette: Look at the person, listen, say "OK."

Staff: (Remains silent)

Bernadette: Avoid making excuses.

Staff: Yes. And if you have any objections, not excuses, you may state them calmly, one time. What if you don't understand the criticism?

Bernadette: I should ask questions.

Staff: Very good. By the way, I don't like the way you're wearing your hair.

Bernadette: What do you mean?

Staff: You're wearing it pinned up with a barrette. I prefer it down.

Bernadette: It's too hot to wear it down.

Staff: OK. Do you see how well you handled that criticism? You asked an appropriate question in a normal voice tone. You stated your objection calmly, and I accepted it.

Bernadette: Uh huh.

Staff: Not all criticisms are that easy, but if you follow the steps, you can keep them from becoming problems. Let's see if we can get some people together for a volleyball game before snacks.

Bernadette: What about my phone call?

Staff: Well . . . are you calm enough to talk on the phone now?

Bernadette: I guess . . . Yes.

Staff: Good. Will you help me get snacks ready after your phone call?

Bernadette: Sure. I mean, I'd be glad to.

Staff: Okay. I'll take Tamika out with us for volleyball.

THE LIFE-SPACE INTERVIEW

The life-space interview is primarily a counseling technique. Staff employ it to promote children's understanding of events that occur around them (information) and to evaluate their responses and the alternative responses they might have employed (guidance, advice, and decision making).

Incidents occur from time to time that are likely to be of interest to a child's therapist, giving additional insight into the child's personality or the child's problems and providing material for the session. However, oftentimes such incidents should not await the next therapy session to receive attention. The opportunity to have an impact on the child may decrease significantly with the passage of even a day or two, or the damage may be done and difficult to reverse by the time the next therapy appointment rolls around. Redl (1966) suggests that a life-space interview may have one or both of two possible goals: "(a.) clinical exploitation of life events and (b.) emotional first aid on the spot" (p. 42).

Clinical Exploitation of Life Events

Clinical exploitation of life events is important in several situations. Children often misinterpret what is happening around them, especially the motivations of others. Questions become accusations; attempts to correct children become vicious attacks. Their own behaviors are defended by rationalizations. "Near-to-delusional misinterpretations of life" may, in time, result in "pictures" that are "hopelessly repainted" (Redl, 1966, p. 44). Persons on the scene may have a distinct advantage over the trained therapist because of their proximity to the events and their ability to work with the child before delusions become memories. Redl terms this "reality rub-in" (Redl, 1966, p. 44).

In some cases, children's egos have "become subservient to the pathological mechanisms they have developed" (Redl, 1966, p. 44). Again, those on the spot have an advantage to "try to pile up evidence that their pathologies really don't pay" (Redl, 1966, pp. 44–45), that their style of handling a given situation creates problems rather than resolving them.

Sometimes children have trouble admitting to sensitivity to the needs of others and to their own needs for love. Redl (1966) terms this "massaging numb value areas" (p. 45), giving attention to little-used values that, nevertheless, are there.

Therapists can advocate the use of new techniques, new behaviors; the life-space interview allows demonstration. When the potential for use of new skills is "liberated in individual therapy," others can use the life-space interview to help children "draw visions of much wider ranges of potential reactions" (Redl, 1966, p. 45) in support of therapy. Redl terms this "new tool salesmanship" (p. 45).

Finally, the life-space interview can be used to expand the child's psychological boundaries. Children can be helped "to expand their selves to include other people, benign adults, their groups, the whole institution to which they feel a sense of belonging" (Redl, 1966, p. 47).

Emotional First Aid

Emotional first aid is likewise beneficial in a variety of circumstances that cannot await a scheduled therapy session with a trained professional. Sometimes, planned activities don't come off as scheduled; other times, scheduling requires the interruption of pleasurable activities. Redl suggests

the need to keep frustration from such situations from (1966) "being added to the original reservoir of hate," of the need to "drain off frustration acidity" (p. 48).

Children need help to manage panic, fury, and guilt that may occur disproportionately to the situations in which they find themselves. "In our overall strategy plan, for instance, we consider it important that an adult always stay with the child, no matter how severe his tantrum attack may become" (Redl, 1966, p. 49).

> There is one reaction of our children that we fear more than any other they may happen to produce— and that is the total breaking off of all communication with us and full-fledged retreat into an autistic world of fantasy into which we are not allowed to penetrate (p. 49).

It is important to keep communication going on any level when a child is in emotional trauma. Redl calls this (1966) "communication maintenance in moments of relationship decay" (p. 49).

The life-space interview may also be used to remind children of rules and regulations and to help them comply. Redl terms this (1966) "regulation of behavioral and social traffic" (p. 49).

Finally, children in a group setting often require help in their interactions with peers. Redl terms this (1966) "umpire services—in decisions as well as in loaded transactions" (p. 52) such as swapping, borrowing, and trading.

Guidelines

Bernstein (cited in Clarizo & McCoy, 1976) offers ten guidelines for using the life-space interview (also referred to as the reality-interview).

1. Be polite to the child. Adults demand good manners from children without always showing children good manners.
2. Get down near the child's level physically. Sit if the child is sitting; kneel if appropriate.
3. While confrontation is not always the best ap-

proach, it may serve to be a relief to the child when you know what happened and you are sure of the facts. It can save the child from denying, lying, or otherwise trying to distort or minimize what happened. On the other hand, confrontation may be very ineffective with children who fear that everyone is an enemy.

4. Don't use "Why?" too much. Reasons and motivations may be very difficult, especially for younger children.
5. Get the child talking about what happened and get a description about what happened. Listen.
6. If you think the child is overwhelmed by guilt or shame, minimize the situation: "This action doesn't bother me too much, but we had better look into it, for it can cause *you* trouble" (Clarizo & McCoy, 1976, p. 492). This can be especially important in instances of sexual exploration or experimentation that may occur among groups of latency-age children or same-sex adolescents.
7. Help the child put feelings into words if the child can't express them accurately.
8. Be aware of the thinking demanded by situations. Bright children may lack the emotional maturity to handle some of the relationships in which they get involved.
9. Help the child to plan specific steps to improve.
10. Give the child an opportunity to ask questions and allow the child to offer statements other than those you have solicited with questions.

TREATMENT OF SIMPLE NOCTURNAL ENURESIS

"*Primary nocturnal enuresis* is the term used to describe simple bedwetting where a child has never had at least a 1-year period of consecutive dry nights" (Houts & Mellon, 1989, p. 60). Since children master bladder control at different ages, the diagnosis is not made until at least age five, according to current diagnostic manuals. Often called simple bedwetting or functional enuresis, the problem is rarely associated with organic problems. When it is associated with emotional problems, it is more likely to be the cause rather than the result of such problems (Houts & Mellon, 1989).

"*Secondary nocturnal enuresis* is the diagnosis made for children who resumed wetting after being dry for a year or more" (Houts & Mellon, 1989, p. 61). Failure to learn daytime control is called diurnal enuresis. Both are more likely to be associated with complex problems, medical or behavioral.

Primary nocturnal enuresis accounts for about 80 percent of all bedwetting. About one out of seven or eight children who wet the bed will remit spontaneously within a year. The theory that such children sleep more soundly than other children cannot be supported; most functional enuretics are no more difficult to rouse from sleep than other children. Bedwetting children tend to have smaller bladders than other children. Heredity may play some part; the problem often occurs in more than one child and several generations in a family. The theory that simple enuresis is a simple problem in learning (that the child fails to learn to attend to the discomfort of a full bladder while sleeping, or learns to sleep in a wet bed) gains credence from the well-documented success of treatment based on learning theory (Houts & Mellon, 1989).

Thus, primary nocturnal enuresis can be viewed as a failure, for whatever reasons, to learn nighttime bladder control. As such, it can be expected to respond to remedial techniques. Urine alarm training utilizes principles of learning to teach the desired control, to help the child to eventually acquire the behavior of awakening prior to wetting to go to the bathroom.

Drug Treatment

Imiprimine hydrochloride, brand name Tofranil, was originally used to treat depression in adults. In 1960, MacLean (cited in Houts & Mellon, 1989) reported that incontinent psychiatric patients often became dry when treated with Tofranil. The drug has been prescribed in smaller doses for bedwetting in children since the 1960s. While the drug often stops bedwetting, the problem usually resumes when the medication is discontinued. The lasting cure rate, defined as one year of successive dry nights, is no higher than would be expected from spontaneous remission.

Possible physical side effects include: increased heart rate, irregular heart beat, increased blood pressure, muscle tremors, profuse sweating, loss of appetite, and retention of urine. Given these side effects, the danger of children or parents exceeding the prescribed dosage to get better results is potentially serious. Tofranil does have positive implications, however, for children experiencing serious social problems due to primary nocturnal enuresis, especially for short-term treatment, as when a child must sleep away from home—for example, summer camp (Houts & Mellon, 1989).

Another drug, Ditropan (oxybutynin chloride), has fewer side effects. It is believed to work directly on the bladder muscle and to increase bladder capacity without the side effects of Tofranil. Its effectiveness in controlling bedwetting, however, has not yet been established (Houts & Mellon, 1989).

Behavioral Treatment

Retention Control Training

Retention control training is designed to increase bladder capacity. It involves a two- to three-hour daily exercise. The child is given eight to sixteen ounces of fluid. When the child first reports having to go to the bathroom, the child is encouraged to wait as long as possible. The child is rewarded for waiting longer and longer periods. Retention control training produces lasting cures in fewer than 30 percent of cases so treated (Houts & Mellon, 1989).

Urine Alarm Training

Mower and Mower (cited in Houts & Mellon, 1989) developed bell and pad, or urine alarm training, in 1938. It is the oldest form of behavioral treatment. An absorbent pad attached to a battery-operated alarm is placed in the bed. The theory is to wake the child as soon as possible after wetting starts. Sears and Roebuck carry such devises as catalog items. A newer device, consisting of a small pad worn in the underwear, the Wet-Stop Alarm, is available from Palco Labs, 5026 Scotts Valley Drive, Scotts Valley, CA 95066 (Houts & Mellon, 1989). Such devices can also be secured from local medical suppliers for costs well under $100.

About 75 percent of children treated with the technique for eight to twelve weeks stop wetting initially, with more than half remaining dry a year later. Failures of the technique are most often due to one or more of three factors:

1. Failure to wake the child every time the alarm sounds, allowing the child to sleep through the alarm.
2. Allowing the child to get up, turn off the alarm, and go back to bed without becoming fully awake and going to the bathroom.
3. Failure to continue the technique long enough, normally twelve to sixteen weeks (Houts & Mellon, 1989).

Children who relapse usually do so within six months. Reapplying the procedure for two to four weeks results in successful retraining in some but not all cases. Children previously treated with Tofranil are more likely to relapse (Houts & Mellon, 1989).

Young and Morgan (cited in Houts & Mellon, 1989) found that overlearning reduces the risk of relapse. Overlearning is begun after the child has remained dry for two weeks. The child is then given a large amount of fluid before bed until the child remains dry for two more weeks. Urine alarm training with overlearning produces a lasting cure rate of more than 60 percent (Houts & Mellon, 1989).

Full Spectrum Home Training

Houts and Mellon (1989) have developed a procedure for parents and the child to follow called Full Spectrum Home Training. It incorporates urine alarm training, retention control training, over-learning, and some aspects of a procedure called Dry-Bed Training developed by Azrin, Sneed, and Foxx (cited in Houts & Mellon, 1989). Dry-Bed Training is a complex procedure that involves waking the child at scheduled times during the night and having the child change wet sheets when necessary, along with the use of the urine alarm (Houts & Mellon, 1989). Houts and Mellon's Full Spectrum Home Training is especially adaptable to residential facilities that have awake staff during the night.

The most important part of the urine alarm training is to awaken the child immediately when the alarm sounds. The child must get out of bed and stand up before turning off the alarm. Only the child may turn off the alarm. Staff should log when wetting occurs. It normally will occur within three hours of going to sleep or within three hours of waking. Children who wet more than once will normally wet in both of these times. With this procedure, most children will require no additional assistance to learn to awaken themselves to the alarm.

Children who fail to awaken themselves to the alarm after five weeks are placed on a wake-up schedule. For children who normally wet during the first three hours, the wake-up time begins three hours after bed time. Each time the child is dry, the time is moved one half hour closer to bed time until the child is being awakened thirty minutes after going to bed, at which time the procedure is discontinued. If the child wets during the procedure, the wake-up time is moved back one half hour, although the three-hour-after-bed-time limit is never exceeded. For children who normally wet during the last three hours, a similar procedure is begun three hours before wake up, and moved thirty minutes forward each night, or back if the child has wet the bed. This procedure helps the child to become sensitized to the alarm.

Retention Control Training is conducted during the alarm training as a two-hour daily exercise. The child is given a large glass of water. When the child has to urinate, the child is asked to wait three minutes, then rewarded. The procedure is moved to a maximum of forty-five minutes by three-minute intervals. It teaches the child to distinguish various bladder sensations and to be able to urinate at specified times.

Cleanliness Training involves having the child change the bed every time the alarm sounds. The Wet-Stop Alarm may react so quickly that urination is stopped before the bed becomes wet. The child should change the bed anyway to insure the child is awake. Alternatives, such as having the child solve a math problem involving thought rather than rote memory, may be employed.

Overlearning involves starting the child with four ounces of water given fifteen minutes before bed time. The amount is increased by two ounces after two consecutive dry nights up to a maximum based on the formula of two ounces plus one additional ounce for each year of age. The child continues the maximum amount until fourteen consecutive dry nights have been achieved. About one-third of the children complete overlearning without further wetting. For the others, if wetting occurs during overlearning, the amount is reduced by two ounces until five consecutive dry nights have been achieved, then the schedule is resumed until the criteria of fourteen consecutive days at the maximum amount is reached.

During this procedure, intake of liquids and fluids should not be restricted. There should be no mention or reference to any inconvenience the procedure may cause others. The child should receive help, praise, encouragement, and support, but should not be urged to try harder or do better. There should be no punishment, scolding, or ridicule for bedwetting. The procedure will do the work.

SUMMARY

The potential of the residential treatment program derives from its ability to meet a variety of needs for its children. These needs range from the age-appropriate, normal developmental needs through needs for counseling and remediation to needs for treatment and therapy.

The child care counselors, by virtue of the amount of time they spend with the children, have the opportunity to address most of the children's normal developmental needs as well as most of their needs for counseling and remediation. Moreover, they can contribute much to treatment and therapy by providing information and by meeting specifically assigned objectives.

Despite their needs for therapy and treatment, children in residential treatment present much that is normal for their age groups. When possible, their normal needs should be met in as normal a fashion as possible. Child care counselors should be able to provide a variety of normal activities with normal supervision.

When trained in techniques for active listening and supported with trained supervision, child care counselors may employ active listening to meet a variety of objectives. Active listening is a counseling technique that facilitates decision making. Helping children to express their emotions verbally, rather than acting them out behaviorally, facilitates treatment objectives as well as the management objective of deescalating potential crises.

The teaching interaction is a remedial technique that is used to teach specific social skills to predefined criteria. Not to be confused with active listening or life-space interviews, it teaches children skills in responding more appropriately to adults and peers.

The life-space interview is a counseling intervention in which child care counselors, on the scene during significant events, may intervene at the most opportune time to facilitate the child's understanding of events and her or his role during an event. Active listening techniques may be employed during a life-space interview. In the next chapter, we will look at the use of a structured life-space interview to complete the process of therapeutic crisis intervention.

Urine alarm training can be used to address a fairly common problem experienced in residential settings—bed wetting, or primary nocturnal enuresis. It can be conceptualized as a remedial technique employing behavior modification to teach the child nighttime bladder control, including awakening before wetting the bed.

While child care counselors may not be the best trained treatment or therapy personnel on staff, they may be among the most effective by virtue of the amount of time they spend with the children and the probability that they will be present in any number of circumstances. In the next chapter, we will look at how child care counselors may be trained to meet treatment, therapeutic, and management needs when a child is in crisis.

Therapeutic Crisis Intervention

RESIDENTIAL treatment programs should expect aggression and violence. These phenomena have become increasingly significant in American life. Society's "response" to crime and criminals is becoming increasingly violent, as is the behavior of criminals. It is interesting to debate whether society is responding to the violence of its criminals, or the criminals to the violence in society. I suspect each is responding to the other. This does not mean that residential treatment programs should tolerate this kind of behavior as an inevitable part of their programs, but that they should be prepared to treat crises involving violent and aggressive behavior as an inevitable part of the job of treating troubled children in this society.

The behavior of a child who is out of control poses some of the most serious problems a residential program may face. Such children may present serious threats to themselves, other children, staff, the facility and equipment, and sometimes the community. I suspect that more allegations of child abuse by agency staff arise from dealing with children in crisis than from all other potential sources of abuse and neglect combined. Thus, the child who is out-of-control is a very serious management issue.

Out-of-control behavior also poses perhaps the most serious problem the child may have in the residential setting. Attempts at self-injury, aggression against peers and staff, and property damage may well account for more unsuccessful discharges

(transfer to a more secure facility, hospital, or juvenile correctional facility) than any other behaviors, except running away in some programs. Children who are out-of-control are extremely vulnerable. Sometimes they invite or provoke abuse. When force is necessary, excessive force may be disguised or rationalized. Further damage may be done to an already damaged child.

Moreover, when children are especially vulnerable, they are not only vulnerable to abuse but also to treatment. Thus, the out-of-control behavior of a child is also a critical issue for treatment. Treatment objectives require that no more damage be done to the child and also that the opportunity for treatment be utilized. It will quickly pass. By the time a child who has had a behavioral crisis gets to her or his therapist, the incident may be so effectively defended and distorted by the child that treatment may be virtually impossible.

Behavioral crises are therefore both treatment and management issues. Child care counselors must be trained to address both sets of issues decisively and effectively. There is no time to plan for either issue once a child enters a behavioral crisis.

Moreover, because crises are so problematic, staff must be trained to identify developing crises and deescalate them therapeutically. Many children who are given to behavioral crises are skilled at manipulating adults into behaviors that help the child to escalate.

Nothing else focuses on the issue of control versus treatment as does a child in crisis. "Often when an individual becomes physically aggressive it is assumed that the therapeutic process should be abandoned. Quite the contrary" (Wyka, 1987, p. 9s). "The therapeutic milieu must be maintained continually, even during the most violent moments" (Wyka, 1987, p. 9s). Crisis produces both the greatest need for control and a heightened opportunity for treatment. The control must be provided; the opportunity for treatment should not be lost.

In this chapter, we will consider mechanical restraints, chemical restraints (sedation), and control (time-out or seclusion) rooms. We shall then consider a model of crisis as an opportunity for treatment, including stages of development, appropriate interventions at each stage, passive physical restraint for control, and the life-space interview for therapeutic recovery.

A SAMPLE "CRISIS"

My first experience with a child in crisis was as a student in a field placement at a juvenile detention home. I taught school in the mornings during the summer along with another student while the regular teacher was on summer break. The incident also provided my first exposure to a control room, a straight jacket, staff escalating a situation, and a child suffering from a long history of multiple placements.

Beverly. Beverly was an attractive and well-developed adolescent of thirteen. Her intelligence was low average; her levels of academic functioning were several grades behind. Beverly had a history of multiple placements beginning at an early age. They included various institutional placements, hospitalizations, and attempts at foster placements. Beverly was temporarily in a juvenile detention home following her most recent failure in a foster home. Beverly had not had a good day. She had not been allowed to attend class, which disappointed her; Friday was movie day. Her probation officer came to visit. After lunch she was locked in her room; all of the children, twelve adolescents in temporary placement awaiting action by the court, were locked in their individual rooms after lunch every day for an hour of "meditation." Her probation officer's car was parked near Beverly's window. As the officer got into the car, Beverly cursed her roundly through the open but securely screened window.

The probation officer returned to the building. She told the houseparents, a young married couple, what Beverly had done. Together, they decided to remove Beverly from her locked room and place her in the padded room, a ten-by-ten room with padded walls and a padded door with a small window for observation. Children who were placed in this room had their clothing removed so that they could not harm themselves with it, even though they had no belts or shoes, only shirts, pants, socks and underwear.

As they brought Beverly from her room, her struggles increased. As they got to the living room, Beverly went to the floor screaming that they were not going to put her in "that room again." Beverly was successful in resisting the attempts of the houseparents and her probation officer to put her into the padded cell. As they struggled with her unsuccessfully on the floor, the female houseparent phoned for assistance. Police officers arrived. Eventually, they secured Beverly in a straight jacket on a stretcher; an ambulance took her to a psychiatric hospital.

Our field placement ended several weeks later. We never head any more about Beverly.

MECHANICAL RESTRAINTS, SEDATION, AND CONTROL ROOMS

The straight jacket, other mechanical restraints, the seclusion or isolation room, and sedation or medication have a long history of use to control people who are out of control. The need for control is obvious; treatment cannot occur without it. Sometimes, however, treatment needs seem to get misplaced, if only for a little while.

Mechanical Restraints

Hospitals may use several techniques of mechanical restraint. The straight jacket was made famous by Houdini. Another technique involves securing the patient in a bed with leather restraints around the midsection, arms, and legs, the five-point restraint. The former may allow the patient to remain ambulatory and verbal. The latter may allow the patient to remain verbal and in his or her own room.

Correctional facilities may use mechanical restraints called shackles. One variation involves securing the hands with handcuffs and the ankles with similar bracelets. Ankle and wrist bracelets are secured together with a chain which is passed through a broad leather belt worn around the waist. The length of the chains between the feet and the length of the chain securing ankles and wrists to the leather belt determine the amount of mobility that is allowed.

All of the above require some means of subduing the child, physically or in combination with sedation. All of the above may be used in conjunction with sedation and/or isolation in a room or solitary cell. They all control behavior. To the extent that the child learns to use different or new behaviors to avoid such consequences (avoidance learning), these techniques may have some treatment value. Such controls, however, are rarely available in settings other than psychiatric hospitals or correctional facilities. Any behaviors that may be learned in response to such techniques may not readily generalize to settings in which such techniques are not employed, such as the home and family, school, a group home, or independent living.

Administrative regulations, laws, and court precedents for any procedures that limit the free-dom of individuals vary from jurisdiction to jurisdiction. Any facilities using such responses to aggressive behavior must be well aware of any legal restrictions, administrative guidelines, or court precedents that apply.

Sedation

Psychiatrists may prescribe and medical personnel may administer medication to control aggressive behavior. Medication may be prescribed situationally, as a response to an outburst. Medication may also be prescribed as preventative treatment for children with a history of aggressive behaviors.

Wishik, Bachman, and Beitsch (1989) report that:

> In our experience, anticholinergics, benzodiazepines, barbiturates, and antihistamines more often serve to aggravate aggressive behavior than alleviate it. Patients can be sedated; however, upon awakening, the agitation and aggression may be worse than prior to treatment. Our opinion is not universally accepted. Other clinicians have reported successfully using these same medications to alleviate aggression. In some cases, they may be accepting a certain degree of sedation to achieve behavioral control. In other cases, perhaps some individual patients may in fact demonstrate a beneficial effect (p. 30).

Use of medication in treatment is considered more fully in chapter 13, ''Professional Interventions.''

Time-Out in Seclusion or Isolation

The concept of time-out, ''short for response-contingent time-out from the availability of positive reinforcement'' (Swartz & Benjamin, 1983, p. 31), has recently been integrated into the use of seclusion to attempt to utilize seclusion in a therapeutic manner. ''Time-out represents an attempt to place the child in an area that is as free of reinforcement as possible in an attempt to eliminate an undesired behavior. It is the assumption that the behavior will be eliminated because the child no longer has access to the reinforcer'' (Swartz & Benjamin, 1983, p. 31).

If we know that behaviors must be reinforced then we also know that a particular behavior can be eliminated by removing the reinforcement. This is the basic assumption underlying the use of time-out. . . [We can] (1) remove the reinforcer from the child, or (2) remove the child from the reinforcer. We choose option two when we cannot identify the reinforcer or for some reason cannot remove it (Swartz & Benjamin, 1983, p. 30).

Variations of Time-Out

Gast and Nelson (cited in Gallagher, Mittelstadt, & Slater, 1988) summarize four classical variations of time-out from the literature:

removal of all sources of reinforcement while the child remains seated, placement as a contingent observer, placement in exclusionary time-out in a contained area in the classroom where observation of others is not possible, and placement in seclusionary time-out in a separate, isolated room (p. 60).

Gutheil and Tardiff (cited in Gallagher et al., 1988) identify three indications for seclusion and restraint: to prevent imminent harm to the patient or other persons when other means of control are ineffective or inappropriate; to prevent serious disruption to the physical environment; and to assist in treatment as part of ongoing behavior therapy (p. 61).

Gallagher et al. (1988) suggest that time-out may be used to comply with a patient's request. They present five levels of seclusionary time-out, from least to most restrictive:

1. In the time-out room with the door ajar and an adult outside the room.
2. In the time-out room with the door closed but unlocked, with an adult outside the room.
3. In the time-out room with the door locked and an adult outside.
4. In the time-out room with an adult in the room with the door closed.
5. In the time-out room physically restrained by an adult until calm.

They note that "low-structured children who are vulnerable to the onset of psychotic processes are not able to tolerate seclusion unless a trusted adult remains with them at all times" (p. 63). Is being placed in a room alone "more restrictive" than being placed in a room with a trusted adult present?

Is Time-Out Punishment?

Swartz and Benjamin (1983) state that:

[C]ontrary to much of the literature, time-out, as a behavioral intervention, does not constitute punishment. Punishment involves the presentation of an aversive stimulus whereas time-out procedures lead to removal of positive reinforcement contingent upon a response (p. 30).

Spitalnik and Drabman, along with Steeves, Martin, and Pear (cited in Swartz & Benjamin, 1984), suggest that time-out is itself aversive, but Holtz, Azrin, and Ayllen (also cited in Swartz & Benjamin, 1983) find that time-out is too mild as an aversive event to be an effective punishment. Smith (cited in Swartz & Benjamin, 1983) presents data on four children treated with time-out procedures. The drop in target behaviors does not produce the sharp curves typically associated with punishment that suppresses behavior; rather, the more gradual curves associated with extinction are produced. "This is to say that appropriate use of time-out results in extinction curves; it does not result in punishment curves" (p. 31).

Effectiveness

In their study on the effects of time-out on children with severe emotional and behavior disorders, Swartz and Benjamin (1983) found that both exclusionary and isolation time-out produced short-term control rather than modification of inappropriate behaviors. Their data indicated that the use of exclusionary time-out increased behaviors that resulted in increased use of isolation time-out:

No final conclusions can be made relative to the use of time-out based on the results of this study. Little is added, however, to recommend it. . . . Expedient methods that effectively control undesirable behaviors might sacrifice long-term outcomes for short-term effectiveness. . . .

The availability of a locked time-out room to control physically aggressive children was an obvious comfort to staff. Reactions from children ranged from considerable fear to dramatically heightened activity levels. It appeared that the time-out room was used more in response to staff losing control of a child rather than a child losing control of his behavior. . . . The treatment philosophy emphasized structure in such a way that the use of time-out appeared to be directly related to attempts to impose stricter limits. The limits took the form of rules that numbered in excess of reasonable short-term memory (pp. 38–39).

Is Time-Out Treatment?

Kelly and Nelson (1979) found in an audit conducted of seclusion procedures for accreditation purposes that time-out in seclusion was used as a reactive measure to deal with incidents. There was no indication that it was used as a treatment modality. It was never discussed in team meetings nor incorporated in treatment plans. "Some children should never be secluded, i.e., a child who deliberately gets himself secluded to escape from an issue he doesn't want to deal with" (p. 284–85). Cates and Cooper (1983) suggest that "from the evidence given, it would appear that if the use of seclusion is to be a therapeutic technique, interaction between staff and patient must occur" (p. 52).

Legal Considerations

While "time-out" is defined in treatment terminology, "seclusion" is a term with legal implications that may be overlooked by clinical staff. Once an "intervention has been classified as seclusion, most jurisdictions place significant restrictions upon its use" (Landau & MacLeish, 1988, p. 33).

Applicable law, court decisions, and administrative regulation vary from state to state. Illinois limits seclusion to use as a therapeutic measure to prevent injury to self or others. States typically require that seclusion may be imposed only by order of a physician, except in an emergency. Illinois

requires the physician to assign someone to observe the patient every fifteen minutes. Most states, however, do allow seclusion in other than dangerous situations when it is incorporated into the treatment plan (Landau & MacLeish, 1988).

Other Considerations

Time-out in isolation (as opposed to a corner of the classroom, at a table, or just sitting off to the side) has been styled as a behavioral intervention in which reinforcement is not possible. Consequently, undesirable behaviors extinguish. It has been argued that it is not punitive or aversive.

In some cases, this may be true. The attitude of the staff and child in approaching time-out will indicate the true nature of the time-out intervention. When staff are gentle and apologetic and the child goes to time-out reluctantly, then time-out may be little more than a temporary loss of positive reinforcement. However, when the child escalates drastically and the staff appear to be angry, aggressive, rough, and punitive, then time-out for that child may have more aversive qualities. In such cases, learning may be more based on principles of avoidance learning, as the child changes behavior to avoid time-out in the future, or escape learning, as the child changes behavior in time-out to get released. In any case, the discrimination cues available in the milieu where time-out is available are substantial; I suspect generalization to other settings is minimal.

CRISIS AS OPPORTUNITY FOR TREATMENT

How can aggressive behavior be handled therapeutically? The Family Life Development Center of Cornell University has developed a training program called Therapeutic Crisis Intervention. The program defines three types of crises:

1. The instructive crisis, in which the child learns something beneficial.

2. The destructive crisis, in which the child is harmed or damaged in some way.
3. The constructive crisis, in which someone helps the child to improve his or her situation (Budlong, Mooney, & the staff of the Family Life Development Center, 1983).

When a child loses self-control, becomes dangerous, and is safely restrained, the child learns that he or she is safe in the program and will not be harmed—an instructive crisis. When the child loses control and is subdued with punitive measures, suffering pain or injury, the child learns that the program is but one more dangerous and hostile place in a violent world—a destructive crisis. When the out-of-control child is restrained without violence and is taught a new way of dealing with his or her anger to avoid a crisis, the crisis is constructive. There is a fourth possibility in which, while the child is not harmed, the child also learns little, such that there is no change. Consequently, crises can be expected to recur whenever similar circumstances present themselves.

Wyka (1987) identifies two types of aggressive behavior that require two different responses. Verbal acting out requires verbal intervention; a premature attempt at physical intervention can readily provoke a physical crisis. On the other hand, physical acting out requires physical intervention; verbal interventions are ineffective responses to someone who is hitting, biting, or choking someone.

Wyka identifies four levels of crisis development:

1. the anxiety level
2. the defensive level (verbal acting out)
3. the acting out level (physical aggression)
4. tension reduction

There are appropriate staff responses to each level.

The Anxiety Stage

Staff who are present at the onset of a crisis and who are in a position to be attentive are likely to observe anxiety—pacing, fidgeting, wringing hands, etc. A supportive response may be effective in averting the crisis. Active listening may be an effective supportive response.

The Defensive Stage

If staff are not present during the anxiety stage, or when supportive responses are not effective, the crisis can be expected to proceed to the defensive stage. The defensive stage is identified by the beginnings of a loss of rationality. It is a highly volatile state that usually includes verbal aggression, threats, and racial, sexual, and personal insults directed at the staff and the program. Children at this level are masters of insult. Telling people where to go and what to do to themselves when they get there is relatively mild. More personal attacks on staff lineage, race, sex, sexual preference, weight, build, and the like can be expected to hit home (Wyka, 1987). "You" or "this place don't really care about us! You're just in it for the money!" can be expected if nothing else works to bring the staff down to the child's level.

According to Wyka, one type of staff response to the defensive stage is illustrated by what occurs on occasion in larger institutions. A crisis alarm summons security to a crisis. When they arrive, security finds two people in a heated argument with one more agitated than the other. Security's first task is to identify which person is the staff, which the client.

The defensive stage requires a directive approach from staff, setting limits. Limits should be simple, clear, and enforceable. Children on the verge of irrationality do not need six or seven options, and they can be expected to test any limits that are set. First, make it clear why limits are being set, for example: "You're disturbing the others." Second, state the alternatives positively, but clearly: "You can stay if you can lower your voice, but we'll have to escort you to your room if you continue to disturb the others." Staff should adopt the attitude that she or he is there merely to enforce the alternatives, not to coerce the child into choosing one option over the other.

The Acting Out Stage

The acting out stage is evidenced by a total loss of control. It may involve any combination of assaultive behaviors including destruction of property, self-destructive behavior, and aggression against peers or staff. Staff may not arrive at the crisis until the child is in this phase, or the child may have been unresponsive to supportive or directive interventions.

Once the child begins acting out physically, verbal interventions will rarely be effective in reducing the crisis, in taking the child back to a previous phase—especially when staff have been present and have attempted verbal interventions during previous phases. On rare occasions, a new person arriving on the scene may be able to interrupt a physically acting out person with a verbal intervention, especially when that person has some significant basis of power, such as an administrator, a physically imposing person, a police officer, or a person with whom the child has a special relationship.

However, when no such miracles appear, the physically acting out person requires physical intervention. Proper physical intervention protects the individual, staff, and others from injury. It protects the client from other serious consequences, such as possible guilt and the legal complications from causing injury to another human being, or the insurmountable indebtedness from extensive property damage. Even two broken windows worth $50 may take a child months to work off if the agency holds the child fully accountable. Such an obstacle can seriously compromise future treatment. Consequently, properly utilized restraint can be a therapeutic necessity.

It is beyond the scope of this text to offer techniques for safely subduing children who are acting out. The National Crisis Prevention Institute (Steiger, 1987) offers such techniques through its Nonviolent Crisis Intervention workshops, as does the Family Life Development Center of Cornell University through its Therapeutic Crisis Intervention training program (Budlong et al., 1983). Both programs offer techniques for staff to avoid injury and escape from various situations without violence towards the child. Such situations include having one's hair pulled, being bitten, being choked, being grabbed in various ways, and being threatened with weapons. Examples include raising one's arms straight overhead and turning 180 degrees to break a choke hold, or pushing into a bite while closing the child's nose to have the child breathe through the mouth and release the bite. In many instances, including the above, the physical intervention techniques taught by the two programs are identical.

Both programs teach staff to be in touch with their own emotions. The physically acting out child has become irrational, with adrenaline pumping. Such situations normally get the adrenaline pumping in staff. While adrenaline may increase one's physical strength and reflexes, adrenaline is not noted for improving one's intellectual reasoning. Responses to an acting out child, therefore, are likely to be reflexive in nature. This is good, since acting out children do not often afford people the opportunity to sit down and develop a treatment plan. On the other hand, it means that staff reflexes must be trained and then maintained with regular practice (Budlong et al., 1983; Wyka, 1987)

If the staff are excited, possibly even fearful in such situations, imagine how the child must feel. Out-of-control people scare virtually everyone, including themselves. The security offered by a staff person who is in control may be the most important factor in resolving a crisis therapeutically.

Therapeutic Crisis Intervention offers specific training for the safe take down and restraint of an out-of-control child. The key to the restraint is that the child is safely controlled in such a manner that virtually all external stimuli are eliminated. An older child is restrained face down on the floor, with the staff member straddling the child. The younger child is also controlled from the rear, with arms crossed in front and staff holding the child from the rear by the wrists (Budlong et al., 1983).

The staff does not respond verbally to the child except when the child demands to be let go or complains of pain or discomfort. When the child demands to be let go, the staff calmly informs the child that he or she will be released when he or she is calm, in control, or something to that effect. This statement is given once clearly, but only once. Further outbursts are ignored. Complaints of pain or discomfort are met with an adjustment in the hold to attempt to alleviate the discomfort, followed by some question as to whether or not that is better. Other staff in the vicinity remain out of sight and do not interact with the child, although they may assist with restraining the legs (Budlong et al., 1983).

Tension Reduction

Some children who are restrained one way or another during a crisis will struggle physically until exhausted; others will avoid the physical struggles, except for an occasional testing of the restraint, but will continue with emotional verbal outbursts until exhausted. In either case, the tension reduction will be both physical and emotional. The tension reduction level, often overlooked, is as critical as any other stage of the crisis if the intervention is to be therapeutic. This is the level at which the individual begins to regain rationality. Individuals in this phase may be emotionally withdrawn, apologetic, or remorseful. The appropriate response from staff is therapeutic rapport (Wyka, 1987).

Therapeutic Crisis Intervention terms this phase of the crisis "recovery"; it offers specific steps for the process of letting go and for utilizing therapeutic rapport to accomplish a therapeutic objective. When the child has calmed down, the staff begins to speak to the child in calm and reassuring tones. The process of letting go is slow and deliberate. The staff informs the child of what is being done (Budlong et al., 1983). "I'm going to let go of your arms now." The staff communicates expectations. "I want you to leave your arms out straight." The staff secures verbal acknowledgement. "Do you understand?" The child must be

appropriately responsive and respond in appropriate voice tones for the process to continue. "Yes," or "OK." "Now I'm going to get off of you. I want you to lie still for a few minutes. OK?" "Yes."

Therapeutic Crisis Intervention has adopted Redl's life-space interview for the final part of therapeutic recovery according to the acronym "I ESCAPE" (Budlong et al., 1983):

I—Isolate the child from the distraction of others and the need to perform for or defend against peers. ("Let's go to your room," or "Let's go to the office.")

E—Explore what happened from the child's perspective. (What others did and what the child did. Possibly what the child felt.)

S—Share your observations of what happened. ("Well, what I saw when I came into the room was . . .")

C—Connect what happened with other real-life situations for the child. ("I think sometimes you have a similar problem in school. Remember when . . .")

A—Help the child look for Alternatives for handling similar situations. ("What else could you have done? What about if you . . .?)

P—Help the child come up with a Plan for handling similar situations in the future. ("OK, so next time that happens, you'll go and tell staff that you're having a problem with Ted.")

E—Exit with the child back into the program. ("OK, it's time for study hall. Are you ready?")

While therapeutic crisis intervention offers this approach to the life-space interview as the final part of the intervention to be used following a restraint, the life-space interview is a verbal tool that may be used to intervene earlier, during the anxiety stage or the defensive stage (if the child responds to the choice of isolating herself or himself) to avoid physical acting out behavior. Very often, isolating the child from others in a neutral area or the child's room, with staff present (as opposed to a seclusion room), will afford greater opportunity for verbal intervention to be effective in avoiding a physical crisis.

There are some similarities between the teaching interaction and the life-space interview as presented in the therapeutic crisis intervention model. Staff sometimes confuse the two. Both are likely to deal with inappropriate behavior. Both will relate the presenting inappropriate behavior to other real-life situations (the "rationale" of the teaching interaction, the "connection" of the life-space interview). Both seek to have the child handle similar situations more effectively (the teaching interaction by teaching predefined social skills, the life-space interview by coming up with a plan). In fact, if the child is familiar with the social skills taught by teaching interactions, the plan might simply be to use the appropriate social skills.

There are, however, some significant differences. The teaching interaction deals with cognitively-learned skills. The life-space interview, while it can deal with the same skills, may also deal more readily with emotional issues. The teaching interaction, with the social skill of temper control, will attempt to teach children how to behave when they are angry; the life-space interview will allow for some exploration of feelings of anger, some exploration of the feelings of other people, in addition to exploring alternatives of how to behave in the presence of those feelings.

Discussion

Anyone who has tried to hold a 135-pound thirteen-year-old child who has absolutely lost it knows the violence, anger, and adrenaline-pumped strength with which such a child can struggle; many older and stronger children do not put up nearly the same fight. When children need control, it's almost as if they're afraid to break out of a reasonable restraint conducted by an adult who is in control.

Byron. **A supervisor of a unit in an adolescent psychiatric facility described an incident with a fifteen-year-old boy weighing in at some 300 pounds. One day the boy become agitated (anxiety stage). He became defiant, challenging staff (defensive stage). He moved almost immediately into the acting out stage. He stood against the wall and defied staff to "take him down." The supervisor (about 5′10″ and 160 pounds) and other staff took the boy down with no problem and secured him in restraints. "He was easy." They then had to call in two "codes" (requests for assistance) to get sufficient personnel to be able to carry the restrained boy to his bed.**

I have noticed that smaller and younger children exhibit the most aggressive behavior towards staff. They punch, kick, scratch, and bite. Older, larger, and potentially more dangerous children do not as readily attack staff physically. They may take aggressive postures and stances and challenge staff; they do not as readily make the first move. Nor do they seem to resist as aggressively as smaller children if staff make appropriate moves to control them. I have developed four hypotheses to explain this observation:

1. Smaller children expect staff to be able to control them safely. They can, therefore, let themselves go without fear of harm coming to themselves, staff, or others, trusting staff to control them safely.
2. Smaller children are younger, less mature, and therefore have less self-control.
3. Staff, out of necessity, are more diligent in avoiding restraints with children they cannot readily control.
4. Larger, more dangerous children who cannot control themselves get placed in correctional or psychiatric facilities; hence, they do not have as much opportunity to act out in residential facilities.

I have no systematized data with which to evaluate these hypotheses. However, in ten years of experience in residential facilities, including one secure correctional facility, I can remember only one child who could not be controlled (or who failed to allow himself to be controlled) by staff. I suspect that hypotheses 1 and 3 are most likely to be the operational factors in most instances.

SUMMARY

Behavioral crises pose some of the most serious problems a residential treatment facility may face. Such crises pose serious managerial problems—the child, other children, staff, the facility, and sometimes the community may be at risk. They also afford excellent opportunities for treatment.

Crises may be classified into four categories according to the outcome:

1. The instructional crisis, in which the child learns something beneficial.
2. The destructive crisis, in which the child is harmed in some way.
3. The constructive crisis, in which the child changes her or his situation for the better.
4. The ineffective crisis, in which the child is neither harmed nor improved.

When a child's behavior is out of control to the point of posing a threat to the child's own safety, or to the safety of others or the facility itself, the child must be controlled in some way. This is a management need. Hospitals and correctional facilities may employ chemical restraints (sedation), mechanical restraints (straight jackets, five-point restraints, or shackles), or isolation or seclusion. They may be used singly or in combination, such as mechanical restraints or sedation along with seclusion, or sedation along with mechanical restraints.

Studies of the uses of such techniques are somewhat contradictory. Some studies indicate that uses of some of these techniques may actually escalate violence or aggression. Studies seem to agree, however, that staff will use whatever techniques are available.

To the extent that such techniques teach children to avoid acting out behavior to avoid these interventions, at least in the institution, such techniques may lead to instructive crises. I suspect, however, that use of such techniques is dehumanizing and damaging to children's self-esteem. To the extent that this may be true, such techniques may lead to destructive crises.

When used as a crisis intervention, time-out, short for response contingent time-out from positive reinforcement, is an attempt to use seclusion in accordance with principles of learning. Given that behavior must be reinforced in order to continue, the application involves removing the misbehaving child from the normal environment so that the child can no longer receive reinforcement. Time-out may be in a neutral area, the child's room, or a specially designated seclusion room for periods of minutes or hours.

Time-out may be an effective application of learning theory when the time-out procedure itself is not aversive to the particular child, when time periods are brief (a few minutes), and when appropriate reinforcements are available in the environment from which the child is removed. It can be very effective when used for inappropriate behaviors that are not of crisis proportions.

When used in crisis response, the child is less likely to go quietly to time-out, and the period of time in time-out is likely to be longer. Consequently, the procedure is more likely to develop punitive aspects.

Wyka (1987) identifies four stages of a crisis and suggests appropriate interventions at each stage.

1. The anxiety stage, evidenced by agitation, pacing, etc. Active listening may be an effective intervention.
2. The defensive stage, characterized by verbal acting out, insults, profanity, threats, and the beginning stages of a loss of rationality. A directive approach in which staff set clear, firm, rational limits and offer clear and simple choices may be successful at this stage.

3. The acting-out stage, characterized by aggression against self, others, or property and full-blown loss of rationality. Prompt, safe physical intervention is called for at this point.
4. The tension reduction stage, which usually occurs when the child (and often the staff) is exhausted. It is characterized by the child's return to rationality. The child may be withdrawn, apologetic, and/or remorseful. Therapeutic rapport is the approach that can help to make the crisis constructive. A structured life-space interview may be especially effective.

Nonviolent Crisis Intervention offers excellent training in techniques for crisis intervention, with careful attention to avoiding crises through early recognition of developing crises and the skillful use of verbal interventions before the crisis reaches a physical level. It also teaches nonviolent techniques for managing a crisis that has reached the level of physical aggression. This is therapeutic in Redl's sense of the milieu: *"don't put poison in their soup"* (Redl, 1972, p. 131), meaning don't cause harm.

Therapeutic Crisis Intervention teaches techniques for managing crises that have reached the physical stage and for using crises to promote therapeutic objectives in the sense of therapy as used in this text—to promote a change in the individual in a desired direction.

Both programs focus on staff attitudes, emotions, and behavior. During pre-physical stages of the crisis, when verbal interventions are called for, both programs teach that communication is only partly verbal. Both teach that persons attempting to intervene verbally should stay out of the child's physical personal space and keep hands open, in sight, and in non-threatening and non-defensive positions, preferably at the sides. Both teach that voice tones, body position, and facial expression are likely to communicate more than words. Both stress the need for staff to attend to their own feelings, emotions, and behavior during the crisis. Both teach that physical interventions must be nonviolent and nonpunitive—yet quick and decisive. Both stress

that physical intervention techniques must be carefully taught with skills maintained through practice. Both stress that what occurs after the crisis is therapeutically important.

Mechanical restraints, sedation, and time-out rooms are effective in managing aggressive behavior. They are unlikely to be effective in the long term as treatment for aggressive behavior in some children; they may actually sacrifice longer term gains for benefits in the short term in some cases. However, such interventions are a comfort to staff. When they are available, they will be difficult to eliminate from the program.

Whatever approach the facility uses towards crisis, there are several critical elements that should be taught to staff:

1. Early recognition of a developing crisis.
2. Appropriate responses and interventions at early stages.
3. Prompt, safe physical interventions for crises that have reached a physical stage.
4. Agency guidelines and expectations that are consistent with legal requirements.
5. Regular practice of physical interventions to keep skills sharp and at the level of "reflexes."
6. Appropriate treatment interventions after the crisis.

According to Bruce Bona (Northrop, 1987):

[R]easonable people seem to do reasonable things in restraint. They don't need to be taught not to hit the child's head on a cement floor. I think the real education comes in realizing that nothing at all happens from the physicalness of the restraint if there isn't more to it than that, if there isn't building of the relationship (p. 50).

Most children need the restraint to be personal (p. 44).

After I go home, I always call him on the phone; even if he is asleep, I ask staff to wake him up. I don't really say anything to him, I just ask him how he's doing or something, but I want him to know I called (p. 39).

13

Professional Interventions

RESIDENTIAL treatment programs may offer a variety of therapies and interventions that require special training and in some cases professional licensure. Other times, residential programs may use outside resources for therapy or treatment, evaluations, medication, and education. When such professional services are offered in coordination with the total treatment milieu, they can be especially effective.

On the other hand, because residential programs are stressful, demand less desirable evening working hours, and frequently offer relatively low pay, they often find much of their professional services provided by recent graduates with limited experience. I have been extremely disappointed with the number of applicants for therapy positions who have difficulty conceptualizing therapy as a goal-directed process with identifiable strategies. Consequently, rather than providing purposeful therapy, such personnel sometimes do little more than counseling, reviewing the child's week, and discussing feelings, consequences, and alternatives, all without the advantage that staff may have—that of being on the scene at the time. While this may have benefit, it is not therapy.

In those instances when professional services are provided by personnel outside of the residential program, through contract or consultant personnel, public mental health centers, or private agencies, such personnel may have limited working knowledge of the residential program and limited time to coordinate with residential staff. Residential personnel must be knowledgeable and realistic about such services if they are to be in a position to maximize benefits for their children and the program.

The techniques and interventions presented in this chapter require professional training, expertise, and in some cases professional credentials and licensure. Some readers may be well-versed on one or more of the techniques I have selected for presentation; they, of course, will find those presentations brief and cursory. I hope they will also find them a reasonably fair summary, should they choose to read them rather than pass over them. Few readers, however, will be well versed in all of these professional interventions.

I have chosen two models of individual therapy: Ellis' Rational Emotive Therapy (RET) and Glasser's Reality Therapy. RET is a cognitive technique that employs some applications of learning theory. It may be utilized in both individual and group settings. It is indicated for many adolescents and families; child care counselors can readily support its use in the living environment. Practitioners, however, sometimes become judgmental of children and families who, having been taught RET principles, still cannot apply them in practice.

I have seen Glasser's Reality Therapy distorted beyond recognition on more than one occasion out of the mistaken belief that allowing a child to suffer natural consequences, a "dose of reality" as it were, is Reality Therapy. Reality Therapy is more and different. It is based on the close relationship that is established between the therapist and the patient. Within that relationship, the therapist helps the patient to face realities in interpersonal relationships that the patient has been denying. Letting a child who has been arrested for shoplifting spend a night in detention, a natural consequence, is indeed reality; it has little to do with Reality Therapy.

I have chosen to present at some length on art therapy. It is an intervention that has considerable potential for children who have problems with verbal communications. It requires more than getting children to draw or color pictures. Few residential programs will have the resources to employ an art therapist. I have devoted considerable space to this modality, however, because it exemplifies the creative use of a modality other than the traditional talking, behavioral, or pharmacological therapies.

Pharmacotherapy requires a licensed psychiatrist, preferably a child psychiatrist, to diagnose the child and prescribe medication. It is most efficacious when it is used in coordination with other treatment modalities. Since many programs do not have psychiatrists on staff but rather rely on mental health centers or consultants when they feel a child may need medication, they must be able to take some initiative in coordinating with the psychiatrist, who may have limited knowledge about the program and its capabilities.

The program must have sufficient knowledge about pharmacological interventions to work efficiently with the psychiatrist, providing appropriate information about the child's response to medication, including side effects, to assist the psychiatrist in finding the best medication and optimum dosage. Pharmacotherapy also poses some serious management problems for smaller facilities related to security of medication, and may be subject to abuse by personnel who attempt to manipulate the psychiatrist, sometimes unconsciously, into prescribing medication they believe is needed.

Education may be the single most important aspect of a child's life, including his or her life in residential treatment. Too often, residential programs and their children are at the mercy of public schools which have little to do with the residential program beyond exhorting staff to have the child behave better in school. Residential programs must have sufficient understanding of educational evaluations, resources, and potential to be able to set realistic goals and effectively plan treatment.

Group therapy, an especially important intervention for adolescents, has different dynamics in the residential setting than in more open settings where the group members do not live together. Consequently, its uses and potential in residential settings are somewhat different than in outpatient groups.

INDIVIDUAL PSYCHOTHERAPY

Individual psychotherapy refers to therapy performed in individual sessions with a trained professional, most often a social worker, psychologist, or psychiatrist. Such professionals may be licensed by the state, or they may work under the supervision of another licensed professional. In residential settings in some states, they may practice without license or licensed supervision.

As defined in this text, therapy requires a goal of some lasting change in the individual. Individual psychotherapy, sometimes referred to as "talking" therapy, seeks to change the individual in some way through sessions with a trained professional. Changes may be sought in some category of ego strength or ego functioning, in personality in some way, or in some other psychodynamic concept. Goals must be fairly clear, despite the fact that such therapies often deal with hypothetical (and therefore unobservable) constructs. Strategies to meet those goals must also be conceptually clear. The Rational Emotive Therapy of Ellis and Glasser's Reality Therapy are two approaches to individual therapy that meet these criteria and may be effectively integrated into residential treatment settings. There are many other approaches.

Rational Emotive Therapy

Ellis began using rational emotive therapy (RET) in 1955 and presented his first paper on the technique at the 1956 annual meeting of the American Psychological Association. It is an approach to therapy that emphasizes both cognitive and behavioral methodology (Ellis, 1977).

According to Ellis (1977), biological inheritance and tendencies of self-learning and social-learning combine to make people human and to provide them with their main goals and satisfactions. He theorizes that when people have an emotional or behavioral problem, it follows an activating event, something that occurs that seems to be unpleasant in some way. This emotional or behavioral problem is a consequence. For example, the consequence that follows the activating event of getting dumped by one's girlfriend or boyfriend may be depression and avoidance of all social contacts. The assumption is that the activating event of being dumped caused the consequence of depression.

Critical to RET theory, however, is the concept of the intervening variable—one's belief about the event that occurred. The person who was not too tied to the girlfriend or boyfriend, who had recently made a new acquaintance and was considering a date, is not likely to be depressed and go into isolation. The emotional and behavioral consequences may quickly follow the activating event, but they are not caused by the event. Rather, they are caused by the beliefs the individual has or forms about the event.

Consider: "Jan was beautiful. She was the only girl for me. I must be awful to have let her get away. There will never be another," to "Bill and I were getting old. It's time for a change," or "There's plenty of other fish in the sea." The first may lead to despair and serious depression; the latter are likely to lead to increased social activity. "Well, it was great, but it just didn't work out" may lead to some disappointment, unhappiness, and regret, but it will not look like the end of the world.

It is the belief about an event that causes behavioral consequences. Irrational beliefs cause serious consequences. Of course, events play a role. If you don't get dumped, there's nothing to get upset about, unless you're afraid about getting dumped. People can make their lives, and the lives of those around them, quite miserable with irrational beliefs about what might happen or with unfounded jealousies, for example.

The role of therapy is to detect and to teach the client to detect irrational beliefs that cause problems. The goal of therapy is a new effect or philosophy that enables the client to think differently about herself or himself, others, and the world.

The theory and process of RET is concisely conceptualized in Ellis' A-B-C framework:

A. Activating event—something occurs.
B. Belief—the person forms a belief about what occurred.
C. Consequence—the person develops a feeling about what occurred, an emotional Consequence, which the person assumes is caused by the Activating event, A.
D. Detecting, Disputing, Debating, Discriminating, and Defining—if the person has a dysfunctional emotional or behavioral Consequence, it almost certainly follows from an irrational Belief that can be Detected by Disputing beliefs through logical and empirical methods. "The scientific method takes any shaky hypothesis, particularly one that leads to poor results, and actively, vigorously disputes it, until it gets surrendered or sustained" (Ellis, 1977, p. 20).
E. new Effect or philosophy—the client eventually ends up with a new Effect or philosophy that results in a semiautomatic way of thinking about self, others, and the world.

Reality Therapy

Glasser's (1975) Reality Therapy operates from the premise that everyone who is experiencing emotional or behavioral problems suffers from one basic inadequacy, the inability to fulfill his or her essential needs. No matter how irrational the problem may appear, it has meaning for the individual in the attempt to fulfill basic needs. The individual, however, denies the reality of the world in which she or he exists. The basic needs are twofold: "the need to love and be loved and the need to feel that we are worthwhile to ourselves and to others" (p. 9).

There are two basic goals of therapy: to help the patient to face reality, and to teach the patient to meet her or his needs within reality. Patients may come for help themselves, be compelled to seek help by family or community, or be placed in a correctional or mental institution because of problems with behavior.

The ability to fulfill these basic needs is learned, beginning in infancy. Failure to learn leads to suffering, which drives people to try unrealistic means to fulfill needs. Those who learn to fulfill needs at an early age may not be able to do so all their lives. When a person comes for therapy, she or he "is lacking the most critical factor for fulfilling [her or] his needs, a person whom [she or] he genuinely cares about and who [she or] he feels genuinely cares about [her or] him" (Glasser, 1975, p. 12). While it may appear that there are plenty of people who care about the patient, there is still something wrong. The patient either cannot accept their love or does not care for them.

The first step of therapy is to get the patient reinvolved with others, beginning with the therapist. The specific goal of therapy is increasing the patient's responsibility. Glasser (1975) defines responsibility as "the ability to fulfill one's needs, and to do so *in a way that does not deprive others of the ability to fulfill their needs*" (p. 13). People who can fulfill their needs are responsible, people who do not have or who have lost the ability to fulfill their needs are irresponsible. Hence, the therapeutic goal of teaching responsibility.

Reality Therapy is a specialized learning situation made up of three interrelated procedures:

1. The therapist and the patient must become involved so that the patient can begin to face reality.
2. The therapist must reject the unrealistic behavior while accepting the patient and maintaining the involvement.
3. The therapist must teach the patient better ways of fulfilling needs within the confines of reality.

The therapist's ability to get involved is the major skill of Reality Therapy. It may take one interview or several months, depending on the patient and on the therapist's skill. The therapist must be responsible and have the strength to become involved, to accept the patient uncritically as he or she is at first, and to understand the behavior, no matter how frightening or aberrant.

Once involvement begins, the therapist insists that the patient face the reality of his or her behavior. This will help to strengthen the relationship as the therapist demonstrates that someone now cares enough to make the patient face a truth she or he has been avoiding for some time: she or he is responsible for her or his own behavior. The therapist confronts the patient with her or his behavior, asking the patient to decide if the behavior is the responsible course of action. The therapist accepts no excuses for the behavior—parents, circumstances, society, feelings of unhappiness, or fears. The therapist cares enough to reject behavior that does not help the patient to fulfill needs. The therapist will discuss attitudes and views of reality, but makes it clear that behavior is the primary concern.

". . . politics, plays, books, movies, sports, hobbies, finances, health, marriage, sex, and religion are all possible topics. . . . When *values, standards, and responsibility are in the background, all discussion is relevant to therapy*" (Glasser, 1975, p. 31). The therapist shares opinions in these discussions, allowing the patient to learn on what kind of a person he or she has come to rely. Further, the patient develops an increased sense of self-worth in the process of parrying opinions with a trusted and respected person.

Relearning, the last phase of therapy, begins when the patient has accepted that her or his behavior is irresponsible. It is not a separate step, but a part of the entire process. Some patients need much help in learning new ways to meet their needs; others require relatively little.

Conclusions

Rational Emotive Therapy may be especially effective with adolescents who are struggling to use their developing powers of reason to make some sense out of life. This is a fairly normal adolescent phase, even for adolescents in treatment. As such, RET may also work well in groups with adolescents, who may be more interested in what their peers say than in what their therapist tells them.

RET also has implications for parents who seem to be always angry with their children. Some parents, when asked for one thing about their child that they would not change, draw a complete blank. RET provides a structured approach to working with the way in which parents perceive their children, think about them, and subsequently feel about them and behave toward them.

With some children, however, feelings run so deeply that they are not readily reached by conscious processes. When such children readily grasp the principles of RET in therapy, but are unable to apply the thinking part in certain situations prior to being engulfed by their emotions, there is sometimes a tendency to blame the child rather than the therapy. While RET may be especially helpful in some situations, other interventions may be more appropriate when a child's anger or sadness is real and justified, as when his mother fails to show for the third weekend in a row.

Reality Therapy may be readily adapted to residential treatment and can be effective with a variety of presenting problems. The theory is relatively simple and does not hinge on technical terminology and unobservable hypothetical constructs of personality. It focuses on present behavior, a primary concern of staff and residents. This does not mean that it is relatively simple to use. It requires training, skill, and experience. It does mean that it can be readily understood and supported by child care staff and that they can be trained to coordinate their daily involvement with residents with ongoing therapy. Further, behavioral management or treatment in the program can be coordinated to facilitate the work of the reality therapist in individual sessions.

However, the principles of Reality Therapy sometimes get simplified to the point that, while little therapy is being done, programs lay claim to offering Reality Therapy as a part of their treatment milieu. When a child misses a home pass because she or he failed to earn enough points according to the point system, when a child spends a night locked up in detention because of a shoplifting charge or a runaway, these may be natural or expected consequences for which the child is indeed responsible. They may even be good for the child on some level. They are reality. They may even be behavior treatment. They are not Reality Therapy.

Reality Therapy involves a relationship. The relationship provides the basis from which the child eventually comes to an understanding that certain behaviors, or misbehaviors, are not meeting her or his needs. The child must then be helped to learn proactive behaviors that will meet her or his interpersonal needs, not merely to withhold behaviors that result in unpleasant consequences.

ART THERAPY

According to Dalley (1984), the main purpose of art is to produce a good work of art that is an end in itself. The creative process is secondary. The purpose of art in a therapeutic setting is different. The person and the process become primary. "[W]ith clear corrective or treatment aims, in the presence of a therapist . . . art activity provides a concrete rather than a verbal medium through which a person can achieve both conscious and unconscious expression, and can be used as a valuable agent for therapeutic change'' (p. xii).

What Art Therapy Is Not

Art therapy is not only for those clients who are talented or interested in art. In fact, those with some skill in art often use their skills to distort or repress unconscious material. "The majority of patients treated successfully in art therapy have neither drawn nor painted before'' (Dalley, 1984, p. xxiii).

Nor are art therapists art teachers. While they may be artists, they must also be trained in awareness of their role in the therapeutic process. Art therapy is not a trivial activity to be played with. Its potential requires training and professional standards (Dalley, 1984), as does any other intervention in a person's life.

Nor is art therapy merely a form of occupational therapy. Occupational therapy works on a conscious level with the goal of making products or teaching skills (Dalley, 1984).

Finally, art therapy is not diagnosis through art. The only person qualified to interpret a work is the artist. "The therapist may speculate, suggest, and connect aspects of the picture, but this occurs within the therapeutic relationship in an environment of trust, openness, and safety, and should not occur outside this context'' (Dalley, 1984, p. xxiv). "Interpretation should be approached with caution, however, for . . . art forms are statements on many different levels, and this tends to exacerbate the risk of error or misunderstanding. For example, a black blob which appears in the corner of a painting may be mistaken for an evil symbol when it is only spilt paint or simply a lack of drawing skill'' (Dalley, 1984, p. xx).

The Scope of Art Therapy

Art therapy creations are concrete and form a permanent record. Creations can be talked about at the time, or at a later time. A series of creations can provide a record of change in attitudes or relationships over time (Birtchnell, 1984).

Art is produced for a particular person or group. It should not be used for other purposes without the permission of the artist. It can also be destroyed. How a subject destroys a creation can provide much insight (Birtchnell, 1984).

Art therapy can permit the fantasy of creating something that has been lost or permit communication with a lost loved one. It can permit the subject to say something to a person that he or she wishes to have said, or to take back something he or she regrets (Birtchnell, 1984).

Art therapy can also permit the creation of something of which the subject is fearful, such as being confined, addressing an audience, or a dream in which she or he appeared naked. Rehearsing fears in pictorial representations may help to reduce those fears (Birtchnell, 1984).

In fantasy, subjects can engage in disapproved or forbidden acts, such as having sexual relations with a parent or sibling, being cruel or punitive, or behaving outrageously. A subject may be irrational, even psychotic on paper. "There are unfortunately still those who use the pictures painted in art therapy sessions as aids to diagnosis and such people may not appreciate that mad pictures are not necessarily painted by mad patients'' (Birtchnell, 1984, p. 39).

Finally, pictures might allude to what might be, as opposed to what is or what was. Subjects might depict a successful outcome, a feared disaster, being tall, thinner, more powerful, famous, of the opposite sex, or anything else (Birtchnell, 1984).

The Practice of Art Therapy

Art therapists can work one-on-one or with groups. They can work as part of a team in an institutional setting or apply techniques in private practice. Sessions are generally divided into two stages. The first stage is a creative activity such as painting or sculpting. During this phase, participants tend to isolate, to think, to withdraw into themselves. Therapists plan sessions, deciding the objective. Materials and themes must be considered, and to what extent the therapist will be directive or nondirective.

The creative phase is followed by a period of discussion. The therapist and client explore the process of creating, how the client felt during the process. They also discuss the work that has been created, how it relates to the individual. This is not done by ''direct analysis or interpretation,'' but by ''mutual suggestion and exploration. . . . The solidity and concrete nature of the art form provides a clear visual arena for therapeutic work and some obvious starting points for interpretation'' (Dalley, 1984, p. xx).

Case Study

Uhlin and De Chiara (1984) present a case study of Mary, who was autistic in infancy. Although the outcome is inconclusive, Mary progressed considerably with an art therapy intervention.

Mary. **Mary was first encountered at the age of eleven. In her classroom, she maintained a collection of bugs, alive and dead, in glass jars at her table. She dumped them out, picked them up and talked to them. Her speech was slurred and difficult to understand. All of her bugs were related to a figure she called ''Shawmite.'' When asked about them, she became anxious, twisted her hair, then clenched it between her teeth.**

Records indicated that Mary's mother gave birth at the age of twenty-two, following a normal pregnancy during which her alcoholic husband abandoned her. Shortly after birth, Mary was given to her maternal grandmother; her grandmother returned her a few months later. Mary's mother carried on a series of affairs, giving birth to Mary's brother when Mary was two. Mary and her brother were locked in a closet for several hours when their mother entertained her male companions. They were removed by welfare authorities when Mary was four. Mary was placed in a succession of foster homes and had not seen her mother or brother since then. Various diagnoses sug-

gested mental deficiency, brain damage, and childhood autism.

Mary was asked to draw a Shawmite. Over two years, Mary drew Shawmites, bug-like figures with eyes that had slits for pupils. For some time she resisted talking about her Shawmites, clenching her hair in her teeth. Eventually, she responded to questions about the Shawmite as she was drawing. She was afraid of him because he was the ''Bad Murderer'' coming to drown her in the water. When asked about the eye, she responded by drawing the eye over and over. She stated, ''This is the eye I'm afraid of. People are born out of the eye'' (Uhlin & De Chiara, 1984, p. 196).

At this point, the form of the Shawmite changed; it began to look like a fetal horse. Mary was also beginning to tear paper into beautiful forms. She was given an ice cream carton from which she created a sculpture of the Shawmite. She created similar sculptures from butcher paper. Her last project was made from an automatic washer carton, out of which she created a human-like figure she called an astronaut. It had eyes with lashes. She placed it in a sitting position in a chair, climbed into its lap, puts its arms around her, and began to suck her thumb. Shortly after this, her foster home released her; she was sent to a state hospital.

Conclusions

Few programs will have the luxury of an art therapist. The art therapist is a highly trained professional whose skills in therapy are more significant than her or his artistic skills. When deep-seated emotional problems that appear to have an early historical origin lead the treatment planner to believe that psychotherapy is indicated, and when verbal skills and potential for insight seem weak or inadequate, art therapy may provide the breakthrough.

With or without an art therapist, art continues to be a valid activity that contributes to the development of skills such as eye-hand coordination, and all of the attendant benefits, including development of confidence, self-esteem, and pride of accomplishment. This is good. It is healthy. But it is not therapy.

Art therapy is more. An art therapist is a professional, trained to work as part of a treatment team. The therapist plans sessions, including the materials and subjects with which to work and how much choice or direction is to be given to the patient or client.

Art therapy can provide a valuable technique especially when the verbal communications, on which most of us depend almost completely, do not serve well for one reason or another. Some clients may not be as verbal as some therapies may require. Some issues may be too primitive to be readily expressed verbally.

As with some other professional interventions, art therapy is subject to misuse. When inexperienced personnel attempt to interpret a child's art work without appropriate interaction with the child, there is the potential for misinterpretation and for decisions or actions that are misguided.

PHARMACOTHERAPY

A wide range of medications are available for children. They work biologically on the child. Medications are available that affect such things as psychotic symptoms (hallucinations and delusions), mood and affect (depression and manic states), aggression, ability to pay attention in class, even urine retention at night. Medication is primarily a treatment or management intervention as the terms are used in this text. It does not generally produce the longer lasting, underlying changes of therapy. Rather, medication may produce a change in the individual's functioning as long as it is continued. Sometimes these changes can be considered treatment; other times they are more closely related to management, as when they are used to control aggression or to help the child to participate to greater advantage in education, therapy, or other treatment modalities.

In addition to their potential beneficial contributions to the treatment of children with problems, many of the medications in use have potential side effects that must be watched for by attentive staff or monitored by medical personnel:

hypotension
bone marrow suppression
tardive dyskinesia (facial tics and other uncontrolled behaviors)
exacerbation of preexisting motor deficits
diminished attention and memory
liver toxicity
tremors
polyuria (frequent urination)
polydipsia (excessive thirst)
nausea and vomiting
diarrhea
encephalopathy (enlargement of the brain or toxicity)
abnormalities in kidney function
abnormalities in thyroid function
anticholinergic side effects (dry mouth, blurred vision, among others)
sedation
cardiac arrhythmia

For some medications, blood pressure and pulse rate must be monitored; for others, blood levels must be taken regularly to monitor levels of medication in the bloodstream to avoid toxic effects (Wishik et al., 1989). Psychiatric medication requires a psychiatrist, preferably a certified child psychiatrist. My strong personal preference is for the prescribing psychiatrist to be actively involved in the child's treatment in the residential program on a near daily basis. When regularly involved, the psychiatrist can both observe the child regularly and get frequent and current reports on the child's behavior, side effects, and progress in other areas, such as school and therapy. This enables the psychiatrist to make first-hand decisions about the appropriateness of the medication, the appropriateness of the dosage, and the indications for continuing the pharmacotherapy.

For many programs, this is not possible. Many

programs must rely on either a contract consultant or a public mental health clinic for psychiatric services. In such cases, the psychiatrist is limited to brief and infrequent observations of the child at an office and is therefore almost totally dependent on reports, often by a single staff member. Residential personnel must be much more knowledgeable about the uses of psychiatric medications if they are to coordinate with the psychiatrist for the most effective use of such medicines for a given child.

Goals for Pharmacotherapy

Dalton and Forman (1992) offer two main purposes for the use of psychiatric medication with children in inpatient psychiatric settings. I believe they apply as well to children in residential settings. The first is to alter internal biological forces that affect behavior to "improve reality testing, observing-ego abilities, and the regulation and modulation of affect" (p. 71). Improvement in these areas may increase impulse control and the ability to adapt to social reality. The second purpose is to assist in behavior control. These two purposes are often related.

The Appropriate Use of Medication in Treatment

It must be emphasized that all aggressive behavior—both "normal" and pathologic—is the end product of an interaction between the brain and the environment. Social, cultural, educational, economic and psychodynamic factors are generally emphasized in most discussions of aggressive behavior, while the contribution of developmental brain defects and acquired brain lesions are all too often unappreciated and ignored. . . . Ultimately, it is the complex interaction of brain, experience, and environment that results in all behavior, including aggression (Wishik, Bachman, & Beitsch, 1989, p. 18).

Wishik et al. (1989), in discussing the use of medication in the treatment of aggressive behavior, offer some guidelines that are relevant to the use of psychotropic medication in residential treatment.

Assessment is important. Family, staff, and possibly other residents should be questioned. The following information should be sought:

1. The clinical state of the child and his or her activity prior to the outburst.
2. The predictability of various environmental factors—time of day, activity, specific places, or specific staff or residents—that may precipitate outbursts.
3. Description of the very first aspects of the outburst.
4. A detailed, blow-by-blow account of the outburst, including the responses of family, staff, or others during the episode.
5. The course of the episode in time.
6. The events that led to the termination of the episode and the child's clinical state at the conclusion of the episode.
7. Historical information, including when such episodes first began. Were they related temporally to illness, injury, family events, or institutionalization?
8. Are behaviors during episodes stereotyped or varied?

For instance, one of us had the opportunity to care for a severely demented, though generally very pleasant man, who became extremely agitated and aggressive when the staff did not appreciate that he had a tack in his slipper. This rather trivial example illustrates the importance of carrying out a complete and detailed evaluation of aggressive behavior for each individual patient. The treatment for a tack in the slipper is not haloperidol (Wishik et al., 1989, p. 21).

According to Wishik et al., medications are often prescribed from one of two extremes, as either the only appropriate treatment or as the treatment of last resort. They believe that neither extreme is correct (1989):

Pharmacologic therapy should be viewed as a useful adjunct to the overall treatment program. The judicious use of the correct medication at an appropriate dosage should leave patients more accessible for other types of behavioral intervention. We have seen therapists struggle hopelessly with a difficult to control patient in the mistaken belief that medication will somehow represent a personal failure. Conversely, in our experience, rarely is medication by itself sufficient to address the needs of a patient with significant behavioral problems (p. 25).

A rich variety of medications are available to treat behavioral disorders. While there are few systematic studies that will help match specific medications to specific individuals and their specific problems, and while "treatment remains largely trial and error" (Wishik et al., 1989, p. 26), there are guidelines for any use of medication for behavior management:

1. An appropriate evaluation as described above should be completed before therapy.
2. Specific goals should be identified for pharmacotherapy.
3. A method should be formulated for determining whether or not those goals have been met.
4. An appropriate medication should be chosen and given at an appropriate dose.
5. Treatment should be continued long enough to determine whether or not the medication has been effective.
6. The decision to medicate should be a consensus agreement of everyone involved in the child's treatment, including the child and the family when appropriate.
7. Ongoing efforts at behavioral treatment should be not only continued but also strengthened.

Potential Problems with Pharmacotherapy

As with just about anything else in the world since the discovery of fire, the wheel, and tools, medication too has beneficial uses and potential for misuse and abuse. Psychotropic medication in residential treatment poses dangers for misuse and abuse in two different areas.

The first is the potential for unauthorized use and abuse by residents and the strain such medication can place on the agency's security procedures. This strain can be especially significant in small facilities that do not routinely use such drugs, and which, therefore, do not have well-established routines for the daily management, administration, and security of dangerous drugs. The second potential for misuse and abuse lies in the area of misuse in treatment: of using such medications inappropriately, of expecting more from medication than medication can deliver, and of overdependence on medication.

Security and the Potential for Misuse by Residents

A resident need only fool staff a few times that he or she has taken a prescribed pill to have a potentially dangerous dosage available for misuse. Palming or under-the-tongue ruses can allow the resident a supply of pills for sale, gift, or personal misuse—including a suicide attempt. Medication prescribed at three times per day allows 90 chances to fool staff in a given month. Residents will soon detect and may readily exploit any weaknesses in staff supervision of the administration of drugs.

In larger facilities, nursing staff are available to administer medications. For nurses, the administration of medication is a primary duty and responsibility. As such, the administration of medication normally receives their full and undivided attention. In smaller facilities, shift personnel or houseparents have a myriad of duties and responsibilities. Administration of medication may readily be perceived as a chore that takes them away from what they perceive, often through the help of training and specific directives, as their primary responsibilities. They may readily be distracted, sometimes by chance, sometimes by deliberate diversion.

Larger facilities with a nursing staff and an infirmary have careful security for medication and medical supplies. Security in this area is a primary responsibility of nursing staff. Smaller facilities may secure medications in a locked area with other items such as petty cash, confiscated contraband, keys to the facility vehicle, etc. Staff going into this area to access the petty cash can be expected to have the security of the agency's money as a primary concern. While attending to the money, they may be inadequately concerned about the medication, which has been exposed while they are counting out allowances, for example.

Moreover, staff have responsibilities in addition to medication. They are responsible for supervising residents. A fight, real or staged, occurring after a cabinet has been opened for cash or medication may require prompt and prolonged attention. A resident who is not distracted by the fight may have access to the medication. If the staff opened the cabinet for cash, the staff may keep an eye on the cash box on the desk while dealing with the fight, but forget about the medication. Upon return, a check of the cash box may satisfy the staff that security was not breached; the theft of medication may go undiscovered until a resident overdoses in an attempt to get high.

Medication and the security of other items. A small, community-based treatment facility had medication administration procedures that had been established by a registered pharmacist to meet the most stringent of hospital standards. All medical supplies were secured in a special cabinet reserved for that purpose. Vehicle keys, cash, and records were secured separately in a padlocked file drawer. One Friday night, a resident violated the rules by playing his large portable radio. Staff eventually confiscated the radio and secured it in the medical supply cabinet since the radio was too large for the file drawer.

Within half an hour, the resident had kicked in the door to the medical cabinet to retrieve his radio. Staff then put the radio in an administrative office that the resident did not dare to enter. The medical cabinet was improperly secured for the remainder of the weekend; fortunately, there were no problems with missing medication.

Potential for Misuse in Treatment

Medication is prescribed by a psychiatrist, often viewed as the final authority in treating children.

Unfortunately, the prescribing psychiatrist is not always fully involved with the treatment of the child. Consequently, there exists some potential for different expectations: the purposes of the psychiatrist in prescribing medication may be very different from the expectations of the staff working with the child.

This is especially notable in situations in which the psychiatrist is not on staff, but is rather a consulting psychiatrist either contracted or utilized through a local public mental health clinic. The psychiatrist prescribes medication to reduce a difficult behavior, often aggression or hyperactivity. The medication might help a little. It might make other treatment modalities just a bit more effective; it might make problems a little less frequent, a little less intense or severe.

Staff, on the other hand, may expect the medication to be the definitive treatment or the treatment of last resort. They may well feel that they have done their job when they have administered the medication as prescribed. When problem behaviors still occur, staff may feel that nothing will work. After all, the psychiatrist has failed.

On the other hand, staff who are frustrated with a particular child may exaggerate their reports of problems to insure that the child is placed on medication at the earliest opportunity. Meanwhile, other treatment interventions that might be more effective and appropriate are not attempted. When medication is prescribed, staff may exaggerate reports in the other direction, minimizing problems to confirm the effectiveness of the medication and their "diagnosis" that medication was the best treatment. Ultimately, the child may go untreated and be recommended for transfer or discharge as untreatable.

In a small facility in which staff have responsibility for administering medication, they occasionally forget a dose. This sometimes results in a temptation to exceed the prescribed dose in response to a later problem.

Conclusions

Clearly, medication for "problem children" should not be taken or given lightly. Some guidelines are indicated:

1. The program must be prepared to maintain the security of the medical supplies.
2. The program must be prepared to maintain security during the administration of medications.
3. The program must be prepared to deal with any emergencies arising from misuse of medications.
4. A thorough assessment of the problems to be treated with medication is required.
5. The prescribing physician should be asked what the goals for the medication are.
6. The prescribing physician should be asked specifically what side effects must be watched for, their probability, and the seriousness of the side effects.
7. The prescribing physician should be asked what the course of treatment with medication can be expected to be. Will the medication be required indefinitely? For life? Until circumstances, behavior, or whatever may change?
8. A plan should be devised to evaluate problems before medication and during medication to determine objectively whether or not the medication is having desired effects.
9. Communications with the treating physician must be free enough and frequent enough to allow the physician to make necessary adjustments to find the most effective medication and the desired therapeutic dosage.
10. All other treatments should continue.
11. The best goal is the ultimate goal of getting the child off of the medication. Little or nothing has been accomplished for a child who is successfully treated (managed?) with medication, but who then discharges to an environment in which the ''necessary'' medication will not be continued.

When used as part of a total treatment regimen, medication can serve to augment other treatment modalities and interventions. It can also undermine the effectiveness of other interventions, as when staff come to believe that the medication is *the* treatment, rely on it to the exclusion of other interventions, blame medication for failures and avoid taking responsibility for their own roles in treatment, or misreport and mistreat in order to manipulate the prescription of medication.

Medication undermines not only other treatment interventions but also normal growth and development when it so sedates the child that he or she falls asleep in class, in group, in staffings, and during free time. I have seen adult mental patients whose mental illness is seriously exacerbated by the fact that they have failed to accomplish some fairly normal developmental tasks, apparently excused from normal responsibilities during developmental years because of their illness and medicated into submission.

EDUCATION

Getting an education is the main business of childhood in our society, whether or not a child is in residential treatment. In fact, problems with school may be the most significant presenting problem for many children in placement. Educational objectives may relate to meeting normal developmental needs, remedial needs, and in cases where especially strong special education programs are available, treatment needs. Larger residential facilities are likely to have trained educators and a school on campus; smaller programs are likely to be heavily or almost totally dependent on public schools for services and expertise.

Assessing the Potential for Success in School

The treatment plan for each resident should contain a long-term educational goal that is appropriate, realistic, and attainable. Success in school is dependent upon several factors:

1. Ability:
   a. Intellectual
   b. Previously learned knowledge and skills

c. Social skills

d. Self-discipline

2. Motivation:

a. Does the child want to do well in school?

b. How much effort must the child invest to do well?

c. What other interests are competing with school for the child's efforts?

d. Does the child believe in his or her ability to achieve?

e. What payoff does the child perceive?

3. Support.

The above all work together towards the child's success in school. The more and greater the strengths, the more likely the child's success in school; the more weaknesses, the more problems the child experiences in school.

Ability

Children have certain natural abilities that are inherited; other abilities are acquired or learned. Both are important to success in school.

Intelligence. The best known measure of intelligence is the IQ test. The *Wechsler Intelligence Scale for Children-Revised* (WISC-R) is commonly used by psychologists with children between the ages of six and sixteen years, eleven months. The test provides verbal and performance scores as well as a combined measure called a full-scale score. There are six verbal subtests: Information, Comprehension, Arithmetic, Similarities, Vocabulary, and Digit Span. The six performance subtests are: Picture Completion, Picture Arrangement, Block Design, Object Assembly, Coding, and Mazes (Otto & Smith, 1980).

"The prime purpose of an intelligence test is to predict. . . . The educator that is knowledgeable about the contents of the subtest may be able to spot a learning disability and proceed with appropriate remediation techniques" (Tarczan, 1972, p. 26). IQ is nothing more than a score on a test, a score that rates the child in comparison with other children of the same age. It is useful for predicting performance in school and in various placements and alternatives within the school.

The evaluating psychologist will normally report three scores from the WISC-R: the verbal IQ, the performance IQ, and the full-scale IQ. The mean IQ for the WISC-R has been established at 100 with a standard deviation of 15 (Tarczan, 1972). This means that scores of between 85 and 115 are within the "normal" range. I suggest the use of "normal" rather than "average" because of the connotations of the terms. While one may like to be of average height or average weight, "average intelligence" conveys something a little less desirable than does "normal intelligence."

While performance, verbal, and full-scale scores that fall between 85 and 115 may be indicative of normal abilities, discrepancies between performance and verbal scores may be indicative of some learning disability. A student whose scores are reported on the WISC-R as Performance 96, Verbal 102, and Full-Scale 98 may be expected to have normal abilities. A student whose scores are reported as Performance 88, Verbal 110, and Full-Scale 97 may have some learning disability. Further testing may be indicated.

Occasionally, psychologists will also report subtest scores. The mean scaled score for each subtest is 10 with a standard deviation of 3. Thus, scores of between 7 and 13 are within the normal range. Scores of 1 to 3 on a subtest are inferior, while scores of 4 to 6 are below average, scores of 14 to 16 are above average, and scores of 17 to 19 are superior (Tarczan, 1972). Scatter among subtest scores may also be indicative of some learning disability.

On the other hand, lower scores on subtests that relate to prior learning such as General Information, Arithmetic, Vocabulary, even Similarities and Picture Completion, as compared with other scores not so dependent on prior experience, may be indicative of some depression of scores due to cultural factors or other problems with opportunities for prior learning. In any case, disparities between subtest scores or performance and verbal scores require further analysis.

Tarczan (1972) describes each subtest briefly and provides examples of the types of questions asked. Examples are fictitious, but they illustrate the extent to which performance on various subtests is dependent upon prior learning as compared to innate ability.

1. Verbal
    a. *Information*. The Information subtest asks questions such as how many months there are in the year and what are the names of the days of the week.
    b. *Comprehension*. The Comprehension subtest asks questions such as what one should do if one is hungry, or what one should do if one wanted to look at a book but had chocolate on one's hands.
    c. *Arithmetic*. The Arithmetic subtest asks questions such as how many pieces one gets if one cuts an orange in half, or how much change one would get from a dollar if one bought two dozen apples at twenty cents a dozen.
    d. *Similarities*. The Similarities subtest deals with analogies or similarities. "Sugar is sweet but limes are _____." "A ruler and a clock both _____." "In what way are an orange and a lemon alike?" "In what way are a cow and a goat alike?" (Tarczan, 1972, p. 37).
    e. *Vocabulary*. The vocabulary subtest asks for definitions of words such as tricycle, pillow, and annoyance.
    f. *Digit Span*. In the Digit Span subtest the child is read series of digits of from three to nine integers and asked to repeat them. The child is also read series of digits of from two to eight integers and asked to repeat them in reverse order.
2. Performance
    a. *Picture Completion*. The Picture Completion subtest consists of showing the child a series of pictures and asking the child what is missing, such as a rabbit without a tail or a buggy without wheels.
    b. *Picture Arrangement*. For the Picture Arrangement subtest, the child is given a series of pictures depicting events such as baking a cake and asked to arrange the pictures in order to make sense.
    c. *Block Design*. In the Block Design test, the child is given blocks with designs on them and a picture; the child is then asked to arrange the blocks like the picture.
    d. *Object Assembly*. Object Assembly consists of having the child place parts of familiar objects, such as animals, into meaningful wholes.
    e. *Coding*. Coding consists of having the child put symbols in correct positions according to a presented pattern.
    f. *Mazes*. The child is asked to find the path out of a series of mazes with a pencil (Tarczan, 1972).

Previous Learning. Previous learning has a marked bearing on a child's ability to perform in school. While we would expect a child with normal intelligence to have the ability to perform on grade level in school, we must also recognize that for a child to function in the eighth grade, the child must have at or near a seventh grade education. Several tests may be used to assess a child's grade level. They are referred to as achievement tests.

The Wide Range Achievement Test (WRAT) is especially popular because of its ease of administration and its reliability. It provides three scores: Reading, Spelling, and Arithmetic. Scores for each area are normally reported in grade-equivalents such as 4.1 (fourth grade, first month), 9.7 (ninth grade, seventh month) or 13.1 (college freshman, first month).

The WRAT consists of three parts. For the Spelling test, the subject is read a list of words and asked to write the correct spelling. The words become increasingly more difficult. The test continues until the child misses five words in succession. The Arithmetic section is a series of math problems that begin with simple addition and proceed with increasing difficulty through long division, algebraic equations, and square root. Finally, in the Reading section, the subject is presented with a list of words to read, beginning with simple three-letter words and progressing through words such as "pusillanimous." The WRAT can be administered in as little as thirty to forty-five minutes.

Other achievement tests include the Stanford Achievement Test (SAT) and the California Achievement Test (CAT). Such tests may take several hours to complete and are often administered in school as part of the regular school program. Scores may be given for a variety of school subjects and may be given in grade equivalents, or in percentiles or stanines with conversion tables for grade equivalents.

Achievement tests are useful for determining placement, such as the grade in which a child should be placed. They are also useful for identifying needs for remediation. Schools use such tests to monitor the effectiveness of their programs.

Social Factors. Children with good social skills (follow instructions, accept criticism, accept "no," accept limits, maintain good peer relations, and maintain good adult relations) tend to do fairly well in school. Such skills may help to some extent to make up for lesser ability or motivation. On the other hand, such children, who do not cause much trouble, may sometimes go unnoticed when they are not learning because of special needs.

Self-Discipline. Self-discipline is the ability to discipline oneself, to make time for responsibilities, to complete tasks and assignments, and to meet deadlines. It is important to success in virtually all phases of school.

Motivation

Motivation was discussed at some length in chapter 7. Education takes a good deal of time, effort, energy, and commitment. I doubt that many of our public school students are pursuing an education because of a clear perception of its importance to their own lives. Motivation can help one to over-

come serious handicaps; lack of motivation can permit unusual talent to lie dormant.

Does the Child Want to Do Well in School? Children want to do well in school for a variety of reasons. Among them are the joy of learning, the sense of accomplishment, pleasing parents, pleasing teachers, gaining status among peers, winning awards and prizes, gaining material rewards that have been offered at home or at school, getting into special advanced classes, getting scholarships, going to certain schools, getting off restrictions imposed by parents, pleasing staff in the residential treatment program, or earning points in the residential program. Some children derive little satisfaction from school, finding it a relatively unpleasant experience to be endured or avoided if possible. Others with learning disabilities and problems with peer relations may find school a singularly unpleasant or even painful experience.

How Much Effort Must the Child Invest? For some children, A's come easily; for other children, A's come only with great effort and difficulty. There are those children for whom C's and D's come only with the greatest of effort. For some children, getting along with others comes naturally; for others, staying out of trouble takes tremendous effort in the face of daily teasing by peers.

What Other Interests Are Competing? Some children are called away from school responsibilities by peers, dating, sports, music, hobbies, jobs, or responsibilities at home. At the other extreme, there are a few children who seem to have no interests apart from school.

Does the Child Believe in Her or His Abilities? Children with a history of success in school are usually confident in their ability to succeed if they choose to invest the effort, to make the commitment. Children with a history of failure in school are afraid to try, to risk more failure.

What Payoff Does the Child Perceive? In the case of an upper-class child who is assured of a college education followed by graduate school or a position in the family business, the payoff of a high school education is especially attractive. It is not only lucrative but also nearly certain. For the lower-class youth in an uncertain environment, the payoff of the same high school education may be much less lucrative and much less certain. For the child in residential treatment who may not even know where he or she will be going to school next year, let alone which or how many high schools he or she may have to attend, the payoff of a high school diploma, attained at great effort, may be quite uncertain. Employment may be doubtful and college is likely to be perceived as out of the question. Consider the role models for such children. How much do the child care staff at the program earn? How satisfied are they with their jobs?

Support

Does the family support the child's efforts and achievements in school? Does the family provide the child with a suitable place to study? Or does the family place obstacles in the child's way? Does the family merely ignore the child's efforts in school, playing the TV too loudly, having guests in, allowing siblings to make too much noise? Does the family gladly provide the child with necessities for school—materials, fees, gym suits, lunch money, supplies? Or does the family complain when they have to make some effort or expenditure? Does the family encourage the child or belittle the child's difficulties? Does the family support the child too much, taking the child's part against a teacher or the school when the child is wrong? Does the family help the child with difficult assignments? Does the family help the child with household responsibilities when the child has a long or difficult assignment? Does the family help the child get to the library for special assignments? Does the child have tutoring, if needed?

Now go back and ask the same questions for the residential treatment program.

Developing Appropriate Educational Goals

A child's success in school depends on a variety of factors, including ability, motivation, and support. A typical child in residential placement will have normal or near normal intelligence, possibly with significant subtest scatter and significant deviation between performance and verbal IQ scores. Achievement scores are likely to be two or three grades below the grade level appropriate for the child's age. There is often a history of failure in school along with a history of behavioral problems. As the child approaches the mid-teens, she or he may have some sense of the importance of her or his education, but little hope of turning things around.

Few children are going to have strengths in all of the areas that are significant for success in school. Some strengths in these areas, however, are necessary for successful completion of high school. With strengths in some of these areas, deficiencies or weaknesses in other areas may be overcome. How can we set a realistic goal for the child's educational future?

High School Graduation

High school graduation requires that the child earn sufficient Carnegie units. Units are earned for passing grades in selected subjects at the rate of .5 units per course per semester. Students passing six courses may earn three units per semester. Two courses may be taken during a summer session (an additional unit may be earned). Requirements vary from state to state, with somewhere between twenty-one and twenty-three units being required for graduation. Carnegie units may only be earned in graded classes. Special education students in ungraded classes do not earn Carnegie units, but some schools may have graded special education classes in which students may earn units towards graduation. Thus, successful completion of high school normally requires that the student enter regular classes at the ninth grade level and proceed through four years of high school.

I suggest the following minimum criteria to

establish high school graduation as a reasonable educational goal:

1. *Ability*.
   a. *Intellectual*. Normal intelligence, with an allowance for 5 percent error (IQ of 80 or above).
   b. *Previous learning*. Achievement test scores to exceed 7.0 by the time the child enters the ninth grade.
   c. *Social skills*. The child must be able to reach the point of managing school without danger of expulsion by the ninth grade.
   d. *Self-discipline*. Lack of self-discipline may be somewhat overcome with externally-imposed discipline if the child is responsive.
   e. *Age*. A highly motivated child who does not fail may complete high school in three years (three units per semester for six semesters, one unit per summer session for three sessions for a total of twenty-one units). Sixteen is the oldest a child may be to begin earning Carnegie units and have a reasonable chance of graduation. A child who enters the ninth grade by the age of sixteen may be able to graduate by the age of nineteen or twenty, if there are no failures or other setbacks.
2. *Motivation*. Motivation can be increased. The child may need to be motivated by rewards for *daily* achievement, measured by daily progress reports from the school, until such time as the child can experience the success of a good report card to create some confidence in her or his abilities. Daily rewards will eventually have to be replaced with the more natural rewards of adult approval, status among peers, and pride in accomplishment. The more deficiencies the child must overcome in other areas, the greater must be the child's motivation.
3. *Support*. The more the child's deficiencies in other areas, the greater the support needed. If a child is entering ninth grade with achievement test scores that are one or two years below grade level, specialized tutoring is strongly in-

dicated. Does the program have high standards for academic achievement? Not only staff but also other residents must share values favorable to education if a child is to overcome deficits in other areas.

A child who is three or more years behind is very unlikely to overcome deficiencies sufficiently to get back on track and complete high school. Strengths in the areas of social skills, self-discipline, and motivation may overcome academic deficiencies with time, but students who are so far behind academically are likely so because of deficiencies in these areas, not strengths.

Graduate Equivalency Diploma

Students who are unable to complete high school because they are too old to realistically complete the necessary Carnegie units, or too far behind academically (achievement test scores three or more years below age-appropriate grade level), may complete the requirements for a Graduate Equivalency Diploma (GED). VoTech schools and adult education classes offer curricula to prepare students for the necessary exam. Students with normal intelligence and achievement test scores of 6.0 or better have a fairly good foundation to pursue a GED. Depending upon motivation, support, self-discipline, social skills, and the extent of academic deficiency, they may be able to pass the exam after six to twenty-four months of study. The following are examples of children who, handicapped by a history of school failures, were nevertheless able to complete requirements for the GED with surprising ease.

Denis. Denis was a sixteen-year-old struggling in the eighth grade. He was able to pass five subjects but was frustrated by an extremely difficult science class that gave most other students trouble. As frustration mounted with the science class, he lost interest in school, passing only four classes at the end of the year, by which time he had turned seventeen. He entered the adult education program at the local high school that summer. He passed his GED the following October.

Gary. Gary had just never been able to get it together in school. With achievement test scores clustering around the sixth grade level and IQ scores in the 90s, Gary entered the VoTech program after turning sixteen in the seventh grade. His problems continued in the VoTech school. He lacked motivation and discipline. After four months, he was faced with juvenile court action for possession and use of marijuana. Transfer to another program far from home was ordered by the court. Such transfers normally took several months. With prompting from staff, Gary began to make sufficient progress in school so that the recommendation could be made to the court to postpone his transfer so that he could complete his work on his GED. Within five months, Gary was ready to pass the GED test. The program recommended discharge since treatment goals had been met; the court approved.

Special Education

Children who are eleven or twelve years of age or older who are functioning at the second to third grade levels are in serious trouble educationally. Likewise, children whose social skills are such that suspensions and expulsion are a strong probability are also in serious trouble educationally. Children with limited intellectual potential, with IQ's in the mentally retarded range (below 70), are also limited educationally. These children require exceptional interventions.

Congress passed the Education for All Handicapped Children Act (P.L. 94–142) in 1975. This act guaranteed the right of all children, regardless of handicap, to a free and public education. Handicapping conditions include physical handicaps, severe emotional disturbance, learning disabilities, and mental retardation or developmental disabilities. Social maladjustment is not covered (Stroul & Friedman, 1986). P.L. 94-142 was superseded by the Individuals with Disabilities Education Act passed by Congress in 1990. The new law added

rehabilitation counseling and social work services to the list of services to be provided.

Multidisciplinary Evaluations. Designating a child as having a handicapping condition requires evaluation by a multidisciplinary team, a process that may take nearly an entire school year. The team may recommend services ranging from a resource room for special tutoring, psychotherapy, placement in a self-contained class, placement in a special school, homebound instruction, and in some cases placement in a residential school or treatment center (Stroul & Friedman, 1986). Some states provide teachers to residential programs under their implementation of Public Law 94-142.

Individual Educational Plans. The law requires that each child have an individual educational plan (IEP) before beginning special services. For emotionally disturbed children, behavioral interventions may be a significant part of the plan. It is important that academics receive attention in the plan, as well as behavior (Stroul & Friedman, 1986). For children in the custody of the state, there is a requirement that a surrogate parent attend the IEP. Surrogate parents may not be employees of the state or of the institution. Natural parents may serve as surrogate parents for their own child. Surrogate parents must, however, complete a brief training program before they can be certified to represent a child as a surrogate parent in an IEP conference.

The residential treatment center should make every effort to have representation at IEP conferences for its children. The goal of special education services should be to get the child back on track for high school graduation when there is any realistic possibility of doing so. This may require improving not only social skills but also academic skills, self-discipline, and motivation, in order to get the child into regular ninth grade classes before the age of sixteen. If that is unrealistic or impossible, then emphasis should be placed on the academic goal of getting the child to a sixth-grade level or better before he or she leaves school. This will give the child a fighting chance at completing GED requirements if she or he decides to do so at some point in the future. The following case is an example of the struggle with special education in a public school.

> *Stanley.* **Stanley came into the group home at the age of eleven. He had been in a special education class for emotionally disturbed children for two years, since the third grade. While at the group home, he continued to attend that same school in that same class. Initially, he was extremely oppositional, refusing virtually all instructions, limits, and consequences, as well as school. After three months, he was transferred to a residential program. He returned to the group home within five months to return to his former school and special education placement in time to start the new school year. This time he performed so well that he completed his projected eighteen-month treatment program in the group home within fifteen months.**
>
> **He had also done well in his special education class, earning good grades in all subjects and in conduct. Just prior to his discharge from the program, he took an achievement test at the school. He earned scores in the mid-second to mid-third grade in all areas, scores that were almost identical to the scores he had earned three years ago, prior to his admission to special education. Apparently, he had learned in regular classes despite his problems with behavior; apparently he had learned little in special education, despite improvements with his behavior and IQ scores of just over 100.**

Conclusions

Education is one of the primary tasks of childhood. It is, therefore, a primary concern in the residential setting. Residential programs are often very dependent upon public schools or personnel supplied by the local school district for their on-grounds school. Residential programs must have some staff with educational expertise to fully utilize these public resources for their children. They must be able to set realistic goals for each child and to advocate for appropriate educational placement and appropriate services. This requires an understanding of Public Law 94-142 and children's rights. It also requires some knowledge of psychological and educational testing to assess the child's potential, as well as some knowledge of the local resources to assess their potential to educate the child.

A child who is inappropriately placed, or who is coerced to pursue unrealistic goals, becomes quickly discouraged with a major portion of his or her life at the residential program, compromising treatment on all levels. A child who is pursuing realistic goals in an appropriate educational setting may well have one of his or her major presenting problems greatly diminished, with an opportunity for success in this important task for the first time in years.

GROUP THERAPY

Not surprisingly, group therapy is popular in residential treatment programs. Some programs utilize treatment groups as a means of deriving maximum benefit (reaching more children) from a limited resource (professional social worker or other professional treatment person). If the children on a living unit attend group three times a week, the program may claim that its children receive three hours of therapy per week. When there are ten children on the living unit, this amounts to thirty hours of therapy; it requires little over three hours of the therapist's time, depending on how much preparation, if any, the therapist does and how much record-keeping. Levine, quoted in Toseland and Rivas (1984), notes that "group therapy can help with almost anything that individual therapy can, providing an appropriate group is available and the individual will accept the group as a mode of treatment" (p. 8). There are other and better reasons for providing group therapy with children.

Therapeutic Advantages

Toseland and Rivas (1984) suggest that group treatment may have advantages over individual treatment. Groups can help members to realize that they are not alone with their problems. They also give members the opportunity to help others by sharing support, suggestions, information, and feedback. As members watch others achieve their goals, they gain what Yalom, cited in Toseland and Rivas (1984), calls an "installation of hope" (p. 8) that is not present in individual therapy. Toseland and Rivas also cite Northern, who argues that group treatment is the preferred modality for clients whose main problem concerns getting along with others, or for clients coerced into treatment who are resistant to suggestions made by the therapist. Feedback from other group members is critical in such cases.

Gardner (1988) suggests that groups may be especially useful for adolescents, least useful for younger children. Adolescents, often resistant to talking with a therapist for an hour in individual sessions, can talk or remain silent at will in group. Possibly distrusting of the therapist, an adult, adolescents are especially accepting of the opinions of their peers. Moreover, the group provides a setting that can bring about a genuine enhancement of self-esteem in at least three ways:

1. Group members learn that their problems are not unique and gain acceptance by other group members.
2. Group members help other group members with their problems and earn respect for their opinions.
3. Group members gain knowledge and skill, learn better ways to handle their own problems, and improve such skills as asserting themselves appropriately.

Groups can provide members with opportunities for role playing, for testing and rehearsing new skills and behaviors in a safe environment. Groups also provide opportunities for vicarious learning, for learning from observing others and hearing about their experiences (Toseland & Rivas, 1984).

Potential Drawbacks

Groups can also encourage undesirable conformity and dependency among members. Members are vulnerable and may be exposed to harm from the responses of others to their disclosures. The problems of quiet members may go unnoticed and untreated when assertive members are allowed to monopolize the group process. Groups are not indicated for people whose behavior is so alien to others that it produces negative reactions to the exclusion of positive reactions, or when it causes others to leave the group (Toseland & Rivas, 1984).

Kernberg and Chazan (1991) suggest that residents with Attention Deficit-Hyperactivity Disorder as the primary diagnosis may not be appropriate for some groups. Children who are severely disturbed, psychotic, or have limited intelligence or severe learning disabilities may be merely tolerated, ignored, or even humiliated in the group (Gardner, 1988).

Special Considerations in the Residential Setting

Groups in the residential setting may differ in some ways from outpatient therapy groups. The main purpose of outpatient group therapy is the treatment of group members within the group. Such groups may on occasion also serve the purpose of providing additional material for individual therapy when a group member is also in individual therapy. In the residential setting, therapy groups may serve an additional purpose, that of providing treatment and management personnel with additional access to the treatment milieu. This may have benefits both for treatment and management purposes.

Moreover, in outpatient settings, therapists often enter sessions with little or no information about what has been happening with their clients at home, in school, and in the community. They are almost totally dependent on their clients for such information at the outset of each session. In the residential setting, therapists often have the opportunity to approach sessions with fairly complete and accurate information about how residents have been performing, at least within the program, and usually at school. Thus, they are in a much better position to anticipate what issues may or should be addressed.

Likewise, in outpatient settings, group members also tend to be dependent for information on what other group members tell them in the group. In the residential setting, group members generally live together and interact regularly outside of the group. They are often well acquainted with the true attitudes, beliefs, and behaviors of other group members. Groups in the residential setting make it difficult for residents to lie to the therapist and also to themselves. Peers sometimes have more information and a different perspective on events than staff do; they are unlikely to let another peer get away with much for long in attempting to evade or distort issues or responsibility.

Access to the Milieu

Group therapy provides a formalized, structured intervention that may address key issues in the treatment milieu, most notably the attitudes, beliefs, values, and behaviors of the residents. Issues such as respecting the property of others, respecting the rights of others, respecting adults, prohibitions against ratting, being macho and not backing down from a challenge, school attendance, attitudes about treatment, and the program in general are all important treatment issues for children. To the extent that group therapy can influence the attitudes, beliefs, and values of members in a positive direction, it enhances the entire treatment program. When group therapy serves to identify serious problems in one or more of these areas, it may identify the need for the treatment team to address those problems with additional interventions.

Groups can also provide a safe forum in which problems or dissatisfaction with the program may be expressed. Such problems may concern food,

programming, staff, or problems with other residents, such as strong-arm activities and intimidation. Problems may be real and serious, such as possible staff abuse or serious misbehavior by other residents. Thus, groups may serve an excellent management purpose, providing information to assist management or supervisory personnel to keep in touch with the overall tone of the milieu and the program, identify potential problems, and plan interventions or take corrective action accordingly.

There is danger in this, as well. Such reports may be merely distractions, ploys to avoid responsibility for individual behavior or attempts to earn sympathy from the therapist. It poses the problem of what, if anything, the therapist is to do about the complaint. If the therapist appears concerned and attentive, she or he may set the tone for future groups, turning them into gripe sessions. It is much easier to complain about things for which one has no responsibility than it is to focus on one's own problems, about which one should do something. However, when allegations are serious, and the therapist appears uninterested or unconcerned, the therapist and the program lose credibility.

Often, the best approach is for the therapist to guide the residents into accepting responsibility for taking appropriate action to resolve the problem: taking the problem to the appropriate staff or supervisor, presenting the problem and following through until some resolution is reached. When allegations are serious, however, the therapist is obligated to report as a mandatory reporter under child protection statutes.

The Therapist as an Informed Group Leader

The therapist in the residential setting should have current information on the progress and problems of each group member. This gives the group therapist in the residential setting an advantage over outpatient therapists—the ability to plan and prepare for group sessions in advance. The therapist knows most of the important issues that may be relevant for a coming group.

Thus, the therapist may be in a position to influence therapeutically what issues may be brought up in group and how and when they are brought up, avoiding the tendency of some clients to save an important issue until group is almost over, then drop it at the last minute. The therapist may also be in a position to work with individual group members in preparation for the group, helping them to prepare for how or when they may present an issue or how they might respond.

The therapist needs these advantages in the residential setting, for the residential therapist also has disadvantages in the residential setting. While the outpatient therapist may on occasion have to deal with conflicts that develop in group, the residential therapist may have to deal with conflicts that originate outside of the therapy group and that will present within the group session. Moreover, residents may also prepare in advance for a group therapy session.

Residents as Knowledgeable Group Members

The fact that group members in the residential setting live together makes the therapy group an especially potent treatment resource. They eat, sleep, and play together. They have conversations, often about things that are important to them, sometimes under staff supervision, oftentimes in private. While the therapist may be knowledgeable about what staff, parents, or school personnel might have reported during the week, the residents may often have more information and a different perspective.

While some children may have some skills that enable them to fool staff and therapists, they can seldom fool their peers. Their peers know when they are really doing well and when they mean what they say. Their peers also know when they are in trouble, when they are trying to manipulate by saying what the therapist wants to hear. Peer confrontation in a residential therapy group can be especially honest and to the point.

General Therapy Groups

Some programs simply assign residents to a given therapy group that meets one or more times per week. Residents continue in an assigned group throughout treatment. Gardner (1988) prefers het-

erogeneous groups, with the exception that children who are more disturbed than other group members or at an intellectual disadvantage may be inappropriate for certain groups. He suggests that while their symptoms may differ significantly, all patients are using those symptoms in attempts to deal with fundamental problems of life. Groups for children with similar symptoms often tend to focus more heavily on symptoms; the cost is that underlying problems receive less attention.

However, I have seen a tendency for such general therapy groups to lose purpose, for sessions to be unplanned, for goals to become lost or not even established. Residents who cannot contribute to or benefit from group treatment tend to be assigned along with everyone else. Residents who are vulnerable may be exposed to harm. These problems may be compounded by an inexperienced therapist who is told to "hold group sessions." For any group, the following questions should be able to be answered readily:

1. What is the purpose of the group?
2. What is the purpose for a given child's being in the group?
3. What is the goal for a given session?
4. What is the plan or strategy for a given session?

Specifically Focused, Time-Limited Groups

The most effective treatment interventions are those that are goal-directed and planned. For groups, this may be easier to accomplish by developing a program that offers a variety of groups for periods of four to twelve weeks, groups with a specific purpose or objective that are offered at different times according to need. Treatment staff of the program are familiar with the types of problems and needs typically presented by the program's residents. They can determine which of these problems may be successfully treated in group settings and plan appropriate groups.

In assessing the needs of an individual resident, treatment staff can identify which specific needs of the individual might best be served in which groups and assign the resident to those groups in the resident's individual treatment plan. Further, the resident's participation in different groups can be scheduled to be most effective in coordination with other groups and other components of the total treatment milieu.

Possible topics include, but are certainly not limited to: orientation, preparation for discharge, school readiness, career planning, goal-setting, sexual abuse survivors, peer relations, play therapy, dating, sex education, substance abuse, physical abuse survivors, children of single-parent families, children with step parents, anger management, managing aggression, assertiveness training, Rational Emotive Therapy, and even self-defense. Such groups and their individual sessions lend themselves readily to goal-directed planning for the individual participants.

Conclusions

Group therapy is a particularly valid and potentially powerful intervention in the residential setting, especially with adolescents. Along with the normal benefits of outpatient group therapy, such therapy in the residential setting offers the advantages of allowing the therapist considerable opportunity to prepare for sessions in advance. It provides meaningful access to the milieu, both allowing the therapist to work on issues that are critical to the milieu and allowing the program to identify problems in the milieu that require attention or corrective action. A skilled therapist may be able to accomplish significant treatment and therapy with general therapy groups to which most residents are assigned. If such groups are unproductive, short-term, time-limited groups focusing on specific issues may be beneficial.

SUMMARY

Therapies and interventions conducted by trained professionals comprise an important part of most residential treatment programs. They are most effective when they are coordinated and fully integrated into the total treatment process.

After behavior modification, individual therapy may be the treatment modality most claimed by residential treatment programs as a major treatment modality. Often, it is in practice little more than counseling, reviewing the child's week, her or his decisions, consequences, and alternatives that may have been chosen. When it is offered in the sense of therapy as proposed in this text, it involves some goal of changing the individual on some level of psychic functioning, ego, personality, etc., along with definitive strategies to meet its goals. Ellis' Rational Emotive Therapy and Glasser's Reality Therapy are two of many possible approaches to therapy with individuals that lend themselves readily to the residential milieu.

Ellis' Rational Emotive Therapy is a technique that can be used effectively with individuals and in groups. It is a cognitive technique that theorizes that events do not cause our emotions. Rather, it is our thoughts and beliefs about events that produce our emotions. When these thoughts or beliefs are irrational, our emotions produce inappropriate behaviors that cause problems. The goal of therapy is to change irrational beliefs and thinking and thereby change subsequent feelings and emotions, leading to behavior that is more productive for the individual. This intervention may be effective with many adolescents and families. It poses problems when clients' feelings and emotions run too deep and fail to be reached by this therapy, leading to blaming of the client rather than alterations to the approach.

Glasser's Reality Therapy stresses the individual's responsibility for meeting her or his own needs. Individual responsibility is a very popular concept in residential programs, which frequently deal with the irresponsible behavior of children. Reality Therapy, however, is much more than holding children responsible for their behavior by allowing them to experience consequences, natural or applied. It begins with the establishment of a relationship. From this relationship, the therapist eventually helps the client to see that her or his behavior has been irresponsible, not just because it leads to some punishment or unpleasant consequence, but because it fails to meet two very basic needs—the need to love and the need to be loved. The client cannot blame parents, others, or society for failure to meet these needs, but must accept responsibility and change behavior appropriately.

Art therapy is an example of a nontraditional therapeutic intervention that may work especially well with children who have difficulty expressing themselves verbally for whatever reason. It is more than having children draw pictures and more than trying to diagnose children from the pictures they draw. It is not a therapy likely to be available in most residential settings. It involves using the artistic creations of children within a relationship to get at primitive material that may be preverbal, or any material with non-verbal clients.

Pharmacotherapy has indications for reducing psychotic symptoms, reducing aggression, changing affect or mood, increasing attention, and even increasing urine retention and bladder control at night. It may have treatment or management objectives. Psychiatric medications also have the potential for considerable undesired side affects. The effectiveness of psychotropic medications with children is less well documented than with adults.

It is preferable that the treating psychiatrist be involved regularly with the treatment of the child and the total treatment program. Often, this is not possible. In any case, communication between the psychiatrist and other program personnel must be attuned to the medication, its desired and actual effects. Sometimes, personnel misreport behavior to influence the psychiatrist's prescribing of a desired medication or to justify a medication that has been prescribed. Moreover, medication poses serious management problems in terms of security of potentially dangerous substances.

Education may be the single most important aspect of childhood for most children; it is very important in residential treatment programs. Education may have normal developmental objectives, remedial objectives, or potential treatment objectives in an especially strong special educational program. Residential programs are often dependent on public schools to meet these needs. Even when on-grounds schools are provided, the public school district may provide most of the personnel.

The most important aspect of educational programming in the residential setting is planning and goal setting. This requires the program to begin with a realistic assessment of the child's potential for high school graduation. Graduation depends on the child's intellectual ability, performance level, and educational placement—all relatively objective criteria. It also depends on the subjective criteria of motivation and support. Motivation is a complex concept that depends on several factors, including desire, self-confidence, confidence in the world, and the sacrifices the child must make in other areas. Realistic goals must be set for graduation, GED, or simply gaining necessary knowledge and skills for survival.

Group therapy in residential settings may be quite different from outpatient group therapy. In the residential setting, where group members live together, group therapy may be especially powerful. When group members know each other intimately, group members cannot fool each other nearly so readily as they might deceive therapists. Group members know their peers' true attitudes and beliefs, not only from their participation in the group, but from out-of-group conversations and observations of behavior. Confrontations may be especially to the point. Moreover, group therapy provides the program with additional access to the milieu, especially the attitudes, values, and beliefs of program residents. This has positive aspects to the extent that the group therapist can influence these to promote treatment objectives. When the therapist and the group get caught up in attitudes that undermine or conflict with treatment, the milieu may be undermined.

14

Family Interventions

Once upon a time, scattered all across this vast land, there existed residential treatment facilities for children [which] shared some common beliefs. Basically, children who demonstrated emotional and behavioral problems could be "cured" by isolating them from their families and community, placing them in a structured facility with other disturbed children, and coercing change by controlling their date of discharge from the facility while inviting them to explore past issues of interest to their therapist (Greene & Holden, 1990, p. 51).

Residential treatment programs typically begin programming for a child by placing the child on a period of orientation during which no home visits are allowed. This is to promote separation and get the child properly installed into the program. Visits by parents may be closely supervised and structured, often limited to interactions in the therapist's office. Later, after thirty or even ninety days, home visits may be earned as a reward for good behavior. Parents are encouraged, required, or coerced to attend counseling or family therapy, and possibly parent education or training sessions.

Needless to say, family members quickly get the message that the parents are incompetent and in need of remediation and education, while the children need the discipline and structure that only the facility can supply. Unfortunately, these messages ultimately undermine and further incapacitate the family system (Greene & Holden, 1990, p. 52).

Children generally come into residential treatment because they cannot live at home. Sometimes they cannot live at home because their own problems are too severe to be treated in the family and community. Other times, children cannot live at home because problems in the family are too severe. In some cases, there is no home. Regardless, if there is family, there are implications for family involvement with the child in residential treatment.

Dalton and Forman (1992) identify the "*improvement of the 'fit' between the child and the interpersonal environment*" (p. 7) as a key element in at least one view of therapy. I believe that this is an excellent philosophy for residential treatment. This suggests three possible approaches:

1. Change the child to fit the environment in which he or she must live.
2. Change the environment in which the child must live to fit the child.
3. Change both the child and the environment so that the fit is improved.

I believe the third alternative offers the most potential for success. To this end, work with the child's family, or the family to whom a child may be discharged, becomes extremely important.

Whether or not the child has a family, and whether or not the child will eventually be discharged home to his or her family, family issues can be expected to be significant issues for treatment. How family issues are treated can have impact on the length of stay, the course of treatment, and success after discharge, whether to home, adoptive home, foster home, or another program.

In this chapter, we will consider a model for parental involvement proposed by Martone, Kemp, and Pearson (1989). Next, we will consider teaching additional skills to parents to empower them to better parent their children at home, especially discipline and communication skills. Third, we will consider family therapy in the residential setting. Finally, we will consider treatment for sexual abuse.

A MODEL FOR PARENT INVOLVEMENT

Martone, Kemp, and Pearson (1989) offer a conceptual model of parental involvement in the residential treatment of a child. The model begins with engagement and progresses through participation and empowerment to discharge. The model is based on their experience with the Evanston Children's Center of Chicago's Children's Aid Society. The program serves up to thirty latency-aged boys and girls whose guardianship has been assumed by the state. The children come from multiple-problem systems; many have experienced multiple failures.

In 1983, six children were discharged after an average length of stay of 5.5 years (65.5 months). Two went home; two went into foster care/adoption; one went to a group home; and the sixth went into a psychiatric hospital. One supervisor presided over the four units in which the children were housed. The three social workers seldom visited the units. Nevertheless, they saw the child as their primary responsibility. Families were "endured" (Martone et al., 1989, p. 13), with occasional family visits occurring in the therapist's office.

At the end of 1983, the program was reorganized. The children were housed in three of the cottages, one for boys and two co-ed. Two additional supervisors were hired so that each cottage had its own supervisor. Each of the three social workers was assigned to a specific cottage, as well. The fourth cottage was used for offices. On Thanksgiving Day in 1983, the program invited families to dinner to participate in the holiday with their children.

During the next four years, the length of stay dropped to 1.9 years (23.6 months). Thirty-eight children were discharged, twenty-two of whom went home to their parents. Six others went to foster care/adoption; four went to group homes; and five went to residential treatment centers, two of which were out of state. During the last two of those four years, eighty-six family members were served in addition to the children. The program had gone from a child-centered institution to a family-centered program in which parents had entered into partnership for the treatment of their children and themselves.

The four stages of Martone et al. (1989) for parental involvement—engagement, participation, empowerment, and discharge—each has its own unique issues. These issues affect the stages that follow.

Engagement

The goal of engagement is to form a partnership in a plan of treatment, an alliance or working relationship. Several problems may be encountered:

1. The state has removed the child. The parents suffer shame, humiliation, and anger. They have difficulty believing that anyone would ask their help in treatment, or that they could contribute anything of value.

2. Many families have had a long history of unpleasant involvement with courts, state agencies, and the like. They may have difficulty seeing the program as separate from other agencies and expect their involvement with the program to be adversarial in nature.
3. The families are likely to be involuntary clients, having been ordered to participate. They may be angry, fearful, resistant, resentful, depressed, and intimidated by the size of the institution and the number of staff with whom they must now interact.
4. Families may be fearful of the agency's power and suspicious of its intentions, since it will be reporting to state agencies and the court.
5. Many families present with psychosocial histories that are similar to that of their children. They may be very focused on their own needs and competitive or jealous of the care and attention their child receives. They may well have insufficient energy to invest in their children.

The initial contact with the family is most often during a preplacement visit to determine whether the child and family need and can benefit from the program. It is important that the social worker and others involved be nonjudgmental and offer empathy, support, and cooperation. The Evanston Children's Center provides food for the child and family during the initial contact as a way of nurturing both the child and the family. This also symbolizes the program's commitment to providing for both during placement.

It is important to have the family present when the child is admitted into the program. This allows the parents to work through separation. It also allows staff to begin to engage the family. The social worker is identified as the primary contact for the family with the program. Staff, however, allow the parent to help the child unpack and arrange the room. "Encouraging the parents to make simple decisions from the beginning can be a stepping stone to future decision-making processes" (Martone et al., 1989, p. 19).

During the first few weeks, the relationship between the family and the social worker is formed as the social worker gathers information. The family is provided with a handbook describing the program and the parents' role within the program. They participate in important plans concerning visits and therapy.

For families who are too resistant to participate in these processes, staff may go to the family. The child may assist in phoning the family and writing letters. The child may invite the family to a special dinner or other activity.

Mrs. R. **Mr. and Mrs. R. had been battling with the system for some three years, during which time they divorced. Mr. R. had been sexually abusing their son and daughter. Moreover, he had coerced Mrs. R. into participating. Both Mr. R. and Mrs. R. had been sexually abused by their fathers.**

Mrs. R. reacted so strongly to the placement of her children that she hospitalized herself for depression shortly after they went into placement. She also had a severe learning disability. She was extremely difficult to engage.

Initially, Mrs. R. was unable to visit her children. Staff took them to visit her, a drive of two hours. These visits helped to develop a relationship between Mrs. R. and the program. She began to call daily to talk about her issues and needs. She was provided with a specific staff contact who was also assigned to supervise home visits. Her calls were limited to twice per week. With time, her conversations began to focus on her children.

After six weeks, Mrs. R. was ready to visit the program. Staff had to go with her to teach her how to take the train and bus. Subsequently, she visited weekly. Even when she didn't feel well, she came because she felt a responsibility. She is described by the child care staff as "a caring mom with potentially good skills" (Martone et al., 1989, p. 20). Both she and her children were working hard on a goal of reunification.

Participation

Parental participation varies, depending upon how well the family has been engaged and the treatment plan. Their participation has some significant therapeutic implications:

1. Regular and predictable participation can begin to repair emotional gaps created by previous placements.
2. Participation can dispel the myths that staff may have about the family, as well as myths the family may have about the program. Without such participation, staff knowledge about the family is based on records, what the child tells them, and inferences from the child's behavior. The parent's knowledge about the program is limited to inferences from past experience with the system and what the child tells them. Children do not always tell the unembellished truth.
3. Many families have chaotic and crisis-oriented days. The program models structure and routine during their participation.
4. Participation may provide fun, relaxation, and humor that may be in short supply in some families.
5. Participation may provide on-the-job training as the family observes child care staff and has opportunity to practice.

Participation also leads to parents meeting other parents and the possible formation of natural support networks. During the stage of participation, issues of competition, competence, and cooperation arise between parents and staff. Activities must be designed to enhance the family's competence, minimize competition with staff, and build cooperation.

Program staff schedule special activities for all of the children in the program and whatever parents can attend. Special attention is given so that children without families will have significant others to attend— relatives, former staff, or volunteers. Two key ingredients are food and activities. Food meets a basic need for parents and may be what hooks them ini-

tially. Activities may include parent-child sack races, softball, singing, or a picnic. Activities should be planned carefully to be sure that they will be something parents will enjoy. Parents may also receive a gift to take home. Photographs or something the child has made for the occasion are appropriate. Eventually, some parents may switch roles and become more active in planing events, even bringing food.

Mrs. C. **Mrs. C. was a single mother who was preoccupied with finding a husband. She had two sons aged ten and five. She did not always arrange the best baby-sitting. Bobby, the five-year-old, was removed and placed when she failed to pick him up from two teenagers with whom she had left him.**

Initially, Mrs. C. was depressed, humorless, and lonely. She was resistant and difficult to engage. She expected her son to relate to her as if he were an adult. Close supervision was required when she came to special events because of her inappropriateness with Bobby. Once staff had established some rapport with her, she was encouraged to participate in the milieu.

At first, she ate dinner with Bobby's unit once per week. Her length of stay was gradually extended into the evening. She learned quickly as staff modeled appropriate ways to play with Bobby and set limits.

She became animated and popular with the other children, achieving some fame for her bedtime stories. She played mom to some of the other children at the Christmas party when their parents couldn't attend. "This was a big change from the woman whose own needs came before meeting the needs of her children. Bobby was able to return home to his mother in less than twelve months after placement in residential treatment" (Martone et al., 1989, p. 25).

Empowerment

"The child's removal from the home, and eventual placement in substitute living situations, disenfranchises the family. The family is divested of their parental rights and responsibilities'' (Martone et al., 1989, p. 26). Some families abdicate totally; others feud with staff over trivial issues. Empowerment is putting parents back in control of normal caretaking and other parental responsibilities. It may begin as early as possible during either of the two previous stages. Martone et al. note the following empowerment issues:

1. Parents can get stuck at the participation stage and remain focused on their own needs. While continuing to nurture the parent, staff must gradually move them towards taking increasing responsibilities for their child.
2. Tasks must be in keeping with the family's current abilities in parenting.
3. Delegation of tasks, no matter how minor, must be carefully orchestrated to help families who attempt to remain in the background take an increasingly active role in decision making.
4. There is a potential for conflict between staff and parents. Delegation must be clearly defined and understood to minimize power struggles and conflict.
5. Children may experience their parents in a parenting role for the first time, causing the child to attempt to provoke conflicts between staff and parents. Staff and parents must address such issues together with the child.
6. As parents are empowered, they will make good and poor decisions. Staff must be prepared to accept both and be empathetic and realistic when failures occur.

Empowerment begins at intake by allowing parents to be involved in simple decision-making which sets the pattern for later. Empowerment reestablishes the parents' right to make decisions that affect their child's life. . . . The challenge to social work and to child care staff is to encourage parents to move ahead in their skills without feeling in competition with them (Martone et al., 1989, p. 28).

Parents begin by making some initial decisions in planning treatment goals. Later, they may become involved in shopping for clothes. Discipline is the most difficult area of empowerment. "Hopefully, staff have taught parents appropriate disciplinary skills before empowering them in this area" (Martone et al., 1989, p. 28). It may begin by calling the parent to discuss consequences when the child has had a difficult day. Later, parents may be expected to follow through with discipline during a home visit. Such involvement should be taken in coordination with the staff who have to deal with the fallout.

Mrs. A. **Tom had been having problems since the age of four. At placement, he was ten, depressed, and having major difficulties with impulse control. He experienced wide mood swings with aggression towards himself and others. Mrs. A., his mother, had divorced Tom's alcoholic father when Tom was seven. Prior to placement, she was unable to control Tom. During placement, she attended weekly family therapy and evening meals; she called Tom and staff regularly, took part in scheduled family activities, and participated in the milieu. However, she rarely intervened, abdicating to staff.**

Mrs. A. came for dinner and family therapy one day per week. After therapy, she assisted Tom with cleaning his room and laying out his clothes for the next day. She also monitored his bath routine and preparation for bed. Her involvement was then increased to twice per week with phone calls to Tom on the other days to monitor his progress. She was given responsibility for all of Tom's clothes shopping.

Before home visits, Mrs. A. was given the responsibility of inspecting his room and of refusing to start the visit until it met her expectations. Further, she carried to the home pass any discipline that Tom might be serving. Eventually, she began confronting Tom on misbehavior, setting limits, and establishing consequences, where previously she had sat by and deferred to staff when Tom verbally abused her or staff.

Discharge

As discharge nears, "families have mastered, although not perfected, numerous parenting skills to allow for family reunification. The family has also gained in the emotional strength necessary to carry out the parenting tasks'' (Martone et al., 1989, p. 30). Both will be tested during discharge, which precipitates regression in both the family and child.

1. As the time for discharge approaches, the eagerness with which the family looked forward to discharge turns to apprehension and a wavering of self-confidence. Discharge brings some elements of loss to the family—loss of the staff and milieu that have become major ''sources of support, structure and self-esteem'' (Martone et al., 1989, p. 30).
2. Families can be expected to employ various means to cope with or defend against impending loss. Some will seek to delay the discharge. Some will begin to deprecate the program, assuming the role of rescuing their child.
3. Regression of the child may also appear in several forms. Previously anxiously awaiting the arrival of parents for a home visit, the child may now not even be ready when they arrive. Aggressive behavior in the program, at school, at home, or elsewhere in the community may occur. The child must also prepare for loss of staff and prepare to leave peers behind, while wondering if the family can indeed provide needed care.
4. Staff likewise have feelings with which to deal. Have they done enough? Can the family deal with the child? Protect the child? Continue the child's growth? Staff need to be aware of their feelings and avoid feeding into regressive maneuvers of the child or family, thinking they all need more time.

As discharge approaches, the role of the social worker and staff is to provide the necessary support to complete the transition home. The social worker and supervisor play key roles in helping the staff, child, and family to say good-bye. Plans and arrangements for school placement, recre-

ation, and follow-up must be made. Meanwhile, the structure of the program should be reduced. Privileges should be more like those at home. Responsibilities such as chores and homework should be accomplished with minimal prompting by staff. One-on-one time with the child should be devoted to exploring what it will be like at home and what resources can be used should problems arise.

At the Evanston Children's Center, staff help the child to prepare a scrapbook of experiences at the program. Gradually, the child moves more and more possessions home. Staff and social workers communicate with the family to try to keep minor incidents from becoming major ones and to provide support. When possible, parents attend a good-bye dinner or discharge party for the child.

Terry. *Terry*. **Terry's mother had been hospitalized twice for depression before Terry was three. His parents divorced when Terry was four; his father was awarded custody because of his mother's serious suicidal condition. His father remarried when Terry was five. Terry had problems from the time he entered school. He became destructive at home. His father was cited three times for physical abuse. His stepmother struck him once, following which she and his father turned themselves in to the police. Terry had been hospitalized three times in less than three years preceding his placement at the age of eight.**

After fourteen months of placement, Terry was ready for discharge. Terry had adjusted quickly to placement and made rapid therapeutic and academic gains. His father and stepmother likewise enjoyed participation and learned. Discharge planning began five months prior to discharge, which was scheduled to coincide with a court review date.

For the first two months, neither Terry nor the family spoke of discharge. The family procrastinated in petitioning the court for unsupervised visits recommended by the agency. Terry became increasingly defiant

with staff and teachers and provoked his peers. The team held fast to the discharge date and made themselves available to the family for support as visits increased, even going to the home to handle crises. Staff increased their one-on-one time with Terry, who was able to express his feelings about discharge. Staff were supportive and helped Terry prepare. He was held increasingly accountable for responsibilities without staff prompting, and his privileges were made more like those he had at home.

The family began pointing out things that the program was doing wrong in an attempt to look like the better parents. The social worker worked closely with the parents to support gains they had made and focus them on necessary tasks related to the discharge. In court, the judge granted approval for Terry to return home that day. Terry and his family returned to the facility for a party the other children and staff had prepared and said their good-byes. The family sent a letter shortly after, ''You've got a really great team . . . we have a way to go, but due to your program, we don't have as far a road to travel'' (Martone et al., 1989, p. 34).

When the Child Is Not Going Home

When parents are unable or unwilling to make the necessary changes, the goal of discharge home may need to be changed. The attempt to fully involve the parent allows for issues to be more quickly sorted out. It enables the child to dispel fantasies of the family and move on to new alternatives if necessary, resulting in a shorter length of stay when foster families are readily available.

When it is clear from the start that the child will not be going home, available family are still an important resource for the child, and should be engaged and provided with some opportunity for participation. It helps provide the child with a sense of identity and connectedness. In the best of cases, the parent or family member may give the child permission to move on to new relationships with other adults (Martone et al., 1989).

SPECIALIZED SKILLS TO EMPOWER PARENTS

The goal of training parents is to empower them to successfully raise their children at home. On occasion, however, the approach taken to parent training may be disempowering to parents in some respects, as when the attitude that the parents must have done something wrong to cause the child's problems permeates the milieu. While this may sometimes be true, it is not always the case. Oftentimes, the parent is simply not doing enough right. Few parents set out to deliberately raise a child to have problems. Also, and again too often, parents find themselves faced with problems and situations that even the best professionals find to be significant challenges. Many parents face these problems without the resources of a stable neighborhood, community, nearby family support, a consistent school environment, or peer groups who share similar values. They face them without a supervisor with whom to consult or the chance to leave at the end of an eight-hour shift.

Once upon a time, when the sense of community was stronger, parents got help from family, neighbors, a ''friendly'' police officer, schools, neighborhood businesses, and others in the community. Children's peers were likely being raised by similar methods to similar standards. Those who were too different were not considered to be peers. Note the presence of drugs and violence in our schools; listen to the debates on sex education and abortion, or environmentalists and Rush Limbaugh. These exemplify the tremendous value clashes in our society. Parents seem to need and want help. Popkin (1990a) lists several reasons he has heard for providing structured education for parents:

Society has changed so much in the last 30 years that the need for new parenting skills has become imperative.

The old autocratic approach seems to foster rebellion in modern children.

The newer permissive style has also been found wanting.

Parents want something that works!

With so much mobility, the informal parenting education of the extended family is missing.

As one mother put it, "Kids don't come with instructions" (p. 7).

What's in a Name?

An instructor teaching police officers about driving safety campaigns suggested that any campaign should be geared towards good drivers. Nearly everyone considers herself or himself to be a good driver; campaigns targeting bad drivers, consequently, don't have much of an audience.

Mateja (1991) reports on a survey of 500 drivers conducted by Valvoline, Inc. While 36 percent rated themselves as excellent drivers, they maintained that only 1 percent of their fellow drivers were as good. On a ten-question test, the average number of correct responses was only five. Only two of the 500 answered all ten questions correctly.

Staff are often required to participate in a driver education course as part of their orientation or inservice training. The course is often entitled "Defensive Driving" rather than driver education. Many accept the training as a matter of course; some resist it as an insult, priding themselves on their driving skill. Consider the likely attitude of a staff person who is required to take such a course because of an accident when the staff feels blameless in that accident.

Few would proudly display a certificate proclaiming their completion of "Driver Education"; they either had it in high school or learned to get along quite well without it (or believe they did). Some would display a certificate for completion of "Defensive Driving." More would display a

certificate proclaiming completion of a course in "Advanced Professional Driving."

I believe the same applies to parents and parenting education. Parent education programs oriented towards poor parents may create some problems. Parents whose children need to be in placement have often suffered serious blows to their egos or self-esteem that should be addressed during preplacement, intake, and early in treatment. The way the agency's staff talk about "parent education" both reflects and affects the way the staff think about the parents of the children. This is a part of the milieu that is likely to impact both the children *and* the parents.

It sometimes appears as though the goal of "parent training" is to get the parents to stop making trouble, to stop undermining the gains that are being made in treatment. Other times, there seems to be a goal of just having the parents become "good" parents, or better parents. Occasionally, there is an expressed goal of having parents support and assist treatment. A few therapists seek to have parents work as co-therapists, which requires more than a course on parenting techniques, however advanced.

Whatever the objectives of teaching, training, or educating parents, I suggest as strongly as possible that the terms "parent education" and "parent training" be eliminated from the program literature and the staff vocabulary. There is no doubt that all parents (and all drivers) can learn more, but give the course a name that doesn't compromise parents' self-esteem, their image to their children, or the way the agency's staff and personnel think about and talk about parents. Give it a name that helps. Give it a name that attracts parents, that excites them, that brings them in with a positive attitude, with the expectation that they will learn something that will enable or empower them to handle the difficulties of raising children in a difficult world. Suggestions include:

Parent Empowerment
Parent Seminar or Seminar for Parents
Advanced Skills for Parents

Child Development and Effective Discipline
How to Raise an Independent Child
Parent Support Group

Active Parenting

Popkin's (1990b; 1993) Active Parenting™ provides an excellent model for empowering parents. Parents are taught clear, easy to understand skills to develop their children's confidence, self-esteem, responsibility, and cooperation. Specific skills include the following:

1. How to identify a failure cycle and interrupt it by becoming a more positive force in a child's life.
2. How to identify the child's goals in misbehaving (contact, power, protection, withdrawal, and challenge) and avoid paying off the respective misbehaviors (pesting, rebellion, revenge, avoidance of responsibility, and thrill-seeking behavior).
3. Skills to avoid power struggles.
4. Skills to teach a child to accept responsibility for his or her own problems.
5. How to use "I" messages ("When you . . . I feel. . . . Therefore, I would like you to . . .).
6. How to help natural consequences work and avoid interfering.
7. How to set appropriate limits and give choices within those limits.
8. How to use logical consequences instead of punishments.
9. Active communication skills (listening for feelings, identifying alternatives, and evaluating and choosing consequences).
10. Family problem-solving skills (Popkin, 1990b; 1993).

Active Parenting offers two courses, Active Parenting of Teens (Popkin, 1990b) and Active Parenting Today for Parents of 2 to 12 Year Olds (Popkin, 1993). Both courses are organized into six two-hour sessions that can be readily adapted to other formats, such as twelve one-hour sessions. Both courses stress family enrichment activities such as teaching skills, taking time for fun, and family talks about drugs. Each course is supported by a detailed, step-by-step guide for leaders, a clear and concise guide for parents, and video tapes in which families model various problems (with plenty of humor) and techniques. Child care counselors and teachers would find portions of the Active Parenting program interesting and useful.

Whatever approach a residential program may take to teaching skills to parents, it should be prepared to offer parents support and encouragement in practicing those skills, and to be patient. Old habits are hard to break and readily resurface in the emotionally-charged atmosphere that children can be masters at creating. The tendency to become judgmental sometimes tends to increase after parents are taught skills, then have trouble using them.

FAMILY THERAPY

"One of the contributions of the family approach when it was developed in the 1950s was the discovery that symptoms could be viewed as appropriate and adaptive behavior" (Haley, 1987, p. 2). It is no wonder that Minuchin observed in the early 1960s that treatment gains evaporated when the children were returned to their families (Colapinto, 1991). Behaviors learned in the residential setting may not be appropriate or adaptive in some homes.

As with individual therapy, there are a number of theories and approaches to family therapy. There are models based on psychoanalytic theory, behavioral theory, systems theory, psychoeducational approaches, or some combination. There are brief therapy models, models based on team intervention in the home, models based on a team approach in a clinical setting, and models in which supervisors observe the family therapy session from behind one-way mirrors, calling the therapist out to discuss strategy (Gurman & Kniskern, 1981–1991; Haley, 1987).

Dalton and Forman (1992) note that there are differences between hospital-based family therapy and outpatient family therapy and that few authors have addressed these differences. When a child is removed from a family for treatment, then outpatient family therapy was most likely either unavailable or inadequate to the task. Moreover, techniques for any approach to family therapy must often be somewhat modified when a key family member is absent most of the time for residential treatment.

Dalton and Forman, based on their experience in psychiatric settings for children, have found that a directive, psychoeducational approach to family therapy is most efficient and least intrusive. When this approach proves insufficient or inadequate, they employ structural and object-relations models. Marital or couples therapy is employed when parental conflicts contribute to the child's problems.

A Psychoeducational Approach

According to McFarlane (1991), family psychoeducation is not a family therapy, but rather a strategy for helping families to treat a disabling mental illness. It was developed to help families who are the caretakers of a family member with schizophrenia. It operates from the assumption that "given information and advice, families will attempt to apply them to aid in the patient's recovery and rehabilitation" (1991, p. 379).

Dalton and Forman (1992) have found that a directive, psychoeducational approach may be the most important approach for children with behavioral disorders, anxiety disorders, and affective disorders. Therapists work with families to establish acceptable standards of behavior, limits, and consequences. They focus on underlying dynamics as necessary to refocus family members on treatment objectives.

Structural Family Therapy

Minuchin's structural family therapy grew out of his work in the early 1960s at the Wiltwyck School for Boys, a correctional facility for boys in the state of New York, and subsequent work at the Philadelphia Child Guidance Clinic beginning in 1965. While more middle-class families deal readily with abstract concepts and respond well to talking therapies, poverty-stricken families tend to be more concrete and action-oriented. Structural family therapy is sensitive to the role of external stressors in creating problems within the family, as well as the role of structure within the family (Colapinto, 1991).

Ironically, the therapist and the family disagree on goals for therapy. The family expects the therapist to focus on the identified patient. They expect the problem to be solved with no change to the family structure. The therapist, on the other hand, seeks to eliminate the problem through transformation of the family structure (Colapinto, 1991).

Structural family therapy focuses on interactions within the family, restating problems in interactional terms. The therapist attends to the family hierarchy and power base and directs parents and children to communicate directly, promoting the understanding of how each family member perceives given problems. The therapist intervenes when parents abrogate their responsibilities or when children attempt to assume parental responsibilities (Dalton & Forman, 1992).

Object-Relations Family Therapy

Dalton and Forman (1992) employ object-relations therapy with the family when the unconscious roles and defense mechanisms of family members influence behavior, especially the problematic behavior of the child. They find this approach necessary when serious character pathology in one or both parents underlies conflicts within the family. Object-relations therapy is a long-term intervention that, in the case of the relatively brief hospitalization of a child, must be continued as part of the post-discharge treatment plan.

Problem-Solving Therapy

Although Haley's (1987) problem-solving therapy is a brief approach to family therapy, the techniques of which generally require the child to be at home, Haley offers some insight into family problems often encountered in residential treatment. Haley's approach depends heavily on the way the therapist defines the problem. Symptoms may be defined in behavioral terms as specific acts, or in more general terms as a state of mind, a character disorder, anxiety, or a feeling of helplessness.

> Even though this approach assumes that the therapist has failed if he or she does not solve the presenting problem, and even though the symptom is defined in operational terms that are as precise as possible, the therapy focus is on the social situation rather than on the person. . . . A problem is defined as a type of behavior that is part of a sequence of acts among several persons. The repeating sequence of behavior is the focus of therapy (p. 2).

"The way one labels a human dilemma can crystallize a problem and make it chronic" (Haley, 1987, p. 3). Giving a child labels (Conduct Disorder, Attention Deficit-Hyperactivity Disorder, Intermittent Explosive Disorder) may result in creating a problem such that change is more difficult.

School refusal may be defined as a problem for therapy. "Yet suppose the school is in a slum and is such a bad school that the therapist can only sympathize with the young person for avoiding it as a waste of time" (Haley, 1987, p. 4). Or suppose the father is chronically unemployed because of economic considerations. Suppose an upper-class child is depressed; suppose her father is totally occupied with a high pressure job and corporate politics. School refusal may be related to a problem school or to a problem family.

According to Haley (1987), the obligation of the therapist:

> is to define the social unit he can change to solve the presenting problem of a client. . . . The most useful point of view for the therapist is the idea that there is sufficient variety in any situation so that some better arrangement can be made (p. 5).

A behaviorally oriented therapist is likely to treat a child's temper tantrums with behavioral techniques to extinguish the tantrums.

> A therapist who thinks in terms of the social context will be concerned about the child's temper tantrums as a response to the child's current relationships. She will also consider the hierarchy in the situation and decide whether she wants to be employed by parents to shape a child in the way they wish. . . . The same concern applies to any coalition of a therapist and a family member when the context is ignored (Haley, 1987, p. 6).

The same can apply in institutions. Is the therapist helping to prepare the patient for life after discharge, or merely creating "better patients for the convenience of staff"? (Haley, 1987, p. 6).

Problem-solving therapy is a relatively short-term therapy. The focus is on the present with little or no attention to historical developments. Helping the family to understand the problem is not relevant; solving the problem is the objective. The therapist working with a problem child may seek to change the child's behavior. The therapist might also think about how to change the responses of others so that the child's behavior must change. In the case of a triad, when two adults are involved with the child, "the child is both a participant and a communication vehicle between them" (Haley, 1987, p. 136). Haley conceptualizes some specific problems that the residential treatment program can expect to encounter, the two-generation problem and the three-generation problem.

The Two-Generation Problem

According to Haley, a classic triangle for family therapy is the case in which one parent is extremely involved with the child while the other is more peripheral. One parent knows all the details about the child's problem, perhaps the child's whole life; the other may not even agree that a problem exists.

A repeating sequence creates this structure. One parent and the child interact intensely. A problem behavior of the child increases, and the other parent is called upon for assistance. The other parent intervenes and is then criticized as not understanding the child. The parent withdraws to avoid conflict with the spouse. The initial parent and child rejoin. The problem behavior again increases and the cycle repeats. The triangle may persist even if parents are divorced.

There are four possible approaches to the therapy, the first three of which have implications for the residential setting.

1. The therapist might direct the more peripheral parent into taking charge.
2. The therapist might direct the more involved parent into taking even greater charge of the child.
3. The therapist may direct both parents to take joint charge by agreeing on what is to be done.
4. The therapist may have the child join with other children in giving the parents a task that they would enjoy, such as going out together.

Entering Through the Peripheral Parent. When this approach is chosen, according to Haley, the therapist must take care to avoid any implication that the peripheral parent is being brought in because of any failure on the part of the more involved parent. For a boy with a dominating mother, the therapist might suggest that the child has now reached an age where he must become more involved with males; therefore, he and his father must do more together. This avoids criticism of the mother's overprotection.

There are three stages. First, the therapist gets involved in an activity with the child and peripheral parent, shifting the dominant parent to the periphery. This creates a new but still abnormal relation. In the second stage, the therapist becomes involved in an activity with both parents, leaving the child free to join peers. Finally, the therapist must disengage, leaving the parents involved with each other and the child involved with peers. This may be readily accomplished when the child is in a residential setting.

Haley suggests that a possible function of a child's problem behavior is to get the peripheral parent more involved. Getting that parent involved in a positive way makes the symptomatic behavior unnecessary. Often when this approach is used, there is a stage of parental conflict, sometimes marital conflict, at which point the therapist might see the family alone.

Entering Through the Involved Parent. Haley suggests that sometimes, what little satisfaction the over-involved parent receives is from the child rather than from the spouse. Without indicating any problems with the over-involvement, which antagonizes the parent and interferes with cooperation, the therapist may seek to get the parent more involved with other, more appropriate activities rather than excessive involvement with the child. Alternatives include work, education, and community involvement. There may be both need and opportunity for this when the child has been removed from the home.

Entering Conjointly Through Both Parents. Haley recommends that this approach receive special consideration when the problems are severe. Both parents are usually involved in cases of a violent youth, psychotic behavior, drug abuse, or suicidal behavior. While one parent may appear to be peripheral, the therapist will usually discover that this parent is very much involved. With such extreme problems, it is best to have the parents reach agreement on what is to be done. Often, parents will report no disagreements about the child, but disagreements surface as plans are made, at which point these disagreements can be resolved.

According to Haley, such cases are often presented in residential treatment. The youth has been out of control to the point that courts and other community agencies have become involved. Parents must plan rules and consequences and work out disagreements, pulling together to plan a homecoming so that the community does not have to become involved again.

The Three-Generation Problem

The three-generation problem may be evident when a grandparent lives in the home, lives very near (next door or just around the corner), or is called upon for extensive child care. It is most often encountered with single parents. It is characterized by the parent's complaint that the grandparent interferes with parental responsibilities, especially those related to discipline, then criticizes the parent for the outcome.

Haley suggests that one approach is to remove the parent from all responsibility, especially for discipline, giving that responsibility to the intrusive grandparent. The parent's role is simply to enjoy the child. After a time, roles are reversed, with the grandparent to have no involvement whatsoever in parental responsibilities, not even to advise. Finally, there is discussion as to which arrangement works best.

According to Haley, the grandparent will usually prefer that the parent be in charge and will agree to communicate through the parent to the child rather than siding with the child. Therapy has presented the threat that the grandparent may be given full responsibility if he or she intrudes. Once the hierarchy is correct, problem behaviors usually subside. If the grandparent prefers full responsibility, and if that is agreeable to all, that too can be a functioning system.

> In this approach, the therapist does not go directly from the malfunctioning structure to the functioning one but as a first step creates a different malfunctional system. This system is only partially different, however, since the grandmother is asked to take charge when she has already been taking charge. However, she is put *fully* in charge. If the therapist attempts to go to the more normal system first, by having the mother take full charge, usually the grandmother will continue to intrude, demonstrating that the mother is not adequate to the task (Haley, 1987, p. 139).

While Haley's approach to the three-generational problem poses some difficulties in applying it while the child is in residential treatment, arrangements can be made. The grandparent can assume responsibility for coming to family sessions and for the child on passes while the mother attends recreational activities and is relieved of disciplinary responsibilities when the child is on pass. Extended passes may be used or the intervention may be planned for a holiday.

Conclusions

There is some disagreement among professionals as to just how much responsibility the family may have for the problems of a disturbed child. Sometimes, as in the case of severe neglect or abuse, the family's role appears to be very clear. Other times, the family's role is not so clear. In any case, I believe that the family should be encouraged to accept as much responsibility as they are able to assist with the child's treatment.

If the goal of the residential program is to prepare the child to succeed in the environment to which he or she will discharge, and if that environment is the family, then the more the family can do for the child, the less needs to be accomplished with the child in residential treatment. When both the child and the family make gains during the child's residence in the program, the chances of success after discharge are improved. When the family has problems that are untreatable (due to resistance or unavailability for treatment due to geographic distances or other factors), then the child must be fully prepared to thrive in the family to which she or he will return.

Often, the family prefers to think of the child as the problem, to deny any responsibility, and to resist any efforts at family treatment. It is sometimes helpful to explain to the family that the program needs their help in order to treat the child. Their attendance at family sessions will help them to keep abreast of the child's treatment and progress. They can provide invaluable information that can assist the program in working with the child. Family sessions can provide a structured format to enable the family to monitor the child's progress in the program. They can learn some of the techniques that the program is using and employ them at home to help their child. They need to know what improvements to expect, as well as what setbacks and regressions can be anticipated and what to do about them.

If individual therapy is complex, family therapy may be even more so. Just as there are a variety of theories and approaches to individual therapy, there are a variety of theories and approaches to family therapy. As with individual therapy, family therapy requires clear goals and deliberate, clearly conceptualized strategies to meet those goals. Anything less is not family therapy.

TREATMENT FOR SEXUAL ABUSE

It is estimated from national statistics that one in every five female children and one in every ten male children will be sexually abused before the age of eighteen. Adult women in therapy reveal a history of childhood sexual abuse, sometimes twenty-five years after the fact (Mason, 1991). However and by whomever the sexual abuse of a child occurs, it has implications for the entire family and is a matter for family therapy that can be expected to be critical for any treatment of a child who has experienced sexual abuse.

Sexual abuse has implications for a child's functioning, surviving, and thriving on a number of levels. First, the child's emotional development is often fixated at the age at which the abuse began. When a child is used as an object for gratification rather than treated as a human being, the child seems to have some difficulty with normal development. Second, the child often feels some responsibility for the abuse, and consequently some shame and guilt. Third, the child has feelings about the perpetrator of the abuse. This is especially significant when the perpetrator is a parent or other adult supposedly in the role of protector; it is less significant but still important when the perpetrator is a sibling, aunt or uncle, or friend of the family. Fourth, the child has feelings about other adults who are in a position to protect the child, especially the mother. The importance of this factor is sometimes underestimated.

Additionally, persons who should protect the child have feelings about the abuse, the perpetrator of the abuse, and the child that affect relationships within the family. Often these persons add to the child's problems by disbelieving the child or by blaming the child rather than holding the perpetrator accountable for the abuse. Finally, the perpetrator's continuing relationship with the child may be significant.

Resolution of the above issues is critical for successful treatment of a child with a history of sexual abuse. Madanes (1991) offers a sixteen-step process for reparation in such cases:

1. Bring the family together and have everyone describe exactly what happened. Encourage the victim to talk, but put no pressure on the victim to do so.
2. Ask each family member, starting with the offender, why what the offender did was wrong. The offender usually has trouble identifying why the behavior was wrong.
3. Agree with all the reasons why it was wrong, then suggest one more reason—the spiritual pain or pain in the heart that it caused.
4. Discuss the spiritual pain the act caused for the perpetrator of the abuse.
5. Step 5 is usually spontaneous. Someone discloses other sexual abuse that has occurred in the family. There is rarely one victim or one victimizer.
6. Point out that the act caused spiritual pain to others in the family who care about the victim. The act was not only against the child but also against all those who care about the child.
7. Ask the offender to apologize to the victim on his or her knees, expressing sorrow and remorse. The offender of course is reluctant. Getting on one's knees is humiliating. The therapist explains that this is exactly why he or she must get on his or her knees. If the offender cannot do this, then therapy cannot proceed and the therapist must report to the court that the offender is not amenable to therapy. This step may need to be repeated several times until

the offender can satisfy the family and the victim that he or she is sincere.

8. Next, other family members must apologize to the victim, also on their knees, for their failure to protect. When the mother explains that she did not know and could not have known, she may apologize for not being available for the child to come to about the problem.

   The apologies are necessary and should be elicited as soon as possible. The victim does not have to accept the apology or offer forgiveness. Nor does the victim have to apologize. The important message is that no one is interested in what the victim may or may not have contributed to the event.

9. Discuss what will happen if more abuse occurs. The harshest penalties should be encouraged—expulsion of the abuser from the family and criminal prosecution.

10. For the tenth step, the therapist meets with the victim alone, encouraging her or him to talk about feelings, fears, and pain. The therapist works to put the abuse in perspective, that it was but a small part of the child's life.

11. The eleventh step involves the therapist's beginning to find a protector for the victim—generally not the mother. In such families, mothers are often weak, although she should become stronger through the course of therapy. A responsible uncle, strong grandmother, or other member of the extended family may be best.

12. Step 12 involves reparation, most often symbolic because there is nothing that can really compensate for the damage such an act causes. The reparation should be beneficial to the victim and involve some longer term sacrifice on the part of the offender.

13. The thirteenth step involves the therapist's spending time with the offender to reorient him or her to normal life, normal activities, normal sex, and what to do if inappropriate sexual urges arise.

14. Restoring love is the fourteenth step. Sometimes mothers turn against the offender, sometimes against the victim. In either case, this is a difficult step.

15. The fifteenth step involves reestablishing the offender's role as a (not "the") protector of the younger children. The therapist might have the offender give some advice about staying out of trouble or danger on the streets, how to refuse drugs, etc.

16. Finally, the therapist must help the offender to forgive him- or herself. This, too, is a difficult step. The offender might be encouraged to do good deeds when he or she begins to feel badly about the offense.

There are other treatment modalities for children with a history of sexual abuse, for families, for individual therapy, and for group therapy with other survivors of sexual abuse. Regardless of the treatment modalities that are used, and even when the child is not expected to go home, family issues remain important in such treatment. At the minimum, the child must be relieved of guilt feelings, must have feelings of humiliation ameliorated, must somehow be empowered in the future, and must come to terms with feelings about the perpetrator and the person who appears somehow to have failed to protect the child.

I have seen too many adults, after years of treatment and hospitalizations, still incapacitated by unresolved issues around childhood abuse. Those issues permeate their relationships with their families, on whom they often continue to be both socially and financially dependent. These issues also seem to impede their ability to function in other areas, to set and achieve goals and move on. One day they are actively forgiving. Later they may be angry. At a later time passive, as if it's just not that important. Then the anger returns. The abuse does not have to involve penile penetration to be potentially serious and disabling; witnessing, or even just knowing about, the abuse of a sibling and being unable to do anything about it, even to talk about it, is problematic.

Conclusions

The residential treatment program must have some capacity to treat victims of sexual abuse in some deliberate way. Children who come to the safety of the residential program may not wish to discuss the abuse. Many of us with normal sex lives don't care to discuss the details with others. Nevertheless, such children are sometimes at risk for further abuse within the program, possibly by other children, on occasion by staff. If the decision is made to not confront abuse issues with a given child at a given time, then that decision should be a deliberate treatment decision, not avoidance on the part of treatment personnel or a failure to recognize the importance of these issues for the child's future. It should include a deliberate plan as to when and how these issues will be addressed. Treatment of a child with a history of sexual abuse that fails to address these issues will be far from complete and, very likely, most unsuccessful.

SUMMARY

Family issues are important in residential treatment. Work with the family, whether it be therapy or merely helping them to learn additional skills and techniques, enhances the probability of success after discharge. If some symptomatic behavior is indeed adaptive in the family setting, then we should expect symptomatic behavior to resume upon the child's return to that same family setting. Even in cases in which the child will not return home or has no family, family issues intrude upon treatment.

Martone, Kemp, and Pearson's model for parent involvement proceeds through four phases: engagement, participation, empowerment, and discharge. Engagement involves overcoming the family's shame, humiliation, and anger at having their child placed and setting the stage for their participation in the treatment of the child. Family participation provides support to the child and dispels myths that the staff may have about the family and myths the family may have about the program. It also provides support for the family. Issues of competition, competence, and cooperation arise.

Empowerment involves putting the family back in control of normal parental responsibilities. They may make good decisions as well as some poor decisions. Empowerment reestablishes the parents' rights and responsibilities. Discharge involves returning the parents to full responsibility. Parents, the child, and staff have feelings at this point. Parents and the child may be fearful. They must deal with the impending loss of the relationships they have established with personnel and the program. Staff must relinquish responsibility to the parents, trusting them and the child to continue with gains made in treatment.

When the child is not going home, involvement of available family members helps the child to dispel myths about the family and contributes to the child's sense of connectedness and identity. Sometimes, the family can give the child a sense of their permission to move on to new relationships with other adults, rather than a sense of abandonment or rejection.

Teaching parents improved or additional skills can be a relatively unintrusive technique to empower them to help their child to learn and grow towards independence. Popkin's Active Parenting™ programs provide an excellent model. In a carefully conceptualized approach to parenting, the programs teach skills of giving the child appropriate choices, determining whether the parent or the child is responsible for managing a problem, active listening, "I" messages, use of natural and logical consequences, and determining a child's goal in misbehavior. Any program that teaches parents skills should be designed to provide encouragement and support as parents practice those skills.

There are any number of theories and approaches to family therapy. There are some differences in family therapy with inpatients, where the program rather than the family has responsibility for the child. Dalton and Forman have found that a directive psychoeducational approach is often helpful. They use an object-relations approach when problematic family relationships appear to be related to the child's symptoms. When marital issues and disagreements appear to be affecting the child's symptomatic behavior, they may employ couple's therapy.

Haley conceptualizes two problems often encountered in residential treatment: the two-generational problem, in which one parent is overly involved with a child, and the three-generational problem, in which a grandparent intrudes into parental responsibilities and interferes. In the two-generational problem, the therapist may enter through the over-involved parent, the peripheral parent, or through both parents. With the intrusive grandparent, the therapist may first have the grandparent assume full parental responsibility, followed by the parent; the family may then negotiate a more realistic and effective arrangement.

When a child has experienced sexual abuse, treatment will not likely be effective unless certain specific issues related to sexual abuse are treated. They may be best treated in family therapy. When the family is unavailable, or when other considerations, such as the child's refusal to meet with certain family members, preclude family therapy, the issues may be treated in individual therapy or in group therapy with other survivors of sexual abuse. Key issues include the humiliation and depersonalization of being treated like an object of gratification rather than as a person; feelings of powerlessness, shame, and guilt; feelings about the perpetrator; and feelings about others who may have been expected to protect the child. Beliefs about responsibility are important. Children often feel responsible for the abuse. Meanwhile, they must be taught how they can become responsible for preventing, avoiding, or stopping such abuse in the future (empowerment).

PART IV

This section is devoted to putting together some of the many subjects that have been covered. In chapter 15, ''Assessment, Treatment Planning, and Progress Review,'' I propose a model for treatment planning that organizes the vast amount of information usually available about an individual child and family, helps to suggest appropriate goals and interventions, facilitates the assigning of goals to appropriate treatment modalities, assigns specific responsibilities to staff, the child, and the family, and facilitates progress reviews and reporting.

In chapter 16, ''Fine Tuning the Milieu,'' we will look at a few final points, specifically, the program's reputation, preplacement, intake, discharge, aftercare, runaways, staff burnout, and the use of computers for statistics and up-to-date emergency information for all staff. In chapter 17, ''Referral: The Continuum of Care Revisited,'' I will suggest some indications and contraindications for each level of intervention in the continuum and some considerations for making referrals.

PUTTING IT

ALL TOGETHER

15

Assessment, Treatment Planning, and Progress Review

A skilled and experienced contractor would not attempt to build a house without a detailed plan. Blueprints for a house detail nearly everything—the size and shape of the foundation, the exact location of exterior and interior walls, the size and location of doors and windows, the exact location of hot and cold water lines, drains, the location of lighting fixtures, switches, and outlets, and more. Plans do not detail where every stud is placed or where each nail is placed, but widely accepted standards provide rules that produce remarkable conformity. The plans and rules help framing carpenters, trim carpenters, roofers, sheetrock hangers, electricians, and plumbers to coordinate efficiently.

Sometimes mistakes are made. A carpenter may line a slab for a wall, then place the wall on the wrong side of the line. This may result in a kitchen that is three-and-one-half inches too small for the cabinets that were planned and ordered. A plumber might misplace the drain in the slab resulting in a toilet that sits against the bath tub. The architect may design a vaulted ceiling that is higher than the roof that she designed on another page of the plan. There may be something wrong with the plan or some problem with the workmanship. When problems are found, they must be corrected or the plan must be changed. Otherwise, the house cannot be finished.

In residential treatment, we often attempt a much more difficult undertaking, the treatment of a child with multiple problems, with a plan that contains only a few goals and brief strategies. As with the construction of a house, the treatment of a child in a residential setting requires the coordinated work of a number of "trades." At the least, child care and education will be involved. More probably, several others will be involved—social work, psychology, psychiatry, medicine, nutrition, recreation. Some of these "trades" may even specialize—individual, group, or family therapy, or behavior modification, for example.

Perhaps we don't develop more detailed plans because we deal with too many variables. Perhaps there is simply too much information to manage. Perhaps we don't feel we need better plans, relying on rules and standards in each discipline. Nevertheless, the better our plan for a child, the better our ability to:

1. Coordinate the approaches of various disciplines.
2. Know when we are on schedule.
3. Identify problems.
4. Determine whether a given problem is with the plan or with the implementation.

In this chapter, I propose a model to facilitate treatment planning for treatment that involves several treatment modalities. First, I offer a form that is designed to help to organize the tremendous amount of information that is typically available about a child in placement and assist in the identification of appropriate goals and treatment strategies. Next, I propose a format for treatment planning that:

1. Enables specific treatment goals and objectives to be assigned to specific treatment modalities or interventions.
2. Provides for a clear statement of strategy to show both how the modality will intervene and how the modality will coordinate with other modalities.
3. Provides for clear assignment of responsibilities, not only to staff but also to children and parents.
4. Generates a quick and easy format for progress evaluation and reporting that should help to make this often dreaded task less tedious and more useful.

Each phase of the process is illustrated with forms completed on John Jones, a fictional thirteen-year-old who is an aggressive, overweight, only child of a married couple. His parents are concerned about his problematic behaviors at home and at school, which include threats of aggression towards parents, teachers, and other children. John appears to be "spoiled," used to getting his own way. His parents appear to be "overindulgent," often giving in to John. They also appear to be somewhat "over-involved" and can be expected to undermine treatment or terminate treatment early. (I have provided blank copies of the various forms in appendix B for those who might wish to try them on a real case.)

ASSESSMENT

Obviously, assessment is important in any type of treatment setting: medical, dental, psychologi-cal, psychiatric, or social. Problems that are improperly identified are not likely to be properly treated. Problems that are unidentified are not likely to be treated at all. Moreover, unidentified problems may interfere with the treatment of problems we have identified.

In residential treatment, information is available from all kinds of sources: social histories, psychiatric evaluations, psychological testing and evaluation, educational testing and evaluation, educational records, physicals, medical records, dental records, speech and hearing evaluations, neurological tests, interviews with parents or foster parents, siblings, and the children themselves, reports from state workers, probation officers, and other professionals involved with the child or family, direct observation of the client and family members, and eventually reports from staff and other residents. Sometimes there is too much information to manage. Other times information is sparse, incomplete, inaccurate, or contradictory. Occasionally, information that is missing, such as a history of sexual abuse or substance abuse by a parent, may be more important than information that is presented in great detail.

Residential treatment programs tend to be very busy with lots of activity and children needing lots of attention. Residential programs also tend to be minimally staffed so that everyone has a full (if not overextended) work load. It is therefore often difficult for staff to find time to concentrate without interruption to effectively sort through information or to pursue additional information, especially if there is no systematic method for managing the tremendous amount of information that may be available. Staff then rely more heavily on intuitive or impulsive decision making.

Residential treatment programs have the potential to bring tremendous resources to bear on a wide variety of problems, provided those problems are identified and goals are established realistically. Moreover, residential treatment programs have the capability of attacking especially difficult problems with a variety of interventions and resources, provided their staff have the time, ability, and tools to plan and coordinate a multidimensional approach.

If problems are difficult to identify clearly and concisely in residential settings, then it is no wonder that strengths often receive the most perfunctory attention. Residential treatment is about problems—problems are what bring clients to treatment. Strengths are important, and every client has them. Strengths are supposed to be what treatment uses to build on to solve problems, provide cures, change behavior, feelings, and attitudes, or whatever the particular modality purports to do. But without a systematic way of identifying strengths and planning around them, strengths tend to be a perfunctorily developed list that heads the treatment plan, if they receive any attention at all.

Assessment Summary for Multi-Modal Treatment

The "Assessment Summary for Multi-Modal Treatment" form proposed in this chapter organizes a comprehensive list of behaviors, abilities, tendencies, attitudes, moods, emotions, and historical events. It provides a format for rating these as:

1. Insufficient information to assess.
2. Relative strengths.
3. Neither significant strengths nor weaknesses.
4. Contributing to some dysfunction or impairment.
5. Contributing to significant dysfunction or impairment.

It also provides a mechanism for identifying goals for each significant item, including goals to utilize identified strengths in treatment and goals for securing any additional information that might be needed. Problems may also be prioritized as requiring immediate attention, requiring significant attention prior to discharge, or optional.

The purpose of the form is not to "do an assessment," but rather to help the worker organize information from assessments that have already been done. It is designed to be used by a treatment professional who is familiar with the child and the family.

A two-page information sheet provides for a summarization of basic data, including name and age, presenting problems, and placement history. It also provides for a brief summary of the most recent formal evaluations—psychiatric diagnosis and recommendations, psychological assessment and recommendations. It concludes with a brief summarization of the most recent performance in school.

The remainder of the form is devoted to a list of phenomena that are organized into several sections. The first section is devoted to biophysical phenomena. It includes topics related to such things as physical health, dental health, intelligence, and organicity.

The next section is devoted to psychosocial development, including infancy, early childhood, latency, adolescence, and developmental milestones. Early problems in psychosocial development may suggest psychotherapy, especially if intelligence and verbal skills also suggest that insight-oriented therapy may be productive. More recent problems may suggest counseling in the milieu and behavioral treatment as primary interventions.

A section on recent and current familial phenomena focuses on current problems that may likely have brought the child into treatment, or which may have implications for the course of treatment. It deals with such things as communication, values, expectations, consistency, and discipline.

A major section of the form is devoted to behavioral phenomena. Subsections are devoted to social skills, temper control, responsibility, behavior towards property, sexual behavior, substance abuse, aggression, and general behaviors such as sleeping, enuresis, and self-injury. It concludes with sections on peer relations and leisure activities.

A section on legal problems, specifically criminal behaviors, is followed by a section on mood, thought, and personality. The latter deals with overall emotions, sense of reality, overall style of relating, motivation, and values.

The second-to-last section is devoted to education. It deals with achievement scores, grades, behavior, motivation, and extracurricular interest.

The final section is devoted to placement, including prior placements, attitude towards placement, discharge resources, sources for support from outside of placement and, finally, possible problematic behaviors to expect during placement.

The checklist can be completed within fifteen to thirty minutes by a worker who is knowledgeable about the child. Stating goals and implications for treatment will take longer. If it takes any longer than developing goals under any other format, however, it may be due to the more comprehensive approach towards goals and strategies. The following form is prepared on the above-mentioned John Jones.

TREATMENT PLANNING

Treatment planning is perhaps the most difficult, yet the most critical aspect of residential treatment. A well-defined treatment plan identifies not only the resident's problems but also the resident's strengths. It establishes goals that will resolve the problems, then provides a strategy for reaching those goals, which utilizes the resources of the program and the strengths of the resident, along with any available family and community resources. It establishes time-limited and measurable objectives that facilitate periodic reviews of progress and evaluation of the effectiveness of the plan. It assigns responsibilities clearly to specific staff, the resident, and the family so that all participants in the plan may be held accountable.

A little extra time spent on the development of a sound and functional treatment plan should save a great deal of time in the future. It should provide a plan that is easy to use, easy to evaluate, and easy to report on. It should effectively focus more time and energy on treatment.

Except for the Initial Treatment Plan, which should be completed on or before intake, the treatment plan outline proposed in this chapter flows from the Assessment Summary for Multi-Modal Treatment. It consists of three possible sections: a

Treatment Goal Summary, a 90 Day Priority Treatment Plan, and the Treatment Plan itself.

Initial Treatment Plan

The initial treatment plan can be completed at intake and might even be completed before intake. It addresses living assignment, staff assigned for orientation, special needs such as medical or dietary needs, needs for special supervision, and educational and other initial assignments.

Treatment Goal Summary

The treatment goal summary flows from the Assessment Summary for Multi-Modal Treatment. It summarizes:

1. Goals to secure additional information.
2. Strengths and how they may be used.
3. Prioritized treatment goals.

In addition, it provides for the assignment of goals to specific treatment modalities according to the overall treatment strategy.

It is designed so that it can be compiled by clerical staff from a carefully completed assessment summary. When there is not sufficient clerical support for this task, the person completing the Assessment Summary may choose to write goals directly on the Treatment Goal Summary rather than on the Assessment Summary.

Additional Information Required
Needs for additional information are summarized along with goals to obtain the information.

Strengths
Strengths are summarized along with goals to use those strengths in treatment.

Priority 1 Goals
Identified problems on the assessment form that are assigned a priority of 1 are those problems that may affect the initial placement of the child.

FIGURE 15.1: Assessment Summary for Multi-Modal Treatment

Assessment Summary for Multi-Modal Treatment

Pre-Admit ___   Admit _X_

Name __John Jones_____   Date __3/3/94___   Admit Date __2/25/92___   Reevaluation ___   Discharge ___

DOB _6/12/80___   Age _13___   Sex _M___   Race/Ethnicity __W_____   Height __5'10"___   Weight ___210 lbs

Presenting   Ideal   Ideal

Problems __John was referred because of serious problems at home and at___   Height __ok___   Weight __155 lbs

school. He does not follow instructions, accept limits, rules, or "no." He uses his size to intimidate others, including his

parents, teachers, and other children. He has never hit an adult, but he has been sent home from school several times for bracing

up to teachers. His father is afraid that they will come to blows in the home.

Referred By: Parents _x_   Juvenile Court ___   State Agency ___   Other Agency ___   Other _____

Prior Placements _1_   Age at First _12_   Foster Families ___   Group Homes ___   Residential ___   Psychiatric ___   Correctional Institution ___   Emergency Shelter _1_

Legal History: Charges/Arrests   Date   Age   Disposition and comments

Child in Need of Supervision_____   _7/15/92__   _12_   2 years probation_____

Psychiatric by __Marian ReDoux, M.D._____   Date 11/12/93____

Impressions _Axis I, Conduct Disorder, solitary aggressive 312.00_   Recommendations __Placement in a structured setting,___

Axis III, Obesity._____   behavioral management and family therapy._____

Psychological by __Frederick Bender, PhD_____   Date _11/14/93___

Verbal IQ __103___   Reading Level __6.1___   Recommendations __Residential placement in a structured_____

Performance _94___   Math Level __5.9___   setting; special education in a self-contained class._____

Full Scale __98___   Spelling Level _5.3___   _____

Comments __John is a personable boy who is used to getting his own way. Parents are often in conflict over what to do with John.__

Limits are often vague, consequences inconsistently applied._____

FIGURE 15.1 *(continued)*

Assessment Summary for Multi-Modal Treatment
Page 2

Name __John Jones_____   Date __3/3/94_____

Education   Current or
              Last School __Martha Price Middle School____   Current   Grade if no
                                                               Grade _7, Sp. Ed._ Failures __7_____

Regular Classes ___   Special Education _x_   Classification _Behavior Disordered_____

Academic Grades Last Report   Extra Curricular Activities __Basketball_____

Reading   _C_   _____

English   _D_   Attendance __OK, except for disciplinary actions_____

Math   _F_   Detentions __about 3/month for refusing class work or homework_____

Science   _D_   Suspensions _None (Sp.Ed.), but sent home repeatedly for fights, refusing detention-authority._

Social Studies _D_   Expulsions __None (Sp.Ed.), but in danger of being put on homebound due to aggression-defiance._

Special Needs _Remediation in all skill areas; behavioral plan._____

Comments _John uses his size to intimidate others and is in danger of being put out of school for the remainder of the year. He_

_has the potential to complete high school with remediation and improved behavior._____

Key for attached assessment:

ISI Insufficient information to evaluate

 +   A strength for this child

 0   Neither poses a problem nor serves as a particular strength

     Put "N/A" in this column (0) if this category is not relevant to this child, i.e., use of makeup for boys,
     absent parent in families where natural parents are still married and living together, etc.

 -   Causes or contributes to some limitation, impairment or dysfunction

 !   Causes or contributes to critical limitation, impairment or dysfunction

Priority 1 Goals - For problems that require prompt and immediate attention. These problems are such that they may place the
                   resident or others in danger, or such that if not promptly addressed and improved, may pose a significant
                   obstacle to further treatment or the resident's continuation in the program.

Priority 2 Goals - These problems are significant to overall functioning and require prompt attention, but not at the expense of
                   Priority 1 problems and goals. Further prioritization depends on factors other than the impact that the area
                   has on functioning, such as ease of accomplishment, timing with program events such as school, and summer
                   programming. These goals must, therefore, be further prioritized during development of the treatment strategy.

Optional 0 Goals - These areas contribute to limitations, impairment, or dysfunction. Improvements in these areas would be
                   beneficial to the child, but they will not be critical to success after discharge. They may be addressed prior
                   to discharge if time and resources permit.

FIGURE 15.1 *(continued)*

Assessment Summary for Multi-Modal Treatment, page 3

BIO-PHYSICAL	ISI	+	0	-	!	Tentative Goal or Implications for Treatment	Priority
General Health			x				
Physical Development			x				
Physical Appearance			x				
Dental Health	x						
Orthodontia	x						
Vision			x				
Hearing			x				
Speech		x				John is quite verbal and a good candidate for talking therapy	
Appetite				x		Put on a weight loss diet	0
Allergies			x				
Birth Complications			x				
Addiction at Birth			x				
Coordination		x				Physical activities will be a potential reinforcement	
Intelligence		x				A good candidate for talking therapy and cognitive treatment	
Hygiene/self-care			x				
Physical Limitations							
1. none			n/a				
2.			n/a				
Organicity			x				
Neurological			x				
Seizures			x				
Medications							
1. none			n/a				
2.			n/a				
3.			n/a				
Other Physical							
1. none			n/a				
2.			n/a				

ISI + 0 - !

FIGURE 15.1 *(continued)*

Assessment Summary for Multi-Modal Treatment, page 4

PSYCHO-SOCIAL DEVELOPMENT	ISI	+	0	–	!	Tentative Goal or Implications for Treatment	Priority
Infancy							
Nurturing			x				
Neglect			x				
Abuse			x				
Trauma			x				
Problems Noted with Infant			x				
Early Childhood							
Security			x				
Neglect/Indulgence				x		History of excessive indulgence will contribute to difficulties with limits. Psychotherapy indicated	Strategy
Abuse			x				
Abandonment or Trauma			x				
Problems with Child			x				
Latency							
Security			x				
Neglect/Indulgence				x		Excessive indulgence by parents. See above	
Abuse			x				
Abandonment or Trauma			x				
Problems with Child			x				
Adolescence							
Stability			x				
Neglect/Indulgence					x	Parents have indulged John. Parents will make favors and privileges more contingent on behavior	2
Abuse				x		Father will learn to deescalate violence	2
Abandonment or Trauma			x				
Problems with Child					x	John will learn to accept limits and "no," and learn to express disagreements without aggression and intimidation	2
Development							
Toilet			x				
Speech			x				
Social			x				
Other 1. none			n/a				
2.			n/a				
	ISI	+	0	–	!		

274

FIGURE 15.1 *(continued)*

Assessment Summary for Multi-Modal Treatment, page 5

RECENT/CURRENT FAMILIAL	ISI	+	0	–	!	Tentative Goal or Implications for Treatment	Priority
Neglect/Indulgence					x	Parents have indulged John. Parents must learn to make privileges, large ticket items more contingent on behavior	2
Abandonment			x				
Emotional Abuse			x				
Physical Abuse				x		Father must learn to deescalate violence and model non-violent behavior	2
Sexual Abuse			x				
In Home Relations	**						
With Mother/Step Mother				x		Mother will learn to set limits and not back down, even when intimidated	2
With Father/Step Father				x		Father will learn to deescalate violence during confrontations	2
With Brothers			n/a				
With Sisters			n/a				
With Other Relatives in Home			n/a				
Out-of-Home Relations	**						
With Out-of-Home Mother			n/a				
With Out-of-Home Father			n/a				
With Other Out-of-Home Relatives	x					Behaves really well with uncle--a possible respite resource	
With Neighbors/Landlord			x				
With Neighborhood Children			X				
Communications	**						
Between Parents				x		Parents must learn to communicate about John before decisions are made and to support each other's decisions	2
Parent/Child				x		John will learn to avoid making threats to parents; parents will learn to refrain from giving in when John makes threats	2
Parental Conflict				x		Parents will learn to communicate about John before decisions are made and to support each other's decisions	2
Parent-Child Conflict					x	Parents will learn to set and enforce limits; John will learn to accept limits	2
Other			x				
	**						
Parental Substance Abuse			x				
Parental Values				x		Father will learn to devalue violence and aggression	2
Parental Expectations				x		Mother will learn to expect age-appropriate behavior from John and stop making excuses for him	2
Consistency				x		Parents will learn to follow through with consequences	2
Discipline (Too Easy/Harsh)				x		Parents will learn to threaten more moderate discipline and follow through	2
	ISI	+	0	–	!		

FIGURE 15.1 *(continued)*

Assessment Summary for Multi-Modal Treatment, page 6

BEHAVIOR	ISI	+	0	-	!	Tentative Goal or Implications for Treatment	Priority
						John will learn to use social skills at home	
Problems in Home					x		2
						John will use social skills at school	
Problems in School					x		2
Problems in Community			x				
Legal Problems			x				
Self-Destructive Behavior			x				
Social Skills	**
						John will learn to follow instructions to program criteria	
Following Instructions			x				2
						John will learn to accept criticism to program criteria	
Accepting Criticism			x				2
Asking Permission			x				
						John will learn to accept "no" to program criteria	
Accepting "No"				x			2
						John will learn to accept and follow limits	
Following Limits			x				2
	**
						John will learn to accept consequences	
Accepting Consequences			x				2
						John will refrain from threats and intimidation	
Adult Relations – Male			x				1 & 2
						John will refrain from threats and intimidation	
Adult Relations – Female			x				1 & 2
						John will refrain from threats and intimidation	
Peer Relations – Male			x				1 & 2
Peer Relations – Female		x					
Temper Control	**
						Program will monitor as a possible problem. John makes so	
Without Striking at Others				x		many threats that he may feel it necessary to follow through	2
						John will learn to refrain from intimidating others	
Without Bracing Up to Others				x			1
						John will learn to refrain from threatening others	
Without Threatening Others				x			1
Without Breaking Things			x				
Without Slamming Things			x				
	**
Without Cursing			x				
						John will learn to maintain appropriate voice tones when	
Without Yelling				x		angry	2
Without Walking Away			x				
Without Crying			x				
Without Pouting			x				
	ISI	+	0	-	!		

FIGURE 15.1 *(continued)*

Assessment Summary for Multi-Modal Treatment, page 7

BEHAVIOR continued	ISI	+	0	–	!	Tentative Goal or Implications for Treatment	Priority
Normal Voice Tone			x				
Normal Language		x					
Manners		x					
Normally Pleasant to be with		x					
Interrupts Others When Talking			x				
Responsibility							
Completes Chores		x				John is a good worker. Extra jobs for pay will be a good reinforcement and source of self-esteem	
Keeps Room Neat		x				Can be used to support self-esteem while he receives criticism in other areas	
Completes Homework				x		John will complete homework	2
Gives Destination When Leaving			x				
Leaves Without Permission			x				
Comes in on Time			x				
Stays Out All Night			x				
Runs Away			x				
Can Stay on the Streets			x				
Can Hide Out with Friends			x				
Property							
Puts Things Away			x				
Breaks/Damages Things			x				
Steals from Family			x				
Steals from Others			x				
Trespasses			x				
Sexual							
Self Sexual Acting Out			n/a				
Is Sexually Active			n/a				
Uses Protection			n/a				
Has Multiple Partners/Promiscuous			n/a				
Is Aggressive or Victimized			n/a				

ISI + 0 – !

FIGURE 15.1 *(continued)*

Assessment Summary for Multi-Modal Treatment, page 8

BEHAVIOR continued	ISI	+	0	–	!	Tentative Goal or Implications for Treatment	Priority
Substance Abuse							
Experimental			n/a				
Recreational			n/a				
Regular			n/a				
Habitual			n/a				
Smoking			n/a				
****
Alcohol			n/a				
Marijuana			n/a				
Other 1. none			n/a				
2.			n/a				
Multiple Habitual Use			n/a				
Physical Aggression	**
With Peers				x		John will refrain from intimidation and fighting	2
With Mother					x	John will express disagreement without intimidating his mother	2
With Father					x	John will express disagreement without intimidating his father	2
With Female Teachers			n/a				
With Male Teachers					x	John will refrain from intimidating teachers	1
****
Likes to Have Weapons			x				
Has Threatened with a Weapon			x				
Has Used a Weapon			x				
Grabs Anything That's Handy			x				
Carries Weapons			x				
General	**
Can't Sit Still			x				
Difficult to Wake Up in Morning			x				
Sleeps During the Day			x				
Does Not Go to Bed			x				
Eating Habits				x		John should lose weight but does not want to	0

ISI + 0 – !

278

FIGURE 15.1 *(continued)*

Assessment Summary for Multi-Modal Treatment, page 9

BEHAVIOR continued	ISI	+	0	–	!	Tentative Goal or Implications for Treatment	Priority
Enuresis			x				
Encopresis			x				
Suicidal Ideation			x				
Suicide Attempt			x				
Other Self-Injurious Behavior			x				
Peer Relations							
Has Good Friends			x				
Has Negative Friends			x				
Follows Others into Trouble			x				
Influences Others into Trouble			x				
Dates			x				
Leisure							
Has Healthy Interests (list)		x				Use as reinforcement	
1. football		x				Use as reinforcement	
2. all sports		x				Use as reinforcement	
3. rides bike		x				Use as reinforcement	
4.			n/a				
Has Problem Interests			x				
Listens to Too Much Music			x				
Watches Too Much TV/Video Games			x				
Stays Alone in Room Too Much			x				
Sleeps Too Much			x				
Leisure Affects Responsibilities				x		John will complete homework	2
Gets into Trouble When Left Alone			x				
Other Behavior							
1. none			n/a				
2.			n/a				
3.			n/a				
	ISI	+	0	–	!		

279

FIGURE 15.1 *(continued)*

Assessment Summary for Multi-Modal Treatment, page 10

LEGAL	ISI	+	0	-	!	Tentative Goal or Implications for Treatment	Priority
Trespassing			n/a				
Shoplifting			n/a				
Theft			n/a				
Car Theft			n/a				
Burglary			n/a				
***							
Armed Robbery			n/a				
Battery				x		John will learn to control aggression before he receives legal charges	1 & 2
Sexual Battery			n/a				
Drug Possession/Use			n/a				
Drug Sales			n/a				
***							
Probation Violation			n/a				
Other 1. none			n/a				
2.			n/a				
3.			n/a				
Incarceration			n/a				
MOOD/THOUGHT/PERSONALITY ***							
Happy		x					
Sad			x				
Angry			x				
Depressed			x				
Satisfied			x				
Sense of Reality **							
Fails to Perceive			n/a				
Distorts Perceptions			n/a				
Distorts Memory			n/a				
Hears Voices			n/a				
Visual Hallucinations			n/a				
	ISI	+	0	-	!		

FIGURE 15.1 (continued)

Assessment Summary for Multi-Modal Treatment, page 11

MOOD/THOUGHT/PERSONALITY Continued	ISI	+	0	–	!	Tentative Goal or Implications for Treatment	Priority
Has Realistic Goals				x		John needs to develop realistic goals and expectations for himself	2
Has Realistic Expectations/Self				x		John should expect more of himself	2
Has Realistic Expectations/Others				x		John needs to learn that others will not always yield to his intimidation	2
Other 1. none			n/a				
2.			n/a				
Style						**	
Assertive/Timid				x		John will learn to control his aggression	1 & 2
Sense of Humor		x				John's sense of humor can be used to improve his insight and help him to learn to accept criticism	
Mean			x				
Violent					x	John will learn to deal with frustration without resorting to intimidation	1 & 2
Selfish			x				
						**	
Impulse Control			x				
Self-Control			x				
Self-Discipline				x		John will complete homework responsibilities	2
Self-Esteem		x				Can withstand criticism even when he doesn't accept it	
Attitude			x				
						**	
Motivation			x				
Goals			x				
Confidence in Self		x				Believes he can do what he wants to do	
Confidence in Others			x				
Seeks Adult Approval		x				Adult approval can be used as reinforcement	
						**	
Seeks Peer Approval			x				
Fears Rejection			x				
Rejects Before Rejected			x				
Isolates from Contact with Others			x				
Imposes Self on Others			x				

ISI   +   0   –   !

281

FIGURE 15.1 *(continued)*

Assessment Summary for Multi-Modal Treatment, page 12

MOOD/THOUGHT/PERSONALITY Continued	ISI	+	0	–	!	Tentative Goal or Implications for Treatment	Priority
Values			X				
Sense of Right and Wrong			X				
Sense of Remorse or Guilt			X				
Honesty with Self			X				
Honesty with Others			X				
***							
Lies to Impress Others			X				
Lies to Get What S/he Wants			X				
Lies to Avoid Admission of Error			X				
Lies to Avoid Consequences			X				
Lies to Protect Self-Image			X				
***							
Deceives without "Lying"			X				
Manipulates			X				
Avoids Meeting Responsibility			X				
Avoids Accepting Responsibility (for Behavior)			X				
Blames Others			X				
***							
Gets Angry with Self			X				
Gets Angry when Denied Own Way					X	John will learn to accept limits. John will learn to accept "no"	2
Gets Angry over Peers' Teasing			X				
Obsessive or Compulsive			X				
Procrastinates			X				
EDUCATION Achievement Scores Reading				X		Provide tutoring if necessary	Strategy
Math				X		Provide tutoring if necessary	Strategy
English/Spelling				X		Provide tutoring if necessary	Strategy
Social Studies	X					Not tested, but it can be expected that John is behind. John will complete class work and homework in SS and pass	2
Science	X					Not tested, but it can be assumed that John is behind. John will complete class work and homework in Sci. and pass	2
	ISI	+	0	–	!		

282

FIGURE 15.1 (continued)

Assessment Summary for Multi-Modal Treatment, page 13

EDUCATION Continued	ISI	+	0	−	!	Tentative Goal or Implications for Treatment	Priority
Academic Grades							
Reading				x		John is somewhat deficient in all academic areas. He should respond to structured study hall and the tutoring that is	2
Math				x		normally available. His grades should improve if he applies himself. John will earn passing grades in all subject areas	2
English/Spelling				x		John will earn passing grades	2
Social Studies				x		John will earn passing grades	2
Science				x		John will earn passing grades	2
Behavior	*****	*****	*****	*****	*****	**	*****
School Attendance			x				
Class Attendance			x				
Tardiness			x				
Class Work				x		John will complete class work	2
Homework				x		John will complete homework	2
	*****	*****	*****	*****	*****	**	*****
Attitude				x		John's attitude towards school should improve with his performance. Individual therapy will support this	Strategy
Motivation				x		John's motivation should improve with success. Individual therapy will be used to support improved motivation	Strategy
Adult/Authority Relations					x	Staff will develop a behavioral plan with the school and John to avoid expulsion. John will use the plan and stop threats	1
Peer Relations				x		John will use skills to avoid fights and arguments with peers	2
Follows Rules				x		John will follow school rules	2
	*****	*****	*****	*****	*****	**	*****
Follows Instructions				x		John will follow instructions at school	2
Accepts Criticism				x		John will accept criticism at school	2
Accepts Consequences				x		John will accept consequences for his behavior	2
Accepts "No"				x		John will accept "no"	2
Controls Temper					x	John will control his temper to avoid threatening teachers	1
	*****	*****	*****	*****	*****	**	*****
Appropriate Language			x				
Stays in Seat			x				
Does Not Talk out of Turn			x				
Does Not Disrupt Class				x		John will avoid disrupting the class by doing his work and following rules and limits	2
Respects Property			x				
	ISI	+	0	−	!		

FIGURE 15.1 *(continued)*

Assessment Summary for Multi-Modal Treatment, page 14

EDUCATION Continued	ISI	+	0	-	!	Tentative Goal or Implications for Treatment	Priority
Appropriate Dress			x				
Grooming			x				
Smoking			x				
Drugs/Alcohol			x				
Fighting				x		John will use social skills to avoid fights with peers	2
Aggression Against Teachers					x	John will use the behavioral plan and social skills to avoid aggression against teachers	1
Threats					x	John will use the behavior plan and social skills to avoid threatening teachers	1
Detentions				x		John will reduce detentions to no more that one in six weeks	2
Suspensions				x		John will use skills to avoid suspensions for 90 days	1 & 2
Expulsions					x	John will use skills and the behavior plan to avoid being put out of school	1
Extra Curricular Interests		x				Participation in basketball will be allowed if John is making satisfactory progress	
Probability of Promotion			x			John can pass if he studies and completes assignments	
Probability of HS Graduation			x			John can be mainstreamed in eighth grade and can complete HS	
Appropriate Placement (present)			x				
Other							
PLACEMENT							
History of Prior Placements				x		John's parents rescued him from a prior placement. They will refrain from rescuing him this time and support treatment	1
Behavior in Prior Placements			x				
Recognizes Problems		x					
Wants to Improve		x					
Has Discharge Resource		x					
Has Out-of-Program Support				x		Parents may undermine treatment and let John fantasize that they will rescue him. Parents will support treatment	1
Family Supports Placement				x		Family is skeptical about placement and having problems with separation	1
Does Not Want to Be in Placement				x		John accepts placement superficially, but may be readily distracted by any possibility of quick discharge	Strategy
Influence on Peers			x				
Influence by Peers			x				
	ISI	+	0	-	!		

FIGURE 15.1 (*continued*)

Assessment Summary for Multi-Modal Treatment, page 15

PLACEMENT Continued	ISI	+	0	-	!	Tentative Goal or Implications for Treatment	Priority
Fights with Peers					x	Because of his size, John's interactions with smaller peers must be supervised. John will refrain from injuring another	1
Victimized by Peers			x				
Runaway by Self			x				
Will Take Peers on Runaway			x				
Will Follow Peers on Runaway			x				
*****	*****	*****	*****	*****	*****	*****	*****
Sexual Assault on Peers			x				
Sexual Assault by Peers			x				
Consenting Sex with Peers			x				
Self Sexual Acting Out			x				
Relations with Opposite Sex			x				
*****	*****	*****	*****	*****	*****	*****	*****
Will Give Drugs to Peers			x				
Will Take Drugs from Peers			x				
Will Use Drugs/Alcohol on Pass			x				
Smoking			x				
Other Substance Problems			x				
*****	*****	*****	*****	*****	*****	*****	*****
Tattoos			x				
Dress			x				
Grooming			x				
Make-up			n/a				
Other			n/a				
*****	*****	*****	*****	*****	*****	*****	*****
Suicide Risk			x				
Needs Physical Control/Restraint					x	John will refrain from behavior which requires physical int. by staff. Criminal charges will be filed for battery	1
Adult Relations					x	John's adult relations are very good, until he is denied something he wants. Aggression will result in legal charges	1
Adult Attachments		x					
Other Issues from Prior Placements			n/a				

ISI + 0 - !

285

Priority 1 problems may be such as to place the child or others at some risk of harm, or problems that may place the child's continued placement in jeopardy. Examples include suicidal behavior, serious aggression, temper control problems involving serious destruction of property, runaway behavior, danger of school expulsion, or parents who can be expected to undermine the program. Goals for such serious problems are to be accomplished during the first ninety days of placement.

Priority 2 Goals

Priority 2 problems are those problems that contribute significantly to the child's dysfunction and must be resolved prior to discharge in order for success after discharge to be probable. Goals for such problems are developed with the placement after discharge clearly in mind. For example, younger children who will be discharging home to a relatively stable family, a family who may be expected to make gains during treatment, may not need to reach the same level of adaptive functioning as might an older adolescent who will be discharging to a less structured family who may not participate in treatment. The latter must be prepared to assume much more responsibility for herself or himself. Goals for priority 2 problems must be completed prior to successful discharge.

Optional Goals

Priority 0 (optional) problems are areas in which the child shows some weakness, but not such as to preclude successful functioning after discharge. Such problems may receive attention during residence, but not at the expense of efforts on priority 2 problems. Failure to achieve goals on priority 0 problems would not delay discharge. Examples include overweight or underweight, some deficiencies in leisure interests or skills, smoking, and minor problems with hygiene or grooming. Goals are, therefore, optional.

The Treatment Plan

The treatment plan flows from the treatment goal summary. Each goal is assigned to one or more treatment modalities on the Treatment Goal Summary form. Each treatment modality receives its own section in the Treatment Plan. Goals for each modality are clearly stated. Each modality has a staff member assigned. Specific interventions are delineated. The treatment strategy is outlined in a brief narrative. Specific responsibilities are clearly delineated for the staff person as well as for the client (child or family). Criteria to measure progress are also clearly delineated.

The Treatment Strategy

Many of the treatment planning formats I have seen and many that I have attempted to use have set rather clear goals for children, but they have failed to communicate just how placement in residential treatment can be expected to help. "John will control his temper without hitting others," or "John will pass to the eighth grade." These are good goals. Someone probably had these goals for John before he came into the program. Maybe even John had these goals in mind for himself before coming into placement—I have not known many children who wanted to fail the seventh grade. Some statement of how placement in residential treatment can be expected to help the child to achieve a goal is in order.

Responsibilities

The responsibilities section is critical. Many of the treatment planning formats I have seen or attempted to use have assigned responsibility for each goal to some person or persons on staff. Then, when the child failed to achieve goals, the child was discharged as "untreatable in this milieu" or with some similar statement suggesting that there was somehow something wrong with the child. Of course there was. That's why the child came into placement.

Residential treatment is a partnership. Staff have responsibilities, children have responsibilities, and parents have responsibilities. Others, including public schools and state workers, may have responsibilities. When responsibilities are carefully and clearly spelled out, then it may be possible to develop a better understanding of why particular treatment objectives are not being realized. Identifying responsibility may, of course, lead to assigning blame. It may also lead to the early identification and correction of problems before the temptation to assign blame becomes almost irresistible.

Staff, resident, and family responsibilities may be found to be fairly standard for many of the treatment modalities or interventions that may be employed. When this is the case, responsibilities may be pre-typed on treatment planning forms for those modalities.

Example

The example of John Jones is designed to operate in conjunction with a point system that has four levels following orientation, much like the one described in chapter 10. The treatment planning format may, of course, be modified to be adapted to other treatment systems. The key is clear and realistic time tables, target dates, criteria, and responsibilities.

The example presented includes a Treatment Goal Summary, a 90 Day Priority Treatment Plan, and a full Treatment Plan. The following list of potential treatment modalities is presented along with an abbreviated code that may be used in the "Treatment Goal Summary." No program will have all of these modalities. A few programs may have modalities that have not been included. I present the comprehensive list to stimulate the reader's awareness of the tremendous potential of residential treatment. I have marked the modalities used in the following example with an asterisk (*).

Treatment Modalities

A. The Therapeutic Milieu
   1. Merit System (MS)*
   2. Individual Behavior Management (IBM)
   3. Individual Behavior Treatment (IBT)
   4. Individual Behavior Therapy (IBTh)
   5. Staff Counseling (SC)*
   6. Teaching Interactions (TI)*
   7. Life-Space Interviews (LSI)*
   8. Therapeutic Crisis Intervention (TCI)
   9. Time-Out (TO)*
  10. Recreational Programming (R)*
  11. Cultural Enrichment (CE)
  12. Milieu Therapy (MT)
  13. Study Hall (SH)*
  14. Free Time (FrT)
  15. Work for Pay (W)
  16. Transportation (T)
  17. Urine Screening (US)
  18. Intensive Supervision (IS)

B. Individual Therapy (IT)*
   1. Traditional Psychotherapy (TP)
   2. Reality Therapy (RT)
   3. Rational Emotive Therapy (RET)
   4. Problem-Solving Therapy (PS)
   5. Substance Abuse Counseling (SA)
   6. Values Clarification (VC)
   7. Contract Therapy Out-of-Program
   8. Play Therapy (PT)

C. Group (G)
   1. Regular Group Therapy (RG)*
   2. Play Therapy (PGT)
   3. Sexual Abuse Group (SXG)
   4. Substance Abuse Group (SAG)
   5. Values Clarification Group (VCG)*
   6. Independent Living Group (ILG)
   7. Orientation Group (OG)
   8. Termination Group (TG)
   9. Student Government (SG)
  10. Management Group (MG)

D. Family
   1. Family Therapy (FT)*
   2. Parent Seminars (PS)*
   3. Structured Home Passes (HP)

E. Health Care
   1. Medical Care (MC)
   2. Dental Care (DC)
   3. Psychotropic Medication (PM)
   4. Physical Therapy (PhT)
   5. Nursing (N)
   6. Sex Education (SE)

F. Education
   1. Public School Regular Classes (PSR)
   2. Public School Special Education (PSS)

FIGURE 15.2: Treatment Goal Summary

Treatment Goal Summary   page _1_ of _5_

Name: John Jones _____   Date: 3/05/94 _____

Strengths:	Goals to Utilize Strengths:
coordination	use skills to maintain self-esteem
intelligence	good candidate for TI, LSI, cog. therapy
relationship with uncle	possible respite resource
keeps room neat	source of positive reinforcement
completes chores	same
athletic interests	use as reinforcement in merit system
probability of promotion	build to mainstream
motivation	use to tackle difficult problems early
pleasant	
happy	
sense of humor	use to improve insight
self-esteem	
verbal skills	good candidate for cognitive therapy
concept skills	good candidate for values clarification
recognizes problems	use to teach solutions
listening skills	will facilitate TI, LSI, & indv. therapy
discharge resource	use passes for motivation
out-of-program support	use in family therapy
adult relations	will respond well to male staff
adult attachments	use to model values
hygiene	

288

FIGURE 15.2 *(continued)*

```
                    Treatment Goal Summary      page  2  of  5

Name:  John Jones                          Date: 3/05/94
Additional Information Needed:
none
_____
_____
_____
_____
_____
_____
_____
_____


Priority 1 Goals - 90 days:                 Modalities:

Resolve parental conflicts about placement    FT

Learn to use staff to avoid fights with peers  TO-TI-LSI-MS-IT-SC

Avoid aggressive posturing with teachers      TI-MS-IT SC

Avoid threatening teachers                    TI-MS-IT-SC

Learn to use time-out to avoid physical       TO-LSI-SC-IT

     intervention by staff
```

FIGURE 15.2 *(continued)*

Treatment Goal Summary   page _3_ of _5_

Name: John Jones _____   Date: 3/05/94 _____

Priority 2 Goals: Modalities:

Parents to learn to make favors, gifts, and treats FT-PS

_____ more contingent on John's behavior _____

Parents to increase expectations of John's behavior FT-PS

_____ at home and school _____

Mother to learn not to back down _____ FT-PS

Father to learn to deescalate confrontations _____ FT-PS

Mother to stop making excuses for John's behavior _ FT-PS

_____ and hold him accountable _____

Parents to increase communication with each other _ FT

_____ about John and other matters _____

John to learn the following social skills _____ MS-TI-LSI-TCI

_____ 1. Following limits _____

_____ 2. Following instructions _____

_____ 3. Accepting "no" _____

_____ 4. Controlling temper w/o aggression _____

_____ 5. Controlling temper w/o threats _____

_____ 6. Controlling temper w/o yelling _____

_____ 7. Peer relations without fighting or _____

_____ intimidation _____

John will apply social skills at home and at school IT-FT-ED

FIGURE 15.2 *(continued)*

Treatment Goal Summary   page __4__ of __5__

Name: John Jones _____   Date: 3/05/94 _____

Priority 2 Goals continued: **Modalities:**

John will learn better study habits   TU-SH _____

John will learn to complete classwork   EC _____

John will learn to complete homework   SH-EC _____

John will learn to complete homework before leisure FT _____

John will improve grades to C or better   EC, possible TU _____

John needs a plan to get into regular classes   EC-IT-SC _____

John will improve his attitude about violence   IT-SC-RG-VC _____

John needs long-term goals for adulthood   IT-SC _____

John needs to learn to tell the truth   IT-SC _____

FIGURE 15.2 *(continued)*

Treatment Goal Summary   page _5_ of _5_

Name: John Jones_____   **Date:** 3/05/94_____

Optional Goals: **Modalities:**

John should lose weight_____   MS-WLD-SC-IT-R_____

_____   _____

_____   _____

_____   _____

_____   _____

_____   _____

_____   _____

_____   _____

_____   _____

_____   _____

_____   _____

_____   _____

_____   _____

_____   _____

_____   _____

Signatures:

Staff_____	date	**Supervisor**_____	date
Resident_____	date	**Parent**_____	date
State Worker_____	date	**Other**_____	date

FIGURE 15.3: 90 Day Priority Treatment Plan

**90 Day Priority
Treatment Plan**

page <u>1</u> of <u>4</u>

Name: John Jones
Date: 3/10/94

Goals Assigned:
1. To resolve parental conflicts about placement.
2. For John to learn to use staff to avoid fights with peers.
3. For John to learn to use Time-Out to avoid physical intervention by staff.
4. For John to avoid physical posturing with teachers.
5. For John to avoid threatening teachers.

Goal #1: Resolve parental conflicts about placement.

Interventions:
Family Therapy

Staff Responsible:
Charlotte Webb, Social Worker

Strategy:
Parental support of placement and treatment will be critical to John's success. The social worker will meet with the family weekly, and more often if necessary, to help parents resolve feelings about John's placement and to answer any questions they may have. The social worker will stay informed about John's adjustment and progress and keep the family informed.

90 Day Criteria:
Parents will support placement and not give John any indications that placement could be terminated early. Parents will discuss any concerns about placement with the social worker. Parents will avoid such discussions with John.

Staff Responsibilities:
Social worker will meet with the family once/wk for 30 min.
Social worker will stay informed of John's progress
Social worker will call family promptly on any unusual events
Social worker will be available by phone for any questions
Social worker will allow family to discuss concerns openly

Resident Responsibilities: (family)
Parents will attend scheduled mtgs. and notify in advance of any need to cancel
Parents will call social worker promptly with any questions, and will ask for a supervisor if social worker is unavailable and it can't wait
Parents will discuss feelings freely and openly
Parents will avoid discussing doubts or questions with John

FIGURE 15.3 (*continued*)

Name: John Jones   **Date:** 3/10/94

Goal #2: John will learn to use staff to avoid fights with peers.

Interventions: **Staff Responsible:**
Time-Out, Teaching Interactions,   Calvin Wright, Supervisor
    Life Space Interviews, Merit
    System, Staff Counseling
Individual Therapy   Charlotte Webb, Social Worker

Strategy:
Due to John's size, fighting cannot be tolerated and may lead to his
transfer to another setting. Staff will teach John techniques to
respond to staff and manage his anger, including Time-Out to regain
self-control.

90 Day Criteria:
John will not injure another resident during the next 90 days. John
will have no more than two instances of aggression or fights with peers
for 90 days, and will avoid fights for 30 consecutive days to make Level
2.

Staff Responsibilities: **Resident Responsibilities:**
To teach John to follow   To listen when staff are teaching
    instructions   To practice what he learns
To provide close supervision of   To follow staff instructions
    John and his peers   To take a Time-Out promptly when
To intervene promptly for any   instructed
    problems   To think when in Time-Out
To teach John to use Time-Out   To keep scheduled appointments and
To keep Time-Out to 5 minutes   meet when asked
To instruct John when Time-Out is To discuss his feelings honestly
    needed   To come to staff immediately with
To teach John to express his anger   any problems
    appropriately
To help John better understand the
    feelings of others
To meet with John twice per week
    for 30 minutes
To respond promptly if John comes
    with a problem

FIGURE 15.3 *(continued)*

90 Day Priority
Treatment Plan   page __3__ of __4__

Name: John Jones   Date: 3/10/94

Goal #3: John will learn to use Time-Out to avoid physical interventions by staff.

Interventions: **Staff Responsible:**
Time-Out, Teaching Interactions,   Calvin Wright, Supervisor
    Crisis Intervention,
    Life-Space Interview
Individual Therapy   Charlotte Webb, Social Worker

Strategy:
Due to John's size, staff will not be able to intervene physically without risk of injury to John. Staff will teach John techniques of self-control, including the use of Time-Out.

90 Day Criteria:
John will have no behaviors that result in injury to himself or others for 90 consecutive days. For 45 consecutive days, John will use Time-Out promptly when instructed and return from Time-Out to discuss problems rationally.

Staff Responsibilities: **Resident Responsibilities:**
To teach John to respond promptly   To learn to respond promptly when
    to instructions to use Time-   instructed to take Time-Out
    Out   To think when in Time-Out
To use Time-Out only when necessary   To return from Time-Out ready to
To limit Time-Out to 5 minutes   talk and listen
To begin to teach John other   To learn and practice other
    techniques of self-control   techniques of self-control
    once he has mastered Time-   when taught
    Out

FIGURE 15.3 *(continued)*

90 Day Priority
Treatment Plan

page __4__ of __4__

Name: John Jones   Date: 3/10/92

Goal #4: To avoid aggressive posturing with teachers.
    #5: To avoid threatening teachers.

Interventions: **Staff Responsible:**
Teaching Interactions, Staff   Calvin Wright, Supervisor
    Counseling, Merit System
Individual Therapy, Education   Charlotte Webb, Social Worker

Strategy:
John is in danger of being put out of school because of his aggression
against teachers and his threats against teachers. Staff will work out
a plan with the school and John to provide an alternative when John is
in conflict with a teacher.

90 Day Criteria:
John will use the plan to avoid threats and aggression. (1) John will
have no instances of hitting a teacher for 90 days, (2) no more than one
incident of threats or aggression in any week, and (3) no more than
three such incidents in 90 days.

Staff Responsibilities: **Resident Responsibilities:**
To meet with school personnel   To meet with staff and school
    to devise an acceptable   personnel to work out a plan
    and workable plan   To learn the plan
To follow their responsibilities   To practice the plan with staff
    under the plan   To review the plan every morning
To make sure John understands   before going to school
    the plan   To review the plan at lunch every
To counsel with John every day   day in school
    before school to remind   To use the plan in school
    him of his responsibilities   To inform staff immediately of any
    under the plan   problems with the plan, or
                                             with anything else in school

Signatures:

Staff _____ date   Supervisor _____ date

Resident _____ date   Parent _____ date

State Worker _____ date   Other _____ date

FIGURE 15.4: Treatment Plan

```
                    TREATMENT PLAN           page _1_ of _13_

   Name: John Jones                            Date: 3/24/94

   Modality:                      Staff Responsible:
   Medical                        Fred Fender, Counselor

   Interventions:                 When to Begin:
   Medical Care                   Immediately
   Dental Care                    When Medicaid Card is received

   Goals Assigned:
   Maintain good health, monitor for problems, secure emergency or other
   treatment as needed.

   Strategy:
   John will receive regular annual physical and dental examinations and
   treatment for any emergencies or other conditions that develop.

   Staff Responsibilities:           Resident Responsibilities:
   To provide for annual physical and  To attend scheduled appointments
       dental examinations           To cooperate with physicians,
   To provide for emergency care when      dentists and nurses and
       necessary                          submit to required tests and
   To provide for needed care for         treatments
       illness or other special needs  To take medication as prescribed
   To provide appropriate medication  To inform staff of any problems or
       as ordered by the physician or      complaints
       dentist                       To follow rules for safety and
   To provide special diets as ordered    practice safety
   To provide or provide for other    To follow medical orders and
       special care as ordered            advice
   To teach good hygiene and health   To learn and practice good health
       habits                             and hygiene
   To provide appropriate supplies
       for self-care and hygiene
   To provide a safe, healthy and
       clean environment

   Criteria for Level 2 (90 days):      Target Date: 6/24/94
   John will receive a dental exam and cooperate with any indicated
   treatment.  John will cooperate with any other treatment or instructions
   from physicians that may become necessary.

   Criteria for Level 3 (9 months):      Target Date: 3/24/95
   John will complete his annual physical by 3/24/95.  John will cooperate
   with any other treatment or instructions from physicians that may become
   necessary.

   Criteria for Level 4 (3 months):      Target Date: 6/24/95
   John will complete his annual dental exam within one year of his first
   exam.  John will cooperate with any other treatment or instructions from
   physicians that may become necessary.

   Criteria for Discharge (3 months):   Target Date: 9/24/95
   John will complete his discharge physical within seven days of
   discharge.  John will cooperate with any other treatment or instructions
   from physicians that may become necessary.
```

297

FIGURE 15.4 *(continued)*

Name: John Jones   Date: 3/24/94

Modality: Staff Responsible:
Medical   Fred Fender, Counselor

Signatures:

Staff	date	Supervisor	date
Resident	date	Parent	date
State Worker	date	Other	date

298

FIGURE 15.4 *(continued)*

```
                        TREATMENT PLAN              page  3  of  13

    Name: John Jones                               Date: 3/24/94

    Modality:                        Staff Responsible
    Milieu                           Fred Fender, Counselor

    Interventions:                   When to Begin:
    Merit System, Teaching           Level I
    Interactions, Life-Space
    Interviews, Crisis Intervention

    Goals Assigned:
    1. Temper Control w/o aggression    6. Asking Permission
    2. Temper Control w/o threats       7. Accepting "No"
    3. Temper Control w/o yelling       8. Following Limits
    4. Following Instructions           9. Peer Relations w/o fights
    5. Accepting Criticism

    Strategy:
    Staff will teach the steps to all social skills while John is on Level
    1.  They will begin holding him accountable for following instructions
    and accepting criticism with one reminder, then use these skills to
    teach other social skills and to intervene in temper control to minimize
    aggression.  John will demonstrate his ability to use these skills at
    home and at school.

    Staff Responsibilities:           Resident Responsibilities:
    To teach appropriate behaviors    To pay attention when staff teach
    To be clear on expectations       To learn expected behaviors
    To explain problems clearly       To do his or her best to use
    To be fair and consistent with       expected behaviors
       consequences                   To accept consequences when
    To award earned privileges fairly    appropriate
    To listen to resident's objections To express disagreements calmly
    To provide an appeal if requested To tell staff before appealing
                                      To use privileges appropriately

    Criteria for Level 2 (90 days):   Target Date: 6/24/94
    1. John will be able to recite the steps to all social skills on
       request.
    2. John will be able to follow instructions with one reminder five
       days per week for four weeks.
    3. John will be able to accept criticism with one reminder five days
       per week for four weeks.
    4. John will earn a total of 7,500 points and 2,500 points during the
       last four weeks to earn Level 2.

    Criteria for Level 3 (9 months):  Target Date: 3/24/95
    1. While on Level 2, John will learn and demonstrate the ability to use
       each of the following social skills to the criteria of no more than
       two problems in 60 days: (Skills may be targeted up to three at a
       time)
       a. Temper Control              d. Accepting "No"
       b. Following Instructions      e. Following Limits
       c. Accepting Criticism         f. Asking Permission
    2. John will use social skills to avoid fights, aggression against
       adults, and making threats for a period of 60 days.
    3. John will maintain his points above 600 for the four weeks prior
       to moving to Level 3.
```

FIGURE 15.4 *(continued)*

```
                    TREATMENT PLAN              page  4  of  13

Name: John Jones                               Date: 3/24/94

Modality:                       Staff Responsible:
Milieu                          Fred Fender, Counselor

Criteria for Level 4 (3 months):      Target Date: 6/24/95
1. Home passes will be increased, and John will use social skills to
   avoid problems on home passes for five out of six passes.
2. John will use social skills to avoid disciplinary action at school
   for a period of 60 days.
3. John will use social skills to avoid discipline in the program for
   60 days and maintain his points above 650 for four consecutive weeks.

Criteria for Discharge (3 months):    Target Date: 9/24/95
1. Using social skills, John will complete three two-day passes during
   the week, attending school from home with no disciplinary problems.
2. John will complete an initial two-week trial discharge with no
   major problems at home and no disciplinary action at school.
3. John will complete a final trial discharge to the same criteria.
4. John will have no disciplinary action in the program for 60 days,
   and no more than three negative comments per week from staff during
   the weeks preceding his final trial discharge.


Signatures:


_____          _____
Staff            date            Supervisor       date

_____          _____
Resident         date            Parent           date

_____          _____
State Worker     date            Other            date
```

FIGURE 15.4 *(continued)*

Name: John Jones   Date: 3/24/94

Modality: Staff Responsible:
Milieu   Fred Fender, Counselor

Interventions: When to Begin:
Staff Counseling   Immediately

Goals Assigned:
1. John needs a plan to get into regular classes.
2. John needs to improve his attitude about violence.
3. John needs long-term goals for adulthood.
4. John needs to learn to tell the truth.

Strategy:
Fred Fender will serve as John's primary counselor and monitor John's progress on behavioral objectives in the program. Fred will be available to John on a daily basis (five days per week) to discuss John's progress and any other issues that may arise. Fred will help John to learn to identify and evaluate alternatives, especially relating to John's use of violence, setting long-term goals for himself, and telling the truth. As John's behavior improves, Fred will work with John on a plan to mainstream into regular classes. Fred will coordinate with the social worker on all counseling issues, and communicate strategies to other staff that help John to manage his aggression.

Staff Responsibilities:	Resident Responsibilities:
To be knowledgeable about the resident's treatment plan	To learn the objectives on the treatment plan
To be knowledgeable about the resident's progress	To meet with staff at least twice per week
To meet with the resident formally at least twice per week for at least 15 minutes	To let staff know when something happens or if he feels a need to talk
To make time to talk each day the resident asks to talk	To wait patiently if staff is busy and has to set a time later in the day
To be honest	To be honest about facts and feelings
To "practice what the staff preaches," at all times modeling appropriate behavior	To try

Criteria for Level 2 (90 days):   Target Date: 6/24/94
John will know the objectives of his Treatment Plan.

Criteria for Level 3 (9 months):   Target Date: 3/24/95
John will be able to talk about some goals for when he grows up, goals that are attractive to him and realistic for him. John will be able to identify alternatives to violence in a variety of situations, alternatives that are appealing to him. John will have a realistic plan for mainstreaming into regular classes.

Criteria for Level 4 (3 months):   Target Date: 6/24/95
John will have no instances of lying to his counselor for 90 days.

Criteria for Discharge (3 months):   Target Date: 9/24/95
John and his counselor will have a plan for maintaining contact after John discharges.

FIGURE 15.4 *(continued)*

TREATMENT PLAN   page 6 of 13

Name: John Jones   **Date:** 3/24/94

Modality: **Staff Responsible:**
Milieu   Fred Fender, Counselor

Signatures:

Staff	date	Supervisor	date
Resident	date	Parent	date
State Worker	date	Other	date

FIGURE 15.4 (*continued*)

Name: John Jones   Date: 3/24/94

Modality: Staff Responsible:
Education   Cheryl Goodheart, Case Manager

Interventions: When to Begin:
Public School, Gr 7 sp. ed.   In progress
Educational Counseling   Immediately
Tutoring, if necessary   When indicated

Goals Assigned:
1. John will learn better study habits.
2. John will learn to complete classwork.
3. John will learn to complete homework.
4. John will improve his grades.
5. John will avoid fights with peers.
6. John will avoid physical confrontations with teachers.
7. John will avoid threatening teachers.
8. Develop a plan for mainstreaming John into regular classes for
   high school.

Strategy:
A 90 Day Priority Treatment Plan has been established to manage
aggressive behavior in school for the remainder of the school year. By
next year, John should learn necessary social skills from the Milieu.
Staff will support his generalization of these skills to the school
setting. Staff will work with John in structured study hall to improve
John's study habits for completion of homework, which should improve his
academic grades. If this proves ineffective, a tutor will be assigned.
When John's behavior, work, and grades improve, staff will meet with
school personnel to develop a plan for mainstreaming.

Staff Responsibilities: Resident Responsibilities:
To arrange an appropriate school   To attend school regularly and on
    placement for the child   time
To meet with teachers, counselors,   To go to all classes on time
    and administrators as necessary   To do class work
    to develop plans and resolve   To bring necessary books and
    problems   materials for homework
To provide the opportunity and   To advise staff of any problems
    appropriate environment for   To do homework
    study   To ask for help when needed
To provide necessary materials   To respect the rights of others in
    promptly   school
To assist the resident when   To learn
    necessary
To protect and advocate for the
    resident's rights in school
To teach the resident good study
    habits and better ways of
    getting along in school
To be available for any problems

Criteria for Level 2 (90 days):   Target Date: 6/24/94
Complete Priority objectives.
Pass to the 8th grade, or begin summer school and earn passing grades
    for the first report.

FIGURE 15.4 *(continued)*

Name: John Jones   Date: 3/24/94

Modality: **Staff Responsible:**
Education   Cheryl Goodheart, Case Manager

Criteria for Level 3 (9 months):   **Target Date:** 3/24/95
Maintain passing grades for the first two report periods.
Improve grades to a C+ average by the third marking period.
Be in no danger of expulsion.
Complete 60 days with no suspensions or being sent home for disciplinary
    reasons.
Complete 30 days with no detentions or other disciplinary action.
Have a realistic plan for mainstreaming to regular classes approved by
    the school.

Criteria for Level 4 (3 months):   **Target Date:** 6/24/95
Pass to the 9th grade and be scheduled for regular classes.
Successfully complete the school year mainstreamed in two regular
    classes.

Criteria for Discharge (3 months):   **Target Date:** 9/24/95
Successfully manage school while on weekday home passes and trial
    discharges, completing assignments and avoiding discipline.

Signatures:

Staff	date	Supervisor	date
Resident	date	Parent	date
State Worker	date	Other	date

FIGURE 15.4 *(continued)*

Name: John Jones   **Date:** 3/24/94

Modality: **Staff Responsible:**
Individual Therapy   Charlotte Webb, Social Worker

Interventions: **When to Begin:**
Reality Therapy   Immediately

Goals Assigned:
1. To develop a plan for mainstreaming into regular classes.
2. To improve John's attitude about violence.
3. To help John develop long-term goals for adulthood.
4. To help John learn to tell the truth.

Strategy:
John's intelligence, verbal skills, and cognitive strengths will be used
to teach John better ways of meeting his needs through weekly individual
sessions.

Staff Responsibilities: **Resident Responsibilities:**
To meet _1_ times/wk. for _45_ mins.   To attend meetings
To prepare for sessions   To complete any assignments
To be honest with the resident   To be honest about feelings and
To be available for special problems   problems
To keep confidential information   To respect other residents' time
    confidential or tell the   with the therapist
    resident if information must
    be passed on and why

Criteria for Level 2 (90 days):   **Target Date:** 6/24/94
John will attend 80 percent of scheduled sessions.
John will honestly discuss his feelings and beliefs.

Criteria for Level 3 (9 months):   **Target Date:** 3/24/95
John will continue with 80 percent attendance.
John will complete 80 percent of assignments on time.
John will have realistic goals and expectations for adulthood.
John will have an approved plan for mainstreaming.
John will be able to discuss violence intelligently and relate it to his
    needs in a realistic way.
John will have no incidents of lying over a three-month period.

Criteria for Level 4 (3 months):   **Target Date:** 6/24/95
John will continue to attend at 80 percent.
John will demonstrate his skills at home, at school, and in the program.

Criteria for Discharge (3 months):   **Target Date:** 9/24/95
John will meet other discharge criteria, or come to the social worker
    with any problems.

Signatures:

_____   _____
Staff   date   Supervisor   date

_____   _____
Resident   date   Parent   date

_____   _____
State Worker   date   Other   date

FIGURE 15.4 (*continued*)

```
                          TREATMENT PLAN              page _10_ of _13_

    Name: John Jones                             Date: 3/24/94

    Modality:                          Staff Responsible:
    Group                              B. Smith, Social Worker

    Interventions:                     When to Begin:
    Regular Group Therapy              Level 1
    Anger Management Group             When announced
    Values Clarification               When announced

    Goals Assigned:
    John needs to improve his attitude about the use of violence.

    Strategy:
    John uses his size to intimidate peers and regularly resorts to violence
    to solve his problems or get what he wants.  In structured group, the
    therapist will devote time to exploring how John's peers feel about his
    intimidation and use of violence and to identifying alternatives to
    these coping strategies that may prove acceptable to John and more
    acceptable to his peers.

    Staff Responsibilities:              Resident Responsibilities:
    To hold group _1_ times/wk. for      To attend group regularly and be
         60 minutes                           on time
    To insure that all members respect   To respect the rights of other
         confidentiality of the group         members to confidentiality
    To maintain order                         with other residents, staff,
    To protect the rights of members          school, and the community
    To be honest                         To respect other members within
    To prepare for each session               the group
    To plan each session in advance,     To be honest
         with the group in the preceding To participate fully
         session when possible           To complete any assignments
                                         To learn
                                         To share with other members


    Criteria for Level 2 (90 days):     Target Date: 6/24/94
    John will attend 80 percent of scheduled groups.  John will listen when
    peers speak.

    Criteria for Level 3 (9 months):    Target Date: 3/24/95
    John will continue to attend 80 percent of scheduled groups.  John will
    respond appropriately to comments made by his peers.  John will express
    his feelings about issues honestly.  John will identify three
    alternatives to violence in interactions with peers.  John will complete
    either the Anger Management Group or the Values Clarification Group.

    Criteria for Level 4 (3 months):    Target Date: 6/24/95
    John will demonstrate some leadership in the group.  John will terminate
    from the group prior to achieving Level 4.

    Criteria for Discharge (3 months):  Target Date: 9/24/95
    None.
```

FIGURE 15.4 *(continued)*

TREATMENT PLAN   page __11__ of __13__

Name: John Jones   Date: 3/24/94

Modality: **Staff Responsible:**
Group   B. Smith, Social Worker

Signatures:

Staff	date	Supervisor	date
Resident	date	Parent	date
State Worker	date	Other	date

FIGURE 15.4 *(continued)*

```
                        TREATMENT PLAN              page _12_ of _13_

    Name: John Jones                              Date: 3/24/94

    Modality:                        Staff Responsible:
    Family                           Charlotte Webb, Social Worker

    Interventions:                   When to Begin:
    Family Therapy                   Immediately
    Structured Home Passes           When John earns Level 1
    Parent Seminars                  9/12/93
```

Goals Assigned:
1. Parents to learn to make favors, gifts, and treats more contingent on John's behavior.
2. Parents to increase expectations of John's behavior at home and at school.
3. Mother to learn not to back down.
4. Father to learn to deescalate confrontations.
5. Mother to stop making excuses for John's behavior and hold him accountable.
6. Parents to increase communication with each other about John and other matters.

Strategy:
John is somewhat spoiled, getting what he wants without any regard for what others may need or want. Parents do not support each other or follow through and let John off easily. Parents need to communicate with each other and support each other. They need to meet each other's needs as well as John's. Frustration leads to confrontations between John and his father, which threaten to get violent. Family therapy will focus on improved communications between parents, then expectations for John, and consistency in holding him accountable for his role in the family. Structured home passes will provide opportunities for practice. Parent Seminars will teach techniques. Since successful discharge depends on both John's improvement and parents' learning ways to help John, and since passes are seen as a means towards successful discharge, passes will be contingent on John's behavior and the parents' participation.

Staff Responsibilities:
To meet with the family _2_ times/ month for _60_ minutes
To prepare for each session, planning with the family in the preceding session when possible
To be honest
To keep the family informed of the progress and any significant problems or developments
To help the family to better understand the child's problems

Family Responsibilities:
To attend scheduled sessions regularly and on time
To notify as far in advance as possible if there is a need to reschedule or cancel
To be honest about feelings, the child's behavior, and child's discipline
To complete any assignments agreed upon to the best of their ability
To learn new techniques for dealing with the child

FIGURE 15.4 *(continued)*

```
                        TREATMENT PLAN               page _13_ of _13_

Name: John Jones                                     Date: 3/24/94

Modality:                              Staff Responsible:
Family                                 Charlotte Webb, Social Worker

Staff Responsibilities cont.:          Family Responsibilities cont.:
To teach the family techniques to      To try those techniques
    help the child                         consistently and report on
To conduct Parent Seminar                  results or problems
    classes at a reasonable time       To attend all Parent Seminar
To schedule home passes in advance         classes
To notify the family in advance if     To be accept the child for
    a pass is canceled                     scheduled home passes
                                       To complete home pass reports
                                           accurately
```

Criteria for Level 2 (90 days):   Target Date: 6/24/94
Parents will attend 80 percent of scheduled sessions.
Parents will complete all home pass reports.

Criteria for Level 3 (9 months):   Target Date: 3/24/95
Parents will complete Parent Seminar classes.
Mother will reduce excuses for John's behavior.
Father will be able to discuss one incident of successfully deescalating
    a confrontation with John.

Criteria for Level 4 (3 months):   Target Date: 6/24/95
Parents and John will successfully complete increased home passes with
    marked decrease in confrontations and problem behaviors.
Parents will successfully manage problems that occur on passes.

Criteria for Discharge (3 months):   Target Date: 9/24/95
John and parents will successfully complete weekday home passes and
    manage any problems which occur at school.
John and parents will successfully complete two 2-week trial discharges
    and manage any problems that occur without violence or threats by
    John or his father.

Signatures:

Staff	date	Supervisor	date
Resident	date	Parent	date
State Worker	date	Other	date

3. On-Grounds School Special Education (OGS)
4. Vocational Technical School (VT)
5. GED Classes (GED)
6. Tutoring (TU)*
7. Educational Counseling (EC)*
8. Career Planning (CP)

G. Dietary (D)
1. Regular Diet (RD)
2. Weight-Loss Diet (WLD)*
3. Weight-Gain Diet (WGD)
4. Special Diet as Ordered (SD)
5. Food and Nutrition Counseling (FNC)
6. Nutritional Education (NE)

H. Employment (E)

I. Special
1. Speech Therapy (ST)
2. Savings Plan (SP)

PROGRESS REPORTING

Progress reporting as required by placement and licensing agencies and courts tends to be a chore that case managers or social workers disdain. The format for progress reporting that is presented here is designed to minimize the time and effort required for progress review and reporting. It provides an easy-to-use format that requires minimal effort and summarizes progress at a glance. Clerical staff can prepare the Progress Report form from the treatment plan, or the form can be handwritten once the treatment plan is completed. Goals are simply taken from the Treatment Plan and placed on the Progress Report. Progress for each goal can then be graded as:

1. not yet targeted (NT)
2. satisfactory (S)
3. achieved (A)
4. some progress (C)
5. unsatisfactory (U)

Once prepared, multiple copies can be made. The form can then be easily used to review progress at any time—for required quarterly reports, for court reviews, when progress is ahead of or behind schedule, monthly or even weekly for staffings, or for clinical sessions with the child or family. The form provides concise, at-a-glance information. The addition of a brief narrative may enhance a report that is being submitted to court or another agency. When appropriate, signatures and comments may be secured from all participants in the treatment plan.

In the following example, progress on John Jones was recorded monthly for three months following implementation of the treatment plan, after which the progress form was combined with a narrative and signature page for submission as a quarterly report. Samples of Progress Report forms as prepared to be used in later phases of treatment are also presented.

SUMMARY

The treatment planning process presented in this chapter, together with the Assessment Summary for Multi-Modal Treatment, appears very intimidating. I do not believe that it is possible to make such a process short and simple in the case of a child with problems that are either so numerous or so severe that residential treatment is indicated. When compared to the drafting of a set of plans for a power plant, or even for a house, however, the process takes on a different perspective.

The Multi-Modal Treatment Assessment Form is designed for use by a professional person who is acquainted with the child, the family, and the treatment program. The checklist can be completed within ten to twenty minutes. Writing goals that are appropriate for the child, the family, and the treatment program, goals that will utilize strengths and correct problems, will take longer—perhaps from one to two hours.

FIGURE 15.5: Progress Report

```
                        Progress Report
Date: 6/02/94                              Page   1   of   4
Name John Jones                    Admit Date 2/25/94
Progress Key:  NT - Goal not yet targeted  A - Goal achieved
               S - Satisfactory progress   C - Some progress
               U - Unsatisfactory progress, explained in narrative

               Date of Evaluation: 3/25  4/22  5/27/94 _____ _____ _____
Goal or Objective:                      Progress:

90 Day Priority Objectives

Parents will support placement          S    S    A   ___  ___  ___

Parents will discuss concerns with

     social worker                      S    S    A   ___  ___  ___

Parents will avoid discussing

     concerns with John                 U    S    A   ___  ___  ___

John will not injure another resident   S    S    A   ___  ___  ___

No more than two instances of

     aggression in first 90 days        C    S    A   ___  ___  ___

No fights for 30 consecutive days       C    S    A   ___  ___  ___

John will use Time-Out promptly when

     instructed for 45 days             U    S    A   ___  ___  ___

No instances of hitting a teacher       S    S    A   ___  ___  ___

No more than 1 incident of threat or

     aggression in any week             C    S    A   ___  ___  ___

No more than 3 incidents in 90 days     U    C    A   ___  ___  ___


Regular 90 Day Objectives for Level 2

John can recite steps to all Social

     Skills                             C    A    A   ___  ___  ___
```

FIGURE 15.5 *(continued)*

Progress Report

Date: 6/02/94

Page __2__ of __4__

Name John Jones

Admit Date 2/25/94

Progress Key: NT – Goal not yet targeted   A – Goal achieved
              S – Satisfactory progress   C – Some progress
              U – Unsatisfactory progress, explained in narrative

Date of Evaluation: 3/25 4/22 5/27/94 ____ ____ ____

Goal or Objective: Progress:

90 Day Goals cont.

Follow instructions w/1 reminder

___ 5 days/week for 4 weeks   S   S   A ____ ____ ____

Accept criticism w/1 reminder

___ 5 days/week for 4 weeks   U   C   A ____ ____ ____

7,500 points   NT NT A ____ ____ ____

2,500 points during last four weeks S   S   A ____ ____ ____

Parents to attend 80% of sessions   S   S   A ____ ____ ____

Parents to complete all home sheets S   S   A ____ ____ ____

Pass to 8th grade or begin summer   C   A   A ____ ____ ____

___ school and pass first report   NT NT NA ____ ____ ____

John to attend 80% of individual

___ sessions   S   S   A ____ ____ ____

Honestly discuss feelings and beliefs C   S   A ____ ____ ____

Dental Exam completed   NT A   A ____ ____ ____

John to cooperate w/dental treatment NT S   A ____ ____ ____

John to cooperate w/doctors' orders   S   S   A ____ ____ ____

John to know all treatment objectives S   S   A ____ ____ ____

FIGURE 15.5 (*continued*)

John and his parents made a good initial adjustment to John's placement and cooperated with the treatment planning process. Both John and his family worked hard to meet their responsibilities during the first 90 days of treatment, including priority objectives. As of 27 July, all objectives have been achieved except for one: John must earn at total of 2,500 points over a four-week period to demonstrate consistency in utilizing social skills. It is expected that John will achieve this goal next week and advance to Level 2.

John's initial physical with Dr. Evelyn Frank on 2/27/94 was normal, except for his obesity and a cold. John was prescribed penicillin and followed through with his medication, needing no further treatment. His initial dental exam with Dr. John Fry on 4/15/94 revealed three cavities. He received porcelain fillings on 4/22 and 5/8/94.

John had two instances of fighting since his arrival, on 4/13 and 4/26/94, both arising from conflicts with peers during activities. On 4/13, staff had to physically intervene to break up the fight; on 4/26, John responded to verbal intervention by staff. There were no injuries in either altercation. John was able to utilize staff to avoid several other fights during this period, one of his priority treatment goals.

John had only one incident of bracing up to a teacher, on 4/15/94. This was another area of priority treatment for John's first 90 days. He was very successful at utilizing the behavioral plan that was worked out with the school, affording him a Time-Out and conference call to the program at either his request, or at the request of school personnel. John will pass to the eighth grade without summer school, grades as follows:

English	C
Reading	D
Math	C
Science	F
Spelling	D
Social Studies	D

John will remain in Special Education with the exceptionality of Behavior Disordered.

John continues on the timetable established for discharge on 9/24/95.

FIGURE 15.5 *(continued)*

Final Page of __4__
                 Progress Report Signatures

I have reviewed the above __3__ pages of the progress report

for resident John Jones _____ dated 6/02/94 _____.

I have been informed that I may make comments in the section provided
before signing. (Comments should be signed)

This report was completed for the following reason:

__X__ Routine Quarterly Review   _____ In preparation for planned
                                                 discharge
_____ In preparation for unplanned discharge due to: _____

_____

_____ Because of special problems or circumstances: _____

_____

Comments: _____

_____

_____

_____

_____

_____

_____

_____

Signatures:

_____   _____
Staff   date   Supervisor   date

_____   _____
Resident   date   Parent   date

_____   _____
State Worker   date   Other   date

FIGURE 15.6: Progress Report for Later Phases of Treatment

```
                        Progress Report
              (for Later Phases of Treatment)  Page ____ of ____

Name John Jones                          Admit Date 2/25/94

Progress Key:  NT - Goal not yet targeted   A - Goal achieved
               S - Satisfactory progress    C - Some progress
               U - Unsatisfactory progress, explained in narrative

                 Date of Evaluation:____ ____ ____ ____ ____ ____
Goal or Objective:                       Progress:

9 Month Objectives for Level 3

Social Skills with no more than

____ 2 problems in 60 days:

____ Temper control              ____ ____ ____ ____ ____ ____

____ Following instructions      ____ ____ ____ ____ ____ ____

____ Accepting criticism         ____ ____ ____ ____ ____ ____

____ Asking permission           ____ ____ ____ ____ ____ ____

____ Accepting "no"              ____ ____ ____ ____ ____ ____

____ Following limits            ____ ____ ____ ____ ____ ____

Use Social Skills to avoid fights,

____ aggression against adults,

____ and threats for 60 days     ____ ____ ____ ____ ____ ____

Points above 600 for 4 weeks     ____ ____ ____ ____ ____ ____

Parents completed Assertive

____ Discipline Course           ____ ____ ____ ____ ____ ____

Mother reduced excuses for John's

____ behavior                    ____ ____ ____ ____ ____ ____

Father reports 1 incident of

____ deescalating violence w/John ____ ____ ____ ____ ____ ____

Passing grades for first 2 reports

____ in 8th grade                ____ ____ ____ ____ ____ ____
```

FIGURE 15.6 *(continued)*

Progress Report
(for Later Phases of Treatment) Page ____ of ____

Name _John Jones_____ Admit Date _2/25/94____

Progress Key: NT – Goal not yet targeted   A – Goal achieved
S – Satisfactory progress   C – Some progress
U – Unsatisfactory progress, explained in narrative

Date of Evaluation: ____ ____ ____ ____ ____ ____

Goal or Objective: Progress:

9 Month Objectives – Level 3 cont.

C+ average on third report card___ ____ ____ ____ ____ ____ ____

In no danger of expulsion___ ____ ____ ____ ____ ____ ____

60 days completed with no_____

_____suspensions/sent home/_____

_____discipline_____ ____ ____ ____ ____ ____ ____

30 days completed no detention or___

_____other discipline_____ ____ ____ ____ ____ ____ ____

Plan for mainstreaming approved____

_____by school_____ ____ ____ ____ ____ ____ ____

80% attendance, individual therapy ____ ____ ____ ____ ____ ____

80% therapy assignments completed_ ____ ____ ____ ____ ____ ____

John has realistic goals for_____

_____adulthood_____ ____ ____ ____ ____ ____ ____

John can discuss violence and_____

_____relate it to his needs___ ____ ____ ____ ____ ____ ____

No incidents of lying for 3 months ____ ____ ____ ____ ____ ____

Complete annual physical_____ ____ ____ ____ ____ ____ ____

_____ ____ ____ ____ ____ ____ ____

_____ ____ ____ ____ ____ ____ ____

_____ ____ ____ ____ ____ ____ ____

316

FIGURE 15.6 *(continued)*

Progress Report
(for Later Phases of Treatment) Page _____ of _____

Name <u>John Jones</u>   Admit Date <u>2/25/94</u>

Progress Key: NT – Goal not yet targeted   A – Goal achieved
                S – Satisfactory progress   C – Some progress
                U – Unsatisfactory progress, explained in narrative

                Date of Evaluation: _____ _____ _____ _____ _____ _____
Goal or Objective: Progress:

<u>Level 4 Objectives 6/24/93</u>

<u>Avoided problems on home pass for</u>

<u>   5 out of 6 weeks</u>   _____ _____ _____ _____ _____ _____

<u>60 days w/no discipline at school</u> _____ _____ _____ _____ _____ _____

<u>60 days w/no discipline in program</u> _____ _____ _____ _____ _____ _____

<u>650 points for 4 consecutive weeks</u> _____ _____ _____ _____ _____ _____

<u>Increased home passes with marked</u>

<u>   decrease in confrontations</u>   _____ _____ _____ _____ _____ _____

<u>   and problems</u>   _____ _____ _____ _____ _____ _____

<u>Parents successfully managed</u>

<u>   problems that occurred</u>   _____ _____ _____ _____ _____ _____

<u>Pass to the 9th grade</u>   _____ _____ _____ _____ _____ _____

<u>Mainstreamed successfully into</u>

<u>   two classes</u>   _____ _____ _____ _____ _____ _____

<u>Complete annual dental exam</u>   _____ _____ _____ _____ _____ _____

<u>Cooperate with medical or dental</u>

<u>   treatment</u>   _____ _____ _____ _____ _____ _____

_____ _____ _____ _____ _____ _____ _____

_____ _____ _____ _____ _____ _____ _____

_____ _____ _____ _____ _____ _____ _____

FIGURE 15.6 *(continued)*

Progress Report
(for Later Phases of Treatment) Page _____ of _____

Name <u>John Jones</u>   Admit Date <u>2/25/94</u>

Progress Key: NT – Goal not yet targeted   A – Goal achieved
                S – Satisfactory progress   C – Some progress
                U – Unsatisfactory progress, explained in narrative

                  Date of Evaluation: _____ _____ _____ _____ _____ _____
Goal or Objective: Progress:

<u>Discharge Criteria</u>

<u>Three weekday passes completed</u>

<u>   with no problems at school</u>   _____ _____ _____ _____ _____ _____

<u>Initial 2-week trial discharge</u>

<u>   completed with no discipline</u>

<u>   at school</u>   _____ _____ _____ _____ _____ _____

<u>Final 2-week trial discharge with</u>

<u>   no discipline at school</u>   _____ _____ _____ _____ _____ _____

<u>60 days, no discipline in program</u> _____ _____ _____ _____ _____ _____

<u>No more than three negatives/week</u>

<u>   prior to discharge</u>   _____ _____ _____ _____ _____ _____

<u>Home passes and trial discharges</u>

<u>   completed without violence or</u>

<u>   threats</u>   _____ _____ _____ _____ _____ _____

<u>School assignments completed while</u>

<u>   on pass</u>   _____ _____ _____ _____ _____ _____

<u>No school discipline while on pass</u> _____ _____ _____ _____ _____ _____

<u>Complete discharge physical within</u>

<u>   7 days prior to discharge</u>   _____ _____ _____ _____ _____ _____

_____ _____ _____ _____ _____ _____ _____

_____ _____ _____ _____ _____ _____ _____

If the program has clerical staff and types its treatment plans, clerical staff can be trained to transfer goals from the assessment form onto the Treatment Goal Summary. If not, the staff completing the checklist may choose to write the treatment goals directly onto the Treatment Goal Summary, eliminating the step of writing treatment goals on the assessment form. In either case, an investment of from one to two hours of professional staff time will produce a comprehensive list of treatment goals that are realistic for the child, family, and residential treatment program, goals to use strengths to resolve problems within the capabilities of the program, the child, and the family. With a few more minutes of professional staff time, goals can be assigned to specific modalities offered by the residential program.

Once goals have been assigned to specific modalities, staff responsible for each modality complete their portion of the Treatment Plan. This includes determining what interventions will be used and writing a brief narrative to outline the treatment strategy. The treatment strategy should delineate how strengths will be used, which goals will be targeted first to be built upon or create a sense of achievement or success, and which goals will be targeted later. It should also note now different modalities might interrelate and coordinate.

This treatment plan format details specific responsibilities, not only for staff but also for the resident and the family. For many modalities, these responsibilities will be similar from case to case; they can be pre-typed on the treatment plan form.

The staff responsible for each modality also establish criteria for assessing progress on assigned goals in accordance with program standards. The sample treatment plan that has been presented is based on a residential program with a normal length of stay of about eighteen months, with five phases or levels:

1. *Adjustment.* Adjustment is a period of orientation and assessment designed to last about thirty days, during which the resident learns expectations of the program, the staff complete assessments, and the staff, resident, and family complete the treatment plan.

2. *Level 1.* On this level, staff get to know the child better. The child can earn all but the more advanced privileges of unsupervised activities in the community. Advancement occurs when the child demonstrates the ability to perform to expectations with some consistency with reminders from staff over a period of about ninety days.

3. *Level 2.* All privileges are available to residents on this level. Most treatment criteria as established in the Treatment Plan must be met prior to advancement to PreTerm. This can be expected to take about twelve months.

4. *PreTerm.* The child must perform to criteria with weekly rather than daily points and reinforcements. Criteria for advancement begin to be more oriented towards family and community.

5. *Term.* Performance must be maintained without points and demonstrated at home during the week as well as on weekends.

The model can be modified to fit programs with different approaches to treatment.

Once a treatment plan has been completed, clerical staff can prepare the Progress Report form to facilitate periodic assessment of progress. The Progress Report form lists all goals and provides a quick and ready assessment tool for evaluating and recording progress. Progress assessment forms may be used weekly or monthly in staffings or as needed if progress is ahead of schedule or when problems develop. The forms can be used by the child, posted in her or his room for self-assessment. They can be used for quarterly progress reporting to courts, state agencies, funding sources, and the family. They may be accompanied by a brief narrative and signature page.

The 90 Day Priority Plan may be used for critical problems that are apparent upon intake and that may be expected to be critical during initial phases of treatment. The 90 Day Priority Plan can also be used later in treatment if critical problems develop, such as excessive aggression, noncompliance that reaches critical proportions, excessive runaways, or lack of progress.

This model generates clear and realistic goals and strategies. It facilitates clear assignment of responsibilities and accountability to the resident, the family, and the staff. It provides for ready assessment of progress and any problems in achieving progress. It requires an initial investment of time and effort, but it helps to focus time and effort later during treatment and reduces time and effort for required reporting. With clerical support, it may require less time and effort overall than less comprehensive formats.

Fine Tuning the Milieu

I N this chapter we will consider a few final factors relating to the milieu. The first is the program's reputation in the community. The program's reputation sets up expectations before the child and family have any contact with the program. It also has implications during treatment, possibly for self-image and self-esteem of the children in the program, possibly for children's interactions in the community, especially for the children's interactions with public school.

Next, we will consider the preplacement process. Preplacement is normally the first contact the child and family have with a residential program. There are several important issues, the most important of which is setting expectations. First impressions that are in error are extremely resistant to change and may seriously compromise future treatment.

Intake is likewise an important process. The child and family are especially vulnerable. Getting off to a good start can jump start treatment; getting off to a poor start can create obstacles that need to be overcome.

Discharge poses some unique problems. In addition to issues of termination that receive lots of attention, there are practical issues in returning a child home that relate to a change in the roles of both parents and the child. We should expect some spontaneous recovery of problem behaviors. So should the child and family. How the family and child are prepared and supported during the transition home can have significant implications for success after discharge.

Aftercare is important. Children and parents require support as roles change and as they practice fairly recently learned skills. While aftercare can be arranged with other agencies in the community, such as mental health, welfare, probation, or case management agencies, aftercare provided by the residential program supplies a key ingredient to the successful functioning of any system: feedback. Without it, systems cannot adjust themselves.

Two additional issues have relevance for the milieu: runaways and staff burnout. We shall consider some types of runaway behavior and consider their implications for the milieu. We shall consider some factors relating to staff burnout and some implications for hiring, orienting, and managing staff and the program. Finally, we shall consider briefly the use of computers to manage data about individual residents and statistical data on residents in the milieu.

REPUTATION

A Christmas Appeal. **Each year, the executive director of a small residential facility went on several local television stations to solicit**

contributions for the children's Christmas. Residents made fun of the appeal. "Send money. Send used items. Send your old clothes. Send your used toothbrushes. No contribution is too small. These children can use anything you can afford to give them." Each year, after the appeal, several children who had earned the privilege of attending public school began to develop attendance problems—children in the public schools also made fun of the appeal.

As with any business, a treatment program's image and reputation in the community have a significant impact on business. In the case of residential treatment, the business is treatment. The agency's image and reputation affect its ability to treat children. Image and reputation affect the child's expectations when referred to the program, before the child even begins treatment. They affect the child's treatment after arrival. They also affect how the child is treated in the community—by local businesspeople, school teachers and principals, and peers. The program's image and reputation are important to the child's identity and self-image, since these are tied, at least for a time, with the program itself.

A program's image in the community is dependent upon a number of factors, including:

1. The conduct of its residents when in the community.
2. The conduct of staff when in the community, whether with children or on other business.
3. The response of the program to community concerns.
4. Publicity.

While few programs can control all of the above with 100 percent efficiency, the better job a program does, the better its reputation.

Conduct in the Community

A poor or a bad reputation is hard to overcome. It takes years. Consequently, activities in the community should be adequately staffed. Staff should be trained in matters relating to the program's image in the community. They should be trained on how to deal with problems children might present in the community. At the first sign of a problem, perhaps the anxiety stage of a child (crisis model, chapter 12), staff must intervene promptly and discreetly. If the child must be removed from an activity, there must be sufficient staff to do so without compromising the activity for other children and members of the community who may have some investment in the activity. Often, providing discreet, one-on-one attention to an anxious child may be sufficient. For potentially sensitive activities in the community, a supervisor should be in attendance and in charge.

Likewise, children should be well prepared in advance for community activities. Staff should communicate expectations clearly before the activity. Follow-up after an activity is equally important, with positive feedback to children who did well. This communicates the importance of community behavior, helps to set the stage for the next activity, and helps to build a positive attitude in the milieu that includes sensitivity on the part of the children towards responsible behavior in the community.

Responsiveness to Community Concerns

From time to time, members of the community may have concerns about the behavior of one or more children or staff. Sometimes the children may be under direct supervision; other times, a child or children may be in the community on their own, in school, on pass, or having earned the privilege of an unsupervised outing. Occasionally a child may be in the community without permission, AWOL or on runaway. Sometimes there are concerns about staff conduct when in the community without children.

The program must appear responsive and responsible. This requires first of all, an apology. Second, it requires some action. Finally, it requires follow-up. Staff on the scene may make an apology. They may also take some initial action. Follow-up should either be done by a supervisor or by staff at the direction of a supervisor. It only takes one dissatisfied person in the community, talking to neighbors, friends, relatives, at the beauty salon or barber shop, to begin a downturn in an agency's reputation. In the following example, all three steps were taken.

> *A complaint about driving.* **A supervisor received a call from a vice-principal. The vice-principal had received a call from a nearby resident stating that the agency's van had passed a school bus that was loading children. The vice-principal said it was OK for the supervisor to call the person making the complaint and gave the phone number. The supervisor called the complainant, thanked her for making the report, apologized, and assured her that he would check into the matter.**
>
> **The driver of the van was puzzled about the incident. He said he had turned a corner and found a school bus stopped with no signs out or lights on and passed it. The supervisor was able to confirm with the bus driver that she was waiting for a child to come out of his house and did not have the lights on. No disciplinary action was called for.**
>
> **The supervisor called the complainant, thanked her again for her interest, and apologized again. He informed her that he had spoken with the bus driver and the agency staff person and taken appropriate action. He asked her to call him personally if she noted any future problems. He did not make any excuses. The complainant was satisfied. The supervisor called a week later to check back. The complainant said there were no further problems.**

Publicity

Publicity is difficult to manage. Positive publicity may be pursued carefully. Special activities, awards, or recognition of staff or residents (with permission of the child, parents, and licensing and placing agencies) may help to build positive publicity credits and a relationship with the local news media. Possible adverse publicity, based on investigation or scandal, is especially difficult to manage. Staff should be trained to refer any questions from media to the administrator and to inform the administrator immediately if they are contacted by the media.

Sometimes, administrators can be successful in requesting the media to hold back on a potential headline story for just a while, explaining the damage that such stories do to the children in placement and attending public school, etc. After a day or two, many potentially sensational stories are no longer sensational and may never appear, as in the following example.

> *The arrest of a staff member.* **A program that had undergone a lengthy and highly publicized investigation into alleged sexual abuse of residents by staff and use of drugs by staff on duty had made significant strides during the following two years, although its reputation still suffered. In fact, it was referred to in the community by a variation of its name which incorporated the word "gay."**
>
> **Then, one night, two boys left to meet an adult friend in the community. They returned to the program with the adult and police, alleging that a staff member had scratched one of them on the back, drawing blood. The police arrested the staff member and took him to jail.**
>
> **The next day, an investigative reporter from a local TV station contacted the executive director. The executive director informed the reporter that a full investigation was being conducted, both internally and by state licensing authorities. He said there were some questions about the veracity of the allegations, pointed out the problems a story would cause for the investigation and for the other children, asked the reporter to hold off, and promised to keep him fully informed. The reporter agreed.**
>
> **The staff member was subsequently cleared and returned to duty. The children and their adult friend had fabricated the incident. The friend wanted custody of the**

boys. The reporter never filed a story on the incident.

The following examples illustrate an additional problem and one success with the reputation of residential programs.

Shoplifting. A few residents of a facility for 120 children were caught shoplifting on several occasions at a nearby supermarket. The supermarket manager sent a letter to the executive director of the program to inform him that all residents of the program would be barred from the store henceforth. Staff on each of the ten units had to inform their children that residents of the program were no longer welcome or permitted in that store.

A small county group home. A county operated two group homes, one for boys, the other for girls. The children had been adjudicated on minor offenses or as children in need of supervision. The program got off to a rough start. Its first residence, a doublewide mobile home, had been burned to the ground by arson just weeks before the first children were to be admitted. A new doublewide was set up and protected by a security agency for a few weeks until the program opened.

During the next ten years, the program paid careful attention to its community relations. It worked with residents to stress appropriate behavior on outings and activities in public. For example, although some residents were allowed to smoke, smoking was discouraged during most activities in the community, on the agency van, and during most activities in which members of the community came into the facility. Staff were specially trained to supervise activities in the community closely, and if necessary to intervene appropriately and decisively, but with discretion. Sensitive community activities were always fully staffed with sufficient child care counselors and a supervisor.

As a result, the program developed a respectable reputation with the various community resources with which it interacted. Its residents generally received first class treatment, even preferential treatment, when scheduling or participating in tours and other activities. Consequently, many residents enjoyed interactions with community people on a level they had not experienced prior to entering the program. They were treated as "special" in a new and different way. They went into the community with a sense of pride. Staff had few problems to handle.

The program had an exciting and busy activity schedule in the community. Its reputation in the community, including public schools, was such that their schoolmates were reported on occasion to threaten their parents with: "I want to go and stay at the group home." After fifteen years of operation, state budget cuts threatened the program. An onslaught of community support, including letters and phone calls to legislators and officials, resulted in full restoration of funding.

PREPLACEMENT

The preplacement visit is the first official contact of a child and his or her family with a residential treatment program. Many programs use such visits to assess the child's appropriateness for placement and to "sell" the program. More importantly, the preplacement process establishes expectations for treatment. First impressions are lasting impressions. First impressions that are in error may pose insurmountable obstacles to treatment.

A program that has some problems with its reputation may try to dispel concerns during preplacement and convince the child and family that it is a good place for children. On the other hand, the above program that had the extensive schedule of activities had to work to focus the child and family on treatment and dispel the image of being primarily a place for children to have fun.

Preplacement issues should include:

1. Assessing the child's appropriateness for treatment in the program.
2. Setting the stage for treatment and creating appropriate and realistic expectations.

The Child's Appropriateness

Unless it is prepared to accept all children referred *and* keep them regardless of behavior or progress, an effective residential treatment program should know what kinds of children or what types of problems it can treat effectively. It should also know what kinds of children and what kinds of problems it cannot treat or manage very well.

The problems with which a child presents should be expected to occur during treatment. The fact that a program has a point system for behavioral management that applies penalties for physical aggression should not lead anyone to believe that such a system will preclude aggression in an aggressive child. It is not reasonable to expect that a child with a primary problem of substance abuse will refrain from substance abuse because he says he wants to and knows that he has to in order to avoid hospitalization or incarceration.

The child may very well want to do better. Doing better, however, will take time and practice. During the time the child is practicing, problems will occur. The child's past behavior is an excellent predictor of the problems that will occur during treatment. Taking a child on a ''trial'' basis (giving the child a chance) is more often giving the child yet another opportunity to fail. The following example illustrates some issues presented during a preplacement visit.

Emilio. **Emilio, nearly fifteen, had been on a locked unit of a residential program for over a year. He had not done well. He had run away several times, often taking other residents with him. He and his girlfriend, also a resident of the institution, had arranged to meet on several of his runaways. A psychiatrist had recommended Emilio for group home placement, suggesting that Emilio might do better in a less structured and more open setting.**

In his preplacement visit, Emilio expressed a strong desire to do well, to complete his GED, get a job, and support himself and his girlfriend when he was old enough to do so. He really wanted a chance and believed he could do what was necessary. He knew that he needed an education. His IQ and achievement test scores indicated that he could probably complete requirements for his GED with a reasonable investment of effort in eight to fifteen months.

In discussing his various runaways, Emilio smiled and displayed obvious pride in his accomplishments. He became quite expansive when relating his abilities to influence other residents, to develop and carry out his plans, and to survive on his own. He was given a three-day preplacement visit over a weekend. By Sunday evening he was questioning staff on the wisdom of some of the routines that had been established in the program over the past several years. He was not accepted for admission. A few weeks later, another group home staffed by a married couple gave him an opportunity. Although he did not run away, he became so aggressive towards the wife that he was removed within the first month.

Emilio, in this example, verbalized appropriate attitudes towards treatment. His affect, however, belied his verbalizations, as did his behavior during an extended preplacement. While there was some possibility that he might have made gains in the program with intensive work and undergone some attitude change, there was a strong indication that he would very quickly pose a real threat to other residents. He was much more focused on peer relations than on adult relations as a source of personal gratification.

Setting the Stage for Treatment— Expectations

Setting treatment expectations is important for both the child and the family. The issues of setting treatment expectations with the child are somewhat different from the issues of setting treatment expectations with the family.

Setting Treatment Expectations with the Child

I have made the mistake of selling the child on the niceties of a program, especially when the not-so-niceties were perhaps a bit too obvious. When I had the luxury of working in a program where there were few not-so-niceties, I soon learned the problems with selling a child on the niceties—the activities, the basketball court, the pool table, and the TV and game room—as the following example illustrates.

> *Bruce.* Bruce was a difficult twelve-year-old who failed to follow instructions or limits at home and at school. He was screened and accepted for the next opening. During the five weeks before he could be scheduled for admission, Bruce called at least once a week to see when he could come into the program. Once he got to the program, Bruce rarely earned the privileges and activities for which he had been so anxious. After six months, he was transferred to a secure facility; he had made no progress on any presenting problem during those six months and presented some evidence of developing even more difficult problems.

If children are indeed coming into placement for treatment, they should come with the expectation of being treated. This may include individual, group, and family therapy, school with regular attendance and homework, household responsibilities in a unit larger than the average family (possibly restaurant-sized pots to wash, bathrooms to clean, and corridors to mop), confrontations by staff and peers, and being held responsible and accountable for problem behaviors. Fun and games are second-

ary. Failure may result in transfer to another program instead of discharge home.

Moreover, children are coming into placement in a somewhat artificial environment, an environment that requires certain rules and expectations simply because it involves a larger than normal group of people living together. For example, few residential programs have the capability of providing teenagers with the amount of time on the telephone that other children may be permitted at home. And other children are often especially interested in the possessions of new residents, often attempting to "borrow," if not steal, unique or valuable items.

Finally, treatment is not magical—it requires hard work not only by staff but also by each child. Children who come with realistic expectations most often have their expectations fulfilled. Children who come with unrealistic expectations are most often disappointed.

Setting Treatment Expectations with the Family

Families who come to preplacement screenings are frequently in crisis. If a crisis has not precipitated the placement, the placement itself may well be traumatic. Families may be upset at interference by a social service agency or court. They may be upset with their child and their own inability to deal with their child. They may feel anger at the child, at an interfering agency or court, or at the program. Parents are often angry with each other. They often feel inadequate and guilty, responsible for the child's placement outside the home. They may expect to be relieved of responsibilities for a problem child who will be "cured" and returned to them in a new state of good health.

The extent to which the parent or parents are responsible for contributing to the cause of the problem is a sensitive and complex treatment issue. The extent to which they are to be held responsible for contributing to the solution of the problem is the more important issue for treatment, and consequently for preplacement. Expectations for parents' participation in therapy and training on "how to raise an independent child" must be made clear during preplacement. Likewise, expectations for accepting their child for home visits and, conversely, having home visits contingent upon treatment, must also be made clear.

Expectations for the course of treatment are important as well. It is not unusual for a child to come into placement and show dramatic improvement. It is not unusual for parents to be hurt by this. Nor is it unusual for a child to come into placement and display marked deterioration, or lay a guilt trip on the parents in hopes of promoting a "rescue." Further, at the end of treatment and following discharge, it is usual for a child to evidence some regression. "Spontaneous recovery" of problem behaviors following discharge is to be expected. Parents must be prepared to manage this normal phenomenon.

Seeking treatment should not be viewed as parents' abdicating their role or responsibility. Rather, seeking treatment is an affirmative action to resolve a problem, a positive step about which parents should have some positive feelings, albeit with some negative feelings. When they have taken the initiative in seeking help, in pursuing placement, they should be helped to feel good about taking a positive step.

Finally, it is a rare parent who does not have some misgivings about the safety of her or his child upon separation. This phenomenon occurs when sending a child off to summer camp. It even occurs when sending a mature child off to college. Most parents know that when going into placement, their child is going into a facility in which children with problems reside. They are most likely aware of the facility's reputation—good, bad, or mixed. Their concerns about the child's safety should be addressed during preplacement and intake. Their opportunities to communicate with the child should be reviewed along with their responsibilities for communicating with the child. They should be introduced to staff. The staff with whom they should communicate about progress, problems, and treatment should be clearly identified, along with parents' responsibilities for communicating with staff and staff's responsibilities for communicating with parents.

INTAKE AND ORIENTATION

A child at intake is especially vulnerable. Most of us can remember our feelings upon attending a new school. The child, at intake, must make new associations. It is the ideal time for staff to establish relationships with the child. It is also the easiest time for the child to form relationships with other residents, and for other residents to take advantage of the child, as the following example suggests.

Scheduling intakes. **While directing two units for adolescent males in a large residential facility, I accepted three boys within a period of a few weeks, all of whom came in on a Thursday or a Friday. Each of these boys failed the program within their first few weeks, either due to running away or serious noncompliant behavior and aggression. I reviewed data on intakes and discharges and found that the program failure rate for boys who come into the program late in the week (Thursdays and Fridays) was over 75 percent.**
Analysis revealed the following:

1. **The major contact of new residents with the program prior to placement was with professional staff. These staff were "the program"—they represented the program almost exclusively during preplacement and much of intake.**
2. **Professional staff—the program director, social worker, case managers, and supervisors—worked Mondays through Fridays and were off on weekends.**
3. **Professional staff were especially busy on Fridays with plans and arrangements for weekend activities.**
4. **Boys who were not doing well in the program, or who were dissatisfied with the program, comprised a disproportionately large number of the boys who were present on the weekends.**
5. **There were fewer staff present on the weekends because of the number of boys who were out on home passes.**

6. Weekends had fewer structured activities (no school or study hall) and more free time for boys to interact.

The treatment team concluded that three things might be occurring, any or all of which might be having a negative impact on residents who were admitted late in the week:

1. Staff had less time for individual boys so that new boys who arrived late in the week were more likely to establish strong relationships with other boys before they established relationships with staff.
2. New boys who were accepted late in the week had more initial exposure to negative or dissatisfied residents since many boys who were doing well were out on home pass.
3. New boys who arrived late in the week, while they might have established a good relationship with professional staff during intake, had to endure their first several days in the program without access to the first staff with whom they had established a relationship and had no one they could comfortably go to with problems.

We suspected that the relevant factors were different for different boys. We established a policy of accepting new residents for intake only on Mondays and Tuesdays, and occasionally on Wednesdays. On two subsequent occasions we had to accept boys on a Friday, one as an emergency and the other due to a contingency of the funding source. Both boys failed the program within their first two months.

DISCHARGE

When a child in residential treatment visits home on weekends, she or he is likely to enjoy the status of a visitor during such visits. This has some advan-

tages. It allows children and parents to relate to each other and to enjoy each other in a new and different way. Expectations for visitors are usually somewhat different from the expectations for children in their own homes. Parents tend to look forward to the visit. Without the distraction that the child used to pose during the week, parents may plan special activities or special meals for the weekend, sometimes with the help of the family therapist. The child may be welcomed home with an affection she or he did not readily perceive during more trying times before placement.

The expectations of the "visitors" are also different from the expectations of children in their own homes. The child, too, may look forward to the visit without the encumbrances of difficulties during the week. Parents may sense an affection from the child that is different from what he or she was able to display prior to placement. Many children offer help as guests much more readily than they perform chores and duties that are expected at home as routine responsibilities. Many of the chores that are expected routinely when the child lives at home change when the child moves out. For example, the child has not been in the home all week to contribute to the trash accumulation, so taking out the garbage on Saturday morning has a much different meaning. The child has not been present all week to contribute to "dirtying" the house. Hence, she or he may not be expected to share as fully in cleaning up. Moreover, the child's room is likely to be already clean in anticipation of the child's arrival.

Finally, the child is not likely to enter the weekend with any disciplinary matters pending from the preceding week. The residential program has assumed much responsibility for the child's discipline, including school, which may have been a major source of conflict in the family. Moreover, the child is likely to have worked for and earned the home pass as a privilege. The idea of home as a privilege is a concept that may attach a special value to time spent at home.

Some or all of these factors may contribute to the improvement upon which parents may remark following a child's placement in a residential facility. These same factors may complicate discharge. Following discharge, the child's role must undergo a significant change, as must that of the parents. The child must accept the role of a functioning and contributing member of the family and forgo the privileged role of weekend guest. The parents must assume full responsibilities for parenting and forgo the roles of host or hostess. Moreover, family routines must be adjusted to accommodate the returning family member. Consider the implications of one more person in line for the bathroom during your morning routine.

Expectations for life after discharge may be very high. In many cases, both the child and family have worked hard for discharge. They have noted gains and improvements in their relationships. Some of these gains are due to their hard work (and the hard work of program staff); other changes may be due simply to a change in roles.

Transition Home

Whenever possible, children who are preparing for discharge should receive home passes on weekdays prior to discharge. This helps the child and family to prepare for the adjustments necessary in both morning and evening routines—getting off to work and school, taking care of supper, homework, and other responsibilities. It allows the parents to begin to reassert themselves during the more structured part of the week in contrast to the more relaxed weekends. It allows the parents to gradually and safely assume more responsibility for their child. It allows the child time to adjust to changes with the safety of returning to the program for support.

Finally, parents and the child should be prepared for problems that normally accompany any change, as well as the normal "spontaneous recovery" of behaviors they might have thought were "extinguished." Problems that surprise the family after discharge lead to discouragement and raise questions about the whole treatment process, including the techniques the parents worked so hard to learn and to implement.

I initially followed the practice of a two-week trial discharge, the "successful" completion of which resulted in the child's continuing at home. Of course, if problems were encountered during these two weeks, the child could be returned to the program for additional treatment. The procedure did not seem to work very well. The child normally took all of his or her possessions home when leaving on the "trial" discharge. No problems were ever reported, by the child or by the family. Aftercare, however, subsequently revealed that problems indeed were occurring during this period.

The treatment team noted that children often enjoy a "honeymoon" during the first few weeks home. Parents often hesitate to report problems during this period. They don't want to appear incompetent. They don't want to accept responsibility for any role in delaying the child's return home.

We amended the procedure. A two-week trial discharge followed by a scheduled and mandatory return to the program allowed the parents and the child more opportunity and freedom to discuss the details of the trial discharge after the child's return, relieving both of the burden of reporting something that might significantly alter the discharge schedule. Final discharge was not scheduled until after the child's return from the trial and full evaluation of the two-week period. This procedure resulted in a dramatic increase in success after discharge.

Timing with the School Year

When school-related problems are significant in the problems that present upon referral, discharge should be carefully timed to the school year. It normally seems desirable for a child to complete a school year at one school and start a new school at the beginning of a new school year. However, habits of attendance, getting up and getting ready, returning, and completing homework may be lost during summer vacation.

It is often a serious disservice to the child and family to discharge a child at the end of a school year. The child works hard, does well, and discharges to a well-deserved summer vacation. Following the summer vacation, the parents then have the responsibility for reestablishing the habits of getting up, getting ready, going to school, and returning to do homework. These habits may have been tenuous at best.

When school has posed a significant problem for the child, it is often best to accelerate or retard discharge a bit so that it falls between the end of September and mid-April. This allows the child to return home in a "school mode." School habits, then, need only be maintained, not reestablished. In terms of learning theory, they may be generalized rather than having to be reacquired.

On the other hand, problems with free time and peers may sometimes appear to be more significant than problems with school. For such children, transition home during the summer may be more appropriate.

AFTERCARE

Professional services after discharge are beneficial in facilitating the transition home and in providing support of gains made during placement. The feedback that aftercare provides to the residential program about the successes and failures in its treatment program, however, may be a much more important benefit of aftercare services, as the following example suggests.

Barry and Jason. **Barry and Jason were model residents on the highest level of a program that served adolescent boys. They had not always been model residents, but had learned and grown during their placement. Both boys had earned the affection and respect of staff. Both boys were admired and respected by other residents. Moreover, Barry's family had participated fully and enthusiastically during treatment.**

Both boys completed their final three months of treatment with near-record per-formance. **They routinely earned all their points. In preparation for discharge, boys on the highest level were eligible to earn home passes every weekend. Both boys earned their passes every week. Barry's only problem seemed to be an obsession with earning points. He would become very angry if he missed points in even one two-point category during the week. However, he controlled his temper. Both boys began their trial discharges at about the same time, completed them successfully, and remained at home. Both boys returned shortly after their discharge for a party to celebrate their success.**

The agency had recently established an aftercare program and promoted a talented staff member to the position of aftercare coordinator. The aftercare coordinator worked closely with both boys and their families following discharge. Within a few weeks, Barry had had several major incidents at home, had moved away, and dropped out of school. Also within a few weeks, Jason had dropped out of school, left his mother, and gone to live with his grandmother.

The agency immediately instituted changes in its programming, including efforts to improve the transition home. Boys on the highest level were taken off the point system and were expected to maintain their behavior and handle their responsibilities and privileges without points. Instead of being eligible for home passes every weekend, boys were required to complete home passes during the middle of the week, meeting responsibilities at home and at school, before they could receive a weekend pass. After several such cycles, boys were scheduled for a two-week trial discharge after which they returned to resume the cycle of weekday and weekend passes until final discharge was scheduled.

The percentage of boys known to be doing well after completing the new discharge program rose to 75.8 percent over a follow-up study covering four years. Doing well was defined as still in school, finished school or

GED, or employed. The program lost contact with 10.3 percent of its graduates. Of the 13.8 percent who were not doing well, 6.9 percent remained in the community while another 6.9 percent were returned to placement or incarcerated (St. Bernard Group Home for Boys, 1989).

As with many studies in residential treatment, it was not possible to isolate and control for all factors that may have been significant in the results. Later changes in other aspects of the program may have had some effect on success after discharge. During this same period, successful discharges rose from a low of 40.0 percent to a high of 90.0 percent (St. Bernard Group Home for Boys, 1989).

In this example, the aftercare position was eliminated after two years due to loss of funding. Nevertheless, success after discharge continued to improve for two years following elimination of the position. The contribution of aftercare towards success after discharge was not so much related to the support provided to the children and their families as to the feedback provided to the program and subsequent changes in treatment.

RUNAWAYS

It is difficult to imagine a child's running away from a situation in which his or her needs are being met. It is also difficult to imagine a situation that has the ability of meeting all of the needs of a variety of children. Different children have different needs.

Children's needs include the basics—food, clothing, and shelter. Children also need love, attention, respect, safety, discipline, security, education, stimulation, opportunity, and sometimes treatment. Some children have needs for which adults cannot or should not provide—such as obsessive needs for drugs, alcohol, or sex.

In my experience, I have observed four basic types of runaways from programs:

1. *The freedom runaway.* The child wants to disappear, to be gone, and to stay gone, and has the ability to do so.
2. *The party runaway.* The child wishes to attend or participate in some activity for which he or she does not expect to be able to get permission, such as a rendezvous with a girlfriend or boyfriend or some other adventure in the community, but the child expects to return or be returned afterwards.
3. *The avoidance runaway.* The child wants to avoid an uncomfortable situation such as confrontation by staff about a wrongdoing, discipline, or problems with peers.
4. *The runaway home.* The child wants to go home but cannot otherwise get there, or the child is unwilling to do what is necessary to go home, such as behave or wait until adults give permission.

The Freedom Runaway

Children who run away for the freedom of being on their own, free from the constraints of adults and society, are the most difficult to manage or treat. They have demonstrated an ability to survive on their own. They may engage in crime sprees—stolen cars and burglaries. They may engage in prostitution—heterosexual or homosexual. They may find accommodations with friends, either peers or adults. They may even support themselves legitimately through bona fide employment.

Such children pose special problems, even for secure facilities. While staff may devote forty-plus hours per week to their jobs, such children can devote 168 hours per week to their "escape." Even in secure settings, they sometimes find ways to breach security. Their preoccupation with their freedom interferes with their treatment. Moreover, while some elope on their own, those who tend to take other peers with them expose more vulnerable children to the dangers of "the streets" and remove them from treatment, only to abandon them at some later point.

I do not know what to do about the children who can "survive" on their own. They usually do little more than survive. They do not grow or mature. They seem to evidence a quasi-maturity that allows them to fend for themselves, but only on a level that is exciting to a child and not likely to lead to lasting satisfaction as an adult. Perhaps the best we can offer is a secure program until they reach adulthood, at which point they can, by definition, no longer "run away," since running away is a juvenile matter and not a crime. During this period, we can hope to advance some of their skills so that when they reach adulthood, their potential to take advantage of the opportunities available to adults is also enhanced. At least we can hope to discourage them from taking peers along for a brief but disruptive and dangerous ride. The following is a case example of a freedom runner.

Raymond. Raymond was a fifteen-year-old from a small, isolated coal mining town in the northeast. The town was poor and somewhat deserted. No coal had been mined for many years. Raymond had a history of running. He stole cars and travelled throughout the northeastern states. He was transferred from a juvenile facility to a small, secure program prior to his release from his latest sentence.

Raymond really wanted to see his family and girlfriend. He gave his word that he would not run if he were taken to see his folks. He had proven himself on several outings where he had clearly had the opportunity to slip away. A supervisor agreed to take him and the visit was arranged. The trip took nearly five hours over rural, isolated roads. While visiting his family, Raymond slipped off with his girlfriend. He kept his word, however, and returned on time for the trip back to the facility.

A few months later, while both staff on the midnight shift dozed, Raymond and another boy lifted the personal car keys of one of the staff from his jacket. However, he had the keys to the facility in his trouser pocket. The other staff had his facility and car keys on the same key ring, near his hand. They took his keys to let themselves out of the locked facility, but left his Thunderbird, even though it was much more stylish and desirable than the Vega driven by the other staff, apparently out of their regard for one staff over the other. They left the car in which they drove off in a ditch three states away.

A few days later, they were caught during a burglary of a residence in a southern state. The boy who ran with Raymond did not put down the gun they had acquired during the burglary. Police shot him in the leg with a shotgun. The wound was not at all serious. The pellets were not removed during the five days they spent in the local jail. When they returned, the facility's physician advised against removing the pellets, since the wounds had healed and probing for the pellets could do considerable damage.

About a year later, Raymond and another inmate seriously injured a guard escaping from the local jail in Raymond's home town.

The Party Runaway

The party runner elopes for fun or adventure, for the stimulation. Such runners may elope out of ennui or for a particularly exciting opportunity. Their elopement may be somewhat planned over a day or two, or be very impulsive. Such runaways may be precipitated by some contact with the community, such as seeing a friend on an outing, receiving a phone call, or making plans for the weekend while attending public school. Such children may be especially vulnerable to the influence of a "freedom runner" planning a "great escape." They are neither able nor desirous of surviving for any length of time on their own and do not intend to remain "at large" for any extended period.

A program that experiences problems with "party" runaways should carefully review its activity schedule during periods when school is out, weekends, long holidays, and the summer. Having stimulating activities to which children look forward interferes with their planning their own activities. Involving children in planning facility activities for the weekend goes even further to promote their investment in weekends with the program.

Possible activities include social events with other youth groups, softball games, dances or other joint activities with another program, activities with community service organizations such as the Kiwanis Club, outings to university gyms, athletic clubs, special local cultural events such as a fairs or free concerts, outings to go-cart tracks, skating rinks, water slides, or amusement parks, or simply outings to a playground in a different part of town or picnics. Much depends on staff enthusiasm for such activities. It is not necessary that special activities occur every weekend. It is important that weekends not be anticipated as boring and repetitious, amounting to nothing more than lots of free time to watch TV, play pool or basketball, or listen to tapes with an occasional movie thrown in.

The above-mentioned program for adolescent boys in need of supervision had only one child discharged on runaway in four years. A sister program for girls, whose regular weekend schedule included shopping for the next week's groceries, had frequent problems with party runaways. The following is an example of a party runner.

Ronald. **Ronald was a fourteen-year-old with elderly adoptive parents. He had been experiencing problems with parental discipline and in school. Ronald struggled with the program initially and had difficulty earning privileges, including home passes and full participation in in-program weekend activities. This was largely due to problems with smoking. Ronald was addicted to smoking when he came into the program, but his father, suffering from emphysema but smoking two packs of cigarettes a day, refused to grant permission for Ronald to smoke.**

The program had numerous activities available to its residents during the week and especially on weekends, some of which were available to all residents and others that had to be earned. Ronald rarely earned the extra privileges because he was always losing points for smoking.

After about two months, Ronald failed to return on the bus from school. He had taken another bus and gone home with a friend. He returned Sunday night, having had some "unearned" fun on the weekend. He served his consequences and began to do well in the program, probably due to the program's finally getting permission from his father for Ronald to smoke. Ronald began earning privileges and had no further problems with running away.

After nearly a year, Ronald got expelled from school just as arrangements were being finalized for his placement in special education. He had "mooned" a teacher. Ronald was transferred to another group home in another school district where he could enroll in school. He had major problems with running away and was transferred to a secure facility. Runaway problems continued, however. He was subsequently discharged from the secure program while on one of his many runaways.

The Avoidance Runaway

Children who run to avoid problems have often demonstrated avoidance as a personal style of managing problems. On the other hand, if other means of handling problems seem inaccessible, running away may appear to be the most desirable alternative. Again, the program must evaluate the extent to which it is meeting the needs of its residents, and the runaway resident in particular. How are staff handling problems? Is discipline (punishment) too harsh or severe? Is the child safe from other residents? Can the child approach staff with problems?

Children who run to avoid problems, confrontations, or accepting responsibility and consequences for their behavior often leave during a crisis. They are upset when they run. When they calm down, they become confused. They may be readily apprehended or call to be returned. Staff who pursue such residents are likely to be successful in talking them down and bringing them back, especially if they are patient and can afford to be so without neglecting the other children. As such children learn better self-control and better ways of dealing with problems, as they become more confident in their abilities and more trusting of others, their runaway behavior decreases markedly.

The Runaway Home

If the parents are supporting the child's treatment, then the runaway home should pose little problem. The program notifies the parent(s) when the child runs away; the parents notify the program when the child arrives home; the child's return to the program is arranged immediately by the adults involved. The child eventually learns other, more productive ways to get home, such as meeting treatment objectives and earning home passes.

In cases in which the parents do not support the child's placement, the runaway home may pose special problems. The lack of parental support of the program is the major problem. It is readily communicated to the child when the parents do not promptly notify the program of the child's arrival. The runaway behavior is reinforced by whatever time the child spends in the home and the support of the parents in their collaboration in the runaway. Unless parental collaboration can be quickly interdicted, successful placement and treatment are unlikely.

Conclusions

Factors relating to the individual child are significant in evaluating any runaway episode. Factors relating to the institution are also significant in evaluating an episode of running away. Factors relating to the institution are most likely critical to the understanding of runaway behavior if a pattern of runaways is evident over a period of time.

STAFF BURNOUT

Raider (1989) notes that research suggests that burnout is related to a breakdown of psychological defenses that workers use to cope with job-related stressors. Stressors include working with the chil-

dren, relating to coworkers, agency rules, role conflict, role ambiguity, job satisfaction, and unrealistic expectations.

"Of the stressors discussed in this article, the only one which cannot be changed derives from working intensely and intimately with residents' problems" (p. 44). Raider notes that there is often no benchmark to measure the success of treatment. In this absence, staff may utilize an unrealistically high standard, feeling a sense of failure when this standard is not met. Excessive rules, regulations, and procedures also create stress. Further, approaches that are directed at teaching staff to deal with or reduce symptoms of stress only delay but do not prevent burnout.

Finch and Krantz (1991) cite Finch, McGowan, and White, noting that stressors experienced by staff in residential settings are primarily attributable to four sources:

1. The demanding, persistent nature of the disabling condition.
2. Deficiencies in staff training and expectations.
3. Frustrating agency policies.
4. Limitations of the larger service system (p. 15).

It is difficult to imagine someone "burning out" in a job he or she enjoys and can do well. If staff are burning out, then something is wrong. Either the staff do not enjoy the work they are required to do or the staff are not able to do their jobs.

Staff Do Not Enjoy Their Work

Staff who want to "help" children are drawn to residential treatment programs. The purpose of these programs is, after all, to help children. But helping children is a process at which we do not seem to be all that good. It is a slow process at best. Staff who expect to share their wisdom with children, to "show them the light" as it were, soon come to realize that children do not readily accept their wisdom. There are few "miracle cures." People have been giving these children the benefit of their wisdom for years—parents, grandparents, teachers, counselors, therapists, school disciplinarians, police, probation officers, clergy, neighbors, and friends. It hasn't worked. Treatment takes time. Progress is slow. Staff who want to help children become easily frustrated when children continue to make mistakes. They then tend to blame the children and the administration, to become angry with either or both. They may do more harm than good.

Staff who genuinely like and enjoy children, even when untrained in helping children, tend to do a lot of good. It is possible to train people to use various techniques that may help children. It is much more difficult to teach people to like and to enjoy children.

The most important criterion for staff, then, is their capacity to enjoy children, to enjoy doing things with children. People who like and enjoy children give children a sense of self-worth and value that is an important ingredient in any child's life—indeed, in anyone's life. Gordon (cited in Finch & Krantz, 1991) refers to the "fit between person and environment" (p. 25). Finch and Krantz refer to "doing with" as opposed to "doing for" (p. 25) as a key difference in a setting in which burnout is low. Staff who enjoy doing things with children are not likely to suffer burnout when they are given the opportunity to do things with children. Staff who want to do things for children, like treatment, often become frustrated with difficult children who do not readily accept their treatment.

Staff Are Not Able to Do Their Work

Staff who cannot do their jobs become frustrated, tense, and anxious. If staff cannot do their jobs because their skills and abilities are not good enough, then their skills can probably be improved with some training—unless we have made serious errors in assessing initial skill levels during preemployment screening. More often, "doing their jobs" is more a matter of definition of the job and opportunity to do the "job" than it is a matter of skill, more a matter of conflicting expectations— of role conflict or confusion.

Staff who come to residential treatment programs generally expect to spend time with children. We tend to talk a lot about children and doing things with children in the interview. After staff start work, they learn about the reports, the documentation, the constant attention that may be needed to maintain the facility, equipment, and vehicles. They learn the frustration when a broken basketball goal or television set may go unrepaired for weeks. The job is not what they expected.

Dealing with troubled children is stressful. It is more stressful for some people than for others. It is more stressful in some programs than in others. Cars that do not start or run properly are stressful for most of us—they are not so stressful for auto mechanics.

What really tends to create stress for staff is the conflict between their perception that they are expected to spend time dealing with children and job expectations that keep them from doing so. I have not found that staff who expect to spend time with children and who enjoy spending time with children develop undue stress when they are allowed to spend time with children, no matter how disturbed the child. They become stressed when they are constantly taken away from the children— meetings, reports, documentation, log entries, shuttling vehicles back and forth to the shop, being denied the necessary supplies and equipment to do their jobs, being criticized for late reports and damages to the facility, being suspect when equipment fails, receiving criticism for "normal wear and tear" when management expects things to hold up in a house full of ten or more active children as if things were being used in a "typical" American family consisting of two children and two adults.

Employment Screening and Expectations

Just as treatment begins during the preplacement interview, dealing with staff burnout begins during the preemployment process. First impressions are lasting impressions. Good staff will attempt to meet expectations. The expectations they develop during the preemployment process will be most lasting. Good staff will often attempt to meet those initial expectations until they are promoted, reassigned, or otherwise leave the job. Any other expectations that may be communicated at some later date are likely to be perceived as "in addition to" initial expectations rather than as "in place of" or superseding initial expectations. If initial expectations as communicated during the preemployment process are somehow in error, they may become a major factor in staff burnout.

Preemployment interviews tend to emphasize dealing with children. This is important. Preemployment interviews, however, should also place proper emphasis on reporting, on supervision of chores and the facility, and other things that the program might also consider to be important. Following employment, emphasis on various "important" aspects of the job should remain in proper perspective. In the following, an apparently carefully screened and oriented new staff member did not work out, leading to changes in hiring and orientation.

> *A new staff.* **Upon accepting a new position supervising a unit for adolescent boys, I immediately began recruiting staff. The program was short two staff, and the supervisor and I had to take turns covering shifts. I interviewed a mature young woman with some related experience and a degree. She was impressive. The supervisor concurred. Following the program's usual procedure, we invited her to come in and spend a few hours with the children in the milieu. She did well. She had dinner with the children. She was engaging. She worked with some of the boys during study hall. She was interested in art and worked with the boys doing some drawing. The boys liked her.**
>
> **After two months on the job, she was a nervous wreck. So were the boys. Several refused to ride with her in the van. She could not manage the boys at any time by herself. She was uncomfortable and awkward. We could find nothing to help her. I had to dismiss her.**
>
> **I noted two significant problems—one in the screening process, the other in the ori-**
> **entation process. While the children liked the new staff as a person, they were extremely uncomfortable with her in a position of authority. She herself was uncomfortable in a position of authority.**
>
> **The agency's practice of having prospective staff "spend time with the kids" set up an artificial situation. Prospective staff, in "spending time with the children," related to the children as a guest in the facility; the children treated them as a guest. Upon starting employment, the new staff had to immediately adopt a new role, that of an authority figure. The two roles had very little to do with each other.**
>
> *Orientation.* **At the urging of other staff, who felt they had had little orientation when they first assumed their positions, we developed a special schedule for this new staff person, making sure that for her first four weeks, she was always paired with an experienced staff and never had to work a shift by herself. After these first four weeks, during which she could always defer to other staff, the children saw her as an "assistant." She never had to assume any authority. She never had to set any limits or apply any consequences. Once her training had been completed and she was expected to assume the responsibilities of a full-time staff person, she was again faced with a major role change.**
>
> *Adjustments.* **We instituted two changes in our hiring procedures. First, rather than have prospective staff "spend time with the children," we instituted a procedure I had used previously with success: we had the children conduct the final interview of prospective candidates and make the final decision. Second, we began orientation of new staff on the midnight shift. We had few problems with new staff afterwards.**

Client Interviews

Allowing children to interview staff provides a number of benefits. First, children need to become acquainted with a new staff person. Allowing them to interview candidates allows them a formal and structured opportunity to do so. When given this opportunity, children ask questions that are important to them. ''What are your interests?'' ''Do you like music?'' ''How would you handle someone who cursed you out?'' (Usually from a child who has a history of losing control with staff and cursing them unmercilessly.) ''How would you react to one of us getting violent or trying to hit you?'' (Usually from a child who has problems with aggression during a crisis.) ''Do you have a boyfriend?'' ''Do you have any plans to get married?'' (after a respected and much-loved staff member got married and gave notice after her honeymoon because her husband had accepted a new job out of state).

Without some structured way of getting to know a new staff person, children have to ''test.'' Allowing the children a structured and formalized opportunity to get to know a new staff reduces (but does not eliminate) the need for testing a new staff member.

Second, it allows the children a formal role in selecting a new staff. It is, after all, the children's home. The staff are perhaps the most significant people in the children's home. When administration selects the staff, one often hears residents, especially experienced residents who have been around, say things like, ''You won't last long,'' or ''We'll run you off in a few weeks.'' When administration hires the new staff, children seem to derive some satisfaction in proving the administration made a mistake. They don't seem to derive the same satisfaction from demonstrating that they themselves have made a poor decision. They thus have some investment in helping the new staff get off to a good start. It doesn't last forever, but it beats having a new staff walk into a hostile environment and gives new staff a good chance to get off to a good start.

Third, it communicates to prospective staff very effectively that children in the program do indeed have certain rights, status, and responsibility. Any applicants who have any problems with respecting children as persons tend to be screened out very quickly.

Finally, it lets the new staff know that he or she is not only welcome and accepted by the children but also has been chosen by the children. It provides new staff with needed confidence when they start work.

Orientation

Providing staff with initial orientation on the midnight shift likewise has some advantages. It allows them to get to know the facility, its security, the program, and the program manual away from the watchful eyes of the residents. The first time the residents see the new staff, he or she is already comfortable with the facility, with the location of supplies, with procedures, and with the keys.

After one or two nights of orientation on the midnight shift and a session or two with the supervisor, we very quickly arranged for the new staff to be alone and in a position of authority with at least some of the children—perhaps taking a few to the store for school supplies or snacks, perhaps supervising others alone in the facility while another staff took some of the children on a brief outing. This was designed so that the children quickly perceived the staff in a role of authority rather than the role of ''trainee.''

These procedures quickly reduced problems with turnover. I have used the procedure of having residents interview staff in every residential setting for children in which I have worked. In some cases, when administrators were skeptical, supervisors sat in on the interviews with the children; in other cases, when I had the freedom, I allowed the children to conduct the interviews in private. My preference is for the latter. However, in both cases, I have found that the children do a remarkable job of hiring people they respect, in almost every case the toughest, most ''hard line'' of the applicants. ''Nice guys'' inevitably finished last.

I never allowed the children to make a mistake I wouldn't make. That is, I never allowed the children to interview someone I wasn't prepared to hire. Prior to involving the children, we completed initial interviews with appropriate supervisors and administrative personnel, preemployment physicals, and reference checks. We refrained from any influence after scheduling interviews by the children. Although I experienced a few mistakes with this procedure, the mistakes never approached the occasional disasters I've seen when the children were not so involved. They may not be capable of conducting the full hiring process, but they invariably contribute something worthwhile to the process when given the opportunity and responsibility.

INFORMATION, STATISTICS, AND COMPUTERS

A tremendous amount of information tends to be available on the children in residential treatment programs. Different information can be important for a variety of reasons, including emergency notifications and statistical analysis of the effectiveness of the program. During emergencies, staff need to know that the information they have available to them is sufficient, accurate, and up-to-date. It adds to their confidence. Emergency phone numbers, special medical information related to special conditions or allergies, Medicaid numbers, and descriptive data needed to report a runaway must be handy, complete, and accurate. Current statistical data about residents helps the treatment team to readily assess progress and problems and institute effective changes.

Several contemporary software programs for personal computers can simplify the management of such data, including spreadsheet programs such as Lotus® or Quattro®, and data base programs such as Q & A®, D-Base®, and Fox-Pro®. Both spreadsheet programs are easy to use and readily adaptable for a variety of data management needs. Agencies that use IBM-compatible personal computers for fiscal management probably have either the Lotus® or Quattro® program for budgeting and expense reporting and the expertise to use them. Data base programs may serve the same purposes, perhaps better, especially in conjunction with a program to generate reports from data base programs, such as R & R®, but they require different training and experience that may not be so readily available.

Emergency Data

Certain information about the children must be readily available to staff in the event of an emergency such as a runaway or a medical emergency. Information that is most often necessary includes date of birth, home address and phone number, an alternate phone number and the name and relationship of the alternate person to contact, custody information and responsible person, physical description (height, weight, hair color and length or style, color of eyes, identifying marks), allergies, medical conditions, and any prescribed medication, Medicaid numbers or other insurance information. It is often necessary to have this information available in more than one location—staff office, social worker's office, with staff on an outing, or with a supervisor on call to staff on duty.

Many agencies maintain this information in card files, with an index card for each resident. For some children, some of this information may change frequently. Index cards become overwritten and scratched out, especially as home or work phone numbers change. It is difficult to update the information readily in all locations where such data may be kept. A busy social worker may become aware of a change in a parent's address or phone number and make note of it in her records, but fail to notify the staff; a staff may become aware of a change and fail to notify the social worker. A supervisor attempting to handle an emergency and aware of different information in the two files can't tell which information is most current.

The Lotus® or Quattro® spreadsheet programs can readily print out an alphabetical listing of program residents with necessary information. Lists can also be arranged by living unit, by age, or by any other criteria deemed helpful. Both spreadsheet programs can sort the data according to any desired criteria with a few strokes of the keys. The list can be printed out weekly as information or residents

FIGURE 16.1: Emergency Data on Residents at the Charity Treatment Center

```
        3/15/95                                    CHARITY TREATMENT CENTER
                                                      RESIDENT ROSTER


                                                                 ADMIT  DAYS  HOME
       NAME                DOB    AGE  R  S  HT.   WT. MEDICAID NUMBER  DATE  SRVC  ADDRESS                    CITY        PHONE
              LITTLE GIRLS COTTAGE
   1  BILLINGSLEY, Joan    01/30/83  12  B  F  5'2"  110                 04/03/94  347  2822 Berwick St.         Lexington   831-4528
   2  BOUDREAUX, Melody    11/03/80  14  B  F  5'5"  161  5503015851901  12/03/94  103  1102 7th St.            Reading     367-2169
   3  BROWN, Charlene      05/04/83  12  W  F  5'3"   95  5506011474632  03/01/94  380  3940 Delaware Ave., #301 Allentown  none
   4  CARLSON, Rachel L.   02/25/84  11  W  F  5'7"  166  5503401984562  03/07/94  374  43 Hennessey Ct.        Lexington   737-9584
   5  KAUCHER, Ruby        11/28/83  11  W  F  5'9"  116  5502934784129  03/14/95    1  1721 Birch St.          Lexington   347-5581
   6  SIMON, Tasha         02/25/84  11  B  F  4'11   97  5502634091837  01/03/95   72  8215 Sesame St.         Princeton   361-5383
   7  STRUNK, Michele      10/25/85   9  B  F  4'9"   74  5503001335005  12/18/93  453  30 Driftwood            Reading     none
              OLDER GIRLS COTTAGE
   1  DORSEY, Pat          05/11/77  18  W  F  5'5"  114  5506027913842  08/21/93  572  1101 Union St.          Nazareth    none
   2  GONZALES, Chastity   04/27/78  17 HS  F  5'5"  137  5507890103291  02/20/94  389  811 Gulf Drive          Georgetown  362-0638
   3  HARVEY, Michelle R.  05/02/78  17  B  F  5'8"  123  5506178354763  07/31/94  228  413 Abbey Way           Reading     737-5403
   4  ISAAC, Desiree       07/03/76  16  B  F  5'10" 135  5502863091864  03/03/94  378  2713 Union St.          Kalamazoo   468-2166
   5  MULDOON, Desiree M.  12/13/74  20  B  F  5'7"  133                 05/02/94  318  2717 Greenwood          Georgetown  461-6117
   6  PURDY, Jennifer      09/16/74  20  B  F  5'4"  117  5503981096345  07/23/94  236  2223 Valley Rd.         Reading     366-3401
   7  ULRICH, Jawanda      05/11/77  18  W  F  5'11" 133  5508639120847  11/23/94  113  4213 Harvard Ct.        Reading     348-8915
   8  WISCZNIEWSKI, Wendy  04/18/78  17  W  F  5'6"  116  5507890573921  09/23/94  174  17 Hastings Rd.         Allentown   736-7001
              LITTLE BOYS COTTAGE
   1  BAKER, Evan          01/14/85  10  B  M  4'11" 110  5504103134501  03/13/94  368  1600 Jerome St.         Nazareth    347-6263
   2  BENNETT, Harry       11/19/82  12  B  M  5'6"  121  5503015609501  02/19/94  390  E. Mary Poppins         Lexington
   3  CACCIACARNE, Joseph  02/10/84  11  W  M  4'7"   83  5503018405002  04/26/94  324  1000 Michael Ct.        Georgetown  466-8918
   4  HINNERSHITZ, David S. 10/22/87  7  W  M  4'7"   91  5507635920391  07/08/94  251  3406 Lime St.           Kalamazoo   899-2548
   5  HOWARD, Richard J.   05/21/82  13  W  M  5'5"  106  5504001855401  04/15/94  335  3940 Delaware Ave., #2  Arlington   none
   6  LAMBERT, Arnold      10/31/84  10  B  M  4'11"  95  5507874839211  01/04/95   71  12 Barrington Pl.       Lexington   434-7576
   7  McQUEEN, Hiram       12/28/83  11  W  M  4'5"   86                 01/17/95   58  8341 Arrowhead Way       Reading     361-6161
   8  SAVANT, Robert       05/20/89   6  B  M  4'3"   74  5503015181202  01/16/94  424  2816 Annette Dr.        Arlington   341-9002
   9  STEVENS, Samuel      07/17/82  13  B  M  5'3"  118  5503009904902  10/11/93  521  2836 Destrehan, Apt. B  Lexington
  10  STUART, Jeremy       03/16/84  11  W  M  4'9"   81  5503005702050  09/13/93  549  1309 Cadiz St.          Princeton   899-4970
  11  WIGGINS, Bernard     06/03/83  12  W  M  5'11" 101                 01/19/95   56  1022 Carver Place       Georgetown  734-7233
              OLDER BOYS COTTAGE
   1  ADAMS, Brad          10/13/79  15  W  M  5'11" 167  5507890834279  08/24/94  204  4213 Howard Ave.        Arlington   361-6082
   2  BROWN, George        04/02/82  13  B  M  5'2"   86  5503003134502  03/13/94  368  1600 Jerome St.         Kalamazoo   347-6263
   3  CUNNINGHAM, Joshua   07/12/80  15  W  M  5'6"  145  5504108638701  10/03/93  529  710 3rd Ave.            Georgetown  347-0425
   4  DUBOIS, Charles      11/10/79  15  W  M  5'8"  177  5503008795201  05/02/94  318  117 8th St.             Lexington   436-2547
   5  HOLLINGSWORTH, Ray J. 10/28/81 13  W  M  5'11" 135  5503018033002  10/10/93  522  5852 Milladorn          Nazareth    341-6485
   6  KOWALSKI, Anthony J. 01/12/79  16  B  M  6'1"  165                 01/30/95   45  7213 Lexington Pl.      Lexington   361-1645
   7  MALONE, Neil         01/19/80  15  W  M  5'2"  120  5507893759287  12/16/94   90  815 Sparrow Lane        Lexington   736-7001
   8  MARTIN, Derrick      12/22/81  13  B  M  5'7"   97  5503005506009  05/23/94  297  6609 Cheneault Dr.      Reading     348-4728
   9  RAND, Jasper         06/03/80  15  B  M  5'7"  144  5503018201101  02/13/94  396  505 George St.          Allentown   436-8852
  10  RUSSELL, Russell R.  11/12/80  14  B  M  5'3"  183  5507897438239  11/30/94  106  12 Madison Place, Apt. 5 Georgetown 341-5413
  11  WELLS, Aaron         06/13/79  16  B  M  6'   177                 02/17/95   27  803 Mulberry St.        Nazareth    736-7003
  12  WHITE, Tyrone        06/22/79  16  B  M  5'9"  133  5522000171601  09/28/93  534  1532 Haydel St.         Reading     341-3751
              SENIOR BOYS COTTAGE
   1  BANG, Phat           05/20/73  18  B  M  5'5"  133                 10/15/94  152  13 General Pershing     Princeton   394-1443
   2  BOURGEOIS, Benny     10/03/76  18  W  M  5'8"  156  5515120040001  11/27/94  109  3330 Merimac Ct., #3    Lexington   347-5581
   3  DELERY, Thomas       06/04/77  18  W  M  6'   185                 11/11/94  125  81331 Bernard Hwy.      Kalamazoo   366-4009
   4  FREEMAN, Charles III 08/20/74  21  B  M  5'10" 148  5522000135701  11/03/94  133  1701 Diedra Rd.         Georgetown  464-0198
   5  JOHNSON, Alton       11/01/78  16  B  M  5'11" 174  5504005512101  02/22/95   22  1013 Avondale Rd.       Georgetown
   6  KOCH, Kennie         07/17/77  18  B  M  5'10" 157  5503032538401  06/18/94  271  2308 36th St.           Arlington   361-1893
   7  MORGAN, James        12/30/78  16  W  M  5'9"  233  5522000205201  02/02/95   42  1611 Harroway Ct.       Princeton   436-9732
   8  RODRIGUEZ, Carlos    06/26/74  21 HS  M  5'7"  144  5504103765201  10/31/94  136  1725 Betty Blvd.        Allentown   368-6962
   9  STEIN, Todd          08/09/77  18  B  M  5'11" 167                 07/06/93  618  403 Amity St.           Lexington   362-9977
  10  WERNER, Terrance     11/13/77  17  W  M  5'7"  165  5507890865321  08/16/94  212  6 Andre Ct.             Lexington   341-6161
  11  WISCZNIEWSKI, Stanley 11/01/77 17  W  M  5'11" 155  1507885714342  10/12/94  155  1112 Henry Clay         Lexington   466-4735
```

change. Copies of the list can readily be distributed to anyone who needs the information. The lists can easily be carried on outings and by persons on call. The spreadsheet programs can be set to automatically print the current date each time a new list is made. Lists can be printed on different colors of paper each week so that updated lists are readily identifiable. Figure 16.1 illustrates readily available data for a fictional program with residents in five cottages.

Statistical Data and Decision Making

Residential programs require countless decisions by treatment and administrative personnel, decisions about individual children and decisions about various aspects of the program. Some decisions are fairly routine: whether or not to accept a particular candidate into the program, whether or not to discharge a child and when, school placements, passes. Other decisions may be more general, possibly more far-reaching: what aspects of the program to maintain, what to cut in a financial crisis, whether or not to continue a particular aspect of the program as is or make changes. The more data that is readily available and organized for use, the more likely that decisions will be based on relevant data and rational criteria.

Usually, when a given decision is called for, it is too late to gather, organize, and analyze data that may be relevant. Consequently, programs should gather various kinds of data in an organized fashion. Programs differ. Data that may be significant may vary from program to program. Some of the following might be significant:

age
sex
race
diagnosis
IQ
history of prior placements
history of substance abuse
history of arrests
years behind in school at admission
referral source
discharge resource
status one, two, or three years after discharge (in school, completed school, employed, still at home, placed with another facility, arrested, living independently, etc.)
treatment interventions used
assigned therapist
assigned living unit
propensity for violence or aggression
school assignment
marital status of parents
history of physical abuse
history of emotional abuse
history of sexual abuse
age at admission
age at discharge
length of stay
frequency of restraints by day of week, time of day, time of year, activity in progress, staff on duty, length of time in the program, etc.
frequency of runaways, as above
average length of stay for successful discharges
average length of stay for unsuccessful discharges

When such information is collected in an organized fashion and available for use, patterns may suggest many things that may be significant for a variety of decisions: With what types of children is the program successful? With what types of children is the program not successful? Do more runaways occur in the evening, overnight, on weekends, during the first few days or weeks of residence, during summers? Do more restraints occur during a specific time of day, during a particular activity, when certain staff are on duty?

What changes can be made to improve success? Changes in admission criteria? Changes in discharge criteria or procedures? Changes in programming? Changes in staff orientation or training? Does a given therapist seem to be more successful (less successful) with certain types of children? Which school placements seem to be most effective for which kinds of children?

Again, various types of computer software programs such as spreadsheets and data base programs are available to readily record vast amounts of data on individual residents and hold the data ready for use. These programs can organize the data to help identify trends and patterns, which may facilitate decision making. However, if the information is not collected routinely, it is not likely to be available when needed and cannot be used. Decisions must then be made in some other way according to some other criteria.

Figures 16.2 to 16.5 illustrate a few easily generated printouts organized to highlight various statistical data for the fictional Charity Treatment Center: Status at Discharge (column 12) by Therapist, Living Unit, Sex, and Length of Stay.

SUMMARY

Each and every aspect of the milieu has implications for treatment, beginning with the reputation of the program. Preplacement, intake, residence, discharge, and aftercare all have implications for the milieu. Very importantly, so do the staff and residents who make up the milieu. Computerized management of information helps the program stay on top of things. When things are not going as well as might be expected, it is necessary to assess the milieu carefully to determine what might be going wrong, what might be improved.

A number of miscellaneous factors have significance for the treatment milieu. The program's reputation in the community has significance for children coming into the program and during treatment. Staff should be trained in the importance of the program's reputation and trained to manage themselves and children accordingly. Children likewise should be sensitized to community issues and have clear expectations set for their behavior in any involvement with the community. Supervisors should be prepared to manage problems in the community effectively, responding appropriately and following up to be sure problems have indeed been resolved.

The preplacement visit is especially important. Programs normally screen children; they should be able to assess children as to whether or not they can treat them successfully. Giving a child a "chance" may be a real disservice to the child, creating one more failure. Further, it is in this initial visit that treatment expectations are set for both the child and the family. False or erroneous expectations take time and considerable effort to overcome and interfere with treatment until they are resolved.

Intake is also important. Children are especially vulnerable at this time. It is at this time that important relationships are begun. Staff must be available and focused on establishing those relationships, or others will—possibly other children whose goals may not be consistent with the objectives of the program at the time.

Discharge is as important to post-discharge success as preplacement and intake can be for the success of treatment. Parents and children must be prepared for changes in roles, from host (hostess) and guest to parent and child. Transitions should include some weekday passes during the normal work and school routine. A trial discharge should include a return to the program for evaluation; then final plans for discharge can be made. Parents and the child should be prepared for problems. Residential treatment cannot be expected to eliminate problems; rather, it should empower families and children to better manage problems when they occur. Problems after discharge (spontaneous recovery) should not surprise anyone—they should be expected. Problems can be minimized when children who have presenting problems in school are discharged during the school year while in a "school mode."

While aftercare is important as a means of supporting children and families in practicing learned skills following the transition home, it may be even more important in providing feedback to the program. Feedback is necessary for any system to adjust itself to meet its goals.

Sometimes, children running away may pose problems for children in the milieu. There are four basic types of runaway: the freedom runaway, the

FIGURE 16.2: Discharge by Therapist at the Charity Treatment Center

CHARITY TREATMENT CENTER
Discharge by Therapist
1994

	NAME	AGE	LIVING UNIT	PRIMARY STAFF	THERAPIST	DOB	RACE	SEX	ADMIT DATE	DISCH DATE	MONTHS SERVICE	DISCHARGE STATUS	DISCHARGE PLACE	AGE ADMIT	AGE DISCH
1	ANTOINE, Charles	15.5	Boys, Oldr	B.J.	Johnson	10/13/79	B	M	11/24/92	05/22/94	17.88	S	at home	13.1	14.6
2	CASTILLE, Juan	14.7	Boys, Oldr	Aaron	Johnson	07/12/80	HS	M	11/01/92	04/27/94	17.82	S	at home	12.3	13.8
3	DUBBINS, Henry	15.4	Boys, Oldr	B.J.	Johnson	11/10/79	W	M	05/02/93	12/01/94	19.00	S	at home	13.5	15.1
4	JOHNSON, Aaron	16.4	Boys, Sr	Ed	Johnson	11/01/78	B	M	08/15/93	11/22/94	15.25	S	at home	14.8	16.1
5	ROBERTS, Matthew	15.7	Boys, Oldr	Mike	Johnson	07/17/79	B	M	11/30/91	02/12/94	26.47	S	at home	12.4	14.6
6	WILLIAMS, Isaac	15.8	Boys, Oldr	Mike	Johnson	06/22/79	B	M	09/28/90	11/30/94	50.10	S	at home	11.3	15.4
7	MONROE, Arthur	16.3	Boys, Sr	Nat	Johnson	12/30/78	W	M	02/02/93	10/15/94	20.38	U	corrections	14.1	15.8
8	DETWEILER, George	17.8	Boys, Sr	Louis	Lewis	06/04/77	W	M	11/11/92	10/15/94	23.11	S	at home	15.4	17.4
9	DORSEY, Darlene	17.9	Grls, Oldr	Jean	Lewis	05/11/77	W	F	08/21/90	04/28/94	44.25	S	at home	13.3	17.0
10	FREEMAN, Barry	20.6	Boys, Sr	Carl	Lewis	08/20/74	B	M	11/03/85	10/10/94	107.28	S	independent	11.2	20.1
11	KAUCHER, John	17.7	Boys, Sr	Ed	Lewis	07/17/77	W	M	05/25/92	06/15/94	24.69	S	at home	14.9	16.9
12	MURDOCK, Deidra	20.3	Grls, Oldr	Jean	Lewis	12/13/74	W	F	05/02/91	11/15/94	42.51	S	independent	16.4	19.9
13	PHONG, Nguyen	19.9	Boys, Sr	Carl	Lewis	05/20/75	A	M	11/15/90	08/12/94	44.91	S	independent	15.5	19.2
14	PURNELL, Judith	20.5	Grls, Oldr	Barbara	Lewis	09/16/74	W	F	07/23/91	09/21/94	38.01	S	independent	16.8	20.0
15	WERNER, Marvin	17.4	Boys, Sr	Carl	Lewis	11/13/77	W	M	08/16/89	11/01/94	62.56	S	at home	11.8	17.0
16	WOJCIECHOWSKI, Stanley	17.4	Boys, Sr	Louis	Lewis	11/01/77	W	M	10/12/91	10/15/94	36.13	S	independent	13.9	17.0
17	BARNES, Ulysses	10.2	Boys, Ltl	Ron	Simmons	01/14/85	B	M	03/13/92	04/26/94	25.45	S	at home	7.2	9.3
18	BROWN, Chris	13.0	Boys, Oldr	George	Simmons	04/02/82	B	M	03/13/93	08/20/94	17.26	S	at home	10.9	12.4
19	HASTINGS, Ronnie	7.4	Boys, Ltl	Robert	Simmons	10/22/87	W	M	07/08/92	02/10/94	19.13	S	at home	4.7	6.3
20	HEFFERNAN, Charles	13.4	Boys, Oldr	George	Simmons	10/28/81	W	M	06/06/93	10/03/94	15.91	S	at home	11.6	12.9
21	MARTIN, Anthony R.	13.3	Boys, Oldr	George	Simmons	12/22/81	W	M	05/23/92	03/13/94	21.67	S	at home	10.4	12.2
22	STEARNS, Jay	11.0	Boys, Ltl	Dan	Simmons	03/16/84	W	M	09/13/92	04/12/94	18.94	S	at home	8.5	10.1
23	CALVIN, Joseph	11.1	Boys, Ltl	James	Simmons	02/10/84	W	M	06/18/93	12/20/94	18.08	U	at home	9.4	10.9
24	LANDRY, John	10.4	Boys, Ltl	Dan	Simmons	10/31/84	B	M	01/04/93	07/01/94	17.85	U	residential	8.2	9.7
25	AARON, Arlene	17.0	Grls, Oldr	Denise	Weinstein	04/18/78	W	F	09/23/91	03/01/94	29.26	S	at home	13.4	15.9
26	BROWN, Ebony	11.9	Grls, Ltl	Brenda	Weinstein	05/04/83	B	F	03/01/93	03/06/94	12.16	S	at home	9.8	10.8
27	HERTZOG, Henrietta	16.9	Grls, Oldr	Barbara	Weinstein	05/02/78	B	F	07/31/91	02/02/94	30.15	S	at home	13.2	15.8
28	KENNEDY, Raenel	11.3	Grls, Ltl	Anne	Weinstein	11/28/83	B	F	03/14/92	02/28/94	23.54	S	at home	8.3	10.3
29	SMITH, Erica	11.1	Grls, Ltl	Brenda	Weinstein	02/25/84	W	F	02/28/93	11/15/94	20.55	S	at home	9.0	10.7
30	STOFFER, Melanie	9.4	Grls, Ltl	Anne	Weinstein	10/25/85	W	F	12/18/92	04/01/94	15.42	S	at home	7.1	8.4
31	WAGNER, Tyra	17.9	Grls, Oldr	Denise	Weinstein	05/11/77	W	F	11/23/92	07/15/94	31.73	S	at home	14.5	17.2
32	CARLETTO, Dolores	14.1	Grls, Ltl	Brenda	Weinstein	02/25/81	HS	F	10/10/94	12/20/94	2.33	U	at home	13.6	13.8
33	GONZALES, Rachel	16.9	Grls, Oldr	Mary	Weinstein	04/27/78	HS	F	02/20/91	07/31/94	41.33	U	runaway	12.8	16.3

Discharge Status: S   Successful   U   Unsuccessful

04/04/95

CHARITY TREATMENT CENTER
Discharge by Living Unit
1994

NAME	AGE	LIVING UNIT	PRIMARY STAFF	THERAPIST	DOB	RACE	SEX	ADMIT DATE	DISCH DATE	MONTHS SERVICE	DISCHARGE STATUS	DISCHARGE PLACE	AGE ADMIT	AGE DISCH
1 BARNES, Ulysses	10.2	Boys, Ltl	Ron	Simmons	01/14/85	B	M	03/13/92	04/26/94	25.45	S	at home	7.2	9.3
2 HASTINGS, Ronnie	7.4	Boys, Ltl	Robert	Simmons	10/22/87	W	M	07/08/92	02/10/94	19.13	S	at home	4.7	6.3
3 STEARNS, Jay	11.0	Boys, Ltl	Dan	Simmons	03/16/84	W	M	09/13/92	04/12/94	18.94	S	at home	8.5	10.1
4 CA,VIN, Joseph	11.1	Boys, Ltl	James	Simmons	02/10/84	W	M	06/18/93	12/20/94	18.08	U	residential	9.4	10.9
5 LANDRY, John	10.4	Boys, Ltl	Dan	Simmons	10/31/84	B	M	01/04/93	07/01/94	17.85	U	residential	8.2	9.7
6 ANTOINE, Charles	15.5	Boys, Oldr	B. J.	Johnson	10/13/79	B	M	11/24/92	05/22/94	17.88	S	at home	13.1	14.6
7 BROWN, Chris	13.0	Boys, Oldr	George	Simmons	04/02/82	W	M	03/13/93	08/20/94	17.26	S	at home	10.9	12.4
8 CASTILLE, Juan	14.7	Boys, Oldr	Aaron	Johnson	07/12/80	HS	M	11/01/92	04/27/94	17.82	S	at home	12.3	13.8
9 DUBBINS, Henry	15.4	Boys, Oldr	B. J.	Johnson	11/10/79	W	M	05/02/93	12/01/94	19.00	S	at home	13.5	15.1
10 HEFFERNAN, Charles	13.4	Boys, Oldr	George	Simmons	10/28/81	W	M	06/06/93	10/03/94	15.91	S	at home	11.6	12.9
11 MARTIN, Anthony R.	13.3	Boys, Oldr	George	Simmons	12/22/81	W	M	05/23/92	03/13/94	21.67	S	at home	10.4	12.2
12 ROBERTS, Matthew	15.7	Boys, Oldr	Mike	Johnson	07/17/79	W	M	11/30/91	02/12/94	26.47	S	at home	12.4	14.6
13 WILLIAMS, Isaac	15.8	Boys, Oldr	Mike	Johnson	06/22/79	B	M	09/28/90	11/30/94	50.10	S	at home	11.3	15.4
14 DETWEILER, George	17.8	Boys, Sr	Louis	Lewis	06/04/77	W	M	11/11/92	10/15/94	23.11	S	at home	15.4	17.4
15 FREEMAN, Barry	20.6	Boys, Sr	Carl	Lewis	08/20/74	B	M	11/03/85	10/10/94	107.28	S	independent	11.2	20.1
16 JOHNSON, Aaron	16.4	Boys, Sr	Ed	Johnson	11/01/78	B	M	08/15/93	11/22/94	15.25	S	at home	14.8	16.1
17 KAUCHER, John	17.7	Boys, Sr	Ed	Lewis	07/17/77	W	M	05/25/92	06/15/94	24.69	S	at home	14.9	16.9
18 PHONG, Nguyen	19.9	Boys, Sr	Carl	Lewis	05/20/75	A	M	11/15/90	08/12/94	44.91	S	independent	15.5	19.2
19 WERNER, Marvin	17.4	Boys, Sr	Carl	Lewis	11/13/77	W	M	08/16/89	11/01/94	62.56	S	at home	11.8	17.0
20 WOJCIECHOWSKI, Stanley	17.4	Boys, Sr	Louis	Lewis	11/01/77	W	M	10/12/91	10/15/94	36.13	S	independent	13.9	17.0
21 MONROE, Arthur	16.3	Boys, Sr	Nat	Johnson	12/30/78	W	M	02/02/93	10/15/94	20.38	U	corrections	14.1	15.8
22 BROWN, Ebony	11.9	Grls, Ltl	Brenda	Weinstein	05/04/83	B	F	03/01/93	03/06/94	12.16	S	at home	9.8	10.8
23 KENNEDY, Raenel	11.3	Grls, Ltl	Anne	Weinstein	11/28/83	B	F	03/14/92	02/28/94	23.54	S	at home	8.3	10.3
24 SMITH, Erica	11.1	Grls, Ltl	Brenda	Weinstein	02/25/84	B	F	02/28/93	11/15/94	20.55	S	at home	9.0	10.7
25 STOFFER, Melanie	9.4	Grls, Ltl	Anne	Weinstein	10/25/85	W	F	12/18/92	04/01/94	15.42	S	at home	7.1	8.4
26 CARLETTO, Dolores	14.1	Grls, Ltl	Brenda	Weinstein	02/25/81	HS	F	10/10/94	12/20/94	2.33	U	at home	13.6	13.8
27 AARON, Arlene	17.0	Grls, Oldr	Denise	Weinstein	04/18/78	W	F	09/23/91	03/01/94	29.26	S	at home	13.4	15.9
28 DORSEY, Darlene	17.9	Grls, Oldr	Jean	Lewis	05/11/77	W	F	08/21/90	04/28/94	44.25	S	at home	13.3	17.0
29 HERTZOG, Henrietta	13.2	Grls, Oldr	Barbara	Weinstein	05/02/78	W	F	07/31/91	02/02/94	30.15	S	at home	13.2	15.8
30 MURDOCK, Deidra	20.3	Grls, Oldr	Jean	Lewis	12/13/74	W	F	05/02/91	11/15/94	42.51	S	independent	16.4	19.9
31 PURNELL, Judith	20.5	Grls, Oldr	Barbara	Lewis	09/16/74	W	F	07/23/91	09/21/94	38.01	S	independent	16.8	20.0
32 WAGNER, Tyra	17.9	Grls, Oldr	Denise	Weinstein	05/11/77	B	F	11/23/91	07/15/94	31.73	S	at home	14.5	17.2
33 GONZALES, Rachel	16.9	Grls, Oldr	Mary	Weinstein	04/27/78	HS	F	02/20/91	07/31/94	41.33	U	runaway	12.8	16.3

Discharge Status   S Successful   U Unsuccessful

FIGURE 16.4: Discharge by Sex at the Charity Treatment Center

04/04/95

CHARITY TREATMENT CENTER
Discharge by Sex
1994

NAME	AGE	LIVING UNIT	PRIMARY STAFF	THERAPIST	DOB	RACE	SEX	ADMIT DATE	DISCH DATE	MONTHS SERVICE	DISCHARGE STATUS	DISCHARGE PLACE	AGE ADMIT	AGE DISCH
1 AARON, Arlene	17.0	Grls, Oldr	Denise	Weinstein	04/18/78	W	F	09/23/91	03/01/94	29.26	S	at home	13.4	15.9
2 BROWN, Ebony	11.9	Grls, Ltl	Brenda	Weinstein	05/04/83	B	F	03/01/93	03/06/94	12.16	S	at home	9.8	10.8
3 DORSEY, Darlene	17.9	Grls, Oldr	Jean	Lewis	05/11/77	W	F	08/21/90	04/28/94	44.25	S	at home	13.3	17.0
4 HERTZOG, Henrietta	16.9	Grls, Oldr	Barbara	Weinstein	05/02/78	W	F	07/31/91	02/02/94	30.15	S	at home	13.2	15.8
5 KENNEDY, Raenel	11.3	Grls, Ltl	Anne	Weinstein	11/28/83	B	F	03/14/92	02/28/94	23.54	S	at home	8.3	10.3
6 MURDOCK, Deidra	20.3	Grls, Oldr	Jean	Lewis	12/13/74	W	F	05/02/91	11/15/94	42.51	S	independent	16.4	19.9
7 PURNELL, Judith	20.5	Grls, Oldr	Barbara	Lewis	09/16/74	W	F	07/23/91	09/21/94	38.01	S	independent	16.8	20.0
8 SMITH, Erica	11.1	Grls, Ltl	Brenda	Weinstein	02/25/84	B	F	02/28/93	11/15/94	20.55	S	at home	9.0	10.7
9 STOFFER, Melanie	9.4	Grls, Ltl	Anne	Weinstein	10/25/85	W	F	12/18/92	04/01/94	15.42	S	at home	7.1	8.4
10 WAGNER, Tyra	17.9	Grls, Oldr	Denise	Weinstein	05/11/77	B	F	11/23/91	07/15/94	31.73	S	at home	14.5	17.2
11 CARLETTO, Dolores	14.1	Grls, Ltl	Brenda	Weinstein	02/25/81	HS	F	10/10/94	12/20/94	2.33	U	at home	13.6	13.8
12 GONZALES, Rachel	16.9	Grls, Oldr	Mary	Weinstein	04/27/78	HS	F	02/20/91	07/31/94	41.33	U	runaway	12.8	16.3
13 ANTOINE, Charles	15.5	Boys, Oldr	B. J.	Johnson	10/13/79	B	M	11/24/92	05/22/94	17.88	S	at home	13.1	14.6
14 BARNES, Ulysses	10.2	Boys, Ltl	Ron	Simmons	01/14/85	B	M	03/13/92	04/26/94	25.45	S	at home	7.2	9.3
15 BROWN, Chris	13.0	Boys, Oldr	George	Simmons	04/02/82	B	M	03/13/93	08/20/94	17.26	S	at home	10.9	12.4
16 CASTILLE, Juan	14.7	Boys, Oldr	Aaron	Johnson	07/12/80	HS	M	11/01/92	04/27/94	17.82	S	at home	12.3	13.8
17 DETWEILER, George	17.8	Boys, Sr	Louis	Lewis	06/04/77	W	M	11/11/92	10/15/94	23.11	S	at home	15.4	17.4
18 DUBBINS, Henry	15.4	Boys, Oldr	B. J.	Johnson	11/10/79	W	M	05/02/93	12/01/94	19.00	S	at home	13.5	15.1
19 FREEMAN, Barry	20.6	Boys, Sr	Carl	Lewis	08/20/74	B	M	11/03/85	10/10/94	107.28	S	independent	11.2	20.1
20 HASTINGS, Ronnie	7.4	Boys, Ltl	Robert	Simmons	10/22/87	W	M	07/08/92	02/10/94	19.13	S	at home	4.7	6.3
21 HEFFERNAN, Charles	13.4	Boys, Oldr	George	Simmons	10/28/81	W	M	06/06/93	10/03/94	15.91	S	at home	11.6	12.9
22 JOHNSON, Aaron	16.4	Boys, Sr	Ed	Johnson	11/01/78	B	M	08/15/93	11/22/94	15.25	S	at home	14.8	16.1
23 KAUCHER, John	17.7	Boys, Sr	Ed	Lewis	07/17/77	W	M	05/25/92	06/15/94	24.69	S	at home	14.9	16.9
24 MARTIN, Anthony R.	13.3	Boys, Oldr	George	Simmons	12/22/81	W	M	05/23/92	03/13/94	21.67	S	at home	10.4	12.2
25 PHONG, Nguyen	19.9	Boys, Sr	Carl	Lewis	05/20/75	A	M	11/15/90	08/12/94	44.91	S	independent	15.5	19.2
26 ROBERTS, Matthew	15.7	Boys, Oldr	Mike	Johnson	07/17/79	W	M	11/30/91	02/12/94	26.47	S	at home	12.4	14.6
27 STEARNS, Jay	11.0	Boys, Ltl	Dan	Simmons	03/16/84	W	M	09/13/92	04/12/94	18.94	S	at home	8.5	10.1
28 WERNER, Marvin	17.4	Boys, Sr	Carl	Lewis	11/13/77	W	M	08/16/89	11/01/94	62.56	S	at home	11.8	17.0
29 WILLIAMS, Isaac	15.8	Boys, Oldr	Mike	Johnson	06/22/79	B	M	09/28/90	11/30/94	50.10	S	at home	11.3	15.4
30 WOJCIECHOWSKI, Stanley	17.4	Boys, Sr	Louis	Lewis	11/01/77	W	M	10/12/91	10/15/94	36.13	S	independent	13.9	17.0
31 CA,VIN, Joseph	11.1	Boys, Ltl	James	Simmons	02/10/84	W	M	06/18/93	12/20/94	18.08	U	at home	9.4	10.9
32 LANDRY, John	10.4	Boys, Ltl	Dan	Simmons	10/31/84	B	M	01/04/93	07/01/94	17.85	U	residential	8.2	9.7
33 MONROE, Arthur	16.3	Boys, Sr	Nat	Johnson	12/30/78	W	M	02/02/93	10/15/94	20.38	U	corrections	14.1	15.8

Discharge Status   S Successful   U Unsuccessful

FIGURE 16.5: Discharge by Length of Stay at the Charity Treatment Center

04/04/95

CHARITY TREATMENT CENTER
Discharge by Length of Stay
1994

NAME	AGE	LIVING UNIT	PRIMARY STAFF	THERAPIST	DOB	RACE	SEX	ADMIT DATE	DISCH DATE	MONTHS SERVICE	DISCHARGE STATUS	PLACE	AGE ADMIT	AGE DISCH
1 BROWN, Ebony	11.9	Grls, Ltl	Brenda	Weinstein	05/04/83	B	F	03/01/93	03/06/94	12.16	S	at home	9.8	10.8
2 JOHNSON, Aaron	16.4	Boys, Sr	Ed	Johnson	11/01/78	B	M	08/15/93	11/22/94	15.25	S	at home	14.8	16.1
3 STOFFER, Melanie	9.4	Grls, Ltl	Anne	Weinstein	10/25/85	W	F	12/18/92	04/01/94	15.42	S	at home	7.1	8.4
4 HEFFERNAN, Charles	13.4	Boys, Oldr	George	Simmons	10/28/81	B	M	06/06/93	10/03/94	15.91	S	at home	11.6	12.9
5 BROWN, Chris	13.0	Boys, Oldr	George	Simmons	04/02/82	B	M	03/13/93	08/20/94	17.26	S	at home	10.9	12.4
6 CASTILLE, Juan	14.7	Boys, Oldr	Aaron	Johnson	07/12/80	HS	M	11/01/92	04/27/94	17.82	S	at home	12.3	13.8
7 ANTOINE, Charles	15.5	Boys, Oldr	B. J.	Johnson	10/13/79	B	M	11/24/92	05/22/94	17.88	S	at home	13.1	14.6
8 STEARNS, Jay	11.0	Boys, Ltl	Dan	Simmons	03/16/84	W	M	09/13/92	04/12/94	18.94	S	at home	8.5	10.1
9 DUBBINS, Henry	15.4	Boys, Oldr	B. J.	Johnson	11/10/79	W	M	05/02/93	12/01/94	19.00	S	at home	13.5	15.1
10 HASTINGS, Ronnie	7.4	Boys, Ltl	Robert	Simmons	10/22/87	W	M	07/08/92	02/10/94	19.13	S	at home	4.7	6.3
11 SMITH, Erica	11.1	Grls, Ltl	Brenda	Weinstein	02/25/84	W	F	02/28/93	11/15/94	20.55	S	at home	9.0	10.7
12 MARTIN, Anthony R.	13.3	Boys, Oldr	George	Simmons	12/22/81	W	M	05/23/92	03/13/94	21.67	S	at home	10.4	12.2
13 DETWEILER, George	17.8	Boys, Sr	Louis	Lewis	06/04/77	W	M	11/11/92	10/15/94	23.11	S	at home	15.4	17.4
14 KENNEDY, Raenel	11.3	Grls, Ltl	Anne	Weinstein	11/28/83	B	F	03/14/92	02/28/94	23.54	S	at home	8.3	10.3
15 KAUCHER, John	17.7	Boys, Sr	Ed	Lewis	07/17/77	W	M	05/25/92	06/15/94	24.69	S	at home	14.9	16.9
16 BARNES, Ulysses	10.2	Boys, Ltl	Ron	Simmons	01/14/85	B	M	03/13/92	04/26/94	25.45	S	at home	7.2	9.3
17 ROBERTS, Matthew	15.7	Boys, Oldr	Mike	Johnson	07/17/79	W	M	11/30/91	02/12/94	26.47	S	at home	12.4	14.6
18 AARON, Arlene	17.0	Grls, Oldr	Denise	Weinstein	04/18/78	W	F	09/23/91	03/01/94	29.26	S	at home	13.4	15.9
19 HERTZOG, Henrietta	16.9	Grls, Oldr	Barbara	Weinstein	05/02/78	W	F	07/31/91	02/02/94	30.15	S	at home	13.2	15.8
20 WAGNER, Tyra	17.9	Grls, Oldr	Denise	Weinstein	05/11/77	B	F	11/23/91	07/15/94	31.73	S	at home	14.5	17.2
21 WOJCIECHOWSKI. Stanley	17.4	Boys, Sr	Louis	Lewis	11/01/77	W	M	10/12/91	10/15/94	36.13	S	independent	13.9	17.0
22 PURNELL, Judith	20.5	Grls, Oldr	Barbara	Lewis	09/16/74	W	F	07/23/91	09/21/94	38.01	S	independent	16.8	20.0
23 MURDOCK, Deidra	20.3	Grls, Oldr	Jean	Lewis	12/13/74	W	F	05/02/91	11/15/94	42.51	S	independent	16.4	19.9
24 DORSEY, Darlene	17.9	Grls, Oldr	Jean	Lewis	05/11/77	W	F	08/21/90	04/28/94	44.25	S	at home	13.3	17.0
25 PHONG, Nguyen	19.9	Boys, Sr	Carl	Lewis	05/20/75	A	M	11/15/90	08/12/94	44.91	S	independent	15.5	19.2
26 WILLIAMS, Isaac	15.8	Boys, Oldr	Mike	Johnson	06/22/79	B	M	09/28/90	11/30/94	50.10	S	at home	11.3	15.4
27 WERNER, Marvin	17.4	Boys, Sr	Carl	Lewis	11/13/77	W	M	08/16/89	11/01/94	62.56	S	at home	11.8	17.0
28 FREEMAN, Barry	20.6	Boys, Sr	Carl	Lewis	08/20/74	B	M	11/03/85	10/10/94	107.28	S	independent	11.2	20.1
29 CARLETTO, Dolores	14.1	Grls, Ltl	Brenda	Weinstein	02/25/81	HS	F	10/10/94	12/20/94	2.33	U	at home	13.6	13.8
30 LANDRY, John	10.4	Boys, Ltl	Dan	Simmons	10/31/84	B	M	01/04/93	07/01/94	17.85	U	residential	8.2	9.7
31 CALVIN, Joseph	11.1	Boys, Ltl	James	Simmons	02/10/84	W	M	06/18/93	12/20/94	18.08	U	at home	9.4	10.9
32 MONROE, Arthur	16.3	Boys, Sr	Nat	Johnson	12/30/78	W	M	02/02/93	10/15/94	20.38	U	corrections	14.1	15.8
33 GONZALES, Rachel	16.9	Grls, Oldr	Mary	Weinstein	04/27/78	HS	F	02/20/91	07/31/94	41.33	U	runaway	12.8	16.3

Discharge Status   S Successful
   U Unsuccessful

party runaway, the avoidance runaway, and the runaway home. Few children will run away from a place in which their needs are being met. However, few places can meet all of a given child's needs all the time. Moreover, a few children seem to have needs that perhaps should not be met—the need for complete freedom from adults or a need for drugs. The freedom runner is especially difficult to treat and may be dangerous to other children. Excessive problems with runaways should prompt a close look at the milieu. Too many runaways indicate that children's needs might not be being met—needs for security, stimulation, respect, nurturance, affection, attention, opportunity, and possibly treatment.

Staff burnout has implications for the milieu as well. Burned out staff are not good for children. They are unenthusiastic, often angry with the children or with the program. Problems with staff burnout suggest attention to hiring procedures and initial expectations as well as to routine responsibilities. Staff who enjoy children and who are allowed to enjoy children in their work are not likely to burn out. Burnout comes from conflict, from conflicting expectations and demands that the individual cannot meet. While problem children (and even normal children) can be expected to pose some stress, stress also derives from the demands of the agency. The agency can do little about stress caused by the children—that's the nature of the job. It can do something to reduce the stress it may cause and hire staff who do not get too stressed by children.

Information is extremely important in residential treatment. In emergencies, staff and supervisors need accurate and up-to-date information about children; treatment and supervisory or administrative personnel need statistical data to monitor the program and make necessary adjustments when treatment is not progressing satisfactorily. Spreadsheet programs, normally used in accounting, can manage a large amount of data and print out up-to-date information weekly or even daily. Data base programs may do an even better job but require different expertise.

17

Referral: The Continuum of Care Revisited

NEXT to the psychiatric hospital and the state juvenile correctional facility, the residential program is the most restrictive and probably the most expensive alternative. The decision to use residential treatment often depends on the alternatives that may be available and their effectiveness. Because of its restrictiveness and expense, residential treatment may not be sought out or recommended until all other options have been exhausted. While this would seem to be appropriately in the best interests of the child, it is not always so. When the decision for residential treatment is delayed too long past the point where it could be most effective, the child may have become so damaged or disturbed that even residential treatment may be hard-pressed to help.

Each failure in less restrictive settings takes its toll on a child. Such children suffer repeated rejections and continued blows to their self-esteem, or they learn that they can escape any unpleasantness or confrontation in any placement by misbehaving their way to another. They learn to avoid or fear commitment, not only to others but also to themselves. Even should they find a placement they like or that is good for them, they cannot feel secure. The need to feel secure is a fairly basic human need.

In order to feel secure, such children seem to have a need, conscious or unconscious, to know at exactly what point they might be removed from a foster home or a program. Their need to find that point sometimes appears to be almost pathologically consuming. They cannot be sure of exactly where that point is until they reach it. They seem almost to search for it by testing with increasingly severe behaviors. Of course, once they reach the point at which they will be thrown out, they get thrown out, or more accurately, thrown away. This is Multiple Placement Syndrome (see appendix A). It is a syndrome that is learned, taught by the system of child care in more than one locality.

In this chapter, we will consider the concepts of the least restrictive environment and permanency planning and how the principle of least restrictive environment sometimes seems to interfere with the permanency of the child's plan. Then we will consider once again the system of care as presented in chapter 4. This time we will consider some aspects of the system that make it more difficult for a child to receive optimum care and treatment. Then, we shall consider each component in terms of indications and contraindications for its usefulness. Not all components or programs are available in all jurisdictions.

Programs that appear to be similar do not all have the same strengths or limitations.

PERMANENCY PLANNING VERSUS THE LEAST RESTRICTIVE ENVIRONMENT

Permanency Planning

One of the most important things we can give a child is a sense of belonging. It is from this sense of belonging that the child develops a sense of identity. It provides a frame of reference from which the child can grow. It provides a base from which the child can begin to prepare and plan for his or her future. Least restrictive is important, but the best place for a child is the one that works, and the sooner we find it the better. If the least restrictive placement is the natural family, one of the qualities of most natural families is that they do not throw their children out. The next least restrictive placement may be the next placement that can manage the child without throwing her or him out, no matter what.

The Least Restrictive Environment

The concept of the least restrictive environment has permeated decisions relating to the care, treatment, and education of children during the past decade. It holds that children should be cared for, treated, and educated in the least restrictive environment that meets their needs. It is a legal concept. The burden of proof rests with the person or agency who has legal responsibility for the child to show that the environment in which the child is placed is the least restrictive environment that will meet the child's needs. The concept applies to the child's placement in school, the use of time-out in the school setting, any placement of the child outside the home, and the use of interventions in that placement. Under the pressure of this legal responsibility, those who make decisions for children tend to pick the least restrictive environment possible for the child. This may appear to be good.

If there is any doubt, the error tends towards the less restrictive rather than the more restrictive. This is very American. We give the child the benefit of the doubt. We give the child a chance. Unfortunately, while we are giving the child a chance to succeed in the least restrictive setting, we may lose sight of the fact that we are at the same time giving the child a chance to fail in that setting.

Failure of a child in a placement such as foster care family often results in another try in a similar setting. This may be tried several times before the child is moved into a "more restrictive" placement. Success in the more restrictive setting may lead to a return of the child to the less restrictive. When the move to the less restrictive setting fails for any reason, the child is faced with yet another failed placement, and very possibly additional less restrictive placements and failures until the child's history is such that only the most restrictive facilities, sometimes only a psychiatric hospital, will accept the child.

Children, no matter what their limitations or handicaps, seem to be able to learn from this process. They learn that they are difficult. They learn that adults cannot be trusted to manage them. They learn that adults will not stick by them. They learn that they have no idea where they will grow up, let alone where they will be next year, or even next month. They learn that they do not have to make any commitments. They learn that if they don't like something about their current home or placement they can change their placement. They learn that some placements are better than others, that no matter how good this placement may be, it's not ideal; the next one may be better, "hoping each time that the next leap will be the leap home" (Bellisario, 1991).

They learn that each placement must be tested to see whether or not it can withstand their difficult behaviors, a test few placements can pass, for each test passed by the placement requires yet another test. Such children have learned that no placement can manage them indefinitely. They learn that no matter what they do, the state will find a place for them. Suddenly, when they reach the age of eighteen, the state no longer provides, and they cannot provide for themselves.

For some children, this learning may be on a very cognitive level. For others, probably for most, it is precognitive, intuitive, almost instinctive. No matter. The results are the same. This is Multiple Placement Syndrome (see appendix A).

THE SYSTEM

If we think of "The System" that deals with children as a system and in terms of systems theory, then one glaring problem should come into focus: feedback. There is very little or no feedback. If we think in terms of management, then another problem comes into focus: accountability. Different agencies and different people within an agency are responsible for different aspects of a child's life at different times. Once a child comes to the attention of state agencies, especially when the child comes into custody, rarely is any one person ever responsible for the child's childhood or growth.

The child protection investigator who decides to remove a child from the home may transfer the case very quickly to another worker: a family caseworker, an adoptions worker, a placement specialist. The investigator is unlikely to get more than short-term feedback. Was the decision to leave the child in the home correct? Is the child better off for the removal?

The next worker places the child, and may stay in touch with the case. However, if the child is placed in an institution at some point, a new worker may become involved, especially if the institution is in another jurisdiction. The worker who places the child in the institution is then unlikely to receive feedback. When the child leaves the institution to return home, go to a foster home, or be placed in another institution, yet another worker may become responsible.

The probation officer works with the child until placement is decided upon. When that happens, a placement specialist handles the placement. Following placement, the case is transferred to the worker assigned as liaison for the particular agency or facility.

If the institution has no aftercare program, and many do not since aftercare is unfunded—only "beds" are funded—then the institution receives no systematic feedback following discharge. Nor does the worker who placed the child in the institution receive feedback after the child's discharge, since the case is likely to be transferred to yet another worker.

Did the institutional placement help? Is the child better off? Systems that receive no feedback cannot adjust themselves to meet their purposes as various factors change. When two or more people or agencies are responsible for the same thing, each may assume that another will do it. When no one does, it is very difficult to hold anyone accountable.

Very often, we don't even talk about children. Nor do we talk about treatment. We talk about "beds" and "placements" and "care." "I need a hospital bed for a twelve-year-old." "We have four boy beds open." Nor do we talk about families. "I need a foster placement for a five-year-old black male."

Of course, when we talk about a hospital bed, we assume the treatment that a hospital bed implies. This is dangerous. All hospital beds may be very much the same. Hospital treatment, on the other hand, may vary greatly from one hospital to another. There are cases in which "hospital mistreatment" might better describe what happens.

What do we mean when we say a child needs hospitalization? Or residential placement? Or group home placement? Or placement in a more structured setting? Does it not make more sense to say that a child needs care, nurturing, help with school, family therapy, treatment for sexual abuse, treatment for aggressive behavior, or treatment to improve self-image? Treatment for substance abuse? Needs to learn social skills? Needs intensive supervision to protect herself? Needs intensive supervision to keep him from harming others? Needs his emotions straightened out? Needs help with peer relations?

If we know what kind of care or treatment we want for a child, we might be able to find it. We might know if and when we get it. We might also know when we don't get it. We might even begin to develop some knowledge about which programs are good at what specific things. We might even improve our abilities to identify the least restrictive setting that can *reasonably* be expected to provide for a child's needs.

Some programs are good at helping children with school. Some are better than others at working with families. Some are very good at supervision and behavior management, others at nurturing. The best program in the country at working with families may not be very good with a poor family with no car who lives sixty miles away, especially when there is no public transportation. An open program near public transportation and a child's home community may not be very effective if the child has a history of running away impulsively and hiding out with friends. A nearby residential program that can facilitate regular family contact may be less restrictive than a group home in a large city ninety miles away when transportation and long distance phone bills are obstacles to regular family contact.

A lightly staffed facility may not be the ideal for a "busy" ten-year-old who requires near constant adult attention and who interacts aggressively with peers to get it. Perhaps a therapeutic foster family with no other children might be more appropriate to his needs. A thirteen-year-old girl who frequently breaks things and punches holes in plaster walls or one who behaves seductively towards men, may not work out well in a family's home; a well-staffed group home might provide the needed supervision and treatment. An acting out fifteen-year-old whose family simply can't seem to manage him might do very well in a therapeutic foster family. But if the therapeutic family program is unable to work effectively with the natural family and the child together, problems should be expected to resume when he returns home.

Outpatient Services: Education, Counseling, or Therapy

A wide variety of programs and services are available in communities for children and families in need. Some are publicly funded, others accept insurance or offer sliding fee scales based on family income.

Education

Under Public Law 94-142, the Education of All Handicapped Children Act, public schools are required to provide a variety of services to educate children with problems. These services may range from resource classrooms and counseling to special education classes and therapy.

Indications. Special education services may be effective when:

1. Problems are primarily school-related—paying attention in class, completing assignments, socialization and peer relations, learning disabilities, adult relations more problematic outside the family than within.
2. Family is supportive of the school and education, or at the least does not actively undermine the school.
3. Peer associations in the school are affecting performance.

Contraindications. Special education services are less likely to be sufficient when:

1. The family actively undermines the school.
2. The family is ineffectual at getting the child to school.
3. The child is evidencing problems with adults, limits, instructions, criticism, etc., in the home and the community as well as in the school.

Parenting Help

Many communities offer programs for parents, from parent education such as Popkin's Active Parenting™ programs to parent support groups and Tough Love.

Indications. Parent support groups and teaching parent skills can be expected to help when:

1. Problems are recent.
2. Problems are minor.
3. The family is seeking help.
4. The family needs to learn better ways in addition to rather than "in place of" what they are already doing with the child.
5. These groups are used in addition to or in conjunction with other interventions.
6. When the parent feels a responsibility for the child, even when the parent may not accept responsibility for the child's problems.

Contraindications. Parent support groups or teaching parent empowerment techniques are less likely to be effective when:

1. The family is abusive rather than "helpless."
2. Problems are severe.
3. Problems are long-standing.
4. No other supports or interventions are being provided.
5. The parent does not accept reasonable responsibility for the child.

Counseling

Outpatient counseling may be available from clergy, community mental health centers, family service agencies, and private practitioners.

Indications. Counseling may be helpful for parents and/or a child when:

1. The individual is failing to identify alternatives and evaluate consequences.
2. The individual would like to do better but doesn't know how.
3. The individual is making poor decisions.

4. Values are in pretty good shape.
5. Feelings are in pretty good shape.

Contraindications. Counseling is less likely to be effective when parents or a child:

1. Seem to care little about consequences.
2. Have little desire to improve, or see no need to improve.
3. Have serious problems with values—lying and deception of others and/or self, theft, aggression and violence, substance abuse, etc.
4. Have serious problems with feelings—poor self-image, anger or rage, strong desire or need for retribution and/or punishment, hate, etc.

Therapy

Therapy may be available from the same sources as counseling, as well as from some psychiatric hospitals.

Indications. Outpatient therapy may be helpful for parents or children when:

1. Severe problems are fairly recent (less than one year).
2. Problems are relatively minor although of longer duration.
3. The individuals involved desire assistance in making changes.
4. It is used in conjunction with or support of more intensive in-home interventions, below.
5. It is used in support of the family and child when the child is returning from out-of-home placement.

Contraindications. Outpatient therapy should not be expected to be sufficient for:

1. Severe problems of a long-standing nature.
2. Families with multiple and interrelated problems, especially when no other interventions are being employed.
3. Families who feel little or no need to change.

4. The situation is extremely volatile and poses some threat to someone's safety.

Probation Services for the Child

Probation services are available when the child has been adjudicated as unruly or ungovernable for status offenses or adjudicated delinquent for criminal behavior.

Indications

Probation services may be helpful:

1. To motivate (coerce) children and parents to do better.
2. To motivate children and parents to participate in available school and educational programs, counseling, or therapy, or to cooperate with in-home services.

Contraindications

Probation may not be effective when:

1. Values are seriously deviant.
2. The child has little or no fear of incarceration.
3. The family has little fear of legal sanctions.
4. Detention and incarceration are available only for the most serious offenses due to overcrowding.
5. Additional services are not available, cannot be arranged, or have been tried and found ineffective.

In-Home Services

Case Management

Case management services may be available from child welfare agencies for children of families who are reported for abuse or neglect, from probation officers, or from community mental health. Mental health case managers generally will have caseloads of ten to thirty, other agencies generally have much larger caseloads of sixty to 120. Case managers visit the family in the home and commu-nity and help children and families to utilize other community resources.

Indications. Case management services can be expected to be effective when:

1. The family would like to do better but is overwhelmed by multiple problems.
2. When sufficient other services are available to be "managed" and coordinated.
3. When the family lacks other support systems.
4. When case managers are not overwhelmed with too many cases.

Contraindications. Case management services are less likely to be effective when:

1. The family has little desire to change.
2. Other needed services are not available.
3. Case loads are large (twenty-five or more).
4. Problems are multiple, severe, and long-standing.

Family Preservation

Family preservation programs may be available through child welfare agencies, juvenile corrections agencies, or mental health agencies. Most programs offer short-term, intensive in-home crisis services for a few weeks' duration when placement of a child appears to be imminent. Such programs seek solutions to practical problems, resolution of family conflicts, and linkage with more long-term support (Hartman, 1993). A few programs are long term.

Indications. Family preservation programs can be expected to be effective when:

1. The family recognizes some need to change.
2. The parents seem frustrated and "helpless."
3. The family has fairly good values but limited skills.
4. The family needs to learn new methods, new ways of managing and relating.
5. It is used in conjunction with other services,

such as in-home crisis intervention, respite care, case management, a parenting program, and outpatient services.

6. An especially difficult child returns from successful out-of-home treatment.
7. Sufficient longer term services such as case management and outpatient services can continue to support gains when the family preservation model is a short-term intervention.
8. The family preservation model is a long-term model (twelve months or more).

Contraindications. Family preservation is less likely to be effective when:

1. Parents are unwilling to accept responsibility or help.
2. Parents seem frustrated and "angry," hostile or vindictive.
3. Deviant values are firmly entrenched in the family system, especially with the parents.
4. Parents have difficulty learning or changing due to mental illness or mental retardation.
5. Parents have entrenched ways of interrelating, of dealing with their children, which they are resistant to giving up.
6. A child with multiple problems needs long-term treatment.
7. A family has multiple problems of a long-standing nature.
8. Substance abuse is present and untreated.
9. The needed longer term services in the continuum of care are not available for the family.

In-Home Crisis Intervention and Respite Care

In-home crisis services may involve an emergency response team that can be sent to a home when a child is experiencing a behavioral crisis. They may be able to provide workers in the home for up to several days or refer the child to a respite family for a few days. They have the ability to secure emergency psychiatric evaluations and emergency hospitalization, if needed.

Indications. In-home crisis intervention and respite care can be expected to be helpful:

1. For a crisis or problem of recent development.
2. In conjunction with other services.
3. As a temporary intervention until other services can be arranged.

Contraindications. In-home services and respite are less likely to be effective when:

1. Problems are multiple or long-standing.
2. Other services cannot be arranged.

Out-of-Home Placement

Inpatient Crisis Intervention in an Acute Care Unit

Although a very restrictive intervention, I have placed the acute care unit here because it is generally designed for brief crisis intervention with the goal of returning the child to the home or prior placement relatively quickly, within a few days or weeks. As such, it may be used to prevent longer term placements in less restrictive settings, but placements that may be more restrictive in that they may result in the child's being in an out-of-home placement for an extended period of time.

Indications. Acute inpatient care can be expected to be necessary and effective for:

1. Acute behavior of recent origin.
2. Suicidal behavior (Gardner, 1988).
3. Homicidal behavior (Gardner, 1988).
4. Substance abuse (Gardner, 1988).
5. Bulimia or anorexia (Gardner, 1988).
6. Establishing a pharmacological regime that cannot be established on an outpatient basis (Dalton & Forman, 1992).
7. Temporary, safe intervention with a seriously disturbed child for assessment, stabilization, and planning for long-term treatment and care.
8. Stabilization of a child with serious problems of a long-standing nature as a prelude to other treatment interventions, such as intensive in-home and outpatient care, group home, or residential placement.

Contraindications. Short-term acute care should not be expected to be effective when:

1. Problems have been long-standing, especially when no other interventions are being planned or when other interventions have been tried and failed.
2. The child is to return home and significant problems in the home cannot be addressed (Gardner, 1988).
3. When the hospital offers little real treatment (Gardner, 1988).
4. When the length of stay and discharge is governed more by financial considerations than by the success of treatment or the needs of the patient (Gardner, 1988).

Placement with Relatives

Very often, relatives can accept a child for a brief period of time in an emergency.

Indications. When short-term placement is necessary until assessments can be completed, or pending other placement decisions or arrangements, placement with relatives in some cases may be preferable to placement with strangers or institutional placements.

Contraindications. When the child is in need of treatment, or when family may resent or interfere with the child's placement with relatives, placement of a child with relatives may be problematic.

Adoption

Public Law 964-272, the Adoption Assistance and Child Welfare Act of 1980, requires states to terminate parental rights and proceed with adoption or some other permanent plan when it is determined that a child cannot return home.

Indications. Adoption may be the best alternative to the natural family when:

1. The child is free for adoption or can be expected to be freed for adoption in a reasonable time.

2. When the adoptive family is fully and accurately apprised of the child's needs and potential problems.
3. When the adoptive family is appropriate.
4. When there are reasonable grounds to believe that the child is not likely to pose problems beyond the abilities or willingness of the adoptive family.

Contraindications. Adoption may be problematic when:

1. A child with serious problems is placed in an adoptive home without reasonable attention to the child's special needs.
2. The adoptive placement serves as yet another failure for the child, delaying needed treatment and the possibility of a more successful adoption in the future.

Foster Care

Children who cannot live at home for a variety of reasons may be placed with a foster family. Foster families are generally recruited by child welfare agencies, given some training, and paid a stipend that offsets expenses of caring for the child.

Indications. Placement with a foster family can be expected to be successful when:

1. The child needs a temporary or permanent home.
2. The child's special needs are not severe and arrangements have been made to provide for those needs.
3. It has not been assumed that the child has no special needs in conjunction with his or her need for a temporary or new home.

Contraindications. Foster placements can be expected to fail, possibly in a manner that may be detrimental to the child, when:

1. The child has noted or unnoted special needs that are not addressed or for which provisions have not been made.

2. The child has a history of serious problems with authority.
3. The child has a history of serious problems with other children, peers or siblings, and other children, natural or foster, are present in the home. When those problems center around competition for adult attention, those problems can be expected to increase in foster placement.
4. The child has special problems that would be difficult for a capable natural family.
5. The foster family is not prepared for the child's special problems or is unwilling to deal with those problems.

Failed foster placement is often the first step in Multiple Placement Syndrome.

Therapeutic Family Care

Therapeutic foster families differ from other foster families in the amount of money, training, and support they receive. They are generally recruited by private agencies that have contracts with the state to provide the service. The agency provides the training, supervision, and on-call support and pays the family a salary.

Indications. Intensive, therapeutic family care can be expected to be of benefit when:

1. A child has special needs beyond the capabilities of the natural family.
2. The agency and family providing the therapeutic family care are prepared to meet the specific special needs of the specific child.
3. The child is to return home and the natural family is supportive of the placement, understands the reasons for the placement, and understands the nature of the "special" home.
4. The child is not expected to return home but may stay with the therapeutic family even after therapeutic purposes have been achieved, or when provisions have been made for the transition to a suitable placement after appropriate gains have been made.

Contraindicatons. Therapeutic family care may fail to achieve the desired results when:

1. The child is to eventually return home and significant problems within the natural family have been overlooked or untreated.
2. The child is not to return home, becomes attached to his or her new home and therapeutic family, then must leave when treatment has been completed to go into regular foster care with a new family. Therapeutic family care and treatment is considerably more expensive than foster care. Further, needs of other children for therapeutic families are likely to create pressure for moving a child who is doing well to foster care to open the treatment slot (bed). The original child is asked to "leave home" through no fault of his or her own, but for doing so well.
3. When the therapeutic family is unprepared for the nature, frequency, or severity of the child's special problems.
4. When the therapeutic family does not receive adequate support for crises, treatment, and possibly respite.
5. When the therapeutic family is new and the parents change their minds after a few weeks with their first child.

Shelter Care

Shelter care can provide for a child who needs immediate and temporary placement pending other arrangements.

Indications. Shelter care is indicated for children who cannot be readily placed with relatives and who do not need immediate specialized services.

Contraindications. Shelter care also poses some problems:

1. By its very nature, it is temporary. This means that it cannot provide security, a sense of belonging, and a foundation from which the child can proceed.

2. Programs that are designed to provide temporary care may not be structured or staffed to manage an aggressive child who may intimidate others or to provide the security an unusually vulnerable child may need.

3. Programs designed to provide temporary care may not be staffed or structured to be able to prevent more "experienced" youth from engaging in mischief or outright criminal behavior.

Runaway Shelters

Runaway shelters can provide a safe haven, crisis counseling, and referral for children that may save them from victimization on the streets or resorting to or continuing crime or prostitution to provide for themselves.

Indications. Runaway shelters may be helpful to youth who leave home because of:

1. Physical or sexual abuse.
2. Neglect.
3. Abandonment.
4. Severe disagreements with their parents.

Contraindications. Children who get caught up in the "adventure" of being free, even those with such home problems as suggested above, may use the shelter as a temporary haven, not from the home but from the street, only to return to the streets after a meal, bath, and safe night's sleep. In such situations, the child may use the shelter to avoid confrontation of more basic issues or problems.

Group Homes

With the variety of services possible under the name of group home, care must be taken in referring a child. Different group homes will have different strengths, capabilities, and limitations. The decision to refer to a group home should be based on the match between the child's needs for care, nurturance, supervision, and treatment, and a particular program's capabilities.

Group Home Staffed with Live-In Married Couple. Indications. Group homes staffed with a married couple have certain advantages and disadvantages. They can be expected to be helpful for:

1. Children who have skills in manipulating adults, playing one off against the other. (Assumes married couple is trained and communicates extremely well, providing a high level of consistency.)
2. Children who need and can benefit from exposure to and interaction with a married couple as a role model.
3. Children who can attach fairly readily to adults.
4. When therapeutic family care is indicated but unavailable.
5. Children who can benefit from and manage interaction with peers, including modeling, support, and possible criticism or confrontation.
6. Children who need and can benefit from interaction with the community.
7. Children who need and can benefit from public education.
8. Children who need some care and consistency for a long term but who are not likely to remain with a foster family for an extended period. Even when the houseparents turn over (job change), the child does not have to leave the home, but merely adjusts to the new houseparents when they arrive.

Contraindications. Group homes staffed by a married couple may not be sufficient for:

1. Children with fairly serious (severe or high frequency) aggressive behaviors against property, peers, or adults, especially females. While relief staff and supervisors may provide some relief to houseparents, the male houseparent can be expected to provide most physical interventions when required. Aggression against the family's natural children or the wife may be especially problematic and require the child's removal.

2. A change in houseparents due to job change may disrupt the program. This may be especially significant for newer residents.

3. Children who require very special services in school, especially when the community school's special educational services are limited.

4. Children who may pose a danger to other residents or the community—burglars, sexual offenders, those who use weapons, armed robbers.

5. Children who require specialized individual therapy when such is not provided as a component of the group home program.

6. Children who are to return home after treatment when the program does not or cannot provide family therapy to the child's family.

7. Children who can be expected to bring contraband into the program from the community, especially alcohol, drugs, or weapons.

8. Children who can be expected to take other children with them on runaway adventures.

9. Children who can be expected to intimidate other children when houseparents are sleeping, children who are especially vulnerable to such intimidation, or who may be seductive.

Group Home Staffed with Shift Personnel. Indications. Group homes staffed with shift personnel, including overnight staff who are awake, offer certain advantages over the houseparent model, yet suffer from certain disadvantages. They can be expected to be helpful for:

1. Children who have problems with aggressive behaviors. A number of staff will be involved at different times in providing necessary physical interventions.

2. Children with strong family ties who might have problems attaching to another couple, especially if natural parents can be expected to interfere.

3. Children who need and can benefit from public school and other community ties.

4. Isolated children who have problems attaching to adults. The number of personnel on staff, different races, sexes, and cultural backgrounds, as well as different interests—sports, academics, cooking, music, crafts, art, drama, and more—make it more possible for a "different" child to find a role model, as well as to expand his or her interests.

5. Children who require individual or family therapy when such is a part of the program.

6. Children who cannot tolerate another loss of a significant adult. Even when one or two staff members leave, four or five, including a supervisor or social worker, will remain, as will administrative continuity and program identity.

Contraindications. Group homes staffed with shift personnel may have difficulties with:

1. Children who are especially good at manipulation. Such children are amazing in their abilities to play off the many adults against each other. Communication from one shift to another, with days off, etc., makes consistency a bit more difficult than with a married couple, although careful supervision and various communication techniques help. Moreover, such children are superb at finding at least one staff to take their side, to advocate for them.

2. Children who can be expected to pose problems because of contact with the community—crime, contraband, etc.

3. Children who can be expected to take others with them on runaway.

4. Children who require psychotropic medication. Such programs may be too small to have staff who have the monitoring of medication as a main and primary responsibility. Too many other responsibilities may interfere, leading to security lapses or too many missed dosages.

5. Children who require more special services from school than the public schools can provide.

Residential Treatment

Given the tremendous variety of programs available under the label of residential treatment, it would be wonderful if one could just ask the residential treatment program what kinds of problems and what kinds of children it treated successfully. Some seem to know exactly, others seem very vague, to have no idea. Still others seem to think they can handle almost anything, then blame the child who has to be removed because "he isn't working out," or "she is not able to benefit from the milieu."

Indications and Contraindications—Some Guidelines.

1. The variety of problems that residential treatment programs can handle successfully is almost endless.
2. The variety of problems a given program can handle is limited.
3. Know what the child needs.
4. Know what problems the child can be expected to pose. Let the program know exactly what they are likely to be. Do not minimize them.
5. Look for a commitment from the program that it *can* manage and treat expected problems. Do not accept "We will accept the child on a trial basis," or "We will give the child a chance."
6. Ask the program what their success rate is. Ask them what it is with children like the one you are referring. If they have no idea, be wary.
7. Ask the program how they measure their success rate. Many programs claim successful discharge when a child goes to a "less restrictive environment." If the child goes to a less restrictive environment and promptly fails, the program did not do its job; it is still likely, however, to count the discharge as a success. If the program provides no follow-up, if it has no idea how a child is doing three to six months after discharge, then the program is getting very little or *no* feedback. Its systems cannot adjust themselves.
8. Ask the program how it manages behavioral problems. If its consequences are "properly" punitive, it may be more oriented towards control rather than teaching, learning, or treatment.
9. Find out what behaviors are stressed or taught.

If the program has a point system, review it. When positive behaviors that are basic and important in all settings, (following instructions, accepting criticism, accepting limits, peer and adult relations, appropriate language, respect of property, etc.), learning and treatment can be expected to generalize, at least somewhat, to other settings after discharge. When the behaviors that are emphasized are negative, or appear to be designed to make good residents (no fighting, no cursing, no stealing, makes bed, does chores, obeys staff, long lists of rules), then learning and treatment are likely to be very specific to the program with little to carry over in other settings after discharge.

10. If the child requires medication, ask how the program will determine if or when the child no longer needs medication. The child or family is very likely to make this determination after discharge if the program cannot. They are very likely to do it in a manner and setting that are not likely to result in a successful discontinuation of medication. If you are satisfied that the program effectively reviews medication, you are more likely to be confident when the program tells you that medication after discharge is required. Do not take medication for granted.
11. If the child is to be returned home, know what the family needs. Find out if the program can provide for any of those needs. Find out how the program transitions a child home, how it prepares the family and the child.
12. If the child is not to be returned home, find out how long the program will care for the child in addition to providing treatment. See whether or not you can get a commitment from the program to accept the child back if a discharge does not work out.
13. Find out what the program's policy and procedures are for discharging a child who poses especially difficult problems, or who fails to progress. How many children are discharged unsuccessfully before 90 days? If the percentage is high (10 or 20 percent), then the program

does not seem to be clear on the kinds of children it can treat and is accepting children it cannot treat. Or the program is giving up too easily on children.

Hospitalization

As with residential programs, psychiatric hospitals providing for longer term treatment (as opposed to acute care units) vary in their abilities and in the treatment they provide. Placement may be funded by the private insurance of parents or by state funds, or the hospital might be operated by the state.

Indications. Hospitals are usually necessary for children who are:

1. Suicidal.
2. Homicidal.
3. Psychotic—out of touch with reality—hearing voices, seeing things, believing people who mean well are out to do them harm.
4. In need of intensive psychotherapy.
5. Abusing substances.
6. Bulimic or anorexic.
7. In need of medication in a closely supervised setting in order to identify appropriate medications and appropriate dosages.

Contraindications.

1. Hospitals are sometimes used for children who pose serious behavioral control problems and who are therefore not accepted by other programs or resources. Hospitals are very good at managing such problems (physical restraints and chemical restraints); some may not be as good at treating such problems; others may be excellent.

    Such problems require not only specific treatment, but also relatively long-term treatment. Hospitals that cannot provide long-term treatment for whatever reasons may be able only to prepare children to better adjust to a facility that can. Private hospitals that dis-

charge children when funds run out after a few months or even a few weeks may not even make preparations for such continued treatment.

2. Hospitals, especially when distant from the child's home and community, may not have the services and resources necessary to assist the child and family in the transition home. Treatment gains in the hospital may sometimes be expected to disintegrate upon the child's return to the pre-hospital environment, unless that environment has somehow changed.
3. For the child who approaches the age of eighteen in the hospital, the hospital may not be equipped to prepare the child/adult for the adult responsibilities of independent living, or arrange supports in the community.

Detention

Detention is a short-term, secure corrections placement for children who have committed a crime and are awaiting trial, for children who are in contempt of court for violating probation, and for children who have been sentenced to a correctional facility and are awaiting transfer.

Indications. Detention can be beneficial for children who have been having difficulties and who need temporary care. It gets their attention and may serve to motivate them to avoid the potential of future incarceration or residential placement.

Contraindications. Placement in detention may be counteproductive when:

1. Used as a threat and not delivered. Such facilities are so often overcrowded or in demand for severe criminal behavior that they are not available and cannot be used for status offenses—truancy, runaway, and violation of probation. They become meaningless and cause the enforcement capabilities of the juvenile justice system to lose credibility.
2. Used as a threat, having been depicted as violent and dangerous, as a place where boys are "turned into little girls." When the child gets

there and finds the facility not only safe but boring, the enforcement capabilities of the juvenile justice system again lose credibility, as do the adults who are attempting to coerce the child.

Corrections

Juvenile correctional facilities may be used only for children convicted of a criminal act and sentenced by the court.

Indications. Sentence to a juvenile correctional facility or training school may be necessary or productive when:

1. The child has committed dangerous criminal acts.
2. The child is not psychotic.
3. The child's behavior is seriously criminal.
4. It has not been used as a threat repeatedly but not delivered; i.e., we have not waited too long.
5. The facility has not only the ability to control but also the capability of providing meaningful educational services, counseling, and treatment.
6. The facility has sufficient controls to keep the child safe from brutalization from other residents and staff, which means also sufficient controls to prevent the child from brutalizing others.

Contraindications. Juvenile incarceration may be problematic for:

1. Children whose family is disinterested, or whose family cannot be involved because the facility is too far away. Such children are especially vulnerable to mistreatment by other residents and even staff.
2. Children who are highly susceptible to peers. Children who are placed in correctional facilities are likely to be exposed to deviant behaviors, attitudes, and values. When controls and supervision in such facilities are inadequate, deviance may be the dominant force in the milieu.

CONCLUSIONS

There are few guidelines for referring or placing children. Moreover, guidelines about what type of placement may be best for what type of child are especially difficult because of the individual differences within "types" of placements, and certainly within "types" of children and families. A given foster parent may offer more skills than a therapeutic family or some group homes. An agency that provides excellent therapeutic family care may place a child with a new family who changes its mind, has to relocate, or doesn't work out for some other reason. A good agency may undergo a major administrative change, with subsequent staff changes at other levels. A group home may have stronger treatment capabilities than available residential programs. Differences are endless.

Moreover, the issue may not be as simple as where to place the child within the continuum of care but rather how much of the continuum of care may be brought to bear for the child at home or in another placement. I suggest the following prioritized guidelines:

1. The needs of the child must come first. A child who does not have a place to stay is most clearly and urgently in need of care. The child most likely also has other needs—treatment needs. Know what they are. Seek placement for the total needs of the child.
2. Whatever treatment needs the child may have, the child's need for stability and a sense of belonging remain critical. The child's commitment to a family or program can be expected to be directly proportional to the commitment of the family or program to the child.
3. Stay one step ahead. What is the next placement going to be
   a. if this one doesn't work out?
   b. if this one works perfectly and the child "must" move to a "less restrictive" setting?
4. Do not err too often on the side of the least

restrictive alternative. Giving a child a "chance" in a less restrictive setting involves both giving the child the chance to succeed *and* giving the child a chance to fail. Children with a long history of failure do not do well with "chances" or opportunities and are extremely difficult to treat.

5. Know the capabilities of various placement and treatment resources.

6. The best placement is the one that can provide for the most of the child's needs—safety, care, security, education, growth, nurturance, development, treatment, a sense of belonging.

7. The poorest placement is the one that not only allows the child's problems to strengthen but also delays the identification of the proper intervention.

8. The most expensive placement is the one that leads to long-term care and a child who is unprepared for meeting adult responsibilities.

9. The most economical placement is the one that meets the child's needs and leads to a successful and lasting return home, when that is possible, or to responsible adult interdependence.

10. The least expensive placement is the one that works when it is found before it is too late.

11. A permanency plan should eventually provide a permanent placement.

SUMMARY

The concept of permanency planning, a legal mandate, requires state agencies to develop a permanency plan for the child's future. The principle of the least restrictive alternative, likewise a legal mandate, requires that a child receive care, treatment, and service in the most natural and family-like setting possible. It is often difficult to reconcile these two mandates in the best interests of the child. Fear of placing the child in a setting that is "too" restrictive often results in a lack of permanency.

Knowing what the child needs in terms of both care and treatment, and knowing the capabilities of the various components of the system of care, as well as the capabilities and limitations of specific programs within the various components, can help those responsible in making reasonable and informed decisions that can promote permanency in the least restrictive setting. These decisions will not be easy in the foreseeable future.

Appendix A

Multiple Placement Syndrome

THE essential feature of this syndrome is a history of three or more placements outside of the natural home with two or more of the most recent placements being of relatively short (six months or less) duration and terminated at least in part due to the child's misbehavior in the placement. Behavior problems may be relatively mild or severe, but they are remarkable for their tendency to increase or escalate over time following a new placement.

Defiant, hostile, or negativistic behaviors may be very similar to those seen in Oppositional Defiant Disorder. The behaviors are not characterized by their frequency so much as by their tendency to increase over time, or increase in intensity during intervention by adults. Behaviors do not involve the more serious violations of the rights of others outside the placement as seen in Conduct Disorder.

Age at onset. Although precursers may appear in early childhood, the syndrome typically appears in latency or early adolescence following two or more placements.

Course. The syndrome typically begins following a child's movement from one placement to another. Initial moves may be caused by factors not related to the child's behavior, such as removal from the natural home due to abuse, neglect, abandonment, or death of a parent. Subsequent moves from foster care may be due to the foster family's moving out of state, pregnancy with their own natural child, or other change in the foster family's living situation. At least one move must be due to the child's posing a behavioral problem that the family, or institution is not willing to accept. Behavior escalates in the new setting until the child is moved again.

The frequent change of placements makes it virtually impossible for the child to complete an education, form long-term attachments, or develop a network of social support. In many cases, the disturbance evolves into Conduct Disorder.

Impairment. While the initial impairment may range from mild to severe, the remarkable feature of this disorder is its progressive nature—behavior continues to escalate until placement is changed. Initial impairment may be greatest within the placement, but eventually occurs in the school setting and possibly in the community.

Complications. Institutional placement almost inevitably becomes necessary. Multiple institutional placement is common. Conduct Disorder is also a common complication.

Predisposing factors and prevalence. Children who have multiple placements are very likely to have some history of neglect, abandonment, or abuse beginning at an early age. Initial placement outside the natural home or a stable foster home is likely to occur prior to the age of eight to ten years.

The primary predisposing factor is two or more changes in primary caretaker causing disruption in the child's life, with the child's perceiving one or more moves as being at least in part due to some behavioral problem or other failing of the child.

Normal adjustment to a new placement may pose some problems for both the child and the family, especially if the family is unprepared for the problems that may be presented normally. Should the child present an Adjustment Disorder, possibly with Disturbance of Conduct or Disturbance of Mood and Conduct, the family may itself suffer unexpected stress.

With the failure of a placement for any reason, the child feels increasingly insecure in subsequent placements. The child needs to know the limits of the new placement, probably on a preconscious level. Can the new placement manage problems the child may present? Most often, the limit of the placement remains vague until the child passes it. The only way the child can find the limit of the new placement in hope of feeling secure is to exceed the limit, thus ending the placement.

The child comes to know that a new placement, possibly a better placement, maybe even return home, is just around the corner. The child has no need to abide by the rules, limits, and instructions of the current placement, for it will not last.

In either case, problem behaviors will escalate. They will be especially resistant to any interventions by adults. Problem behaviors often escalate during adult intervention to the point of destruction of property or physical aggression. Such children are very good at reading people and situations. They have a need to find the limit and the ability to identify the most sensitive areas.

They readily identify and test the most vulnerable areas: valued property, the family pet, the family's natural children, disrespect of adult authority, problems at school necessitating foster parent's missing work, running away, embarrassing the family in the community, disrespect of staff, excessive noncompliance, or aggression against staff in an institution.

It is a rare family that can withstand and outlast the escalating behavior of a child with Multiple Placement Disorder. Most group homes and many institutions are hard-pressed to maintain and treat such children. If the disorder is interrupted by a successful institutional placement, there is a tendency to seek to return the child to foster care, at which time the disorder resumes.

Due to the lack of stability and frequent disruption in their lives, such children reach adulthood with few social supports, minimal education, and few social skills, although their interpersonal skills on a superficial level are likely to be deceptively good.

Sex ratio. The pattern is more prevalent among boys than among girls because of the larger number of boys in placement. When adjustments are made for the higher numbers of boys in placement, differences according to sex disappear.

Familial pattern. A familial pattern such that the child cannot return home is typical—death of parents, incarceration, abandonment, severe dysfunction due to alcoholism or drug abuse, patterns of sexual abuse, or physical abuse.

Differential diagnosis. In Multiple Placement Syndrome all of the features of an Adjustment Disorder or Oppositional Defiant Disorder are likely to be present. For that reason, Multiple Placement Syndrome preempts those diagnoses. If the antisocial behavior meets the criteria for Conduct Disorder, a diagnosis of Conduct Disorder preempts a diagnosis of Multiple Placement Syndrome.

Any other diagnoses, such as Attention Deficit-Hyperactivity Disorder or Specific Developmental Disorders, should also be noted when present.

DIAGNOSTIC CRITERIA FOR MULTIPLE PLACEMENT SYNDROME

1. A history of two or more placements outside the natural home during which any of the following have occurred:
   a. Two or more placements ending in the past twelve months.
   b. Placement terminated within the past twelve months due to the child's behavior.

c. Two or more placements within the past three years of less than six months' duration.

2. Disturbance of conduct during the last six months during which at least five of the following have been present and at least one of which has been increasing in frequency or intensity:

   a. Often loses temper.
   b. Often argues with adults.
   c. Often refuses to follow instructions.
   d. Often refuses to follow rules or limits.
   e. Often refuses to accept criticism.
   f. Often refuses to accept ''no.''
   g. Often refuses to accept consequences.
   h. Has become physically aggressive with adults in the placement on two or more occasions.
   i. Has picked up a weapon in the home.
   j. Has been physically aggressive with other children in the placement three or more times.
   k. Has deliberately injured another child in the placement.
   l. Has deliberately destroyed property of others in the placement.
   m. Has often been in trouble in school, requiring parents or staff to go to the school.
   n. Often refuses school.
   o. Frequently withdraws from contact with others in the placement, refusing to communicate.
   p. Often does things to deliberately annoy others in the placement.
   q. Often blames others for his or her mistakes.
   r. Has run away two or more times, or one time but failed to return.
   s. Has stolen in the home.

CRITERIA FOR SEVERITY OF MULTIPLE PLACEMENT SYNDROME

Mild. Few conduct problems in excess of those required to make the diagnosis *and* problems cause only minor harm or inconvenience to others; little sign of escalation.

Moderate. Number of problems and effect on others intermediate with some escalation.

Severe. Many conduct problems in excess of those required to make the diagnosis, *or* problems that cause injury to others, significant damage to property or significant disruption of the placement, *or* marked escalation of a given problem.

Appendix B

Forms

Initial Treatment Plan

Name _____   Date _____

Admit Date _____   Living Unit _____

Staff Assigned _____   Room Assignment _____

Special Needs: _____

Medical _____

Medication _____   Dosage _____

_____   _____

_____   _____

Clothing _____

Diet: Regular _____   Special _____

Reason _____

Activity: Regular _____   Restricted _____

Reason _____

Special Concerns for Supervision _____

_____

Programming:

Educational Placement _____

Home Passes _____

Individual Therapy _____   Group _____   Family _____

Other _____

_____

Signatures:

Staff	date	Supervisor	date
Resident	date	Parent	date
State Worker	date	Other	date

FIGURE B.2: Assessment Summary for Multi-Modal Treatment

Assessment Summary for Multi-Modal Treatment

Pre-Admit ___   Admit ___

Name _____   Date _____   Admit Date _____   Reevaluation ___   Discharge ___

DOB _____   Age _____   Sex _____   Race/Ethnicity _____   Height _____   Weight _____
Presenting   Ideal   Ideal
Problems _____   Height _____   Weight _____

_____

_____

_____

                     Juvenile   State   Other
Referred By: Parents ___   Court ___   Agency ___   Agency ___   Other _____
Prior   Age at   Foster   Group   Correctional   Emergency
Placements ___   First ___   Families ___   Homes ___   Residential ___   Psychiatric ___   Institution ___   Shelter ___

Legal History: Charges/Arrests   Date   Age   Disposition and comments

_____   _____   ____   _____

_____   _____   ____   _____

_____   _____   ____   _____

Psychiatric by _____   Date _____

Impressions _____   Recommendations _____

_____   _____

_____   _____

_____   _____

_____   _____

Psychological by _____   Date _____

Verbal IQ _____   Reading Level _____   Recommendations _____

Performance _____   Math Level _____   _____

Full Scale _____   Spelling Level _____   _____

Comments _____

_____

_____

Assessment Summary for Multi-Modal Treatment
Page 2

Name _____   Date _____

Education   Current or   Current   Grade if no
              Last School _____   Grade _____   Failures _____

Regular Classes ___   Special Education ___   Classification _____

Academic Grades Last Report   Extra Curricular Activities _____

Reading   ___   _____

English   ___   Attendance _____

Math   ___   Detentions _____

Science   ___   Suspensions _____

Social Studies ___   Expulsions _____

Special Needs _____

Comments _____
_____

Key for attached assessment:

ISI   Insufficient information to evaluate

+   A strength for this child

0   Neither poses a problem nor serves as a particular strength

      Put "N/A" in this column (0) if this category is not relevant to this child, i.e., use of makeup for boys,
      absent parent in families where natural parents are still married and living together, etc.

-     Causes or contributes to significant limitation, impairment or dysfunction

!   Causes or contributes to critical limitation, impairment or dysfunction

Priority 1 Goals - For problems that require prompt and immediate attention. These problems are such that they may place the
                   resident or others in danger, or such that if not promptly addressed and improved, may pose a significant
                   obstacle to further treatment or the resident's continuation in the program.

Priority 2 Goals - These problems are significant to over all functioning and require prompt attention, but not at the expense of
                   Priority 1 problems and goals. Further prioritization depends on factors other than the impact that the area
                   has on functioning, such as ease of accomplishment, timing with program events such as school and summer
                   programming. These goals must, therefore, be further prioritized during development of the treatment strategy.

Optional 0 Goals - These areas contribute to limitations, impairment or dysfunction. Improvements in these areas would be
                   beneficial to the child, but will not be critical to success after discharge. They may be addressed prior to
                   discharge if time and resources permit.

Assessment Summary for Multi-Modal Treatment, page 3

BIO-PHYSICAL	ISI	+	0	-	!	Tentative Goal or Implications for Treatment	Priority
General Health							
Physical Development							
Physical Appearance							
Dental Health							
Orthodontia							
Vision							
Hearing							
Speech							
Appetite							
Allergies							
Birth Complications							
Addiction at Birth							
Coordination							
Intelligence							
Hygiene/self-care							
Physical Limitations							
1.							
2.							
Organicity							
Neurological							
Seizures							
Medications							
1.							
2.							
3.							
Other Ohysical							
1.							
2.							
	ISI	+	0	-	!		

Assessment Summary for Multi-Modal Treatment, page 4

PSYCHO-SOCIAL DEVELOPMENT	ISI	+	0	-	!	Tentative Goal or Implications for Treatment	Priority
Infancy							
Nurturing							
Neglect							
Abuse							
Trauma							
Problems Noted with Infant							
Early Childhood							
Security							
Neglect/Indulgence							
Abuse							
Abandonment or Trauma							
Problems with Child							
Latency							
Security							
Neglect/Indulgence							
Abuse							
Abandonment or Trauma							
Problems with Child							
Adolescence							
Stability							
Neglect/Indulgence							
Abuse							
Abandonment or Trauma							
Problems with Child							
Development							
Toilet							
Speech							
Social							
Other 1.							
2.	ISI	+	0	-	!		

FIGURE B.2 *(continued)*

Assessment Summary for Multi-Modal Treatment, page 5

RECENT/CURRENT FAMILIAL	ISI	+	0	-	!	Tentative Goal or Implications for Treatment	Priority
Neglect/Indulgence							
Abandonment							
Emotional Abuse							
Physical Abuse							
Sexual Abuse							
In Home Relations							
With Mother/Step Mother							
With Father/Step Father							
With Brothers							
With Sisters							
With Other Relatives in Home							
Out-of-Home Relations							
With Out-of-Home Mother							
With Out-of-Home Father							
With Other Out-of-Home Relatives							
With Neighbors/Landlord							
With Neighborhood Children							
Communications							
Between Parents							
Parent/Child							
Parental Conflict							
Parent-Child Conflict							
Other							
Parental Substance Abuse							
Parental Values							
Parental Expectations							
Consistency							
Discipline (Too Easy/Harsh)							

ISI + 0 - !

FIGURE B.2 *(continued)*

Assessment Summary for Multi-Modal Treatment, page 6

BEHAVIOR	ISI	+	0	-	!	Tentative Goal or Implications for Treatment	Priority
Problems in Home							
Problems in School							
Problems in Community							
Legal Problems							
Self-Destructive Behavior							
Social Skills	**							
Following Instructions							
Accepting Criticism							
Asking Permission							
Accepting "No"							
Following Limits	**							
Accepting Consequences							
Adult Relations - Male							
Adult Relations - Female							
Peer Relations - Male							
Peer Relations - Female							
Temper _Control_	**							
Without Striking at Others							
Without Bracing Up to Others							
Without Threatening Others							
Without Breaking Things							
Without Slamming Things	**							
Without Cursing							
Without Yelling							
Without Walking Away							
Without Crying							
Without Pouting							
	ISI	+	0	-	!		

373

FIGURE B.2 *(continued)*

Assessment Summary for Multi-Modal Treatment, page 7

BEHAVIOR continued	ISI	+	0	-	!	Tentative Goal or Implications for Treatment	Priority
Normal Voice Tone							
Normal Language							
Manners							
Normally Pleasant to be with							
Interrupts Others When Talking							
Responsibility							
Completes Chores							
Keeps Room Neat							
Completes Homework							
Gives Destination When Leaving							
Leaves Without Permission							
Comes in on Time							
Stays Out All Night							
Runs Away							
Can Stay on the Streets							
Property							
Puts Things Away							
Breaks/Damages Things							
Steals from Family							
Steals from Others							
Trespasses							
Sexual							
Self Sexual Acting Out							
Is Sexually Active							
Uses Protection							
Has Multiple Partners/Promiscuous							
Is Aggressive or Victimized							

ISI + 0 - !

Assessment Summary for Multi-Modal Treatment, page 8

BEHAVIOR continued	ISI	+	0	–	!	Tentative Goal or Implications for Treatment	Priority
Substance Abuse							
Experimental							
Recreational							
Regular							
Habitual							
Smoking							
**							
Alcohol							
Marijuana							
Other 1.							
2.							
Multiple Habitual Use							
Physical Aggression	**						
With Peers							
With Mother							
With Father							
With Female Teachers							
With Male Teachers							
**							
Likes to Have Weapons							
Has Threatened with a Weapon							
Has Used a Weapon							
Grabs Anything That's Handy							
Carries Weapons							
General	**						
Can't Sit Still							
Difficult to Wake Up in Morning							
Sleeps During the Day							
Does Not Go to Bed							
Eating Habits							
	ISI	+	0	–	!		

375

Assessment Summary for Multi-Modal Treatment, page 9

BEHAVIOR continued	ISI	+	0	–	!	Tentative Goal or Implications for Treatment	Priority
Enuresis							
Encopresis							
Suicidal Ideation							
Suicide Attempt							
Other Self-Injurious Behavior							
Peer Relations							
Has Good Friends							
Has Negative Friends							
Follows Others into Trouble							
Influences Others into Trouble							
Dates							
Leisure							
Has Healthy Interests (list)							
1.							
2.							
3.							
4.							
Has Problem Interests							
Listens to Too Much Music							
Watches Too Much TV/Video Games							
Stays Alone in Room Too Much							
Sleeps Too Much							
Leisure Affects Responsibilities							
Gets into Trouble When Left Alone							
Other Behavior							
1.							
2.							
3.							
	ISI	+	0	–	!		

FIGURE B.2 (continued)

Assessment Summary for Multi-Modal Treatment, page 10

LEGAL	ISI	+	0	-	!	Tentative Goal or Implications for Treatment	Priority
Trespassing							
Shoplifting							
Theft							
Car Theft							
Burglary							
Armed Robbery							
Battery							
Sexual Battery							
Drug Possession/Use							
Drug Sales							
Probation Violation							
Other 1.							
2.							
3.							
Incarceration							
MOOD/THOUGHT/PERSONALITY							
Happy							
Sad							
Angry							
Depressed							
Satisfied							
Sense of Reality							
Fails to Perceive							
Distorts Perceptions							
Distorts Memory							
Hears Voices							
Visual Hallucinations							
	ISI	+	0	-	!		

377

Assessment Summary for Multi-Modal Treatment, page 11

MOOD/THOUGHT/PERSONALITY Continued	ISI	+	0	–	!	Tentative Goal or Implications for Treatment	Priority
Has Realistic Goals							
Has Realistic Expectations/Self							
Has Realistic Expectations/Others							
Other 1.							
2.							
Style	**						
Assertive/Timid							
Sense of Humor							
Mean							
Violent							
Selfish	**						
Impulse Control							
Self-Control							
Self-Discipline							
Self-Esteem							
Attitude	**						
Motivation							
Goals							
Confidence in Self							
Confidence in Others							
Seeks Adult Approval	**						
Seeks Peer Approval							
Fears Rejection							
Rejects Before Being Rejected							
Isolates from contact with Others							
Imposes on Other							
	ISI	+	0	–	!		

FIGURE B.2 *(continued)*

Assessment Summary for Multi-Modal Treatment, page 12

MOOD/THOUGHT/PERSONALITY Continued	ISI	+	0	−	!	Tentative Goal or Implications for Treatment	Priority
Values							
Sense of Right and Wrong							
Sense of Remorse or Guilt							
Honesty with Self							
Honesty with Others							
**							
Lies to Impress Others							
Lies to Get What S/he Wants							
Lies to Avoid Admission of Error							
Lies to Avoid Consequences							
Lies to Protect Self-Image							
**							
Deceives without "Lying"							
Manipulates							
Avoids Meeting Responsibility							
Avoids Accepting Responsibility (for Behavior) Blames Others							
**							
Gets Angry with Self							
Gets Angry when Denied Own Way							
Gets Angry over Peers' Teasing							
Obsessive or Compulsive							
Procrastinates							
EDUCATION Achievement Test Scores Reading							
**							
Math							
English/Spelling							
Social Studies							
Science							
	ISI	+	0	−	!		

379

Assessment Summary for Multi-Modal Treatment, page 13

Education Continued Academic Grades	ISI	+	0	–	!	Tentative Goal or Implications for Treatment	Priority
Reading							
Math							
English/Spelling							
Social Studies							
Science							
Behavior							
School Attendance							
Class Attendance							
Tardiness							
Class Work							
Homework							
Attitude							
Motivation							
Adult/Authority Relations							
Peer Relations							
Follows Rules							
Follows Instructions							
Accepts Criticism							
Accepts Consequences							
Accepts "No"							
Controls Temper							
Appropriate Language							
Stays in Seat							
Does Not Talk out of Turn							
Does Not Disrupt Class							
Respects Property							
	ISI	+	0	–	!		

Assessment Summary for Multi-Modal Treatment, page 14

Education <u>Continued</u>	ISI	+	0	–	!	Tentative Goal or Implications for Treatment	Priority
Appropriate Dress							
Grooming							
Smoking							
Drugs/Alcohol							
Fighting							
Aggression Against Teachers							
Threats							
Detentions							
Suspensions							
Expulsions							
Extra Curricular Interests							
Probability of Promotion							
Probability of HS Graduation							
Appropriate Placement (present)							
Other							
<u>PLACEMENT</u>							
History of Prior Placements							
Behavior in Prior Placements							
Recognizes Problems							
Wants to Improve							
Has Discharge Resource							
Has Out-of-Program Support							
Family Supports Placement							
Does Not Want to Be in Placement							
Influence on Peers							
Influence by Peers							

ISI + 0 – !

Assessment Summary for Multi-Modal Treatment, page 15

PLACEMENT continued	ISI	+	0	-	!	Tentative Goal or Implications for Treatment	Priority
Fights with Peers							
Victimized by Peers							
Runaway by Self							
Will Take Peers on Runaway							
Will Follow Peers on Runaway							
Sexual Assault on Peers							
Sexual Assault by Peers							
Consenting Sex With Peers							
Self Sexual Acting Out							
Relations with Opposite Sex							
Will Give Drugs to Peers							
Will Take Drugs from Peers							
Will Use Drugs/Alcohol on Pass							
Smoking							
Other Substance Problems							
Tattoos							
Dress							
Grooming							
Make-up							
Other							
Suicide Risk							
Needs Physical Control/Restraint							
Adult Relations							
Adult Attachments							
Other Issues from Prior Placements							

ISI + 0 - !

FIGURE B.3: Treatment Goal Summary

Treatment Goal Summary   page _1_ of ___

Name: _____   Date: _____

Strengths: Goals to Utilize Strengths:

_____   _____

_____   _____

_____   _____

_____   _____

_____   _____

_____   _____

_____   _____

_____   _____

_____   _____

_____   _____

_____   _____

_____   _____

_____   _____

_____   _____

_____   _____

_____   _____

_____   _____

Treatment Goal Summary
cont.

page ___ of ___

Name: _____

Date:_____

Additional Information Needed:

_____

_____

_____

_____

_____

_____

_____

_____

Priority 1 Goals – 90 days:

Modalities:

_____ _____

_____ _____

_____ _____

_____ _____

_____ _____

_____ _____

_____ _____

_____ _____

_____ _____

_____ _____

Treatment Goal Summary
cont.

page ____ of ____

Name: _____

Date:_____

Priority 2 Goals:

Modalities:

_____ _____

_____ _____

_____ _____

_____ _____

_____ _____

_____ _____

_____ _____

_____ _____

_____ _____

_____ _____

_____ _____

_____ _____

_____ _____

_____ _____

_____ _____

_____ _____

_____ _____

_____ _____

_____ _____

_____ _____

Treatment Goal Summary
cont.

Final
page of ___

Name: _____

Date:_____

Optional Goals:

Modalities:

_____   _____

_____   _____

_____   _____

_____   _____

_____   _____

_____   _____

_____   _____

_____   _____

_____   _____

_____   _____

_____   _____

_____   _____

_____   _____

_____   _____

Signatures:

_____		_____	
Staff	date	Supervisor	date
Resident	date	Parent	date
State Worker	date	Other	date

**90 Day Priority
Treatment Plan**   page __1__ of ___

Name: _____   Date: _____

Goals Assigned:

1.

2.

3.

4.

Goal # :

Interventions: Staff Responsible:

Strategy:

90 Day Criteria:

Staff Responsibilities: Resident Responsibilities:

```
                        90 Day Priority
                     Treatment Plan cont.        page ___ of ___


Name: _____        Date: _____


Goal # :



Interventions:                     Staff Responsible:




Strategy:




90 Day Criteria:



Staff Responsibilities:            Resident Responsibilities:
```

```
                        90 Day Priority        Final
                       Treatment Plan cont.    page of ___

Name: _____         Date: _____

Goal #  :



Interventions:                         Staff Responsible:






Strategy:




90 Day Criteria:




Staff Responsibilities:                Resident Responsibilities:




Signatures:

_____        _____
Staff                    date          Supervisor                 date
_____        _____
Resident                 date          Parent                     date
_____        _____
State Worker             date          Other                      date
```

TREATMENT PLAN page ___ of ___

Name: _____ Date: _____

Modality: _____ Staff
Responsible:_____

Interventions: When to Begin:

Goals Assigned:

Strategy:

Staff Responsibilities: Resident Responsibilities:

TREATMENT PLAN cont.   page ___ of ___

Name: _____   Date: _____

Modality: Staff
                                           Responsible:

Criteria for Level 2 (90 days):   Target Date:

Criteria for Level 3   Target Date:
(9 months after Level 2):

Criteria for Level 4   Target Date:
(3 months after Level 3):

Criteria for Discharge   Target Date:
(3 months after Level 4):

Signatures:

Staff	date	Supervisor	date
Resident	date	Parent	date
State Worker	date	Other	date

FIGURE B.6: Progress Report

```
                         Progress Report

Date: _____                        Page ___ of ___
                                             Admit
Name: _____          Date: _____

Progress Key:   NT – Goal not yet targeted   A – Goal achieved
                S – Satisfactory progress    C – Some progress
                U – Unsatisfactory progress, explained in narrative

                Date of Evaluation: ____ ____ ____ ____ ____ ____
Goal or Objective                            Progress

_____    ____ ____ ____ ____ ____ ____

_____    ____ ____ ____ ____ ____ ____

_____    ____ ____ ____ ____ ____ ____

_____    ____ ____ ____ ____ ____ ____

_____    ____ ____ ____ ____ ____ ____

_____    ____ ____ ____ ____ ____ ____

_____    ____ ____ ____ ____ ____ ____

_____    ____ ____ ____ ____ ____ ____

_____    ____ ____ ____ ____ ____ ____

_____    ____ ____ ____ ____ ____ ____

_____    ____ ____ ____ ____ ____ ____

_____    ____ ____ ____ ____ ____ ____

_____    ____ ____ ____ ____ ____ ____

_____    ____ ____ ____ ____ ____ ____

_____    ____ ____ ____ ____ ____ ____

_____    ____ ____ ____ ____ ____ ____

_____    ____ ____ ____ ____ ____ ____

_____    ____ ____ ____ ____ ____ ____
```

Progress Report Signatures   Final
                                  Page of ____

        I have reviewed the above ____ pages of the progress report

for resident _____ dated _____.

I have been informed that I may make comments in the section provided
before signing or attach a separate sheet. (Comments should be signed)

This report was completed for the following reason:

____ Routine Quarterly Review   ____ In preparation for planned
                                          discharge
____ In preparation for unplanned discharge due to: _____

_____

____ Because of special problems or circumstances: _____

_____

Comments: _____

_____

_____

_____

_____

_____

_____

_____

Signatures:

_____   _____
Staff   date   Supervisor   date

_____   _____
Resident   date   Parent   date

_____   _____
State Worker   date   Other   date

Appendix C

Urine Testing for Substance Abuse

THE collecting and testing of urine to detect drug use is being used in more and more settings and situations. It is widely practiced in Federal prisons and community programs of the Federal Bureau of Prisons. Federal Probation and Parole offices also use urine screening extensively. State and local authorities use the procedure to varying degrees. Child protective services may require parents with substance abuse problems to attend substance abuse clinics and submit ''clean'' urine specimens as a condition of getting their children back. Employers are requiring employees in ''sensitive'' jobs to submit to urine tests. Other employers are requiring all job applicants to submit urine specimens for drug testing prior to employment.

Most abused substances remain in the system for many days, often up to one week. The exception is alcohol, which is quickly metabolized and does not last in the urine sample long enough to be detected during testing. Most labs that screen urine specimens for drugs are highly reliable. Their results, however, are only as reliable as the specimens that are submitted. Breakdowns may occur during collection as well as during the chain of custody from the person collecting, storage of samples, packaging for shipment, and delivery to the lab.

Experienced substance users are likely to know how to beat the system.

One technique is to carry a small squeeze bottle in one's underwear. The bottle has previously been filled with urine from someone who does not use drugs. Unless the urine collection is observed very closely, a specimen bottle can readily be filled from such a container without the awareness of the person supervising the collection. The specimen will be near body temperature. Properly supervised collection of urine specimens for drug screening is therefore a very intrusive procedure. The passage of the urine from the penis or urethra to the specimen bottle must be completely observed.

The chain of custody of urine specimens must be carefully documented. A simple error due to accidental mislabeling can have serious consequences for an innocent party who will likely have no recourse or appeal for a positive report that is in error. When urine collection is done routinely, persons who handle specimens at any point from collection to shipment may be subject to bribes, intimidation, or blackmail. The more people who have access to the place in which the urine is stored, the greater the risk of tampering. If urine storage is not properly secured, anyone might gain access.

Worse, custodians might not even be aware that someone has gained unauthorized access and switched labels, resulting in a positive report for someone who has not used drugs.

The risk is less when the consequences for detected drug use are minimal. The risk increases with the consequences. When the consequences are serious, such as incarceration or loss of employment, procedures should be extremely well-controlled. I have seen a man returned to prison protesting his innocence, later to learn that a secretary who had access to urine specimens had taken bribes to switch labels. I suspect that the urine collecting procedures of some employers are adequate to catch recreational users of marijuana who smoked two joints last Friday night and who never worked under the influence, while inadequate to catch the more sophisticated addict for whom the procedures were instituted.

A well-run urine screening program may serve to discourage drug use or to detect substance abuse problems to facilitate treatment. A poorly operated program is likely to provide little discouragement for substance abuse while promoting other problems, such as selling and buying of urine among residents, coercing clean specimens to be substituted for dirty specimens, or blackmailing staff who may be abusing residents, sleeping on duty, etc. If urine screening is done for any reason, the process requires constant vigil and scrutiny.

REFERENCES

Preface

Bandler, R., & Grinder, J. (1979). *Frogs into Princes*. Moab, UT: Real People Press.

Chapter 1

Adler, J. (1981). *Fundamentals of Group Child Care: A Text Book and Instructional Guide for Child Care Workers*. Cambridge, MA: Ballinger Publishing Company.

Alt, H. (1960). *Residential Treatment for the Disturbed Child: Basic Principles in Planning and Design of Programs and Facilities*. New York: International Universities Press.

Heads, T. B. (1978). Ethical and legal considerations in behavior therapy. In D. Markholin, II (Ed.), *Child Behavior Therapy* (pp. 416–433). New York: Gardner Press.

Hoffman, M. S. (1992). *The World Almanac and Book of Facts 1993*. New York: Pharos Books.

Mayer, M. F., Richman, L. H., & Balcerzak, E. A. (1978). *Group Care of Children: Crossroads and Transitions* (2nd ed.). New York: Child Welfare League of America.

Schaefer, C. E., & Swanson, A. J. (Eds.). (1988). *Children in Residential Care: Critical Issues in Treatment*. New York: Van Nostrand Reinhold Company.

Weber, G. H., & Haberlein, B. J. (1972). *Residential Treatment of Emotionally Disturbed Children*. New York: Behavioral Publications.

Chapter 2

Adler, J. (Ed.). (1981). *Fundamentals of Group Child Care: A Textbook and Instructional Guide for Child Care Workers*. Cambridge, MA: Balinger Publishing Company.

Alt, H. (1960). *Residential Treatment for the Disturbed Child: Basic Principles in Planning and Design of Programs and Facilities*. New York: International Universities Press.

Boys Town. (undated). *Questions and Answers: Father Flanagan's Boys' Home*. Boys Town, NE: Boys Town.

Bremner, R. H. (Ed.). (1970). *Children and Youth in America: A Documentary History* (Vol. I). Cambridge, MA: Harvard University Press.

Bremner, R. H. (Ed.). (1971). *Children and Youth in America: A Documentary History* (Vol. II). Cambridge, MA: Harvard University Press.

Cavan, R. S. (1969). *Juvenile Delinquency: Development, Treatment, Control* (2nd ed.). Philadelphia: J. B. Lippincott Company.

Gill, H. (1979). State prisons in America: 1787–1937. In G. G. Killinger, P. F. Cromwell, Jr., & J. M. Woods (Eds.), *Penology: The Evolution of Corrections in America* (2nd ed., pp. 60–97).

Heads, T. B. (1978). Ethical and legal considerations in behavior therapy. In D. Markholin, II (Ed.), *Child Behavior Therapy* (pp. 416–433). New York: Gardner Press.

Healy, W., & Bronner, A. F. (1915). An outline for institutional education and treatment of young offenders. *Journal of Educational Psychology, 6,* 301–316.

Levine, M., & Levine, A. (1970). *A Social History of Helping Services: Clinic, Court, School and Community*. New York: Appleton-Century-Crofts.

Mayer, M. F., Richman, L. H., & Blacerzak, E. A. (1978). *Group Care of Children: Crossroads and Transitions* (2nd ed.). New York: Child Welfare League of America.

Sarri, R. C. (1985). Juvenile justice as child welfare. In J. Laird, & A. Hartman (Eds.), *A Handbook of Child Welfare: Context, Knowledge, and Practice* (pp. 489–513). New York: The Free Press.

Stroul, B. A. (1989). *Series on Community Based Services for Children & Adolescents Who Are Severely Emotionally Disturbed: Volume III: Therapeutic Foster Care*. Washington, DC: CASSP Technical Assistance Center.

Stumphauzer, J. S. (1986). *Helping Delinquents Change: A Treatment Manual of Social Learning Approaches*. New York: The Haworth Press.

Taylor, R. B. (1981). *The Kid Business: How It Exploits the Children It Should Help*. Boston: Houghton Mifflin Company.

Tiffin, S. (1982). *In Whose Best Interest: Child Welfare Reform in the Progressive Era*. Westport, CT: Greenwood Press.

Trattner, W. I. (1984). *From Poor Law to Welfare State: A History of Social Welfare in America* (3rd ed.). New York: The Free Press.

VisionQuest, (undated). *VisionQuest: The New Direction* (Brochure). Tucson, AZ: Author.

Weber, G. H., & Haberlein, B. J. (1972). *Residential Treatment of Emotionally Disturbed Children*. New York: Behavioral Publications.

Whittaker, J. K. (1985). Group and institutional care: An overview. In J. Laird, & A. Hartman (Eds.), *A Handbook of Child Welfare: Context, Knowledge, and Practice* (pp. 617–637). New York: The Free Press.

Wiley House. (undated). *Program profiles*. Bethlehem, PA: Wiley House.

Yelton, S. (1993). Children in residential treatment—Policies for the 90's. In *Children and Youth Services Review, 15*(3), 173–193.

Chapter 3

Boys Town. (undated a). *Boys Town 1989 Annual Report: Destination: America*. Boys Town, NE: Author.

Boys Town. (undated b). *Come Teach Our Children* (Brochure). Boys Town, NE: Author.

Boys Town. (undated c). *Questions and Answers: Father Flanagan's Boys' Home* (Brochure). Boys Town, NE: Author.

Buckel, L. (1990, Nov. 28). Personal communication.

Considine, J. W., Jr. (Producer), & Taurog, N. (Director). (1938). *Boys Town* (Film). Hollywood: Metro-Goldwyn-Mayer.

Dennis, K. (1992, June 1). Training presentation on children's services in Metairie, LA.

Kaleidoscope. (undated a). *Fact Sheet*. Chicago: Author.

Kaleidoscope. (undated b). *Kaleidoscope, Inc*. Chicago: Author.

Kaleidoscope. (undated c). *Satellite Family Outreach Program*. Chicago: Author.

Kaleidoscope. (undated d). *Therapeutic Foster Family Programs*. Chicago: Author.

Kaleidoscope. (undated e). *Youth Development Program*. Chicago: Author.

Powers, W. M (1994, May 17). Personal communication.

Snyder, D. (1988a, June 12). Children's home residents missing. *The Times-Picayune*, pp. A-1, A-4.

Snyder, D. (1988b, May 1). Church home accused of child labor abuses. *The Times-Picayune*, pp. A-1, A-6.

Snyder, D. (1988c, June 14). Cops remove 35 from youth home, arrest leader. *The Times-Picayune*, pp. A-1, A-4.

Snyder, D. (1988d, June 19). Fountain: Bible backs tough home. *The Times-Picayune*, p. A-2.

Snyder, D. Two girls detail abuses at Miss. youth home. (1988e, June 15). *The Times-Picayune*, p. A-4.

Snyder, D. (1989, July 3). Mississippi moves to regulate wayward children homes. *The Times-Picayune*, pp. A-1, A-6.

VisionQuest. (1989a, September). *Group Home Program* (Program manual, 1517). Tucson: Author.

VisionQuest. (1989b, September). *HomeQuest* (Program manual, 1519). Tucson: Author.

VisionQuest. (1989c, September). *The HomeQuest Plus Program* (Program manual, 1518). Tucson: Author.

VisionQuest. (1989d, September). *The Impact Camp* (Program manual, 1502). Tucson: Author.

VisionQuest. (1989e, September). *OceanQuest*. (Program manual, 1516). Tucson: Author.

VisionQuest. (1989f, September). *Quests* (Program manual, 1503–1509). Tucson: Author.

VisionQuest. (1989g, September). *The Wagon Train Program* (Program manual, 1515). Tucson: Author.

VisionQuest. (1990, March). *The VisionQuest Program* (Program manual, 1202). Tucson: Author.

VisionQuest. (undated a). *VisionQuest Clarifier*. Tucson: Author.

VisionQuest. (undated b). *VisionQuest: The New Direction* (Brochure). Tucson: Author.

Wiley House. (undated a). *Accreditations/Associations* (Brochure). Bethlehem, PA: Author.

Wiley House. (undated b). *Program Profiles* (Brochure). Bethlehem, PA: Author.

Wiley House. (undated c). *Programs and Services* (Brochure). Bethlehem, PA: Author.

Chapter 4

Cavan, R. S. (1969). *Juvenile Delinquency: Development, Treatment, Control* (2nd ed.). Philadelphia: J. B. Lippincott.

Costin, L. B. (1985). The historical context of child welfare. In J. Laird, & A. Hartman (Eds.), *A Handbook of Child Welfare: Context, Knowledge, and Practice* (pp. 34–60). New York: The Free Press.

Dalton, R., & Forman, M. A. (1992). *Psychiatric Hospitalization of School-Age Children*. Washington, DC: American Psychiatric Press.

Giovannoni, J. M. (1985). Child abuse and neglect: An overview. In J. Laird, & A. Hartman (Eds.), *A Handbook of Child Welfare: Context, Knowledge, and Practice* (pp. 193–212). New York: The Free Press.

Hardin, M. (1985). Families, children and the law. In J. Laird, & A. Hartman (Eds.), *A Handbook of Child Welfare: Context, Knowledge, and Practice* (pp. 213–236). New York: The Free Press.

Hartman, A. (1993). Family preservation under attack. *Social Work: Journal of the National Association of Social Workers, 38*(5), 509–512.

Kohan, J., Pothier, P., & Norbeck, J. S. (1987). Hospitalized children with a history of sexual abuse: incidence and care issues. *The American Journal of Orthopsychiatry, 57,* 258–264.

Mason, M. J. (1991). Family therapy as the emerging context for sex therapy. In A. S. Gurman, & D. P. Kniskern (Eds.), *Handbook of Family Therapy* (Vol. II, pp. 479–507). New York: Brunner/Mazel.

Sarri, R. C. (1985). Juvenile justice as child welfare. In J. Laird, & A. Hartman (Eds.), *A Handbook of Child Welfare: Context, Knowledge, and Practice* (pp. 489–513). New York: The Free Press.

Yelton, S. (1993). Children in residential treatment—Policy for the 90's. In *Children and Youth Services Review, 15,*(3), 173–193.

Chapter 5

American Psychiatric Association. (1987). *Diagnostic and Statistical Manual of Mental Disorders (3rd ed.—revised): DSM-III-R.* Washington, DC: Author.

Anderson, R. E., & Carter, I. (1984). *Human Behavior in the Social Environment: A Social Systems Approach,* (3rd ed.). New York: Aldine De Gruyter.

Beck, M., and Cowley, G. (1990, March 26) Beyond lobotomies: Psychosurgery is safer—but still a rarity. *Newsweek,* p. 44.

Ellis, A. (1977). The basic clinical theory of rational-emotive therapy. In A. Ellis, & R. Grieger (Eds.), *Handbook of Rational Emotive Therapy* (Vol. 1, pp. 3–34). New York: Springer.

Gelman, D. (1990, March 26). Drugs vs. the couch. *Newsweek,* pp. 42–43.

Glasser, W. (1975). *Reality Therapy: A New Approach to Psychiatry.* New York: Harper & Row.

Millon, T. (1990). *Toward a New Personality: An Evolutionary Model.* New York: John Wiley & Sons.

Staff. (1990, March 26). Shock therapy returns. *Newsweek,* p. 44.

Wishik, J., Bachman, D. L., & Beitsch, L. M. (1989). A neuro-

behavioral perspective of aggressive behavior: Implications for pharmacological management. In *Residential Treatment for Children and Youth, 7*(2), 17–35.

Chapter 6

Dalton, R., & Forman, R. A. (1992). *Psychiatric Hospitalization of School-Age Children.* Washington, DC: American Psychiatric Press.

Feist, J., Slowiak, C., & Colligan, R. (1985). Beyond good intentions: Applying scientific methods to the art of milieu therapy. *Residential Group Care and Treatment, 3*(1), 13–32.

Morse, W. (1991). Introduction. *Residential Treatment for Children & Youth, 8*(4), 1–10.

Ott, J. N. (1976). Influence of fluorescent lights on hyperactivity and learning disabilities. *Journal of Learning Disabilities, 9*(7), 417–422.

Redl, F. (1972). The concept of a "therapeutic milieu." In G. H. Weber, & B. J. Haberlein (Eds.), *Residential Treatment of Emotionally Disturbed Children* (pp. 127–148). New York: Behavioral Publications.

Chapter 7

Birnbrauer, J. S. (1978). Some guides to designing behavioral programs. In D. Markholin, II (Ed.), *Child Behavior Therapy* (pp. 37–81). New York: Gardner Press.

Burghardt, G. M. (1973). Instinct and innate behavior: Toward an ethological psychology. In J. A. Nevin, & G. S. Reynolds (Eds.), *The Study of Behavior: Learning, Motivation, Emotion, and Instinct.* Glenview, IL: Scott, Foresman and Company.

Deese, J., & Hulse, S. H. (1967). *The Psychology of Learning* (3rd ed.). New York: McGraw-Hill.

Gambrill, E. D. (1977). *Behavior Modification: A Handbook of Assessment, Intervention and Evaluation.* San Francisco: Jossey-Bass.

Hill, W. F. (1963). *Learning: A Survey of Psychological Interpretations.* San Francisco, CA: Chandler Publishing Company.

Horton, P. B., & Hunt, C. L. (1976). *Sociology* (4th ed.). New York: McGraw-Hill.

Houts, A. C., & Mellon, M. W. (1989). Home-based treatment for primary enuresis. In C. E. Schaefer, & J. M. Briesmeister (Eds.), *Handbook of Parent Training: Parents as Co-Therapists for Children's Behavior Problems* (pp. 60–79). New York: John Wiley & Sons.

Krasner, L. (1970). Behavior modification, token economies and training in clinical psychology. In C. Neuringer, & J. L. Michael (Eds.), *Behavior Modification in Clinical Psychology*. New York: Appleton-Century-Crofts.

Lawson, R. (1960). *Learning and Behavior*. New York: Macmillan.

Munn, N. L. (1961). *Psychology: The Fundamentals of Human Adjustment*. Cambridge, MA: The Riverside Press.

Neuringer, C. (1970). Behavior modification as the clinical psychologist views it. In C. Neuringer, & J. L. Michael (Eds.), *Behavior Modification in Clinical Psychology*. New York: Appleton-Century-Crofts.

Neuringer, C., & Michael, J. L. (Eds.). (1970). *Behavior Modification in Clinical Psychology*. New York: Appleton-Century-Crofts.

Nevin, J. A. (1973). Conditioned reinforcement. In J. A. Nevin, & G. S. Reynolds (Eds.), *The Study of Behavior: Learning, Motivation, Emotion, and Instinct*. Glenview, IL: Scott, Foresman and Company.

Pavlov, I. P. (1966). The psychical secretion of the salivary glands (Complex nervous phenomena in the work of the salivary glands). In T. Verhave (Ed.), *The Experimental Analysis of Behavior*. New York: Appleton-Century-Crofts.

Taber, S. M. (1981). Cognitive behavior modification treatment of an aggressive 11-year-old boy. *Social Work Research & Abstracts, 17*(2), 13–23.

Tighe, T. J. (1982). *Modern Learning Theory: Foundations and Fundamental Issues*. New York: Oxford University Press.

Verhave, T. (1966). *The Experimental Analysis of Behavior*. New York: Appleton-Century-Crofts.

Chapter 8

Allport, F. (1924). *Social Psychology*. Boston: Houghton Mifflin Company.

Bandura, A. (1977). *Social Learning Theory*. Englewood Cliffs, NJ: Prentice-Hall, Inc.

Cartwright, D., & Zander, A. (Eds.). (1960). *Group Dynamics: Research and Theory* (2nd ed.). New York: Harper & Row.

Hare, A. P. (1962). *Handbook of Small Group Research*. New York: The Free Press.

Horton, P. B., & Hunt, C. L. (1976). *Sociology* (4th ed.). New York: McGraw-Hill.

Jackson, J. M. (1960). Reference group processes in a formal organization. In D. Cartwright, & A. Zander (Eds.),

Group Dynamics: Research and Theory (2nd ed.). New York: Harper & Row.

Kirscht, J. P., Lodahl, T. M., & Haire, M. (1960). Some factors in the selection of leaders by members in small groups. In D. Cartwright & A. Zander (Eds.), *Group Dynamics: Research and Theory* (2nd ed.). New York: Harper & Row.

Lewin, K. (1951). *Field Theory in Social Science*. New York: Harper & Row.

Schachter, S. (1960). Deviation, rejection, and communication. In D. Cartwright & A. Zander, (Eds.), *Group Dynamics: Research and Theory* (2nd ed.). New York: Harper & Row.

Secord, P. F., & Backman, C. W. (1964). *Social Psychology*. New York: McGraw-Hill.

Sherif, M. (1936). *The Psychology of Social Norms*. New York: Harper & Row.

Siegel, A. E., & Siegel, S. (1960). "Reference groups, membership groups, and attitude change." In D. Cartwright & A. Zander (Eds.), *Group Dynamics: Research and Theory* (2nd ed.). New York: Harper & Row.

Thrasher, F. (1927). *The Gang*. Chicago: University of Chicago Press.

Toseland, R. W., & Rivas, R. F. (1984). *An Introduction to Group Work Practice*. New York: Macmillan Publishing Company.

Chapter 9

Gardner, R. A. (1988). *Psychotherapy with Adolescents*. Cresskill, NJ: Creative Therapeutics.

Help wanted. (1971, February 17). *The Times Picayune*, p. I–16.

Neuringer, C. (1970). Behavior modification as the clinical psychologist views it. In C. Neuringer & J. L. Michael (Eds.), *Behavior Modification in Clinical Psychology* (pp. 1–9). New York: Appleton-Century-Crofts.

Popkin, M. H. (1993). *Active Parenting™ Today for Parents of 2 to 12 Year Olds: Parent's Guide*. Atlanta: Active Parenting.

Chapter 10

Feindler, E. L., Ecton, R. B., Kingsley, D., & Dubey, D. R. (1986). Group anger-control training for institutionalized psychiatric male adolescents. *Behavior Therapy, 17*(2), 109–123.

Neuringer, C. (1970). Behavior modification as the clinical psychologist views it. In C. Neuringer, & J. L. Michael (Eds.), *Behavior Modification in Clinical Psychology* (pp. 1–9). New York: Appleton-Century-Crofts.

Taber, S. M. (1981). Cognitive behavior modification of an aggressive 11-year-old boy. *Social Work Research & Abstracts, 17*(2), 13–22.

Wolpe, J. (1962). The experimental foundations of some new psychotherapeutic methods. In A. J. Bachrach (Ed.), *Experimental Foundations of Clinical Psychology* (pp. 554–575). New York: Basic Books.

Chapter 11

Clarizo, H. F., & McCoy, G. F. (1976). *Behavior Disorders in Children* (2nd ed.). New York: Harper & Row.

Hourts, A. C., & Mellon, M. W. (1989). Home-based treatment for primary enuresis. In C. E. Schaefer, & J. M. Briesmeister (Eds.), *Handbook of Parent Training: Parents as Co-Therapists for Children's Behavior Problems* (pp. 60–79). New York: John Wiley & Sons.

Popkin, M. H. (1993) *Active Parenting™ Today: For Parents of 2 to 12 Year Olds.* Atlanta: Active Parenting Publishers.

Redl, F. (1966). *When We Deal with Children: Selected Writings.* New York: The Free Press.

Weber, D. E., & Burke, W. H. (1986). An alternative approach to treating delinquent youth. *Residential Group Care & Treatment, 3*(3), 65–85.

Chapter 12

Budlong, M. J., Mooney, A., and the staff of the Family Life Development Center, Department of Human Development and Family Studies, New York State College of Human Ecology, Cornell University. (1983). *Therapeutic Crisis Intervention for the Child Care Worker: Instructor's Manual.* Ithaca, NY: Family Life Development Center.

Cates, J. A., & Cooper, G. D. (1983). Characteristics of secluded children in a residential treatment center. *Residential Group Care & Treatment, 1*(3), 43–54.

Gallagher, M. M., Mittelstadt, P. A., & Slater, B. R. (1988). Establishing time-out procedures in a day treatment facility for young children. *Residential Treatment for Children & Youth, 5*(4), 59–68.

Kelly, K. E., & Nelson, R. H. (1979). Audit review of seclusion procedures. *Residential and Community Child Care Administration, 1*(3), 277–286.

Landau, R. J., & MacLeish, R., Jr. (1988). When does time-out become seclusion, and what must be done when this line is crossed? *Residential Treatment for Children & Youth, 6*(2), 33–38.

National Crisis Prevention Institute. (1987). *Nonviolent Crisis Intervention: Participant Workbook.* Brookfield, WI: Author.

Northrup, G. (1987). Restraints: An interview with Bruce Bona. *Residential Treatment for Children & Youth, 5*(2), 25–50.

Redl, F. (1972). The concept of a "therapeutic milieu." In G. H. Weber, & B. J. Haberlein (Eds.), *Residential Treatment of Emotionally Disturbed Children* (pp. 127–148). New York: Behavioral Publications.

Steiger, L. K. (Ed.). (1987). *Nonviolent Crisis Intervention: Participant Workbook.* Brookfield, WI: National Crisis Prevention Institute.

Swartz, S. L., & Benjamin, C. (1983). The use of time-out in a residential treatment program for emotionally disturbed children. *Residential Group Care & Treatment, 1*(3), 29–40.

Wishik, J., Bachman, D. L., & Beitsch, L. M. (1989). A neurobiological perspective of aggressive behavior: Implications for pharmacological management. *Residential Treatment for Children & Youth, 7*(2), 17–35.

Wyka, G. T. (1987). Nonviolent crisis intervention: A practical approach for managing violent behavior. In L. K. Steiger (Ed.), *Nonviolent Crisis Intervention: Participant Workbook* (pp. 1s–9s). Brookfield, WI: National Crisis Prevention Institute.

Chapter 13

Birtchnell, J. (1984). Art therapy as a form of psychotherapy. In T. Dalley (Ed.), *Art as Therapy: An Introduction to the Use of Art as a Therapeutic Technique* (pp. 30–44). London: Tavistock.

Dalley, T. (Ed.). (1984). *Art as Therapy: An Introduction to the Use of Art as a Therapeutic Technique.* London: Tavistock.

Dalton, R., & Forman, M. A. (1992). *Psychiatric Hospitalization of School-Age Children.* Washington, D.C.: American Psychiatric Press.

Ellis, A. (1977). The basic clinical theory of rational-emotive therapy. In A. Ellis, & R. Grieger (Eds.), *Handbook of Rational Emotive Therapy* (Vol. 1, pp. 3–34). New York: Springer.

Gardner, R. A. (1988). *Psychotherapy with Adolescents.* Cresskill, NJ: Creative Therapeutics.

Glasser, W. (1975). *Reality Therapy: A New Approach to Psychiatry.* New York: Harper & Row.

Kernberg, P. F., & Chazan, S. E. (1991). *Children with Conduct Disorders: A Psychotherapy Manual.* United States: Basic Books.

Otto, W., & Smith, R. J. (1980). *Corrective and Remedial Teaching* (3rd ed.). Boston: Houghton Mifflin Co.

Stroul, B. A., & Friedman, R. M. (1986, July). *A System of Care for Severely Emotionally Disturbed Children and Youth.* Washington, DC: CASSP Technical Assistance Center, Georgetown University.

Tarczan, C. (1972). *An Educator's Guide to Psychological Tests.* Springfield, IL: Charles C. Thomas.

Toseland, R. W., & Rivas, R. F. (1984). *An Introduction to Group Work Practice.* New York: Macmillan.

Uhlin, D. M., & De Chiara, E. (1984). *Art for Exceptional Children* (3rd ed.). Dubuque, IA: Wm. C. Brown.

Wishik, J., Bachman, D. L., & Beitsch, L. M. (1989). A neurobehavioral perspective of aggressive behavior: Implications for pharmacological management. In *Residential Treatment for Children and Youth. 7*(2), 17–35.

Chapter 14

Colapinto, J. (1991). Structural family therapy. In A. S. Gurman, & D. P. Kniskern (Eds.), *Handbook of Family Therapy* (Vol. 1, pp. 417–443). New York: Brunner/Mazel.

Dalton, R., & Forman, M. A. (1992). *Psychiatric Hospitalization of School-Age Children.* Washington, DC: American Psychiatric Press.

Greene, J. R., & Holden, M. M. (1990). A strategic-systemic family therapy model: Rethinking residential treatment. *Residential Treatment for Children & Youth, 7*(3), 51–61.

Gurman, A. S., & Kniskern, D. P. (Eds.). (1981–1991). *Handbook of Family Therapy* (Vols. 1–2). New York: Brunner/Mazel.

Haley, J. (1987). *Problem-Solving Therapy* (2nd ed.). San Francisco: Jossey-Bass.

Madanes, C. (1991). Strategic family therapy. In A. S. Gurman, & D. P. Kniskern (Eds.), *Handbook of Family Therapy* (Vol. 1, pp. 396–416). New York: Brunner/Mazel.

Martone, W. P., Kemp, G. F., & Pearson, S. J. (1989). The continuum of parental involvement in residential treatment: Engagement—participation—empowerment—discharge. *Residential Treatment for Children & Youth, 6*(3), 11–37.

Mason, M. J. (1991). Family therapy as the emerging context for sex therapy. In A. S. Gurman, & D. P. Kniskern (Eds.), *Handbook of Family Therapy* (Vol. II, pp. 479–507). New York: Brunner/Mazel.

Mateja, J. (1991, September 27). Test how good a driver you are. *The Times-Picayune,* p. F-2.

McFarlane, W. R. (1991). Family psychoeducational treatment. In A. S. Gurman, & D. P. Kniskern (Eds.), *Handbook of Family Therapy* (Vol. 1, pp. 363–395). New York: Brunner/Mazel.

Popkin, M. H. (1990a). *Active Parenting™ of Teens: Leader's Guide.* Atlanta: Active Parenting.

Popkin, M. H. (1990b). *Active Parenting™ of Teens: Parent's Guide.* Atlanta: Active Parenting.

Popkin, M. H. (1993). *Active Parenting™ Today for Parents of 2 to 12 Year Olds: Parent's Guide.* Atlanta: Active Parenting.

Chapter 16

Finch, E. S., & Krantz, S. R. (1991). Low burnout in a high-stress setting: A study of staff adaptation at Fountain House. *Psychosocial Rehabilitation Journal, 14*(3), 15–26.

Raider, M. C. (1989). Burnout in children's agencies: A clinician's perspective. *Residential Treatment for Children & Youth, 6*(3), 43–50.

St. Bernard Group Home for Boys. (1989). *Annual Report.* Meraux, LA: Author.

Chapter 17

Bellisario, D. P. (Executive Producer). (1991). *Quantum Leap* (Television series). New York: NBC.

Dalton, R., & Forman, M. A. (1992). *Psychiatric Hospitalization of School-Age Children.* Washington, D.C.: American Psychiatric Press.

Gardner, R. A. (1988). *Psychotherapy with Adolescents.* Cresskill, NJ: Creative Therapeutics.

Hartman, A. (1993). Family preservation under attack. *Social Work: Journal of the National Association of Social Workers, 38*(5), 509–512.

INDEX

ABOUT THE AUTHOR

J OHN STEIN began his career in human services as a police officer in Bethlehem, PA, while working on his bachelor's degree in psychology at Lehigh University. He completed his studies while working as a community organizer in neighborhood centers and urban renewal project areas. He completed his master's degree in education, specializing in social restoration, also at Lehigh, while teaching college-level courses in accounting and economics to inmates in a maximum security prison.

In 1975, he opened Pennsylvania's first secure community-based program for treatment of hard-core juvenile offenders under Dr. Jerome Miller's deinstitutionalization of the state's juvenile justice system. In 1980, he directed the first correctional program in the State of Louisiana to receive accreditation from the American Correctional Association.

He has directed both secure and community-based residential programs for boys and girls and has taught courses in corrections and sociology. He has consulted with several residential programs. Presently, he is the director of Adult Services for United Cerebral Palsy of Greater New Orleans, Inc.